EXPLANATION

OF THE

PSALMS AND CANTICLES

IN THE

DIVINE OFFICE.

BY

S. ALPHONSUS LIGUORI,

DOCTOR OF THE CHURCH.

TRANSLATED BY

The Rev. T. LIVIUS, C.SS.R.

WITH A PREFACE BY

HIS EMINENCE CARDINAL MANNING.

LONDON : BURNS AND OATES, Ltd.
NEW YORK : CATHOLIC PUBLICATION SOCIETY CO.

Permissu Superiorum.

Nihil Obstat.

T. E. Bridgett, C.SS.R.,

Censor Deputatus.

Imprimatur.

Henricus Eduardus,

Card. Archiepiscopus.

In Festo Assumptionis B.M.V., 1887.

TO THE

Right Rev. Robert Cornthwaite,

LORD BISHOP OF LEEDS.

MY DEAR LORD,

I DEEM MYSELF HAPPY IN DEDICATING THIS "EXPLANATION OF THE PSALMS" BY MY HOLY FATHER S. ALPHONSUS TO YOUR LORDSHIP, WHO WELL-NIGH A QUARTER OF A CENTURY AGO EXPRESSED TO ME YOUR EARNEST DESIRE THAT ITS ITALIAN ORIGINAL SHOULD BE RENDERED INTO ENGLISH, AS BEING, IN YOUR OPINION, AMONGST ALL HIS WORKS, THAT ONE WHICH WOULD BE ESPECIALLY OF INTEREST AND PROFIT TO THE CLERGY, RELIGIOUS, AND THE FAITHFUL IN GENERAL ; AND WHO YOURSELF SOON AFTERWARDS COMMENCED ITS TRANSLATION, WHICH THE PRESSURE OF YOUR MORE IMMEDIATE EPISCOPAL DUTIES ALONE PREVENTED YOU FROM COMPLETING.

I AM, WITH MUCH RESPECT,

YOUR DEVOTED SERVANT IN CHRIST,

T. LIVIUS, C.SS.R.

BISHOP ETON, LIVERPOOL,
THE CENTENARY FEAST OF S. ALPHONSUS, AUG. 2, 1887.

ISBN: 978-1-7371910-0-1

Published by:

St Athanasius Press
133 Slazing Rd
Potosi, WI 53820
melwaller@gmail.com
www.stathanasiuspress.com

Specializing in reprinting Catholic Classics!

TRANSLATOR'S PREFACE.

S. Alphonsus, in a letter to Don Xavier Mattei, to whose Metrical Version of the Psalter and Commentary he so often refers with such great praise, speaks of his own book as his little work on the Psalms, composed under the pressure of heavy episcopal cares, old age, and much bodily infirmity. He did not propose it as an exhaustive volume for learned students in Biblical science; but, urged by charitable zeal, wrote it for the benefit of such as were on this matter the most in need of instruction: as he says himself in his Dedication to Clement the Fourteenth.

However, this unpretending little work of the Saint, on its first appearance, met at once in Italy with a universal welcome, and received the highest commendation from all the theologians and learned men of the day for its wide and solid erudition, its spirit of piety, and its great utility, not only to Ecclesiastics and Religious, but also to all Catholics in general. It has merited, moreover, to obtain the special eulogium and approbation of the Holy See, through the particular mention made of it in the Decree of March 23rd, 1871, which conferred on S. Alphonsus the glorious title of Doctor of the Church. It is there spoken of in the following terms :—" Lastly, he unlocked the hidden secrets of the Sacred Scriptures, as well in his Ascetical treatises, which are full of a peculiar heavenly sweetness, as in that most sound and wholesome Commentary, wherein, to aid the devotion and spiritual instruction of ecclesiastics, he has explained the Psalms and Canticles which they have to recite in the Divine Office." This work of S. Alphonsus on the Psalms is one that has hitherto been almost unknown in these countries ; and its translation has been long desired by several Bishops and Priests, as well as by many Religious. It will serve for the profit of all the devout Faithful, and will, we would fain hope, supply a want that is very generally felt by Catholics to exist in English Sacred literature.

In rendering into English the original work of the holy Doctor, we have found it necessary to modify to some extent the arrangement of the Italian text, in which the Saint's literal translation at one time, or his paraphrase at another, of the Latin, is for the most part not continuous, but interrupted by frequent parenthetical remarks of comment or criticism; whilst sometimes he does not give any translation, strictly speaking, of a verse at all, but enters at once into explanation or paraphrase.

On this account, then, after taking mature advice, we have judged it best, for the convenience and profit of the reader, to set by the side of the Latin the literal

English version.[1]   Hence, we have not repeated so
much of the text of S. Alphonsus as is simply iden-
tical with that translation; but, at the same time,
we have been very careful not to omit anything that
the holy Doctor himself says in each verse by way of
different rendering, paraphrase, or explanatory comment.

For much in this method, and for many of the foot-
notes, which are added for the reader's profit, but are
all wholly distinct from the Saint's Commentary, we
are indebted to the French translation of the work by
the late Père Dujardin, C.SS.R.[2]   The few notes by
the Translator have *Tr.* appended to them.

The present year 1887 has been especially chosen
for our Translation, as that in which falls (August 2nd)
the first Centenary Anniversary of the holy death of
the Saint : and this little work is intended as a slight
tribute of honour and filial piety to their Father on
the part of all his children in these lands, in commemoration of that blessed event.

---

[1] For this, we have adopted the Douay Version of the Psalms, as
revised by the late Archbishop Kenrick, of Baltimore, and Cardinal
Wiseman, and especially approved of by His Eminence Cardinal
Manning. (*The Book of Psalms.* Burns & Oates, 1878.) We have,
at the same time, reproduced the Titles of the Psalms and several
of the Notes given in that Edition.

[2] *Œuvres Complétes de S. Alphonse de Liguori.*   Tome xv.
Tournai, 1875.

O Doctor optime,
Ecclesiæ Sancte Lumen,
Beate Alphonse Maria,
Divinæ legis Amator,
Deprecare pro nobis
Filium Dei.
Amen.

O most admirable Doctor,
Light of the Holy Church,
Blessed Alphonsus Mary,
Lover of the Divine Law,
Pray for us to the
Son of God.
Amen.

PREFACE BY HIS EMINENCE
CARDINAL MANNING.

S. AUGUSTINE says that all the history and the prophecy of the Old Testament is to be found in the Book of Psalms. It contains also the theology which, from Adam to Abraham and from Abraham to the Incarnation, was the inheritance of all who lived by faith. In the midst of the theosophies of the East and the idolatries of the West, the pure theism of Israel ran as the river of life. The knowledge of the One True God, Whom no man had ever seen, or could see, in all the fulness of His perfections of holiness, justice, truth, mercy, wisdom, and power, elevated and unfolded the spiritual life of the Hebrew race above all nations of the world. When our Divine Lord said, " God is a Spirit, and they that adore Him must adore Him in spirit and in truth," He was not revealing a new and unknown truth, but appealing to the pure and primeval conception of God, inherited by Israel, and even by Samaria. "The Lord is my light," and " Taste and see that the Lord is sweet," are a theology so perfect, that it has run on into the Catholic Church as the river that makes glad the City of God. Even now in the full light of the Incarnation, and of the Holy Trinity,

the Church makes the Book of Psalms the chief
devotion of its priests and people. Seven times a
day we give thanks and offer praise to God, in union
with the Heavenly Court; but it is chiefly in the very
words of the Book of Psalms. No song of praise and
thanksgiving more perfect has ever been found. In
this the Church of Israel and the Church of Christ
are one. The words of the Holy Ghost abide for ever.

For all who are bound to the daily recital of the
Divine Office, it is of vital interest that they should
be able to give not only a material, but also an
intellectual, attention to the Psalms. It is indeed
true that the fervent intention of the simple will
prevail with God, even when the intellectual apprehension of the Psalms may be imperfect. It is with
all a question of degree. The most learned will
not apprehend all, and the least learned will apprehend much of the inspired words.

Nevertheless, the work of bringing the Psalms
home to us in English, as S. Alphonsus did in their
vernacular to Italians, is of the highest utility. It
will greatly help our intellectual attention in reciting
the Office, and thereby make it the source of light
and of sweetness in various measures both to the
simple and to the learned. F. Livius has therefore,
by his patient industry, bestowed upon us a gift for
which we all owe him cordial thanks.

HENRY EDWARD,
Cardinal Archbishop.

EXPLANATION

OF THE PSALMS AND CANTICLES IN THE
DIVINE OFFICE.

TO HIS HOLINESS POPE CLEMENT XIV.

Most Holy Father,

As the present work has been composed in the last years of my life,—for I am now decrepit and in daily expectation of death,—and as it treats of the Psalms of David, the recitation of which, after the ministration of the sacraments and of the divine word, is the holiest occupation of persons consecrated to God ;—since to celebrate the praises of the Lord is to do here below what the Angels are doing in heaven ; —I have thought that to no one could I more appropriately dedicate this book than to Your Holiness, who is the Head of the Church, and holds on earth the place of Jesus Christ. I will not here pause to enumerate all the many encomiums which Your Holiness deserves by a thousand titles ; hence, to spare Your modesty, I refrain from praising in particular the bright examples of virtue You have shown before the whole world by Your mortified life, Your detachment from relatives, and Your freedom from all human respect; but I cannot pass over in silence that most admirable prudence of which Your Holiness has given proof, through the adoption of so many wise measures, whereby You have succeeded in allaying the differences that were troubling the friends of the Church's weal.

I venture to hope that Your Holiness will be pleased graciously to accept this my work, as one that may be useful to all those who recite the Divine Office; amongst whom there are many who, from their little knowledge of the Latin language, understand imperfectly the meaning of the words, and still less the sense of the Psalms; and this all the more, because the greater number of them are so difficult of comprehension that it is only with much pains even the learned arrive at their right meaning.

It is true that many commentators have already undertaken to explain the Psalms; but because they have either written in Latin, or in a not sufficiently simple style, their works are not found so generally useful as might be wished. For this reason I have done my best to render their sense intelligible, so that all in reciting the Canonical Hours may understand well what they say, and may consequently recite them with more attention.

I lay, then, this my book at the feet of Your Holiness, praying You to correct it, if it merits correction, and to bless it if You think it may be of any service to the Faithful.

Prostrate at Your Pontifical throne, I devoutly

kiss Your feet, and humbly ask Your holy benediction.

Remaining always

Your Holiness' humble, devoted, and obedient
son and servant,

ALFONSO MARIA,

Bishop of S Agatha of the Goths.

INTRODUCTION.

DESIGN OF THE WORK.

1. The Fruit to be derived from the Recitation of the Psalms.

Cardinal Bellarmine, in the preface to his Commentary on the Psalms, says that the Psalter is a compendium of the whole of the Old Testament; for whatever Moses has written with regard to Sacred History and the Law, and whatever the other Prophets have said, all is found in the Psalms, as S. Augustine observes: "The Book of Psalms contains whatever things are useful in all (the Canonical Books), and is a sort of common treasury of good devotion, well suited to supply what is necessary to everyone." [1]

It needs indeed but slight attention for us to see that the Psalms are full of divine lights, of holy instructions, of fervent prayers, and of special prophecies, relating particularly to the Redemption wrought by Jesus Christ. We draw attention to the Psalms II., XV., XXI., XLIV., LXVIII., and to other Psalms also, in which the Psalmist clearly foretells the reign of Jesus

[1] *Præf. in Ps.*

b

Christ, His Birth, His preaching, His miracles, His Passion, His Resurrection, His Ascension into heaven, and the propagation of the Church, according to what He Himself declared to His disciples: "All things must needs be fulfilled, which are written in the Law of Moses, and in the Prophets, and in the Psalms, concerning Me" (*Luke* xxiv. 44).

The Psalms breathe throughout sentiments of divine love, of patience, of humility, of meekness, of forgetfulness of injuries, of strength of soul, and of confidence in God; hence in reciting the Office we should apply to ourselves all the sentiments and all the acts that the Psalmist elicits of holy fear, of confidence in God, of thanksgiving, of good desires, of humility, of offering, of love, and of praise; and especially all the prayers that he makes for pardon, light, and help; for the Lord, having destined the Psalms to be recited by the whole Church, certainly intended that everyone in reciting them should apply to his own particular case the acts and prayers which the Psalmist made for himself.

With regard to the prayers which the Royal Prophet addressed to God for the Hebrew people, we should have the intention of offering them up for all Christians. When David speaks of his enemies, he is generally understood, according to the literal sense, to refer to those who persecuted him; but for ourselves we should apply these words to the evil spirits who are our worst enemies, since they seek to deprive us not only of the life of the body, but also of the life of the soul.

2. THE DIFFICULTIES TO BE FOUND IN THE PSALMS.

Many of the Psalms are easy to understand; but many others are difficult and obscure. Hence the Holy Fathers gave all their attention to render them intelligible, as well for the explanation of dogmas and moral precepts, as for preaching, and for the general profit of all the faithful.

For myself, in the present work, where the verses are more easy, I shall give a simple translation, in order that those who are bound to recite the Canonical Hours, understanding what they say and savouring the heavenly maxims and holy affections contained in the Psalms, may thus recite them with more attention, and with greater spiritual profit. Oh! how great is the merit of a single Office recited with devotion!

With regard to the obscure passages, I own that when I first thought of undertaking this work, I looked upon it as an easy task, considering the abundant provision I had made of excellent commentators; but when once I set to work, I found it very difficult and laborious: so much so, that in several places I was at times embarrassed and undecided as to which amongst the different explanations given by the commentators I ought to adopt. Sometimes I spent a whole hour in interpreting a verse, and after consulting a great number of authors, I remained more perplexed than ever at seeing before me so many different opinions.

At length, not to give up the work altogether, I resolved not to state in it all the various explanations of commentators, nor all the questions raised by the

learned, but to confine myself to the interpretations
which seemed to me most commonly adopted and were
most in conformity with the Vulgate : this is the rule
that I have followed. Xavier Mattei, in his learned
and laborious metrical translation of the Psalms, justly
remarks that modern critics, especially Protestants,
no sooner find some version differing from the Vulgate,
than they eagerly embrace it, without examining into
its merits or demerits.

Some, no doubt, will say, that after so many explanations of the Psalms given by commentators, this
work of mine appears superfluous. I confess, however,
that it has been of great benefit, at least to myself;
for since making this translation, I find that I recite
the Office with more attention than formerly, when I
used to read many passages without understanding
their meaning; and this makes me hope that others
may derive from it the same profit. I have, moreover,
thought it desirable to arrange my translation according to the order, not of the Psalter, but of the Breviary,
for the greater convenience of those who have to recite
the Divine Office.

3. The Hebrew Text and the Versions.

There can be no doubt that, strictly and ante-
cedently speaking (*per se*), the Hebrew text, being the
original, is to be preferred to all the Versions; but
according to the teaching of the greater number of the
learned, the original Hebrew is not wholly free from
corruption : some say, with Salmeron and Morinus,
that it was corrupted by the Jews, out of hatred to

the Christian religion; others, with Cardinal Bellarmine, that many errors crept in, whether through
ignorance, or by carelessness of copyists; and especially
because, since the fifth century, the Masorite Jewish
doctors, have added to it the vowel points, which were
not there before, and these points have given occasion
for many equivocal and various interpretations. It
was for this reason the Council of Trent would not
declare the Hebrew text authentic, as it did the Latin
text of the Vulgate, by saying that this latter is exempt
from all error, at least in what concerns the dogmas
of Faith and Moral precepts. Hence, Xavier Mattei,
in his dissertation on the Tradition and Preservation
of the Sacred Books, concludes that when there is any
disagreement between the Hebrew text and the Vulgate, we should keep to the latter: " Not," says he,
" that this version is more authentic than the original,
but because it may be presumed that the original in
the ancient manuscripts was different in such a
passage from what it is now, and that the genuine
text was that which was made use of by the Author
of the Vulgate, which has merited to be approved by
the Church." We should, moreover, be persuaded
that there are in the Psalms many verses so
obscure, that it is impossible, whatever pains one
takes, to discover their certain meaning, without an
extraordinary divine illumination.

It is, then, admitted on all hands, as we have just
said, that the Versions ought, properly speaking, all to
be corrected according to the Hebrew text, as being
the original, and yet that this rule at the present day

is anything but a safe one, because this text, as we now have it, is full of faults in transcription or impression, and because the vowel points introduced into the orthography by the Rabbinists have given room for many ambiguities, and even for errors. The result of this is : (1) That the Hebrew text is variously interpreted, by some in one way, by others in another ; (2) that the sense of the Psalms, as several commentators justly observe, is less discoverable from the original text than from the versions that have been made of it, particularly the Septuagint, which is considered to be the most exact, because it was made at the time when the Hebrew text was more pure.

Besides, the Latin Version of the Vulgate, which S. Augustine[1] calls *Itala*, and S. Gregory *Vetus* (Ancient), though unadorned in style, is nevertheless the best; and its excellence is enhanced from the fact of its having been in use in the primitive Church after it had been corrected by S. Jerome from the Septuagint version. It is well to remark here that S. Jerome afterwards made another translation of the Psalms directly from the Hebrew text; but this second translation, as Estius[2] remarks, was not received by the faithful, especially the Monks, from their objecting to change the ancient Psalmody. Hence it has been the practice ever since, to recite the Psalms according to the first translation, corrected by the holy Doctor. We have, moreover, in these later times, the Decree of the Council of Trent,[3] which has declared that the

---

[1] *De Doctr. chr.* l. ii. c. 5.   [2] *In Ps.* i.   [3] *Sess.* iv.

Vulgate is free from all substantial error; so that this version is for us the safest; the Council having said: "If anyone will not receive as sacred and canonical the entire Books themselves with all their parts, as they have been used to be read in the Catholic Church, and are found in the ancient Latin Vulgate edition, . . . and should knowingly and of afore-thought contemn them, let him be anathema." And afterwards, in the Decree: "The Holy Synod rules and declares, that this same ancient and Vulgate edition, which by long use of so many centuries has been approved of in the Church herself in her public lections, is to be accounted authentic, and no one, for any pretext whatever, may dare or presume to reject it."

Consequently, in the present Translation we shall, for the most part, keep closely to the Vulgate version, which is for us, undoubtedly, the most safe, as being exempt from all error in what is substantial; and we shall do so the more, because the Vulgate is often in accordance with the Septuagint version, the authors of which had at the time they wrote the Hebrew text in a purer state than we have now. I say this for yet another reason: my object, as I explained in the beginning, is to enable those who say the Office to understand as well as possible the Psalms they recite; and these are found in the Divine Office exactly as they are in the Vulgate, as Urban VIII. says in his Bull *Divinam Psalmodiam*, the summary of which stands at the head of the Breviary. For this reason I shall keep, as a rule, closely to the letter of the

Psalms as they are in the Divine Office ; nevertheless, in certain passages where the sense of the letter or of the text seems difficult to understand, I shall endeavour to explain it in other terms.

4. CERTAIN PRELIMINARY QUESTIONS.

Commentators discuss several other preliminary questions, viz.: (1) the authorship of the Psalms; (2) their titles ; (3) the way in which they were composed, whether in verse or in prose. As regards these controverted points, I will now set forth in a few words the opinions most generally received, leaving the reader free to study the questions more at length in order to arrive at their truth so far as it may be ascertainable.

I. As to the authorship of the Psalms, it is undeniable that the holy king David composed at least a great part of them ; for the Bible says expressly that the hymns sung by the Levites in the Temple were the work of David, and it is evident that these hymns were the Psalms : " And the priests stood in their offices : and the Levites with their instruments of music of the Lord, which king David made to praise the Lord : because His mercy endureth for ever, singing the hymns of David by their ministry."[1] Several of the Holy Fathers, as S. Augustine,[2] S. Chrysostom, Theodoret, and others, would make David the sole author of the Psalms ; but S. Hilary,[3] S. Athanasius,[4] S. Isidore of Pelusium, &c., are of opinion

[1] 2 *Par.* vii. 6.   [2] *De Civ. D.* l. xvii. c. 14.
[3] *In Lib. Ps. prol.*   [4] *Syn. S. Script.* l. xiii.

that many of the Psalms belong to other authors,
especially those that bear in their titles the names of
different personages, such as Asaph, Idithun, Ethan,
&c.   S. Jerome writes : " We affirm that all the Psalms
have for their authors those whose names are placed
in the several titles." [1]   But, according to S. Augustine
and Theodoret, these names were not the names of
the authors, but rather the names of the chief singers
or musicians.   Nevertheless S. Jerome maintains his
opinion and says : " Know that they err who think
that all the Psalms were by David, and not by those
with whose names they are inscribed." [2]   And S.
Augustine himself had no objection to say : " Not all
the Psalms were put forth by David." [3]   Hence we
may well conclude with Calmet,[4] and according to the
opinion most common, that the greater number of the
Psalms are David's, but not all.   Before we take leave
of this point, let us recall what Theodoret says with
much wisdom : " What much doth it profit me to
know who were the several authors of different Psalms,
since it is certain that all composed them by the power
of the Spirit of God." [5]   S. Gregory the Great thus
admirably expresses the same thought : " Since we
hold the Holy Ghost to be the Author here, in our
questions about the writer, what else are we doing but,
whilst reading our letters, going in search after the
pen ? " [6]   We read, says he, the letters, and we know

[1] *Præf. in L. Ps. juxta Heb. ver.*   [2] *Ep. ad Cyprian.*
[3] *In Ps.* i. *adnot.*   [4] *Préf. gén. sur les Ps.* n. 2.
[5] *In omnes Ps. prol.*   [6] *Præf. in Job*, c. 1.

that they are divine : what boots it, then, thus to
perplex ourselves by trying to find out the particular
pen that wrote them ?

II. With regard to the *Titles* of the Psalms, I may
observe that this subject is so confused that the commentators, notwithstanding all their endeavours, have
not been able to clear it up ; for many of these Titles
are ancient ; some of them were added before the collection of Esdras without its being known by whom,
and others were added in later times. It is for this
reason that in the Septuagint version and in the
Vulgate we read Titles that are not to be found in the
Hebrew text. Moreover, it is doubtful whether the
names given in the Titles are the names of the authors
or those of the Cantors of the Psalms. In the face of
these difficulties, I do not undertake to explain the
Titles ; but I shall set forth at the head of each Psalm
a short summary of what it contains.

III. Lastly, the question is discussed among the
learned whether the Psalms were composed in verse or
in prose. Joseph Scaliger, in his Notes on the Chro-
nicle of Eusebius, thinks, with other authors, that the
Psalms are not rhythmical verse, but only an ornate
prose, written, as he says, in a poetic style, and Calmet
is also of this opinion ; but more commonly the learned
hold with S. Jerome that the Psalms were composed
in verse. As to the form given to this verse, whether
the metre had to have a certain fixed number of
syllables, whether it was with or without rhyme—these
are points which it is impossible now to determine,
since we no longer know with any certainty what was

the character of ancient Hebrew poetry, and have in these days, at the most, but a very imperfect and no intimate knowledge at all of the Hebrew language ; besides, we are ignorant of its right pronunciation, because, through the introduction by the Rabbinists of the use of points in the copies of the Bible, vowels are added or taken away, so that thereby the number of syllables has been increased or diminished. Xavier Mattei is of opinion that the poetical compositions of the Hebrews were in verses of free rhythm, without any fixed number of syllables or connecting link, and that they resembled the Choruses of the Greek Tragedies.

5. The Attention and Devotion which the Recitation of the Divine Office demands.

Before beginning the explanation of the Psalms, I have thought that it will be useful for those who are bound to the recitation of the Divine Office, to offer here some reflections which may help much to recite it well ; that is, with attention and devotion.

All men ought to be continually occupied during the present life in praising the Lord, in thanking Him for His benefits, and in asking of Him the graces necessary for obtaining eternal salvation ; but because seculars live distracted with worldly affairs, the Church wills that ecclesiastics and religious of both sexes should be employed, at least at certain hours of the day, in praising God and praying to Him for all the faithful, as well as for the interests of the Holy Church.

For this reason, S. Thomas says that the Divine

Office is a common prayer which is offered to God on
the part of the Church by her ministers in the name
of the whole Christian people:[1] *Communis quidem
oratio est, quæ per ministros Ecclesiæ, in persona totius
fidelis populi, Deo offertur.* Elsewhere he says that the
recitation of the Office is a public work laid upon the
clergy for the edification of the Church, that is, for its
conservation and increase: *Orationibus et Psalmis vacare
in Ecclesia, Divinum Officium celebrando, est quoddam opus
publicum ad Ecclesiæ ædificationem ordinatum.* And
before him S. Bernard had already written that the
three chief duties of ecclesiastics are to preach the
word of God, to give good example to others, and to
pray for all; but he adds that the duty of prayer is
greater than the other two: *Manent tria hæc: verbum,
exemplum, oratio ; major autem his est oratio.*[2] We may
hence infer how great will be the punishment those
will receive from God in the next life who, being bound
to the recitation of the Office, neglect this obligation,
whether from wearisomeness, or in order to give themselves to worldly amusements. But I am not now
speaking of these; I speak of those who say the Office,
but say it ill. It is a pity to see with what irreverence
some recite the Canonical Hours, saying them in the
streets, or in view of everybody at a window looking
at what passes below, or in conversation with friends,
laughing and jesting, intermingling trifling words and
jokes with the divine praises, without paying any
attention to what they recite. If anyone behaved

[1] 2. 2. q. lxxxiii. a. 12.   [2] *Epist.* cci. n. 3.

thus when speaking to a prince, he would certainly be at once driven away and punished; and yet there are those who dare thus to treat God, so that one would suppose they meant to dishonour rather than to honour Him!

On the other hand, very great is the merit, and the profit also, which they derive who say the Divine Office with attention. What lights are then obtained from the word of God, with what holy maxims is the soul penetrated! How many good acts may one not make—acts of love, of confidence, of humility, of contrition—by paying attention to the verses one recites! Above all, how many beautiful prayers are found in the Office, prayers which, if said with faith and fervour, will obtain for us treasures of grace, according to the infallible promise of our Lord that He will hear whoever prays to Him: "Ask, and it shall be given you. For everyone that asketh, receiveth." [1]

I may add that when the Office is said without devotion, and with no other thought than to get over it as quickly as possible, it becomes a very heavy and wearisome burden, and seems as though it would never come to an end; but, on the contrary, when it is recited with devotion, and with the desire to derive profit from it, by applying the mind and the heart to what the lips pronounce, its burden becomes light and sweet: of this the Saints made good experience, who found more pleasure in saying the Divine Office than worldlings find in all their pastimes and amusements.

[1] *Matt.* vii. 7 ; *Luke* xi. 10.

One single Office recited with devotion may gain for us many degrees of glory; what abundance of merits will not they, then, have acquired who thus recite it for thirty or forty years! This thought has led me to undertake the labour of the present Translation : the end I have had in view is to help those who, by the duty of their state, are bound to recite the Divine Office, to do so with merit and profit to their souls, and not with demerit, and a conscience continually burdened with remorse and fear at the thought of having one day to render an account before the divine tribunal of their Office ill-said, and of having to be punished for this in the next life.

MATINS FOR SUNDAY.

MATINS FOR SUNDAY.

INVITATORY.—PSALM XCIV.

SEVERAL corrections have been made in this Psalm as it is found in the Psalter, which do not appear here in the Breviary, where it still remains as it was anciently recited. The Psalm, as S. Paul declares (*Heb.* iii. 7, iv. 7), directly refers to Jesus Christ, Who in it is set forth as God, Creator, and Saviour of the world : hence we are exhorted to praise Him, and to hearken to Him as our Supreme Pastor.

Praise of a canticle for David himself.[1]

1. Venite, exultemus Domino, jubilemus Deo salutari nostro : præoccupemus faciem ejus in confessione, et in psalmis jubilemus ei.

O come, let us exult in the Lord : let us rejoice before God our Saviour. Let us come into His presence with thanksgiving ; and rejoice before Him with psalms.

"*Venite* . . ." O come, let us rejoice in the Lord, and sing with jubilee the praises of God our Saviour. Before the rising of the sun let us be found in His presence, praising Him and confessing our faults : let us rejoice exceedingly as we sing to His glory.——"*In confessione.*" S. Augustine says : *Est confessio laudantis, est confessio gementis :* "There is the confession of him who praises, and the confession of him who mourns".

2. Quoniam Deus magnus Dominus, et Rex magnus super omnes deos : quoniam non repellet Dominus plebem suam, quia in manu ejus sunt omnes fines terræ, et altitudines montium ipse conspicit.

For the Lord is a great God ; and a great King above all gods. For in His hand are all the ends of the earth : and the heights of the mountains are His.

"*Omnes deos.*" All the false gods, and all the kings of earth.——"*Altitudines montium.*" *Earthly powers,* according to S. Augustine. That is to say : The Lord regards alike the height of the mountains and the depth of the valleys, that is, as much the powerful of the world, as the poor whom the

[1] *For David,* or *to David :* that is, inspired to David himself, or to be sung by him.

1

world despises: for all is in His power, as sovereign Lord: and therefore He does not reject any one of His people.

3. Quoniam ipsius est mare, et ipse fecit illud, et aridam fundaverunt manus ejus: venite adoremus, et procidamus ante Deum: ploremus coram Domino, qui fecit nos, quia ipse est Dominus Deus noster: nos autem populus ejus, et oves pascuæ ejus.

For the sea is His, and He made it: and His hands formed the dry land. O come, let us worship and fall down: and weep before the Lord that made us. For He is the Lord our God: and we are the people of His pasture and the sheep of His hand.

4. Hodie si vocem ejus audieritis, nolite obdurare corda vestra, sicut in exacerbatione secundum diem tentationis in deserto: ubi tentaverunt me patres vestri, probaverunt, et viderunt opera mea.

To-day if ye shall hear His voice, harden not your hearts. As in the provocation, and in the day of temptation in the wilderness: where your fathers tempted Me, proved Me, and saw my works.[1]

"*Sicut in exacerbatione...*" We must here observe that this passage is in the Office, as anciently it was read in the Psalter. But it was afterwards corrected, as it is now in the Psalter, where we read: *Sicut in irritatione, secundum diem tentationis in deserto, ubi tentaverunt me patres vestri, probaverunt me, et viderunt opera mea.* This version, with which the English translation accords, better explains the text: its sense is as follows: God is here speaking to the Hebrews, and He says to them: Harden not your hearts, as you did of old time, by provoking Me to anger in the wilderness, where your fathers willed to tempt Me, to see if I were the true God, when in that place of barrenness and utter destitution, they sought for water, bread, and flesh: and they found by experience, at the sight of My wondrous works, that I can do all things according as it pleaseth Me.

5. Quadraginta annis proximus fui generationi huic, et dixi: Semper hi errant corde: ipsi vero non cognoverunt vias meas, quibus juravi in ira mea, si introibunt in requiem meam.

Forty years long was I offended with that generation, and said: They do always err in their heart. And they have not known My ways; so I sware in My wrath that they shall not enter into My rest.[2]

"*Proximus.*" In place of this word the corrected version of the Psalter has *Offensus.* Where S. Paul quotes this verse (*Heb.* iii. 10), the Vulgate has *Infensus.* But the meaning is the same, as Du Hamel and Bellarmine remark, if *Proximus*

---

[1] See *Ps.* lxxvii. 21.

[2] See *Heb.* iii. and iv., where S. Paul comments on these two last verses.

is taken for *Proximus ad ulciscendum:* Near to take vengeance on.——"*Semper . . . meas.*" They have always their heart perverse : they would not know My righteous judgments.—— "*Requiem meam.*" My rest, that is, the land which I promised to them.

THE FIRST NOCTURN.

PSALM I.

DAVID's object in this Psalm is to convince us that God bestows happiness only upon the just; and that consequently he who would be happy must seek after justice.

1. Beatus vir, qui non abiit in consilio impiorum, et in via peccatorum non stetit : et in cathedra pestilentiæ non sedit.

Blessed is the man who hath not walked in the counsel of the ungodly, nor stood in the way of sinners : nor sat in the chair of pestilence.

"*Beatus . . .*" Blessed is the man who gives no ear to the counsels of the wicked, and goes not in the way of sinners, and who sits not in the chair of pestilence, that is, who does not teach false and pernicious doctrines.——"*Et in cathedra . . .*" In place of the word *Pestilentiæ,* S. Jerome has *Derisorum,* according to the sense of the Hebrew ; Scoffers, impostors who teach falsehood. The sense of the Septuagint rendering is *Cathedra pestium:* the chair of pests, or the pestilential chair. These various renderings, however, come to much the same sense : for the impious, such as atheists and heretics, are, as S. Athanasius, S. Augustine, and S. Basil show, the pest of the world by the false and pernicious doctrines which they teach.[1]

2. Sed in lege Domini voluntas ejus : et in lege ejus meditabitur die ac nocte.

But his will is in the law of the Lord : and on His law shall he meditate day and night.

The just man wills that which God ordains in His law, and therefore he meditates on it continually.

---

[1] In this first verse we may note a triple gradation : 1. *Abiit,* turning aside from good ; *Stetit,* taking part in evil ; *Sedit,* settling down in it through habit ; 2. *Consilio,* temptation ; *Via,* straying away ; *Cathedra,* giving scandal ; 3. *Impiorum,* bad principles ; *Peccatorum,* bad conduct ; *Pestilentiæ,* utter corruption.

3. Et erit tamquam lignum, quod plantatum est secus decursus aquarum : quod fructum suum dabit in tempore suo.

And he shall be like a tree which is planted by the running waters : which shall bring forth its fruit in due season.

4. Et folium ejus non defluet : et omnia quæcumque faciet, prosperabuntur.

And his leaf shall not fall off : and all whatsoever he doeth, it shall prosper.[1]

Such a tree will not lose, but will keep its leaves, which will help to ripen the fruit : in like manner whatsoever the just man shall do will all go on prosperously.

5. Non sic impii, non sic : sed tamquam pulvis, quem projicit ventus a facie terræ.

Not so the wicked, not so : but they are like the dust, which the wind driveth from the face of the earth.

"*Non sic...*" But not so shall it be with the wicked ; they shall be scattered even as the dust which is driven over the earth by the wind.——"*Pulvis.*" Pagnini's translation of the Hebrew word is *Gluma:* Husk, that is, the fine chaff which the wind carries away, when the grain is sifted on the threshing-floor.

6. Ideo non resurgent impii in judicio : neque peccatores in concilio justorum.

Therefore the wicked shall not rise again in judgment : nor sinners in the counsel of the just.

"*Non resurgent.*" That is, according to the Hebrew text : *Non stabunt, non subsistent ; Shall not stand, shall not keep their ground.* In the Chaldee version it is : *Non justificabuntur : Shall not be justified* (Bossuet). This means that the wicked at the last judgment will not be able to withstand the just vengeance of Jesus Christ.——S. Augustine explains this verse by saying that "the ungodly will not rise again to be judged because they are already condemned to punishment". We should, however, here remark that the words *Non resurgent* do not mean that the wicked will not really rise again at the last judgment ; since we read in S. Matthew (xxv. 31-46) that all men, just and sinners, must then rise ; and this S. Paul affirms still more clearly : "We shall all stand before the judgment seat of Christ" (*Rom.* xiv. 10). The Apostle himself elsewhere explains how we are to understand this expression, "*Non resurgent,*" in the Psalms, where he says : "We shall all indeed rise again : but we shall not all be changed" (1 *Cor.* xv. 51) : meaning thereby to say, that

[1] *Jer.* xvii. 8.

though all will rise again, all will not obtain the happiness of having a spiritual and heavenly body, such as the just will receive, according to what he had written just before in verses 44-49 : "It is sown a natural body, it shall rise a spiritual body. . . . Therefore, as we have borne the image of the earthly, let us bear also the image of the heavenly." The words *Non resurgent*, then, being thus understood, accord very well with the Hebrew text and with the Chaldee version. Hence the two verses 5 and 6, taken together, may be easily explained in this sense : that the wicked, as the dust or fine chaff that is borne away by the wind, will be separated from the just, who are the good grain ; according to what we read in the Gospel : "Gather up first the cockle . . . to burn, but the wheat gather ye into my barn. The Angels shall go out and shall separate the wicked from among the just." (*Matt.* xiii. 30, 49).

| 7. Quoniam novit Dominus viam justorum : et iter impiorum peribit. | For the Lord knoweth the way of the just : and the way of the wicked shall perish. |

"*Novit.*" That is, approves and blesses.——"*Peribit.*" Shall be reprobated.[1]

PSALM II.

THE whole of this Psalm is, in its literal sense, a prophecy of the reign of Jesus Christ, as is clearly shown by the Apostles themselves in their prayer (*Acts* iv. 24) : "Lord, . . . Who by the Holy Ghost, by the mouth of our father David, Thy servant, hast said, Why have the Gentiles raged, and the people meditated vain things ? The kings of the earth stood up, and the princes assembled together against the Lord and against His Christ," &c. They then go on to say that Herod and Pilate, the people of Israel and the Gentiles, had conspired against our Saviour Jesus Christ. Several Protestant and also Catholic Authors, however, apply this Psalm, in its literal sense, to the reign of David ; but, as Xavier Mattei judiciously remarks, this is a novel opinion prevailing principally amongst Protestants, and ought to be rejected. We should then hold by what is written in the Acts of the Apostles, and which we

[1] To be known by God, says S. Augustine, is to live ; to be ignored by Him is to perish.—See *Ps.* xxxvi. 18. Jesus Christ has also said in the same sense : "I know you not" (*Matt.* xxv. 12).

have just cited. Besides, this Psalm cannot be applied to
King David without doing great violence to the text, which
speaks in the clearest terms of the reign of Jesus Christ.
Mattei says, moreover, that sometimes (as he proves in his
Preface), in Scripture, the spiritual sense is the one alone to
be taken as the literal sense, and beyond this we are not to
suppose any other hidden sense. When then, he says, we read
in this Psalm so clear a prophecy of the reign of Jesus Christ,
and find the explanation of it given by the Apostles, what
reason is there to apply it to the reign of David ? S. Jerome,
speaking of this very Psalm, says that it would be rash indeed
to do so. " It would be presumptuous," he writes, " to wish to
interpret this Psalm after Peter has already done so, or even
to hold an opinion on it, other than that which Peter has
given utterance to in the Acts of the Apostles." Such is also
the sentiment of Cardinal Bellarmine : " They are evidently
quite wrong who seek to explain this Psalm literally of David".

1. **Quare fremuerunt Gentes: et**   Why have the Gentiles raged :
populi meditati sunt inania ?   and the people devised vain things ?

It is here foretold that it will be all in vain that so many
enemies conspired against the Messias. S. Jerome translates
the verbs *Fremuerunt* and *Meditati sunt* in the future tense ;
but Bellarmine well remarks that the rendering of the Vulgate,
which here follows the Septuagint, is to be preferred, since in
the Acts of the Apostles, as we have already seen, these verbs
are in the past tense.——It is said : " *Meditati sunt inania*,"
because these enemies, while seeking to destroy Christ's kingdom, were in fact really co-operating in its establishment.

2. **Astiterunt reges terræ, et prin-**   The kings of the earth stood up
cipes convenerunt in unum : adversus   and the princes have met together :
Dominum, et adversus Christum ejus.   against the Lord and against His
                                           Christ.

" *Reges terræ et principes.*" By these kings and princes are
meant not only Herod, Pilate, and the Chief Priests of the
Jews, but also all the emperors and kings of the Gentiles who
have persecuted the Church of Jesus Christ.——" *Adversus
Dominum, et adversus Christum ejus.*" By these words the
Psalmist intimates that these enemies, in persecuting Christ,
made war also against God ; for the Messias, by His miracles,
had plainly proved Himself to be the Son of God. The first
word of the verse, " *Astiterunt*," according to the sense of the
Hebrew text is to be understood properly of the counsel which

the Jews took among themselves to compass the seizure and the death of Jesus Christ.

3. Dirumpamus vincula eorum: et projiciamus a nobis jugum ipsorum.　Let us break their bonds asunder: and cast away their yoke from us.

David here makes the enemies of God and of Christ speak. They say : Let us free ourselves from Their rule and from Their laws.——"*Jugum.*" S. Jerome here has *Laqueos:* their snares. The sense in the Hebrew is *Funes:* their cords. The wicked hate the laws of God, as an intolerable yoke, and galling chains.

4. Qui habitat in cœlis, irridebit eos: et Dominus subsannabit eos.　He that dwelleth in heaven shall laugh them to scorn : and the Lord shall have them in derision.

But David predicts that God will bring to nought and confound all their plots, and have their designs in derision. This was accomplished by the destruction of idolatry, the dispersion of the Jews, and the conversion of the Gentiles to the Faith.

5. Tunc loquetur ad eos in ira sua : et in furore suo conturbabit eos.　Then shall He speak to them in His anger : and trouble them in His rage.[1]

God spoke to them and confounded them, not by words, but by the terrible punishments which He inflicted on them. ——"*In ira . . . suo.*" It is well to remark that when Holy Scripture speaks of God's anger, we must understand that God never does anything in anger, as men do, who act through passion and with trouble of mind : since the Lord disposes and does everything with perfect calm : "Thou judgest with tranquillity" (*Wisd.* xii. 18). When, then, God is said to be angry, we are to understand that He is chastising sinners, not now with a view to their eternal salvation, as He often does with those whom He chastises in order to bring them to repentance, but that that He is punishing them solely to punish them, and to give free course to His justice.

6. Ego autem constitutus sum Rex ab eo super Sion montem sanctum ejus : prædicans præceptum ejus.　But I am appointed by Him King over Sion His holy mountain : preaching His commandments.

Here it is Jesus Christ Who speaks : He will say to them, I have been made King, not by men, but by God, My Father,

[1] See *Ps.* vi. 1.

over His holy mountain of Sion, that is, over the Church,
which, as S. Augustine says, was typified by the city of
Jerusalem, of which Mount Sion was the principal part, and
that most beloved by God.——"*Prædicans præceptum ejus.*"
Hereby is meant: I have been made King, that I might
publish His commandment. According to the Hebrew, we
read here : "*Narrabo ad decretum*" : I will declare for a decree.
However, the words *Præceptum* and *Decretum* mean substantially the same thing : viz., the decree whereby God established the Kingdom of Jesus Christ to be spread abroad
through the whole world. The terms of this decree are as
follows (v. 7).

7. Dominus dixit ad me : Filius   The Lord hath said unto Me :
meus es tu, ego hodie genui te.   Thou art My Son, this day have I
                           begotten Thee.

The literal sense of these words which the Eternal Father
speaks to Jesus Christ here is, in the mind of the Holy Ghost,
threefold, as Cardinal Bellarmine and Menochius well remark :—The first sense is that of the eternal generation of
Jesus Christ as the Word and Eternal Son of God, according
to what S. Paul writes : "Being made so much better than
the Angels, as He hath inherited a more excellent name than
they. For to which of the Angels hath He said at any time :
Thou art My Son, to-day have I begotten Thee ?" Hence
rightly says S. Augustine, this passage is to be understood in
its literal sense of the eternal generation whereby the Word
was begotten of the Father from all eternity, in contradistinc-
tion to the Angels, who are the ministers of God created in
time. It is said : "*Hodie genui te*" : To-day have I begotten
Thee ; because eternity is a duration always actually present,
without beginning and without end, as S. Augustine well explains, commenting upon this Psalm : "In eternity nothing is
either past or future, but only the present : since what is
eternal, always *is*". Bossuet (*Suppl. in Ps.* ii. 7) says that it
would be difficult to find in the Psalms another passage where
Jesus Christ is so expressly affirmed to be the true Son of God
as He is here.——The second literal sense refers to the Resurrection of Jesus Christ, according to what we read in the
Acts of the Apostles : "And we declare unto you that the
promise which was made to our fathers, this same God hath
fulfilled to our children, raising up Jesus again, as in the
second Psalm also is written : Thou art my Son, this day

have I begotten Thee" (*Acts* xiii. 32, 33). The Resurrection is, in fact, a sort of regeneration, according to what we read in S. Matthew (xix. 28) : " In the regeneration when the Son of Man shall sit," &c.——The third sense, also literal, has in view the temporal generation of Jesus Christ according to the flesh. Thus, S. Cyprian (*Testim. adv. Jud.* §. ii. c. 8) and S. Fulgentius (*Contra Arian. resp.* 5) explain it : and this sense has good confirmation in the words of the Apostle : " So Christ also did not glorify Himself that He might be made a high-priest : but He that said unto Him, Thou art My Son, this day have I begotten Thee" (*Heb.* v. 5). The Church, moreover, in the Introit of the first Mass on Christmas night, applies these words of the Psalm to the Mystery of the Nativity. We may here add that the Holy Fathers understand those words of Isaias (liii. 8) : " Who shall declare His generation ?" to refer not only to the divine, but also to the human generation of Jesus Christ.

| 8. Postula a me, et dabo tibi Gentes hereditatem tuam : et possessionem tuam terminos terræ. | Ask of Me, and I will give Thee the Gentiles for Thine inheritance : and the uttermost parts of the earth for Thy possession. |

The Eternal Father continues to speak to Jesus Christ. Since Thou art My Son by nature, it is just that Thou shouldst have dominion over all the nations and over the whole earth, as Thy inheritance and possession. ——S. Augustine understands this of the spiritual rule Christ has over the Church which through His merits was to be spread throughout the world, according to what our Saviour has Himself said : " All power is given to Me in heaven and on earth " (*Matt.* xxviii. 18).

| 9. Reges eos in virga ferrea : et tamquam vas figuli confringes eos. | Thou shalt rule them with a rod of iron : and shalt break them in pieces like a potter's vessel. |

These words denote the power which Jesus Christ has to reward the good and to punish the wicked, as easily as the potter can break with a rod of iron his vessels of clay. The iron rod signifies, moreover, the righteous and inflexible justice of Jesus Christ, which none can resist.

| 10. Et nunc reges intelligite : erudimini qui judicatis terram. | And now, O ye Kings, understand : be instructed, ye that judge the earth. |

You then who are kings, and as such hold the office of judges on earth, understand what is your duty, and learn to perform it well.

11. Servite Domino in timore : et exultate ei cum tremore.	Serve the Lord with fear : and rejoice unto Him with trembling.

"*Exultate ei cum tremore.*"   S. Augustine comments upon these words thus : "In rejoicing, that we may give thanks ; in trembling, lest we fall " (*In Ps.* l. n. 4).——By the word "*Timore,*" according to the Hebrew, is meant the piety of children towards their father, that is, that filial love with which kings and judges should serve God.   Hence, the verse may be thus explained : Serve the Lord with filial fear and with joy, hoping for the reward if you observe justice, and fearing the punishment, if you observe it not.

12. Apprehendite disciplinam, ne- quando irascatur Dominus: et pereatis de via justa.	Embrace discipline : lest at any time the Lord be angry, and ye perish from the just way.

Accept lovingly the divine law, and keep it ; lest if you fail to observe it, the Lord be angry, and permit you to stray away from the path of justice.

13. Cum exarserit in brevi ira ejus: beati omnes, qui confidunt in eo.	When His wrath shall be kindled in a short time : blessed are all they that trust in Him.

Unhappy they who offend against justice, and so cause God to be angry with them, and make haste to punish them. Blessed, on the other hand, are they who trust in God, for He will grant them light and strength not to turn aside from the right way.

PSALM III.

This Psalm, from its title, is commonly understood, according to the literal sense, of David flying before his son Absalom, who was persecuting him : but according to the mystical sense, S. Jerome, S. Augustine, S. Bede, Theodoret, and other commentators say that, in the person of David, we are to recognise the person of Jesus Christ, with reference to His Passion and Resurrection.   We would here once more remark, that in all the Psalms when they speak literally of the enemies who persecuted David on earth, we are to understand spiritually all our own enemies, whether internal or external, and especially the devils, who are ever plotting against our eternal salvation, and are of all our enemies the most powerful and the most dangerous.

The Psalm of David when he fled from the face of his son Absalom.— 2 Kings xv.[1]

1. Domine quid multiplicati sunt qui tribulant me? multi insurgunt adversum me.

How are they multiplied, O Lord, that afflict me : many are they that rise up against me.

2. Multi dicunt animæ meæ : Non est salus ipsi in Deo ejus.

Many say to my soul : There is no salvation for him in his God.

They tell me that there is no salvation for me even though I trust in my God.[2]

3. Tu autem Domine susceptor meus es : gloria mea, et exaltans caput meum.

But Thou, O Lord, art my protector : my glory, and the lifter up of my head.

"*Gloria . . . meum.*" That is, the cause of my glory. Thou art He who consolest me : I went of late my head bowed down with sadness, and Thou hast now enabled me to lift it up again with joy.

4. Voce mea ad Dominum clamavi: et exaudivit me de monte sancto suo.

I have cried to the Lord with my voice : and He hath heard me from His holy hill.

"*De monte sancto suo.*" That is, from His high heaven.

5. Ego dormivi, et soporatus sum : et exsurrexi, quia Dominus suscepit me.

I have slept and taken my rest : and I rose up, for the Lord protected me.

In the midst of persecution I slept tranquilly with a sweet repose, whereon I awoke in peace, seeing that the Lord had taken me under His protection. This verse is mystically applicable to Jesus Christ when He willed to lie down upon the Cross and there resign His life, and then willed to rise again from death by the power of His divinity.

[1] Bellarmine observes that the word *David* is here in the dative case, as is proved by the Greek version ; these words consequently signify : A Psalm inspired by God to David. He adds that the principal object the Holy Ghost has in view in this Psalm appears to be Jesus Christ Himself, of whom David was the figure.

[2] "*Ipsi . . . Ejus.*" According to the Greek these pronouns are masculine.—— Striking features of resemblance : David is betrayed by Achitophel, who ends by hanging himself (2 *Kings* xvii. 23); Jesus Christ is betrayed by Judas, who ends the same way. David is persecuted by his own people ; Jesus hears the Jews crying out to Pilate : "Away with Him, away with Him, crucify Him. . . . We have no king but Cæsar" (*John* xix. 15). David hears these words : "There is no salvation for Him in His God ". Jesus hears these other words : "He trusted in God : let Him now deliver Him if He will have Him " (*Matt.* xxvii. 43).

6. Non timebo millia populi circumdantis me: exurge Domine, salvum me fac Deus meus.

I will not fear thousands of the people surrounding me : arise, O Lord ; save me, O my God.

7. Quoniam tu percussisti omnes adversantes mihi sine causa : dentes peccatorum contrivisti.

For Thou hast struck all them that are mine adversaries without cause : Thou hast broken the teeth of sinners.

"*Sine causa.*" According to the Hebrew it is : "*In maxilla*" : On the jaw, or the cheek-bone. The Septuagint, however, has : *Sine causa*. And this rendering, says Bellarmine, was due to a Hebrew text more pure than any we now possess.

8. Domini est salus : et super populum tuum benedictio tua.

Salvation is of the Lord : and Thy blessing is upon Thy people.

It is for the Lord to give salvation to whom He will. Let Thy blessing, O Lord, descend upon Thy people.—— "*Domini est salus.*" According to the Hebrew it is *Domino salus*. That is, salvation is to be referred to God, and from Him alone must we hope for it. This salvation, then, is the blessing which God gives to His servants, for to be blessed by God is to become blessed.

PSALM VI.

This Psalm, according to the most probable opinion of the learned, refers properly, in the literal sense, to the penitence of David. Its main burden, therefore, is the prayer of the sinner, who dreads the judgments of God and seeks to be reconciled to Him.[1]

Unto the end in verses. A Psalm for David. For the octave.[2]

1. Domine, ne in furore tuo arguas me : neque in ira tua corripias me.

O Lord, rebuke me not in Thine anger : nor chastise me in Thy wrath.

Punish me, O Lord if Thou wilt, but reprove me not in Thine anger ; that is to say : Chastise me as a father and not as a judge. Not to be punished here on earth, after having

[1] The first Penitential Psalm.

[2] *Unto the end*, or, as S. Jerome renders it, *to him that overcometh* (*Victori*) ; which may be understood to refer to Christ, Who is the *end of the Law*, and the *great conquerer* of death and hell, and to the New Testament.——*In verses*, *In carminibus*. In the Hebrew it is *neghinoth*, supposed by some to be a musical instrument with which this Psalm was to be sung.——*For the octave*. That is, to be sung on an instrument of eight strings. S. Augustine understands it mystically of the resurrection at the last day, and the world to come, which is, as it were, the octave or eighth day after the seven days of this mortal life.

offended Thee, would be to me the greatest of punishments ;
wherefore, chastise me, I beseech Thee, that Thou mayest see
me amended and not lost. (See what is said on this point at
Ps. ii. 5.)

2. Miserere mei, Domine, quoniam infirmus sum : sana me, Domine, quoniam conturbata sunt ossa mea. Have mercy on me, O Lord, for I am weak : heal me, O Lord, for my bones are troubled.

Have pity on me, O Lord, for I am full of infirmities :
do Thou heal me by strengthening me with Thy grace, for
my very bones are troubled ; that is, are all trembling with
weakness.

3. Et anima mea turbata est valde : sed tu Domine usquequo ? My soul also is troubled exceedingly : but Thou, O Lord, how long ?

My soul also is troubled, and *that* much more than my
body. O Lord, wilt Thou delay to succour me ?

4. Convertere Domine, et eripe animam meam : salvum me fac propter misericordiam tuam. Turn Thee, O Lord, and deliver my soul : O save me for Thy mercy's sake.

Deliver my soul from the manifold miseries and dangers
that threaten it : out of Thy pure mercy save me, for I deserve
nothing but punishment, and even hell itself.

5. Quoniam non est in morte qui memor sit tui : in inferno autem quis confitebitur tibi ? For in death there is no one that is mindful of Thee : and who will give Thee thanks in hell ?

He who incurs the penalty of eternal death, remembers
Thee no longer : and who, while falling into hell, shall sing
Thy praises ?

6. Laboravi in gemitu meo lavabo per singulas noctes lectum meum : lacrymis meis stratum meum rigabo. I have laboured in my groanings, every night will I wash my bed : and water my couch with my tears.

"*Laboravi . . . meo.*" I feel wearied, O Lord, with my
lamentations. I will not cease to weep.

7. Turbatus est a furore oculus meus; inveteravi inter omnes inimicos meos. Mine eye is troubled through indignation : I have grown old amongst all mine enemies.

I have conceived a great indignation against myself, at
the thought of the deformity of my sins ; and in seeing how
I have grown old amongst my enemies, which are my vices
and my bad habits.[1]

[1] To these we may add the devil and sinners who had led him to offend
God, and from whom he is resolved henceforth to keep aloof (v. 8).

8. Discedite a me omnes qui operamini iniquitatem : quoniam exaudivit Dominus vocem fletus mei.

Depart from me, all ye workers of iniquity : for the Lord hath heard the voice of my weeping.

" *Qui operamini iniquitatem.*" My perverse enemies who would also pervert me.

9. Exaudivit Dominus deprecationem meam : Dominus orationem meam suscepit.

The Lord hath heard my supplication : the Lord hath received my prayer.

10. Erubescant, et conturbentur vehementer omnes inimici mei : convertantur et erubescant valde velociter.

Let all mine enemies be put to shame, and be sore troubled : let them be turned back, and put to shame very speedily.

PSALM VII.

In this Psalm David represents to Almighty God his innocence, and the trials he has had to endure from the persecution either of Saul or of Absalom, most probably of Saul. He exhorts at the same time all his enemies to be converted, and forewarns them of the chastisement they will receive if they do not repent.[1]

The Psalm of David, which he sang to the Lord, for the words of Chusi, the son of Jemini.—2 *Kings* xvi.

1. Domine Deus meus in te speravi: salvum me fac ex omnibus persequentibus me, et libera me.

O Lord my God, in Thee have I put my trust : save me from all them that persecute me, and deliver me.

2. Nequando rapiat ut leo animam meam : dum non est qui redimat, neque qui salvum faciat.

Lest at any time he seize upon my soul like a lion: while there is no one to redeem me, nor to save.

"*Animam meam.*" My life.

3. Domine Deus meus, si feci istud: si est iniquitas in manibus meis.

O Lord my God, if I have done this thing : if there be iniquity in my hands.

" *Si feci istud.*" If I have done the evil that is laid to my charge. This may mean that David's enemies accused him of wishing to usurp the throne of Saul.——" *In manibus meis.*" In my actions.

4. Si reddidi retribuentibus mihi mala : decidam merito ab inimicis meis inanis.

If I have made a return to them that did evils to me : let me deservedly fall empty before mine enemies.

[1] In the prophetical sense, says Bellarmine, David represents the person of Jesus Christ, and that of all the just who are persecuted and calumniated.

If out of revenge I have rendered evil to those who wrought me evil, deservedly may I be left conquered, to my shame, by my enemies.

5. Persequatur inimicus animam meam, et comprehendat, et conculcet in terra vitam meam : et gloriam meam in pulverem deducat.

Let the enemy pursue my soul, and take it, and tread down my life on the earth : and bring down my glory to the dust.

"*Conculcet . . . meam.*" May he trample upon the earth stained with my blood in the place where he hath taken away my life.

6. Exurge Domine in ira tua : et exaltare in finibus inimicorum meorum.

Rise up, O Lord, in Thine anger : and be Thou exalted in the borders of mine enemies.

But if I am innocent, O Lord, arise, and show forth Thy just indignation, by punishing my enemies : make Thy power to shine gloriously in their land, by chastising them as they deserve. We should not here reproach David as though he sought vengeance upon his enemies, for we must understand him as either speaking prophetically, foretelling the chastisements with which God would punish them, or as praying God to visit them with temporal punishment with a view to their amendment.

7. Et exurge Domine Deus meus in præcepto quod mandasti : et synagoga populorum circumdabit te.

And arise, O Lord my God, in the precept which Thou hast commanded : and a congregation of people shall surround Thee.

Arise, my God, save innocence according as Thou hast given the command to others to defend the innocent ; then shall all the people gather together around Thee, to praise the justice of Thy judgments. —"*Et synagoga.*" According to the Hebrew : *Congregatio tribuum* : The congregation of the tribes.

8. Et propter hanc in altum regredere : Dominus judicat populos.

And for their sakes return Thou on high : the Lord judgeth the people.

And therefore do Thou ascend Thy throne, for to Thee does it belong, as Lord of all, to judge the people.

9. Judica me Domine secundum justitiam meam : et secundum innocentiam meam super me.

Judge me, O Lord, according to my justice : and according to my innocence in me.

10. Consumetur nequitia peccatorum, et diriges justum : scrutans corda et renes Deus.

The wickedness of sinners shall be brought to nought, and Thou shalt direct the just : O God Who searchest the hearts and reins.

The craftiness of sinners shall not avail them, for Thou Who art God, to Whom are open the secrets of their hearts, well knowest how to direct the just man, so that he may remain unharmed by their wiles.

11. Justum adjutorium meum a Domino: qui salvos facit rectos corde.

Just is my help from the Lord : Who saveth the upright of heart.

The Lord will not fail to give me His just help, for He saves all such as act with an upright heart.

12. Deus judex justus, fortis, et patiens : numquid irascitur per singulos dies ?

God is a just judge, strong and patient : is He angry every day ?

It must be here observed that the Hebrew text has a contrary sense, viz. : *Deus justus, fortis, comminans, irascens tota die* : God is just, strong, threatening, angry all the day. According, then, to the present Hebrew text, God threatens and is angry every day : while in the Vulgate it is said that God does not threaten and is not angry every day. This latter reading is also that of the Septuagint,[1] and with Bellarmine I prefer to keep to it, for the reason already given, viz., that it is believed that, at the time when the Septuagint version was made, the Hebrew text was more correct than that which we now have ; moreover, as Bellarmine remarks, the sense as it is in the Vulgate agrees better with the following verse.

13. Nisi conversi fueritis, gladium suum vibrabit : arcum suum tetendit, et paravit illum.

Except ye be converted, He will brandish His sword : He hath bent His bow, and made it ready.

This verse, taken in connection with the preceding one, signifies that God is not always angry and in the mind to punish sinners as they deserve, but, when they are obstinate and will not be converted, He will brandish His sword, and will chastise them according to His justice ; for this purpose He holds in readiness and has bent His bow, to let fly the arrow of His just vengeance.

14 Et in eo paravit vasa mortis : sagittas suas ardentibus effecit.

And in it He hath prepared the instruments of death : He hath made ready His arrows for them that burn.[2]

[1] The literal translation from the Greek is : *Justus, et fortis, et patiens, et non iram adducens omni die.*

[2] That is, against the persecutors of His saints.

"*Vasa mortis.*" That is, the weapons that bring death.[1]
——"*Sagittas* . . ." By this is meant, thunderbolts. This
is precisely the explanation given by S. Jerome: *Sagittas suas
ad comburendum ignitas effecit:* He hath set His arrows on fire
to burn.

15. Ecce parturiit injustitiam : concepit dolorem, et peperit iniqui-tatem.	Behold, he hath been in travail with injustice : he hath conceived sorrow, and brought forth iniquity.

The sinner first of all conceives in his heart grief, that
is to say, hatred against the just man, called grief because it
afflicts the soul of him who cherishes it ; he then gives birth
to his iniquity by seeking to oppress the person hated.

16. Lacum aperuit, et effodit eum : et incidit in foveam, quam fecit.	He hath opened a pit and dug it : and he is fallen into the hole that he hath made.

He has opened and dug out a pit-fall, or a covered trap,
but has succeeded in falling himself into the hole he has made.

17. Convertetur dolor ejus in caput ejus : et in verticem ipsius iniquitas ejus descendet.	His sorrow shall be turned on his own head : and his wickedness shall come down upon his own pate.

The sorrow which he willed to bring down upon others
shall fall upon himself ; and the evil result of his wickedness
shall descend upon his own head.

18. Confitebor Domino secundum justitiam ejus : et psallam nomini Domini altissimi.	I will give glory to the Lord ac-cording to His justice : and will sing to the name of the Lord Most High.

I, however, will praise the justice of the Lord : and in
psalms I will praise the name of the Most High.

PSALM VIII.

THE argument of this Psalm is praise to God for His power,
wisdom, and goodness ; especially for the goodness He has
shown to man. In explaining this Psalm of the benefits
vouchsafed to man, we are following the more common opinion
of commentators ; but others, also with probability, apply it
to Jesus Christ, on the authority of S. Paul (*Heb.* ii. 9).

---

[1] In Holy Scripture the word *Vas* is often used to mean Instrument.—*Ps.*
lxx. 24 ; *Is.* xxii. 24 ; *Jer.* l. 25, i. 20.

Unto the end, for the presses.[1]   A Psalm for David.

1. Domine Dominus noster: quam admirabile est nomen tuum in universa terra!

O Lord our Lord : how admirable is Thy name in the whole earth !

2. Quoniam elevata est magnificentia tua : super cœlos.

For Thy magnificence is elevated : above the heavens.

"*Super cœlos.*"   Since the whole world cannot contain it.

3. Ex ore infantium et lactentium perfecisti laudem propter inimicos tuos : ut destruas inimicum et ultorem.

Out of the mouth of babes and sucklings Thou hast perfected praise because of Thine enemies : that Thou mayest destroy the enemy and the avenger.

Even babes and sucklings at the breast praise Thee perfectly, to the confusion of Thy enemies ; and thus dost Thou overthrow Satan, Thy chief enemy, and the avenger (*ultorem*) of all Thy enemies. Some explain this verse, not according to the Vulgate, which has followed the Septuagint, but according to the Hebrew text which, in place of "*Perfecisti laudem*": Thou hast perfected praise, signifies : *Fundasti fortitudinem*—Thou hast ordained strength. But, be this as it may, we have interpreted the passage in the sense given above : Even the very infants at the breast praise Thee perfectly, and confound Thy enemies. Nor should we depart from this interpretation, which is that of the Vulgate : since Jesus Christ Himself gave to it His own authentic sanction, on the occasion of His public entry into Jerusalem, when, as we read in S. Matthew, the children cried in the Temple, saying, Hosanna to the Son of David (*Matt.* xxi. 15). And on the Pharisees murmuring at this praise offered to our Saviour, He said to them : " Yea, have you never read: Out of the mouth of infants and of sucklings Thou hast perfected praise ?" He did not say : *Fundasti fortitudinem :* Thou hast ordained strength. Xavier Mattei justly remarks that in all those passages of the Psalter, and indeed of the whole of the Old Testament, which are cited in the New Testament according to the Septuagint version, this version must be regarded as the true and incontestably genuine text ; and that if the Hebrew text differs from it, it ought to be corrected according to the Septuagint version. He adds that it is an act of temerity to interpret such passages in a sense different from that given to them in the New Testament, save only certain passages which the Church has explained otherwise according to the Hebrew text, and which are interpretable in divers literal senses.

---

[1] *The presses.* Supposed to be a musical instrument

4. Quoniam videbo cœlos tuos, opera digitorum tuorum : lunam et stellas, quæ tu fundasti.

For I will behold Thy heavens, the works of Thy fingers : the moon and the stars which Thou hast set.

5. Quid est homo, quod memor es ejus? aut filius hominis, quoniam visitas eum?

What is man that Thou art mindful of him? or the son of man that Thou visitest him.

4, 5. " *Quoniam visitas eum ?* " That is to say : When I consider all these marvels and other beautiful things which Thou hast created in favour of man, how can I refrain from praising Thee and from crying out : What then is this creature man for whom Thou hast so great mindfulness, and whom Thou deignest to favour with Thy visit?——This accords with what is said in the Canticle of Zachary : "Blessed be the Lord God of Israel : because He hath visited and wrought the redemption of His people ". The Son of God comes Himself to visit man, to take human flesh, and to redeem him from the slavery of the devil.

6. Minuisti eum paulo minus ab Angelis, gloria et honore coronasti eum : et constituisti eum super opera manuum tuarum.

Thou hast made him a little less than the Angels, Thou hast covered him with glory and honour : and hast set him over the works of Thy hands.

Although, O Lord, Thou has made him a little less than the Angels, yet Thou hast crowned him with glory and with honour, and hast set him over all the rest of Thy creatures.[1]

7. Omnia subjecisti sub pedibus ejus, oves et boves universas : insuper et pecora campi.

Thou hast put all things under his feet : all sheep and oxen, yea, and all the beasts of the field.

8. Volucres cœli, et pisces maris : qui perambulant semitas maris.

The birds of the air and the fishes of the sea : that pass through the paths of the sea.

7, 8. Thus, an honour is given to men which was not given to the angels. As saith S. Paul : "For God hath not subjected to the angels the world " (*Heb.* ii. 5).

[1] This passage has a two-fold signification. In the literal sense it is applicable to men, whom God has made masters over all earthly things : "The heaven of heavens is the Lord's, but the earth hath He given to the children of men" (*Ps.* cxiii. 16). But in the figurative sense it applies to Jesus Christ, as S. Paul attests (*Heb.* ii. 6). God deigned to visit the human race by the Incarnation of the Word, Who appeared then in some sort inferior to the Angels, especially in His Passion, but who afterwards was crowned with glory in His Resurrection and Ascension, when were submitted to His dominion all things—Angels, men, and devils, who, according to S. Augustine and Bellarmine, are figured by the animals which people the air, the earth, and the sea. "Knowing that the Father had given Him all things into His hands " (*John* xiii. 3). "For He hath put all things under His feet " (1 *Cor.* xv. 26).

9. Domine Dominus noster : quam admirabile est nomen tuum in universa terra !

O Lord our Lord : how admirable is Thy name in all the earth.

PSALM IX.

COMMENTATORS are of opinion that the literal sense of this Psalm regards David, who in it gives thanks to God for having given him the victory over his enemy ; but that the spiritual sense refers to Jesus Christ, Who by the work of Redemption has subdued the devil, the enemy of the human race. Others think, and also with probability, that the Psalm describes the unhappy end of the prosperous wicked man, and the glorious end of the persecuted just man.

Unto the end, for the hidden things of the Son.[1] A Psalm for David.

1. Confitebor tibi Domine in toto corde meo : narrabo omnia mirabilia tua.

I will give praise to Thee, O Lord, with my whole heart : I will relate all Thy wonders.

2. Lætabor et exultabo in te : psallam nomini tuo Altissime.

I will be glad and rejoice in Thee : I will sing to Thy name, O Thou Most High.

3. In convertendo inimicum meum retrorsum: infirmabuntur, et peribunt a facie tua.

When mine enemy shall be turned back : they shall be weakened, and perish before Thy face.

Grant that my enemy be defeated and put to flight : once defeated, all his followers will be weakened and destroyed before Thy face.

4. Quoniam fecisti judicium meum et causam meam : sedisti super thronum qui judicas justitiam.

For Thou hast maintained my judgment and my cause : Thou hast sat on the throne, Who judgest justice.

Thou Who judgest according to justice hast already ascended Thy throne : Thou hast given judgment on me, and hast decided my cause.

5. Increpasti Gentes, et periit impius : nomen eorum delesti in æternum, et in sæculum sæculi.

Thou hast rebuked the Gentiles, and the wicked one hath perished : Thou hast blotted out their name for ever and ever.

Thou hast confounded the wicked nations and hast laid them low : Thou hast blotted out their name for ever : it shall be buried in eternal oblivion.

[1] *The hidden things of the Son.* The humility and sufferings of Christ, the *Son* of God ; and of good Christians, who are His *sons* by adoption ; are called *hidden things*, with regard to the children of this world, who know not the value and merit of them.

6. Inimici defecerunt frameæ in finem: et civitates eorum destruxisti.

The swords of the enemy have failed for ever : and their cities Thou hast destroyed.

7. Periit memoria eorum cum sonitu : et Dominus in æternum permanet.

Their memory hath died away like a sound : but the Lord remaineth for ever.

6, 7. The word "*Inimici*," as Menochius and Mattei observe, is here in the genitive.——"*In finem*" : Unto the end —*i.e.*, utterly.——"*Cum sonitu.*" With a noise. This, according to Bossuet, means : *Cum ingente rerum gestarum fama :* Together with the mighty fame of all their exploits. ——The Psalmist says more, that not only their fame, but even the very memory of them has perished. But the Lord continues the same for ever and ever.

8. Paravit in judicio thronum suum : et ipse judicabit orbem terræ in æquitate, judicabit populos in justitia.

He hath prepared His throne in judgment : and He shall judge the world in equity, He shall judge the people in justice.

"*In judicio.*" According to the Hebrew : *Ad judicium.* He has established and keeps open His tribunal to judge : and He will judge all the nations of the earth with equity and with justice.

9. Et factus est Dominus refugium pauperi: adjutor in opportunitatibus, in tribulatione.

And the Lord is become a refuge for the poor : a helper in due time in trouble.

10. Et sperent in te qui noverunt nomen tuum : quoniam non dereliquisti quærentes te, Domine.

And let them trust in Thee who know Thy name : for Thou hast not forsaken them that seek Thee, O Lord.

9, 10. The Lord has become Himself the refuge of the afflicted poor. He is their protector in their need, in time of tribulation.——Therefore they who know and adore Thy name have great reason to trust in Thee, O Lord, Who never forsakest those who seek Thee in truth.

11. Psallite Domino, qui habitat in Sion : annuntiate inter Gentes studia ejus :

Sing ye to the Lord, Who dwelleth in Sion : declare His ways among the Gentiles :

12. Quoniam requirens sanguinem eorum recordatus est : non est oblitus clamorem pauperum.

For seeking after their blood He hath remembered them : He hath not forgotten the cry of the poor.

11, 12. Praise then the Lord Who dwells in Sion, where He is adored as true God, and not as the idols that are found in the temples of the Gentiles.——Even amongst the most barbarous nations publish abroad His wonderful works, that these

too may praise Him ; for in searching into the unjust deeds
of men, He has had in remembrance the blood of the poor,
and their lamentations.

13. Miserere mei Domine : vide humilitatem meam de inimicis meis.

Have mercy on me, O Lord : behold
my humiliation by mine enemies.

14. Qui exaltas me de portis
mortis : ut annuntiem omnes laudationes tuas in portis filiæ Sion.

Thou that liftest me up from the
gates of death : that I may declare
all Thy praises in the gates of the
daughter of Sion.

13, 14. David here turns to God in prayer—"*Humilitatem
... meis.*" The state of abjection to which my enemies
have reduced me.——"*De portis mortis.*" The perils of
death.——"*Filiæ Sion.*" That is : Jerusalem.[1]

15. Exultabo in salutari tuo : infixæ
sunt Gentes in interitu, quem fecerunt.

I will rejoice in Thy salvation : the
Gentiles have stuck fast in the destruction which they prepared.

I will rejoice in the salvation which Thou hast given
me, since my enemies have fallen into the pit of death, which
they had prepared for me.——"*In interitu.*" The sense of
the Hebrew is : *In fovea* : In a pit ; with which agrees well
the word *Infixæ.* The meaning, then, according to Menochius,
would be : These Gentiles, my enemies, have fallen into a pit
of mud, a slough from which, when once in, it is very difficult
to get out again.

16. In laqueo isto : quem absconderunt : comprehensus est pes eorum.

Their foot hath been taken : in the
very snare which they hid.

" *Quem absconderunt.*" Which they had laid in secret to
catch me.

17. Cognoscetur Dominus judicia
faciens : in operibus manuum suarum
comprehensus est peccator.

The Lord shall be known when He
executeth judgments : the sinner
hath been caught in the works of his
own hands.

The Lord shall make Himself known for the great God
that He is, by the just vengeance He takes on the wicked, in
causing the sinner to be caught in the same toils which his
hands had laid for others.

18. Convertantur peccatores in infernum : omnes Gentes quæ oblivi-
scuntur Deum.

The wicked shall be turned into
hell : all the people that forget God.

[1] At the gates of the city, where ordinarily was assembled a crowd of
people.—See *Ps.* lxxii. 28.

According to Malvenda the meaning of *Convertantur in infernum* is : Shall perish miserably. "*Quasi dicat: Male peribunt.*" Menochius is of opinion that by the word *Infernum*, we must here understand hell, properly so called, the place destined for the punishment of the wicked : " By the word Hell, in this passage, not only is meant the grave, but also the place of punishment ". This is also the sentiment of Gordona. The sense then of the verse is : Those who forget God during their life will make a bad death, and will be sent to hell.

19. Quoniam non in finem oblivio erit pauperis: patientia pauperum non peribit in finem.	For the poor man shall not be forgotten utterly : the patience of the poor shall not perish for ever.

While, on the other hand, God will not in the end forget the poor ; the patience of the poor shall not utterly perish, *i.e.*, shall not remain always without reward.

20. Exurge Domine, non confortetur homo : judicentur Gentes in conspectu tuo.	Arise, O Lord, let not man be strengthened : let the Gentiles be judged in Thy sight.

Arise, O Lord, and show forth Thy power : let not sinful man prevail ; let all the nations be judged in Thy sight according to their merit.

21. Constitue Domine legislatorem super eos : ut sciant Gentes quoniam homines sunt.	Appoint, O Lord, a law-giver over them : that the Gentiles may know themselves to be *but* men.[1]

Give them, O Lord, a legislator, who, by the severity of his punishments, will curb and subdue them ; that so they may learn that they are men, that is, weak and mortal, bound to obey Thee.

22. Ut quid Domine recessisti longe : despicis in opportunitatibus, in tribulatione ?	WHY, O Lord, hast Thou retired afar off : why dost Thou slight us in our wants, in the time of trouble?

"*Despicis . . . tribulatione.*" Why dost Thou appear to despise me, by not consoling me in seasonable time, when I am troubled ?

23. Dum superbit impius, incenditur pauper : comprehenduntur in consiliis quibus cogitant.	Whilst the wicked man is proud, the poor is set on fire : they are caught in the counsels which they devise.

[1] Here the late Hebrew doctors divide this Psalm into two, making verse 22 the beginning of *Psalm* x. And again they join the *Psalms* cxlvi. and cxlvii. into one, in order that the whole number of Psalms should not exceed 150. And in this manner the Psalms are numbered in the Protestant Bible.

Whilst the wicked man grows proud, the poor man grieves, but both one and the other err in their thoughts ; for in vain does the proud man make a boast of his prosperity, and in vain does the poor man complain of his poverty.

24. Quoniam laudatur peccator in desideriis animæ suæ: et iniquus benedicitur.

For the sinner is praised in the desires of his soul: and the unjust man is applauded.

For the sinner glories in, and boasts of his evil desires.

25. ExacerbavitDominum peccator: secundum multitudinem iræ suæ non quæret.

The sinner hath provoked the Lord : in the greatness of his wrath he will not seek Him.

The sinner has aroused the indignation of God, and whereas he ought to seek to be reconciled with the Lord, yet on account of the multitude of his anger, *i.e.*, the greatness of his pride, which blinds him ; *non quaeret*, he will not seek to appease Him.

26. Non est Deus in conspectu ejus : inquinatæ sunt viæ illius in omni tempore.

God is not before his eyes : his ways are defiled at all times.

"*Inquinatae...*" All the actions of his life are constantly stained with sin.

27. Auferuntur judicia tua a facie ejus : omnium inimicorum suorum dominabitur.

Thy judgments are removed from his sight : he will lord it over all his enemies.

He thinks no longer, O Lord, of Thy judgments, *i.e.*, of Thy precepts, nor of the punishments with which Thou threatenest him, and therefore he seeks to lord it over, *i.e.*, to oppress, all his enemies.

28. Dixit enim in corde suo : non movebor a generatione in generationem sine malo.

For he hath said in his heart : I shall not be moved from generation to generation, *and I shall be* without harm.

"*Non movebor.*" I shall never fall from my happy state.

29. Cujus maledictione os plenum est, et amaritudine, et dolo : sub lingua ejus labor et dolor.

His mouth is full of cursing, and of bitterness, and of deceit : under his tongue *are* labour and sorrow.

"*Sub lingua...*" His tongue serves only to bring sorrow and distress on others.

30. Sedet in insidiis cum divitibus in occultis: ut interficiat innocentem.

He sitteth in ambush with the rich in secret places : that he may kill the innocent.

He associates with the rich and powerful ; to lay hidden snares for the ruin of the innocent.

31. Oculi ejus in pauperem respiciunt : insidiatur in abscondito, quasi leo in spelunca sua.

His eyes are set upon the poor man : he lieth in wait in secret like a lion in his den.

He keeps his eye upon the poor man : he lurks in ambush like the lion that hides in his den to devour the passer by.

32. Insidiatur ut rapiat pauperem: rapere pauperem, dum attrahit eum.

He lieth in ambush that he may catch the poor man : to catch the poor, whilst he draweth him to him.

33. In laqueo suo humiliabit eum: inclinabit se, et cadet cum dominatus fuerit pauperum.

In his net he will bring him down: he will crouch and fall, when he shall have power over the poor.

Having taken him in his snare, he will seek to torment him ; and having got him under, he will do as he will with him, whilst he has him in his power.

34. Dixit enim in corde suo: Oblitus est Deus : avertit faciem suam, ne videat in finem.

For he hath said in his heart : God hath forgotten : He hath turned away His face that He may not see at all.

For he has said within himself : God has no care for His creatures ; when once He has created them, He forgets them, and turns away His face that He may see them no more.

35. Exurge Domine Deus, exaltetur manus tua : ne obliviscaris pauperum.

Arise, O Lord God, let Thy hand be exalted : forget not the poor.

" *Exaltetur manus tua.*" Let Thy power be exalted against the wicked.

36. Propter quid irritavit impius Deum? dixit enim in corde suo : Non requiret.

Wherefore hath the wicked provoked God? for he hath said in his heart: He will not look after it.

" *Dixit enim.*" He does so, because he says in his heart : God has no care for human things, and does not trouble Himself about them.

37. Vides, quoniam tu laborem et dolorem consideras : ut tradas eos in manus tuas.

Thou seest *it*, for Thou considerest labour and sorrow : that Thou mayest deliver them into Thy hands.

Already, O Lord, dost Thou look upon and consider the distresses and afflictions of the poor, so that, when the time comes, Thou causest the wicked to fall into Thy hands to punish them.

38. Tibi derelictus est pauper: orphano tu eris adjutor.

To Thee is the poor man left: Thou wilt be a helper to the orphan.

To Thy care is the poor man left; Thou Who art the protector of orphans, who are destitute of any help.

39. Contere brachium peccatoris et maligni : queretur peccatum illius, et non invenietur.

Break Thou the arm of the sinner and of the malignant: his sin shall be sought, and shall not be found.

40. Dominus regnabit in æternum, et in seculum seculi : peribitis Gentes de terra illius.

The Lord shall reign for ever, yea for ever and ever : ye Gentiles shall perish from His land.

39, 40. "*Contere brachium*"—*i.e.*, Bring down the power.—— S. Augustine explains "*Quæretur . . . invenietur*" thus : He shall be judged for his sin, and he shall be lost on account of his sin. This interpretation seems to accord with what follows : *Peribitis Gentes de terra illius.* Ye Gentiles shall perish from His land—shall be exterminated from the land consecrated to Himself.——The sense, then, of the words *Quæretur peccatum,* &c., is : The sinner shall be judged according to his sin, and he shall be no more found, because he will be for ever lost.

41. Desiderium pauperum exaudivit Dominus : præparationem cordis eorum audivit auris tua.

The Lord hath heard the desire of the poor : Thine ear hath heard the preparation of their heart.

The Lord will always graciously hear the desire of the just in their afflictions : nay, Thou, O God of goodness, wilt hearken even to the preparation of their heart—that is to say, the interior disposition which precedes their prayers.

42. Judicare pupillo et humili : ut non apponat ultra magnificare se homo super terram.

To judge for the fatherless and for the humble : that man may no more presume to magnify himself upon earth.

Judge, O Lord, in favour of the orphan and the humble, so that men here on earth may no longer exalt themselves, that is, grow proud, against Thee and against their neighbour.

PSALM X.

An exhortation to the just to trust in God in time of persecution.

. Unto the end. A Psalm for David.

1. In Domino confido ; quomodo dicitis animæ meæ : Transmigra in montem sicut passer ?

In the Lord put I my trust : how say ye then to my soul : Get thee hence to the mountain like a sparrow ?

This verse is a difficult one, but it may be thus explained: In the Lord have I put my trust; why, then, do you come to me and say :[1] Fly to the mountain, as a sparrow, to escape the annoyances of the place where thou art? The just man is here rejecting the suggestions of the devil, who says to him : Leave this place where you find so much that is trying, and betake yourself, like the sparrow, to the mountain. Sparrows, when afraid of being taken in the nets of the fowler, fly away to the mountains, as to places more safe for them ; but the just man, who trusts in God, seeks no change of place, knowing that in every place there are temptations of the enemy, and that in every place there is the help of God for those who trust in Him.

2. Quoniam ecce peccatores intenderunt arcum, paraverunt sagittas suas in pharetra : ut sagittent in obscuro rectos corde.	For lo, the wicked have bent their bow; they have made ready their arrows in the quiver : that they may shoot in the dark them that are upright of heart.

"*In obscuro*," that is, in the darkness of the night, as the Greek text explains it, to indicate that such attacks are with difficulty guarded against.

3. Quoniam quæ perfecisti, destruxerunt : justus autem quid fecit ?	For they have destroyed the things which Thou hast made : but what has the just man done ?

The wicked, O Lord, says the Psalmist, have set at nought the laws which Thou hast made, by persecuting the just, without their having given them any cause.

4. Dominus in templo sancto suo : Dominus in cœlo sedes ejus.	The Lord *is* in His holy temple : the Lord's throne is in heaven.

5. Oculi ejus in pauperem respiciunt : palpebræ ejus interrogant filios hominum.	His eyes look on the poor man : His eyelids try the sons of men.

4, 5. The Lord sits as judge in His holy Temple, which is Heaven ; and thence His eyes look upon the poor man, and see all things ; so that the Lord knows all that passes, as though by asking questions of men He had to learn, and thus gained His knowledge of what is done. It is in this way Menochius explains the passage, he says : Just as though He were putting questions to them, and they were giving answer what was done.

[1] "*Animæ meæ*". A Hebraism for *Mihi.*

6. Dominus interrogat justum et impium : qui autem diligit iniqui-tatem, odit animam suam.

The Lord trieth the just and the wicked : but he that loveth iniquity hateth his own soul.

The Lord puts questions to the just and to the wicked ; that is, He knows the just to reward him, and He knows the wicked to punish him ; hence, says the Psalmist, he that loves iniquity hates himself, because he thus draws upon himself the divine vengeance.

7. Pluet super peccatores laqueos : ignis, et sulphur, et spiritus procel-larum pars calicis eorum.

He shall rain snares upon sinners : fire and brimstone and storms of wind *shall be* the portion of their cup.

The Lord will shower down upon sinners in this life snares, through which they will involve themselves in greater sins :[1] and in the next life, He will rain upon them fire and sulphur and the spirit of storms, that is, most baneful winds ; all which things shall be the portion of their chalice, that is, of their eternal punishment : and such shall be the fruit of their sins.

8. Quoniam justus Dominus, et justitias dilexit : æquitatem vidit vultus ejus.

For the Lord is just, and hath loved justice : His countenance hath beheld righteousness.

For the Lord is just, and loves His justice : and according to it does He punish the wicked and reward the good.

PSALM XI.

THIS Psalm speaks of the confidence we ought to have in the mercy of God, and of the fear we ought ever to have of His justice.

Unto the end ; for the octave. A Psalm for David.

1. Salvum me fac Domine, quoniam defecit sanctus : quoniam diminutæ sunt veritates a filiis hominum.

Save me, O Lord, for there is no godly man left : truths are failing from among the children of men.

Save me, O Lord, for even those who are reputed holy have failed in keeping Thy precepts, and are found liars.

2. Vana locuti sunt unusquisque ad proximum suum : labia dolosa, in corde et corde locuti sunt.

They have spoken vain things every one to his neighbour : *with* deceitful lips, *and* with a double heart have they spoken.[2]

---

[1] Bellarmine thus explains : He will permit them to be daily involved in more and greater sins, by striking them with blindness, and delivering them over to a reprobate sense.

[2] *Ps.* xxxvii. 4.

Every one speaks, with a view to deceive his neighbour, words that are nought but vanity and guile: for every one has a double heart. They mean one thing and say another. This is what is signified by the words: "*In corde et corde locuti sunt*".

3. Disperdat: Dominus universa labia dolosa: et linguam magnilo- quam.

May the Lord destroy all deceitful lips: and the tongue that speaketh proud things.

Here the Psalmist would strike terror into the impious, by threatening that the Lord will bring to destruction those deceitful lips and those vain-glorious tongues that are ever boasting of merits which they do not possess.

4. Qui dixerunt: Linguam nostram magnificabimus, labia nostra a nobis sunt: quis noster Dominus est?

Who have said, We will magnify our tongue: our lips are our own; who is Lord over us?

"*Linguam nostram magnificabimus.*" That is : We will make the most of our tongues, so that they be thought much of, and have weight. This accords with the Hebrew, which may be thus rendered : *Linguæ nostræ vires addemus* : We will add strength to our tongue.——"*Labia nostra a nobis sunt.*" We have our own lips to defend ourselves with.——"*Quis noster Dominus est?*" What master have we over us, who is to stop our mouth ?

5. Propter miseriam inopum et gemitum pauperum : nunc exurgam, dicit Dominus.

Because of the misery of the needy, and the groans of the poor : now will I arise, saith the Lord.

6. Ponam in salutari : fiducialiter agam in eo.

I will set him in safety : I will deal confidently in his regard.

I will set the just in a place of safety. Herein I will act freely, so that no one may resist Me.

7. Eloquia Domini, eloquia casta : argentum igne examinatum, proba- tum terræ, purgatum septuplum.

The words of the Lord are pure words : *as* silver tried by the fire, purged from the earth, refined seven times.

The words and the promises of the Lord are chaste, *i.e.*, pure and sincere, free from all falsehood and deceit : they are as silver tried with fire in the crucible, and refined seven times, so as to be purified from the earth, that is, from the dross.——"*Probatum terræ.*" S. Jerome's rendering is : *Separatum a terra.*

8. Tu Domine servabis nos : et custodies nos a generatione hac in æternum.

Thou, O Lord, wilt preserve us : and keep us fiom this generation for ever.

Thou, O Lord, wilt ever save and preserve us from this race
of proud and deceitful men.

9. In circuitu impii ambulant: secundum altitudinem tuam multiplicasti filios hominum.

The wicked walk round about: according to Thy high counsel, Thou hast multiplied the children of men.

The wicked circumvent the good that they may oppress
them : and Thou, in the depth of Thy judgments, permittest
the wicked to increase in numbers, and to take their delight
in the good things of this world. The sense of the Hebrew
here is, *Epulari fecisti :* hast made them to banquet.

PSALM XII.

This Psalm contains a prayer, which the just man makes to
God in time of tribulation, and in temptations of the enemy.

Unto the end. A Psalm for David.

1. Usquequo Domine oblivisceris me in finem? Usquequo avertis faciem tuam a me ?

How long, O Lord, wilt Thou forget me unto the end ? how long dost Thou turn away Thy face from me ?

2. Quamdiu ponam consilia in anima mea : dolorem in corde meo per diem ?

How long shall I take counsels in my soul : with sorrow in my heart all the day ?

How long shall I remain agitated, taking counsel with
myself, to discover the means of deliverance from my enemies,
suffering meanwhile as I do with continual sorrow in my
heart ?

3. Usquequo exaltabitur inimicus meus super me ? respice, et exaudi me Domine Deus meus.

How long shall mine enemy be exalted over me ? Consider, and hear me, O Lord my God.

How long shall my enemies take delight in tormenting
me ? My Lord and my God, look down upon my affliction,
and graciously hearken to my prayers.

4. Illumina oculos meos, ne umquam obdormiam in morte: nequando dicat inimicus meus : Prævalui adversus eum.

Enlighten mine eyes, that I sleep not ever in death : lest mine enemy say at any time, I have prevailed against him.

" *Ne umquam . . . morte.*" That I may never consent to
temptations, which would bring death to the soul.

5. Qui tribulant me, exultabunt si motus fuero : ego autem in misericordia tua speravi.

They that trouble me will rejoice when I am moved : but I have trusted in Thy mercy.

They who lie in wait for me, will rejoice should I fall beneath their attack : but I have placed all my trust in Thy mercy, and Thou wilt not permit it.

6. Exultabit cor meum in salutari tuo : cantabo Domino qui bona tribuit mihi ; et psallam nomini Domini altissimi.

My heart shall rejoice in Thy salvation ; I will sing unto the Lord, Who hath given me good things ; yea I will sing unto the name of the Lord Most High.

I will rejoice in the salvation which I have received from Thee : for ever will I thank Thee, my Lord, for having succoured me.

PSALM XIII.

THIS Psalm deplores the blindness and corruption of the wicked, and especially of infidels.[1]

Unto the end. A Psalm for David.

1. Dixit insipiens in corde suo : Non est Deus.

The fool hath said in his heart : There is no God.

"*Insipiens.*" The fool ; for the infidel who denies God is not only impious, but also is bereft of reason, since the existence of God is evident for every one who has the use of reason.——It is said, moreover : *In corde suo :* In his heart ; because he does not dare to say it to others, lest he should be laughed at as a fool.

2. Corrupti sunt, et abominabiles facti sunt in studiis suis : non est qui faciat bonum, non est usque ad unum.

They are corrupt, and are become abominable in their ways : there is none that doeth good, no not one.

The wicked say that there is no God, because they have become corrupt, first in their will, and then in their understanding ; nay, so abominable have they come to be by following their passions, that amongst them there is not even one who does good.

3. Dominus de cœlo prospexit super filios hominum: ut videat si est intelligens, aut requirens Deum.

The Lord hath looked down from heaven upon the children of men : to see if there be any that understand and seek after God.

4. Omnes declinaverunt, simul inutiles facti sunt : non est qui faciat bonum, non est usque ad unum.

They are all gone aside, they are become worthless altogether : there is none that doeth good, no not one.

[1] See *Ps.* lii.

3, 4. The Lord from heaven has cast His eyes on these wicked men, to see if any of them knows God, and seeks Him to obey and to love Him ; but no, all have wandered from the right path, and all are good for nothing, so that there is not one amongst them who does good.

5. Sepulchrum patens est guttur eorum ; linguis suis dolose agebant : venenum aspidum sub labiis eorum.

Their throat is an open sepulchre ; with their tongues they acted deceitfully : the poison of asps *is* under their lips.

"*Sepulchrum patens.*" An open sepulchre, which reeks with corruption.——"*Venenum aspidum sub labiis eorum.*" They seem to keep beneath their tongue the venom of asps, to defame and injure others.

6. Quorum os maledictione et amaritudine plenum est : veloces pedes eorum ad effundendum sanguinem.

Their mouth is full of cursing and bitterness : their feet are swift to shed blood.

7. Contritio et infelicitas in viis eorum, et viam pacis non cognoverunt : non est timor Dei ante oculos eorum.

Destruction and unhappiness are in their ways ; and the way of peace they have not known : there is no fear of God before their eyes.

6, 7. Miserable that they are ! their whole life is but affliction and sadness, because they did not wish to know the way to find peace, which is to have ever before one's eyes the fear of God ; but this they did not do.[1]

8. Nonne cognoscent omnes qui operantur iniquitatem : qui devorant plebem meam sicut escam panis ?

Shall not all they know that work iniquity : who devour My people as they eat bread ?

Will they never know the truth, then, all these wicked men, who oppress My people, with as little remorse as they eat their bread ?

9. Dominum non invocaverunt : illic trepidaverunt timore, ubi non erat timor.

They have not called upon the Lord : there have they trembled for fear, where no fear was.

This obstinacy of theirs arises from their unwillingness to call upon the Lord for help, and to pray that He would give them His holy fear. They do fear, indeed ; but they fear

These three verses, 5, 6, and 7, are not found in the Hebrew nor in the Greek : they are, however, cited as they here stand by S. Paul (*Rom.* iii. 10, 18 ; see also *Ps.* v. 2, cxxxix. 4, ix. 29 ; *Prov.* i. 16 ; *Isa.* lix. 7, 8 ; *Ps.* xxxv. 1). "*Contritio et infelicitas in viis eorum.*" Bellarmine and Menochius understand these words in the active sense, so as to mean : They spread everywhere ruin and desolation, and leave no one in peace.

where there is nothing to fear : they fear the loss of some earthly good, and they fear not to lose divine grace, which brings with it every good.

10. Quoniam Dominus in generatione justa est, consilium inopis confudistis : quoniam Dominus spes ejus est.

For the Lord is in the just generation : ye have confounded the counsel of the poor man, but the Lord is his hope.

For the Lord does not forsake the just. Alas for you, who have ridiculed the poor, because they had placed their hope in God !

11. Quis dabit ex Sion salutare Israel ? cum averterit Dominus captivitatem plebis suæ, exultabit Jacob, et lætabitur Israel.

Who shall give the salvation of Israel out of Sion ? when the Lord shall have turned away the captivity of His people, Jacob shall rejoice, and Israel shall be glad.

But say the wicked : Who will come from Sion to give salvation to Israel ? Know, then, that when the Lord shall deliver His people from bondage, then shall Jacob exult with joy, and Israel shall be glad.

PSALM XIV.

In this Psalm is described the character of a worthy minister of the Tabernacle, and at the same time that of a predestined soul, whose lot will be to dwell in heaven, his true country, for all eternity.

A Psalm for David.

1. Domine quis habitabit in tabernaculo tuo: aut quis requiescet in monte sancto tuo?

Lord, who shall dwell in Thy tabernacle ? or who shall rest on Thy holy hill ?

Who, O Lord, shall be worthy to dwell in Thy house, and to have his abode in peace upon Thy holy mountain of heaven ?

2. Qui ingreditur sine macula: et operatur justitiam :

He that walketh without blemish: and worketh justice :

He who enters without stain of sin, and acts as a just man.

3. Qui loquitur veritatem in corde suo: qui non egit dolum in lingua sua :

He that speaketh truth in his heart: who hath not used deceit in his tongue :

He who in his heart adheres to the truth, and who does not employ his tongue to deceive others.

3

4. Nec fecit proximo suo malum : et opprobrium non accepit adversus proximos suos.

Nor hath done evil to his neighbour : nor taken up a reproach against his neighbours.

He who does no evil to his neighbour, and gives no ear to to the calumnies uttered against him.

5. Ad nihilum deductus est in conspectu ejus malignus : timentes autem Dominum glorificat :

In his sight the wicked is despised : but he honoureth them that fear the Lord.

In whose eyes the malicious are utterly contemptible ; whilst he honours all those that fear the Lord.

6 Qui jurat proximo suo, et non decipit: qui pecuniam suam non dedit ad usuram, et munera super innocentem non accepit.

He that sweareth to his neighbour, and deceiveth not : he that hath not put out his money to usury, nor taken bribes against the innocent :

He who makes a promise to his neighbour on oath, and does not deceive him ; who lends not his money usuriously, nor receives bribes to injure the innocent.

7. Qui facit hæc: non movebitur in æternum.

He that doeth these things : shall not be moved for ever.

He who does these things shall dwell securely in heaven for ever and ever.

THE SECOND NOCTURN.

PSALM XV.

THIS Psalm is a prayer of Jesus Christ to His Father when His most holy Body was lying in the Sepulchre, as the Apostle S. Peter testifies (*Acts* ii. 25-32).[1] According to this authority, Mattei rightly observes, and F. Rotigni agrees with him, that the literal sense of this Psalm is no other than the only spiritual sense, that, namely, of Jesus Christ speaking in the Sepulchre.

The inscription of a title to David himself.[2]

1. Conserva me, Domine, quoniam speravi in te : Dixi Domino, Deus meus es tu, quoniam bonorum meorum non eges.

Preserve me, O Lord, for in Thee have I put my trust : I have said to the Lord, Thou art my God, for Thou hast no need of my goods.

[1] S. Paul also (*Acts* xiii. 35). Bellarmine says that, as all this Psalm is one continuous prayer, the four last verses cannot be understood of Jesus Christ, without applying to Him the entire Psalm.

[2] *The inscription of a title.* That is, of a pillar or monument, which is as much as to say, that this Psalm is most worthy to be engraved on an everlasting monument.

"*Bonorum meorum non eges.*" Thou hast no need of my goods. This means that God is the sovereign master of all things.

2. Sanctis, qui sunt in terra ejus : mirificavit omnes voluntates meas in eis.

To the saints who are in His land : He hath made wonderful all my desires in them.

According to commentators, Jesus Christ is here speaking, and says : God, My Father, wills that My will should tend in a marvellous way to benefit the saints who live on earth.

3. Multiplicatæ sunt infirmitates eorum : postea acceleraverunt.

Their infirmities were multiplied afterwards they made haste.

Our Lord still continues to speak. Their ancient spiritual infirmities, that is, their sins, have been many, but afterwards, when through My merits they were healed, they were able to hasten to God.

4. Non congregabo conventicula eorum de sanguinibus : nec memor ero nominum eorum per labia mea.

I will not gather together their meetings for blood-offerings : nor will I make mention of their names with my lips.

I will never approve of the assemblies which they before held in the state of their infirmity, to celebrate sacrifices of blood, nor will I so much as make mention of their names.—— S. Jerome renders the Hebrew thus : *Non libabo libamina eorum de sanguine.* Their libations of blood I will not offer.

5. Dominus pars hereditatis meæ, et calicis mei : tu es qui restitues hereditatem meam mihi.

The Lord is the portion of my inheritance and of my cup : Thou art He that will restore my inheritance unto me.

God is the portion of My inheritance and of My chalice. An allusion to the custom of old for him who presided at a banquet to assign to the different guests the portion of wine for their use.——Thou art He, O My God, Who will restore to Me My inheritance.——Jesus Christ speaks these last words to His Eternal Father in reference to His Resurrection.

6. Funes ceciderunt mihi in præclaris : etenim hereditas mea præclara est mihi.

The lines are fallen unto me in goodly places : for my inheritance is goodly unto me.

Here it must be observed that in ancient times the fields were measured with cords, as well as the portion which fell to the lot of each. The sense of the verse, therefore, is as follows : The portion which has fallen to My lot is excellent (*in præclaris*) : excellent therefore is my inheritance.

7. Benedicam Dominum, qui tribuit mihi intellectum : insuper et
usque ad noctem increpuerunt me
renes mei.

I will bless the Lord, Who hath
given me understanding : moreover
my reins also have corrected me even
till night.

I will bless the Lord who has given Me the understanding to choose Himself for My inheritance all days, even unto
this night of My death : and all the affections of My heart
(*renes mei*) have excited Me to suffer for Him with patience
even death itself.

8. Providebam Dominum in conspectu meo semper: quoniam a
dextris est mihi, ne commovear.

I set the Lord always in my sight :
for He is at my right hand, that I be
not moved.

I have kept the Lord always before My eyes, being fully
assured that at My right hand He assists Me, that I be not
shaken in My desire and in the hope which I have placed in
Him.

9. Propter hoc lætatum est cor
meum, et exultavit lingua mea: insuper et caro mea requiescet in spe.

Therefore my heart hath been
glad, and my tongue hath rejoiced :
moreover my flesh also shall rest in
hope.

Wherefore, My heart hath rejoiced, and My tongue hath
praised the Lord ; for My body, separated from My soul, shall
rest in hope, that is, in hope of the resurrection and of the
glory which He hath prepared for Me.

10. Quoniam non derelinques animam meam in inferno: nec dabis
sanctum tuum videre corruptionem.

For Thou wilt not leave my soul
in hell : nor wilt Thou give Thy holy
one to see corruption.

For Thou, O Lord, wilt not allow My soul to remain
long in hell, that is, in the limbo of the fathers ; nor wilt
Thou suffer My holy body in the sepulchre to undergo corruption.

11. Notas mihi fecisti vias vitæ,
adimplebis me lætitia cum vultu tuo:
delectationes in dextera tua usque in
finem.

Thou hast made known unto me
the ways of life : Thou shalt fill me
with joy with Thy countenance ; at
Thy right hand are delights for evermore.

Right soon wilt Thou make Me to know the way of life,
that is, of My Resurrection. Thou wilt overwhelm Me with
joy at the sight of Thy face ; and at length Thou wilt give Me
with Thee to enjoy Thy own glory, by placing Me at Thy
right hand for evermore.

PSALM XVI.

A PRAYER which the just man in persecution makes to the Lord for deliverance.

The prayer of David.

1. Exaudi Domine justitiam meam: intende deprecationem meam.　Hear, O Lord, my justice : attend unto my cry.

Show favour to my innocence, O Lord, by hearkening to me ; lend a gracious ear to my prayer.

2. Auribus percipe orationem meam: non in labiis dolosis.　Give ear unto my prayer : *which proceedeth* not from deceitful lips.

Give ear to my petitions which I lay before Thee, not in words of falsehood, but of sincerity.

3. De vultu tuo judicium meum prodeat ; oculi tui videant æquitates.　Let my judgment come forth from Thy countenance : let Thine eyes behold the things that are just.

I beseech Thee, O Lord, that the judgment of my cause may proceed from Thy mouth, and from no other. Have respect to justice, and according to justice judge me.

4. Probasti cor meum, et visitasti nocte : igne me examinasti, et non est inventa in me iniquitas.　Thou hast proved my heart, and visited it by night : Thou hast tried me by fire ; and iniquity hath not been found in me.[1]

Thou hast proved my heart, by visiting me at night, that is, in the dark time of my desolation. Thou hast examined and put me to the proof in the penetrating fire of tribulation, and hast not found iniquity in me.

5. Ut non loquatur os meum opera hominum : propter verba labiorum tuorum ego custodivi vias duras.　That my mouth may not speak the works of men : for the sake of the words of Thy lips, I have kept hard ways.

In restraining my tongue from speaking ill of those who persecute me, and in so obeying Thy command to keep silence, I have had to walk in hard and very toilsome ways, and have had much to suffer.

6. Perfice gressus meos in semitis tuis : ut non moveantur vestigia mea.　Perfect Thou my goings in Thy paths ; that my footsteps be not moved.

Do Thou, O Lord, make perfect, that is, do Thou continue to direct my steps in Thy ways, by which Thou wouldst

[1] See *Ps.* lxv. 9, 10.

have me journey, that my footsteps be not moved, nor turn
aside from the right path.

7. Ego clamavi,quoniam exaudisti me Deus : inclina aurem tuam mihi, et exaudi verba mea.

I have cried *unto Thee*, for Thou, O God, hast heard me : O incline Thine ear unto me, and hear my words.

I have cried out to Thee, O my God, and Thou hast
heard me : cease not still, O Lord, to incline Thy ear towards
me, by graciously hearkening to all the prayers that I make
to Thee.

8. Mirifica misericordias tuas : qui salvos facis sperantes in te.

Show forth Thy wonderful mercies: Thou who savest them that trust in Thee.

Show forth Thy wondrous mercies towards me, Thou who
savest all that put their trust in Thee.

9. A resistentibus dexteræ tuæ : custodi me ut pupillam oculi.

From them that resist Thy right hand : keep me as the apple of Thine eye.

Guard me as the apple of Thine eye, *i.e.*, with great care—
from those that resist Thy right hand, which is raised to defend
me.

10. Sub umbra alarum tuarum protege me : a facie impiorum qui me afflixerunt.

Protect me under the shadow of Thy wings: from the face of the wicked who have afflicted me.[1]

Protect me, by keeping me beneath the shadow of Thy
wings ; and hide me from the face (*i.e.*, from the eyes) of
the wicked, who seek to oppress me.

11. Inimici mei animam meam circumdederunt, adipem suum concluserunt : os eorum locutum est superbiam.

Mine enemies have surrounded my soul : they have shut up their fat ; their mouth hath spoken proudly.

My enemies have surrounded me to take away my
life.——" *Adipem suum concluserunt.*" S. Jerome, following
the Hebrew text, translates : *Adipe suo concluserunt—viscera*
being understood : With their fat they have closed up their
bowels.——The meaning, then, of the passage is : that as fat
in the human body closes the bowels, so the wicked, filled with
pride, through the abundance of their riches, keep their bowels

---

[1] "Under the shadow of Thy wings." The Psalmist often employs this
metaphor which so well depicts the tenderness and goodness of the Lord
towards His faithful servants. Our Saviour Himself explains this touching
signification in those words addressed to Jerusalem : "How often would I
have gathered together thy children, as the hen doth gather her chickens
under her wings" (*Matt.* xxiii. 39).

of compassion closed against others. And their mouth knows not how to speak, except with pride.

12. Projicientes me nunc circum- dederunt me : oculos suos statuerunt declinare in terram.	They have cast me forth, and now they have surrounded me : they have set their eyes bowing down to the earth.

Having thrown me to the ground, my enemies now come about me again to repeat their outrages. Miserable men ! they are determined not to lift up their eyes from the earth, to which they keep their hearts attached.

13. Susceperunt me sicut leo para- tus ad prædam : et sicut catulus leonis habitans in abditis.	They have taken me, as a lion pre- pared for the prey : and as a young lion dwelling in secret places.

"*In abditis:*" hiding in secret places to devour the passer by.——F. Rotigni remarks that this verse applies better to Jesus Christ than to David, who was never taken by his enemies.

14. Exurge Domine, præveni eum, et supplanta eum : eripe animam meam ab impio, frameam tuam ab inimicis manus tuæ.	Arise, O Lord, prevent him, and cast him down : deliver my soul from the wicked one : Thy sword from the enemies of Thy hand.

"*Eripe animam meam.*" And thus deliver my life.—— "*Frameam tuam ab inimicis manus tuæ.*" Take away Thy sword, that is to say, the power to harm which comes from Thee, from the enemies of Thy hand, that is, from those who abuse the gifts of Thy hand.

15. Domine a paucis de terra divide eos in vita eorum : de absconditis tuis adimpletus est venter eorum.	O Lord, divide them from the few of the earth n their life : their belly is filled from thy hidden *stores.*[1]

Some, as Bellarmine, Gordona, and Lallement, explain the first clause of this verse thus : Separate, O Lord, the multitude of the ungodly from the little number of Thy servants who live upon earth.——Others, as Bossuet, Tirinus, and Mattei, expound it as follows : Separate, that is, detach, O Lord, the ungodly, during their life from that little portion

[1] *Divide them from the few, etc.* That is, cut them off from *the earth*, and the *few* trifling things thereof, of which they are so proud, or *divide them from the few;* that is, from Thy elect, who are but *few;* that they may no longer have it in their power to oppress them. It is not meant by way of a curse or imprecation : but, as many other passages in the Psalms, by way of a prophecy of what should come upon them, in punishment of their wicked- ness.—*Thy hidden stores.* Thy secret treasures, out of which Thou furnishest those earthly goods, which Thou hast distributed both to the good and the bad.

of earthly goods which they possess and which renders them
so proud. This latter interpretation seems to me to be the
more probable ; for S. Jerome translates the Hebrew : *Quorum
pars in vita sua :* Whose portion is in their life ; the meaning
of which is, that in such goods they make all the happiness of
the present life consist. So that, according to S. Jerome, and
also according to the Hebrew text, the words : *"A paucis"* :
From the few—refer not to the number of the just, but
to the goods which the wicked have in this life. In any case
the passage is very obscure.——*" De absconditis tuis adimpletus
est venter eorum."* They have their belly or their heart filled
with their goods of earth which they keep hidden, carefully
laid by : but in reality these goods are all Thine.——This is
the explanation given of these most obscure words : *De absconditis tuis.*——According then to this latter interpretation, the
general sense is : O Lord, separate the wicked from (that
is, take away from them) the few earthly goods to which they
are attached.

16. Saturati sunt filiis : et dimise-
runt reliquias suas parvulis suis.

They are full of children : and they
have left to their little ones the rest
of their substance.

They see themselves surrounded by a numerous offspring,
to whom at death they leave their remaining goods. By
" Parvulis," Bossuet understands grandchildren.

17. Ego autem in justitia apparebo
conspectui tuo : satiabor cum appa-
ruerit gloria tua.

But as for me, I will appear before
Thy sight in justice : I shall be satisfied when Thy glory shall appear.

But I hope to appear just in Thy eyes, on the day when
I am judged, that I may be admitted into Heaven, where
I shall be satiated by beholding Thy glory.

PSALM XVII.

THIS is a Psalm of thanksgiving, which David offers to God
for having delivered him from the hands of his enemies, and
especially from Saul. It is very applicable to every faithful
servant of God who finds himself delivered, through the divine
assistance, from any grievous persecution or temptation of the
devil.[1]

[1] See 2 *Kings* xxii., where this Psalm is found almost in the same words.

Unto the end, for David the servant of the Lord, who spoke to the Lord the words of this canticle, in the day that the Lord delivered him from the hand of all his enemies, and from the hand of Saul.

1. Diligam te Domine fortitudo mea: Dominus firmamentum meum, et refugium meum, et liberator meus.	I will love Thee, O Lord, my strength : the Lord is my rock, my refuge, and my deliverer.
2. Deus meus adjutor meus : et sperabo in eum.	My God is my helper : and in Him will I put my trust.
3. Protector meus, et cornu [1] salutis meæ : et susceptor meus.	My protector and the horn of my salvation : and my support.
4. Laudans invocabo Dominum : et ab inimicis meis salvus ero.	I will call upon the Lord and give praise : and I shall be saved from mine enemies.

1-4. O Lord, I will love none other but Thee, Who art my strength. The Lord is my firm support, my refuge, and my deliverer from all evils. My God is my defender, in Him will I place all my hope. For He it is Who protects me, He is the strength that secures my salvation, He defends me as His own. Therefore I will do nought but praise the Lord, and call upon Him in all my wants ; and thus doing, I am certain that I shall be ever safe from all my enemies.

5. Circumdederunt me dolores mortis : et torrentes iniquitatis conturbaverunt me.	The sorrows of death surrounded me : and the torrents of iniquity troubled me.

The sorrows of death have encompassed me, for my enemies have filled me with terror, and have rushed upon me like a furious torrent.——" Conturbaverunt:" Have troubled. S. Jerome, according to the Hebrew, translates : Terruerunt : Have terrified.

6. Dolores inferni circumdederunt me : præoccupaverunt me laquei mortis.	The sorrows of hell encompassed me : and the snares of death prevented me.

I am overwhelmed with the horrors of the tomb, that is, with the sadness which he feels who knows that he must soon be carried to the grave : since the snares which my enemies

[1] Holy Scripture frequently employs the word *Cornu* as signifying strength or power, a metaphor taken from animals with horns. The Psalmist began by calling God his strength, " *Fortitudo mea*": he then explains (verses 1-3) in what way the Lord is his strength. In the Hebrew, as Bellarmine observes, the expressions are more figurative and energetic : where instead of " *Firmamentum*," " *Refugium*," " *Adjutor*," " *Protector*," and " *Susceptor*," the several words signify, *Petra*, Rock ; *Arx*, Fortress ; *Rupes*, high and craggy Rock ; *Clypeus*, Shield or Buckler ; *Propugnaculum*, Bulwark or Rampart. The following verse is a kind of conclusion to this exordium ; after that comes the description of the help received from the Almighty.

have laid to take away my life have preoccupied me, or have filled my soul with terror.

7. In tribulatione mea invocavi Dominum: et ad Deum meum clamavi:

In my affliction I called upon the Lord: and I cried unto my God:

8. Et exaudivit de templo sancto suo vocem meam: et clamor meus in conspectu ejus introivit in aures ejus.

And He heard my voice from His holy temple: and my cry came before Him into His ears.

9. Commota est, et contremuit terra: fundamenta montium conturbata sunt, et commota sunt, quoniam iratus est eis.

The earth shook and trembled: the foundations of the mountains were troubled and were moved, because He was angry with them.

God, aroused to anger against His enemies, has manifested His indignation by making the earth to tremble and the mountains to shake from their very foundations.

10. Ascendit fumus in ira ejus, et ignis a facie ejus exarsit: carbones succensi sunt ab eo.

There went up a smoke in His wrath; and a fire flamed forth from His face: coals were kindled by it.

When God is angry, there exhales from the gaping earth a terrific smoke, and from the breath of His wrath fire is kindled, with lightnings and thunders which fall like burning coals.

11. Inclinavit cœlos, et descendit: et caligo sub pedibus ejus.

He bowed the heavens, and came down: and darkness was under His feet.

He has bowed down the heavens and has descended upon the clouds.——The meaning is, that when the clouds are near to the earth it seems as though the heavens were being lowered and that God Himself were descending upon these clouds.

12. Et ascendit super Cherubim, et volavit: volavit super pennas ventorum.

And He rode upon the Cherubim, and did fly: He flew upon the wings of the winds.

Mounted upon the wings of the cherubim, He flies: He soars upon the wings of the wind.

13. Et posuit tenebras latibulum suum, in circuitu ejus tabernaculum ejus: tenebrosa aqua in nubibus aeris.

And He made darkness His covert, His pavilion round about Him: dark waters in the clouds of the air.

God has hidden Himself under the darkness which surrounds Him, and which forms His pavilion, where He fills the clouds with the dark waters.——When the clouds are more charged with water, they become darker, and then they bring the rain. It is, so to speak, herein, as in a closed pavilion, that God hides Himself.——Commentators explain this image, in a mystical sense, thus : The Lord, in this present life, does not make His presence sensible ; He hides His Majesty, as within black clouds laden with dark rain : that is to say, from the depth of this obscurity He will shower down rich graces upon His faithful souls. This is especially to be understood of souls that have arrived at the prayer of contemplation, and who, the more united they are to God, find themselves all the more involved in great obscurity.

14. Præ fulgore in conspectu ejus nubes transierunt: grando et carbones ignis. At the brightness *that was* before Him the clouds passed: hail and coals of fire.

Before the splendour of the face of the Lord the clouds passed, dissolving into hailstones, lightnings, and thunders. Such is the meaning of coals of fire.

15. Et intonuit de cœlo Dominus, et Altissimus dedit vocem suam: grando et carbones ignis. The Lord thundered from heaven, and the Highest gave His voice : hail and coals of fire.

The hail, the lightning, and the thunder are the voice of the Lord, by which He makes us know that He is the Most High.

16. Et misit sagittas suas, et dissipavit eos : fulgura multiplicavit, et conturbavit eos. And He sent forth His arrows, and scattered them : He cast many lightnings, and discomfited them.

17. Et apparuerunt fontes aquarum ; et revelata sunt fundamenta orbis terrarum. Then the springs of waters were seen : and the foundations of the world were discovered :

18. Ab increpatione tua Domine : ab inspiratione spiritus iræ tuæ. At Thy rebuke, O Lord : at the blast of the breath of Thy wrath.

17, 18. Thus also has God in His anger brought to light, at times, the fountains, that is, the hidden sources of the waters, and has laid bare the innermost bowels of the earth.

19. Misit de summo et accepit me: et assumpsit me de aquis multis. He sent from on high, and took me : and drew me out of many waters.

The Lord, from His high heaven, has sent, that is, has stretched out His hand, and has received me into His arms, and has thus withdrawn me from the many dangers and tribulations which, as a deluge of waters, were overwhelming me.

20. Eripuit me de inimicis meis fortissimis, et ab iis qui oderunt me : quoniam confortati sunt super me. He delivered me from my strongest enemies, and from them that hated me : for they were too strong for me.

"*Confortati sunt super me.*"   S. Jerome's translation is: *Robustiores me erant.*   They were stronger than me.

21. Prævenerunt me in die afflictionis meæ: et factus est Dominus protector meus.

They prevented[1] me in the day of my affliction: and the Lord became my protector.

"*Prævenerunt me.*"   That is, they sought to take me by surprise.

22. Et eduxit me in latitudinem: salvum me fecit quoniam voluit me.

He brought me forth into a large place: He saved me, because He was well pleased with me.

And He has set me at liberty: He has saved me from their hands, because He wished me for Himself.

23. Et retribuet mihi Dominus secundum justitiam meam: et secundum puritatem manuum mearum retribuet mihi:

The Lord will reward me according to my justice: and will repay me according to the cleanness of my hands:

The Lord has already rewarded, as He will in future reward me, according to the uprightness of my heart and the purity of my deeds.

24. Quia custodivi vias Domini: nec impie gessi a Deo meo.

Because I have kept the ways of the Lord: and have not done wickedly against my God.

25. Quoniam omnia judicia ejus in conspectu meo: et justitias ejus non repuli a me.

For all His judgments are in my sight: and His precepts I have not put away from me.

For all His laws are ever before my eyes, and I have never repelled from my heart His just commandments.

26. Et ero immaculatus cum eo: et observabo me ab iniquitate mea.

And I shall be spotless with Him: and shall keep myself from mine iniquity.

And I hope with His help to remain faithful to Him, and to preserve myself from all sin.

27. Et retribuet mihi Dominus secundum justitiam meam: et secundum puritatem manuum mearum in conspectu oculorum ejus.

The Lord will reward me according to my justice: and according to the cleanness of my hands before His eyes.

And the Lord in His goodness will grant me His graces, according to the uprightness of my intention, and according to my actions found free from defect, because done in His presence.

---

[1] *Prevented.* They attacked me unexpectedly.

28. Cum sancto sanctus eris : et cum viro innocente innocens eris.

With the holy Thou wilt be holy : and with the innocent man Thou wilt be innocent.

29. Et cum electo electus eris : et cum perverso perverteris.

With the elect Thou wilt be elect : and with the perverse Thou wilt deal perversely.

28, 29. With the merciful, O Lord, Thou wilt be merciful (the Hebrew word here for Holy is merciful), and upon him who does no evil to others Thou wilt inflict no evil. With the elect, that is, with the good (as the word is in the Hebrew), Thou wilt be good : and the perverse man Thou wilt treat as his perversity deserves.

30. Quoniam tu populum humilem salvum facies : et oculos superborum humiliabis.

For Thou wilt save the humble people : but wilt bring down the eyes of the proud.

For Thou wilt save the humble, and Thou wilt humble the proud.——The text has " the eyes of the proud," because it is especially by their eyes that the proud show forth their pride.

31. Quoniam tu illuminas lucernam meam Domine : Deus meus illumina tenebras meas.

For Thou, O Lord, doth light my lamp : enlighten my darkness, O my God.

Do Thou, O Lord, give light to my lamp, that is, to my mind, which without Thee would be ever deprived of light : enlighten my darkness, O my God, with the light of Thy truth.

32. Quoniam in te eripiar a tentatione : et in Deo meo transgrediar murum.

For by Thee I shall be delivered from temptation : and by the help of my God I shall leap over a wall.

Because through Thy help, I hope to be delivered from temptation : in Thy strength, O my God, and fortified by Thy grace, I shall leap over the wall, that is, I shall be able to overcome all the difficulties I may have to encounter in Thy service.

33. Deus meus impolluta via ejus : eloquia Domini igne examinata : protector est omnium sperantium in se.

As for my God, His way is undefiled, the words of the Lord are firetried : He is the protector of all that trust in Him.

The path which my God teaches me to keep is free from every defect, that is, from all stumbling-blocks : His promises are purified with fire, that is, are sincere and true. For He is in truth the protector of all that put their trust in Him.

34. Quoniam quis Deus præter Dominum? aut quis Deus præter Deum nostrum?

For who *is* God but the Lord? or who *is* God but our God.

Where indeed shall we find a God so faithful as our God ? nay, what other God is there at all besides our God ?—— In the Hebrew, instead of the second *Quis Deus*, the words are : Who is a rock, save our God ? meaning, Where shall we find a support so firm as that which we have in our God ?

35. Deus qui præcinxit me virtute: et posuit immaculatam viam meam.

God Who hath girt me with strength : and made my way to be without spot.

He it is Who has indued me with strength, and has enabled me to pass my days free from all stain of sin.

36. Qui perfecit pedes meos tamquam cervorum : et super excelsa statuens me.

Who hath made my feet like the feet of harts : and Who setteth me upon high places.

He has perfected my feet by rendering them swift like those of the hart : He has placed me on the tops of the mountains, in order to set me beyond the reach of my enemies.

37. Qui docet manus meas ad prælium : et posuisti, ut arcum æreum, brachia mea.

Who teacheth my hands to war : Thou hast made mine arms like a brazen bow.

He has instructed me how to fight, and He has so strengthened my arms that they have become as a bow of brass.

38. Et dedisti mihi protectionem salutis tuæ : et dextera tua suscepit me.

And Thou hast given me the protection of Thy salvation : and Thy right hand hath held me up.

Thou, by Thy protection, hast saved me : and Thy right hand has supported me.

39. Et disciplina tua correxit me in finem : et disciplina tua ipsa me docebit.

Thy discipline hath corrected me unto the end : and Thy discipline itself shall teach me.

Thy instruction has guided me hitherto, and will teach me to persevere in the time yet to come.

40. Dilatasti gressus meos subtus me : et non sunt infirmata vestigia mea.

Thou hast enlarged my steps under me : and my feet are not weakened.

Thou hast enlarged my steps under me, that is, the way wherein I ought to walk : and my feet have not been weakened, that is, have not failed of strength. S. Jerome's rendering is : *Non deficient tali mei.* My ankles shall not fail.

41. Persequar inimicos meos, et comprehendam illos: et non convertar donec deficiant.

I will pursue after mine enemies, and overtake them: and I will not turn again till they are consumed.

Relying upon Thy help, O Lord, I have said : I will pursue my enemies, and will get them within my power ; and I will not turn from the combat until they are defeated.

42. Confringam illos, nec poterunt stare : cadent subtus pedes meos.

I will strike them, and they shall not be able to stand : they shall fall under my feet.

I will break them to pieces, so that they cannot rise again to stand : I shall have the satisfaction of seeing them fallen at my feet.

43. Et præcinxisti me virtute ad bellum : et supplantasti insurgentes in me subtus me.

Thou hast girded me with strength unto battle : and hast subdued under me them that rose up against me.

44. Et inimicos meos dedisti mihi dorsum: et odientes me disperdidisti.

And Thou hast made mine enemies to turn their back before me : and hast destroyed them that hated me.

45. Clamaverunt, nec erat qui salvos faceret, ad Dominum: nec exaudivit eos.

They cried, but there was none to save them : even unto the Lord, but He heard them not.

They sought succour from the Lord, but no one was found to save them : for the Lord would not hear them.

46. Et comminuam eos ut pulverem ante faciem venti : ut lutum platearum delebo eos.

And I shall beat them as small as the dust before the wind : I shall bring them to nought, like the dirt in the streets.

I will scatter them as dust that is driven by the wind, and will utterly destroy them, that they may be no better than the mud in the streets, which is trodden down by every passer by.

47. Eripies me de contradictionibus populi : constitues me in caput Gentium.

Thou wilt deliver me from the contradictions of the people : Thou wilt make me head of the Gentiles.

48. Populus, quem non cognovi, servivit mihi : in auditu auris obedivit mihi.

A people, which I knew not, hath served me : at the hearing of the ear they have obeyed me.

These two last verses, and those that follow, are more properly applicable to our Divine Redeemer, Who here speaks and says : A people (that is, the Gentiles), which hitherto I have not acknowledged as Mine, has served Me faithfully, and at the sound of My voice has promptly obeyed Me.

49. Filii alieni mentiti sunt mihi: filii alieni inveterati sunt, et claudi-caverunt a semitis suis.

The children that are strangers have lied unto me: strange children have faded away, and have halted from their paths.

My natural subjects, whom I called My children, are alienated from Me, and have deceived Me by pretending to serve Me ; they have become strangers to Me, and are grown old, like dry withered leaves (according to the Hebrew), and thus have turned aside from the straight paths that once they trod.   This may be well understood of Jesus Christ speaking of the Jewish people who had proved unfaithful to Him.

50. Vivit Dominus, et benedictus Deus meus : et exaltetur Deus salutis meæ.

The Lord liveth, and blessed be my God : and let the God of my sal-vation be exalted.

May the Lord live, and may my God be for ever blessed : may that God be for ever exalted, Who is the whole hope of my salvation.

51. Deus, qui das vindictas mihi, et subdis populos sub me ; liberator meus de inimicis meis iracundis.

O God, Who avengest me, and subduest the people under me : my deliverer from mine enemies.

Mayest Thou, O my God, be for ever praised, Who avengest the injuries done to Me, and subduest the people to Me, by delivering Me from the fury of my enemies.

52. Et ab insurgentibus in me exaltabis me : a viro iniquo eripies me.

And Thou wilt lift me up above them that rise up against me : from the unjust man Thou wilt deliver me.

Thou wilt make Me superior in strength to those that shall rise up against Me, and wilt deliver Me from the wicked.

53. Propterea confitebor tibi in nationibus Domine : et nomini tuo psalmum dicam.

Therefore will I give glory to Thee, O Lord, among the nations : and I will sing a psalm to Thy name.

Therefore, I will praise Thee, O Lord, among the nations, and everywhere will I sing to Thy great name.——Here it is evidently Jesus Christ Who is speaking of His victories over the world and the devil.

54. Magnificans salutes Regis ejus, et faciens, misericordiam christo suo David, et semini ejus usque in sæcu-lum.

Giving great deliverance to His king, and showing mercy to David His anointed : and to his seed for ever.

Glorifying ever the favours granted and the mercies vouchsafed to David, His anointed king, and to all his posterity.——We should here remark that Jesus Christ is called David by Ezeckiel and other Prophets: and this is why the Psalmist concludes by thanking the Eternal Father for all the graces bestowed upon His Son, and upon all the faithful, His followers.

THE THIRD NOCTURN.

PSALM XVIII.

PRAISE of God's perfections, of His holy law, and of His admirable works. In the spiritual sense, this Psalm is applicable to Jesus Christ and to His Apostles ; and is in this way applied by S. Augustine, Bellarmine, Rotigni, Malvenda, Tirinus, and Gordona.

Unto the end. A Psalm for David.

1. Coeli enarrant gloriam Dei: et opera manuum ejus annuntiat firmamentum.

The heavens show forth the glory of God : and the firmament declareth the works of His hands.

The heavens proclaim the glory of God ; He is made manifest in the marvellous works of His hands.——By the word *Heavens*, the above mentioned Commentators understand the Apostles, by whose preaching of the Gospel, and miracles, the faith of Jesus Christ was propagated throughout the earth.

2. Dies diei eructat verbum: et nox nocti indicat scientiam.

Day unto day uttereth speech : and night unto night showeth knowledge.

Each day uttereth, that is, communicates to the following day, the praises of God : and night announces to succeeding night the science of how to praise Him : so that the heavens are unceasingly publishing the glory of the Most High.

3. Non sunt loquelæ neque sermones: quorum non audiantur voces eorum.

There are neither speeches nor languages : where their voices are not heard.

There is no nation, whatsoever its language, which does not hear these voices of the heavens ; that is, of the Apostles, according to the interpretation of S. Paul, as will be remarked in the following verse.

4. In omnem terram exivit sonus eorum : et in fines orbis terræ verba eorum.

Their sound hath gone forth into all the earth : and their words unto the ends of the world.

4

Their sound, that is, their voice, has made itself heard
over the whole earth, even unto its farthest limits.——This
accords with the command which our Lord gave to His
Apostles: "Going, therefore, teach ye all nations" (*Matt.*
xxviii. 19). And S. Paul, speaking of the preaching of the
New Law by means of the Apostles, refers to this verse of the
Psalm, saying: "Have they not heard? Yea, verily: their
sound hath gone forth into all the earth, and their words unto
the ends of the whole world" (*Rom.* x. 18).

5. In sole posuit tabernaculum suum: et ipse tamquam sponsus procedens de thalamo suo.

He hath set His tabernacle in the sun: and as a bridegroom coming out of his bride chamber.

"*In sole posuit tabernaculum suum.*" The Lord has placed
His Tabernacle in the sun, as being the principal site in the
heavens. From the east the sun goes forth resplendent with
light as a spouse from his nuptial chamber.——Mattei is not
content with this explanation, which is that of Bellarmine :
he prefers the sense of the Hebrew text, viz., *Soli posuit
tentorium in eis:* In them, *i.e.*, in the heavens, He has set a
tabernacle for the sun. But Bellarmine observes that the
Septuagint version, which the Vulgate has followed, says, as
above, that God has placed His tabernacle in the sun ; and
that we ought here to follow the Septuagint, because there is
good reason for believing that at the time that translation was
made, the Hebrew text then was more correct than it is in the
present day.

6. Exultavit ut gigas ad currendam viam: a summo cœlo egressio ejus,

He hath rejoiced as a giant to run his course : his going out is from the end of heaven,

7. Et occursus ejus usque ad summum ejus : nec est qui se abscondat a calore ejus.

And his circuit even to the end thereof: and there is no one that can hide himself from his heat.

6, 7. The sun goes forth meanwhile to make his rapid course ;
taking his departure from one end of heaven, that is, the east,
he reaches even to its other furthest bound, so that there is no
one hidden from his heat.

8. Lex Domini immaculata, convertens animas : testimonium Domini fidele, sapientiam præstans parvulis.

The law of the Lord is without spot, converting souls : the testimony of the Lord is faithful, giving wisdom to little ones.

The law of the Lord is beautiful, fair without flaw,
converting, that is, freeing the soul from evil and from error.

It is His testimony, that is to say, it testifies to us what is the Divine will : it is faithful in its promises, and gives wisdom to little children, that is, to those who are docile and submit themselves willingly to its precepts.

9. Justitiæ Domini rectæ, lætificantes corda: præceptum Domini lucidum, illuminans oculos.

The precepts of the Lord are right, rejoicing hearts : the commandment of the Lord is lightsome, enlightening the eyes.

The justices, that is, the commandments of the Lord, are right, and rejoice the hearts of the faithful : they are full of light, of divine light, and enlighten the mind. For the mind is the eye of the soul.

10. Timor Domini sanctus, permanens in sæculum sæculi : judicia Domini vera, justificata in semetipsa.

The fear of the Lord is holy, enduring for ever and ever : the judgments of the Lord are true, justified in themselves.

The fear of the Lord is holy and endures for ever : that is, the divine law which teaches holy fear is enduring, in regard to the eternal reward, which it promises to those that keep it.

11. Desiderabilia super aurum et lapidem pretiosum multum : et dulciora super mel et favum.

More to be desired are they than gold and many precious stones : and sweeter than honey and the honeycomb.

By holy souls they are held more precious than gold or costly gems, and sweeter far than honey.

12. Etenim servus tuus custodit ea : in custodiendis illis retributio multa.

For Thy servant keepeth them: and in keeping them there is great reward.

13. Delicta quis intelligit ? ab occultis meis munda me : et ab alienis parce servo tuo.

Who can understand his offences from my secret ones cleanse me, O Lord : and from those of others spare Thy servant.

But what man is there who knows all the sins, or, according to S. Jerome's translation, all the errors, into which he may perchance fall, so as to be able to avoid them ? Wherefore, O Lord, purify me from those stains of mine that are hidden from me, and spare Thy servant ; that is : Suffer me not to join the company of those who are of strange manners, that is to say, the wicked. According to S. Jerome, it is : *A superbis libera servum tuum :* From the proud deliver Thy servant.

14. Si mei non fuerint dominati, tunc immaculatus ero : et emundabor a delicto maximo.

If they shall have no dominion over me, then shall I be without spot: and I shall be cleansed from the greatest sin.

If I do not let my sins[1] get the mastery over me, then I shall be free from all fault, and pure, especially from grievous sins.

15. Et erunt ut complaceant eloquia oris mei : et meditatio cordis mei in conspectu tuo semper.

And the words of my mouth shall be such as may please : and the meditation of my heart *shall be* always in Thy sight.

Then the words of my mouth, that is, my prayers, will be pleasing to Thy heart, as well as my meditations, which I shall ever make in Thy presence.

16. Domine adjutor meus : et redemptor meus.

O Lord, my helper : and my Redeemer.

Thou, O Lord, art my helper in needs, and my deliverer from danger.

PSALM XIX.

This Psalm is a prayer of the people for the success of the arms of David : but Bellarmine and F. Rotigni are of opinion that it, as well as the two following Psalms, refer to the victories of Jesus Christ over the devil, and the persecutors of the Church.

Unto the end. A Psalm for David.

1. Exaudiat te Dominus in die tribulationis : protegat te nomen Dei Jacob.

May the Lord hear thee in the day of trouble : may the name of the God of Jacob protect thee.

2. Mittat tibi auxilium de sancto : et de Sion tueatur te.

May He send thee help from the sanctuary : and defend thee out of Sion.

" *De Sion.*" That is, from the heavenly Sion.

3. Memor sit omnis sacrificii tui : et holocaustum tuum pingue fiat.

May He be mindful of all thy sacrifices : and may thy whole burnt offerings be made fat.

" *Holocaustum tuum pingue fiat.*" May thy holocaust be acceptable to the Lord, as are the sacrifices of fat animals (*Dan.* iii. 40).

---

[1] Or, These strangers (*alieni*, v. 13) who live far from Thee and Thy law.

4. Tribuat tibi secundum cor tuum: et omne consilium tuum confirmet.

May He give unto thee according to thine own heart: and confirm all thy counsels.

May the Lord grant thee prosperous success according to the desires of thy heart, and Himself bring to good effect every work of thy hand.

5. Lætabimur in salutari tuo: et in nomine Dei nostri magnificabimur.

We will rejoice in thy salvation: and in the name of our God we shall be exalted.

We shall rejoice in thy safety and victory.——*"Magnificabimur."* Here the sense of the Hebrew is, *Vexillum attollemus:* We shall lift up our banner, that is, we shall celebrate the victory that saves and exalts us, by proclaiming the glory of our God, to Whom it is due.

6. Impleat Dominus omnes petitiones tuas : nunc cognovi quoniam salvum fecit Dominus Christum suum.

The Lord fulfil all thy petitions : now have I known that the Lord hath saved His anointed.

"Christum suum." His Christ, that is, the King Whom He hath anointed with His grace.

7. Exaudiet illum de cœlo sancto suo : in potentatibus salus dexteræ ejus.

He will hear him from His holy heaven : the salvation of His right hand *is* powerful.

" In potentatibus salus dexteræ ejus." S. Jerome's translation is : *In fortitudine salutis dexteræ ejus.* By the strength of the salvation of His right hand ; which means : God will save him with the strength of His right hand.

8. Hi in curribus, et hi in equis : nos autem in nomine Domini Dei nostri invocabimus.

Some *trust* in chariots, and some in horses : but we will call upon the name of the Lord our God.

Our enemies put their trust in the goods of earth, in chariots and in horses ; but we will invoke the name of the Lord our God, Who gives victory to those who trust in Him.

9. Ipsi obligati sunt, et ceciderunt: nos autem surreximus et erecti sumus.

They are entangled and have fallen : but we are risen, and stand upright.

"Obligati." That is, *Colligati,* bound as though by cords. They are tied down by earthly affections, as by so many fetters, and have fallen ; but we are risen and are lifted up above the earth.

10. Domine salvum fac regem, et exaudi nos in die, qua invocaverimus te.

O Lord, save the king : and hear us in the day that we shall call upon Thee.

PSALM XX.

This is a Psalm of thanksgiving on the part of the people, for the good success of the arms of David. But in the spiritual sense, according to Bellarmine, it proclaims the victory of Jesus Christ over sin and hell, through the merits of His Passion.

Unto the end. A Psalm for David.

1. Domine in virtute tua lætabitur rex : et super salutare tuum exultabit vehementer.

In Thy strength, O Lord, the king shall joy : and in Thy salvation he shall rejoice exceedingly.

"*Super salutare tuum.*" On account of the salvation he has has received from Thee.

Desiderium cordis ejus tribuisti ei : et voluntate labiorum ejus non fraudasti eum.

Thou hast given him his heart's desire : and hast not withholden from him the request of his lips.

"*Voluntate labiorum ejus non fraudasti eum.*" That is : Thou hast not failed to graciously hear his prayer.

3. Quoniam prævenisti eum in benedictionibus dulcedinis : posuisti in capite ejus coronam de lapide pretioso.

For Thou hast prevented him with blessings of sweetness : Thou hast set a crown of precious stones on his head.

"*In benedictionibus dulcedinis.*" With the sweetness of Thy benedictions.

4. Vitam petiit a te : et tribuisti ei longitudinem dierum in sæculum, et in sæculum sæculi.

He asked life of Thee : and Thou hast given him length of days for ever and ever.

"*Longitudinem dierum . . .*" That is, Eternal life.

5. Magna est gloria ejus in salutari tuo : gloriam et magnum decorem impones super eum.

His glory is great in Thy salvation: glory and great beauty shalt Thou lay upon him.

"*In salutari tuo.*" In the salvation He hath received from Thee. "*Gloriam . . .*" And Thou wilt increase his glory and majesty.

6. Quoniam dabis eum in benedictionem in sæculum sæculi : lætificabis eum in gaudio cum vultu tuo.

For Thou shalt give him to be a blessing for ever and ever : with Thy countenance Thou shalt make him exceeding glad.[1]

"*Dabis eum in benedictionem.*" According to the Hebrew: *Posuisti eum benedictiones :* Thou hast set him to be blessings.

[1] Others understand : Thou wilt cause him to be blessed in all ages.

These words can only be verified in Jesus Christ, and may be thus paraphrased: Thou, O Lord, hast constituted Him an everlasting source of blessings, whereof all shall receive through means of Him.——"*Lætificabis* . . ." Thou wilt make Him blessed for ever by giving Him to enjoy the vision of Thy beautiful Face (*Isa.* xxxiii. 17).

7. Quoniam rex sperat in Domino: et in misericordia Altissimi non commovebitur.

For the king hopeth in the Lord: and through the mercy of the Most High he shall not be moved.

The king puts his whole confidence in Thee, as his Lord; and thus he will be always secure, trusting in the mercy of the Most High.

8. Inveniatur manus tua omnibus inimicis tuis: dextera tua inveniat omnes, qui te oderunt.

Let Thy hand be felt by all Thine enemies: let Thy right hand find out all them that hate Thee.

According to the Hebrew, the first clause of this verse is: *Inveniet manus tua omnes inimicos tuos:* Thy hand shall find all Thy enemies.——"*Dextera* . . ." Thy right hand shall make its force felt by all Thy enemies, who hate Thee.

9. Pones eos ut clibanum ignis in tempore vultus tui: Dominus in ira sua conturbabit eos, et devorabit eos ignis.

Thou shalt make them as a fiery oven, in the time of Thine anger: the Lord shall trouble them in His wrath, and fire shall devour them.

"*In tempore vultus tui.*" In the time of Thy countenance. That is, when Thy angry face shall make all see Thy just wrath.

10. Fructum eorum de terra perdes: et semen eorum a filiis hominum.

Their fruit shalt Thou destroy from the earth: and their seed from among the children of men.

And here on earth Thou wilt destroy the fruits of their labour, together with their offspring, so that their posterity shall no more be found amongst men.

11. Quoniam declinaverunt in te mala: cogitaverunt consilia, quæ non potuerunt stabilire.

For they have intended evils against Thee: they have devised counsels which they have not been able to perform.

And most justly wilt Thou thus deal with them, since they have striven to work Thee evil by the many outrages they have done Thee. Poor miserable creatures! they made a multitude of schemes, and then were unable to carry them out.

12. Quoniam pones eos dorsum ; in reliquiis tuis præparabis vultum eorum.

For Thou shalt make them turn their back : Thine arrows Thou shalt make ready against their face.

This very obscure verse is variously interpreted. Theodoret and Euthymius explain it thus : "*Pones eos dorsum.*" Thou shalt make them turn their back, or put them to flight.——"*In reliquiis tuis.*" That is : In their children.—— "*Præparabis vultum.*" Thou wilt show Thy angry face.—— Bellarmine explains it thus : "*Pones eos dorsum*". Thou shalt make them as though nothing but back, or all back : thereby signifying the part of the body exposed to the scourges.—— "*In reliquiis tuis præparabis vultum eorum.*" Thou wilt cause that their sight, for their greater punishment, be fixed in considering Thy elect, who are Thy remnant reserved and saved by Thee.——Mattei, Menochius, Bossuet, and Tirinus explain this whole verse all in one sense, thus : Thou wilt discharge Thy arrows so thick in their face, that they will be forced to turn and take to flight.——Let the reader choose whichever of these interpretations he pleases : the last, however, agrees best with the Hebrew text, according to which, instead of *In reliquiis tuis*, it is, *In nervis:* signifying the string of the bow on which the arrow is placed.

13. Exaltare Domine in virtute tua : cantabimus et psallemus virtutes tuas.

Be Thou exalted, O Lord, in Thine own strength : we will sing and praise Thy power.

O Lord, show forth Thy strength, and we will praise and ing of Thy might, even the admirable works of Thy power.

LAUDS FOR SUNDAY.

PSALM XCII.

THE Psalmist exalts the power of God, manifested in the creation of heaven and earth. The Lord is represented in the first moment of creation, as though come forth from the hidden depths of His own Eternal Being, and revealing Himself by the production of creatures.

Praise *in the way* of a canticle, for David himself, on the day before the Sabbath, when the earth was founded.[1]

1. Dominus regnavit: decorem indutus est: indutus est Dominus fortitudinem et præcinxit se.

The Lord hath reigned: He is clothed with beauty: the Lord is clothed with strength, and hath girded Himself.

The Lord has established His reign over the whole universe ; He has clothed Himself with majesty ; He has girt Himself ready to govern the world, and to fill it with His benefits.

2. Etenim firmavit orbem terræ; qui non commovebitur.

For He hath established the world : which shall not be moved.

3. Parata sedes tua ex tunc : a sæculo tu es.

Thy throne is prepared of old : Thou art from everlasting.

S. Jerome translates thus : *Firmum solium tuum ex tunc : ab æterno tu es :* Thy throne is firm from then ; from eternity

[1] By this title we see that formerly this Psalm was sung on the eve of the Sabbath, the day when the work of creation was completed by the formation of man, whose dominion the earth was to be. On this same day the world was renewed and restored by the Passion of our Divine Saviour, to which mystery interpreters likewise apply this Psalm ; but the Holy Church sings it at day-break on Sunday, at Lauds, because, if Jesus Christ redeemed the world by His Passion and Death on the eve of the Sabbath, it was at the earliest dawn of Sunday that He took possession of His kingdom by His glorious Resurrection : *Dominus regnavit,* &c., a song of triumph, which placed at the beginning, characterises perfectly the entire Office.

Thou art. Thy seat, O Lord, that is, the throne of Thy kingdom, or Thy reign, was established from all eternity, since Thou hast existed eternally before all creatures.

4. Elevaverunt flumina Domine: elevaverunt flumina vocem suam.	The floods have lifted up, O Lord: the floods have lifted up their voice.

5. Elevaverunt flumina fluctus suos: a vocibus aquarum multarum.	The floods have lifted up their waves: with the noise of many waters.

4, 5. The rivers, O Lord, the rivers seem to have raised their voice to praise Thee : they have lifted up their waves, and the sound of their many waters has served them for voice to give Thee glory.

6. Mirabiles elationes maris, mirabilis in altis Dominus.	Wonderful are the surges of the sea: wonderful is the Lord on high.

Marvellous are the heavings of the waves of the sea when agitated by the winds ; and yet more marvellous is the Lord, Who, from the height of heaven, bridles the rage of the billows, and governs all things.

7. Testimonia tua credibilia facta sunt nimis : domum tuam decet sanctitudo, Domine, in longitudinem dierum.	Thy testimonies are made exceedingly credible: holiness becometh Thy house, O Lord, unto length of days.

The tokens of Thy goodness and grandeur, which are proclaimed from Thy House, that is, from the Church, are but too clear and evident : it is fitting, then, that this Thy House, O Lord, should be ever kept holy, and pure of all stain.

PSALM XCIX.

AN exhortation to the faithful to praise and thank God for having created them, and made them children of the Church, wherein He feeds them as His sheep.

A Psalm of praise.

1. Jubilate Deo omnis terra : servite Domino in lætitia.	Sing joyfully unto God, all the earth : serve ye the Lord with gladness.

2. Introite in conspectu ejus : in exultatione.	Come in before His presence : with exceeding joy.

1, 2. All ye people of the earth, let all your joy and gladness be to praise your God, and to serve Him as is meet : enter, then, joyfully to adore His presence.

3. Scitote, quoniam Dominus ipse est Deus: ipse fecit nos, et non ipsi nos.

Know ye that the Lord He is God: He hath made us, and not we ourselves.

Keep ever before the eyes of your mind that the Lord is the true God: we did not of ourselves come into the world, nor did we make ourselves—it is God that gave us our being.

4. Populus ejus, et oves pascuæ ejus: introite portas ejus in confessione, atria ejus in hymnis: confitemini illi.

We are His people and the sheep of His pasture: go ye into His gates with praise, and into His courts with hymns: and give glory unto Him.

We are His people, and the sheep whom He feeds: enter, then, my brothers, within the gates of His tabernacle, confessing yourselves unworthy to stand in His presence : sing ye His praises, and acknowledge that all that you have has been given you by Him.

5. Laudate nomen ejus: quoniam suavis est Dominus, in æternum misericordia ejus, et usque in generationem et generationem veritas ejus.

Praise ye His name: for the Lord is gracious, His mercy is everlasting, and his truth endureth from generation to generation.

Praise ye the glories of His name, for He is all sweetness: His mercy shall endure for ever : and the truth of His teaching and of His promises shall never fail.

PSALM LXII.

A PRAYER of David, when he was in the desert, pursued by his enemies: in it he thanks God for His protection, and places his confidence in the divine mercy.

A Psalm of David, when he was in the desert of Edom.

1. Deus Deus meus ad te de luce vigilo.

O God, my God, to Thee do I watch at break of day.

2. Sitivit in te anima mea: quam multipliciter tibi caro mea !

For Thee my soul hath thirsted: for Thee my flesh longeth, O how exceedingly !

1, 2. My God, at break of day I wake from sleep, and come to Thee. My soul hath so great thirst for Thee, that my body also feels the ardour.[1]

---

[1] Or else with Bellarmine : My soul desires Thee ardently as its food and its drink, its light and its joy. Even my body sighs after Thee, on account of its numberless necessities and many miseries, which Thou alone canst remedy.

3. In terra deserta, et invia, et inaquosa: sic in sancto apparui tibi, ut viderem virtutem tuam, et gloriam tuam.

In a desert and pathless land where no water is: so have I come before Thee in Thy holy place, that I might see Thy power and Thy glory.

In this desert land, where is no way nor water, I present myself to Thee, as though I were standing in Thy holy Temple, to contemplate Thy power and Thy glory.

4. Quoniam melior est misericordia tua super vitas: labia mea laudabunt te.

For Thy mercy is better than life: my lips shall praise Thee.

For Thy mercy is dearer to me than a thousand lives: O my God, my lips shall never cease to praise Thee.

5. Sic benedicam te in vita mea: et in nomine tuo levabo manus meas.

Thus will I bless Thee all my life long: and in Thy name I will lift up my hands.

Thus, throughout my life, I will do nought but bless Thee; and I will lift up my hands continually to invoke Thy name.

6. Sicut adipe et pinguedine repleatur anima mea: et labiis exultationis laudabit os meum.

Let my soul be filled as with marrow and fatness: and my mouth shall praise Thee with joyful lips.

Let my soul be filled with the fatness—the richness—of Thy grace and consolations: and my mouth shall praise Thee with the voice of gladness.

7. Si memor fui tui super stratum meum, in matutinis meditabor in te: quia fuisti adjutor meus.

If I have remembered Thee upon my bed, on Thee will I meditate in the morning: because Thou hast been my helper.

If in the time of my repose, and when in my bed, I was mindful of Thee, much more when day comes will I meditate upon Thy goodness in having thus protected me.

8. Et in velamento alarum tuarum exultabo, adhæsit anima mea post te: me suscepit dextera tua.

And I will rejoice under the covert of Thy wings: my soul hath cleaved unto Thee: Thy right hand hath upheld me.

I will rejoice at seeing that Thou coverest me with Thy wings:[1] my soul cleaves closely to Thee; and Thy hand has laid hold on me to protect me.

9. Ipsi vero in vanum quæsierunt animam meam, introibunt in inferiora terræ: tradentur in manus gladii, partes vulpium erunt.

But they have sought my soul in vain: they shall go into the lower parts of the earth: they shall be delivered into the hands of the sword: they shall be the portions of foxes.

[1] See *Ps.* xiv. 10.

My enemies have sought in vain to take my life : they shall lose their own instead, and shall be buried in the abyss of hell : they shall be given into the hand of the avenging sword of God : they shall be the prey of foxes, that is, of devils, who, as foxes, deceive men by their cunning.

10. Rex vero lætabitur in Deo, laudabuntur omnes qui jurant in eo : quia obstructum est os loquentium iniqua.	But the king shall rejoice in God, all they that swear by Him shall be praised : because the mouth of them that speak wicked things is stopped.

But the king (David is speaking of himself) shall rejoice in his God ; and all who, after his example, adore the Lord, shall be praised : whereas, on the other hand, the mouths of the wicked shall be stopped.——"*Qui jurant in eo.*" Some refer these words to David, and to the oath of fidelity which had to be made to him when he came to the throne. But Rotigni and Lallement say, with greater probability, that they refer to God, or rather to the Messias, the King of the world and true God : for it is one thing to swear allegiance to a king, and another to swear by the name of a king. And this is the sense of the words, "*Qui jurant in eo* ".

PSALM LXVI.

A PRAYER full of zeal, in which the Psalmist beseeches God that He will make Himself known and adored by all nations, by sending the Messias.

Unto the end, in hymns. A Psalm of a canticle for David.

1. Deus misereatur nostri, et benedicat nobis: illuminet vultum suum super nos, et misereatur nostri.	God be merciful unto us, and bless us : cause the light of His countenance to shine upon us, and have mercy on us.

May God have pity on us and bless us : may He illuminate us by the splendours of His presence, and pour down His mercies upon us.

2. Ut cognoscamus in terra viam tuam : in omnibus gentibus salutare tuum.	That we may know Thy way upon earth : Thy salvation in all nations.

Make us, O Lord, to know here on earth the way to please Thee : and cause that amongst all the nations the Saviour, Thy Son, be known.

3. Confiteantur tibi populi Deus: conflteantur tibi populi omnes.

Let the people praise Thee, O God: let all the people praise Thee.

May all the nations thus enlightened confess that Thou art their God. May they praise and give Thee thanks.

4. Lætentur et exultent gentes: quoniam judicas populos in æquitate, et gentes in terra dirigis.

O let the nations be glad and re-joice: for Thou dost judge the people with justice, and govern the nations upon earth.

Let the nations rejoice and exult in knowing that Thou judgest the people with equity, and directest them here on earth in the right path.

5. Confiteantur tibi populi Deus: confiteantur tibi populi omnes : terra dedit fructum suum.

Let the people praise Thee, O God: let all the people praise Thee: the earth hath yielded her fruit.

May all the people praise Thee, O my God, and thank Thee for all Thy benefits ; and especially because the earth, that is, the most pure womb of a Virgin such as Mary, by the operation of the Holy Ghost, has brought forth the Fruit so greatly desired, the Saviour of the world. Wherefore, Jesus was called by the Angel the Blessed Fruit of Mary.[1]

6. Benedicat nos Deus, Deus nos-ter, benedicat nos Deus : et metuant eum omnes fines terræ.

May God, even our own God, bless us, may God bless us : and may all the ends of the earth fear Him.

"*Deus, Deus noster . . . Deus.*" In this triple repetition of the name of God, commentators recognise a sufficiently clear indication of the Mystery of the Most Blessed Trinity.——
"*Metuant eum omnes fines terræ.*" May all men on earth, even to its furthest limits, fear and adore Him.

CANTICLE OF THE THREE CHILDREN.

A HYMN sung by the three young Israelites, Ananias, Misael, and Azarias, whilst they were in the midst of the fiery fur-nace, wherein king Nabuchodonosor had condemned them to die for having refused to adore his statue (*Dan.* iii. 57-88). This Canticle, in which all creatures are called upon to bless God, is very simple and easy to understand. We therefore

---

[1] "*Dedit.*" The past instead of the future, according to the custom of the Prophets.——"*Fructum suum.*" Its fruit by excellence beyond all comparison. See Psalm lxxxiv. 13 ; also the text of Isaias : "The bud of the Lord shall be in magnificence and glory, and the fruit of the earth shall be high (*Is.* iv. 2)

omit to explain it; because to do so, instead of being agreeable or instructive, would rather be wearisome to the reader.[1]

1. Benedicite omnia opera Domini Domino : laudate et superexaltate eum in sæcula.

O all ye works of the Lord, bless ye the Lord : praise and exalt Him above all for ever.

2. Benedicite Angeli Domini Domino : benedicite cœli Domino.

O ye Angels of the Lord, bless ye the Lord: bless the Lord, ye heavens.

3. Benedicite aquæ omnes, quæ super cœlos sunt, Domino : benedicite omnes virtutes Domini Domino.

O all ye waters that are above the heavens, bless ye the Lord : bless the Lord, all ye powers of the Lord.

4. Benedicite sol et luna Domino : benedicite stellæ cœli Domino.

O ye sun and moon, bless ye the Lord : bless the Lord, ye stars of heaven.

5. Benedicite omnis imber et ros Domino : benedicite omnes spiritus Dei Domino.

O all ye showers and dew, bless ye the Lord : bless the Lord, all ye spirits of God.

6. Benedicite ignis et æstus Domino : benedicite frigus et æstus Domino.

O ye fire and heat, bless ye the Lord : bless the Lord, ye winter and summer.

7. Benedicite rores et pruina Domino : benedicite gelu et frigus Domino.

O ye dews and hoar frost, bless ye the Lord : bless the Lord, ye frost and cold.

8. Benedicite glacies et nives Domino : benedicite noctes et dies Domino.

O ye ice and snow, bless ye the Lord : bless the Lord, ye nights and days.

9. Benedicite lux et tenebræ Domino : benedicite fulgura et nubes Domino.

O ye light and darkness, bless ye the Lord : bless the Lord, ye light-nings and clouds.

10. Benedicat terra Dominum : laudet et superexaltet eum in sæcula.

O let the earth bless the Lord : let it praise and exalt Him above all for ever.

11. Benedicite montes et colles Domino : benedicite universa germin-antia in terra Domino.

O ye mountains and hills, bless ye the Lord : bless the Lord, all things that spring forth upon the earth.

[1] This Canticle is abridged from the one found in the Prophet Daniel (Ch. iii.), of thirty-eight verses. In it the three young martyrs, under the inspira-tion of the Holy Ghost, call first (v. 1) upon all creatures in general, animate and inanimate, to bless the Lord; then (vv. 2-14) they address themselves to the several kinds of creatures in particular, beginning with the Angels in the heavens above, and descending by degrees down to earth ; then (vv. 15-17) they encourage all the servants of God, and lastly (v. 18) their own selves, to praise Him. The two concluding verses have been added by the Holy Church ; the last one being formed from the verses 52 and 56 of Daniel.

REMARKS.—Verse 3. *"Aquæ omnes quæ super cœlos sunt."* See *Ps.* cxlviii. 4.——*"Virtutes Domini."* This expression is variously understood; it seems to denote the angelic hosts charged with executing the intimations of God's will throughout the whole universe. See *Ps.* cii. 19-22.——Verse 5. *"Spiritus Dei."* The winds.——Verse 6. *"Frigus et æstus."* Some understand hereby, winter and summer.

12. Benedicite fontes Domino: benedicite maria et flumina Domino.

O ye fountains, bless ye the Lord: bless the Lord, ye seas and floods.

13. Benedicite cete, et omnia quæ moventur in aquis, Domino: benedicite omnes volucres cœli Domino.

O ye whales, and all that move in the waters, bless ye the Lord: bless the Lord, all ye fowls of the air.

14. Benedicite omnes bestiæ et pecora Domino; benedicite filii hominum Domino.

O all ye beasts and cattle, bless ye the Lord: bless the Lord, ye sons of men.

15. Benedicat Israel Dominum; laudet et superexaltet eum in sæcula.

Let Israel bless the Lord: let him praise and exalt Him above all for ever.

16. Benedicite sacerdotes Domini Domino: benedicite servi Domini Domino.

O ye priests of the Lord, bless ye the Lord: bless the Lord, ye servants of the Lord.

17. Benedicite spiritus, et animæ justorun Domino: benedicite sancti et humiles corde Domino.

O ye spirits and souls of the just, bless ye the Lord: bless the Lord, all ye that are holy and humble of heart.

18. Benedicite Anania, Azaria, Misael Domino: laudate et super-exaltate eum in sæcula.

O Ananias, Azarias, Misael, bless ye the Lord: praise and exalt Him above all for ever.

19. Benedicamus Patrem et Filium cum Sancto Spiritu: laudemus et superexaltemus eum in sæcula.

Let us bless the Father, and the Son, with the Holy Ghost: let us praise and exalt Him above all for ever.

20. Benedictus es Domine in fir-mamento cœli: et laudabilis, et glori-osus, et superexaltatus in sæcula.

Blessed art Thou, O Lord, in the firmament of heaven: worthy to be praised, and glorious, and exalted above all for ever.

PSALM CXLVIII.

This Psalm, as well as the two that follow (cxlix. and cl.), contains an exhortation to all creatures to praise the Lord, and at the same time to give Him thanks for victory over the enemy. Allegorically, Christians are called on to bless God for having made them triumph over the devil, the world, and the flesh : a victory for which they will be honoured by being constituted judges at the day of judgment.

Alleluia.

1. Laudate Dominum de cœlis: laudate eum in excelsis.

Praise ye the Lord from the hea-vens: praise Him in the heights.

2. Laudate eum omnes Angeli ejus: laudate eum omnes virtutes ejus.

Praise Him, all ye His Angels: praise ye Him, all His hosts.

1, 2. Praise the Lord of heaven, all ye spirits on high: praise Him in the heaven of heavens, where He makes His abode.

3. Laudate eum sol et luna : laudate eum omnes stellæ, et lumen.

Praise Him, O ye sun and moon :
praise Him, all ye stars and light.

4. Laudate eum cœli cœlorum : et
aquæ omnes, quæ super cœlos sunt,
laudent nomen Domini.

Praise Him, O ye heaven of heavens : and let all the waters that are
above the heavens, praise the name
of the Lord.

"*Aquæ omnes quæ super cœlos sunt.*" That is, above the atmosphere of air, which is near to the earth.——With regard to
these waters, there are various opinions. Some, as S. Bona-
venture and Catharinus, say that they are the crystalline
heaven. Others, as S. Athanasius (*Cont. Arian. Or.* 2, n. 28),
S. Basil (*In Hexam. Hom.* 3), S. Ambrose (*Hexam.* 1. 2, c. 2-3),
S. Chrysostom (*In Genes. Hom.* 4), and S. Bede (*In Hexam.*),
believe that these waters are above the firmament or starry
heavens, and they cite for this opinion *Genesis* i. 7, where we
read : "And God made a firmament, and divided the waters
that were under the firmament from those that were above
the firmament". And S. Augustine, who holds the same
view, says : "The authority of this Scripture is greater than
all the capacity of the human mind" (*De Gen. ad litt.* 1. 2, c.
5, n. 9). Several modern commentators also, cited by Tirinus,
follow this opinion. Others, in fine, as Rupert, Lorinus,
Mariana, and Valentia, with the greatest number of modern
commentators, understand by these waters the clouds that
are suspended above the earth.

5. Quia ipse dixit, et facta sunt :
ipse mandavit, et creata sunt.

For He spake, and they were
made : He commanded, and they
were created.

6. Statuit ea in æternum, et in
sæculum sæculi : præceptum posuit,
et non præteribit.

He hath established them for ever,
and for ages of ages : He hath made
a decree, and it shall not pass away

"*Ea.*" That is, the Angels and the heavenly bodies.

7. Laudate Dominum de terra :
dracones, et omnes abyssi.

Praise the Lord from the earth : ye
dragons, and all ye deeps.

Praise the Lord, you also, all ye creatures of the earth :
praise Him, ye dragons, or sea-monsters, and all ye abysses—
that is, the deep waters.

8. Ignis, grando, nix,glacies, spiritus procellarum : quæ faciunt verbum
ejus :

Fire, and hail ; snow, and ice :
and stormy winds, which fulfil His
word :

9. Montes, et omnes colles : ligna
fructifera, et omnes cedri :

Mountains, and all hills : fruitful
trees, and all cedars :

5

10. Bestiæ et universa pecora : serpentes, et volucres pennatæ :

Beasts, and all cattle : creeping things, and feathered fowls :

"*Bestiæ et pecora.*" That is, wild and domestic animals.——
"*Serpentes.*" Living creatures that crawl upon the earth.——
"*Volucres pennatæ.*" Birds that fly through the air.

11. Reges terræ, et omnes populi : principes et omnes judices terræ :

Kings of the earth, and all people : princes and all judges of the earth :

12. Juvenes, et virgines : senes cum junioribus laudent nomen Domini : quia exaltatum est nomen ejus solius.

Young men and maidens, old men and children, let them praise the name of the Lord : for His name alone is exalted.

"*Exaltatum . . .*" He alone is the Most High : to Him alone all glory belongs.

13. Confessio ejus super cœlum et terram : et exaltavit cornu populi sui.

His praise is above heaven and earth : and He hath exalted the horn of His people.

Let, then, the praises of the Lord resound through heaven and earth, since He has willed to exalt, by His power, His faithful people : in giving them Jesus Christ, Who has made His servants victorious over the devils.

14. Hymnus omnibus sanctis ejus : filiis Israel, populo appropinquanti sibi. Alleluia.

A song of praise to all His saints : to the children of Israel, a people drawing nigh unto Him. Alleluia.

Let praise be given at the same time to all His Saints, and to all the true children of Israel, who form the people that, by their faith and virtue, are brought nigh to Him.

PSALM CXLIX.

Alleluia.

1. Cantate Domino canticum novum : laus ejus in ecclesia Sanctorum.

Sing unto the Lord a new song : let His praise be in the Church of the Saints.

Sing to the Lord a new canticle for all the new benefits He has bestowed upon us, and especially for having given us Jesus Christ for our Redeemer : it is just that in the Church of the Saints, that is, of Christians, should ever resound the praises of the Lord.

2. Lætetur Israel in eo, qui fecit eum : et filii Sion exultent in rege suo.

Let Israel rejoice in Him that made him : and let the children of Sion be joyful in their king.

Let Israel rejoice in the God Who has created him; and let the children of the heavenly Sion, that is, the Holy Church exult in their God, Who reigns in them by His grace.

3. Laudent nomen ejus in choro : in tympano et psalterio psallant ei :

Let them praise His name in the choir : let them sing unto Him with timbrel and psaltery :

Let them praise His name, singing together in united chorus, with the sound of the timbrel and the psaltery.

4. Quia beneplacitum est Domino in populo suo : et exaltabit mansuetos in salutem.

For the Lord is well pleased with His people : and He will exalt the meek unto salvation.

For the Lord takes pleasure in His people ; and He will exalt the meek by giving them eternal salvation.

5. Exultabunt sancti in gloria : lætabuntur in cubilibus suis.

The saints shall rejoice in glory : they shall be joyful in their beds.

The saints shall exult with jubilee in the glory of heaven ; and, seated on their thrones, shall enjoy eternal gladness.

6. Exaltationes Dei in gutture eorum : et gladii ancipites in manibus eorum :

The high praises of God shall be in their mouth : and two-edged swords in their hands :

7. Ad faciendam vindictam in nationibus : increpationes in populis ;

To execute vengeance upon the nations : and chastisements among the people ;

Wherewith to execute a just vengeance upon the nations who had persecuted them; by reproaching them with their iniquities.

8. Ad alligandos reges eorum in compedibus : et nobiles eorum in manicis ferreis.

To bind their kings with fetters and their nobles with chains of iron·

They shall bind with fetters the tyrant kings, and with manacles of iron the nobles of these people that persecuted them.

9. Ut faciant in eis judicium conscriptum : gloria hæc est omnibus sanctis ejus. Alleluia.

To execute upon them the judgment that is written : this glory have all His saints. Alleluia.

And so shall they execute against these persecutors the judgment spoken of in Holy Scripture. "They shall judge nations, and rule over people." (*Wisdom* iii. 8.)—— —And this glory God reserves for all His Saints.

PSALM CL.

Alleluia.

1. Laudate Dominum in sanctis ejus: laudate eum in firmamento virtutis ejus.

Praise the Lord in His holy places: praise Him in the firmament of His power.

"*In sanctis ejus.*" According to the Hebrew : *In sanctuario ejus.* In His sanctuary, which is principally heaven.——"*In firmamento virtutis ejus.*" S. Jerome translates : *In fortitudine potentiæ ejus.* In the strength of His power.——The almighty power of God shines forth in a special manner in the firmament, or in the heavens, as is the meaning given of the word in the first chapter of Genesis.——The sense of the verse, then, is : Praise the Lord, Who dwells in His sanctuary of heaven : praise Him seated on the firm throne of His Omnipotence.

2. Laudate eum in virtutibus ejus : laudate eum secundum multitudinem magnitudinis ejus.

Praise Him in His mighty acts : praise Him according to the multitude of His greatness.

"*In virtutibus ejus.*" In the effects of His power, or in the marvels that He works.——"*Multitudinem.*" The immensity.

3. Laudate eum in sono tubæ : laudate eum in psalterio, et cithara.

Praise Him with the sound of the trumpet : praise Him with psaltery and harp.

4. Laudate eum in tympano, et choro : laudate eum in chordis, et organo.

Praise Him with timbrel and choir : praise Him with strings and organs.

"*Choro.*" Some think that hereby is meant some musical instrument, now unknown to us : others, a concert of voices. ——We are ignorant as to what instruments correspond to those mentioned by the Psalmist. Calmet has treated this subject in a special dissertation.

5. Laudate eum in cymbalis bene-sonantibus : laudate eum in cymbalis jubilationis : omnis spiritus laudet Dominum. Alleluia.

Praise Him upon the high-sounding cymbals : praise Him upon cymbals of joy : let every spirit praise the Lord. Alleluia.

Praise Him on cymbals well attuned, and which give forth a joyous sound ; let every spirit praise the Lord.

THE CANTICLE OF ZACHARY (Luke i. 68).

In this Canticle the Prophet Zachary praises and gives thanks to the Messias, who comes to save mankind: he then announces the office of his son, S. John the Baptist, who was to be Precursor of our Divine Redeemer.

1. Benedictus Dominus Deus Israel: quia visitavit, et fecit redemptionem plebis suæ:

Blessed be the Lord God of Israel : for He hath visited and wrought the redemption of His people :

"*Fecit redemptionem.*" Has commenced the work of man's redemption.

2. Et erexit cornu salutis nobis: in domo David pueri sui :

And hath raised up a horn of salvation to us: in the house of His servant David :

"*Cornu salutis nobis.*" For us, the strength of salvation, that is, our Saviour.

3. Sicut locutus est per os sanctorum: qui a sæculo sunt, prophetarum ejus :

As He spake by the mouth of His holy prophets : who are from the beginning :

4. Salutem ex inimicis nostris : et de manu omnium, qui oderunt nos :

Salvation from our enemies : and from the hand of all that hate us :

3, 4. Who have already foretold our salvation, which is deliverance from our enemies, &c.

5. Ad faciendam misericordiam cum patribus nostris : et memorari testamenti sui sancti.

To perform mercy to our fathers · and to remember His holy testament.

"*Testamenti sui sancti.*" That is, the promise or covenant which He made to Abraham.

6. Jusjurandum, quod juravit ad Abraham patrem nostrum : daturum se nobis :

The oath that He sware to Abraham our father; that He would grant unto us :

7. Ut sine timore, de manu inimicorum nostrorum liberati : serviamus illi.

That being delivered from the hand of our enemies : we may serve Him without fear.

8. In sanctitate et justitia coram ipso : omnibus diebus nostris.

In holiness and justice before Him : all the days of our life.

7, 8. "*In sanctitate et justitia coram ipso.*" That is to say, not merely with external worship, but also with piety and interior justice, which renders us likewise interiorly just in the sight of God.

9. Et tu puer, Propheta Altissimi vocaberis : præibis enim ante faciem Domini parare vias ejus :

And thou, child, shalt be called the Prophet of the Highest, for thou shalt go before the face of the Lord to prepare His ways :

Thou shalt be the Prophet of the Lord : for before He manifests Himself on earth, thou shalt go forth to prepare souls to follow His teaching.

10. Ad dandam scientiam salutis plebi ejus: in remissionem peccatorum eorum :

To give knowledge of salvation unto His people : for the remission of their sins :

11. Per viscera misericordiæ Dei nostri : in quibus visitavit nos, Oriens ex alto :

Through the bowels of the mercy of our God : whereby the Orient from on high hath visited us :

" *Per viscera misericordiæ.*" That is : Through the immense and tender pity coming from His inmost heart.——" *Oriens ex alto.*" That is : The Incarnate Word coming down from the height of heaven. The word *Oriens* is not the participle of the verb *Orior:* to rise ; but, according to the Hebrew and the Greek texts, is a noun substantive, which, as explained by S. Jerome, S. Cyril, and others cited by Tirinus in his comments on *Zachary* iii. 8, denotes the Eternal Word begotten by God. And the Church, amongst the greater Antiphons, which are recited on the days immediately preceding our Lord's nativity, in the fifth, salutes Him thus : *O Oriens, Splendor lucis æternæ, et Sol justitiæ! veni, et illumina sedentes in tenebris et umbra mortis:* O Orient, Splendour of Eternal light, and Sun of justice, come and enlighten those who sit in darkness and in the shadow of death.

12. Illuminare his, qui in tenebris, et in umbra mortis sedent: ad dirigendos pedes nostros in viam pacis.

To enlighten them that sit in darkness, and in the shadow of death : to direct our feet into the way of peace.

Enlighten, O Divine Saviour, all those who lie buried in darkness and in the shadow of death, that is, who are destitute of divine grace (the absence of which is the shadow of eternal death), and guide our steps into the path of everlasting peace.

PRIME, TERCE, SEXT, NONE.

PRIME.

PSALM LIII.

A PRAYER of David asking God to deliver him from the soldiers of Saul, by whom he was surrounded.[1] It may serve for all Christians who find themselves assailed by the temptations of the devil. Cardinal Bellarmine remarks that the Holy Church, in her choice of this Psalm for the Hour of Prime, admonishes us to fortify ourselves betimes by prayer against the tribulations and temptations that we may have to meet with in the course of the day.

Unto the end, in verses, understanding for David. When the men of Ziph had come, and said to Saul: Is not David hidden with us? (1 *Kings* xxiii. 19).

1. Deus in nomine tuo salvum me fac : et in virtute tua judica me.

Save me, O God, by Thy name : and judge me in Thy strength.

Save me, O my God, for the glory of Thy name, from the danger I am in ; and judge me according to my innocence, and according to Thy power, which protects the innocent.

2. Deus exaudi orationem meam : auribus precipe verba oris mei.

Hear my prayer, O God : give ear unto the words of my mouth.

3. Quoniam alieni insurrexerunt adversum me, et fortes quæsierunt animam meam : et non proposuerunt Deum ante conspectum suum.

For strangers have risen up against me, and the mighty have sought after my soul : and they have not set God before their eyes.

For my own fellow-countrymen have turned against me ; and, as foreign enemies, have armed themselves in force against me, and seek to take away my life, having no longer God before their eyes.

[1] *Ps.* lxxxv. 13.

4. Ecce enim Deus adjuvat me : et Dominus susceptor est animæ meæ.

For behold, God is my helper : and the Lord is the protector of my soul.

"*Ecce enim.*" But, lo, I know that God, &c.——"*Animæ meæ.*" My life.

5. Averte mala inimicis meis : et in veritate tua disperde illos.

Turn back evil upon mine enemies : and destroy Thou them in Thy truth.

"*Averte mala.*" According to the Hebrew : *Revertatur malum.* May evil return to.——Make to retort upon my enemies, O Lord, the evil which they have planned for me ; scatter them according to Thy promises, which are always faithful and true.

6. Voluntarie sacrificabo tibi : et confitebor nomini tuo Domine, quoniam bonum est :

I will freely sacrifice unto Thee, and will praise Thy name, O Lord : for it is good :

Then, with ready heart, will I offer Thee sacrifices, O Lord; and I will praise Thy holy name, so full of goodness to him who invokes Thee.

7. Quoniam ex omni tribulatione eripuisti me : et super inimicos meos despexit oculus meus.

For Thou hast delivered me out of all my trouble : and mine eye hath looked down upon mine enemies.

For through Thy mercy I find myself delivered by Thy hand from all anxiety : and my eyes shall be able to see, with scorn, my enemies cast down.

Here follow the Psalms next severally said at Prime on the different days of the week, except Saturday. To this second Psalm at Prime succeeds that first portion of Psalm cxviii., which invariably forms a part of this Hour.

NOTE.—*The only Psalms for Saturday's Prime are, as on feasts, Psalm liii. and the portion of Psalm cxviii.*

PSALM CXVII.

(ON SUNDAY.)

A PSALM of thanksgiving which David offers to God for having accorded him victory over his enemies, and for all His other benefits, especially for His having given to the world Jesus Christ our Saviour.

Alleluia.

1. Confitemini Domino quoniam bonus : quoniam in sæculum misericordia ejus.

O praise the Lord, for He is good : for His mercy endureth for ever.

2. Dicat nunc Israel, quoniam bonus: quoniam in sæculum misericordia ejus.

Let Israel now say, that He is good: that His mercy endureth for ever.

3. Dicat nunc domus Aaron: quoniam in sæculum misericordia ejus.

Let the house of Aaron now say: that His mercy endureth for ever.

4. Dicant nunc qui timent Dominum: quoniam in sæculum misericordia ejus.

Let them that fear the Lord now say: that His mercy endureth for ever.

1-4. The Psalmist begins by inviting all men to praise the Lord for the mercy He continually exercises towards them. He then calls specially on the Israelites, among whom were all the Apostles; he next invites all the Priests, who were to propagate the holy Faith; and lastly, all the faithful.

5. De tribulatione invocavi Dominum: et exaudivit me in latitudine Dominus.

In my trouble I called upon the Lord: and the Lord heard me, and set me at large.

"*Exaudivit me in latitudine.*" He hath heard me by succouring me abundantly.[1]

6. Dominus mihi adjutor: non timebo quid faciat mihi homo.

The Lord is my helper: I will not fear what man can do unto me.

7. Dominus mihi adjutor: et ego despiciam inimicos meos.

The Lord is my helper: and I will look down upon mine enemies.

The Lord is my protector, so that I fear not aught of all the evils that men think to do me: I will despise all the efforts and snares of my enemies.

8. Bonum est confidere in Domino: quam confidere in homine.

It is better to trust in the Lord: than to put confidence in man.

9. Bonum est sperare in Domino: quam sperare in principibus.

It is better to trust in the Lord: than to put confidence in princes.

It is far better to trust in the Lord than in men, or in the power of princes of the earth.

10. Omnes Gentes circuierunt me: et in nomine Domini quia ultus sum in eos.

All nations compassed me round about: and in the name of the Lord have I been revenged upon them.

11. Circumdantes circumdederunt me: et in nomine Domini quia ultus sum in eos.

Surrounding me, they compassed me about: and in the name of the Lord have I been revenged upon them.

[1] Another very general interpretation is: By drawing me out of distress, and placing me at ease in perfect liberty.

12. Circumdederunt me sicut apes, et exarserunt sicut ignis in spinis : et in nomine Domini quia ultus sum in eos.

They gathered about me like bees, and burned like fire among thorns : and in the name of the Lord I have been revenged upon them.

10-12. "*Ultus sum.*" I have been revenged. It must be observed that this expression is not to be understood here of vengeance properly speaking, but of a victory gained over the enemy. It applies especially to Jesus Christ triumphing over His enemies, and to all the faithful who, by His help, overcome their temptations. We may, then, take these three verses together, and explain them thus : All my enemies have closed in around me from every side, as an angry swarm of bees, or as a burning flame in a bundle of thorns ; but, thanks to the protection of the Lord, I have been avenged on them, that is, I have overcome them all.

13. Impulsus eversus sum ut cade- rem : et Dominus suscepit me.

I was sore pressed, and overthrown that I might fall : but the Lord held me up.

Thrust sore by their assaults, I was on the point of falling, but the Lord kept me up.

14. Fortitudo mea, et laus mea Dominus : et factus est mihi in salutem.

The Lord is my strength and my praise : and He is become my salvation.

The Lord is my strength and the one object of my praise, and He has become my Saviour.

15. Vox exultationis, et salutis : in tabernaculis justorum.

The voice of joy and salvation : is in the tabernacles of the just.

In the tabernacles or tents of the just no voices were heard but of gladness and victory in thanksgiving to God for having saved me, and caused me to triumph over my enemies.

16. Dextera Domini fecit virtutem: dextera Domini exaltavit me, dextera Domini fecit virtutem.

The right hand of the Lord hath done mightily ; the right hand of the Lord hath exalted me : the right hand of the Lord hath wrought strength.

The hand of the Lord hath shown forth its strength ; and in raising me up, has made all to see how great was His power.

17. Non moriar, sed vivam : et narrabo opera Domini.

I shall not die, but live : and shall declare the works of the Lord.

"*Non moriar.*" I shall not die, as my enemies had hoped.

18. Castigans castigavit me Domi- nus : et morti non tradidit me.

The Lord hath chastened and corrected me : but He hath not given me over unto death.

"*Castigans castigavit me.*" He hath chastised me, but with the tender compassion of a father.

19. Aperite mihi portas justitiæ, ingressus in eas confitebor Domino : hæc porta Domini, justi intrabunt in eam.

Open unto me the gates of justice: I will go into them, and give praise unto the Lord. This is the gate of the Lord : the just shall enter into it.

"*Aperite justitiæ.*" Open to me the gates of justice, that is, the gates of heaven; for justice is the gate of the kingdom of God, as we read in *S. Matt.* vi. 33. "Seek first the kingdom of God and His justice." And since justice is the only gate by which we can come to God, it is only the just who enter through it: "*Justi intrabunt in eam*". Such is the sense given to this passage by S. Jerome, S. John Chrysostom, and S. Augustine.——"*Ingressus in eas.*" Once entered therein, I will sing the glory of my Lord. (This is continued in the next verse.)

20. Confitebor tibi quoniam exaudisti me : et factus es mihi in salutem.

I will praise Thee, for Thou hast heard me : and art become my salvation.

I will praise Thee always, O Lord, and give Thee thanks for having heard my prayer, and for having become my Saviour.

21. Lapidem, quem reprobaverunt ædificantes : hic factus est in caput anguli.

The stone which the builders rejected : the same is become the head of the corner.

This verse is to be understood only of Jesus Christ and His Church ; and in this sense S. Peter explains it to the Jews: "This is the stone which was rejected by you, the builders, which is become the head of the corner "[1] (*Acts* iv. 11). God sent upon earth this most precious Stone, His own beloved Son ; but the Jews, who at that time formed the Church, rejected Him. This Stone, nevertheless, became the head of the corner, joining together the two walls ; to wit, the Hebrew and the Gentile nations into one Church.

22. A Domino factum est istud : et est mirabile in oculis nostris.

This is the Lord's doing : and it is wonderful in our eyes.

This great work is the Lord's: a work worthy of our admiration throughout eternity.

---

[1] We may add that our Saviour applied to Himself this and the next verse (*Matt.* xxi. 42).

23. Hæc est dies, quam fecit Dominus : exultemus, et lætemur in ea.

This is the day which the Lord
hath made : let us be glad and rejoice
in it.

This is the happy day: a day especially made by God; let
us ever be glad and rejoice therein, for the immense benefits
to-day received.[1]

24. O Domine salvum me fac, O
Domine bene prosperare : benedictus
qui venit in nomine Domini.

O Lord, save me ; O Lord, give
good success: Blessed be he that
cometh in the name of the Lord.

Save me, O Lord, and be ever gracious to me, so that I
never may cease to repeat: Blessed be He that has come in
the name of the Lord to save us.——This precisely was the
cry of the multitude when Jesus Christ made His triumphant
entry into Jerusalem : " *Hosanna Filio David ! benedictus, qui
venit in nomine Domini !*" (*Matt.* xxi. 9).

25. Benediximus vobis de domo
Domini: Deus Dominus, et illuxit
nobis.

We have blessed you out of the
house of the Lord : the Lord is God,
and He hath shone upon us.

We wish and bespeak you a thousand blessings, you who
are of the house of the Lord; for He is the true God; and
He hath manifested Himself to us by taking to Him our
human flesh.

26. Constituite diem solemnem in
condensis : usque ad cornu altaris.

Appoint a solemn day, with shady
boughs : even unto the horn of the
altar.

Celebrate, then, this solemn day, by adorning the temple,
even to the altar, with green and leafy boughs.

27. Deus meus es tu, et confitebor tibi : Deus meus es tu, et
exaltabo te.

Thou art my God, and I will praise
Thee : Thou art my God, and I will
exalt Thee.

Thou art my God, for ever will I praise Thee and proclaim
Thy glory.

28. Confitebor tibi quoniam exaudisti me : et factus es mihi in
salutem.

I will praise Thee, for Thou hast
heard me : and art become my salvation.

For ever will I thank Thee, for Thou hast heard my prayers,
and hast become my Saviour.

---

[1] The Office of Easter, in which this verse is frequently repeated, attests
that the day here spoken of is that of the Resurrection of Jesus Christ,
when, having been rejected by the Jews in His Passion, He was established
and recognised as the Corner Stone of the great edifice of the universal
Church. According to Bellarmine the following verse joins on in sense,
thus : Let us then rejoice, saying : O Domine ! &c.

29. Confitemini Domino quoniam bonus: quoniam in sæculum misericordia ejus.

O praise ye the Lord, for He is good: for His mercy endureth for ever.

Praise, then, the Lord, ye faithful, for His goodness to His servants, and for His mercy, which we hope for, for ever.

(*Here follows part of the Psalm CXVIII. See p. 91.*)

PSALM XXIII.
(ON MONDAY.)

DAVID predicts in this Psalm, according to the literal sense, the principal mysteries of the New Law: he foretells the vocation of the Gentiles; he describes the character of the predestined; he foresees the interior justice which the faithful will receive through the grace of Jesus Christ, Whose divinity he declares; in fine, he prophesies of the victories of our Saviour, and His glorious Ascension into heaven.

On the first day of the week. A Psalm for David.

1. Domini est terra, et plenitudo ejus: orbis terrarum, et universa, qui habitant in eo.

The earth is the Lord's, and the fulness thereof: the world and all they that dwell therein.

2. Quia ipse super maria fundavit eum: et super flumina præparavit eum.

For He hath founded it upon the seas: and hath prepared it upon the rivers.

For in creating it from nothing, He founded it upon the seas and on the rivers, and prepared it to be the habitation of man.

3. Quis ascendet in montem Domini? aut quis stabit in loco sancto ejus?

Who shall ascend into the mountain of the Lord? or who shall stand in His holy place?

Heaven is called a mountain, by reason of its elevation; and it is the holy place or sanctuary of God, where He has His throne.

4. Innocens manibus et mundo corde: qui non accepit in vano animam suam, nec juravit in dolo proximo suo.

He that hath clean hands and a pure heart: who hath not taken his soul in vain, nor sworn deceitfully to his neighbour.

He shall ascend thither who has not sinned in his works, and has kept his heart pure, that is, detached from creatures; "who has not received his life in vain," that is, who has not only avoided evil, but has also fulfilled what God has enjoined on him; he who loves truth, and has not sworn falsely to deceive his neighbour.

5. Hic accipiet benedictionem a Domino: et misericordiam a Deo salutari suo.

He shall receive a blessing from the Lord: and mercy from God his Saviour.

"*Misericordiam* . . ." The mercy of eternal salvation from his God, Who has saved him.

6. Hæc est generatio quærentium eum : quærentium faciem Dei Jacob.

This is the generation of them that seek Him : of them that seek the face of the God of Jacob.

This is the happy generation of those who seek God by being attentive here on earth to serve Him, and who long to go to see in heaven the God of Jacob.——According to the Hebrew text, we read : *Quærentium faciem tuam, O Jacob!* Bellarmine says that this phrase is very obscure, and hence the Septuagint interpreters supplied here the word "*God,*" and have rendered the verse as we have it in the Vulgate; for it is God alone Who makes the joy of the Saints.

7. Attollite portas principes vestras, et elevamini portæ æternales: et introibit rex gloriæ.

Lift up your gates, O ye princes, and be ye lifted up, O eternal gates: and the King of Glory shall enter in.

O Angels, Princes of the heavenly city, lift up, open the gates which have been given you to guard ; and yourselves, "O eternal gates," that is, you who have been shut from all eternity, as Rotigni explains it, be ye lifted up, be ye opened, and the King of Glory shall enter in.

8. Quis est iste rex gloriæ? Dominus fortis et potens, Dominus potens in prælio.

Who is this King of Glory? the Lord strong and mighty: the Lord mighty in battle.

"*In prælio.*" In the battle with His enemies, whom He has conquered and discomfited.

9. Attollite portas principes vestras, et elevamini portæ æternales : et introibit rex gloriæ.

Lift up your gates, O ye princes, and be ye lifted up, O eternal gates: and the King of Glory shall enter in.

10. Quis est iste rex gloriæ? Dominus virtutum ipse est rex gloriæ.

Who is this King of Glory? the Lord of Hosts, He is the King of Glory.

PSALM XXIV.

(ON TUESDAY.)

DAVID begs God's help in his afflictions: and looking on them as a just punishment for his sins, he renews his acts of repentance. We may apply this Psalm to ourselves when we are troubled and afflicted by temptations, whether from men or from evil spirits.

Unto the end.   A Psalm for David.

1. Ad te Domine levavi animam meam : Deus meus in te confido, non erubescam :

To Thee, O Lord, have I lifted up my soul. In Thee, O my God, I put my trust ; let me not be ashamed :

"*Non erubescam.*" I hope, by Thy help, that I shall not have the confusion of seeing myself conquered by my enemies.

2. Neque irrideant me inimici mei : etenim universi, qui sustinent te, non confundentur.

Neither let mine enemies laugh at me : for none that wait on Thee shall be confounded.

Suffer not that they have me in derision by gaining a victory over me.——"*Sustinent te.*" Wait on Thee for succour.

3. Confundantur omnes : iniqua agentes supervacue.

Let all them be confounded : that transgress without cause.

Let all the wicked rather be speedily put to confusion at seeing how they have worked their iniquity in vain, without the fruit they hoped for.

4. Vias tuas, Domine, demonstra mihi : et semitas tuas edoce me.

Show me Thy ways, O Lord : and teach me Thy paths.

Show me, O Lord, the ways by which Thou wouldst have me walk : teach me to keep the paths that lead to Thee.

5. Dirige me in veritate tua, et doce me : quia tu es Deus salvator meus, et te sustinui tota die.

Direct me in Thy truth, and teach me : for Thou art God my Saviour, and on Thee have I waited all the day long.

"*In veritate tua.*" In the straight way of Thy law.—— "*Te sustinui tota die.*" From Thee I continually look for succour.

6. Reminiscere miserationum tuarum Domine : et misericordiarum tuarum, quæ a sæculo sunt.

Call to remembrance, O Lord, Thy compassion : and Thy mercies which are of old.

"*Quæ a sæculo sunt.*" Which Thou showest to the world for so many ages.

7. Delicta juventutis meæ : et ignorantias meas ne memineris :

Remember Thou not the sins of my youth, and mine ignorances :

8. Secundum misericordiam tuam memento mei tu : propter bonitatem tuam Domine.

According to Thy mercy remember Thou me : for Thy goodness' sake, O Lord.

9. Dulcis et rectus Dominus : propter hoc legem dabit delinquentibus in via.

The Lord is sweet and righteous : therefore He will give a law to sinners in the way.

"*Legem . . .*" To those who have sinned in this life He will give the true rule to follow, for returning to the right way.

10. Diriget mansuetos in judicio: docebit mites vias suas.

The meek will He guide in judgment: the gentle He will teach His ways.

He will guide the gentle by the straight paths of His law, which in the Scriptures is called Judgment, "*Judicium*"; and He will teach the docile of heart to walk in His ways.

11. Universæ viæ Domini, misericordia et veritas: requirentibus testamentum ejus, et testimonia ejus.

All the ways of the Lord are mercy and truth: unto such as seek after His covenant and His testimonies.

The whole conduct of the Lord is to show mercy and faithfulness to His promises towards His servants, who keep before their eyes the covenant made between God and those who are faithful to observe His precepts.

12. Propter nomen tuum Domine propitiaberis peccato meo : multum est enim.

For Thy name's sake, O Lord, Thou wilt pardon my sin : for it is great.

Thou wilt show mercy, O Lord, with regard to my sins, and their pardon will cause Thy glory to shine forth all the more brightly, because they have been grievous and many.

13. Quis est homo qui timet Dominum? legem statuit ei in via, quam elegit.

Who is the man that feareth the Lord? He hath appointed him a law in the way he hath chosen.

Who is the man that truly fears God ? It is he to whom the Lord has taught the way, by which he has thenceforth chosen to walk.

14. Anima ejus in bonis demorabitur: et semen ejus hereditabit terram.

His soul shall dwell in good things: and His seed shall inherit the land.

His soul shall dwell in good things, that is, it shall continually be enriched with goods spiritual and temporal ; and his children, following his good example, shall be heirs of the Promised Land, that is, of heaven.

15. Firmamentum est Dominus timentibus eum : et testamentum ipsius ut manifestetur illis.

The Lord is a support to them that fear Him : and His covenant that it may be manifest unto them.

The Lord is a firm support to those who fear Him, to those to whom He manifests the covenant He has made to protect His faithful servants.

16. Oculi mei semper ad Dominum: quoniam ipse evellet de laqueo pedes meos.

Mine eyes are ever toward the Lord : for He shall pluck my feet out of the snare.

I will keep, then, my eyes ever fixed upon the Lord, for He it is Who shall deliver me from the snares which my enemies lay for me.

17. Respice in me, et miserere mei : quia unicus et pauper sum ego.

Look Thou upon me, and have mercy on me : for I am alone and poor.

Turn Thine eyes towards me, O my God, and have pity upon me, for I am alone and poor, and my enemies are many and powerful.

18. Tribulationes cordis mei multiplicatæ sunt : de necessitatibus meis erue me.

The troubles of my heart are multiplied : deliver me out of my necessities.

"*De necessitatibus.*" According to the Hebrew : *De pressuris.* Distresses.

19. Vide humilitatem meam, et laborem meum : et dimitte universa delicta mea.

Look upon my lowliness and my labour : and forgive me all my sins.

Behold my weakness and the troubles I endure, whereof my sins, I know, are the cause; therefore, grant me for them all a full pardon.

20. Respice inimicos meos, quoniam multiplicati sunt : et odio iniquo oderunt me.

Consider mine enemies, for they are multiplied : and have hated me with an unjust hatred.

21. Custodi animam meam, et erue me : non erubescam, quoniam speravi in te.

Keep Thou my soul, and deliver me : I shall not be ashamed, for I have hoped in Thee.

"*Non erubescam . . . te.*" Verily I shall not be confounded, after having placed all my confidence in Thee.

22. Innocentes et recti adhæserunt mihi : quia sustinui te.

The innocent and the upright have cleaved unto me : because I have waited on Thee.

The just and the upright of heart have united to defend me, seeing that I have put my trust in Thee.

23. Libera Deus Israel : ex omnibus tribulationibus suis.

Deliver Israel, O God : out of all his troubles.

PSALM XXV.

(ON WEDNESDAY.)

AN instruction for all those who are persecuted wrongfully, showing the virtues they should practise in such circumstances. Especially, too, may we see in this Psalm the dis-

6

positions the faithful should have in approaching the **Altar**, whether to communicate or to offer the Holy Sacrifice.

Unto the end. A Psalm for David.

1. Judica me Domine, quoniam ego in innocentia mea ingressus sum : et in Domino sperans non infirmabor.

Judge me, O Lord, for I have walked in mine innocence : I have put my trust in the Lord, and I shall not be weakened.

Be Thou, O Lord, my judge against my persecutors, since I present myself before Thee with an unblemished conscience, which in nothing reproaches me : I hope that Thou wilt not permit that I be declared guilty.

2. Proba me, Domine, et tenta me : ure renes meos et cor meum.

Prove me, O Lord, and try me : try with fire my reins and my heart.

Prove me, and try my fidelity : put to the test, in the fire of tribulations, my heart and all its most secret folds.

3. Quoniam misericordia tua ante oculos meos est : et complacui in veritate tua.

For Thy mercy is before mine eyes : and I am well pleased with Thy truth.

Thy faithfulness to Thy promises makes me abide in peace, as I think that I have lived according to Thy truth.

4. Non sedi cum concilio vanitatis : et cum iniqua gerentibus non introibo.

I have not sat with the council of vanity : neither will I go in with them that do unjustly.

I have avoided the company of vain and lying men, and I will ever guard against entering the society of the wicked.

5. Odivi ecclesiam malignantium : et cum impiis non sedebo.

I have hated the assembly of the wicked : and with the ungodly I will not sit.

"*Malignantium.*" Malicious persons, who turn even good actions to evil.

6. Lavabo inter innocentes manus meas : et circumdabo altare tuum Domine.

I will wash my hands among the innocent : and I will compass Thine altar, O Lord.

7. Ut audiam vocem laudis : et enarrem universa mirabilia tua.

That I may hear the voice of praise : and tell of all thy wondrous works.

6, 7. I will seek to wash my hands, that is, to purify myself, together with the just ; and so united with them, I also will join in surrounding Thy altar : that there I may hear the voices of those that praise Thee ; and that I may publish all the marvels which Thou hast wrought.

8. Domine dilexi decorem domus tuæ: et locum habitationis gloriæ tuæ.

O Lord, I have loved the beauty of Thy house: and the place where Thy glory dwelleth.

"*Locum* ..." Wherein Thou dost make Thy abode, and dost cause Thy glory to shine forth.

9. Ne perdas cum impiis, Deus, animam meam: et cum viris sanguinum vitam meam:

Take not away my soul, O God, with the wicked: nor my life with men of blood:

Condemn me not to death, O Lord, with impious men and murderers.

10. In quorum manibus iniquitates sunt: dextera eorum repleta est muneribus.

In whose hands are iniquities: their right hand is filled with gifts.

To have their hands full of gifts, or bribes, they commit acts of injustice against their neighbour.

11. Ego autem in innocentia mea ingressus sum: redime me, et misere mei.

But as for me, I have walked in my innocence: redeem me, and be merciful unto me.

I, on the contrary, have entered upon judgment with a clear conscience: therefore, have pity on me, and deliver me from my persecutors.

12. Pes meus stetit in directo: in ecclesiis benedicam te Domine.

My foot hath stood in the right way: in the churches I will bless Thee, O Lord.

My foot hath stood firm in the right way of Thy precepts: wherefore, I hope to bless Thee always, O my Lord, in the company of the just.

PSALM XXII.

(ON THURSDAY.)

IN this Psalm God is principally considered as a good Shepherd, Whose whole care is to provide His servants with all the helps and graces that are necessary for their eternal salvation, especially with the Holy Communion of His Body and Blood, clearly indicated in verses 1, 2, 6, and 7.

A Psalm for David.

1. Dominus regit me, et nihil mihi deerit; in loco pascuæ ibi me collocavit.

The Lord ruleth me; and I shall want nothing: He hath set me in a place of pasture.

2. Super aquam refectionis edu-
cavit me : animam meam convertit.

He hath brought me to the waters
of refreshment : He hath converted
my soul.

He has nourished me near waters that flow in the very place
of my pasturage : and when my soul, like a silly, wayward
sheep, went away from Him, He brought it back again to His
Fold.

3. Deduxit me super semitas justitiæ ; propter nomen suum.

He hath led me on the paths of
justice : for His own name's sake.

He hath led me back to the paths of justice, from which I
had strayed.

4. Nam etsi ambulavero in medio
umbræ mortis, non timebo mala :
quoniam tu mecum es.

For though I should walk in the
midst of the shadow of death, I will
fear no evils : for Thou art with me.

"*In medio umbræ mortis.*" In the midst of a thousand
dangers, which seem to me to be the figure of death.

5. Virga tua, et baculus tuus : ipsa
me consolata sunt.

Thy rod and Thy staff : they have
comforted me.

The shepherd's crook, and the staff which Thou hast in
hand, console me; for with the crook Thou correctest me
when I go out of the path, and with the staff Thou dost drive
away the wolves that seek to devour me.——"*Virga.*" Some
commentators by this understand the Blessed Virgin Mary,
who was called "*Virga de radice Jesse*" (*Is.* xi. 1). From
whom came forth the Flower—"Of whom was born Jesus"
(*Matt.* i. 16).[1]

6. Parasti in conspectu meo mensam : adversus eos, qui tribulant me.

Thou hast prepared a table before
me : against them that afflict me.

Thou hast prepared before me a table, where I shall take a
food that will make me strong against my enemies.——By
this table we may well understand the altar, where we receive
as food the Body of Jesus Christ, which renders us strong
against all the assaults of hell.

7. Impinguasti in oleo caput
meum : et calix meus inebrians quam
præclarus est !

Thou hast anointed my head with
oil : and my cup which inebriateth
me, how goodly it is !

[1] In the same mystical sense, by "Baculus" is understood the Cross,
which was the instrument of our salvation.——Here ends the allegory of the
Shepherd and the Sheep.

"*In oleo.*" With the unction of Thy grace.[1]——"*Calix meus . .*. *præclarus est !*" The chalice which Thou offerest me contains a wine that holily inebriates him who drinks it, making him forget the world to remember Thee alone and Thy love. Oh, how noble and precious is it !

8. Et misericordia tua subsequetur me : omnibus diebus vitæ meæ.

And Thy mercy will follow me : all the days of my life.

9. Et ut inhabitem in domo Domini : in longitudinem dierum.

And that I may dwell in the house of the Lord : unto length of days.

And Thy mercy will, I hope, be favourable to me all the days of my life, and will bring me at length to dwell in the house of the Lord, there to live for all eternity.

PSALM XXI.

(ON FRIDAY.)

THIS Psalm is to be understood literally of Jesus Christ, speaking at the time of His Passion and Death ; and is also to be understood of His glorious Resurrection. Bellarmine says that it would be an act of temerity to seek to turn it to any other sense. This Psalm, then, is an express prophecy of what our Saviour suffered when dying upon the Cross.

Unto the end, for the morning protection. A Psalm of David.

1. Deus Deus meus respice in me : quare me dereliquisti? longe a salute mea verba delictorum meorum.

O God my God, look upon me ; why hast Thou forsaken me? far from my salvation are the words of my sins.

My God, My God, look upon the affliction that I am in : why hast Thou abandoned Me ? I see well that My sins,[2] that is, the sins of My people, which I have taken upon Myself to expiate, as though they were my own, keep Me far from My salvation; that is, make it impossible for Me not to

---

[1] Amongst the ancients it was the custom, as Bellarmine remarks, to provide at feasts precious unguents for the guests, as an attention especially grateful ; hence our Lord, when reproaching Simon for his discourtesy, said, "My head with oil thou didst not anoint" (*Luke* vii. 46).——It would seem that in these two verses, 6 and 7, the Psalmist employs another allegory, and speaks to God as to a generous host who treats him magnificently.

[2] "*Verba delictorum meorum.*" According to Bellarmine and Menochius, a Hebraism for *Delicta mea.* That is, the sins of the world, which I have taken upon Myself, which as words cry out against Me, and are the cause of all My sufferings.

die.——We make here the following observation on the abandonment of Jesus Christ. It is certain that the Divine Word did not abandon the Sacred Humanity of Jesus Christ when He was dying upon the Cross. Why, then, did our Saviour say: "My God, My God, why hast Thou forsaken Me?" (*Matt.* xxvii. 46). S. Leo replies as follows (*Serm.* 16 *de Pass*): *Vox ista doctrina est, non querela* ; That voice utters teaching, not complaint. Jesus Christ did not thus speak to the Eternal Father to be delivered from death, nor was He speaking of His own abandonment, but of the abandonment of grace, of which all men would have remained deprived if He had not died for our salvation. He was praying, then, in our name, that we might be delivered from eternal death; in our name, also, He prayed for His Resurrection, to make us also have a share therein. So that He then put Himself in our place, and thus prayed not to be abandoned ; whilst, at the same time, He offered up His own death in order to save us from the abandonment we had deserved; and He did not die Himself until He had first made our salvation secure. This is why, towards the end of the Psalm, He gives thanks to His Father, and sings the fruits of His victory.

2. Deus meus clamabo per diem, et non exaudies: et nocte, et non ad insipientiam mihi.

O my God, I shall cry by day, and Thou wilt not hear: and by night, and it shall not be reputed as folly in me.

" *Et non . . . mihi.*" Ah! attribute not my prayers to imprudence and indiscretion.

3. Tu autem in sancto habitas : laus Israel.

But Thou dwellest in the holy place : the praise of Israel.

" *Laus Israel.*" Thou art the praise of Israel, for the many great graces Thou hast vouchsafed to him ; but now it seems, for Me, that Thou wilt not listen to Me.

4. In te speraverunt patres nostri : speraverunt, et liberasti eos.

In Thee have our fathers hoped : they hoped, and Thou didst deliver them.

Our Lord is here speaking of the deliverance which the Holy Fathers under the old law were to obtain by His death.

5. Ad te clamaverunt, et salvi facti sunt : in te speraverunt, et non sunt confusi.

They cried unto Thee, and they were saved : they trusted in Thee, and they were not confounded.

6. Ego autem sum vermis, et non homo: opprobrium hominum, et abjectio plebis.

But I am a worm, and no man: the reproach of men, and the outcast of the people.

Behold! I am no longer looked upon as a man, but as a worm of earth.

7. Omnes videntes me deriserunt me: locuti sunt labiis, et moverunt caput.

All they that saw me laughed me to scorn: they spoke with their lips, and shook their head.

All seeing Me reduced to this miserable plight have set themselves to mock Me : they speak against Me, and insult Me by wagging their heads.——An allusion to the words : "And they that passed by blasphemed Him, wagging their heads " (*Matt.* xxvii. 39).

8. Speravit in Domino, eripiat eum: salvum faciat eum, quoniam vult eum.

He hoped in the Lord, let Him deliver him: let Him save him, seeing He delighteth in him.

They have said : He put His hope in the Lord; let, then, the Lord deliver Him, since He has a will for Him and protects Him. These words correspond to those of *S. Matthew* xxvii. 43 : " He trusted in God ; let Him now deliver Him, if He will have Him ".

9. Quoniam tu es, qui extraxisti me de ventre : spes mea ab uberibus matris meæ. In te projectus sum ex utero.

For Thou art He that drew me out of the womb : my hope from my mother's breasts ; I was cast upon Thee from the womb.

10. De ventre matris meæ Deus meus es tu : ne discesseris a me.

From my mother's womb Thou art my God : depart not from me.

9, 10. "*In te projectus sum . . . ne discesseris a me.*" It was Thou, O Lord, Who hast drawn Me out of the womb of My mother, and from her breasts, and since then I have placed in Thee all My hopes; from the time that I came forth from My mother's womb I have always acknowledged Thee for My God ; in mercy, then, do not abandon Me.

11. Quoniam tribulatio proxima est : quoniam non est qui adjuvet.

For trouble is very near : for there is none to help *me*.

Bellarmine says that Jesus Christ is speaking here of His approaching death. This appears from the verses soon to follow, in which He speaks of His crucifixion and of the division of His garments.

12. Circumdederunt me vituli multi : tauri pingues obsederunt me.

Many calves have surrounded me : fat bulls have beset me around.

By the calves (those, viz., that were already growing their horns), and by the bulls, are meant the chief priests and Pharisees, who, by their sharp words and mocking jeers, as though with thrusts of horns, insulted Jesus Christ, saying : "He saved others: Himself He cannot save; if He be the King of Israel, let Him now come down from the cross, and we will believe Him " (*Matt.* xxvii. 42).

13. Aperuerunt super me os suum: sicut leo rapiens et rugiens.

They have opened their mouths against me : as a lion ravening and roaring.

"*Sicut leo ...*" Like so many famished lions greedy to devour Me, roaring with rage. Such were the Jews, when they cried out to Pilate: "Away with Him, away with Him, crucify Him " (*John* xix. 15).

14. Sicut aqua effusus sum: et dispersa sunt omnia ossa mea.

I am poured out like water : and all my bones are scattered.

I am spent of all My strength through the shedding of My blood, which has poured forth from My body like water from a vase.——"*Dispersa.*" According to the Hebrew *Divulsa :* Torn from their sockets, out of joint.

15. Factum est cor meum tamquam cera liquescens: in medio ventris mei.

My heart is become like wax : melting in the midst of my bowels.

Spite of all this, My heart, far from being hardened against My enemies, has become soft like melted wax, through the compassion that I have for their evils.[1]

16. Aruit tamquam testa virtus mea, et lingua mea adhæsit faucibus meis : et in pulverem mortis deduxisti me.

My strength is dried up like a potsherd, and my tongue hath cleaved to my jaws : and Thou hast brought me down into the dust of death.

"*Et in pulverem ...*" In short, Thou hast, O my God, brought Me to lie beneath the dust of the tomb that covers the dead.

17. Quoniam circumdederunt me canes multi : concilium malignantium obsedit me.

For many dogs have encompassed me : the council of the wicked hath besieged me.

"*Obsedit me.*" Besieged Me to take away My life.

18. Foderunt manus meas, et pedes meos : dinumeraverunt omnia ossa mea.

They have pierced my hands and feet : they have numbered all my bones.

---

[1] *Luke* xxiii. 34.

They have pierced My hands and My feet with nails; and they have so stretched my body upon the Cross, that they can count all My bones.—In these words, David clearly describes the crucifixion of Jesus Christ; and thus S. Jerome, S. Augustine, Theodoret, and Euthymius explain the passage.

19. Ipsi vero consideraverunt et inspexerunt me: diviserunt sibi vestimenta mea, et super vestem meam miserunt sortem.

And they have looked and stared upon me: they parted my garments amongst them; and upon my vesture they cast lots.

My executioners, after crucifying Me, have set themselves to watch Me with contempt, and to gaze upon my sufferings with complacency; they have parted My garments amongst them, and for my under-tunic, which was woven entire, and without seam, they have cast lots.——This text is quoted in the Gospel, where we read: "That it might be fulfilled which was spoken by the Prophet, saying: They divided My garments," &c. (*Matt.* xxvii. 35).

20. Tu autem, Domine ne elongaveris auxilium tuum a me: ad defensionem meam conspice.

But Thou, O Lord, remove not Thy help far from me: look towards my defence.

21. Erue a framea Deus animam meam: et de manu canis unicam meam.

Deliver, O God, my soul from the sword: my only one from the power of the dog.

Save My life speedily from the sword of death, by raising up My body after I shall be dead. Cause that My soul, which appears now left alone and abandoned, triumph over the infernal dog.

22. Salva me ex ore leonis: et a cornibus unicornium humilitatem meam.

Save me from the lion's mouth; and my lowliness from the horns of the unicorns.

Save Me from the lion, which keeps its mouth open to devour Me; and protect My weakness from the assaults of these ferocious unicorns.

23. Narrabo nomen tuum fratribus meis: in medio Ecclesiæ laudabo te.

I will declare Thy name to my brethren: in the midst of the church will I praise Thee.

The Psalmist here speaks more expressly of the Resurrection of our Lord, and of the fruit it would produce, viz.: the conversion of the Gentiles. He says: I will publish the glory of Thy name by means of My brethren the Apostles, &c.[1]

[1] *Heb.* ii. 11.

24. Qui timetis Dominum, laudate eum : universum semen Jacob glorificate eum.

Ye that fear the Lord, praise Him: all ye the seed of Jacob, glorify Him.

"*Semen Jacob.*" By this is meant Christians who have the faith of Jacob.

25. Timeat eum omne semen Israel : quoniam non sprevit, neque despexit deprecationem pauperis.

Let all the seed of Israel fear Him: because He hath not slighted nor despised the cry of the poor.

"*Pauperis.*" This poor man is Jesus Christ Himself, Who died upon the Cross naked and abandoned by all.

26. Nec avertit faciem suam a me: et cum clamarem ad eum, exaudivit me.

Neither hath He turned away His face from me : and when I cried to Him He heard me.

27. Apud te laus mea in ecclesia magna : vota mea reddam in conspectu timentium eum.

To Thee is my praise in the great assembly : I will pay my vows in the sight of them that fear Him.

I will praise Thee, O Lord, in the great assembly, the Church of the faithful gathered together from all the nations. In their presence will I pay My vows, renewing My sacrifice, by the ministry of My priests.

28. Edent pauperes et saturabuntur : et laudabunt Dominum qui requirunt eum : vivent corda eorum in sæculum sæculi.

The poor shall eat and shall be filled ; and they shall praise the Lord that seek Him : their hearts shall live for ever and ever.

The poor in spirit, who are conscious of their spiritual misery, shall feed upon and be satiated with grace : they that seek the Lord shall praise Him, and hence their souls shall live eternally.

29. Reminiscentur et convertentur ad Dominum : universi fines terræ :

All the ends of the earth shall remember, and shall be converted to the Lord :

30. Et adorabunt in conspectu ejus : universæ familiæ Gentium.

And all the kindreds of the Gentiles shall adore in His sight.

29, 30. All the nations even to the furthest bounds of the earth shall call to mind the benefits of God, and the mysteries of Redemption which shall be preached to them, and they shall be converted to the Lord : so that all the nations of the Gentiles shall enter into the Church to adore the true God.

31. Quoniam Domini est regnum : et ipse dominabitur Gentium.

For the kingdom is the Lord's : and He shall have dominion over the nations.

For to the Lord belongs the government of the world; and to Him, therefore, it appertains to exercise dominion over all the nations.

32. Manducaverunt et adoraverunt omnes pingues terræ : in conspectu ejus cadent omnes qui descendunt in terram.

All the fat ones of the earth have eaten and worshipped : all they that go down to the earth shall fall before Him.

Not only the poor, but also "*Pingues terræ*," the great and powerful of the earth, who abound in riches, shall eat at the table of the Lord, and shall adore Him ; and in bowing down to adore, they shall humble themselves even to the earth.——"*Qui descendunt in terram.*" According to the Hebrew : "*Qui descendunt in pulverem*" : Who go down to the dust. Hence this other interpretation, which is also probable: All men, who, since they are mortal, must return to dust, shall prostrate themselves before Him.

33. Et anima mea illi vivet: et semen meum serviet ipsi.

And to Him my soul shall live : and my seed shall serve Him.

My soul shall live only for My God, and the posterity of My children and of believers shall be faithful in serving Him.

34. Annuntiabitur Domino generatio ventura : et annuntiabunt cœli justitiam ejus populo qui nascetur, quem fecit Dominus.

There shall be declared to the Lord a generation to come : and the heavens shall show forth His justice to a people that shall be born, which the Lord hath made.

The generation [1] to come of believers shall receive the good tidings of the Lord, that is to say, the knowledge of the Faith ; and the heavens, or heavenly men, shall publish the justice of God, or the justice of Faith, which makes men just, —to the new people that shall be born to the life of grace: a people which the Lord hath made, that is, a special people of God created in Jesus Christ.

PSALM CXVIII.

In the Hebrew text this Psalm is divided into twenty-two portions of eight verses, each of which begins with a letter of the alphabet; thus the first portion begins with the first letter, the second with the second letter, and so on with the twenty-

---

[1] "*Annuntiabitur Domino generatio ventura.*" Bellarmine thus explains this phrase : *Annuntiabitur Dominus generationi venturæ.*

two letters. This seems to have been done to help the
memory. The learned say that the Psalm is so long because
it was composed with the view of giving profitable and pious
occupation to the people, who were used to sing or recite it on
their way as they went up to the Tabernacle or to the Temple
three times in the year; and that when this Psalm was
finished, they sang the Gradual Psalms as they ascended the
steps of the Tabernacle, or afterwards of the Temple. It is
filled with praises of the divine law,[1] with prayers for grace to
observe it perfectly, and with petitions for help in the dangers
that beset us, whether on the part of men, or especially of the
evil spirits who seek to destroy the life of our soul. In the
Divine Office the Psalm is divided into eleven parts of sixteen
verses each, distributed among the Little Hours, viz.: Prime,
Terce, Sext, and None. As the Little Hours are always the
same, and have to be recited daily, it will be of much help
when reciting them to give the attention of the mind to the
petitions which the several verses contain.

Alleluia.

ALEPH.

1. Beati immaculati in via : qui
ambulant in lege Domini.

Blessed are the undefiled in the
way : who walk in the law of the
Lord.

"*Immaculati in via.*" Those who keep themselves without
stain in the course of their life.——"*In lege.*" Without devi-
ating from the law.

2. Beati, qui scrutantur testimonia
ejus : in toto corde exquirunt eum.

Blessed are they that search [2] His
testimonies : that seek Him with
their whole heart.

"*Testimonia ejus.*" That is : His divine precepts, which
testify what is the will of God.

[1] This holy law is designated in almost every verse of this Psalm under
various names, which express its different characteristics ; these names are :
Eloquium, repeated five times ; *Eloquia,* four times ; *Judicium,* twice ;
Judicia, thirteen times ; *Justificationes,* twenty-eight times ; *Lex,* twenty-
seven times ; *Mandatum,* twice ; *Mandata,* thirty-six times ; *Sermones,* four
times ; *Testimonia,* twenty-two times ; *Verbum,* once ; *Verba,* four times ;
Veritas, once ; *Via,* once ; *Viae,* three times. Moreover, it is noteworthy
that several of these words are employed here and there in the sense of a
Promise, viz. : *Eloquium,* ten times ; *Eloquia,* once : *Judicium,* twice ; *Sermones,* once ; *Verbum,* seven times ; *Verba,* once. They refer to the
promise of help and of reward, and this also relates to the fulfilment of the
law.

[2] *Search.* This word means to observe or watch, and sometimes to keep.
As here applied, it means to attend to the Law as a rule of conduct.

3. Non enim qui operantur iniquitatem : in viis ejus ambulaverunt.

For they that work iniquity: have
not walked in His ways.

"*In viis ejus.*" According to His laws, which are the way
to go in order to find Him.

4. Tu mandasti : mandata tua cus-
todiri nimis.

Thou hast commanded that Thy
commandments be kept most dili-
gently.

5. Utinam dirigantur viæ meæ : ad
custodiendas justificationes tuas !

O that my ways may be so directed:
that I may keep Thine ordinances! [1]

Grant, then, O God, I beseech Thee, that my life may be
always so directed that I keep Thy precepts.

6. Tunc non confundar : cum per-
spexero in omnibus mandatis tuis.

Then shall I not be confounded :
when I shall have regard to all Thy
commandments.

Then I shall not be confounded at Thy judgment, if I have
always the intention to observe all Thou hast commanded me.

7. Confitebor tibi in directione
cordis: in eo quod didici judicia
justitiæ tuæ.

I will praise Thee with uprightness
of heart : when I shall have learned
the judgments of Thy justice.

I will give thanks to Thee for having given me an upright
heart, when I shall have learnt to observe Thy just commandments.

8. Justificationes tuas custodiam :
non me derelinquas usquequaque.

I will keep Thine ordinances : O
forsake me not utterly.

I hope, with Thy help, to observe them faithfully : Lord,
cease not to assist me.

BETH.

9. In quo corrigit adolescentior
viam suam ? in custodiendo sermones
tuos.

By what doth a young man correct
his way? even by keeping Thy words.

How else can a young man correct the errors of his way of
life than by observing Thy teachings ?

10. In toto corde meo exquisivi te:
ne repellas me a mandatis tuis.

With my whole heart have I
sought after Thee : let me not stray
from Thy commandments.

---

[1] *Ordinances.* The word thus rendered is in the Vulgate *justificationes.*
S. Jerome translates it *præcepta.* The Hebrew term signifies *statutes,* for
which the French translation gives *ordonnances,* the Spanish *mandamientos*
and *leyes,* and the German, specially sanctioned by the Apostolic Nuncio,
has *gebote* and *satzungen.* It may be taken to mean either the law of God in
general, the conformity to which constitutes man's justice ; or more specially
the Sacraments and Sacrifice, which are the appointed means of justification.

11. In corde meo abscondi eloquia tua : ut non peccem tibi.

Thy words have I hidden within my heart : that I may not sin against Thee.

I have striven to impress Thy law deeply on my heart, in order to avoid in any wise offending Thee.

12. Benedictus es Domine : doce me justificationes tuas.

Blessed art Thou, O Lord : O teach me Thine ordinances.

Blessed art Thou, O Lord, by all Thy creatures, for the graces Thou vouchsafest them. Grant me the grace of learning to know Thy commandments.

13. In labiis meis : pronuntiavi omnia judicia oris tui.

With my lips have I declared : all the judgments of Thy mouth.

My voice has published all the laws that have come from Thy mouth.

14. In via testimoniorum tuorum delectatus sum : sicut in omnibus divitiis.

I have had delight in the way of Thy testimonies : even as in all riches.

I have found delight in walking by the way of Thy precepts, as though I had been enriched with all riches.

15. In mandatis tuis exercebor : et considerabo vias tuas.

I will meditate on Thy commandments : and I will consider Thy ways.

"*Considerabo vias tuas.*" I will always keep before my eyes the way to please Thee.

16. In justificationibus tuis meditabor : non obliviscar sermones tuos.

I will think upon Thine ordinances : I will not forget Thy words.

I will meditate always upon Thy law : and I will never forget Thy instructions.

GHIMEL.

17. Retribue servo tuo, vivifica me : et custodiam sermones tuos.

Deal bountifully with Thy servant : quicken Thou me, and I shall keep Thy words.

Restore to me, Thy servant, the life which I have lost through sin ; and thus I shall be faithful in keeping Thy commandments.

18. Revela oculos meos : et considerabo mirabilia de lege tua.

Open Thou mine eyes : and I shall see the wondrous things of Thy law.

Enlighten me with Thy light, and thus I shall see how admirable is Thy law.

19. Incola ego sum in terra : non abscondas a me mandata tua.

I am a sojourner upon earth : O hide not Thy commandments from me.

I am a pilgrim here on earth; wherefore, conceal not from me Thy precepts, by the observance of which I hope to arrive at the heavenly country.

20. Concupivit anima mea: desiderare justificationes tuas in omni tempore.

My soul hath longed greatly : to desire Thine ordinances at all times.

My soul longs with its every affection to keep Thy commandments now and for ever.

21. Increpasti superbos: maledicti qui declinant a mandatis tuis.

Thou hast rebuked the proud: cursed are they that do err from Thy commandments.

" *Superbos.*" Those who, through pride, refuse to obey Thee.

22. Aufer a me opprobrium, et contemptum: quia testimonia tua exquisivi.

O take from me shame and contempt: for I have sought after Thy testimonies.

Deliver me, O Lord, from the reproach of seeing myself despised and cursed by Thee, so that the devil should be able to say of me: I have conquered him, I have made him to fall. Thus we read in *Ps.* xii. 4 : " *Lest mine enemy say at any time, I have prevailed against him*".——Preserve me, O Lord, from this misery, because I wish to accomplish in all things Thy holy will.

23. Etenim sederunt principes, et adversum me loquebantur: servus autem tuus exercebatur in justificationibus tuis.

Princes also did sit and speak against me: but Thy servant was occupied in Thy statutes.

The powerful ones of the earth have designedly set themselves to speak evil of me; but Thy servant, nevertheless, has not ceased to exercise himself in all Thy just ordinances.

24. Nam et testimonia tua meditatio mea est: et consilium meum justificationes tuæ.

For Thy testimonies are my meditation: and Thine ordinances are my counsel.

For I meditate ever upon these testimonies of Thy will: they counsel me how to conduct myself.

DALETH.

25. Adhæsit pavimento anima mea: vivifica me secundum verbum tuum.

My soul hath cleaved to the earth: O quicken Thou me according to Thy word.

" *Pavimento.*" According to the Hebrew : *Pulveri :* To the dust.——My soul has become attached to the earth, and thus has lost the life of Thy grace. Restore to me, O Lord, this

life, according to the promise Thou hast made to hear him
who prays.[1]

26. Vias meas enuntiavi, et exaudisti me: doce me justificationes
tuas.

I have declared my ways, and
Thou heardest me: teach me Thy
statutes.

O my God, to Thee I have exposed the disorders of my life,
and my needs; and when imploring Thy mercy, Thou didst
hear me. Deign, then, to teach me what I must do in future
to observe all Thy precepts.

27. Viam justificationum tuarum
instrue me : et exercebor in mirabilibus tuis.

Make me to understand the way
of Thine ordinances: and I will
meditate on Thy wondrous works.

Instruct me how to walk always in the way of Thy commandments, and so shall I exercise myself in keeping Thy
precepts, which are wonderful, that is, difficult, nay, impossible, to observe without Thy help, but easy with Thy grace.

28. Dormitavit anima mea præ
tædio : confirma me in verbis tuis.

My soul hath slumbered through
weariness : strengthen Thou me in
Thy words.

My soul has slumbered, that is, has become lukewarm in
Thy service, through the weariness I found therein: give me
strength to fulfil whatever Thou commandest me.

29. Viam iniquitatis amove a me :
et de lege tua miserere mei.

Remove from me the way of iniquity : and have mercy on me in
Thy law.

" *Et de lege ...*" According to the Hebrew : *Et legem tuam
dona mihi* : And give me Thy law.——Draw me out of the
path of sin; and in Thy mercy grant me the grace to keep
Thy law.

30. Viam veritatis elegi : judicia
tua non sum oblitus.

I have chosen the way of truth: I
have not forgotten Thy judgments.

I have chosen to walk in the way of truth, that is, of faith,
and of Thy holy precepts, which I have not forgotten.

31. Adhæsi testimoniis tuis Domine : noli me confundere.

I have cleaved unto Thy testimonies : O Lord, put me not to shame.

O Lord, by Thy gift I have become enamoured of Thy commandments : suffer me not to merit the shame of transgressing
them.

---

[1] " *Vivifica ...*" This is also interpreted : Grant that I may live conformably to Thy law.

32. Viam mandatorum tuorum cucurri : cum dilatasti cor meum.

I have run in the way of Thy commandments : when Thou didst enlarge my heart.

Whenever, O Lord, Thou hast enlarged my heart by Thy grace, inflaming it with Thy holy love, I have always made rapid progress in the way of Thy commandments.

TERCE.

HE.

33. Legem pone mihi Domine viam justificationum tuarum : et exquiram eam semper.

Set before me, O Lord, for a law the way of Thy statutes : and I will alway seek after it.

"*Legem pone mihi.*" According to the Hebrew : Teach me the way of Thy precepts. The passage is thus explained : Make a law for me, O Lord, to follow the way, that is, the rule of Thy commandments. As though he had said : Grant that I take not pleasure in the law of the world or of the flesh, but only in Thy law; and thus I shall always seek to put it in practice.

34. Da mihi intellectum, et scrutabor legem tuam : et custodiam illam in toto corde meo.

Give me understanding, and I will search Thy law : and I will keep it with my whole heart.

35. Deduc me in semitam mandatorum tuorum : quia ipsam volui.

Lead me into the path of Thy commandments : for I have longed for it.

"*Ipsam volui.*" For therein alone do I wish to walk.

36. Inclina cor meum in testimonia tua ; et non in avaritiam.

Incline mine heart unto Thy testimonies : and not to covetousness.

Incline my heart towards the observance of Thy law by means of Thy holy love, which by the weight of its influence inclines hearts to Thee ; and deliver it from avarice, that is, from the concupiscence of earthly goods.

37. Averte oculos meos ne videant vanitatem : in via tua vivifica me.

Turn away mine eyes lest they behold vanity : quicken Thou me in Thy way.

Turn away my eyes from looking at the vanities of the world, that I may avoid loving them; grant that I may live only for Thee, and that my life may consist in walking by the way that leads to Thee.

38. Statue servo tuo eloquium tuum ; in timore tuo.

Establish Thy word unto Thy servant : in Thy fear.

Establish Thy law in the heart of Thy servant, so that he may pay attention to observe it, through fear of displeasing Thee.

39. Amputa opprobrium meum quod suspicatus sum: quia judicia tua jucunda.

Turn away my reproach, of which I am afraid: for Thy judgments are pleasant.

Take from me the reproach which I dread, viz., of transgressing Thy precepts, which are so pleasant to those who observe them.

40. Ecce concupivi mandata tua: in æquitate tua vivifica me.

Behold, I have longed after Thy precepts: quicken Thou me in Thy justice.

I have set my heart upon Thy law; it is just then that Thou shouldst give me strength to observe it.

VAU.

41. Et veniat super me misericordia tua Domine: salutare tuum secundum eloquium tuum.

Let Thy mercy also come upon me, O Lord: and Thy salvation according to Thy word.

Let Thy mercy, O Lord, come upon me, and Thy saving help, according to the promise Thou hast made to him who prays to Thee in the name of the Saviour.

42. Et respondebo exprobrantibus mihi verbum: quia speravi in sermonibus tuis.

So shall I answer them that reproach me: that I have trusted in Thy words.

To those who reproach me for living in this state of humiliation, I will answer that I hope in Thy promises, which can never fail.

43. Et ne auferas de ore meo verbum veritatis usquequaque: quia in judiciis tuis supersperavi.

And take not Thou the word of truth utterly out of my mouth: for in Thy words I have hoped exceedingly.

Permit not, O Lord, that I ever fail of saying the truth, for I have placed all my hopes in Thy judgments, which are full of mercy.

44. Et custodiam legem tuam semper: in sæculum et in sæculum sæculi.

So shall I alway keep Thy law: yea for ever and ever.

45. Et ambulabam in latitudine: quia mandata tua exquisivi.

And I walked at large: because I have sought after Thy commandments.

I have walked in the wide breadth of Thy love, which enlarges hearts in the way of Thy precepts, for I have sought to observe them with exactness.[1]

46. Et loquebar in testimoniis tuis in conspectu regum: et non confundebar.

And I spake of Thy testimonies before kings: and I was not ashamed.

"*Loquebar.*" I spoke in praise of.

47. Et meditabar in mandatis tuis: quæ dilexi.

I meditated also on Thy commandments: which I loved.

48. Et levavi manus meas ad mandata tua, quæ dilexi: et exercebar in justificationibus tuis.

And I lifted up my hands unto Thy commandments, which I have loved: and I meditated on Thine ordinances.

ZAIN.

49. Memor esto verbi tui servo tuo: in quo mihi spem dedisti.

Be mindful of Thy word unto Thy servant: in which Thou hast given me hope.

"*Verbi tui . . .*" The promise made to Thy servant upon which Thou hast founded my hope.

50. Hæc me consolata est in humilitate mea: quia eloquium tuum vivificavit me.

This hath comforted me in my humiliation: for Thy word hath quickened me.

This hope has consoled me in my tribulations, for Thy promise has given me strength to suffer them with patience.

51. Superbi inique agebant usquequaque: a lege autem tua non declinavi.

The proud have acted wickedly altogether: but I declined not from Thy law.

My enemies, proud of their power, have hitherto unjustly persecuted me, but I have never failed in the observance of Thy law.

52. Memor fui judiciorum tuorum a sæculo Domine: et consolatus sum.

I remembered, O Lord, Thy judgments of old: and I was comforted.

I have ever borne in mind Thy eternal judgments, and by them I have been consoled.——Let us here remark that we ought to fear the judgments of God if we are unfaithful to Him; but when we are faithful to Him, with His help, which we shall certainly obtain if we are careful to ask it of Him by prayer, the judgments of God should not terrify, but should rather console us; for these judgments are full of joy and comfort, because full of mercy, as David says in verse 39 :

[1] According to Bellarmine, this and the three following verses are as verse 44, in the future.

"Thy judgments are pleasant". This is why he adds in verse 43, that in his confidence in these same judgments he places all his hope of salvation. "For in Thy judgments I have hoped exceedingly."

53. Defectio tenuit me : pro pecca-toribus derelinquentibus legem tuam.   Fainting hath laid hold upon me : because of the wicked that forsake Thy law.

I have felt myself as though fainting away for sorrow at the sight of so many sinners, who despise Thy law.

54. Cantabiles mihi erant justifi-cationes tuæ : in loco peregrinationis meæ.   Thine ordinances were the subject of my song : in the place of my pilgrimage.

For myself, whilst here on earth in the place of my pilgrimage, I have ever praised Thy ordinances.

55. Memor fui nocte nominis tui, Domine : et custodivi legem tuam.   In the night have I remembered Thy name, O Lord : and have kept Thy law.

During the night I have been mindful of Thy name : I have invoked it, and so have had strength to keep Thy law.

56. Hæc facta est mihi : quia justificationes tuas exquisivi.   This happened to me : because I sought after Thine ordinances.

All this has happened to me because I have striven to obey Thy just commands.[1]

HETH.

57. Portio mea Domine : dixi cus-todire legem tuam.   Thou art my portion, O Lord : I have said that I would keep Thy law.

I have said : Lord, my portion, my riches, is to keep Thy law.[2]

58. Deprecatus sum faciem tuam in toto corde meo : miserere mei se-cundum eloquium tuum.   I entreated Thy face with my whole heart : have mercy upon me according to Thy word.

In Thy divine presence I have besought Thee with all my heart to have pity on me, according to Thy promise.

59. Cogitavi vias meas : et con-verti pedes meos in testimonia tua.   I have thought upon my ways : and turned my feet unto Thy testimonies.

I have considered the way which I ought to keep, and have directed my steps in the path of Thy commandments.

[1] "*Hæc facta est.*" S. Jerome renders it : *Hoc factum est.* In Hebrew, for want of the neuter gender, the feminine is employed.

[2] Following the Hebrew and the Greek, many understand this verse as if it were : *Portio mea es :* Lord, Thou art my inheritance and my only good ; therefore I have resolved to keep Thy law.

60. Paratus sum, et non sum turbatus: ut custodiam mandata tua.

I am ready, and am not troubled:
to keep Thy commandments.

I have prepared myself to suffer all tribulations, and am
not troubled at the sight of them, if so I may keep Thy
precepts.

61. Funes peccatorum circumplexi
sunt me: et legem tuam non sum
oblitus.

The cords of the wicked have encompassed me: but I have not forgotten Thy law.

Sinners have sought to ensnare me in their toils, but I have
not forgotten Thy law.

62. Media nocte surgebam ad confitendum tibi: super judicia justifica-
tionis tuæ.

At midnight have I risen to give
praise unto Thee: because of the
judgments of Thy justice.

"*Judicia . . .*" Thy just judgments, decrees, ordinances.

63. Particeps ego sum omnium
timentium te: et custodientium mandata tua.

I am a partaker with all them that
fear Thee: and that keep Thy commandments.

64. Misericordia tua Domine
plena est terra: justificationes tuas
doce me.

The earth, O Lord, is full of Thy
mercy: teach me Thine ordinances.

"*Justificationes . . .*" Teach me Thy just law, and give me
strength to observe them.

TETH.

65. Bonitatem fecisti cum servo
tuo Domine: secundum verbum
tuum.

Thou hast dealt well with Thy
servant, O Lord: according unto Thy
word.

Thou hast shown goodness to Thy servant, O Lord, according as Thou hast promised.

66. Bonitatem, et disciplinam et
scientiam doce me: quia mandatis
tuis credidi.

Teach me goodness, and discipline
and knowledge: for I have believed
Thy commandments.

Deign to teach me, after Thy example, the goodness I should
show forth to others; instruct me in the rule of how to live
well, and give me the science of the Saints, which consists in
knowing how to love Thee, for I have placed all my hopes in
the fulfilment of Thy precepts.

67. Priusquam humiliarer ego
deliqui: propterea eloquium tuum
custodivi.

Before I was humbled, I did
wickedly: therefore have I kept Thy
word.

I sinned before I was humbled by Thee with tribulations
these have taught me to keep Thy law.

68. Bonus es tu : et in bonitate tua doce me justificationes tuas.

Thou art good : in Thy goodness teach me Thine ordinances.

Thou, my God, art good; and by this, Thy goodness, I pray Thee to instruct me in Thy holy ordinances.

69. Multiplicata est super me iniquitas superborum : ego autem in toto corde meo scrutabor mandata tua.

The iniquity of the proud hath been multiplied over me : but I will seek Thy commandments with my whole heart.

The iniquity of the proud—and these foes are especially the infernal spirits—is multiplied against me, to make me transgress Thy law; but I will ever study, with all my heart, to enter into the purposes of Thy holy will concerning me, that I may accomplish them.

70. Coagulatum est sicut lac cor eorum : ego vero legem tuam meditatus sum.

Their heart is curdled like milk ; but I have meditated on Thy law.

"*Coagulatum ... lac.*" Is hardened like curdled milk.

71. Bonum mihi quia humiliasti me : ut discam justificationes tuas.

It is good for me that Thou hast humbled me : that I may learn Thine ordinances.

We may here remark how necessary it is to keep ourselves humble before God and before men ; for the Lord, as He did with David, is wont to chastise the proud, by permitting them to fall into shameful sins, such as they had previously held in abhorrence.

72. Bonum mihi lex oris tui : super millia auri, et argenti.

The law of Thy mouth is good unto me : above thousands of gold and silver.

It is well for me that Thy law has been dear to me beyond a thousand treasures of gold and silver.

JOD.

73. Manus tuæ fecerunt me, et plasmaverunt me : da mihi intellectum, et discam mandata tua.

Thy hands have made me and fashioned me : O give me understanding, and I will learn Thy commandmandments.

Thy hands have formed me, so that I am the work of Thy hands : but by sin I have lost the knowledge and the love of Thy law; give me, then, understanding to know it, and love to keep it.

74. Qui timent te videbunt me, et lætabuntur : quia in verba tua supersperavi.

They that fear Thee shall see me, and shall be glad : because I have greatly hoped in Thy words.

Those who fear Thee will rejoice to see that I keep Thy law, and that I have put all my hopes in Thy promises.

75. Cognovi, Domine, quia æquitas judicia tua : et in veritate tua humiliasti me.

I know, O Lord, that Thy judgments are just: and in Thy truth Thou hast humbled me.

" *Æquitas.*" Most just.——" *In veritate tua.*" In Thy justice, most justly.

76. Fiat misericordia tua ut consoletur me : secundum eloquium tuum servo tuo.

O let Thy mercy be my comfort according unto Thy word unto Thy servant.

"*Secundum eloquium tuum.*" According to the promises Thou hast made.

77. Veniant mihi miserationes tuæ, et vivam : quia lex tua meditatio mea est.

Let Thy tender mercies come unto me, and I shall live : for Thy law is my meditation.

Make me to feel the effects of Thy mercy, and then I shall live always in Thy grace, for I meditate only upon Thy law in order not to transgress it.

78. Confundantur superbi, quia injuste iniquitatem fecerunt in me : ego autem exercebor in mandatis tuis.

Let the proud be put to shame, for they have dealt unjustly with me : but I will be occupied in Thy commandments.

79. Convertantur mihi timentes te : et qui noverunt testimonia tua.

Let them that fear Thee, turn unto me : and they that know Thy testimonies.

Let all unite themselves to me who fear Thee, and who know how just are Thy precepts.

80. Fiat cor meum immaculatum in justificationibus tuis : ut non confundar.

Let my heart be undefiled in Thine ordinances : that I be not confounded.

May my heart become pure through the observance of Thy precepts, that I may not one day incur the confusion of having transgressed them.

S E X T.

81. Defecit in salutare tuum anima mea : et in verbum tuum supersperavi.

My soul hath fainted after Thy salvation : and in Thy word have I hoped exceedingly.

O Lord, my soul has fainted away for desire to see myself saved from so many anguishes and fears that torment me.

82. Defecerunt oculi mei in eloquium tuum, dicentes : Quando consolaberis me ?

Mine eyes have failed for Thy word, saying : O when wilt Thou comfort me ?

My eyes, too, have grown faint through keeping them fixed on Thee, expecting the effect of Thy word, saying : When, O my God, wilt Thou console me ?

83. Quia factus sum sicut uter in pruina : justificationes tuas non sum oblitus.

For I am become like a bottle in the frost : I have not forgotten Thine ordinances.

" *Pruina.*" This word has given rise to different interpretations. Mattei thinks that it is put in place of *Fumo :* In the smoke; because the Hebrew word is thus rendered by S. Jerome in *Genesis* xix. 28: and Emmanuel Sa explains it in the same sense, according to the Chaldee : *Ad fumum.* So that thus the meaning of the passage would be : By reason of my sufferings, I am become like a skin shrivelled and blackened by the smoke. (*Conf. Job* xxx. 30.)——But others, keeping to the Vulgate, which has "*In pruina*" : In the frost ; explain it thus: The sufferings I have endured have made me to become like a skin, or bladder, that has grown slack by the damp, and then is contracted and hardened by the frost ; that is to say, have made me to become tepid.——Of these two interpretations, the reader can choose the one which most approves itself to him. For my part, I prefer the second, because it is in conformity with the letter of the Vulgate, and is the one most commonly received.

84. Quot sunt dies servi tui : quando facies de persequentibus me judicium ?

How many are the days of Thy servant : when wilt Thou execute judgment on them that persecute me ?

How many days, O Lord, must Thy servant remain thus tried ? When wilt Thou pass judgment on my persecutors, and punish them as they deserve ?

85. Narraverunt mihi iniqui fabulationes : sed non ut lex tua.

The wicked have told me false things : but *they are* not as Thy law.

These wicked men have set before my eyes the goods of this world, which in truth are all deceitful fables when confronted with Thy law, which alone satisfies him who keeps it.

86. Omnia mandata tua veritas : inique persecuti sunt me, adjuva me.

All Thy statutes are truth : they have persecuted me wrongfully ; help Thou me.

All Thy precepts are the very truth, which gives true peace to him who fulfils them : the wicked cease not to persecute me ; but do not Thou, O Lord, cease to succour me.

87. Paulo minus consummaverunt me in terra: ego autem non dereliqui mandata tua.

They had almost made an end of me upon earth: but I have not forsaken Thy commandments.

They had all but ruined me here on earth with their temptations, but with Thy help I have not ceased to obey Thy precepts.

88. Secundum misericordiam tuam vivifica me: et custodiam testimonia oris tui.

O quicken me according to Thy mercy: and I shall keep the testimonies of Thy mouth.

In Thy mercy give me strength, and so I shall be faithful to Thy commandments.

LAMED.

89. In æternum, Domine: verbum tuum permanet in cœlo.

O Lord, Thy word: endureth for ever in heaven.

90. In generationem et generationem veritas tua: fundasti terram, et permanet.

Thy truth *also* unto all generations: Thou hast founded the earth, and it abideth.

91. Ordinatione tua perseverat dies: quoniam omnia serviunt tibi.

By Thine ordinance the day continueth: for all things serve Thee.

92. Nisi quod lex tua meditatio mea est: tunc forte periissem in humilitate mea.

If Thy law had not been my meditation: I might haply have perished in my trouble.

89-92. These four verses are variously interpreted; but the most suitable and the best explanation appears to me to be that given by Mattei, with Bossuet and several others, according to which David means here to say: "O Lord, the heavens obey Thee, by remaining always in the state wherein Thou hast placed them; in like manner, the earth remains the same as when Thou didst first establish it; so, too, the day and all irrational creatures obey Thee.——After this the Psalmist concludes: If I had not obeyed Thee myself, by meditating upon and observing Thy law in the numerous persecutions I have suffered, I should have perished through my weakness.[1]

93. In æternum non obliviscar justificationes tuas: quia in ipsis vivificasti me.

Thine ordinances I will never forget: for by them Thou hast given me life.

" *Vivificasti me.*" Thou hast preserved my life.

94. Tuus sum ego, salvum me fac: quoniam justificationes tuas exquisivi.

I am Thine, O save me: for I have sought Thine ordinances.

[1] " *Meditatio.*" According to the Hebrew, *Delectatio:* My delight. ——" *In humilitate.*" According to the Hebrew, *In afflictione.* S. Jerome translates, *In pressura.*

I have given myself to Thee, and Thou hast to save me, for I have striven to obey Thy ordinances.

95. Me expectaverunt peccatores ut perderent me : testimonia tua intellexi.

The wicked have waited for me, to destroy me : but I have understood Thy testimonies.

Sinners watched their opportunity to strike me down, but I have taken care not to withdraw from Thy precepts.

96. Omnis consummationis vidi finem : latum mandatum tuum nimis.

I have seen an end of all perfection : Thy commandment is exceeding broad.

I have seen that all things come to an end, but the law which Thou hast given us will endure for ever. Thus, Mattei and Bossuet explain this verse after Theodoret.

MEM.

97. Quomodo dilexi legem tuam Domine : tota die meditatio mea est.

How have I loved Thy law, O Lord : it is my meditation all the day long.

In what way, O Lord, have I loved Thy law ? I have loved it by meditating upon it every day.[1]

98. Super inimicos meos prudentem me fecisti mandato tuo : quia in æternum mihi est.

Through Thy commandment, Thou hast made me wiser than mine enemies : for it is ever with me.

"*Mandato tuo.*" Not by craft, but by means of Thy law, which is full of wisdom, since I have it always before my eyes.

99. Super omnes docentes me intellexi : quia testimonia tua meditatio mea est.

I have had more understanding than all my teachers : for Thy testimonies are my meditation.

I have understood Thy law better than my masters, because I have constantly meditated upon Thy precepts.

100. Super senes intellexi : quia mandata tua quæsivi.

I have had understanding above the aged : because I sought after Thy commandments.

101. Ab omni via mala prohibui pedes meos : ut custodiam verba tua.

I have refrained my feet from every evil way : that I may keep Thy words.

102. A judiciis tuis non declinavi : quia tu legem posuisti mihi.

I have not turned aside from Thy judgments : for Thou hast appointed for me a law.

---

1 " *Quomodo?* " S. Jerome translates : *Quam!* and Bellarmine explains : *Quam vehementer!* How exceedingly ! Hence this other interpretation of the verse : Oh ! how I love Thy law : it is unceasingly the subject of my meditation.

"*Quia*..." Since these are the laws which Thou hast given me.

103. Quam dulcia faucibus meis eloquia tua : super mel ori meo !

How sweet are Thy words unto my taste : yea, sweeter than honey unto my mouth.

How sweet it is to speak of Thy precepts! Thy words are sweeter than honey to my mouth.

104. A mandatis tuis intellexi : propterea odivi omnem viam iniquitatis.

By Thy commandments I have had understanding : therefore have I hated every evil way.

"*Intellexi.*" I have received the true understanding of my duties.

NUN.

105. Lucerna pedibus meis verbum tuum : et lumen semitis meis.

Thy word is a lamp unto my feet : and a light unto my paths.

Thy words are to me as a torch, which makes me see where I have to place my steps; and as a light, which shows me the way which I have to keep.

106. Juravi, et statui : custodire judicia justitiæ tuæ.

I have sworn, and am steadfastly purposed : to keep the judgments of Thy justice.

107. Humiliatus sum usquequaque Domine : vivifica me secundum verbum tuum.

I have been humbled, O Lord, exceedingly : O quicken me according unto Thy word.

I have been, O Lord, everywhere afflicted and persecuted : do not fail, I beseech Thee, to give me strength, as Thou hast promised.

108. Voluntaria oris mei beneplacita fac Domine : et judicia tua doce me.

Let the free-will offerings of my mouth be pleasing unto Thee, O Lord : and teach me Thy judgments.

Graciously accept, O my God, the free offerings of my mouth, and teach me to observe Thy laws.

109. Anima mea in manibus meis semper : et legem tuam non sum oblitus.

My soul is continually in my hands : and I have not forgotten Thy law.

"*Anima...meis.*" That is : My life is in danger.——In the same way, it is said of David when he went against Goliath : "*He put his life in his hand*" (1 *Kings* xix. 5). The proper interpretation, therefore, of the present verse is as follows : My life is always in danger, because I wish to keep Thy law; but I will never forget it.

110. Posuerunt peccatores laqueum mihi : et de mandatis tuis non erravi.

The wicked have laid a snare for me : but I have not erred from Thy precepts.

111. Hereditate acquisivi testimonia tua in æternum : quia exultatio cordis mei sunt.

Thy testimonies have I taken for an heritage for ever : for they are the joy of my heart.

I have chosen for my heritage to accomplish always Thy will, for it is the joy of my heart.

112. Inclinavi cor meum ad faciendas justificationes tuas in æternum : propter retributionem.

I have inclined my heart to fulfil Thine ordinances for ever : because of the reward.

" *Propter retributionem.*" Mindful of the recompense Thou hast promised to Thy faithful servant.[1]

SAMECH.

113. Iniquos odio habui : et legem tuam dilexi.

I have hated the unjust : and Thy law have I loved.

114. Adjutor et susceptor meus es tu : et in verbum tuum superspe- ravi.

Thou art my helper and my protector : and in Thy word have I greatly hoped.

" *Et in verbum . . .*" In Thy promise I have placed all my confidence.

115. Declinate a me maligni : et scrutabor mandata Dei mei.

Depart from me, ye wicked : and I will meditate on the commandments of my God.

Come not near to disturb me : I wish to give myself to search into the precepts of my God, that I may observe them with exactness.

116. Suscipe me secundum eloquium tuum, et vivam : et non confundas me ab expectatione mea.

Uphold me according unto Thy word, and I shall live : and let me not be confounded in my hope.

O Lord, take me under Thy protection, as Thou hast promised, that I may live to Thee; do not, I beseech Thee, permit me to fall into the confusion of being deprived of the help which I expect from Thee.

117. Adjuva me, et salvus ero : et meditabor in justificationibus tuis semper.

Help me and I shall be saved: and I will alway think on Thine ordinances.

---

[1] S. Jerome renders it : *Propter æternam retributionem:* Because of the eternal reward. De Muis interprets the Hebrew text : *Usque ad finem:* Even to the end. (*Tr.*) See also *Ps.* xv. 5, and *Ps.* lxxii. 24-25.

118. Sprevisti omnes discedentes a judiciis tuis : quia injusta cogitatio eorum.

Thou hast despised all them that err from Thy judgments : for their thoughts are unjust.

"*Injusta ...*" They give themselves to thoughts contrary to justice.

119. Prævaricantes reputavi omnes peccatores terræ : ideo dilexi testimonia tua.

I have accounted as unjust all the sinners of the earth : therefore have I loved Thy testimonies.

"*Prævaricantes.*" That is : Transgressors of God's law.——— Sinners are such only in so far as they transgress the Divine Law, for where there is no law there is no sin.

120. Confige timore tuo carnes meas : a judiciis enim tuis timui.

Pierce Thou my flesh with Thy fear : for I am afraid of Thy judgments.

Pierce through and restrain my flesh, that is, my carnal appetites, with Thy holy fear, for Thy judgments make me tremble.

121. Feci judicium et justitiam : non tradas me calumniantibus me.

I have done judgment and justice : give me not up to them that speak against me unjustly.

I have always taken care to observe justice : suffer not that I remain abandoned in the hands of my calumniators.

122. Suscipe servum tuum in bonum : non calumnientur me superbi.

Uphold Thy servant unto good : let not the proud speak evil of me.

123. Oculi mei defecerunt in salutare tuum : et in eloquium justitiæ tuæ.

Mine eyes have failed for Thy salvation : and for the word of Thy justice.

"*Oculi.*" See verses 81 and 82.

124. Fac cum servo tuo secundum misericordiam tuam : et justificationes tuas doce me.

Deal with Thy servant according unto Thy mercy : and teach me Thine ordinances.

"*Justificationes ...*" Teach me how I ought to obey Thy commandments.

125. Servus tuus sum ego : da mihi intellectum, ut sciam testimonia tua.

I am Thy servant : O give me understanding that I may know Thy testimonies.

I am Thy servant, bound to obey Thee ; make me to well understand Thy commands, that I may know them and put them in execution.

126. Tempus faciendi Domine: dissipaverunt legem tuam.

It is time, O Lord, to act: they have made void Thy law.

It is time, O Lord, to make known Thy justice against those who destroy Thy law.

127. Ideo dilexi mandata tua: super aurum et topazion.

Therefore have I loved Thy commandments: above gold and the topaz.

For my part, this shameful conduct of theirs moves me to love Thy precepts more than gold and precious stones.

128. Propterea ad omnia mandata tua dirigebar: omnem viam iniquam odio habui.

Therefore have I followed all Thy commandments: and I have hated every evil way.

Therefore, I have set myself not to transgress any one of Thy precepts; and I have abhorred not iniquity only, but also every occasion which might lead me to sin.

NONE.

129. Mirabilia testimonia tua: ideo scrutata est ea anima mea.

Thy testimonies are wonderful: therefore hath my soul sought them.

Thy law and all the truths which Thou hast revealed are indeed worthy of our admiration; therefore, has my soul studied to penetrate them.

130. Declaratio sermonum tuorum illuminat: et intellectum dat parvulis.

The declaration of Thy words giveth light: it giveth understanding unto little ones.

When the hidden sense of Thy divine Scriptures is made clear by Thy holy Doctors, there arises a light that dispels the darkness, and gives to the humble the true intelligence, in which the proud can have no part.

131. Os meum aperui, et attraxi spiritum: quia mandata tua desiderabam.

I opened my mouth, and drew in my breath: for I longed for Thy commandments.

I opened my mouth in prayer to Thee, and have received from Thee the good spirit,[1] that is, the help to keep Thy commandments, for my desire is to fulfil them exactly.

---

[1] "*Attraxi spiritum.*" Literally, I inhaled the air, or drew in my breath. S. Jerome translates: *Respiravi.* Meaning, says Bossuet: I sighed deeply with desire of Thy commandments. So also De Muis.—*Tr.*

132. Aspice in me, et miserere mei : secundum judicium diligentium nomen tuum.

Look Thou upon me, and be merciful unto me : as Thou usest to do unto them that love Thy name.

"*Secundum judicium.*" According as Thou art wont to deal with.

133. Gressus meos dirige secundum eloquium tuum : et non dominetur mei omnis injustitia.

Direct my steps according to Thy word : and let not any iniquity have dominion over me.

"*Eloquium tuum.*" Thy commandments.——"*Non dominetur . . .*" Permit not that any unjust passions whatsoever have dominion over me.

134. Redime me a calumniis hominum : ut custodiam mandata tua.

Redeem me from the oppression of men : that I may keep Thy commandments.

135. Faciem tuam illumina super servum tuum : et doce me justificationes tuas.

Make Thy face to shine upon Thy servant : and teach me Thine ordinances.

Look upon Thy servant, O Lord, with a gracious eye, and enlighten him ; teach him to be faithful to Thy law.

136. Exitus aquarum deduxerunt oculi mei : quia non custodierunt legem tuam.

Mine eyes have sent forth springs of water : because they have not kept Thy law.

My eyes have shed floods of tears when thinking that in the past I did not keep Thy law.[1]

SADE.

137. Justus es Domine : et rectum judicium tuum.

Thou art just, O Lord : and Thy judgment is right.

Thou, O Lord, art just by essence ; Thou art justice itself, and Thy judgments are rectitude itself.

138. Mandasti justitiam testimonia tua : et veritatem tuam nimis.

The testimonies Thou hast commanded : are justice and Thy very truth.

Whatsoever Thou hast commanded and attested, all is justice, and most clear and evident truth.

139. Tabescere me fecit zelus meus : quia obliti sunt verba tua inimici mei.

My zeal hath made me to pine away : because mine enemies have forgotten Thy words.

"*Zelus meus.*" My zeal for Thy glory.

---

[1] "*Non custodierunt . . .*" Some refer these words to "*Oculi mei*" (see *Deut.* xv. 39); others to the wicked, or to David's enemies (vv. 134, 139). Thus Bossuet, who says: Behold David's charity towards his enemies ; he pines away, and is all melted to tears in sorrow for their sins.—*Tr.*

140. Ignitum eloquium tuum vehementer : et servus tuus dilexit illud.   Thy word is as a very fire : and Thy servant hath loved it.

"*Ignitum.*" According to the Hebrew : *Probatum et examinatum igne:* Proved and tried in the fire. The sense is : Thy law is most pure, as gold refined by fire, and it enflames hearts exceedingly with holy love ; therefore it is that Thy servant has ever loved it.

141. Adolescentulus sum ego, et contemptus : justificationes tuas non sum oblitus.   I am little and despised : but I have not forgotten Thine ordinances.

"*Adolescentulus sum.*" [1] I am a youth of but few years.——"*Justificationes.*" Commandments.

142. Justitia tua, justitia in æternum : et lex tua veritas.   Thy justice is an everlasting justice : and Thy law is the truth.

Thy justice is eternal and unchangeable, and Thy law is truth itself.

143. Tribulatio et angustia invenerunt me : mandata tua meditatio mea est.   Trouble and anguish have found me : yet are my thoughts upon Thy commandments.

In these pains that afflict me, my comfort is to meditate on Thy commandments.

144. Æquitas testimonia tua in æternum : intellectum da mihi, et vivam.   The testimonies are justice for ever : O give me understanding, and I shall live.

Thy precepts are and will be ever just ; grant that I understand them well, and thus I shall always live faithful to Thee.

КОPH.

145. Clamavi in toto corde meo, exaudi me Domine: justificationes tuas requiram.   I cried with my whole heart, hear me, O Lord : I will seek Thine ordinances.

"*Justificationes...*" And thus shall I strive to discover what, in all things, is Thy holy and just will, that I may accomplish it.

146. Clamavi ad te, salvum me fac : ut custodiam mandata tua.   I cried unto Thee, O save me : that I may keep Thy commandments.

"*Salvum me fac.*" Save me, by giving me needful help.

---

[1] S. Jerome has : *Parvulus sum ego, et contemptibilis :* I am little and contemptible.—*Tr.*

147. Præveni in maturitate, et clamavi : quia in verba tua super-speravi.

I prevented the dawning of the day, and cried : for in Thy words have I hoped exceedingly.

"*In maturitate.*" According to the Hebrew and the Greek : *In crepusculo :* At the dawn.——I have begun at break of day to call upon Thee, O my Lord, because I have much hoped in Thy promise.

148. Prævenerunt oculi mei ad te diluculo : ut meditarer eloquia tua.

Mine eyes have looked unto Thee before the morning : that I might think upon Thy words.

"*Prævenerunt.*" Have anticipated the ordinary time of praying to Thee.

149. Vocem meam audi secundum misericordiam tuam Domine : et secundum judicium tuum vivifica me.

Hear my voice, O Lord, according to Thy mercy : and quicken me according to Thy judgment.

"*Secundum judicium...*" According to Thy promise, give me strength to be faithful.

150. Appropinquaverunt perse-quentes me iniquitati : a lege autem tua longe facti sunt.

They that persecute me have drawn nigh unto iniquity : they have gone far off from Thy law.

My persecutors have made themselves friends of iniquity, by seeking to pervert others. But woe to them! the nearer they approach to iniquity, the further do they depart from Thy law.

151. Prope es tu Domine : et omnes viæ tuæ veritas.

Thou art near, O Lord : and all Thy ways are truth.

Thou art ever at hand to succour him who loves Thy law, which is all just and faithful.

152. Initio cognovi de testimoniis tuis : quia in æternum fundasti ea.

From the beginning have I known concerning Thy testimonies : that Thou hast founded them for ever.

From the first beginning that I knew Thy commandments, I knew at the same time that they are eternal, that is, un-changeable.

RESH.

153. Vide humilitatem meam, et eripe me : quia legem tuam non sum oblitus.

Look upon my lowliness and deliver me : for I have not forgotten Thy law.

154. Judica judicium meum et redime me : propter eloquium tuum vivifica me.

Judge Thou my cause and redeem me : quicken Thou me for Thy word's sake.

Judge Thou my cause, and rescue me from the hands of my enemies; give me strength against them as Thou hast promised me.

8

155. Longe a peccatoribus salus : quia justificationes tuas non exquisierunt.

Salvation is far from sinners : because they have not sought Thine ordinances.

Sinners are far from salvation, for they do not care even to know Thy laws.

156. Misericordiæ tuæ multæ Domine : secundum judicium tuum vivifica me.

Many, O Lord, are Thy mercies : quicken me according to Thy judgment.

Misericordiæ. See verse 149.

157. Multi qui persequuntur me, et tribulant me ; a testimoniis tuis non declinavi.

Many are they that persecute me, and trouble me : *but* I have not turned aside from Thy testimonies.

158. Vidi prævaricantes, et tabescebam : quia eloquia tua non custodierunt.

I beheld the transgressors, and I pined away : because they have not kept Thy word.

I saw sinners transgress Thy law, and I pined away with fretting, observing the little account they make of Thy commandments. See verses 53 and 139.

159. Vide quoniam mandata tua dilexi Domine : in misericordia tua vivifica me.

Behold, O Lord, I have loved Thy commandments : quicken Thou me in Thy mercy.

"Vivifica me." In Thy mercy, give me strength to continue so to love them.

160. Principium verborum tuorum, veritas : in æternum omnia judicia justitiæ tuæ.

The beginning of Thy words is truth : all the judgments of Thy justice are for evermore.

Thy words proceed from truth, as from their source : Thy decrees, therefore, can never be wanting in justice.

SHIN.

161. Principes persecuti sunt me gratis ; et a verbis tuis formidavit cor meum.

Princes have persecuted me without cause : but my heart stood in awe of Thy word.

The great ones of the earth have persecuted me without cause, but I have had no other fear than to violate Thy ordinances.

162. Lætabor ego super eloquia tua : sicut qui invenit spolia multa.

I will rejoice at Thy words : as one that hath found great spoil.

I shall rejoice over Thy promises, as the soldier, after a victory gained over the enemy, rejoices when he finds rich and abundant spoils.

163. Iniquitatem odio habui, et abominatus sum : legem autem tuam dilexi.

I have hated and abhorred iniquity : but Thy law have I loved.

164. Septies in die laudem dixi tibi : super judicia justitiæ tuæ.

Seven times a day have I given praise unto Thee : because of the judgments of Thy justice.

"Septies." Frequently.[1]——*"Super judicia ..."* At seeing how just are Thy judgments.

165. Pax multa diligentibus legem tuam : et non est illis scandalum.

Great peace have they that love Thy law : and for them there is no stumbling-block.

" Non est illis scandalum." To such Thou givest strength to avoid the snares of the enemy, and to escape all danger.

166. Expectabam salutare tuum Domine : et mandata tua dilexi.

I looked for Thy salvation, O Lord : and I loved Thy commandments.

167. Custodivit anima mea testimonia tua : et dilexit ea vehementer.

My soul hath kept Thy testimonies : and hath loved them exceedingly.

168. Servavi mandata tua, et testimonia tua : quia omnes viæ meæ in conspectu tuo.

I have kept Thy commandments and Thy testimonies : for all my ways are in Thy sight.

I have fulfilled Thy commandments and Thy will, for I have ever walked in Thy presence.

TAU.

169. Appropinquet deprecatio mea in conspectu tuo Domine : juxta eloquium tuum da mihi intellectum.

Let my cry come near before Thee, O Lord : give me understanding according to Thy word.

" Juxta eloquium tuum ..." According to Thy promise, make me well understand what Thou willest of me.

170. Intret postulatio mea in conspectu tuo : secundum eloquium tuum eripe me.

Let my supplication come before Thee : deliver me according to Thy word.

" Secundum ..." Deliver me from my afflictions, according to Thy promise to me.

171. Eructabunt labia mea hymnum : cum docueris me justificationes tuas.

My lips shall break forth into song : when Thou shalt teach me Thine ordinances.

---

[1] Some commentators explain "Septies" here as denoting what amongst the Hebrews was the number of perfection. Others, again, think that it is here used in a definite sense, and that the Psalmist actually prayed seven times in the day, and that so the Church understood in primitive times, since she appointed for every day the Seven Canonical Hours, without counting the one at night, which is Matins ; for the Psalmist, besides these seven times of prayer, had already said that he prayed at midnight.—*Tr.*

My lips shall give utterance to words of praise, when Thou shalt have instructed me in Thy ordinances.

172. Pronuntiabit lingua mea eloquium tuum: quia omnia mandata tua æquitas.

My tongue shall declare Thy word: for all Thy commandments are justice.

My tongue shall publish Thy law, for all Thy commands are just and holy.

173. Fiat manus tua, ut salvet me: quoniam mandata tua elegi.

Let Thine hand save me: for I have chosen Thy commandments.

"Manus tua." Thy power.——*"Elegi."* I have resolved to always keep.

174. Concupivi salutare tuum Domine: et lex tua meditatio mea est.

I have longed for Thy salvation, O Lord: and Thy law is my meditation.

I much desired, O Lord, Thy grace, which is to save me; and, therefore, do I meditate solely upon Thy law.

175. Vivet anima mea, et laudabit te: et judicia tua adjuvabunt me.

My soul shall live, and shall praise Thee: and Thy judgments shall help me.

I hope that my soul will live always united to Thee, and will ever praise Thee; and Thy judgments, which are full of mercy, will help me to be faithful to Thee.

176. Erravi sicut ovis quæ periit: quære servum tuum, quia mandata tua non sum oblitus.

I have gone astray like a sheep that is lost: O seek Thy servant, for I have not forgotten Thy commandments.

In time past, alas! I have gone astray, like a sheep that, through leaving its shepherd, was lost. Deign, O Lord, to seek Thy lost servant, for in all my wanderings away from Thee I have not forgotten Thy commandments.

MATINS FOR MONDAY.

PSALM XXVI.

DAVID, persecuted by Saul, and surrounded by dangers of every kind, shows great courage by the confidence he has in the divine protection; at the same time, he sighs after the sight of the Tabernacle. He is a figure of the just man who, in the midst of the enemies of his salvation, longs to leave this world, and to enter into the heavenly kingdom.

The Psalm of David before he was anointed.

1. Dominus illuminatio mea et salus mea : quem timebo.

The Lord is my light and my salvation : whom shall I fear ?

2. Dominus protector vitæ meæ : a quo trepidabo ?

The Lord is the protector of my life : of whom shall I be afraid ?

3. Dum appropiant super me nocentes : ut edant carnes meas ;

Whilst the wicked draw near against me : to eat my flesh ;

4. Qui tribulant me inimici mei : ipsi infirmati sunt, et ceciderunt.

Mine enemies that trouble me : have themselves been weakened, and have fallen.

3, 4. My enemies advance against me, like ferocious beasts to devour my body; but those who ill-treat me, I have seen weakened and cast down.[1]

5. Si consistant adversum me castra : non timebit cor meum.

If armies in camp should stand together against me : my heart shall not fear.

6. Si exurgat adversum me prælium : in hoc ego sperabo.

If battle should rise up against me : in this will I be confident.

Though I saw the battle already risen up against me, I would still hope in my Lord.

7. Unam petii a Domino, hanc requiram : ut inhabitem in domo Domini, omnibus diebus vitæ meæ.

One thing have I asked of the Lord, this will I seek after : that I may dwell in the house of the Lord all the days of my life.

1 Bellarmine says that the past is here employed for the future, according to the custom of the Prophets, to show the certainty of the event.

8. Ut videam voluptatem Domini: et visitem templum ejus.

That I may see the delight of the Lord : and may visit His temple.

And that when I visit His Temple, I may taste the sweetness which the Lord vouchsafes to those who love Him.

9. Quoniam abscondit me in tabernaculo suo : in die malorum protexit me in abscondito tabernaculi sui.

For He hath hidden me in His tabernacle : in the day of evils, He hath protected me in the secret place of His tabernacle.

In this His tabernacle He hides me during the time of my persecutions, and protects me from the snares of my enemies.

10. In petra exaltavit me : et nunc exaltavit caput meum super inimicos meos.

He hath set me up upon a rock : and now He hath lifted up my head above mine enemies.

He has placed me as upon a high rock, so that now I hold my head above my enemies; that is to say, I have overcome them.[1]

11. Circuivi, et immolavi in tabernaculo ejus hostiam vociferationis : cantabo, et psalmum dicam Domino.

I have gone round, and have offered up in His tabernacle a sacrifice of praise : I will sing and speak praise unto the Lord.

"*Circuivi, et immolavi.*" The Hebrew has this in the future, which agrees better with the rest of the verse. The sense, then, is : United with the priests I also will go round the altar, and will offer in His tabernacle a sacrifice of praise, and will sing psalms in honour of the Lord.

12. Exaudi Domine vocem meam qua clamavi ad te : miserere mei, et exaudi me.

Hear, O Lord, my voice, with which I have cried unto Thee : have mercy on me, and hear me.

"*Vocem ... te.*" The urgent supplication I address to Thee.

13. Tibi dixit cor meum, exquisivit te facies mea : faciem tuam Domine requiram.

My heart hath said to Thee ; my face hath sought Thee : Thy face, O Lord, will I seek.

In the past, my heart, that is, the desire of my heart, which is well known to Thee, has already told Thee that my eyes have sought to find Thee: for the future, I will strive to be always in Thy presence, to obey Thee and to love Thee.

14. Ne avertas faciem tuam a me : ne declines in ira a servo tuo.

Hide not Thy face from me : turn not in Thy wrath from Thy servant.

"*In ira.*" In wrath, as a punishment for my sins.

15. Adjutor meus esto : ne derelinquas me, neque despicias me Deus salutaris meus.

Be Thou my helper, forsake me not : neither despise me, O God, my Saviour.

[1] See *Ps.* lx. 2.

16. Quoniam pater meus, et mater mea dereliquerunt me : Dominus autem assumpsit me.

For my father and my mother have forsaken me : but the Lord hath taken me up,

"*Assumpsit me.*" Hath taken me lovingly into His arms.

17. Legem pone mihi, Domine, in via tua : et dirige me in semitam rectam propter inimicos meos.

Set me, O Lord, a law in Thy way: and guide me in the right path, because of mine enemies.

Teach me, O God, to walk according to Thy law, guide me in the right path that leads to Thee, lest I fall into the hands of my enemies.

18. Ne tradideris me in animas tribulantium me : quoniam insurrexerunt in me testes iniqui, et mentita est iniquitas sibi.

Deliver me not over to the will of them that trouble me : for unjust witnesses have risen up against me ; and iniquity hath lied to itself.

"*Mentita ...*" Their iniquity has lied, that is, has done injury to their own selves.

19. Credo videre bona Domini : in terra viventium.

I believe that I shall see the good things of the Lord : in the land of the living.

I hope to enjoy in the land of the living, that is, in the kingdom of the blessed, where death has no place, the good things which the Lord has prepared for those that love Him.

20. Expecta Dominum, viriliter age : et confortetur cor tuum, et sustine Dominum.

Wait on the Lord, do manfully, and let thy heart take courage : and wait thou on the Lord.

Expect, then, my soul, the mercy of the Lord, and fight with courage : let thy heart be of good cheer, and wait for thy help from God, Who will never fail thee.

PSALM XXVII.

DAVID, in his persecutions, implores the help of God, and foretells his deliverance.[1] This Psalm is applicable to all the faithful, who live here on earth in the midst of so many temptations and dangers.

A Psalm for David himself.

1. Ad te Domine clamabo, Deus meus ne sileas a me : nequando taceas a me, et assimilabor descendentibus in lacum.

Unto Thee will I cry, O Lord ; O my God, be not Thou silent to me : lest if Thou be silent to me, I become like them that go down into the pit.

[1] This Psalm is also mystically applied, according to S. Augustine and S. Jerome, to Jesus Christ upon the Cross. It is, says Bellarmine, an abridgment of *Ps.* xxi.

"*Ad te Domine clamabo.*"   O Lord, I will not cease to cry to Thee for help.——"*Ne sileas a me.*"   Keep not silence, as though Thou didst not hear my prayers.——"*Assimilabor . . .*" I become like to those who should find themselves shut up in the tomb, whence their voice can be no more heard.

2. Exaudi Domine vocem deprecationis meæ dum oro ad te : dum extollo manus meas ad templum sanctum tuum.

Hear, O Lord, the voice of my supplication when I cry to Thee : when I lift up my hands to Thy holy temple.

3. Ne simul trahas me cum peccatoribus : et cum operantibus iniquitatem ne perdas me.

Draw me not away together wit the wicked : and with the workers of iniquity destroy me not.

"*Ne simul trahas me.*"   Do not permit me to fall into precipices.

4. Qui loquuntur pacem cum proximo suo : mala autem in cordibus eorum.

Who speak peace with their neighbour : but evils *are* in their hearts.

"*Mala autem . . .*"   But in their hearts they plot his ruin.

5. Da illis secundum opera eorum : et secundum nequitiam adinventionum ipsorum.

Give them according to their works : and according to the wickedness of their inventions.

Give them the punishment that is due to their deeds, and to their malice, which invents artifices to injure others.

6. Secundum opera manuum eorum tribue illis : redde retributionem eorum ipsis.

According to the works of their hands give Thou unto them : render to them their reward.

"*Redde . . .*"   Cause that the evil which they are plotting for others fall upon themselves.[1]

7. Quoniam non intellexerunt opera Domini, et in opera manuum ejus : destrues illos, et non ædificabis eos.

Because they have not understood the works of the Lord, and the operations of His hands : Thou shalt destroy them, and shalt not build them up.

"*Non intellexerunt.*"   They would not understand.[2]—— "*Non ædificabis eos.*"   Thou wilt not restore them to their former state.

---

[1] "*Da . . . Tribue . . . Redde . . .*" These words are not an imprecation but a prophecy, as the following verse explains and proves.

[2] "*Et in opera.*" Judging by the Hebrew and Greek version, the preposition *in* is redundant. S. Jerome's translation has : *Et opus.*——Bellarmine makes an excellent reflection on this passage ; All our evils, he says, come from our not applying ourselves to know and understand the wonders worked by God in the creation, redemption, and government of the human

8. Benedictus Dominus : quoniam exaudivit vocem deprecationis meæ.

Blessed be the Lord : for He hath heard the voice of my supplication.

9. Dominus adjutor meus, et protector meus : in ipso speravit cor meum, et adjutus sum.

The Lord is my helper and my protector : my heart hath trusted in Him, and I have been helped.

10. Et refloruit caro mea : et ex voluntate mea confitebor ei.

And my flesh hath flourished anew : and willingly will I give praise unto Him.

And through His help, my flesh, that is, my weakness, has regained its vigour;[1] therefore, I will sing even with all my heart the praises of my Saviour.

11. Dominus fortitudo plebis suæ ; et protector salvationum Christi sui est.

The Lord is the strength of His people : and the protector of the salvation of His anointed.

David thus calls himself " Christi sui " : Christ, or the anointed of the Lord, as having received from God the royal unction.

12. Salvum fac populum tuum Domine, et benedic hæreditati tuæ : et rege eos, et extolle illos usque in æternum.

Save, O Lord, Thy people, and bless Thine inheritance : rule them and set them up for ever.

PSALM XXVIII.

THE Psalmist invites the people to come and adore God in His Temple. Under this figure, the Gentiles are invited to receive the Gospel, which was preached in the midst of persecutions, here represented by the winds, the tempests, and the thunders.

A Psalm at the finishing of the tabernacle.[2]

1. Afferte Domino filii Dei : afferte Domino filios arietum :

Bring unto the Lord, O ye children of God : bring unto the Lord the offspring of rams :

race. If we considered these things attentively, we could scarcely refrain from loving God. Hence those words of our Saviour to Jerusalem : " If thou also hadst known, and that in this thy day, the things that are to thy peace ! . . . They shall not leave in thee a stone upon a stone ; because thou hast not known the time of thy visitation " (Luke xix. 42). And S. Paul says ; " If they had known it, they would never have crucified the Lord of glory " (1 Cor. ii. 8). Hence also : " With desolation is all the land made desolate : because there is none that considereth in the heart " (Jer. xii. 11).

[1] " Refloruit caro mea." These words, applied to Jesus Christ, admirably foretell His Resurrection.

[2] From this title S. Jerome infers that David composed this Psalm at the time that he caused the Ark of the Covenant to be placed in the tabernacle erected on Mount Sion (2 Kings vi. 17). This tabernacle being a figure of the Church, the Psalmist raises his thoughts from the figure to the reality, and announces the preaching of the Gospel by the Voice of the Lord, which nothing can resist. Thus Bellarmine explains in detail this Psalm.

"*Filios arietum.*" Young rams, to offer them to Him in sacrifice.

2. Afferte Domino gloriam et honorem, afferte Domino gloriam nomini ejus: adorate Dominum in atrio sancto ejus.

Bring unto the Lord glory and honour ; bring unto the Lord glory unto his name : worship the Lord in His holy court.

3. Vox Domini super aquas, Deus majestatis intonuit : Dominus super aquas multas.

The voice of the Lord *is* upon the waters : the God of Majesty hath thundered, the Lord is upon many waters.

The Lord hath made His voice heard upon the storm of waters : in the sound of many waters, together with peals of thunder, does He make heard the voice of His Majesty.

4. Vox Domini in virtute : vox Domini in magnificentia.

The voice of the Lord *is* powerful : the voice of the Lord is full of majesty.

"*In virtute.*" According to the Hebrew: *In potentia.* In power. The Lord makes His voice known in His power and in His grandeur; for when He wills He makes the earth and sea to tremble.

5. Vox Domini confringentis cedros : et confringet Dominus cedros Libani :

The voice of the Lord breaketh the cedars : yea, the Lord shall break the cedars of Libanus :

The voice of the Lord makes itself heard in crashing and shivering the loftiest and strongest cedars of Libanus, by the violence of the tempest.

6. Et comminuet eas tamquam vitulum Libani: et dilectus quemadmodum filius unicornium.

And shall split them as a calf of Libanus : and as the beloved son of unicorns.[1]

"*Comminuet.*" According to the Hebrew : *Saltare faciet :* He shall make them to leap. He shall break them and make them to leap like a calf that goes bounding over the mountain of Libanus, and they shall be seen to leap as the fondled foal of the unicorn. The word "*Dilectus*" is used because the unicorn, when little, is admired and petted for its beauty.

7. Vox Domini intercidentis flammam ignis : Vox Domini concutientis desertum, et commovebit Dominus desertum Cades.

The voice of the Lord divideth the flame of fire : the voice of the Lord shaketh the desert : and the Lord shall shake the desert of Cades.

---

[1] In Hebrew : *Shall make them to skip like a calf.* The Psalmist here describes the effects of thunder (which he calls the voice of the Lord), which sometimes breaks down the tallest and strongest trees, and makes their broken branches skip, &c. All this is to be understood mystically of the powerful voice of God's word in His Church, which has broken the pride of the great ones of this world, and brought many of them meekly and joyfully to submit their necks to the sweet yoke of Christ.

"*Intercidentis flammam.*" S. Jerome's translation is: *Dividens flammam:* Dividing the flame. Thus the sense is: The voice of the Lord, that is, the thunder, divides the flames of fire, by darting a number of lightning flashes one after the other, and so dividing them, or making the intervals between them.——"*Commovebit...*" The voice of the Lord shakes the wilderness, and throws into confusion the desert of Cades. Cades is a vast desert of Arabia.

8. Vox Domini præparantis cervos, et revelabit condensa: et in templo ejus omnes dicent gloriam.

The voice of the Lord prepareth the stags, and He will lay open the thickets: and in His temple all shall speak His glory.

"*Præparantis cervos.*" This means, according to some interpreters, that the thunder terrifies to such a degree the deer, that they bring forth before their time. Authors in favour of this interpretation cite the Hebrew text, which is thus rendered: *Vox Domini parere faciens cervas.* The voice of the Lord makes the hinds to bring forth. But I prefer the interpretation of Mattei, who says that the voice of the Lord, or the thunder, so alarms the deer as to drive them from their thickets; and he observes that in the Vulgate it is *Cervos*, and not *Cervas.*——"*Et revelabit...*" That is to say, the Lord lays open to daylight the thick forests, by shivering and uprooting the trees with His thunderbolts; and thereupon men will all go to render homage to the glory, that is, to the power, of the Lord in His Temple.

9. Dominus diluvium inhabitare facit: et sedebit Dominus rex in æternum.

The Lord maketh the flood to dwell: and the Lord shall sit king for ever.

The Lord makes the deluge of waters which flood the earth to dwell, that is, to abide or last; and Himself, as Lord and eternal King seated upon the clouds, will dispose of everything for His own glory.

10. Dominus virtutem populo suo dabit: Dominus benedicet populo suo in pace.

The Lord will give strength unto His people: the Lord will bless His people with peace.

The Lord, meanwhile, will give to His people the virtue of trusting in His protection; and so blessing them, He will fill them with peace.

PSALM XXIX.

DAVID returns thanks to God for having delivered him from a
dangerous sickness. This Psalm may be fitly used by the
Christian who, assailed by his passions and by temptation, is
in danger of falling into sin.

A Psalm of a Canticle, at the dedication of David's house.[1]

1. Exaltabo te Domine quoniam
suscepisti me : nec delectasti inimicos
meos super me.

I will extol Thee, O Lord, for
Thou hast lifted me up : and hast
not made my foes to rejoice over me.

I will praise Thee, O Lord, by giving Thee thanks, because
Thou hast taken me under Thy protection, and hast not
allowed my enemies to sing victory over me.

2. Domine Deus meus clamavi ad
te : et sanasti me.

O Lord my God, I have cried unto
Thee : and Thou hast healed me.

3. Domine eduxisti ab inferno
animam meam : salvasti me a descendentibus in lacum.

Thou hast brought forth, O Lord,
my soul from hell : Thou hast saved
me from them that go down into the
pit.

"*Eduxisti . . . meam.*" Thou hast brought me back from the
tomb.[2]

4. Psallite Domino sancti ejus : et
confitemini memoriæ sanctitatis ejus.

Sing unto the Lord, O ye His
saints : and give praise at the remembrance of His holiness.

"*Sancti ejus.*" You that are His servants.——"*Memoriæ...*"
For His holy remembrance which He has of you, to do you
good.

5. Quoniam ira in indignatione
ejus : et vita in voluntate ejus.

For wrath is in His indignation :
and life in His *good* will.

The wrath of God, that is, divine punishment, proceeds
from His indignation, which He conceives against the sinner

---

[1] Some think, from this title, that David composed this Psalm for the
ceremony of his entrance into the palace he had built at Jerusalem (*2 Kings*
v. 11). As to the words "*Sanasti me*" (v. 2), they understand them of the
Psalmist's deliverance from the mental sufferings which afflicted him
amidst the mortal dangers he had encountered. According to many Holy
Fathers it is applicable to our Saviour in His Resurrection ; hence it forms
part of the Office for Holy Saturday.

[2] This verse may signify : Thou hast preserved me from death, or, in a
spiritual sense, from sin. When applied to Jesus Christ it describes His
Resurrection, His soul coming forth from Limbo and His body from the
tomb.

on account of his sin; whereas life, that is, salvation, proceeds from the will of God, Who, in His goodness, desires to save man.

6. Ad vesperum demorabitur fletus: et ad matutinum lætitia. — In the evening weeping shall have place: and in the morning gladness.

"*Demorabitur.*" Pagnini's translation is *Pernoctabit.*——The sense of the verse is: Though the Lord cause us to pass the night in sorrow, in the morning He will give us joy.[1]

7. Ego autem dixi in abundantia mea : non movebor in æternum. — In my abundance I said : I shall never be moved.

Finding myself in an abundance of consolations, I said : I shall never be removed from my happiness.

8. Domine in voluntate tua : præstitisti decori meo virtutem. — O Lord, in Thy favour : Thou hast given strength unto my beauty.

Thou, O Lord, in Thy good pleasure, hast given to my glory and happiness strength, that is, solidity.

9. Avertisti faciem tuam a me : et factus sum conturbatus. — Thou didst turn away Thy face from me : and I became troubled.

10. Ad te Domine clamabo : et ad Deum meum deprecabor. — Unto Thee, O Lord, will I cry: and I will make supplication unto my God.

Nevertheless, O Lord, I will not cease ever to cry to Thee, Who art my God, and to pray to Thee to succour me.[2]

11. Quæ utilitas in sanguine meo : dum descendo in corruptionem ? — What profit is there in my blood : whilst I go down to corruption ?

What fruit, indeed, couldst Thou draw from my blood, that is to say, as S. Augustine explains the passage, applying it to Jesus Christ, from the shedding of My blood, or from My death ?——But literally it is better understood of David himself, who fears not being able to do after death the good which he can do in life, as he explains in the following verse.

12. Numquid confitebitur tibi pulvis : aut annuntiabit veritatem tuam? — Shall the dust praise Thee : or shall it declare Thy truth ?

Will, then, perchance, dust, that is, this body of mine reduced to dust, be able after death any more to praise Thee, and to publish the faithfulness of Thy promises?

[1] By the night may be understood the present life ; by the morning the entrance into a blessed eternity.

[2] According to Bellarmine and Bossuet, the future is used instead of the past in this passage ; for the Psalmist relates what he said then, and this agrees better with verse 13.

13. Audivit Dominus, et misertus est mei : Dominus factus est adjutor meus.	The Lord hath heard, and hath had mercy upon me : the Lord is become my helper.
14. Convertisti planctum meum in gaudium mihi: conscidisti saccum meum, et circumdedisti me lætitia :	Thou hast turned my mourning into joy : Thou hast cut off my sackcloth, and encompassed me with gladness :

"*Conscidisti*..." Thou hast torn to pieces my garment of mourning and humiliation, and hast clothed me with a robe of gladness.

15. Ut cantet tibi gloria mea, et non compungar ; Domine Deus meus in æternum confitebor tibi.	That my glory may sing unto Thee, and that I be not sorrowful : O Lord my God, I will give praise unto Thee for ever.

To the end that I may place my glory in singing Thy praises, and that I may no longer be hindered therefrom by sadness.——"*Non compungar.*" According to the Hebrew : *Non taceat.* That is : Let not my glory cease to praise Thee. ——"*In æternum*..." I will never cease to sing Thy glories, and I will ever thank Thee for Thy benefits.

PSALM XXX.

DAVID, driven out of Jerusalem by his son Absalom, begs succour from God. This Psalm may be well applied to the Christian who, when tormented by temptations, puts his confidence in God, and implores His help.[1] We should add that our Divine Redeemer, Jesus Christ, applies to Himself the sixth verse of this Psalm, teaching us thereby that the persecution of David was a figure of that which He Himself suffered at the hands of the Jews.

Unto the end, a Psalm for David, in an ecstasy.

1. In te Domine speravi, non confundar in æternum : in justitia tua libera me.	In Thee, O Lord, have I hoped, let me never be confounded : deliver me in Thy justice.

"*In justitia*..." Deliver me from confusion by Thy justice, according to which Thou dost punish the guilty and protect the innocent.

2. Inclina ad me aurem tuam : accelera ut eruas me.	Bow down Thine ear unto me : make haste to deliver me.

Incline Thy ear to my prayers, and make haste to deliver me from the danger I am in.

[1] The subject is the same as that of *Ps.* lxx.

3. Esto mihi in Deum protectorem: et in domum refugii : ut salvum me facias.

Be Thou unto me a God, a protector : and a house of refuge to save me.

4. Quoniam fortitudo mea, et refugium meum es tu : et propter nomen tuum deduces me, et enutries me.

For Thou art my strength and my refuge : and for Thy name's sake Thou wilt lead me, and nourish me.

For Thou art my strength in temptations, and my refuge in persecutions; in Thee do I hope that, for the glory of Thy name, Thou wilt lead me safe through all dangers, and provide for me in all my wants.

5. Educes me de laqueo hoc, quem absconderunt mihi : quoniam tu es protector meus.

Thou wilt bring me out of this snare, which they have hidden for me : for Thou art my protector.

6. In manus tuas commendo spiritum meum : redemisti me Domine Deus veritatis.

Into Thy hands I commend my spirit : Thou hast redeemed me, O Lord God of Truth.

Into Thy hands I commit my life; many other times Thou hast delivered me from death; for Thou art my Lord and my God, faithful to Thy promises.——Some think that these words, and indeed the whole Psalm, are to be understood of Jesus Christ, since before expiring on the Cross He said : "*Father, into Thy hands I commend My spirit*" (*Luc.* xxiii. 46). Bellarmine, however, justly observes that our Lord, in dying, might well make use of these words, but not of those which follow—"*Redemisti . . .*" "Thou hast redeemed me, O Lord God of truth"; since Jesus Christ was Himself the Redeemer, and not the redeemed.

7. Odisti observantes vanitates supervacue.

Thou hast hated them that regard vanities : to no purpose.

S. Jerome translates the passage thus: *Odisti custodientes vanitates frustra.* Thou, O Lord, dost hate those who keep, that is, who love, vanities, the vain goods of the world; which, indeed, they do uselessly, for they will never find in them the peace that they hope for.

8. Ego autem in Domino speravi : exultabo, et lætabor in misericordia tua.

But I have hoped in the Lord : I will be glad and rejoice in Thy mercy.

But I have put my trust in the Lord; I hope, therefore, through His mercy, to be at peace, and to find therein my joy.

9. Quoniam respexisti humilitatem meam : salvasti de necessitatibus animam meam.

For Thou hast regarded my humiliation : Thou hast saved my soul out of distresses.

For Thou hast looked upon my weakness, and hast saved my life from many dangers.

10. Nec conclusisti me in manibus inimici : statuisti in loco spatioso pedes meos.

And Thou hast not shut me up in the hands of the enemy : Thou hast set my feet in a large place.

Nor hast Thou suffered that I should remain shut up in the hands of my enemies, but hast set my feet in a spacious place; that is, Thou hast given me a large field, plenty of room for making my escape from my enemies, who would close the way against me.

11. Miserere mei Domine, quoniam tribulor : conturbatus est in ira oculus meus, anima mea, et venter meus :

Have mercy on me, O Lord, for I am afflicted : mine eye is troubled with wrath, my soul, and my belly :

Have pity on me, O Lord, for I see myself troubled by the remembrance of my sins; and hence, my eyes, my soul, and my bowels, that is, all my powers, exterior and interior, are troubled at the sight of Thy anger, provoked by my infidelity. Such is the explanation which Bellarmine gives, following S. Augustine.

12. Quoniam defecit in dolore vita mea : et anni mei in gemitibus.

For my life is wasted with grief ; and my years in sighs.

13. Infirmata est in paupertate virtus mea : et ossa mea conturbata sunt.

My strength is weakened through poverty: and my bones are troubled.

"*In paupertate.*" In my tribulation.——"*Conturbata sunt,*" *i.e.*, by losing their strength.

14. Super omnes inimicos meos factus sum opprobrium et vicinis meis valde : et timor notis meis.

I am become a reproach among all mine enemies, and especially to my neighbours: and a fear to mine acquaintance.

"*Valde.*" Still more.——"*Et timor . . .*" Also to my friends I am become an object of horror, so that they are afraid of being known to be my friends.

15. Qui videbant me foras fugerunt a me : oblivioni datus sum, tamquam mortuus a corde.

They that saw me without fled from me : I am forgotten as one dead, out of mind.

They who beheld me in the streets fled from me ; I am clean gone out of their remembrance as a dead man from the memory of hearts : so that in their hearts they hold me as one dead.

16. Factus sum tamquam vas perditum : quoniam audivi vituperationem multorum commorantium in circuitu :

I am become like a broken vessel : for I have heard the rebuke of many that dwell round about :

I have become as a broken vessel, that is, now good for nothing ; since I have to hear myself reviled by all those who come about me.

17. In eo dum convenirent simul adversum me : accipere animam meam consiliati sunt.

While they assembled together against me : they plotted to take away my life.

18. Ego autem in te speravi Domine : dixi : Deus meus es tu : in manibus tuis sortes meæ.

But in Thee, O Lord, do I put my trust ; I said, Thou art my God : my lot is in Thy hands.

19. Eripe me de manu inimicorum meorum : et a persequentibus me.

Deliver me out of the hands of mine enemies ; and from them that persecute me.

20. Illustra faciem tuam super servum tuum, salvum me fac in misericordia tua : Domine non confundar quoniam invocavi te.

Make Thy face to shine upon Thy servant : O save me in Thy mercy. Let me not be confounded, O Lord : for I have called upon Thee.

" *Illustra . . . tuum.*" Turn Thy gracious eyes upon me.——
" *Non confundar.*" I hope that I shall not, to my confusion, be abandoned by Thee.

21. Erubescant impii, et deducantur in infernum : muta fiant labia dolosa.

Let the wicked be ashamed, and be brought down to hell : let deceitful lips be made dumb.

" *Erubescant . . . infernum.*" May the confusion fall rather upon the wicked, and may they be buried in eternal oblivion.

22. Quæ loquuntur adversus justum iniquitatem : in superbia, et in abusione.

Which speak iniquity against the just : with pride and abuse.

" *In abusione.*" According to the Hebrew and Greek : *In contemptu.* With contempt.

23. Quam magna multitudo dulcedinis tuæ Domine : quam abscondisti timentibus te !

O how great is the multitude of Thy sweetness, O Lord : which Thou hast hidden for them that fear Thee!

" *Abscondisti.*" Thou storest up for. This word is used, because such consolations are hidden from the wicked, who do not fear God.

24. Perfecisti eis, qui sperant in te : in conspectu filiorum hominum.

Which Thou hast wrought for them that hope in Thee : in the sight of the sons of men.

Thou hast reserved these perfect consolations of sweetness, for all those who hope in Thee, in the sight of men too.

25. Abscondes eos in abscondito faciei tuæ: a conturbatione hominum.

Thou shalt hide them in the secret of Thy face: from the disturbance of men.

Thou wilt make them enjoy in secret Thy sensible presence ; as God vouchsafes to certain favoured souls. In this secret place they are in security, and sure not to be disturbed by men of the world, or by human passions.

26. Proteges eos in tabernaculo tuo: a contradictione linguarum.

Thou shalt protect them in Thy tabernacle: from the strife of tongues.

27. Benedictus Dominus: quoniam mirificavit misericordiam suam mihi in civitate munita.

Blessed be the Lord : for He hath shown His wonderful mercy in a fortified city.

" *In civitate munita.*" By placing them in a well-fortified city.

28. Ego autem dixi in excessu mentis meæ : projectus sum a facie oculorum tuorum.

But I said in the transport of my mind : I am cast away from before Thine eyes.

" *In excessu.*" According to the Hebrew : *In stupore.* In the excess of my tribulation, which held me stupified as though I had lost my senses.——"*A facie . . .*" That is, from Thy presence.

29. Ideo exaudisti vocem orationis meæ : dum clamarem ad te.

Therefore Thou hast heard the voice of my prayer ; when I cried unto Thee.

30. Diligite Dominum omnes sancti ejus : quoniam veritatem requiret Dominus, et retribuet abundanter facientibus superbiam.

O love the Lord, all ye His saints : for the Lord will seek after truth, and will abundantly requite them that act proudly.

" *Veritatem requiret.*" According to the Hebrew : *Sinceros tuetur.* He protects the sincere.——The sense of the verse is : All you who serve the Lord, love Him, for He will test and show forth your innocence, and He wells know how to defend those who love Him, as He knows how to punish the proud with terrible torments.

31. Viriliter agite, et confortetur cor vestrum : omnes qui speratis in Domino.

Do ye manfully, and let your heart be strengthened : all ye that hope in the Lord.

PSALM XXXI.

The happiness of the really repentant sinner, and the unhappiness on the other hand of the obstinate sinner who goes on in sin.

1 The second penitential Psalm.

To David himself, understanding.

1. Beati, quorum remissæ sunt iniquitates: et quorum tecta sunt peccata.	Blessed are they whose iniquities are forgiven: and whose sins are covered.

"*Quorum tecta sunt peccata.*" Whose sins have been covered, that is, blotted out. Protestants make use of these words, as a proof that sins, though forgiven by God, are yet not removed from the soul, but are only covered, so that the stain of guilt remains there ; and that God sees it, but remits the penalty due, as though He did not see it. They add that God remits the sin only so far as He does not impute it to the sinner, according to what we read in the next verse : "*Blessed is the man to whom the Lord hath not imputed sin*". But all this is false ; for God, in forgiving sins, does not merely cover, but for the merits of Jesus Christ, takes them away from the penitent's soul, as Holy Scripture expresses it : "The Lord also hath taken away thy sin" (2 *Kings* xii. 13). "Behold the Lamb of God, behold Him Who taketh away the sins of the world" (*John* i. 29). Moreover, as the Council of Trent has declared, man is not justified solely by the remission of sin, but by grace and inherent justice. And if God is said not to impute sin, this is, so far as He remits and blots it out, as the same Council also teaches. (*Sess.* 6 *De Justif.* cap. 7, can. 11.)

2. Beatus vir, cui non imputavit Dominus peccatum : nec est in spiritu ejus dolus.	Blessed is the man to whom the Lord hath not imputed sin : and in whose spirit there is no guile.

"*Non imputavit peccatum.*" Has not imputed his sin, because He has forgiven it him.——"*Nec est . . .*" And who has sincerely repented of his fault.[1]

3. Quoniam tacui, inveteraverunt ossa mea : dum clamarem tota die.	Because I was silent, my bones grew old : whilst I cried out all the day long.[2]

Because I was silent, and did not confess my sins, this silence made me lament all the day long, so that my bones grew old ; that is to say, my continual tears have weakened me, as if my bones had become old, or had lost their strength

---

[1] Thus most interpreters understand this second verse as though pretty much a repetition of the first ; but some, with Bellarmine, who gives a detailed explanation of it, prefer the following meaning : Blessed is the man to whom the Lord hath not imputed sin, &c., that is, Blessed is he who has preserved his innocence. S. Paul cites these two verses (*Rom.* iv. 7).

[2] *Because I was silent*, &c. That is, whilst I kept silence, by concealing, or refusing to confess my sins, Thy hand was heavy upon me, &c.

and were broken.——S. Jerome's translation is : *Ossa mea attrita sunt:* My bones are bruised, *in rugitu meo, tota die,* so that the whole day I cried out through pain.

4. Quoniam die ac nocte gravata est super me manus tua : conversus sum in ærumna mea, dum configitur spina. — For day and night Thy hand was heavy upon me : I am turned in my anguish, whilst the thorn is fastened.[1]

Thou hast afflicted me with justice, and hence, when tribulation was piercing me like a sharp thorn, the only course I took was to return to Thee, my God, beseeching Thee to have mercy on me.

5. Delictum meum cognitum tibi feci : et injustitiam meam non abscondi. — I have acknowledged my sin unto Thee : and mine iniquity I have not concealed.

6. Dixi : Confitebor adversum me injustitiam meam Domino : et tu remisisti impietatem peccati mei. — I said I will confess against myself mine iniquity unto the Lord : and Thou hast forgiven the wickedness of my sin.

When I had resolved to confess against myself, my injustice to Thee, O my God, Thou didst thereupon at once forgive me the enormity of my guilt.

7. Pro hac orabit ad te omnis sanctus : in tempore opportuno. — For this shall every one that is holy pray to Thee : in a seasonable time.

"*Pro hac.*" This means, according to Bellarmine and Mattei : For this reason, on account of my confusion and sorrow.——"*Omnis sanctus.*" According to the Chaldee : *Omnis pius.* That is to say, every sinner truly penitent. Such a one is called holy and pious, because, in stripping himself of the impiety he has committed, he clothes himself with holiness by means of sanctifying grace.——"*In tempore opportuno.*" In this life, when we can obtain forgiveness of our sins, before death comes.

8. Verumtamen in diluvio aquarum multarum : ad eum non approximabunt. — And yet in a flood of many waters : they shall not come nigh unto him.

But in the flood of many waters, that is, at death and at judgment, when scourges shall fall as a great deluge upon the

---

[1] *I am turned,* &c. That is, I turn and roll about in my bed, to seek for ease in my pain, whilst the thorn of Thy justice pierces my flesh, and sticks fast in me. In the Hebrew it is, *My moisture is turned into the droughts of the summer.*

wicked, they shall then no more come nigh to God, for then no more will they find place of repentance or pardon.[1]

9. Tu es refugium meum a tribulatione, quæ circumdedit me : exultatio mea, erue me a circumdantibus me.

Thou art my refuge from the trouble which hath encompassed me : my joy, deliver me from them that surround me.

10. Intellectum tibi dabo, et instruam te in via hac, qua gradieris : firmabo super te oculos meos.

I will give thee understanding, and I will instruct thee in this way, in which thou shalt go : I will fix Mine eyes upon thee.

David here makes the Lord speak to the penitent sinner.——
"*Firmabo*..." I will continue to look with gracious eye upon thee, and to protect thee.

11. Nolite fieri sicut equus et mulus : quibus non est intellectus.

Be not as the horse and the mule : that have no understanding.

The Lord addresses these words to obstinate sinners.

12. In camo et freno maxillas eorum constringe : qui non approximant ad te.

With bit and bridle bind fast their jaws : who come not near unto Thee.

Restrain, O Lord, so powerfully, those who keep far from Thee, that they may be forced to obey Thee.[2]

13. Multa flagella peccatoris ; sperantem autem in Domino misericordia circumdabit.

Many are the scourges of the sinner : but mercy shall encompass him that hopeth in the Lord.

Many are the chastisements reserved for sinners, but he who hopes in the Lord shall be so surrounded by His mercy, that he will not be able to go beyond its reach and be lost.

14. Lætamini in Domino, et exultate justi : et gloriamini omnes recti corde.

Be glad in the Lord, and rejoice, ye just : and be joyful, all ye that are right of heart.

"*Gloriamini.*" Let your glory be to serve and love Him.

---

[1] The sense which is very obscure, leaves room for various interpretations. Bellarmine finds the following more conformable to the letter of the Vulgate and to the Hebrew text : Certainly, when the mighty waters come, that is, sufferings of all sorts which, at the last day, must fall as a deluge on the wicked, they shall not approach him, that is, the man who was converted in time.

[2] "*In camo et freno.*" By the evils and afflictions which withdraw or remove the soul from sin.

PSALM XXXII.

The Psalmist exhorts the just to praise the Lord, to fear His judgments, and to have confidence in His mercy.

A Psalm for David.

1. Exultate justi in Domini : rectos decet collaudatio.

Rejoice in the Lord, O ye just : praise becometh the upright.

"*Collaudatio.*" To unite in praising God.

2. Confitemini Domino in cithara : in psalterio decem chordarum psallite illi.

Praise the Lord upon the harp : sing unto Him with the psaltery of ten strings.

3. Cantate ei canticum novum ; bene psallite ei in vociferatioue.

Sing unto Him a new song : play well unto Him with a loud noise.

" *Bene psallite . . .*" Bossuet understands the word " *Psallite*" to mean playing on a musical instrument, and not singing. Thus the sense of the passage would be : Let your voices be in good accord with the music.

4. Quia rectum est verbum Domini : et omnia opera ejus in fide.

For the word of the Lord is right : and all his works are *done* with faithfulness.

For the Lord is sincere in His words, and all His works are faithful, that is, stable.

5. Diligit misericordiam et judicium : misericordia Domini plena est terra.

He loveth mercy and judgment : the earth is full of the mercy of the Lord.

He loves mercy and justice ; but the earth is full of mercy rather than of justice.

6. Verbo Domini cœli firmati sunt : et spiritu oris ejus omnis virtus eorum.

By the word of the Lord were the heavens established : and all the host of them by the breath of His mouth.

The Lord, by one single word, has established the heavens. ——" *Virtus.*" S. Jerome's translation is : *Ornatus.* Adornment, by which is meant the stars.——The sense, then, of this latter clause of the verse is, that God, by a breath of His mouth, or by another single word, adorned the heavens with stars.

7. Congregans sicut in utre aquas maris : ponens in thesauris abyssos.

He gathereth together the waters of the sea as in a vessel : He layeth up the depths in storehouses.

"*Sicut in utre.*" As easily as anyone might put water into a vessel.——"*Ponens in thesauris abyssos.*" The Lord holds the abysses, or the deep waters of the sea, in His treasures, that is, in reserve, to dispose of them according to His good pleasure, whether for doing good to men, or for punishing them.

8. Timeat Dominum omnis terra : ab eo autem commoveantur omnes inhabitantes orbem.	Let all the earth fear the Lord : and let all the inhabitants of the world stand in awe of Him.

"*Ab eo commoveantur.*" S. Jerome's translation is : *Ipsum formident.* Let them fear Him.

9. Quoniam ipse dixit, et facta sunt : ipse mandavit et creata sunt.	For He spake, and they were made : He commanded, and they were created.

Whatsoever God said or willed was done.

10. Dominus dissipat consilia Gentium : reprobat autem cogitationes populorum, et reprobat consilia principum.	The Lord bringeth to nought the counsels of nations : and He defeateth the devices of peoples, and casteth away the counsels of princes.

11. Consilium autem Domini in æternum manet : cogitationes cordis ejus in generatione et generatione.	But the counsel of the Lord endureth for ever : the thoughts of His heart unto all generations.

But every counsel, that is, everything ordained by the Lord, endures for ever; and all the thoughts of His mind, which are hidden to us, shall always have their fulfilment.

12. Beata gens, cujus est Dominus, Deus ejus : populus, quem elegit in hæreditatem sibi.	Blessed is the nation whose God is the Lord : the people whom He hath chosen for His own inheritance.

Blessed is the nation that has the Lord for their God, that is, that makes God and not creatures its last end : this is the people whom God has chosen for His inheritance.

13. De cœlo respexit Dominus : vidit omnes filios hominum.	The Lord hath looked down from heaven : He hath beheld all the sons of men.

14. De præparato habitaculo suo : respexit super omnes, qui habitant terram.	From His habitation which He hath made : He hath looked upon all that dwell on the earth.

"*De præparato habitaculo suo*" : viz., Heaven, which He has prepared for Himself.

15. Qui finxit singillatim corda eorum : qui intelligit omnia opera eorum.	He Who hath made the hearts of every one of them : Who understandeth all their works.

He it is Who created their hearts, or their souls.——*"Singil-latim."* One by one, as Bellarmine, Menochius, and Tirinus explain it.——*"Intelligit . . ."* He well understands and pene-trates all the motives of their actions.

16. Non salvatur rex per multam virtutem : et gigas non salvabitur in multitudine virtutis suæ.

No king is saved by a great army : nor shall a giant be saved by the greatness of his own strength.

17. Fallax equus ad salutem : in abundantia autem virtutis suæ non salvabitur.

Vain is the horse for safety : neither shall he be saved by the abundance of his strength.

No one can be secure of his safety, however fleet, strong, steady, or sagacious the horse that carries him may be ; all this is fallacious.

18. Ecce oculi Domini super metu-entes eum : et in eis, qui sperant super misericordia ejus.

Behold, the eyes of the Lord are upon them that fear Him ; and upon them that hope in His mercy.

19. Ut eruat a morte animas eorum : et alat eos in fame.

To deliver their souls from death : and to feed them in the time of dearth.

20. Anima nostra sustinet Domi-num : quoniam adjutor et protector noster est.

Our soul waiteth for the Lord : for He is our helper and protector.

21. Quia in eo lætabitur cor nos-trum : et in nomine sancto ejus speravimus.

For in Him shall our heart rejoice: and in His holy Name we have trusted.

22. Fiat misericordia tua Domine super nos : quemadmodum speravi-mus in te.

Let Thy mercy, O Lord, be upon us : as we have hoped in Thee.

PSALM XXXIII.

The Psalmist invites us constantly to praise the Lord, for the care and continual providence with which He watches over His servants, and for the assistance which He gives them in their tribulations.

For David, when he changed his countenance before Achimelech, who dismissed him, and he went his way (1 *Kings* xxi.).

1. Benedicam Dominum in omni tempore : semper laus ejus in ore meo.

I will bless the Lord at all times : His praise shall be always in my mouth.

2. In Domino laudabitur anima mea : audiant mansueti, et lætentur.

My soul shall glory in the Lord : let the meek hear and rejoice.

"*Laudabitur.*" According to the Hebrew : *Gloriabitur.* Shall glory.——"*Audiant* . . ." Let the meek and the devout listen to the account of the benefits He has done to me, and let them rejoice thereat.

3. Magnificate Dominum mecum : et exaltemus nomen ejus in idipsum.

O magnify the Lord with me : and let us extol His name together.

4. Exquisivi Dominum, et exaudivit me : et ex omnibus tribulationibus meis eripuit me.

I sought the Lord, and He heard me : and He delivered me from all my troubles.

"*Exaudivit.*" He heard me, by giving me grace to find Him.

5. Accedite ad eum, et illuminamini : et facies vestræ non confundentur.

Come ye to Him and be enlightened : and your faces shall not be confounded.

"*Facies vestræ* . . ." Your faces shall not be made to blush with shame by the refusal of what you ask and hope for.

6. Iste pauper clamavit et Dominus exaudivit eum : et de omnibus tribulationibus ejus salvavit eum.

This poor man cried, and the Lord heard him : and saved him out of all his troubles.

"*Iste pauper.*" In proof of which, this man poor in merit.

7. Immittet Angelus Domini in circuitu timentium eum : et eripiet eos.

The Angel of the Lord shall encamp round about them that fear Him : and shall deliver them.

"*Immittet,*" *se* understood. Shall set himself.

8. Gustate, et videte quoniam suavis est Dominus : beatus vir, qui sperat in eo.

O taste, and see that the Lord is sweet : blessed is the man that hopeth in Him.

"*Gustate.*" Taste, or savour, the Lord, by applying yourselves to contemplate His goodness.——"*Videte quoniam suavis est.*" You will know by experience how sweet He is to him who seeks and tastes Him.

9. Timete Dominum omnes sancti ejus : quoniam non est inopia timentibus eum.

Fear the Lord, all ye His saints : for there is no want to them that fear Him.

"*Timete . . . ejus.*" O all ye servants of the Lord, fear Him.——A filial fear is intended here, and not a servile fear.

10. Divites eguerunt et esurierunt : inquirentes autem Dominum non minuentur omni bono.

The rich have wanted, and have suffered hunger : but they that seek the Lord shall not be deprived of any good.

The rich ones of this world, though possessing in abundance the goods of this earth, are left to suffer hunger and thirst, because they find in them neither peace nor satisfaction ; but those that seek the Lord, though poor, shall be filled with every good.

11. Venite filii, audite me: timorem Domini docebo vos.

Come, ye children, hearken unto me : I will teach you the fear of the Lord.

12. Quis est homo qui vult vitam : diligit dies videre bonos ?

Who is the man that desireth life : who loveth to see good days.

The sense is : What is the way to enjoy the true life, true happiness ? The answer is given in the following verses.

13. Prohibe linguam tuam a malo : et labia tua ne loquantur dolum.

Keep thy tongue from evil: and thy lips from speaking guile.

14. Diverte a malo, et fac bonum : inquire pacem, et persequere eam.

Turn away from evil, and do good: seek peace, and pursue it.

" *Inquire pacem ...*" Seek true peace, and never give over seeking it.

15. Oculi Domini super justos : et aures ejus in preces eorum.

The eyes of the Lord are upon the just : and His ears *are open* unto their prayers.

16. Vultus autem Domini super facientes mala : ut perdat de terra memoriam eorum.

But the countenance of the Lord is against them that do evil things : to cut off the remembrance of them from the earth.

" *Vultus ... mala.*" On the contrary, He keeps His eyes upon the wicked to punish them.

17. Clamaverunt justi, et Dominus exaudivit eos : et ex omnibus tribulationibus eorum liberavit eos.

The just cried, and the Lord heard them : and delivered them out of all their troubles.

18. Juxta est Dominus iis qui tribulato sunt corde : et humiles spiritu salvabit.

The Lord is nigh unto them that are of a contrite heart : and He will save the humble of spirit.

19. Multæ tribulationes justorum : et de omnibus his liberabit eos Dominus.

Many are the afflictions of the just : but the Lord will deliver them out of them all.

20. Custodit Dominus omnia ossa eorum : unum ex his non conteretur.

The Lord keepeth all their bones : not one of them shall be broken.

Hence, at the general resurrection, they will be all found whole and sound.

21. Mors peccatorum pessima : et qui oderunt justum delinquent.

The death of the wicked is very evil : and they that hate the just shall be guilty.

On the contrary, sinners will have a most miserable death, and they that hate the just shall come to ruin.——"*Delinquent.*" According to the Hebrew : *Devastabuntur.* Shall be laid desolate.

22. Redimet Dominus animas servorum suorum : et non delinquent omnes qui sperant in eo.

The Lord will redeem the souls of His servants : and none of them that trust in Him shall offend.[1]

The Lord shall rescue from every danger the souls of His servants, and will not let any of them who trust in Him fail in their duties.

PSALM XXXIV.

THE just man in this life, tempted by the devil, and persecuted by men, seeks help from God.[2]

For David himself.

1. Judica Domine nocentes me : expugna impugnantes me.

Judge Thou, O Lord, them that wrong me : overthrow them that fight against me.

"*Judica.*" That is, punish as they deserve.

2. Apprehende arma et scutum : et exurge in adjutorium mihi.

Lay hold of arms and shield : and rise up to help me.

"*Apprehende . . . scutum.*" Take Thy arms to strike my enemies, and Thy shield to protect me.[3]

3. Effunde frameam, et conclude adversus eos, qui persequuntur me : dic animæ meæ, Salus tua ego sum.

Bring forth the spear, and stop the way against them that persecute me : say unto my soul, I am thy salvation.

"*Effunde.*" S. Jerome's translation is : *Evagina.* Unsheath.

4. Confundantur et revereantur : quærentes animam meam.

Let them be confounded and put to shame : that seek after my soul.

"*Quærentes . . .*" Those who seek to take away my life.

1 *Offend.* The Hebrew term means *perish.*

2 This Psalm is admirably suited to Jesus Christ, the Just by excellence : Bellarmine even thinks, with S. Augustine and S. Jerome, that this is its principal meaning.

3 The shield of God is His goodness, His benevolence. "Thou hast crowned us as with a shield of Thy goodwill" (*Ps.* v. 13). It is also equity or justice. "He will take equity for an invincible shield" (*Wisdom* v. 20).

5. Avertantur retrorsum, et confundantur : cogitantes mihi mala.

Let them be turned back, and brought to confusion : that devise evil against me.

6. Fiant tamquam pulvis ante faciem venti : et Angelus Domini coarctans eos.

Let them become as dust before the wind : and let the Angel of the Lord straiten them.

"*Angelus . . . eos.*" Let the Angel, the minister of the Lord's justice, press on to discomfit them.

7. Fiat via illorum tenebræ et lubricum : et Angelus Domini persequens eos.

Let their way become dark and slippery : and let the Angel of the Lord pursue them.

"*Fiat . . . lubricum.*" That is to say : Let them fall into a precipice.———He who goes by night along a slippery path can hardly avoid meeting with a dangerous fall.———"*Angelus Domini.*" The avenging Angel of the Lord.

8. Quoniam gratis absconderunt mihi interitum laquei sui: supervacue exprobraverunt animam meam.

For without cause they have hidden their net for my destruction : without cause they have upbraided my soul.

For without cause on my part they have set their snares, or laid ambush, to take my life ; and have, at the same time, gratuitously loaded me with unmerited injuries.

9. Veniat illi laqueus, quem ignorat : et captio, quam abscondit, apprehendat eum : et in laqueum cadat in ipsum.

Let the snare which he knoweth not of come upon him : and let the net which he hath hidden catch himself, and into that very snare let him fall.

"*Laqueus.*" According to the Hebrew : *Calamitas.*———The meaning is : Let a calamity come upon him which he did not expect.———"*Captio.*" According to the Hebrew : *Retis.* A net.

10. Anima autem mea exultabit in Domino : et delectabitur super salutari suo.

But my soul shall rejoice in the Lord : and shall be delighted in His salvation.

"*Super salutari suo.*" At the salvation received from **Him.**[1]

11. Omnia ossa mea dicent: Domine, quis similis tibi ?

All my bones shall say : Lord, who is like unto Thee ?

"*Omnia ossa mea.*" All parts even of my body, to my very bones.

---

[1] Or, according to S. Augustine and conformably with verse 3 : In his Salvation, his Saviour Who is God Himself.

12. Eripiens inopem de manu fortiorum ejus: egenum et pauperem a diripientibus eum.

Who deliverest the poor from the hand of them that are stronger than he : the needy and the poor from them that strip him.

13. Surgentes testes iniqui ; quæ ignorabam, interrogabant me.

Unjust witnesses rising up : have charged me with things that I knew not.

"*Quæ ignorabam . . .*" They asked me about things of which I was ignorant, in order to find matter for accusation against me.

14. Retribuebant mihi mala pro bonis : sterilitatem animæ meæ.

They have repaid me evil for good : to the depriving me of my soul.

"*Sterilitatem.*" According to the Hebrew : *Orbitatem.* Privation, despoiling.——The meaning is : They sought to strip my life (me) of everything.

15. Ego autem cum mihi molesti essent : induebar cilicio.

But as for me, when they molested me : I was clothed with hair-cloth.

16. Humiliabam in jejunio animam meam : et oratio mea in sinu meo convertetur.

I humbled my soul with fasting : and my prayer shall be turned into my bosom.

15, 16. For my part, seeing myself thus tormented by them, I clothed myself with sackcloth, and afflicted myself with fasting, humbling myself before God, as one deserving such ill-treatment, and praying for my persecutors : if my prayer does not benefit them, it will turn at least to my own profit.

17. Quasi proximum, et quasi fratrem nostrum, sic complacebam : quasi lugens et contristatus sic humiliabar.

I behaved as though he were a neighbour and a brother : as one mourning and sorrowful, so was I humbled.

I loved to pray for him who persecuted me, as though he had been my friend and my brother ; and I suffered for him, weeping and afflicting myself with his miseries, even as a mother weeps for the sorrows of her children. Such is the sense of the Hebrew, according to the translation of S. Jerome : *Quasi mater lugens tristis, sic incedebam.* As a mother mourning and sad, so did I go my way.

18. Et adversum me lætati sunt, et convenerunt : congregata sunt super me flagella, et ignoravi.

But they rejoiced against me, and came together : scourges were gathered together upon me, and I knew it not.

They, on the contrary, rejoiced at my ills ; yet more, they conspired against me, and, when I least thought of it, the scourges were gathered together over me.

19. Dissipati sunt, nec compuncti, tentaverunt me, subsannaverunt me subsannatione: frenduerunt super me dentibus suis.

They were separated, and they repented not, they tempted me, they scoffed at me with scorn: they gnashed upon me with their teeth.

They have been scattered by the Lord, yet still they have not repented ; on the contrary, they have continued to tempt me, now mocking at me in scorn, and now gnashing their teeth at me in rage.

20. Domine quando respicies? restitue animam meam a malignitate eorum, a leonibus unicam meam.

Lord, when wilt Thou look upon me? rescue Thou my soul from their malice, my only one from the lions.

When, O Lord, wilt Thou look upon me with an eye of pity? Ah! deliver me from the malice of those who, like lions, lie in wait for my life.[1]

21. Confitebor tibi in ecclesia magna : in populo gravi laudabo te.

I will give thanks to Thee in a great assembly : I will praise Thee in a strong people.

If Thou wilt be propitious to my prayer, I will give Thee thanks on the solemn days, when the nation is assembled, and there in the presence of a great people I will praise Thy mercy.

22. Non supergaudeant mihi, qui adversantur mihi inique : qui oderunt me gratis et annuunt oculis.

Let not them that are my enemies wrongfully rejoice over me : who have hated me without a cause, and wink with the eyes.

"*Annuunt oculis.*" To deceive me, they pretend to look upon me with a good eye, or with favour.——On these words S. Augustine thus comments : *Quid est, Annuentes oculis? Pronuntiantes vultu, quod corde non gestant.* What is, Winking with the eyes? Expressing by look what one has not got in the heart.

23. Quoniam mihi quidem pacifice loquebantur : et in iracundia terræ loquentes, dolos cogitabant.

For they spake indeed peaceably unto me : and speaking in the anger of the earth they devised guile.

"*In iracundia terræ loquentes.*" But inwardly speaking according to the anger of an earthly heart. Thus Bellarmine and Bossuet explain the words.

24. Et dilataverunt super me os suum : dixerunt, Euge, euge, viderunt oculi nostri.

And they opened their mouth wide against me : they said, Aha, aha, our eyes have seen it.

"*Euge...*" What joy, what joy ; we have seen what we wished to see.

[1] "*Unicam meam.*" My soul, or my life, which is my only one. According to Bellarmine : "Rightly it is called the only one, as being the one alone beloved". See the same expression *Ps.* xxi. 21.

25. Vidisti Domine, ne sileas: Domine ne discedas a me.

Thou hast seen, O Lord, be not Thou silent : O Lord, depart not from me.

" *Ne sileas.*" Do not fail to punish them.

26. Exurge et intende judicio meo : Deus meus, et Dominus meus in causam meam.

Arise, and be attentive unto my judgment : unto my cause, my God and my Lord.

27. Judica me secundum justitiam tuam Domine Deus meus : et non supergaudeant mihi.

Judge me, O Lord my God, according unto Thy justice : and let them not rejoice over me.

" *Non ...*" Let not my enemies have any more to rejoice over my misfortunes.

28. Non dicant in cordibus suis, Euge, euge, animæ nostræ : nec dicant, Devoravimus eum.

Let them not say in their hearts, Aha, aha, it is as we wished : neither let them say, We have swallowed him up.

29. Erubescant et revereantur simul : qui gratulantur malis meis.

Let them blush, and be ashamed together : who rejoice at my misfortunes.

30. Induantur confusione et reverentia : qui magna loquuntur super me.

Let them be clothed with confusion and shame : who speak great things against me.

31. Exultent et lætentur qui volunt justitiam meam : et dicant semper, Magnificetur Dominus, qui volunt pacem servi ejus.

Let them rejoice and be glad who are well pleased with my justice : and let them that delight in the peace of His servant say always, The Lord be magnified.

" *Qui ... meam.*" Who rejoice in my innocence.——
" *Pacem.*" The prosperity. Thus Bellarmine, Malvenda, and others, following S. Jerome, explain the verse.

32. Et lingua mea meditabitur justitiam tuam : tota die laudem tuam.

And my tongue shall speak of Thy justice : *and of* Thy praise all the day long.

PSALM XXXV.

THE Psalmist shows us how great is the malice of sinners, and the mercy of God towards them ; he speaks, at the same time, of His goodness towards the just.

Unto the end, for the servant of God, David himself.

1. Dixit injustus, ut delinquat in semetipso : non est timor Dei ante oculos ejus.

The unjust hath said within himself, that he would sin : there is no fear of God before his eyes.

The wicked man has said in his heart, or has resolved (as
Bellarmine and Mattei explain it), to sin freely ; and he acts
thus because he has no longer the fear of God before his eyes.

2. Quoniam dolose egit in conspectu ejus : ut inveniatur iniquitas
ejus ad odium.

For in His sight he hath done
deceitfully : that his iniquity may be
found unto hatred.[1]

This is a very difficult verse. S. Augustine explains it
thus : *In odio, persequente iniquitate sua, dolose egit coram Deo.*
Out of hatred, pursuing his path of crime, he acts deceitfully
before God ; words well applicable to sacrilegious confessions.
The Rabbinists, in their comments upon the Hebrew text,
explain it thus : The wicked man sins, flattering himself that
God does not see and does not abhor his iniquity.——But
Mattei believes that some words are wanting in the Hebrew
text : his opinion is that the Psalmist is not speaking here of
deceitful hypocrites, but of obstinate sinners ; and he explains
the passage as follows : The sinner acts perversely before the
eyes of God, to the end that his iniquity may draw down the
divine hatred upon himself ; and thus sins to be hated by
God.——It is proper to the obstinate sinner that he should
will to perish. Such is also the explanation of Bellarmine
and Bossuet.

3. Verba oris ejus iniquitas, et
dolus : noluit intelligere ut bene
ageret.

The words of his mouth are
iniquity and guile : he would not
understand that he might do well.

"*Noluit* . . ." He is unwilling to understand what is good,
that he may not be obliged to practise it.

4. Iniquitatem meditatus est in
cubili suo : astitit omni viæ non
bonæ, malitiam autem non odivit.

He hath devised iniquity on his
bed : he hath set himself on every
way that is not good : but evil he
hath not hated.

On his bed he premeditates to do evil, and he gives himself
to every wicked means ; for so far from hating evil, he loves it.

5. Domine in cœlo misericordia
tua : et veritas tua usque ad nubes.

O Lord, Thy mercy is in the
heavens : and Thy truth reacheth
even unto the clouds.

That is, Thy mercy and Thy faithfulness to Thy promises
are immense and infinite.

6. Justitia tua sicut montes Dei :
judicia tua abyssus multa.

Thy justice is as the mountains of
God : Thy judgments are a great
deep.

[1] *Unto hatred.* That is, hateful to God.

Thy justice is great as a mountain, and that mountain a divine mountain which is high beyond our sight in this life; and Thy judgments are to us abysses very obscure and impenetrable.

7. Homines, et jumenta salvabis Domine: quemamodum multiplicasti misericordiam tuam Deus.

Men and beasts Thou wilt preserve, O Lord: O how hast Thou multiplied Thy mercy, O God!

Bellarmine explains this by saying that God wishes to save not only good men, but those who, by following their sensual appetites, make themselves like the brute beasts. So greatly, O my God, hast Thou multiplied Thy mercies to men.

8. Filii autem hominum : in tegmine alarum tuarum sperabunt.

But the children of men shall put their trust : under the covert of Thy wings.

"*Autem.*" Hence it comes that.——"*In tegmine alarum tuarum.*" That is, securely relying on the protection of Thy providence.

9. Inebriabuntur ab ubertate domus tuæ : et torrente voluptatis tuæ potabis eos.

They shall be inebriated with the plenteousness of Thy house : and Thou shalt make them drink of the torrent of Thy pleasure.

"*Ab ubertate...*" With the abundant delights of Thy house ; for Thou wilt give them to taste, in part, of that same infinite joy which Thou dost Thyself enjoy.

10. Quoniam apud te est fons vitæ : et in lumine tuo videbimus lumen.

For with Thee is the well of life : and in Thy light shall we see light.

"*In lumine...*" Illumined by Thy divine light, we shall see Thyself, Who art the Light by essence.

11. Prætende misericordiam tuam scientibus te : et justitiam tuam his, qui recto sunt corde.

Stretch forth Thy mercy unto them that know Thee : and Thy justice unto them that are right of heart.

"*Justitiam tuam.*" The just reward which Thou hast prepared for each according to his deserts.

12. Non veniat mihi pes superbiæ : et manus peccatoris non moveat me.

Let not the foot of pride come unto me : and let not the hand of the sinner move me.

S. Augustine explains this verse thus : O Lord, suffer not that pride set its foot on me (gain dominion over me), nor that the hand of the sinner, that is, of the devil, or of any of his followers, detach me from Thy service.

13. Ibi ceciderunt qui operantur iniquitatem : expulsi sunt, nec potuerunt stare.	There are the workers of iniquity fallen : they are cast out, and they could not stand.

"*Ibi.*" There, in pride.——"*Expulsi* . . ." They have been driven out of heaven, and it is precisely on account of their pride that they were not able to remain there.

PSALM XXXVI.

THE Psalmist exhorts the just to persevere in virtue, and to trust in the divine mercy, without allowing themselves to be moved by the prosperity of the wicked in this world.[1]

A Psalm for David himself.

1. Noli æmulari in malignantibus : neque zelaveris facientes iniquitatem.	Be not jealous of evil-doers : nor envy them that work iniquity.

Do not thou become the rival, that is, the imitator of the wicked : by allowing thyself to be moved by zeal, that is, by envy of their happiness.——Another sense is : Be not inflamed with zeal against sinners on account of their happiness, as though complaining to God for prospering them as He does.

2. Quoniam tamquam fœnum velociter arescent : et quemadmodum olera herbarum cito decident.	For they shall shortly wither away as the grass : and as the green herbs they shall quickly fall.

For they shall soon wither as the grass that falls under the scythe : they shall fall as the herb cut off at the root.

3. Spera in Domino, et fac bonitatem : et inhabita terram, et pasceris in divitiis ejus.	Trust in the Lord, and do good : and dwell in the land, and thou shalt be fed with its riches.

"*Inhabita* . . ." And so dwell in this land, fully assured that God will feed thee with His delights.——Or, as others understand it : Cultivate the land, and thou shalt be abundantly provided with its fruits.

4. Delectare in Domino : et dabit tibi petitiones cordis tui.	Delight in the Lord : and He will give thee the desires of thy heart.

Make thy happiness consist in pleasing God : or, make the Lord thy delight and He will satisfy all thy requests, all the desires of thy heart.

[1] Bellarmine remarks that this Psalm does not form a consecutive discourse ; it is a collection of detached sentences, to the number of 22, and in the Hebrew they are arranged alphabetically, according to the first letter of each. The other Alphabetic Psalms are xxiv. xxxiii. cx. cxi. cxviii. and cxliv.

5. Revela Domino viam tuam, et spera in eo : et ipse faciet.

Commit thy way unto the Lord: and trust in Him, and He will do it.

Lay before God all the wants and desires of thy life : put thy trust in Him and He will do whatever thou desirest.

6. Et educet quasi lumen justitiam tuam : et judicium tuum tamquam meridiem ; subditus esto Domino, et ora eum.

And He will bring forth thy justice as the light, and thy judgment as the noon-day : be subject to the Lord, and pray to Him.

He will even draw forth from the darkness thy innocence, as a torch of flame, and He will cause it to shine as the sun at noonday : be obedient to the Lord, and be attentive to pray for His help.

7. Noli æmulari in eo, qui prosperatur in via sua : in homine faciente injustitias.

Envy not the man who prospereth in his way : the man who doeth unjust things.

"*In via sua.*" In his evil way.

8. Desine ab ira, et derelinque furorem : noli æmulari ut maligneris.

Cease from anger, and forsake wrath : be not zealous to do evil.

Refrain from anger, and much more from rage : do not emulate the wicked, by becoming wicked like them.

9. Quoniam qui malignantur, exterminabuntur : sustinentes autem Dominum, ipsi hereditabunt terram.

For evil-doers shall be cut off : but they that wait upon the Lord, they shall inherit the land.

"*Sustinentes* ..." They who expect, with patience, help from the Lord, shall inherit the land of promise, which is heaven.

10. Et adhuc pusillum, et non erit peccator : et quæres locum ejus, et non invenies.

For yet a little while, and the wicked shall not be : and thou shalt seek his place, and shalt not find it.

Wait a little while, and thou wilt see that the sinner, now so puffed up with pride about his goods, shall be no more : thou wilt seek his place, that is, the prosperous state in which he lived, and thou wilt no longer find it.

11. Mansueti autem hereditabunt terram : et delectabuntur in multitudine pacis.

But the meek shall inherit the land : and shall delight in abundance of peace.

On the contrary, the meek, as are the humble, shall possess the land which was destined to them for their inheritance, and shall enjoy a great peace.[1]

---

[1] *Matth.* v. 4.

12. Observabit peccator justum : et stridebit super eum dentibus suis.

The sinner shall watch the just man : and shall gnash upon him with his teeth.

The sinner will look with contempt on the life of the just man ; and from the hatred he feels, will gnash on him with his teeth, in his desire to oppress him.

13. Dominus autem'irridebit eum : quoniam prospicit quod veniet dies ejus.

But the Lord shall laugh at him : for He foreseeth that his day shall come.

" *Quoniam . . ."* Knowing that one day he will be punished as he deserves.

14. Gladium evaginaverunt peccatores : intenderunt arcum suum.

The wicked have drawn out the sword : they have bent their bow.

15. Ut dejiciant pauperem et inopem : ut trucident rectos corde.

To cast down the poor and needy : to slay the upright of heart.

16. Gladius eorum intret in corda ipsorum : et arcus eorum confringatur.

Let their sword enter into their own hearts : and let their bow be broken.

God grant that, &c.[1]

17. Melius est modicum justo : super divitias peccatorum multas.

Better is a little to the just : than the great riches of the wicked.

The just man is more content with the little that he possesses, than are sinners with all their great wealth.

18. Quoniam brachia peccatorum conterentur : confirmat autem justos Dominus.

For the arms of the wicked shall be broken in pieces : but the Lord strengtheneth the just.

For all the power of sinners shall be destroyed : whilst that of the just shall be strengthened by the Lord.

19. Novit Dominus dies immaculatorum : et hereditas eorum in æternum erit.

The Lord knoweth the days of the undefiled : and their inheritance shall be for ever.

" *Novit . . . immaculatorum."* The Lord notes with care and approval the days and the steps of the innocent.[2]

20. Non confundentur in tempore malo, et in diebus famis saturabuntur : quia peccatores peribunt.

They shall not be confounded in the evil time : and in the days of famine they shall be filled ; for the wicked shall perish.

" *In tempore malo."* In the time of divine vengeance.——

---

[1] Or else : Divine justice will cause.——An ordinary prediction under the form of imprecation.

[2] See *Ps.* i. 7.

"*In diebus famis saturabuntur.*" When every one shall ardently desire his eternal salvation, they shall be satiated with joy by the benediction of God.

21. Inimici vero Domini mox ut honorificati fuerint et exaltati : deficientes, quemadmodum fumus deficient.

And the enemies of the Lord, soon after they are honoured and exalted : shall come to nothing, and vanish like smoke.

But on the other hand, the enemies of the Lord shall hardly have been honoured and exalted in the world when they shall disappear from the eyes of men, as smoke vanishes that is dispersed in the air.

22. Mutuabitur peccator, et non solvet : justus autem miseretur et tribuet.

The sinner shall borrow, and not pay again : but the just showeth mercy, and shall give.

"*Justus* . . ." But the just, who has compassion on the poor, helps them, and will always have means to help them.

23. Quia benedicentes ei hereditabunt terram : maledicentes autem ei disperibunt.

For such as bless Him shall inherit the land : but such as curse Him shall perish.

For those who bless God, as S. Augustine understands it, shall be blessed by God, and shall inherit the land of the living : but those who curse Him with blasphemies, shall be cursed and brought to ruin.

24. Apud Dominum gressus hominis dirigentur : et viam ejus volet.

By the Lord shall the steps of a man be ordered : and He shall approve his way.

"*Hominis.*" Of the just man.——"*Viam* . . ." He approves of his ways, his conduct.

25. Cum ceciderit, non collidetur : quia Dominus supponit manum suam.

When he shall fall, he shall not be bruised : for the Lord putteth His hand under him.

If the just man should at any time stumble, the Lord will not allow him to suffer hurt : for, putting His hand under him, He will hold him up.

26. Junior fui, etenim senui : et non vidi justum derelictum, nec semen ejus quærens panem.

I have been young, and now am old : and I have not seen the just forsaken, nor his seed begging bread.

27. Tota die miseretur et commodat : et semen illius in benedictione erit.

He showeth mercy, and lendeth all the day long : and his seed shall be in blessing.

All the day long having compassion on the poor, he relieves them, at least by lending to them ; and, therefore, his family shall see itself always blessed by God.

28. Declina a malo, et fac bonum : et inhabita in sæculum sæculi.

Turn away from evil, and do good : and dwell for evermore.

And thou wilt be happy wherever thou shalt dwell.

29. Quia Dominus amat judicium, et non derelinquet sanctos suos : in æternum conservabuntur.

For the Lord loveth judgment, and He will not forsake His saints : they shall be preserved for ever.

"*Judicium.*" Justice.——"*Sanctos suos.*" His servants.

30. Injusti punientur : et semen impiorum peribit.

The unjust shall be punished : and the seed of the wicked shall perish.

On the contrary, etc.

31. Justi autem hereditabunt terram : et inhabitabunt in sæculum sæculi super eam.

But the just shall inherit the land : and shall dwell therein for evermore.

"*Terram.*" The land of the blessed.

32. Os justi meditabitur sapientiam : et lingua ejus loquetur judicium.

The mouth of the just shall meditate wisdom : and his tongue shall speak of judgment.

"*Os . . . sapientiam.*" The words of the just man are all well-considered, prudent, and wise.——"*Judicium.*" Only what is in accordance with justice.

33. Lex Dei ejus in corde ipsius : et non supplantabuntur gressus ejus.

The law of his God is in his heart : and his footsteps shall not slip.

The law of God remains fixed in his heart : and his steps shall not slip, go wrong.

34. Considerat peccator justum : et quærit mortificare eum.

The wicked watcheth the just man : and seeketh to put him to death.

The wicked man reflects on the life of the just, so unlike his own ; and through the hatred he bears him, he seeks to do him evil.[1]

35. Dominus autem non derelinquet eum in manibus ejus : nec damnabit eum cum judicabitur illi.

But the Lord will not leave him in his hands : nor condemn him when he shall be judged.

But the Lord will not abandon the just man to the hand of the wicked man, nor when He has to judge the just will He condemn Him, however great the calumnies laid to his charge by the wicked.

36. Expecta Dominum, et custodi viam ejus : et exaltabit te, ut hereditate capias terram : cum perierint peccatores, videbis.

Wait on the Lord, and keep His way : and He shall exalt thee to inherit the land : when the wicked perish, thou shalt see it.

[1] The same as verse 12 ; but there it was by violence, here it is by craft, as the Jews acted towards Jesus Christ.

Wait then for the Lord, and continue to walk in the path by which He has led thee : and He will exalt thee in such-wise, as to make thee come to possess for thy inheritance the land that thou desirest : and when the wicked shall be lost, then shalt thou see the recompense which shall be given thee according to His promise.

37. Vidi impium superexaltatum : et elevatum sicut cedros Libani.	I have seen the wicked highly exalted : and lifted up like the cedars of Libanus.

"*Superexaltatum.*" Above other men.

38. Et transivi, et ecce non erat : et quæsivi eum, et non est inventus locus ejus.	And I passed by, and lo, he was not : I sought him, and his place was not found.

"*Locus ejus.*" His greatness, whereof no more trace remained than if it had never been.

39. Custodi innocentiam, et vide æquitatem : quoniam sunt reliquiæ homini pacifico.	Keep innocence, and behold just-ice : for the posterity of the peace-able man continues.[1]

" *Vide.* " Always observe. —— " *Sunt . . . pacifico.* " S. Jerome's translation is : *Quia erit ad extremum viro pax :* Because the man shall have peace at the last. This comes nearer to the Hebrew, which may be rendered : *Novissimum viro pax :* The end of the man is peace.——Accordingly, the sense is : The remainder of the life of the meek man will be a true peace, which will accompany him even unto death.—— Others explain the passage thus : His virtuous actions, besides his good name, will leave a good example, which even after his death will continue to help others, and be a consolation to the virtuous.——Both explanations are good.

40. Injusti autem disperibunt simul : reliquiæ impiorum interi-bunt.	But the unjust shall be destroyed together : the posterity of the wicked shall perish.

"*Simul reliquiæ . . .*" And together with them, their riches and their glory, which they thought were to last here on earth, all shall perish.

41. Salus autem justorum a Do-mino : et protector eorum in tempore tribulationis.	But the salvation of the just is from the Lord : and He is their pro-tector in the time of trouble.

[1] The Hebrew word, in this and the following verse, as also the Vulgate, bear the meaning, which is conformable to the context.——This may be understood also, and in a higher sense, of eternal reward, according to the text : " Their works follow them " (*Apoc.* xiv. 13).

42. Et adjuvabit eos Dominus, et liberabit eos : et eruet eos a peccatoribus, et salvabit eos : quia speraverunt in eo.

And the Lord will help them and deliver them : and He will deliver them from the wicked, and save them, because they have hoped in Him.

PSALM XXXVII.

DAVID bewails his sins. This Psalm is suitable for every penitent who looks upon his infirmities and tribulations as just chastisements of his sins, for which he begs pardon from God.

A Psalm for David, for a remembrance of the Sabbath.[1]

1. Domine ne in furore tuo arguas me : neque in ira tua corripias me.

Rebuke me not, O Lord, in Thine indignation : neither chasten me in Thy sore displeasure.

That is to say : Chastise me as a father, not as a judge ; chastise me that I may amend, instead of being lost.——See here what was said at *Ps.* ii. 5 and *Ps.* vi. 1.

2. Quoniam sagittæ tuæ infixæ sunt mihi : et confirmasti super me manum tuam.

For Thine arrows are fastened in me : and Thy hand presseth heavily upon me.

" *Sagittæ tuæ.*" Thy chastisements.——" *Confirmasti* . . ." Justly hast Thou pressed heavily Thy hand upon me, loading me with trials.

3. Non est sanitas in carne mea a facie iræ tuæ : non est pax ossibus meis a facie peccatorum meorum.

There is no health in my flesh, because of Thy wrath : there is no rest for my bones, because of my sins.

At the sight of Thy anger, I have lost my health of body : and at the sight of my sins, I have lost peace, so that my very bones are all trembling.

4. Quoniam iniquitates meæ supergressæ sunt caput meum : et sicut onus grave gravatæ sunt super me.

For mine iniquities are gone over my head : and as a heavy burden are become heavy upon me.

For my iniquities are so many that they rise higher even than my head : and so grievous that they weigh me down as a heavy burden.

5. Putruerunt, et corruptæ sunt cicatrices meæ : a facie insipientiæ meæ.

My sores have rotted and are corrupt : because of my foolishness.

[1] *For a remembrance,* viz., of their miseries and sins, and to be sung on the *Sabbath day.*——The third Penitential Psalm.

" *A facie ...*" Owing to my sad carelessness in not applying a timely remedy.

6. Miser factus sum, et curvatus sum usque in finem : tota die contristatus ingrediebar.

I am become miserable, and am greatly bowed down : I went about sorrowful all the day long.

" *Curvatus ... finem.*" I have remained utterly bent down towards the earth, so that I am scarcely able to raise up my eyes to heaven.

7. Quoniam lumbi mei impleti sunt illusionibus : et non est sanitas in carne mea.

For my loins are filled with illusions : and there is no soundness in my flesh.

" *Lumbi mei.*" That is, my concupiscence.—— " *Illusionibus.*" According to the Chaldee : *Ardore:* A malignant, dangerous heat.

8. Afflictus sum, et humiliatus sum nimis : rugiebam a gemitu cordis mei.

I am afflicted, and humbled exceedingly : I have roared with the groaning of my heart.

I have been so afflicted and cast down, that the groans of my heart to heaven were like to the roarings of a lion.

9. Domine, ante te omne desiderium meum: et gemitus meus a te non est absconditus.

Lord, all my desire is before Thee: and my groaning is not hid from Thee.

" *Ante te.*" Thou knowest.

10. Cor meum conturbatum est, dereliquit me virtus mea : et lumen oculorum meorum, et ipsum non est mecum.

My heart is troubled, my strength hath forsaken me : and the light of mine eyes itself is not with me.

My heart, that is, my will, has continued in trouble, since all strength has left me : and my eyes, that is, my mind, have lost the light, which made me see the truth.

11. Amici mei, et proximi mei : adversum me appropinquaverunt, et steterunt.

My friends and my neighbours have drawn near : and stood against me.

They have drawn near and stayed with me, not to help, but to oppress me.

12. Et qui juxta me erant, de longe steterunt : et vim faciebant qui quærebant animam meam.

And they that were near me stood afar off : and they that sought after my soul used violence.

My near kinsmen have gone away from me, and have left me in the hands of those who strove to take away my life.

13. Et qui inquirebant mala mihi, locuti sunt vanitates : et dolos tota die meditabantur.

They that sought my hurt spoke vain things : and thought upon deceits all the day long.

"*Locuti sunt vanitates.*" Spoke falsehoods, calumnies, against me, to destroy me.

14. Ego autem tamquam surdus non audiebam : et sicut mutus non aperiens os suum.

But I, as a deaf man, heard not : and I was as a dumb man that doth not open his mouth.

"*Non audiebam.*" I gave no ear to them.

15. Et factus sum sicut homo non audiens : et non habens in ore suo redargutiones.

And I became as a man that heareth not : and that hath no reproofs in his mouth.

"*Non audiens...*" One who has lost his hearing, and has no longer a mouth wherewith to reply and give his reasons.

16. Quoniam in te Domine speravi: tu exaudies me Domine Deus meus.

For in Thee, O Lord, have I hoped: Thou wilt hear me, O Lord my God.

17. Quia dixi : Nequando supergaudeant mihi inimici mei : et dum commoventur pedes mei, super me magna locuti sunt.

For I said, Lest at any time mine enemies rejoice over me : and whilst my feet slip, they glory over me.

I said within myself : Ah ! may my enemies not have to rejoice over my ruin : since as soon as my feet began to be unsteady, and they saw me tottering and likely to fall, they said great things at my expense, predicting my final overthrow.

18. Quoniam ego in flagella paratus sum : et dolor meus in conspectu meo semper.

For I am ready for scourges : and my sorrow is continually before me.

Lord, I am prepared to suffer every scourge which Thou mayest send upon me ; for my sorrow, that is, my sin which is the object of my sorrow, is ever before my eyes.

19. Quoniam iniquitatem meam annuntiabo : et cogitabo pro peccato meo.

For I will declare mine iniquity : and I will be thoughtful of my sin.

For I know and will always confess my fault : I will ever think on my sin, that I may satisfy, as far as I can, my offended Lord, in order to obtain His forgiveness.

20. Inimici autem mei vivunt et confirmati sunt super me : et multiplicati sunt qui oderunt me inique.

But mine enemies live, and are stronger than I : and they that hate me wrongfully are multiplied.

My enemies, however, still continue to live, and are preparing to arm themselves against me : the number of those who hate me unjustly has ever increased.

21. Qui retribuunt mala pro bonis, detrahebant mihi : quoniam sequebar bonitatem.

They that render evil for good, have slandered me : because I followed goodness.

They are such as return evil for good, and so lay themselves out to slander me, because I endeavoured to act rightly.

22. Ne derelinquas me Domine Deus meus : ne discesseris a me.

Forsake me not, O Lord my God : do not Thou depart from me.

23. Intende in adjutorium meum: Domine Deus salutis meæ.

Give heed unto my help, O Lord : Thou God of my salvation.

Continue, I beseech Thee, to help me, Thou Who art my Lord, and the God of my salvation.

LAUDS FOR MONDAY.

PSALM L.

David penitent bewails his sins. This Psalm expresses well the sorrow for his sins which a contrite sinner feels who humbly asks God's forgiveness.[1]

Unto the end a Psalm of David, when Nathan the prophet came to him, after he had sinned with Bethsabee (2 *Kings* xii.).

1. Miserere mei Deus : secundum magnam misericordiam tuam.

Have mercy upon me, O God: according to Thy great mercy.

Since I am a great sinner, show to me great mercy.

2. Et secundum multitudinem miserationum tuarum : dele iniquitatem meam.

And according to the multitude of Thy tender mercies : blot out my iniquity.

"*Dele . . .*" Blot out from my soul all my sins.

3. Amplius lava me ab iniquitate mea : et a peccato meo munda me.

Wash me yet more from my iniquity : and cleanse me from my sin.

"*A peccato . . .*" Cleanse me from the filthiness of my sins.

4. Quoniam iniquitatem meam ego cognosco : et peccatum meam contra me est semper.

For I acknowledge my iniquity : and my sin is always before me.

For I well know the enormity of my sin : which is continually before my eyes, reproaching me with the evil I have done.

5. Tibi soli peccavi, et malum coram te feci : ut justificeris in sermonibus tuis, et vincas cum judicaris.

Against Thee only have I sinned, and done evil in Thy sight : that Thou mayest be justified in Thy words, and mayest overcome when Thou art judged.

[1] The fourth Penitential Psalm.

O Lord, against Thee alone, I have sinned, and I have dared to do evil before Thy eyes ; but I hope to receive from Thee the pardon, which Thou hast promised to repentant sinners ; so, "*that Thou mayest be justified in Thy words*" ; and thus Thou wilt verily be justified "*in Thy words*," in regard, viz., to Thy promises to pardon him who repents : so, too, that "*Thou mayest overcome when Thou art judged*" : and thus Thou wilt verily overcome, that is, Thou wilt shut the mouth of my enemies, who think and dare to say that it is not just that I should receive pardon for so great a sin, when Thou shalt judge me.——This verse, we must remark, is variously explained by authors. Bellarmine, Tirinus, and Mattei, following the commentary of S. Cyril and of S. Gregory, explain thus : "*Against Thee only have I sinned as Judge*"*:* I have sinned against Thee alone, in this sense, that Thou alone art to judge me ; for though it is true that I have sinned also against my neighbour, by causing the death of Urias and by scandalising the people, nevertheless, I am afraid of Thee alone ; because, as king, I have no one on earth to judge me, and yet I have to be judged, and by Thee alone must I be judged, and by Thee alone be punished, and not by men.—— This commentary is beautiful, but the interpretation given above appears to me more simple and more appropriate : "*Lord, against Thee alone I have sinned*," for it was God's law alone which David transgressed. It is no objection that he had also offended against Urias and the people ; for these offences were sins only so far as they were transgressions of the law of God, since all the malice of sin consists in the transgression of the divine law, according to what the Apostle says : "*But I did not know sin, but by the law*" (*Rom.* vii. 7) : Hence, David said with good reason : Against Thee only have I sinned ; for Thy law alone I have transgressed.——"*Ut justificeris.*"[1] Theodoret says that the conjunction *Ut* does not signify here cause, but consequence.——"*Judicaris.*" According to the Hebrew this is not passive, but active : it is the same as "*Judicaveris*" : Thou shalt judge.

6. Ecce enim in iniquitatibus con- For behold, I was conceived in
ceptus sum : et in peccatis concepit iniquities: and in sins did my mother
me mater mea. conceive me.

[1] This part of the verse is cited by S. Paul (*Rom.* iii. 4).

Miserable man that I am, I was conceived in sin; when my mother conceived me, I appeared in the world already a sinner. As though he would say: What, O Lord, couldst Thou expect from a man conceived in sin.——Grotius explains it thus: I was guilty from my birth. But such an interpretation seems to favour the opinion of Socinus, who denied original sin, and its being contracted from the moment of conception; whereas this text proves perhaps more clearly than any other that all men are conceived in original sin.

7. Ecce enim veritatem dilexisti: incerta et occulta sapientiæ tuæ manifestasti mihi.

For behold, Thou hast loved truth: the secret and hidden things of Thy wisdom Thou hast made manifest unto me.

Thou lovest truth, and him also who confesses his fault: I confess my ingratitude, inasmuch as Thou hast favoured me by making known to me the secrets of Thy wisdom, secrets uncertain and hidden to others.

8. Asperges me hyssopo, et mundabor: lavabis me, et super nivem dealbabor.

Thou shalt sprinkle me with hyssop, and I shall be cleansed: Thou shalt wash me, and I shall be made whiter than snow.

Allusion is here made to the sprinkling of the blood of the victims, which was made over the lepers with hyssop to purify them (Lev. xiv. 6).——Hence, the Psalmist means to say: Cleanse me, O Lord, ever more and more.

9. Auditui meo dabis gaudium et lætitiam: et exultabunt ossa humiliata.

Thou shalt make me hear of joy and gladness: and the bones that were humbled shall rejoice.

In making me hear that Thou hast pardoned me, Thou wilt give to my soul a joy and a gladness so great, that my very bones, that is, all my interior powers, which have been so greatly afflicted, shall leap for joy.

10. Averte faciem tuam a peccatis meis: et omnes iniquitates meas dele.

Turn away Thy face from my sins: and blot out all my iniquities.

My God, turn, then, Thy face from my sins, that is, look no longer upon them; and blot out from my soul all my faults, which gave Thee horror.

11. Cor mundum crea in me Deus: et spiritum rectum innova in visceribus meis.

Create in me a clean heart, O God: and renew a right spirit within me.

Change my heart, O my God, and give me a pure heart, that loves none but Thee : and renew within my bowels, that is, in my interior, that right spirit, which I had lost by sin.

12. Ne projicias me a facie tua: et spiritum sanctum tuum ne auferas a me.

Cast me not away from Thy face : and take not Thy Holy Spirit from me.

13. Redde mihi lætitiam salutaris tui : et spiritu principali confirma me.

Restore unto me the joy of Thy salvation: and strengthen me with a perfect spirit.

Restore to me the joy of the salvation which Thou hast given me ; and confirm me in good, by means of a *principal* spirit, one, viz., that is strong, inspired by Thee.

14. Docebo iniquos vias tuas: et impii ad te convertentur.

I will teach the unjust Thy ways : and the wicked shall be converted unto Thee.

I promise Thee, on account of the scandal I have given, to instruct sinners in Thy law, and I hope that they will be converted to Thee.

15. Libera me de sanguinibus Deus, Deus salutis meæ : et exultabit lingua mea justitiam tuam.

Deliver me from sins of blood, O God, Thou God of my salvation : and my tongue shall extol Thy justice.

" *Sanguinibus.*" Rotigni and Lallement give a sense that is very probable to this word, by explaining it to refer to the remorse of conscience with which David was tormented, on account of the blood of Urias,[1] which he had caused to be shed.——" *Justitiam tuam.*" Bellarmine says that the pardon of sin is mercy with respect to us ; but that it is justice with respect to Jesus Christ, Who, by His death, has merited for us pardon; and this is the divine justice of which David meant to speak.——The sense of the verse then is : O God of my salvation, deliver me from remorse, on account of the blood that I unjustly caused to be shed ; and my tongue shall exult with joy in praising Thy mercy.

16. Domine, labia mea aperies : et os meum annuntiabit laudem tuam.

Thou shalt open my lips, O Lord : and my mouth shall declare Thy praise.

17. Quoniam si voluisses sacrificium, dedissem utique : holocaustis non delectaberis.

For if Thou hadst desired sacrifice, I would surely have given it ; with burnt-offerings Thou wilt not be delighted.

1 *Sanguinibus.* The plural instead of the singular, a hebraism, to denote the abundance of the blood shed, and the enormity of the crime : besides Urias, David had caused a considerable number of his bravest soldiers to be destroyed (2 *Kings* xi. 17).

If, to satisfy for my sin, Thou hadst willed of me sacrifices, I would willingly have offered them to Thee; but I well know that with holocausts Thou art not satisfied.

18. Sacrificium Deo spiritus contribulatus : cor contritum, et humiliatum Deus non despicies.

A sacrifice unto God is a troubled spirit : a contrite and humble heart, O God, Thou wilt not despise.

The sacrifice that is pleasing to Thee, O my God, is a soul afflicted on account of its sin : a contrite and humbled heart Thou knowest not how to despise.[1]

19. Benigne fac, Domine, in bona voluntate tua Sion : ut ædificentur muri Jerusalem.

Deal favourably, O Lord, in Thy goodwill with Sion : that the walls of Jerusalem may be built up.

As though he would say : If I do not deserve to be heard, look, O Lord, with a gracious eye upon Thy city Sion, and according to Thy good will, that is, in accordance with the purpose of Thy good pleasure, which Thou hadst in choosing it as Thy dwelling-place, show to it Thy favour, so that the walls of Jerusalem, now fallen in ruins, may be rebuilt.

20. Tunc acceptabis sacrificium justitiæ, oblationes, et holocausta : tunc imponent super altare tuum vitulos.

Then shalt Thou accept the sacrifice of justice, oblations and whole burnt-offerings : then shall they lay calves upon Thine altar.

Then wilt Thou accept with joy my sacrifices of justice, that is, as Bellarmine understands it, my homage justly due to Thee, and all my offerings and holocausts : and then many, after my example, will offer to Thee, upon Thy altar, calves, that is, excellent, choice victims, amongst which the calf was the noblest.

PSALM V.

This Psalm is suitable for the just man. It teaches him how he should behave in adversity, and console himself by confidence in God. It then speaks of the happiness of the heavenly country, where the patience of the afflicted finds its reward.

---

[1] What is said in these two verses, 18 and 19, does not mean that the victims offered on the altar were in no way pleasing to God, but simply that He did not accept them when those who offered them had not the requisite interior dispositions. See *Ps.* xlix. 9-16.

Unto the end, for her that obtained the inheritance. A Psalm for David.[1]

1. Verba mea auribus percipe Domine : intellige clamorem meum.

Give ear, O Lord, unto my words : understand my cry.

2. Intende voci orationis meæ : Rex meus, et Deus meus.

Hearken unto the voice of my prayer : O my King and my God.

1, 2. God hears everything and understands everything ; but sometimes He seems not to perceive, or not to comprehend, because the prayer we make to Him is either not just, or because it is ill-made. This is why David says : Give ear, O Lord, unto my words, that is, to my prayer. Hearken unto the voice of my prayer, to that which I ask.

3. Quoniam ad te orabo : Domine, mane exaudies vocem meam.

For unto Thee will I pray, O Lord : in the morning Thou shalt hear my voice.

I will always have recourse to Thee ; and I know of a certainty, according to Thy promises, that Thou wilt always hearken to my prayer.

4. Mane astabo tibi, et videbo : quoniam non Deus volens iniquitatem tu es.

In the morning I will stand before Thee, and will see : for Thou art not a God that willest iniquity.

From the early morning I will place myself in Thy presence to pray to Thee : and I will always have before my eyes that Thou hatest all iniquity.

5. Neque habitabit juxta te malignus : neque permanebunt injusti ante oculos tuos.

Neither shall the wicked dwell near Thee : nor shall the unjust abide before Thine eyes.

The wicked shall not find place near to Thee : and they shall not dwell in Thy presence.

6. Odisti omnes, qui operantur iniquitatem : perdes omnes, qui loquuntur mendacium.

Thou hatest all the workers of iniquity : Thou wilt destroy all that speak a lie.

7. Virum sanguinum et dolosum abominabitur Dominus : ego autem in multitudine misericordiæ tuæ,

The bloody and the deceitful man the Lord will abhor : but as for me, in the multitude of Thy mercy,

8. Introibo in domum tuam : adorabo ad templum sanctum tuum in timore tuo.

I will come into Thy house : in Thy fear will I worship towards Thy holy temple.

7, 8. "*Ego autem ...*" But I, favoured by the abundance

---

[1] *For her that obtained the inheritance.* That is, for the Church of God.

of Thy mercy.——"*Adorabo* . . ." Full of reverential fear, will adore Thee in Thy holy temple.

9. Domine deduc me in justitia tua : propter inimicos meos dirige in conspectu tuo viam meam.

Lead me, O Lord, in Thy justice because of mine enemies : direct my way in Thy sight.

"*Propter inimicos* . . ." To confound my enemies, so direct me, that I may walk always in Thy presence.

10. Quoniam non est in ore eorum veritas : cor eorum vanum est.

For there is no truth in their mouth : their heart is vain.

11. Sepulchrum patens est guttur eorum, linguis suis dolose agebant : judica illos Deus.

Their throat is an open sepulchre, they dealt deceitfully with their tongues : judge them, O God.

Their mouth is an open sepulchre, reeking with malignant infection, for they use their tongues to weave deceits ; judge them, O my God, and punish them.

12. Decidant a cogitationibus suis, secundum multitudinem impietatum eorum expelle eos : quoniam irrita-verunt te Domine.

Let them fall from their devices ; according to the multitude of their iniquities cast them out : for they have provoked Thee, O Lord.

Let all their designs fall to the ground, and, according to the multitude of their iniquity, drive them from Thee : for they have had, O Lord, the audacity to provoke Thee to anger.

13. Et lætentur omnes, qui sperant in te : in æternum exultabunt, et habitabis in eis.

But let all them that hope in Thee be glad : they shall rejoice for ever, and Thou shalt dwell in them.

On the other hand, let all that hope in Thee rejoice, and always exult with gladness, for Thou wilt dwell in them.

14. Et gloriabuntur in te omnes, qui diligunt nomen tuum : quoniam tu benedices justo.

And all they that love Thy name shall glory in Thee : for Thou wilt bless the just.

Well may they glory in Thee, all those who love the glory of Thy name, for Thou wilt bless every just man.

15. Domine, ut scuto bonæ volun-tatis tuæ : coronasti nos.

O Lord, Thou hast crowned us : as with a shield of Thy goodwill.

Thou hast surrounded us, O Lord, on every side with the shield of Thy goodwill, which renders us secure from all the assaults of our enemies.

PSALMS LXII. AND LXVI.

CANTICLE OF THE PROPHET ISAIAS (Ch. xii.).

THE Prophet Isaias, after having predicted the coming of the Messias, the call of the Gentiles, and the return of the Jews from Babylon to the Land of Promise, composed this Canticle for them in thanksgiving to the Lord. The Church appoints it to be sung, in memory of the Law of Grace, which Jesus Christ has given us, whereby He has delivered us from the slavery of the devil.

1. Confitebor tibi Domine, quoniam iratus es mihi : conversus est
furor tuus, et consolatus es me.

I will give thanks to Thee, O Lord,
for Thou wast angry with me : Thy
wrath is turned away and Thou hast
comforted me.

I will ever thank Thee, O Lord, because, after being justly angry with me for my sins, Thy wrath is turned to clemency, and has consoled me.

2. Ecce Deus salvator meus : fiducialiter agam, et non timebo.

Behold, God is my Saviour: I will
deal confidently and will not fear.

3. Quia fortitudo mea, et laus mea
Dominus : et factus est mihi in salutem.

Because the Lord is my strength,
and my praise : and He is become my
salvation.

Behold, my God has come Himself to save me : I shall live, then, from henceforward in confidence and without fear : for the Lord will be my strength and the object of my praise, since He hath willed to become my Saviour.

4. Haurietis aquas in gaudio de
fontibus Salvatoris, et dicetis in illa
die : Confitemini Domino, et invocate
nomen ejus.

You shall draw waters with joy
out of the Saviour's fountains, and
you shall say in that day : Praise ye
the Lord, and call upon His name.

5. Notas facite in populis adinventiones ejus : mementote quoniam
excelsum est nomen ejus.

Make His works known among the
people: remember that His name is
high.

The Prophet here addresses his words to the faithful, and says : O blessed Faithful, you will draw with joy from the very fountains of the Saviour the waters of salvation ; that is, according to S. Cyril and S. Jerome, His holy doctrine ; or, according to S. Ambrose and Origen, the Sacraments ; or, according to S. Bernard, the gifts of the Holy Ghost. And in that day you will say one to another : Give praise to the

Lord, and call upon His name.——Make known to the people the inventions of His love, and remember always to praise Him, for His name is exceedingly great, even high above all praise.

6. Cantate Domino, quoniam magnifice fecit : annuntiate hoc in universa terra.

Sing ye to the Lord, for He hath done great things : show this forth in all the earth.

Give honour to the Lord for the magnificence He hath wrought in making us pass from death to life : preach this in all the earth.

7. Exulta et lauda habitatio Sion : quia magnus in medio tui sanctus Israel.

Rejoice and praise, O thou habitation of Sion : for great is He that is in the midst of thee, the Holy One of Israel.

" *Habitatio Sion* " : O habitation of Sion, O assembly of the Faithful, O Holy Church.——" *Quia magnus . . .* " For the great God, the Holy One of Israel, that is, Emmanuel, the expected of Israel, is in thy midst, perpetually present to enrich Thee with His graces.

PSALMS CXLVIII., CXLIX., CL.

THE CANTICLE OF ZACHARY.

MATINS FOR TUESDAY.

PSALM XXXVIII.

DAVID sets forth how much he had to endure, and the silence
he kept when he was insulted,: he exposes at the same time
the reflections he made upon his own sins and upon the vain
cares of men. The Psalmist then goes on to speak of himself
as a pilgrim here on earth, and points out to repentant sinners
what sentiments they ought to nourish in their hearts.

Unto the end, for Idithun himself, a Canticle of David.[1]

**1. Dixi, Custodiam vias meas : ut
non delinquam in lingua mea.**

I said, I will take heed unto my
ways : that I sin not with my tongue.

I said, that is, I have resolved within myself, that I will
watch my ways, that is, do my actions well : and therefore I
have determined to be attentive not to sin with my tongue.

**2. Posui ori meo custodiam : cum
consisteret peccator adversum me.**

I have set a guard unto my mouth :
when the sinner stood against me.

I have placed a guard upon my mouth, in order not to speak
when some insolent person sets to provoke me with injurious
words.

**3. Obmutui, et humiliatus sum, et
silui a bonis : et dolor meus renovatus
est.**

I was dumb, and was humbled,
and kept silence from good things :
and my sorrow was renewed.

" *Silui a bonis.*" I refrained from reproaching my enemies
with the good that I had done them.——" *Dolor . . .*" I felt
my grief renewed in thinking that I had well deserved their
injuries by my sins.

[1] Idithun was the chief of the singers of the family of Merari (1 *Par.* vi. 44).

4. Concaluit cor meum intra me : et in meditatione mea exardescet ignis.

My heart grew hot within me : and in my musing a fire shall flame out.

At this remembrance, my heart within me glowed with confusion, and in my meditation the heat of my pain was still increased.

5. Locutus sum in lingua mea : notum fac mihi Domine finem meum:

I spake with my tongue : O Lord, make me to know mine end :

6. Et numerum dierum meorum quis est : ut sciam quid desit mihi.

And what is the number of my days : that I may know what remaineth unto me.

5, 6. I said, Lord, make me to know when Thy anger against me shall have an end : or, as others explain it, how near my end is. Make known to me the number of my days, that I may see what is wanting to my penitence : or, according to others, how much longer I have to live.

7. Ecce mensurabiles posuisti dies meos : et substantia mea tamquam nihilum ante te.

Behold, Thou hast made my days of short measure : and my substance is as nothing before Thee.

" *Mensurabiles.*" S. Jerome's translation is : *Breves:* Short. Measurable, or so short that they are easy to count.——"*Et substantia mea . . .*" According to S. Jerome : *Vita.* Nay, my life is as nothing before Thee.

8. Verumtamen universa vanitas : omnis homo vivens.

And indeed all things are vanity : every man living.

It is indeed true that every man who lives here on earth, with all the riches and honours he possesses, is but mere vanity.

9. Verumtamen in imagine pertransit homo ; sed et frustra conturbatur.

Surely man passeth as an image : yea, and he is disquieted in vain.

Verily, man passes his life in an unreal semblance ; that is, all the joys he thinks to find on earth, turn out to be empty : it is in vain, then, that he troubles himself about them, and labours to acquire such goods as will never satisfy his heart.

10. Thesaurizat : et ignorat cui congregabit ea.

He storeth up : and he knoweth not for whom he shall gather these things.

He heaps up treasures, without knowing for whom he shall have gathered them when he shall be dead.

11. Et nunc quæ est expectatio mea? nonne Dominus? et substantia mea apud te est.

And now what is my hope? is it not the Lord? and my reliance is upon Thee.

"*Substantia . . .*" All that I have, all my good, subsists in Thee, and depends on Thee, in Whom are all my hopes. According to the Hebrew text : *Spes mea apud te est.* My hope is with Thee.

12. Ab omnibus iniquitatibus meis erue me : opprobrium insipienti de- disti me.

Deliver Thou me from all my ini- quities : Thou hast made me a re- proach unto the foolish.

It is supposed that Semei is here meant, who treated David as a usurper of the throne.

13. Obmutui, et non aperui os meum, quoniam tu fecisti : amove a me plagas tuas.

I was dumb, and I opened not my mouth, because Thou hast done it : O remove Thy scourges from me.

I was silent, and did not open my mouth to complain, because it was Thou who didst it, that is, Thou didst permit it for my just punishment : I beseech Thee now to remove from me the other scourges that I have deserved.

14. A fortitudine manus tuæ ego defeci in increpationibus : propter iniquitatem corripuisti hominem.

Thy strong hand hath made me faint in rebukes : Thou hast cor- rected man for iniquity.

I fainted away under the weight of the chastisements of Thy strong hand : justly dost Thou thus punish the man who offends Thee by his wicked life.

15. Et tabescere fecisti sicut ara- neam animam ejus : verumtamen vane conturbatur omnis homo.

And Thou hast made his soul to waste away like a spider : surely in vain is any man disquieted.

Thou makest him to wear away his life as the spider spends herself in forming her fragile web ; wherefore, it is in vain that any man should trouble himself to lay up the goods of this earth.

16. Exaudi orationem meam Do- mine, et deprecationem meam : auri- bus percipe lacrymas meas.

Hear my prayer, O Lord, and my supplication : give ear unto my tears.[1]

17. Ne sileas ; quoniam advena ego sum apud te, et peregrinus : sicut omnes patres mei.

Be not silent ; for I am a stranger with Thee : and a sojourner, as all my fathers were.

My God, be not with me as one deaf : for Thou knowest already that I am a stranger upon this earth and a pilgrim, as all my fathers have been before me.

---

[1] *My tears, i.e.,* prayer accompanied by sorrow and weeping.

18. Remitte mihi, ut refrigerer priusquam abeam : et amplius non ero.

O forgive me, that I may be refreshed, before I go hence : and be no more.

Before, then, I leave this world, where one day I shall be no longer, I beseech Thee to appease Thy just anger against me, that so I may find refreshment and relief.

PSALM XXXIX.

S. Ambrose, S. Jerome, S. Augustine, and Euthymius apply the whole of this Psalm directly to Jesus Christ and to the Church, that is, to the Head and to the mystical Body; so that all along it is Jesus Christ Who speaks, first in the person of His mystical Body and then in His own person. And, in fact, S. Paul (*Heb.* x. 5) applies to Jesus Christ several verses of this Psalm, which are quite inapplicable to David; and there are in it other things besides, which it would be difficult to refer to the person of the Royal Prophet. Our Saviour speaks in it according to His human nature, showing Himself full of humility and gratitude towards God : He speaks in it also as the Head of the predestined, and as having taken upon Himself, as man, our obligations towards the Divine Majesty. He, therefore, prays, humbles Himself, and trembles as charged with our sins, and as Mediator between us and God.

Unto the end, a Psalm for David himself.

1. Expectans expectavi Dominum:[1] et intendit mihi.

With expectation I waited for the Lord : and He was attentive unto me.

Long time have I waited for the Lord as liberator and redeemer of His people.——"*Intendit mihi.*" According to the Hebrew : He hath inclined Himself to me, that is, He hath inclined His ear to listen to me.

2. Et exaudivit preces meas: et eduxit me de lacu miseriæ, et de luto fæcis.

And He heard my prayers : and brought me out of the pit of misery, and out of the miry clay.

"*De lacu* . . . " These expressions denote, according to the Hebrew text, as Bellarmine remarks, a deep abyss, without light, filled with filthy mud, in which have fallen and flounder confusedly a miserable multitude : such are those who are plunged in the mire of their carnal appetites.

[1] A Hebraism signifying a prolonged waiting, accompanied by an ardent desire.

3. Et statuit super petram pedes   He set my feet also upon a rock :
meos : et direxit gressus meos.   and directed my steps.

" *Super petram.*" That is, upon Myself, Who am the
foundation-rock of the Church. " *The Rock was Christ* " (1
Cor. x. 4).——"*Et direxit . . .*" He hath established My feet
in a way, not only solid, but also straight ; and thus He hath
guided My steps.

4. Et immisit in os meum canti-   And he put a new song into my
cum novum : carmen Deo nostro.   mouth : *even* a hymn unto our God.

" *Canticum novum, carmen.*" A new canticle, a canticle of
love, of thanksgiving and of praise—according to the Hebrew,
which would be *Laudem* : Praise, instead of *Carmen.*

5. Videbunt multi, et timebunt :   Many shall see it, and shall fear :
et sperabunt in Domino.   and they shall hope in the Lord.

Many shall see, that is, shall come to know the misery of
the pit in which they are, and shall have fear or horror of it :
they shall then see their deliverer, and shall put their trust in
the Lord.

6. Beatus vir, cujus est nomen   Blessed is the man whose trust is
Domini spes ejus : et non respexit in   in the name of the Lord : and who
vanitates et insanias falsas.   hath not had regard to vanities and
    lying follies.

" *Vanitates.*" Human supports, which are all vain.——
" *Insanias falsas.*" Earthly goods, from which it is only folly
to hope for happiness.

7. Multa fecisti tu Domine Deus   Many *are* Thy wonderful works
meus miribilia tua : et cogitationibus   *which* Thou hast done, O Lord my
tuis non est qui similis sit tibi.   God : and in Thy thoughts there is
    none that is like unto Thee.

My Lord and my God, Thou hast wrought many marvels
for our good : and who could ever be like to Thee in Thy
thoughts, that is, in the inventions of Thy love, which Thou
hast conceived and brought to effect for our sakes ?

8. Annuntiavi, et locutus sum :   I have declared, and I have spoken:
multiplicati sunt super numerum.   they are multiplied above number.

I have preached Thy marvels and the benefits done to men :
they are multiplied above number who have been converted
from infidelity to follow Jesus Christ.——"*Multiplicati.*"
Bellarmine thinks, according to the Hebrew text, that perhaps
an error has here crept in, and that it should be : *Multiplicatæ*
(*cogitationes tuæ*) : Thy thoughts are multiplied : or, *Multiplicata* (*mirabilia tua*) : Thy marvels are multiplied. But S.

Ambrose, S. Jerome and S. Augustine say that the verse is to
be read as it stands, and explain *Multiplicati* as we have done.

9. Sacrificium et oblationem
noluisti : aures autem perfecisti
mihi.

Sacrifice and offering Thou didst
not desire : but ears Thou hast perfected unto me.

10. Holocaustum et pro peccato
non postulasti: tunc dixi, Ecce
venio.

Burnt offering and sin offering
Thou didst not require : then said I,
Behold I come.

9, 10. Thou hast refused the sacrifices and the offerings of
the Law, which could not avail to purify the conscience.
This means, that God did not accept those sacrifices as sufficient to expiate for sin and to remove it from the soul ; but
that he accepted them only as figures of the Sacrifice of Jesus
Christ upon the Cross. And hence the Redeemer says :
" *Aures . . .* " which words S. Paul thus expresses : " *A body
Thou hast fitted to Me*" (*Heb.* x. 5). We must not swerve from
this text of the Apostle, who by it explains that of David. So
that it means : Thou hast formed for Me a body fitted to
suffer and to die. Then follow the words—" *Tunc dixi: Ecce
venio* ". Then, that is, on hearing Thy decree that I should
take human flesh and sacrifice Myself on the Cross to atone
for the sins of men, I said : Behold I come to obey Thee.[1]

---

[1] " *Sacrificium.*" St. Paul (*Heb.* x. 5) says : *Hostiam.* In the following
verse we read : " Holocaust for sin ". These words designate the different
sacrifices, or rather the bloody victims, such as bulls and lambs, which,
in the Old Law, were offered on the altar to expiate sin (*Lev.* i., v., vi., vi.).
——" *Oblationem.*" By this may be understood offerings of inanimate gifts,
such as flour, bread, oil, &c. (*Lev.* ii. 6)——"*Aures autem perfecisti mihi.*"
The Septuagint renders the passage in the same words as those of S.
Paul (*Heb.* x. 5). The Hebrew and S. Jerome's translation have : *Aures
autem fodisti mihi :* Thou hast dug or bored my ears. According to Menochius and others these different versions may be reconciled thus : The ears
by a figure of speech, viz., of using a part for the whole, signify the *body* ;
and the part chosen is well suited to denote attention and readiness to obey,
as we read in *Ps.* xvii. 44 : " At the hearing of the ear he has obeyed me ".
——Here we should not fail to note that it was the practice amongst the
Jews, according to the prescription of the law (*Exod.* xxi. 6 ; *Deut.* xv. 17),
to bore the ears of a servant, on his giving himself up voluntarily to the
entire and perpetual service of his master. This custom, as we learn from
classical authors, obtained of old amongst other nations. The boring of the
ear, then, was a token of complete subjection (the ear being the organ through
which commands are received and the medium of obedience), most aptly
expressive of the humiliation and obedience of the Divine Eternal Word, Who
" being in the form of God," by assuming a human body in His Incarnation,
" debased Himself, taking the form of a servant, being made in the likeness
of men, and in habit found as a man " (*Philip.* ii. 6, 7). Thus the meaning of
the two renderings, so diverse in letter as are the Septuagint and the Vulgate,
is really one and the same (see Estius in *Heb.* xv.).—*Tr.*

| 11. In capite libri scriptum est de me ut facerem voluntatem tuam : Deus meus volui, et legem tuam in medio cordis mei. | In the head of the book it is written of me that I should do Thy will : O my God, I have desired it, and Thy law is in the midst of my heart. |

"*In capite libri.*" According to the Hebrew : *In volumine libri.* That is, in the volume of the law. By this, S. Ambrose understands the beginning of Genesis, where we read: "*Wherefore, a man shall leave father and mother, and shall cleave to his wife, and they shall be two in one flesh (Gen.* ii. 24), a passage on which S. Paul thus comments : "*This is a great sacrament, but I speak in Christ and in the Church (Eph.* v. 32).——According to S. Jerome, it refers to the Gospel of S. John, which commences with these words: "*In the beginning was the Word . . . and the Word was made flesh*".——But Bellarmine thinks that the expression, *In volumine Libri,* denotes rather the whole volume of the Bible, which speaks throughout of the Messias Who was to come, as says S. John Chrysostom and Theodoret, because Jesus Christ is the end of the law.[1]——Therefore, the Redeemer turns to His Father, and says to Him : In the head of the Book it is written of Me that I should do Thy will.—— "*Deus meus volui.*" I accept, My God, what Thou willest of Me.——"*Et legem tuam (posui* being understood) *in medio cordis mei.*" And I have placed Thy law in the midst of My heart, that is, of My will.——S. Paul, after having said that God did not accept the ancient sacrifices that were offered for sin, quotes this text : "*Then said I : Behold I come,*" &c. He then adds : "*He taketh away the first, that He may establish that which followeth : in the which will we are sanctified by the oblation of the body of Jesus Christ once*" (*Heb.* x. 7-10). He thus gives us to understand that by the one Sacrifice of the Cross, by which Jesus Christ delivered us from sin and sanctified us, all the ancient sacrifices were abolished.

| 12. Annuntiavi justitiam tuam in ecclesia magna : ecce labia mea non prohibebo, Domine tu scisti. | I have declared Thy justice in the great congregation : lo, I will not restrain my lips ; O Lord, Thou knowest it. |

I have made known Thy just law in a great assembly, that is, to a numerous people ; and Thou knowest that I have done it, and that I shall continue to do it by Myself until My death, and after My death, by means of My disciples.

[1] "*Legem tuam in medio cordis mei.*" *Posui* : I have placed, understood. That is : I have resolved, from the bottom of My heart, to execute all Thou hast ordained.

13. Justitiam tuam non abscondi in corde meo : veritatem tuam et salutare tuum dixi.

I have not hid Thy justice within my heart : I have declared Thy truth and Thy salvation.

14. Non abscondi misericordiam tuam, et veritatem tuam : a concilio multo.

I have not concealed Thy mercy and Thy truth : from the great assembly.

13, 14. I have not concealed in My heart, but have preached publicly to a great multitude of people Thy justice and Thy truth, by which Thou renderest to every one according to his works, as well as the salvation which Thou hast promised to him who hopes in Thee.——"*Non abscondi in corde meo.*" In contrast to those who keep the truth shut up in their heart, and do not preach it through some human respect.

15. Tu autem Domine ne longe facias miserationes tuas a me : misericordia tua et veritas tua semper susceperunt me.

Withhold not Thou Thy tender mercies from me, O Lord : Thy mercy and Thy truth have always upheld me.

"*Veritas tua.*" Thy faithfulness.

16. Quoniam circumdederunt me mala, quorum non est numerus : comprehenderunt me iniquitates meæ, et non potui ut viderem.

For evils without number have surrounded me : mine iniquities have overtaken me, and I was not able to see.

"*Comprehenderunt...*" My sins[1] have laid hold of Me to afflict Me with remorse, so that I am unable to look at them for horror.

17. Multiplicatæ sunt super capillos capitis mei : et cor meum dereliquit me.

They are multiplied above the hairs of my head : and my heart hath failed me.

"*Cor meum...*" My heart has abandoned, or failed Me from sorrow.

18. Complaceat tibi Domine ut eruas me : Domine, ad adjuvandum me respice.

Be pleased, O Lord, to deliver me : look down, O Lord, to help me.

---

[1] My iniquities : that is (since it is Jesus Christ Who speaks) : The sins of all men which I have taken on Me to expiate. Our Divine Saviour, having accepted the sacrifice of His Passion to redeem the human race, by supplying the insufficiency of all other sacrifices, according to the will of His Father, vv. 9, 10, 11, says that in spite of persecutions He publishes His mercy and His justice, vv. 12, 13, 14. He then begs of His Father not to abandon Him in His Passion and Death, but to hasten the moment of His Resurrection ; vv. 15 to 18 : finally, in the form of a prayer, He predicts on one side the confusion of His enemies, vv. 19, 20, 21, and on the other the triumph of His faithful friends, v. 22. The two last verses are a summary of the entire Psalm with regard to the person of Jesus Christ and His mystical Body, the Holy Church.

Be pleased, O Lord, to deliver Me from so many pains : look upon Me with an eye of pity, and succour Me.

19. Confundantur, et revereantur simul, qui quærunt animam meam : ut auferant eam.

Let them be confounded and ashamed together : that seek after my soul to take it away.

20. Convertantur retrorsum, et revereantur : qui volunt mihi mala.

Let them be turned backward, and put to shame : that wish me evil.

21. Ferant confestim confusionem suam : qui dicunt mihi, Euge, euge.

Let them at once be put to confusion : that say unto me, Aha, aha.[1]

"*Euge, euge.*" Well done, well done, we have made an end of Him. (See *Ps.* lxix. 4.)

22. Exultent, et lætentur super te omnes quærentes te : et dicant semper, Magnificetur Dominus : qui diligunt salutare tuum.

Let all those that seek Thee rejoice and be glad in Thee : and let such as love Thy salvation say always, The Lord be praised.

"*Magnificetur Dominus.*" May the Lord be glorified, who defends us.——"*Salutare tuum.*" The salvation which they hope from Thee.

23. Ego autem mendicus sum, et pauper : Dominus solicitus est mei.

But as for me I am poor and needy : but the Lord is careful for me.

But I, miserable and poor though I see myself to be, console myself with the thought that the Lord is solicitous for me, that is, for my salvation.

24. Adjutor meus, et protector meus tu es : Deus meus ne tardaveris.

Thou art my helper and my protector : O my God, make no delay.

"*Ne tardaveris.*" Be not slow to succour me when Thou seest me in danger.

PSALM XL.

This Psalm, like the preceding, refers to the Passion of Jesus Christ : it is so interpreted by S. Jerome, S. Ambrose, S. Augustine, and especially by S. John Chrysostom, who says that it would be rash to interpret it otherwise, because Jesus Christ Himself (*John* xiii. 18) cites a verse of this Psalm to signify that the treason of Judas had long before been foretold by the Psalmist. This Psalm speaks also of the mystical Body of Jesus Christ.

[1] *Aha.* The Hebrew here is an interjection of insult and derision, like the Vah (*Matt.* xxvii. 40).

Unto the end, a Psalm for David himself.

1. Beatus qui intelligit super egenum et pauperem : in die mala liberabit eum Dominus.

Blessed is he that considereth the needy and poor : the Lord will deliver him in the evil day.

Happy the man who is careful to help the poor[1] or whoever is in need of assistance : in the evil day, that is, the day of his death, the Lord will deliver him from all his straits.

2. Dominus conservet eum et vivificet eum, et beatum faciat eum in terra : et non tradat eum in animam inimicorum ejus.

The Lord preserve him and give him life, and make him blessed upon the earth : and deliver him not up to the will of his enemies.

The Lord will preserve him in the midst of dangers, and will so fortify him that he will come safe out of them.[2]—— "*In animam.*" According to some Greek copies, as S. Ambrose remarks, it is : *In manus.* But Bellarmine justly observes that the sense is almost the same, except that the expression *In animam,* that is, *voluntatem, arbitrium :* to the will, or good pleasure, is more expressive than, *In manus :* to the power.

3. Dominus opem ferat illi super lectum doloris ejus : universum stratum ejus versasti in infirmitate ejus.

The Lord help him on his bed of sorrow : Thou hast turned all his bed in his sickness.

At the time of his last sickness, the Lord will bring him help as he lies upon his bed of pain : Thou, O Lord, wilt in Thy goodness Thyself make up his bed, and smooth down his pillow, for his greater consolation in his last hour.

4. Ego dixi : Domine miserere mei : sana animam meam, quia peccavi tibi.

I said : O Lord, be Thou merciful unto me : heal my soul, for I have sinned against Thee.

"*Sana.*" Heal my soul, which has become sick through the offences I have committed against Thee.[3]

5. Inimici mei dixerunt mala mihi : Quando morietur, et peribit nomen ejus ?

Mine enemies have spoken evil against me : When shall he die, and his name perish ?

[1] This poor and indigent man is Jesus Christ, suffering in His own person or in the members of His mystical Body.

[2] A prediction or promise in form of prayer.—"*In terra.*" Here on earth, and hereafter in the land of the living.

[3] In this and the following verses it is Jesus Christ Who speaks.——If He says that He has sinned, it must be understood of our iniquities which He took upon Himself.

6. Et si ingrediebatur ut videret, vana loquebatur : cor ejus congregavit iniquitatem sibi.

And if he came in to see me, he spoke vain things : his heart gathered together iniquity to itself.

"*Vana.*" Words of pretended kindness and compassion. ——"*Cor ejus.*" But he consoled himself in his own mind by redoubling his wicked hope of seeing Me dead.[1]

7. Egrediebatur foras : et loquebatur in idipsum.

He went out : and spoke to the same purpose.

He then went out to make others take part in his wickedness.

8. Adversum me susurrabant omnes inimici mei : adversum me cogitabant mala mihi.

All mine enemies whispered together against me : against me have they devised evils.

On this, My enemies united together to speak ill of Me, to plot against Me, and to wish Me all the evil that could befall Me.

9. Verbum iniquum constituerunt adversum me : Numquid qui dormit, non adjiciet ut resurgat ?

They sent forth an unjust word against me : shall he that sleepeth rise again no more?

They are confirmed in their design upon My life, saying : What ! Shall then He who dies think to return to life again ?

10. Etenim homo pacis meæ, in quo speravi : qui edebat panes meos, magnificavit super me supplantationem.

For even the man of my peace, in whom I trusted, who ate my bread : hath greatly sought to overthrow me.

This verse alludes to the treason of Judas, according to what we read in the Gospel of St. John (xiii. 18). "*That the Scripture may be fulfilled : He that eateth bread with Me shall lift up his heel against Me.*"——"*Homo pacis meæ*": The man with whom I was at peace.——"*In quo speravi*": In whom I had confided.——"*Qui edebat panes meos*": Who ate of the same bread that I Myself did eat.——"*Magnificavit . . .*" Has made it his boast to complete My ruin, by offering to give Me up into the hands of My enemies.

11. Tu autem Domine miserere mei, et resuscita me : et retribuam eis.

But do Thou, O Lord, have mercy upon me, and raise me up again : and I will requite them.

"*Resuscita . . .*" Jesus Christ here predicts His Resurrection. After I shall be dead upon the Cross, do Thou make Me to rise again : and then, as Judge, I shall render to them the just

---

[1] This verse and the following one apply to Judas—"*Ut rideret*". In order to find a favourable occasion for the execution of his project.

punishment they deserve.——The Son of God here prays His Father to raise Him up again, because He is praying as a servant : but He was well able, for that matter, to raise up His body again by His own power, as the Word of the Father, and true God equal to His Father : and this was what in fact happened, according as He Himself declared : "*I have power to lay down My life: and I have power to take it up again*". (*John* x. 18.)

12. In hoc cognovi, quoniam voluisti me : quoniam non gaudebit inimicus meus super me.	By this I know that Thou hast wished well to me : because mine enemy shall not rejoice over me.

"*Voluisti.*" Thou lovest Me.——"*Super me.*" Over Me, on account of My death.

13. Me autem propter innocentiam suscepisti : et confirmasti me in conspectu tuo in æternum.	But Thou hast upheld me because of mine innocence : and Thou hast set me before Thy face for ever.

On account of My innocence, Thou hast defended Me from the hands of My enemies, and hast placed Me in heaven at Thy right hand for ever : as happened at the Ascension of Jesus Christ.

14. Benedictus Dominus Deus Israel a sæculo : et usque in sæculum. Fiat. Fiat.	Blessed be the Lord, the God of Israel : from eternity and to eternity. Amen. Amen.

"*Fiat, fiat.*" In the Hebrew, *Amen, Amen.* So be it : Let all be for His praise and glory.

PSALM XLI.

DAVID, in flying from Saul, is full of sadness at finding himself so far from the Tabernacle : he consoles himself with the hope of soon seeing it again, and this fosters the desire of enjoying the sight of God in the temple of Heaven, after his exile upon earth. This should be the desire of every Christian who lives in this world at a distance from his heavenly country : he ought to be always sighing to leave the earth, that he may go to see God face to face.[1]

Unto the end, understanding for the Sons of Core.[2]

1. Quemadmodum desiderat cervus ad fontes aquarum : ita desiderat anima mea ad te Deus.	As the hart panteth after the water-springs: so panteth my soul after Thee, O God.

[1] See on the same subject *Ps.* lxxxiii.

[2] *Sons of Core*, a band of musicians (1 *Par.* ix. 19).

2. Sitivit anima mea ad Deum fortem vivum : quando veniam, et apparebo ante faciem Dei ?

My soul hath thirsted after the strong living God; when shall I come, and appear before the face of God?

"*Deum fortem.*" The God Almighty.——"*Vivum.*" The living God, very different from the gods of the Gentiles who are dead gods.——"*Quando veniam ...*" When shall I come to see Thee, and find myself enjoying the sight of Thy face ?

3. Fuerunt mihi lacrymæ meæ panes die ac nocte : dum dicitur mihi quotidie, Ubi est Deus tuus ?

My tears have been my bread day and night : whilst it is said to me daily, Where is Thy God ?

"*Dum dicitur ...*" As I hear my enemies saying to me continually, when they see me in affliction : Where then is now thy God, in Whom thou so much hopest, to console thee.

4. Hæc recordatus sum, et effudi in me animam meam : quoniam transibo in locum tabernaculi admirabilis, usque ad domum Dei.

These things I remembered, and I poured out my soul in me : for I shall go over into the place of the wonderful tabernacle, even unto the house of God.

Such reproaches I remembered, and I poured out my soul, that is, I emptied or stripped it of all earthly affections, with the sweet thought that I should one day pass from this exile to the admirable tabernacle of the House of God.

5. In voce exultationis, et confessionis : sonus epulantis.

With the voice of joy and praise ; the noise of one feasting.

Thither shall I go, and with voice of gladness I shall praise the Lord : then I shall take part in the banquet of the blessed, whose voices resound with ceaseless songs of joy and thanksgiving.

6. Quare tristis es anima mea ? et quare conturbas me ?

Why art thou sad, O my soul ? and why dost thou disquiet me ?

7. Spera in Deo, quoniam adhuc confitebor illi : salutare vultus mei, et Deus meus.

Hope thou in God, for I will yet praise Him : *Who is* the salvation of my countenance, and my God.

Have confidence in God, for with His help I hope to go one day to heaven, there to give Him praise and say to Him : Thou art my God and the salvation of my face, that is, my Saviour always present to my eyes : Thou causest my face to see Thy Face. (See *Ps.* xlii. 6.)

8. Ad meipsum anima mea conturbata est : propterea memor ero tui de terra Jordanis, et Hermoniim a monte medico.

My soul is troubled within myself : therefore will I remember Thee from the land of Jordan and Hermoniim, from the little hill.

12

My soul, however, is inwardly troubled.——"*Memor ero tui* . . ." To console myself I will think always of Thee, in whatever place I am; whether it be in the Land of Jordan, or, &c.

9. Abyssus abyssum invocat: in voce cataractarum tuarum.

Deep calleth on deep: at the noise of Thy flood-gates.

One abyss of ills invites another, which pours down upon me with a crash.——David here speaks of the tribulations or temptations which came upon him like billows raised by a storm with terrific roaring.

10. Omnia excelsa tua, et fluctus tui : super me transierunt.

All Thy waves and Thy billows: have passed over me.

Alas! all the waters of the heavens, and all the floods of ill with which Thou triest Thy servants, seem to have passed over me.

11. In die mandavit Dominus misericordiam suam : et nocte canticum ejus.

In the daytime the Lord hath commanded His mercy : and a song to Him in the night.

In the daytime, or at the time of my consolations, the Lord hath made me to taste of the sweetness of His mercy : but now in this night of tribulations He wills that, resigned to His will, I cease not to sing His praises and to bless Him.

12. Apud me oratio Deo vitæ meæ: dicam Deo, Susceptor meus es.

With me *is* prayer to the God of my life : I will say unto God, Thou art my support.

My prayer, therefore, to the God of my life shall be perpetual : always will I say to Him : Lord, Thou art my protector, do not abandon me.

13. Quare oblitus es mei ? et quare contristatus incedo, dum affligit me inimicus ?

Why hast Thou forgotten me ? and why go I mourning whilst mine enemy afflicteth me ?

But why dost Thou now deal towards me as though Thou hadst forgotten me ?

14. Dum confringuntur ossa mea : exprobraverunt mihi qui tribulant me inimici mei :

Whilst my bones are broken : mine enemies who trouble me have reproached me :

15. Dum dicunt mihi per singulos dies : Ubi est Deus tuus ? quare tristis es anima mea ? et quare conturbas me ?

Whilst they say to me day by day : Where is Thy God? why art thou cast down, O my soul? and why dost thou disquiet me ?

Repetition of verses **3** and **6.**

16. Spera in Deo, quoniam adhuc confitebor illi : salutare vultus mei, et Deus meus.

Hope thou in God, for I will yet praise Him : *Who is* the salvation of my countenance, and my God.

Repetition of verse 7.

PSALM XLIII.

This Psalm, speaking generally, alludes to the sentiments of the just under the trials of life : the Psalmist then suggests to them the matter for prayer when under affliction.

Unto the end, for the Sons of Core for understanding.

1. Deus auribus nostris audivimus: patres nostri annuntiaverunt nobis,

We have heard with our ears, O God : our fathers have declared unto us,

2. Opus quod operatus es in die-bus eorum : et in diebus antiquis.

The work Thou hast wrought in their days : and in the days of old.

1, 2. With our own ears we have heard, O great God, what our fathers have related of the wonderful works Thou didst of old in their lifetime.

3. Manus tua gentes disperdidit, et plantasti eos : afflixisti populos, et expulisti eos.

Thy hand destroyed the nations, and Thou plantedst them : Thou didst afflict the people and cast them out.

Thy powerful arm scattered the idolatrous nations that dwelt in the Land of Promise, and in their place Thou didst establish our fathers, &c.[1]

4. Nec enim in gladio suo possed-erunt terram : et brachium eorum non salvavit eos :

For they got not the land in pos-session by their own sword : neither did their own arm save them :

5. Sed dextera tua, et brachium tuum, et illuminatio vultus tui : quoniam complacuisti in eis.

But Thy right hand and Thine arm, and the light of Thy counte-nance : because Thou wast pleased with them.

But all was the work of Thy power : for Thou didst look upon them with a gracious eye, and Thou wast well-pleased to favour and do them good.

6. Tu es ipse Rex meus et Deus meus : qui mandas salutes Jacob.

Thou art Thyself my King and my God : Who commandest the saving of Jacob.

[1] *Plantasti eos.* A significant metaphor, more fully developed, *Ps.* lxxix 10, 11, 12.

"*Qui mandas...*" Thou Who providest for the salvation of Jacob, that is, of Thy people who descend from Jacob.

7. In te inimicos nostros ventilabimus cornu : et in nomine tuo spernemus insurgentes in nobis.

Through Thee will we push down our enemies with the horn : and through Thy name will we despise them that rise up against us.

"*In te ... cornu.*" In Thee, that is, in the strength we shall derive from Thee, we shall scatter our enemies.[1]

8. Non enim in arcu meo sperabo : et gladius meus non salvabit me.

For I will not trust in my bow : neither shall my sword save me.

9. Salvasti enim nos de affligentibus nos : et odientes nos confudisti.

But Thou hast saved us from them that afflict us : and hast put them to shame that hate us.

10. In Deo laudabimur tota die : et in nomine tuo confitebimur in sæculum.

In God shall we glory all the day long : and in Thy name we will give praise for ever.

"*Laudabimur.*" Delivered by Thy hand, we shall glory.

11. Nunc autem repulisti et confudisti nos : et non egredieris Deus in virtutibus nostris.

But now Thou hast cast us off, and put us to shame : and Thou, O God, wilt not go forth with our armies.

"*Et non...*" Nor do we look upon Thee as our God, Who goes out with our armies to fight for us.

12. Avertisti nos retrorsum post inimicos nostros : et qui oderunt nos diripiebant sibi.

Thou hast made us to turn our backs to our enemies : and they that hated us spoiled for themselves.

"*Avertisti...nostros...*" Thou hast subjected us to our enemies, so that they have made us their prisoners, and we are forced to follow them.

13. Dedisti nos tamquam oves escarum : et in gentibus dispersisti nos.

Thou hast given us up like sheep to be eaten : Thou hast scattered us among the nations.

14. Vendidisti populum tuum sine pretio : et non fuit multitudo in commutationibus eorum.

Thou hast sold Thy people for no price : and there was no reckoning in the exchange of them.

Thou hast allowed Thy people to be sold for nothing : nor was there one amongst all the multitude who offered a price for the men of Thy people, for they despised them as not worth buying.

---

[1] " *Ventilabimus cornu.*" We will scatter them, as a bull when infuriated casts into the air with his horn earth or straw. (See Bellarmine.)

15. Posuisti nos opprobrium vicinis nostris : subsannationem et derisum his, qui sunt in circuitu nostro.

Thou hast made us a reproach unto our neighbours : a scoff and derision to them that are round about us.

16. Posuisti nos in similtudinem Gentibus : commotionem capitis in populis.

Thou hast made us a by-word among the Gentiles : a shaking of the head among the peoples.

Thou hast made us to be an example for terror among the nations, so that the people shake their heads at us in derision.

17. Tota die verecundia mea contra me est : et confusio faciei meæ cooperuit me.

All the day long my shame is before me : and the confusion of my face hath covered me.

18. A voce exprobrantis, et obloquentis : a facie inimici, et persequentis.

At the voice of him that reproacheth and revileth me : at the face of the enemy and persecutor.

19. Hæc omnia venerunt super nos, nec obliti sumus te : et inique non egimus in testamento tuo.

All these things have come upon us, yet we have not forgotten Thee : and we have not done wickedly in Thy covenant.

20. Et non recessit retro cor nostrum : et declinasti semitas nostras a via tua :

And our heart hath not turned back : neither hast Thou turned aside our steps from Thy way:

"*Declinasti...*" It is generally thought that the negative particle, *Non*, which is found in the first part of the verse, should be supplied here. S. Jerome translates the passage thus : *Non declinaverunt semitæ nostræ a via tua.* Accordingly the meaning of the verse is : And our hearts have not receded, that is, we have not turned our backs upon Thee ; and Thou hast not permitted our steps to wander from Thy way.

21. Quoniam humiliasti nos in loco afflictionis : et cooperuit nos umbra mortis.

For Thou hast humbled us in the place of affliction: and the shadow of death hath covered us.

"*Humiliasti... afflictionis.*" Thou hast abandoned us to the depth of misery.——S. Jerome's translation, according to the Hebrew, is : *In locum draconum.* To a place of dragons, meaning a place of horrors.——"*Umbra mortis.*" The shadow of death, after which darkness alone remains : this denotes a great obscurity.

22. Si obliti sumus nomen Dei nostri : et si expandimus manus nostras ad deum alienum:

If we have forgotten the name of our God : and if we have spread forth our hands unto a strange god :

23. Nonne Deus requiret ista? ipse enim novit abscondita cordis.

Shall not God search out these things ? for He knoweth the secrets of the heart.

22, 23. Had we ever forgotten the name of our God, or raised up our hands to strange gods : could we hope that the Lord would not call us to account, He Who knows the most secret thoughts of our hearts ?

24. Quoniam propter te mortifica-
mur tota die : æstimati sumus sicut
oves occisionis.

Because for Thy sake we are killed
all the day long : we are counted as
sheep for the slaughter.

Every day, for love of Thee, we suffer such pains, that we are looked upon as sheep, that is, as victims destined to death.

25. Exurge, quare obdormis Domine ? exurge, et ne repellas in finem.

Arise, why sleepest Thou, O Lord?
arise, and cast us not off for ever.

" *Quare obdormis.*" Why dost Thou make as though Thou sleepest, and takest no more care of us ?

26. Quare faciem tuam avertis :
oblivisceris inopiæ nostræ et tribulationis nostræ ?

Why turnest Thou away Thy face:
and forgettest our want and trouble ?

27. Quoniam humiliata est in
pulvere anima nostra : conglutinatus
est in terra venter noster.

For our soul is humbled down
unto the dust : our belly cleaveth
unto the earth.

We see ourselves humbled, and despised as the dust that is trodden under foot : wherefore prostrate with our faces to the earth, we implore Thy mercy.

28. Exurge Domine, adjuva nos :
et redime nos propter nomen tuum.

Arise, O Lord, and help us : and
redeem us for Thy name's sake.

" *Redime . . .*" Deliver us from so many evils for the glory of Thy name.

PSALM XLIV.

A CANTICLE of praise in honour of Jesus Christ, and the Church, His spouse. The Prophet announces plainly in this Psalm the mystery of the Incarnation of the Word, and the victory of the Divine Redeemer over the world.

Unto the end, for them that shall be changed, for the Sons of Core, for understanding : a song for the beloved.[1]

1. Eructavit cor meum verbum
bonum : dico ego opera mea Regi.

My heart hath uttered a good
word : I speak of my works for the
King.

[1] *For them that shall be changed*, that is, For souls happily changed by being converted to God. *The beloved*, that is, Our Lord Jesus Christ.

My heart, full of divine illuminations, breaks out into holy words, and utters this hymn in honour of my King, Who is the Messias.

2. Lingua mea calamus scribæ : velociter scribentis.

My tongue *is* the pen : of a writer that writeth swiftly.

My tongue is as the pen in the hand of a rapid writer, who writes all that is dictated to him by the Holy Spirit.

3. Speciosus forma præ filiis hominum, diffusa est gratia in labiis tuis : propterea benedixit te Deus in æternum.

Thou art beautiful above the sons of men, grace is poured abroad in Thy lips : therefore God hath blessed Thee for ever.

Thou, my King and my Saviour, &c.

4. Accingere gladio tuo super femur tuum : potentissime.

Gird Thy sword upon Thy thigh : O Thou most mighty.

5. Specie tua et pulchritudine tua : intende, prospere procede, et regna.

With Thy comeliness and Thy beauty : go forth, advance prosperously, and reign.

"*Specie tua ... tua.*" S. Jerome translates : *Gloria tua et decore tuo.*——"*Intende ...*" Go forward, advance from victory to victory, and establish Thy reign in the world.

6. Propter veritatem, et mansuetudinem, et justitiam : et deducet te mirabiliter dextera tua.

Because of truth and meekness and justice : and Thy right hand shall lead Thee wondrously.

Reign with truth, that is, with fidelity to Thy promises, together with that gentle meekness which Thou usest towards sinners, and with the justice which Thou exercisest in judging the obstinate : thus will Thy power lead Thee on wonderfully to extend Thy kingdom.

7. Sagittæ tuæ acutæ, populi sub te cadent : in corda inimicorum regis.

Thine arrows are sharp, under Thee shall the people fall : into the hearts of the king's enemies.

The peoples, conquered by Thy arrows, that is, by the rays of Thy light, which has power to penetrate hearts, will fall and submit themselves to Thee, so that the hearts of Thy enemies, which before despised Thee, shall be brought to adore Thee.

8. Sedes tua Deus in sæculum sæculi : virga directionis virga regni tui.

Thy throne, O God, is for ever and ever : the sceptre of Thy kingdom is a sceptre of uprightness.

And thus, O God, Saviour of the world, Thy throne, or Thy reign, unlike the temporal reigns of other sovereigns, shall be

eternal in the Church ; and Thy rod, that is, Thy sceptre or
Thy government, shall ever be most just.——" *Virga directionis* " means the same as *Virga rectissima :* A most righteous
sceptre.[1]

9. Dilexisti justitiam, et odisti
iniquitatem : propterea unxit te
Deus, Deus tuus, oleo lætitiæ præ
consortibus tuis.

Thou hast loved justice and hated
iniquity : therefore God, Thy God,
hath anointed Thee with the oil of
gladness above Thy fellows.

" *Præ consortibus tuis.*" That is, Exalting Thee, so as to
make Thee sit at His right hand, a glory which surpasses that
of all the men and Angels who shall be Thy companions in
heaven.——It is here said that Jesus Christ is anointed or
constituted King of the world. This is to be understood, not
of His Divinity, but of His Humanity. We are to understand
also by these words that He is anointed with the unction of
grace as Head of the faithful, who, through His merits, shall
receive graces from God.

10. Myrrha, et gutta, et casia a
vestimentis tuis, a domibus eburneis :
ex quibus delectaverunt te filiæ regum
in honore tuo.

Myrrh and aloes and cassia per-
fume Thy garments, from the ivory
palaces : whence the daughters of
kings have made Thee glad in Thine
honour.

" *A vestimentis . . . eburneis.*" Here, by the garments and
the ivory houses, is to be understood the most sacred Humanity
of the Redeemer. Hence the verse is thus explained : From
Thy Humanity comes the odour of most pure and sweet per-
fumes, which leads the daughters of kings, that is, great souls,
to rejoice Thee by running to adore Thee.

11. Astitit regina a dextris tuis in
vestitu deaurato : circumdata varie-
tate.

On Thy right hand stood the
queen, in golden raiment : wrought
about with variety.

By this Queen is understood the Church : it may also be
referred to the holy Mother of God, and to every just soul,
which is the spouse of Jesus Christ, and therefore a queen, as
S. Bernard says : *Singulæ animæ, singulæ sponsæ :* Every soul,
a spouse.

12. Audi filia, et vide, et inclina
aurem tuam : et obliviscere populum
tuum, et domum patris tui.

Hearken, O daughter, and consider, and incline thine ear : forget
also thine own people and thy
father's house.

Then is said to this Queen : Hearken, My daughter, and
behold the honour to which thou art raised, and listen to that
which thou hast to do.

[1] *Heb.* i. 8, 9.

13. Et concupiscet Rex decorem tuum : quoniam ipse est Dominus Deus tuus, et adorabunt eum.

And the King shall greatly desire thy beauty : for He is the Lord thy God, and Him they shall adore.

And the King shall love thy beauty, He Who is thy Spouse, Whom alone thou oughtest to love, since He is thy Lord and thy God, Whom, in the end, all men must adore.

14. Et filiæ Tyri in muneribus vultum tuum deprecabuntur: omnes divites plebis.

And the daughters of Tyre with gifts shall entreat thy face : all the rich among the people.

This is addressed to the Church alone. The daughters of Tyre, that is, the Gentile nations, shall honour thee, with gifts and offerings : and among them shall be seen all the great ones of the people, humbly prostrating themselves before thee, to implore thy protection.

15. Omnis gloria ejus filiæ Regis ab intus : in fimbriis aureis circum- amicta varietatibus.

All the glory of the king's daughter is from within : in fringes of gold wrought with divers colours.

All the glory of the King's daughter should be from within, that is, should consist in interior virtue of the soul, more than (" *in fimbriis aureis circumamicta varietatibus* ") in those various exterior ornaments which are manifest to others.[1]

16. Adducentur Regi virgines post eam : proximæ ejus afferentur tibi.

After her shall virgins be brought unto the King : her neighbours shall be brought unto Thee.

17. Afferentur in lætitia et exulta- tione : adducentur in templum Regis.

With joy and gladness shall they be brought : they shall be brought into the temple of the King.

16, 17. In the train of the Spouse, many virgins shall be brought to the King in His temple, but they shall be those only who are her nearest, that is, united to the Queen and Spouse, who is the Church ; according to the explanation of S. Basil and S. Augustine.

18. Pro patribus tuis nati sunt tibi filii : constitues eos principes super omnem terram.

Instead of thy fathers, sons are born to thee : Thou shalt make them princes over all the earth.

According to S. Basil, S. Jerome, S. John Chrysostom, and S. Augustine, these words are addressed to the Church : their sense is : O Spouse of the Saviour, instead of the fathers of old, the patriarchs and the prophets who are now no more,

---

[1] *Ejus.* According to Bellarmine and other interpreters, this pronoun is redundant.——" *Filiæ Regis.*" The Spouse of the King is also the King's daughter : this is very applicable to the Church and to other significations.

there are born to thee sons, the Apostles, the disciples and
their successors, whom thou hast constituted princes over
the whole earth, for by their preaching of the Gospel thou
hast subjected all the nations to thy obedience.

19. Memores erunt nominis tui: They shall be mindful of Thy
in omni generatione et generationem. name: from generation to generation.

O Lord, these Apostles, these disciples and their successors,
in every age, shall continue to preach throughout all generations Thy Name, that is, Thy power and Thy mercy towards
men.——"*Memores erunt.*"   Many, according to the present
Hebrew text and the Septuagint, read : *Memor ero:* I shall
remember.   But S. Jerome and S. Augustine follow the
Vulgate.

20. Propterea populi confitebun-   Therefore shall the people praise
tur tibi in æternum: et in sæculum Thee for ever : yea for ever and ever.
sæculi.

And therefore the nations, converted to the faith, will never
cease to adore Thee.

PSALM XLV.

S. Ambrose, S. Jerome, S. Augustine, S. Chrysostom, Theodoret, and Euthymius concur in teaching that this Psalm is to be
understood of the Catholic Church with regard to the victories
she has gained over her persecutors, and her stability under
the protection of God.

Unto the end, for the Sons of Core, for the hidden.

1. Deus noster refugium, et virtus: Our God is our refuge and
adjutor in tribulationibus, quæ in- strength : a helper in troubles, which
venerunt nos nimis.   have come upon us heavily.

2. Propterea non timebimus dum   Therefore will we not fear, when
turbabitur terra : et transferentur the earth shall be troubled : and the
montes in cor maris.   mountains shall be removed into the
                                     heart of the sea.

3. Sonuerunt, et turbatæ sunt   Their waters roared, and were
aquæ eorum : conturbati sunt montes troubled : the mountains were
in fortitudine ejus.   troubled at the violence thereof.

"*Eorum.*" Bossuet with S. Jerome, following the Hebrew,
reads : *Ejus.*——We should not lose courage though we beheld
all the waters of the sea agitated with such violence that rocks
as high as mountains were moved by them.

4. Fluminis impetus lætificat civitatem Dei ; sanctificavit tabernaculum suum Altissimus.

The stream of the river maketh glad the city of God: the Most High hath sanctified His own tabernacle.

But in the midst of all these storms, the Lord will cause to flow down a river of peace, which shall rejoice the city of God, that is, the Holy Church, which the Most High has chosen for His temple, by sanctifying it with His grace.

5. Deus, in medio ejus, non commovebitur : adjuvabit eam Deus mane diluculo.

God is in the midst of her, she shall not be moved : God shall help her in the morning early.

God will never depart from her midst, assisting her from the first dawn of the morning, that is, from the first moment of her birth.

6. Conturbatæ sunt gentes et inclinata sunt regna : dedit vocem suam, mota est terra.

Nations were troubled, and kingdoms bowed down : He gave forth His voice, the earth was moved.

"*Inclinata.*" S. Jerome has *Concussa* : Shaken.——At the establishment of the Church, the nations were troubled and the kingdoms were shaken.

7. Dominus virtutum nobiscum : susceptor noster Deus Jacob.

The Lord of Hosts is with us : the God of Jacob is our helper.

But for ourselves we have no cause to fear, privileged as we are.

8. Venite, et videte opera Domini, quæ posuit prodigia super terram : auferens bella usque ad finem terræ.

Come ye, and behold the works of the Lord : what wonders He hath wrought upon the earth, making wars to cease even to the ends of the earth.

9. Arcum conteret, et confringet arma : et scuta comburet igni.

He shall break the bow and snap the weapons in sunder : and the shields shall He burn with fire.

10. Vacate, et videte quoniam ego sum Deus : exaltabor in gentibus, et exaltabor in terra.

Be still and see that I am God : I will be exalted among the nations, and I will be exalted in the earth.

"*Vacate.*" According to the Hebrew : *Cessate.*——Therefore, you who are My servants, leave alone your earthly cares and employ yourselves in reflecting that I alone Myself am God, for Whom all things exist, and upon Whom all things depend : a day will come when I shall be exalted, that is, acknowledged as the sovereign Lord of the universe, by the nations, and throughout the whole earth.

11. Dominus virtutum nobiscum : susceptor noster Deus Jacob.

The Lord of Hosts is with us : the God of Jacob is our helper.

Repetition of verse 7 for the conclusion. As much as to say : Let us then once more rejoice that we, His faithful servants, have this great, all-powerful God on our side to protect us.

PSALM XLVI.

THIS Psalm may be explained in two literal senses : in the first, it alludes to the triumph of the Ark, when it was carried to Mount Sion (2 *Kings* vi. 15) ; in the second sense, it is applied, according to several of the Holy Fathers, to the glorious Ascension of Jesus Christ into heaven.

Unto the end, for the Sons of Core.

1. Omnes gentes plaudite mani- bus : jubilate Deo in voce exultationis.

O clap your hands, all ye nations : shout unto God with the voice of joy.

2. Quoniam Dominus excelsus, terribilis : Rex magnus super omnem terram.

For the Lord is high and terrible : a great King over all the earth.

For He is the Lord, supreme above all by His majesty, and terrible by His power : He is the great Monarch who holds dominion over the whole earth.

3. Subjecit populos nobis : et gentes sub pedibus nostris.

He hath subdued the people under us : and the nations under our feet.

4. Elegit nobis hereditatem suam : speciem Jacob, quam dilexit.

He hath chosen His inheritance for us : the beauty of Jacob which He hath loved.

Amongst all the nations, He has chosen us to be His especial inheritance, because we are the seed of Jacob, whom He so much loved.

5. Ascendit Deus in jubilo : et Dominus in voce tubæ.

God is gone up with a shout of joy : and the Lord with the sound of the trumpet.

"*Ascendit Deus.*" Our Saviour ascends to heaven, by His own power, since He is God.

6. Psallite Deo nostro, psallite : psallite Regi nostro, psallite.

Sing praises unto our God, sing praises : sing praises unto our King, sing praises.

7. Quoniam Rex omnis terræ Deus : psallite sapienter.

For God is the King of all the earth : sing ye praises wisely.

Because He is King of the whole earth, and most high God : sing to Him, then ("*Sapienter*": Wisely), the praises He deserves, and as He deserves.

8. Regnabit Deus super gentes: Deus sedet super sedem sanctam suam.	God shall reign over the nations: God sitteth upon His holy seat.

Over all the nations He shall reign as God, and as God He shall sit upon His holy throne, at the right hand of the Father.

9. Principes populorum congregati sunt cum Deo Abraham: quoniam dii fortes terræ, vehementer elevati sunt.	The princes of the people are gathered together, with the God of Abraham: for the strong gods of the earth are exceedingly exalted.

"*Principes* . . . *Abraham.*" According to the Hebrew : *Congregati sunt, populus Dei Abraham.* The princes of the Gentile people are united to the people of the God of Abraham.——— "*Quoniam* . . ." This passage is very obscure. Some, as Mattei and Genebrard, say that by the Hebrew word *Elohim* (the plural for the singular) is here to be understood God Himself, and they explain the words thus : *Deus victoria elevatus est:* God is exalted in victory.———But S. Cyril, Theodoret, and Didymus understand by the words "*Dii fortes terræ*": The princes of the earth. This agrees with the translation of S. Jerome : *Dii scuta terræ.* The gods, the shields of the earth, that is, Protectors, those who have subjects under them.——— "*Elevati sunt.*" Have become exalted, by being united in worshipping the true God.———This last explanation the more pleases me, because it is most in conformity with the Vulgate and the Septuagint. The passage, therefore, may thus be explained : The princes, who are the protectors and rulers of the earth, have been greatly elevated by uniting in the worship of the true God.

PSALM XLVII.

THE protection of God, in the literal sense, over the earthly Jerusalem ; and, in the figurative sense, over the spiritual Jerusalem, which is His Church.

A Psalm of a Canticle, for the Sons of Core, on the second day of the week.

1. Magnus Dominus, et laudabilis nimis : in civitate Dei nostri, in monte sancto ejus.	Great is the Lord, and greatly to be praised : in the city of our God, even upon His holy mountain.

"*In civitate* . . ." In the city of Jerusalem, and especially on the holy mountain of Sion, where our God makes His glory to shine forth.

2. Fundatur exultatione universæ terræ mons Sion : latera Aquilonis, civitas Regis magna.

With the joy of the whole earth is Mount Sion founded : on the sides of the north, the city of the great King.

3. Deus in domibus ejus cognosce- tur : cum suscipiet eam.

In her houses shall God be known: when He shall protect her.

God shall be known amongst the inhabitants of this city, when He shall defend her against the attacks of her enemies.

4. Quoniam ecce reges terræ con- gregati sunt : convenerunt in unum.

For behold, the kings of the earth assembled themselves : they gathered together.

"*Convenerunt in unum.*" They have united together with design to lay it waste.

5. Ipsi videntes sic admirati sunt : conturbati sunt, commoti sunt : tre- mor apprehendit eos.

So they saw, and they wondered : they were troubled and were moved : trembling took hold upon them.

"*Ipsi . . . admirati sunt.*" On seeing that the hand of the Omnipotent protects her, they are seized with great astonish- ment.

6. Ibi dolores ut parturientis : in spiritu vehementi conteres naves Tharsis.

There were pains as of a woman in labour : with a vehement wind Thou shalt break in pieces the ships of Tharsis.

They shall suffer pains like those which a woman endures in child-birth : Thou, O Lord, wilt raise stormy winds, which shall break in pieces the ships of Tharsis, *i.e.*, the largest ships, such as those that sailed to Tharsis.[1]

7. Sicut audivimus, sic vidimus in civitate Domini virtutum, in civitate Dei nostri : Deus fundavit eam in æternum.

As we have heard, so have we seen, in the city of the Lord of Hosts, in the city of our God : God hath founded it for ever.

Mark now what the inhabitants of Jerusalem will say : What was promised we have seen with our own eyes verified in the city of our Lord, the God of Hosts, Who has made its foundations everlasting.——This has been indeed verified in the Church, of which it is said : "*The gates of hell shall not prevail against her*" (*Matt.* xvi. 18).

8. Suscepimus Deus misericordiam tuam : in medio templi tui.

We have received Thy mercy, O God : in the midst of Thy temple.

"*In medio . . .*" In Thy Church, and in sight of all the world.

---

[1] "*Tharsis.*" It is not known what this name designates : it is supposed to be India.

9. Secundum nomen tuum Deus, sic et laus tua in fines terræ : justitia plena est dextera tua.

According to Thy name, O God, so also *is* Thy praise unto the ends of the earth : Thy right hand is full of justice.

As Thou hast made known, O Lord, Thy great Name throughout the earth, so everywhere has Thy glory been proclaimed : and so also has Thy power been praised, which is always full of justice, in rewarding the good and in punishing the wicked.

10. Lætetur mons Sion, et exultent filiæ Judæ : propter judicia tua Domine.

Let Mount Sion rejoice, and the daughters of Juda be glad : because of Thy judgments, O Lord.

" *Propter* . . ." On account of the just judgments which Thou, O Lord, dost exercise upon earth.

11. Circumdate Sion, et complectimini eam : narrate in turribus ejus.

Walk round about Sion, and encompass her : tell ye of her towers.

Come, O nations, come all of you to dwell round about Sion, and let her be in the midst of you : and then preach the Gospel from her towers, that is, publicly.——"*Narrate* . . ." According to the Hebrew : *Numerate turres ejus:* Count the high towers that defend her.

12. Ponite corda vestra in virtute ejus : et distribuite domos ejus : ut enarretis in progenie altera.

Set your hearts on her strength : and distribute her houses ; that ye may relate it in another generation.

Apply yourselves to consider her strength, and distribute or mark out for the different citizens, or workmen, the spaces upon which to erect their houses, that is, the particular churches, so that, when the city is built up, and filled with a faithful people, we may transmit to posterity the knowledge of the true God.

13. Quoniam hic est Deus, Deus noster in æternum, et in sæculum sæculi : ipse reget nos in sæcula.

For this is God our God unto eternity, and for ever and ever : He shall rule us for evermore.

For he is the true God, and He shall be our God for ever : Who shall rule us always and world without end.

PSALM XLVIII.

An instruction to the faithful that they may learn to despise the goods of this world ; to fear only a bad death, which must be followed by a severe judgment ; and to consider that in God alone can true happiness be found. These things are set forth obscurely, but the light of the Gospel makes us see the thought of the Prophet.

Unto the end, a Psalm for the Sons of Core.

1. Audite hæc omnes gentes : auribus percipite omnes, qui habitatis orbem :

Hear these things, all ye nations : give ear, all ye inhabitants of the world :

2. Quique terrigenæ, et filii hominum : simul in unum dives et pauper.

All ye that are earth born, and ye sons of men : both rich and poor together.

3. Os meum loquetur sapientiam : et meditatio cordis mei prudentiam.

My mouth shall speak wisdom : and the meditation of my heart understanding.

My mouth shall speak to you of those things only which it is necessary to know ; I will tell you what I have meditated in my own heart, that you may know how to act prudently in all you do.

4. Inclinabo in parabolam aurem meam : aperiam in psalterio propositionem meam.

I will incline mine ear unto a parable : I will open my saying upon the harp.

I shall be attentive to listen to the truths that are told me in parable, that is, in enigma : and this enigma I will explain to you, accompanied with the sound of the psaltery.——"*Propositionem meam.*" According to the Hebrew : *Ænigma meum.*

5. Cur timebo in die mala ? iniquitas calcanei mei circumdabit me :

Why shall I fear in the evil day ? the iniquity of my heel shall encompass me :[1]

Why should I fear on the evil day, that is, at the day of my judgment ? My wickedness alone makes me fear, especially that of my heel, that is, that which shall follow me unto death, which is the end of my life, as the heel is the extremity of the body.

6. Qui confidunt in virtute sua : et in multitudine divitiarum suarum gloriantur.

They that trust in their own strength : and glory in the multitude of their riches.[2]

The great ones of this world trust in their power, and the wealthy glory in their riches.

[1] *The iniquity of my heel.* That is, the iniquity of my *steps* or *ways.* The meaning of this verse is, why should I now indulge those passions, or commit those sins, which will cause me so much anguish when the sorrows of death shall compass me.

[2] *They that trust, &c.* That is, let them fear that trust in their strength or riches : since no brother or friend can by any price rescue them from death.

7. Frater non redimit, redimet homo : non dabit Deo placationem suam.

A brother redeemeth not, nor shall man redeem : he shall not give to God his ransom.

"*Frater . . . homo . . .*" *Non* is understood again before *homo:* such omission is common in Scripture, as Bellarmine remarks. The sense, then, is : At the moment of death their brother will be unable to deliver them from the peril ; and much less will any other man be able to do so.——"*Non dabit . . .*" No other man will be able to appease God for them.

8. Et pretium redemptionis animæ suæ : et laborabit in æternum, et vivet adhuc in finem.

Nor the price of the redemption of his soul : and shall labour for ever, and shall still live unto the end.[1]

And no one will be able to give a price sufficient to redeem his soul ; so that his labour, that is, his penalty, shall be eternal, and thus he shall live for ever unhappy.

9. Non videbit interitum, cum viderit sapientes morientes : simul insipiens, et stultus peribunt :

He shall not see destruction, when he shall see the wise dying : the senseless and the fool shall perish together :[2]

"*Non videbit interitum.*" These words, according to Bossuet, are spoken ironically, as though the Prophet said : *An putavit se non visurum interitum ?* Will he suppose that he will not see death ?——Others explain them thus : He shall not see death, that is, he shall not die, until he has completed the natural course of his life, although he sees wise men die.—— Or, as Bellarmine says, we may understand the passage to mean : He shall not see death, that is, he shall neglect to provide for death, which is waiting for him at its time ; for the wicked avoid thinking of their death : but alike for the fool as for the wise man, there must come a day when they must die.

10. Et relinquent alienis divitias suas : et sepulchra eorum domus illorum in æternum.

And they shall leave their riches to strangers : and their sepulchres shall be their houses for ever.

11. Tabernacula eorum in progenie, et progenie : vocaverunt nomina sua in terris suis.

Their dwelling-places to all generations : they have called their lands by their names.

[1] *And shall labour for ever*, &c. This may be understood of the eternal sorrows and dying *life* of hell, which is the dreadful consequence of dying in sin.

[2] *He shall not see destruction.* However thoughtless he may be of his death, he must not expect to escape : when even the wise and the good are not exempt from dying.

These shall still be their dwellings after many generations, so that there shall be nothing left of them in their lands but their names, inserted on tablets of marble, or on the walls of their houses.

12. Et homo, cum in honore esset, non intellexit: comparatus est jumentis insipientibus, et similis factus est illis.

And man when he was in honour did not understand : he is compared unto senseless beasts, and is become like unto them.

"*Non intellexit.*" Did not understand what he should understand as man. (See *Ps.* xxvii. 7.)

13. Hæc via illorum scandalum ipsis : et postea in ore suo complacebunt.

This their way is their ruin : and afterwards they shall delight in their mouth.[1]

"*Hæc ... ipsis.*" Such is their way, that is, their life, in which they find many dangerous occasions to bring them to ruin.——"*Et postea ...*" And this is the life in which they continue to take so much pleasure, and of which they make their boast.

14. Sicut oves in inferno positi sunt: mors depascet eos.

They are laid in hell like sheep : death shall feed upon them.

Miserable men, living like animals without reason, they will one day find themselves, as though so many animals, victims of the divine justice, cast into hell, where death shall feed upon them, that is, where their death will be eternal. As sheep feed upon the blades of grass, and leave the roots to sprout forth again, so death torments unceasingly the reprobate, still leaving them life, that they may go on suffering eternally.

15. Et dominabuntur eorum justi in matutino : et auxilium eorum veterascet in inferno a gloria eorum.

And the just shall have dominion over them in the morning: and their help shall decay in hell from their glory.

At the general resurrection, which is "morning," or the beginning of the age to come, the wicked shall see the just set to be their masters and their judges : and then the power which they had in this world will be seen shattered and destroyed in hell, after all the empty glory of which they boasted during their life.

16. Verumtamen Deus redimet animam meam de manu inferi : cum acceperit me.

But God will redeem my soul from the hand of hell : when He shall receive me.

[1] *They shall delight in their mouth.* Notwithstanding their death, their children adopt the same views, and approve their sayings.

"*Cum acceperit me.*" When He shall receive me amongst His servants, after having completed the work of Redemption.

17. Ne timueris cum dives factus fuerit homo: et cum multiplicata fuerit gloria domus ejus.

Be not thou afraid, when a man shall be made rich: and when the glory of his house shall be increased.

"*Ne timueris* . . ." Faithful soul, be not afraid of the sinful man whom thou shalt see, &c.

18. Quoniam cum interierit, non sumet omnia : neque descendet cum eo gloria ejus.

For when he dieth he shall take nothing away : nor shall his glory descend with him.

"*Non sumet omnia.*" A Hebraism. He shall take nothing away with him.

19. Quia anima ejus in vita ipsius benedicetur : confitebur tibi cum benefeceris ei.

For in his lifetime his soul will be blessed : and he will praise thee when thou shalt do well to him.

The sinner shall be blessed, that is, applauded by worldlings during his life upon earth : whilst he will not praise you, save when you shall load him with earthly goods.

20. Introibit usque in progenies patrum suorum : et usque in æternum non videbit lumen.

He shall go into the generations of his fathers : and shall never see light.

And behold, after his wicked life, the miserable man shall go into the abode of his ancestors, whose bad example he has followed, and there will he remain for ever, never more to see the light.

21. Homo cum in honore esset, non intellexit : comparatus est jumentis insipientibus, et similis factus est illis.

Man when he was in honour did not understand : he hath been compared unto senseless beasts, and made like unto them.

Repetition of verse 12 for the conclusion. See then the end of him, who, though a man, chose to become like the beasts, who live and work without reason, just as he himself lived.

PSALM XLIX.

THE second coming of Jesus Christ, which will be public and full of majesty, in contrast with His first coming, which was hidden and in humility.

A Psalm for Asaph.[1]

1. Deus deorum Dominus locutus est : et vocavit terram.

The God of gods, the Lord hath spoken : and He hath called the earth.

[1] Asaph was one of the chief singers (1 *Par.* xxv.).

The God of gods,[1] that is, the true God, the Sovereign
Master of all created powers, has spoken, and has cited all
men of the earth to give an account of their lives before His
divine tribunal.

2. A solis ortu usque ad occasum : ex Sion species decoris ejus.	From the rising of the sun unto the going down thereof : out of Sion is the loveliness of His beauty.

He will make His voice heard from one extremity of the
world to the other ; and He shall come down from the
Heavenly Sion adorned with His glory and majesty.

3. Deus manifeste veniet : Deus noster, et non silebit.	God shall come manifestly : our God *shall come*, and shall not keep silence.

Our God shall come in sight of all the world, and then He
shall be recognised as the great God that He is : He shall then
no longer be silent, as He has been in the past, seeing the sins
of the wicked, whilst seeming not to notice the injury He
received.

4. Ignis in conspectu ejus exardes-cet : et in circuitu ejus tempestas valida.	A fire shall burn before Him : and a mighty tempest *shall be* round about Him.

The fire at His presence will burn with greater force,
reducing the world to ashes, according to the words of S.
Peter : " *The earth and the works which are in it shall be burnt
up* ". (2 *Pet.* iii. 10.) And around Him there shall be a great
and universal tempest, which shall throw everything into
confusion on earth, in the sea, and in the air.

5. Advocabit cœlum desursum : et terram discernere populum suum.	He shall call the heaven from above : and the earth to judge His people.

He will then call the heavens above and the earth beneath,
that is, all the Angels and all men, to assist at the judgment
He will make of His people, by separating the elect from the
reprobate.

6. Congregate illi sanctos ejus : qui ordinant testamentum ejus super sacrificia.	Gather ye together His saints unto Him : who seal His covenant by sacrifices.

---

[1] Bellarmine observes that many are called gods by different rights, viz.:
by a false creed, as the pagan divinities or the demons ; by the grace of
adoption, as the Angels and Saints ; by similitude, as princes and judges.
But all these gods are subject to one alone Who is the true God, called
therefore the God of gods. (See *Ps.* lxxxi. 1, 6.)

Angels of heaven, gather together around the Judge His Saints, that is, the elect, who, besides sacrifices, that is, besides external worship, have kept His covenant by obeying His law.

7. Et annuntiabunt cœli justitiam ejus : quoniam Deus judex est.

And the heavens shall declare His justice : for God is judge.

"*Deus judex est.*" The Judge is God, Who cannot be deceived.

8. Audi populus meus, et loquar : Israel, et testificabor tibi : Deus Deus tuus ego sum.

Hear, O My people, and I will speak ; O Israel, and I will testify unto thee : I am God thy God.

Here it is Jesus Christ Who speaks. He says : Listen, My people, to what I shall say to thee : listen, Israel, that is, all the true faithful, to what I shall testify to thee, that is, to all that I shall make known to thee, through My inspirations and by My ministers : and believe Me, for I am thy true God, Who knows all things, and Who loves thee.

9. Non in sacrificiis tuis arguam te : holocausta autem tua in conspectu meo sunt semper.

I will not reprove thee for thy sacrifices : and thy burnt-offerings are always in My sight.

My people, I will not reproach thee for the sacrifices thou hast neglected to offer to Me : for those which thou hast offered suffice Me, and they are ever before My eyes.

10. Non accipiam de domo tua vitulos : neque de gregibus tuis hircos.

I will not take calves out of thine house : nor he-goats out of thy flocks.

"*Non accipiam.*" I am not seeking to have.

11. Quoniam meæ sunt omnes feræ silvarum : jumenta in montibus et boves.

For all the beasts of the woods are Mine : the cattle on the hills and the oxen.

12. Cognovi omnia volatilia cœli : et pulchritudo agri mecum est.

I know all the fowls of the air : and with Me is the beauty of the field.

I know well that all the birds of the air are Mine, and that what gives richness and beauty to the fields is Mine.

13. Si esuriero, non dicam tibi : meus est enim orbis terræ, et plenitudo ejus.

If I were hungry, I would not tell thee : for the world is Mine, and the fulness thereof.

14. Numquid manducabo carnes taurorum ? aut sanguinem hircorum potabo ?

Shall I eat the flesh of bullocks ? or shall I drink the blood of goats ?

"*Numquid manducabo.*" What ! dost thou think that for my sustinence I have any need to eat ?

15. Immola Deo sacrificium laudis: et redde Altissimo vota tua.

Offer unto God the sacrifice of praise : and pay thy vows unto the Most High.

If thou wouldest please Me, offer to Me, thy God, a sacrifice of praise, which comes not alone from the lips, but from a heart that loves Me, and fulfil the promises thou hast made to the Most High.

16. Et invoca me in die tribulationis : eruam te, et honorificabis me.

And call upon me in the day of trouble : I will deliver thee, and thou shalt glorify Me.

And call upon Me in the day of affliction : for I will deliver thee, and " *Honorificabis me* ". Thou shalt honour Me by returning Me thanks.

17. Peccatori autem dixit Deus : Quare tu enarras justitias meas, et assumis testamentum meum per os tuum ?

But to the sinner hath God said : Why dost thou declare My laws, and take My covenant in thy mouth?

S. Jerome thus translates the passage : *Quid tibi est cum narratione præceptorum meorum, ut assumas pactum meum in ore tuo ?* The verse, therefore, may be thus explained : The Lord says, on the contrary to the sinner : What good is it for thee to talk about My precepts, when thou dost not observe them ? and of My covenant, when thou art wanting to it on thy part ?

18. Tu vero odisti disciplinam : et projecisti sermones meos retrorsum.

Seeing thou hast hated discipline : and hast cast My words behind thee.

" *Disciplinam.*" That is, My teaching.

19. Si videbas furem, currebas cum eo : et cum adulteris portionem tuam ponebas.

If thou sawest a thief, thou didst run with him : and thou hast been partaker with adulterers.

20. Os tuum abundavit malitia : et lingua tua concinnabat dolos.

Thy mouth hath abounded with evil : and thy tongue framed deceits.

21. Sedens adversus fratrem tuum loquebaris : et adversus filium matris tuæ ponebas scandalum : hæc fecisti, et tacui.

Thou didst sit and speak against thy brother : and didst lay a stumbling-block for thy mother's son : these things hast thou done, and I was silent.

" *Ponebas scandalum.*" S. Jerome's translation is : *Fabricabaris opprobrium.*——The sense of the verse is : Sitting in company with others, thou hast spoken ill of thy neighbour ; thou hast sought to take away the good name even of thy brother : this hast thou done, and I have been silent.

22. Existimasti inique quod ero tui similis : arguam te, et statuam contra faciem tuam.

Thou thoughtest unjustly that I shall be like unto thee : *but* I will reprove thee, and set *them* before thy face.

Didst thou think, O wicked man, that I was like to thee? and that I should take no account of thy offences against Me? In due time I will bring up against thee thy wicked life, and I will take care that thy crimes are ever before thy eyes, that their very hideousness may ever be thy torment.

23. Intelligite hæc qui oblivisci-mini Deum : nequando rapiat et non sit qui eripiat.

Understand these things, ye that forget God : lest He snatch you *away*, and there be none to deliver you.

" *Nequando rapiat.*" That so you may avoid being made one day the prey of the devil.

24. Sacrificium laudis honorifica-bit me : et illic iter, quo ostendam illi salutare Dei.

The sacrifice of praise shall glorify Me : and that is the way by which I will show him the salvation of God.

Remember that the sacrifice of praise, that is, a good life, is the only sacrifice which honours Me : this is the way by which I give thee to understand thou wilt obtain salvation, which consists in the enjoyment of the sight of God, and in loving Him for all eternity.

PSALM LI.

In the literal sense, a reproach which David makes to Doeg the Edomite, who had excited the anger of Saul against him-self and the priest Achimelech, and had thus caused the ruin of many others (1 *Kings* xxii.). In the person of Doeg we may understand all the wicked who persecute the good.

Unto the end, understanding for David, when Doeg the Edomite came and told Saul, *saying :* David went to the house of Achimelech (1 *Kings* xxii. 9).

1. Quid gloriaris in malitia : qui potens es in iniquitate?

Why dost thou glory in malice : thou that art mighty in iniquity?

" *In iniquitate.*" In doing injury to others.

2. Tota die injustitiam cogitavit lingua tua : sicut novacula acuta fecisti dolum.

All the day long thy tongue hath devised injustice : as a sharp razor, thou hast wrought deceit.

All the day long thou hast employed thy tongue for nought else but to offend others unjustly : thou hast used it as a well-sharpened razor to deceive.

3. Dilexisti malitiam super benig- | Thou hast loved malice more than
nitatem : iniquitatem magis quam | goodness : and iniquity rather than
loqui æquitatem. | to speak righteousness.

Thou hast better loved to do evil to thy neighbour than to
do him good : and hast sought to speak more readily to his
damage than to his advantage.

4. Dilexisti omnia verba præcipi- | Thou hast loved all the words of
tationis : lingua dolosa. | ruin : O deceitful tongue.

Thou hast done thy best constantly to speak words that
might destroy and bring ruin upon thy neighbour, thou
slanderous tongue.

5. Propterea Deus destruet te in | Therefore shall God destroy thee
finem : evellet te, et emigrabit te de | for ever : He shall pluck thee out,
tabernaculo tuo : et radicem tuam de | and remove thee from thy dwelling-
terra viventium. | place : and thy root out of the land
| of the living.

"*In finem.*" Utterly.——"*Radicem tuam.*" He will make
thee to disappear with all thy race, even as a tree is felled,
and pulled up with all its roots.

6. Videbunt justi, et timebunt, et | The just shall see and fear, and
super eum ridebunt et dicent : Ecce | shall laugh at him, and say : Behold
homo, qui non posuit Deum adju- | the man that made not God his
torem suum : | helper :

The just shall see all this, and they will have horror thereat ; they will laugh at his ruin, and will say : Behold the
man who refused to put his trust in God, as though he did
not need His help.

7. Sed speravit in multitudine | But trusted in the abundance of
divitiarum suarum : et prævaluit in | his riches : and strengthened himself
vanitate sua. | in his vanity.

"*Prevaluit...*" He reckoned on his vain supports, which
gave him a promise of happiness.

8. Ego autem, sicut oliva fructi- | But I, as a fruitful olive-tree in
fera in domo Dei : speravi in miseri- | the house of God : have hoped in the
cordia Dei in æternum, et in sæculum | mercy of God for ever, yea for ever
sæculi. | and ever.

9. Confitebor tibi in sæculum quia | I will praise Thee for ever, because
fecisti : et expectabo nomen tuum, | Thou hast done it : and I will wait on
quoniam bonum est in conspectu | Thy name, for it is good in the sight
sanctorum tuorum. | of Thy saints.

I will never cease to thank Thee, O Lord, for the graces
with which Thou hast favoured me, and in all my tribulations
I will wait for the help of Thy goodness, which never fails to
succour Thy servants.

LAUDS FOR TUESDAY.

PSALM L.

PSALM XLII.

DAVID begs of God to be delivered from his enemies, and consoles himself with the hope of again seeing the Tabernacle. In the spiritual sense this Psalm applies to the just man, who, in the trials of the present life, longs to leave this earth, and to go to his heavenly country.

A Psalm for David.

1. Judica me Deus, et discerne causam meam de gente non sancta : ab homine iniquo et doloso erue me.

Judge me, O God, and distinguish my cause from the nation that is not holy: deliver me from the unjust and deceitful man.

"*De gente non sancta.*" Against the wicked, who persecute me.

2. Quia tu es Deus fortitudo mea : quare me repulisti ? et quare tristis incedo, dum affligit me inimicus ?

For Thou art God my strength : why hast Thou cast me off ? and why go I sorrowful whilst the enemy afflicteth me ?

"*Quare me repulisti ?*" Why dost Thou seem to have cast me off ?

3. Emitte lucem tuam et veritatem tuam : ipsa me deduxerunt, et adduxerunt in montem sanctum tuum, et in tabernacula tua.

Send forth Thy light and Thy truth : they have led me, and brought me unto Thy holy hill, and into Thy tabernacles.

Send forth Thy light, and make me enjoy Thy promises : they will bring me out of sadness, and will lead me to Thy holy mountain of Sion, and to Thy tabernacle.——"*De-*

duxerunt, et adduxerunt." According to the Hebrew, these verbs are not in the past but in the future tense.

4. Et introibo ad altare Dei: ad Deum, qui lætificat juventutem meam.   And I will go in unto the altar of God: unto God Who giveth joy to my youth.

Having entered therein, I will draw near to the divine altar, and even to my God, Who will restore to me the gladness that rejoiced my youth.

5. Confitebor tibi in cithara Deus Deus meus: quare tristis es anima mea? et quare conturbas me?   I will praise Thee upon the harp, O God my God: why art thou sad, O my soul? and why dost thou disquiet me?

"*Confitebor tibi.*" There I will sing Thy praises."——- "*Quare...*" Why, my soul, having such a hope, art thou sad?

6. Spera in Deo, quoniam adhuc confitebor illi: salutare vultus mei, et Deus meus.   Hope thou in God, for I will yet praise Him: *Who is* the salvation of my countenance, and my God.

Put, then, thy trust in God, for I hope to go one day to bless Him, and to thank Him for ever in heaven: since Thou, O Lord, art my God, and the salvation of my face, that is, Thou, my Saviour, wilt be ever present to my eyes, and to see Thy beautiful Face will be my salvation and beatitude.

PSALMS LXII and LXVI.

THE CANTICLE OF EZECHIAS (*Is.* xxxviii. 10, 20).

THE title of this Canticle sufficiently explains its contents: it runs thus: "*The writing of Ezechias, king of Juda, when he had been sick, and was recovered of his sickness*". The first part expresses the laments of Ezechias, and the second his thanksgiving for the recovery of his health. This Canticle may well be applied to the Christian who bewails his spiritual infirmities, and then thanks God for the help He has vouchsafed to him.

1. Ego dixi: In dimidio dierum meorum: vadam ad portas inferi.   I said: In the midst of my days:[1] I shall go to the gates of hell.

[1] Ezechias was then thirty-nine years old (4 *Kings* xviii. 2, xx. 6).

It is, then, in the middle of my life's course that I shall enter into the tomb.

2. Quæsivi residuum annorum meorum : dixi : Non videbo Dominum Deum in terra viventium.

I sought for the residue of my years : I said : I shall not see the Lord God in the land of the living.

I set myself to consider the rest of the years which I might have lived, and I said : So here on earth I shall not any more have the joy of going to the temple, there to visit and to adore my Lord and my God.

3. Non aspiciam hominem ultra : et habitatorem quietis.

I shall behold man no more: nor the inhabitant of rest.

I shall see no more the inhabitants of my kingdom, who now live in peace.

4. Generatio mea ablata est, et convoluta est a me : quasi tabernaculum pastorum.

My generation is at an end, and it is rolled away from me as a shepherd's tent.

Behold I remain deprived of all posterity, and my family will be destroyed, as is the wont to destroy a shed of shepherds. ——Such is the explanation of S. Jerome, S. Thomas, and others.[1]

5. Præcisa est velut a texente vita mea : dum adhuc ordirer, succidit me : de mane usque ad vesperam finies me.

My life is cut off as by a weaver : whilst I was but beginning, He cut me off : from morning even till night Thou wilt make an end of me.

My life is being cut off, like a web that is cut off by the weaver : I was still weaving it when the Lord cut it off : thus, my God, from morning to eve, Thou wilt make an end of me, that is, within the space of one day Thou wilt bring my life to a close.

6. Sperabam usque ad mane : quasi leo sic contrivit omnia ossa mea.

I hoped till morning : as a lion so hath he broken my bones.

7. De mane usque ad vesperam finies me : sicut pullus hirundinis sic clamabo, meditabor ut columba.

From morning even till night Thou wilt make an end of me : I will cry like a young swallow, I will meditate like a dove.

6, 7. I hoped to live until the morning of the second day, but the violence of the disease, like a lion, has broken all my

[1] As Ezechias had as yet no child, it grieved him to think that the promised Messias would not be in his line. However, according to the Hebrew, the word *Generatio* means here : life, age, or time of life ; hence the words are more commonly interpreted, My life has been taken away.

bones, that is, has taken away all my strength, so that I
cannot now last out to see the evening. Like a little callow
swallow that is in the nest, without feathers, suffering from
cold and hunger, I cry out and beg for pity: and, like a
plaintive dove, so do I meditate upon my miseries, and implore
for help by my moanings.

8. Attenuati sunt oculi mei: suspicientes in excelsum.

My eyes are weakened: with looking upward.

"*In excelsum.*" Upwards to heaven.

9. Domine vim patior, responde pro me: Quid dicam, aut quid respondebit mihi, cum ipse fecerit?

Lord, I suffer violence, answer Thou for me. What shall I say, or what shall He answer for me, whereas He Himself hath done it?

O Lord, I am oppressed by evil, do Thou answer for me.
But what is it I ask for, or what will the Lord reply to me,
since it is He Himself Who has done it, that is, it is He Who
has reduced me to the state in which I am?

10. Recogitabo tibi omnes annos meos: in amaritudine animæ meæ.

I will recount to Thee all my years: in the bitterness of my soul.

It being as it is, I will go over in thought all my past years,
in bitterness of soul for the sins I have committed.

11. Domine si sic vivitur, et in talibus vita spiritus mei, corripies me, et vivificabis me: Ecce in pace amaritudo mea amarissima.

O Lord, if man's life be such, and the life of my spirit be in such things as these, Thou shalt correct me, and make me to live: Behold in peace is my bitterness most bitter.

If this, O God, be man's life, that is, a life of sin; and if
thus my life has been passed, punish me, O Lord, and thus
preserve my life. Behold, in the time even of my great
bitterness, I have regained peace.

12. Tu autem eruisti animam meam ut non periret: projecisti post tergum tuum omnia peccata mea.

But Thou hast delivered my soul that it should not perish: Thou hast cast all my sins behind Thy back.

But Thou, my God, hast delivered me from death; and, in
order to deliver me therefrom, Thou hast cast all my sins
behind Thy back, no more to behold them.

13. Quia non infernus confitebitur tibi, neque mors laudabit te: non expectabunt qui descendunt in lacum veritatem tuam.

For hell shall not confess to Thee, neither shall death praise Thee: nor shall they that go down into the pit look for Thy truth.

For he who is dead in the tomb can no longer praise Thee, nor can he hope to see the fulfilment of Thy promises.[1]

14. Vivens vivens ipse confitebitur tibi, sicut et ego hodie : pater filiis notam faciet veritatem tuam.

The living, the living, he shall give praise to Thee, as I do this day : the father shall make Thy truth known to the children.

The living alone are they who sing Thy praises as I am doing this day ; and so fathers shall recount to their children Thy fidelity to the promises Thou hast made to them.

15. Domine salvum me fac : et psalmos nostros cantabimus cunctis diebus vitæ nostræ in domo Domini.

O Lord, save me: and we will sing our psalms all the days of our life in the house of the Lord.

Save me, O Lord : and so I shall then, in Thy temple, sing Thy glory all the days of my life.

PSALMS CXLVIII., CXLIX., CL.

THE CANTICLE OF ZACHARY.

[1] Bellarmine (*Ps.* vi. 5) thinks, with S. Jerome and other Fathers, that Ezechias speaks here of eternal death and hell, as the preceding verse would seem to indicate.

MATINS FOR WEDNESDAY.

PSALM LII.

THE Psalmist deplores the corruption of mankind, and prays God to deliver His people from the persecution of the wicked. He speaks also of God's goodness in waiting for sinners to do penance ; and at the same time he sighs for the coming of the Redeemer to set man free from the slavery of the devil, typified by the Captivity of Babylon.[1]

Unto the end, for Maeleth,[2] understandings to David.

1. Dixit insipiens in corde suo : Non est Deus.

The fool hath said in his heart : There is no God.

"*Insipiens.*" The impious man become a fool by his impiety. A man must have lost his reason to think that there is no God.

2. Corrupti sunt, et abominabiles facti sunt in iniquitatibus: non est qui faciat bonum.

Corrupt are they, and become abominable in iniquities : there is none that doeth good.

Miserable men ! living a life of moral corruption, they have become abominable by their iniquity before God and before men : there is not one among them who does a good action.

3. Deus de cœlo prospexit super filios hominum : ut videat si est intelligens, aut requirens Deum.

God looked down from heaven upon the children of men : to see if there were any that did understand, or did seek God.

"*Intelligens...*" Who understands his duty, and seeks to please God.

[1] All the verses of this Psalm, except v. 7, and some differences of expression, are found in *Ps.* xiii.

[2] *Maeleth.* A musical instrument, or a chorus of musicians : for S. Jerome renders it, *per chorum.*

4. Omnes declinaverunt, simul inutiles facti sunt: non est qui faciat bonum, non est usque ad unum.

All have gone aside, they are become worthless together: there is none that doeth good, no not one.

"*Omnes ... sunt.*" All are wanting to their duty, and thus render themselves useless to God and to men.

5. Nonne scient omnes qui operantur iniquitatem: qui devorant plebem meam ut cibum panis?

Shall not all the workers of iniquity know: who eat up my people as they eat bread?

Will all these unhappy men then never know their perversity, and will they continue to oppress My people with as much ease as one eats bread?

6. Deum non invocaverunt; illic trepidaverunt timore, ubi non erat timor.

They have not called upon God: there have they trembled for fear, where no fear was.

All their evil life comes from their unwillingness to call upon the Lord in the dangers of offending Him; they fear where there is no cause for fear, that is, they fear to lose some earthly good, and they are not afraid of losing the grace of God.

7. Quoniam Deus dissipavit ossa eorum qui hominibus placent: confusi sunt, quoniam Deus sprevit eos.

For God hath scattered the bones of them that please men: they have been confounded, because God hath despised them.[1]

But God will utterly destroy those who displease Him in order to please men; they shall be confounded; for as they despise God, so also shall they be despised by Him.

8. Quis dabit ex Sion salutare Israel? cum converterit Deus captivitatem plebis suæ, exultabit Jacob, et lætabitur Israël.

Who will give out of Sion the salvation of Israel? when God shall bring back the captivity of His people, Jacob shall rejoice, and Israel shall be glad.

The fools will say : Who will come from Sion to save Israel ? ——But when God shall turn the slavery of His people into a glorious liberty, then this same people shall be glad and exult for joy.

PSALM LIV.

In the literal sense, David implores the help of God against the persecution of his son Absolom. But S. Hilary and S. Jerome apply the Psalm to Jesus Christ betrayed by Judas

---

[1] *God hath scattered the bones,* &c. That is, God hath brought to nothing the strength of all those that seek to please men to the prejudice of their duty to their Maker.

and persecuted by the Jews. Generally speaking, it may be applied to all the just, persecuted in this life by men or devils.

Unto the end, in verse, understanding for David.

1. Exaudi Deus orationem meam, et ne despexeris deprecationem meam: intende mihi, et exaudi me.

Hear my prayer, O God, and despise not my supplication: be attentive unto me, and hear me.

"*Intende mihi.*" Consider my tribulation.

2. Contristatus sum in exercitatione mea: et conturbatus sum a voce inimici, et a tribulatione peccatoris.

I am grieved in my prayer:[1] and am troubled at the voice of the enemy, and at the tribulation of the sinner.

I am afflicted in applying myself to consider my sufferings, and I am troubled at hearing of the persecution which my perverse enemy is plotting against me.

3. Quoniam declinaverunt in me iniquitates: et in ira molesti erant mihi.

For they have cast iniquities upon me: and in wrath they were grievous unto me.

My enemies have accused me of crimes which I have not committed ; and, moved by anger, they seek all means to annoy me.

4. Cor meum conturbatum est in me: et formido mortis cecidit super me.

My heart is disquieted within me: and the fear of death is fallen upon me.

5. Timor et tremor venerunt super me: et contexerunt me tenebræ :

Fear and trembling are come upon me: and darkness hath covered me :

Hence I am filled with fear and trembling ; and I am encompassed all around with darkness, so that I am unable to see any escape from the dangers that threaten me.

6. Et dixi : Quis dabit mihi pennas sicut columbæ : et volabo, et requiescam ?

And I said: Who will give me wings like a dove: and I will fly and be at rest ?

In this state I said : Who will give me wings, that, like a timid dove, as I am at present, I may be able to fly and seek repose in some secure place ?

7. Ecce elongavi fugiens : et mansi in solitudine.

Lo, I have gone far off flying away: and I remained in the wilderness.

I would take flight and be far away, if I could, and I should be content to remain in some unknown desert.——This is the explanation given by Rotigni and Lallemant.

---

[1] *Prayer.* S. Jerome has *meditation*: the Latin word is *exercitatio.*

8. Expectabam eum qui salvum me fecit: a pusillanimitate spiritus et tempestate.

I waited for him that hath saved me : from fearfulness of spirit, and from the storm.

There I would wait for Him Who has so often delivered me from my great fear of soul, and from the tempest which arose against me.

9. Præcipita Domine, divide linguas eorum : quoniam vidi iniquitatem et contradictionem in civitate.

Cast down, O Lord, *and* divide their tongues: for I have seen iniquity and gainsaying in the city.

Cast down, O Lord, those who seek to oppress me ; confound their tongues, that is, put discord between them, so that their designs become fruitless ; for I see their iniquity, I see the city in contradiction, that is, all in disorder and confusion.

10. Die ac nocte circumdabit eam super muros ejus iniquitas: et labor in medio ejus, et injustitia.

Day and night shall iniquity go round about it upon its walls : and in the midst thereof are labour and injustice.

I see that the city will be encompassed with iniquity, and that its walls will be occupied with evil, so that it will be infested on all sides with affliction and injustice.

11. Et non defecit de plateis ejus : usura, et dolus.

And usury and deceit : have not departed from its streets.

And, for its greater ruin, there will not be wanting in its streets usury and deceit.

12. Quoniam si inimicus meus maledixisset mihi : sustinuissem utique.

For if mine enemy had reviled me : I would verily have borne it.

13. Et si is, qui oderat me, super me magna locutus fuisset ; abscondissem me forsitan ab eo.

And if he that hated me had spoken great things against me : I would perhaps have hidden myself from him.

14. Tu vero homo unanimis : dux meus, et notus meus.

But it was thou, a man of one mind with me : my guide, and mine acquaintance.

But the man who persecutes me, who is he ? It is thou, my guide and my friend, who I believed had but one and the same heart with me.[1]

15. Qui simul mecum dulces capiebas cibos : in domo Dei ambulavimus cum consensu.

Who didst take sweet meats together with me : in the house of God we walked with consent.

1 See *Ps.* xl. 10.

Thou, who with me didst feed sweetly at my table, and with me didst join company to go to the House of God.

16. Veniat mors super illos: et descendant in infernum viventes.

Let death come upon them: and let them go down alive into hell.[1]

Let death come upon such workers of iniquity, and may they go buried alive in an underground pit.

17. Quoniam nequitiæ in habita-culis eorum : in medio eorum.

For there is wickedness in their dwellings : in the midst of them.

Since their houses as well as their hearts are full of iniquity.

18. Ego autem ad Deum clamavi : et Dominus salvabit me.

But I have cried unto God : and the Lord will save me.

But I have cried and had recourse to my God, and He will save me.

19. Vespere, et mane, et meridie narrabo et annuntiabo : et exaudiet vocem meam.

Evening and morning and at noon I will speak and declare ; and He shall hear my voice.

In the morning, at midday, and in the evening, that is, at all times, I will recount and publish the mercy of my Lord in succouring me : and I hope that He will ever graciously hearken to my prayers.[2]

20. Redimet in pace animam meam ab his qui appropinquant mihi : quoniam inter multos erant mecum.

He shall redeem my soul in peace from them that draw near against me : for among many they were with me.

He will establish me again in my former peace, and will deliver my life from those who draw near to oppress me, for they are come in great numbers against me to cast me down. ——This is according to the translation of S. Jerome, who has : *Multi enim fuerunt adversum me.*

21. Exaudiet Deus, et humiliabit illos : qui est ante sæcula.

God shall hear and shall bring them down : even He who is from everlasting.

" *Qui est ante sæcula.*" He who is the Eternal.

---

[1] *Let death,* &c. This, and such like expressions, which occur in the Psalms are delivered prophetically, and not by way of ill-will, which the law of God disallows.

[2] " *Vespere, et mane, et meridie.*" It was the custom to pray at three special times in the day (*Don.* vi. 10). The evening is put first, because then the celebration of the feasts began (*Lev.* xxiii. 32). Hence the first Vespers, in the Office of the Holy Church.

22. Non enim est illis commutatio, et non timuerunt Deum : extendit manum suam in retribuendo.

For there is no change with them, and they have not feared God : He hath stretched forth His hand to repay.

For the Lord sees that for them there is no change, that is, He sees that they are obstinate, and that they have no fear of God ; and for this reason He has already raised His hand to punish them according to their malice.

23. Contaminaverunt testamentum ejus, divisi sunt ab ira vultus ejus : et appropinquavit cor illius.

They have defiled His covenant, they are dispersed at the wrath of His countenance : and His heart hath drawn near.

"*Contaminaverunt testamentum ejus.*" They have violated His covenant.——S. Jerome's translation is : *Contaminavit pactum ejus.* That is, they have broken their given faith.—— "*Divisi sunt ab ira vultus ejus.*" But they have been scattered at the sight of the anger which the Lord showed against them. ——"*Appropinquavit cor illius.*" The heart of God hath drawn near, that is, is set to take on them His just vengeance. ——Others refer the words "*Cor illius,*" not to God, but to the rebellious : They say that such a rebel or traitor has one thing on his lips and another in his heart.[1] But Bellarmine, explaining the Hebrew text, is of opinion that here is signified the heart of God aroused to anger.

24. Molliti sunt sermones ejus super oleum : et ipsi sunt jacula.

His words are smoother than oil : and yet they are very darts.

Their words are softer and sweeter than oil, but in reality they are sharp arrows shot when least expected.

25. Jacta super Dominum curam tuam, et ipse te enutriet : non dabit in æternum fluctuationem justo.

Cast thy care upon the Lord, and He shall nourish thee : He shall not give over the just to the waves for ever.

But the Lord encourages me to leave to His goodness the care of my salvation, and thus He will take thought to preserve my life : He will not permit that the just man should be always tossed about on the billows of fear.

26. Tu vero Deus deduces eos : in puteum interitus.

But Thou, O God, shalt bring them down : into the pit of destruction.

As for my enemies, on the contrary, O Lord, Thou wilt cast them down into the pit of death, that is, into hell, where has

[1] This explanation is doubtless taken from the Hebrew text : S. Jerome thus translates this passage ; His mouth is smoother (*nitidius*) than butter ; but his heart is at war. A meaning which agrees with the following verse.

to be endured a never-ending death.——Hell is called a pit because it has a mouth to receive the damned, but has no door by which they can go out.

27. Viri sanguinum et dolosi non dimidiabunt dies suos: ego autem sperabo in te Domine.

Bloody and deceitful men shall not live out half their days: but I will trust in Thee, O Lord.

PSALM LV.

DAVID, flying from the presence of Saul, who was seeking his death, retires amongst the Philistines: but when recognised by them who he was, he finds himself in great danger (1 *Kings* xxi. 10). Under these circumstances he composes this prayer, which every Christian can use when he sees himself in danger of falling into sin and becoming the prey of the devil.[1]

Unto the end, for a people that is removed at a distance from the sanctuary: for David, for an inscription of a title, when the Philistines held him in Geth.

1. Miserere mei Deus, quoniam conculcavit me homo: tota die impugnans tribulavit me.

Have mercy upon me, O God, for man hath trodden me under foot: fighting against me all the day long hath he afflicted me.

The man, who is my enemy, has sought to tread me under foot: and therefore, persecuting me all the day, he has striven to afflict me.

2. Conculcaverunt me inimici mei tota die: quoniam multi bellantes adversum me.

Mine enemies have trodden upon me all the day long: for they are many that make war against me.

All my enemies have united to plot continually my ruin.

3. Ab altitudine diei timebo: ego vero in te sperabo.

From the height of the day I shall fear: but I will trust in Thee.[2]

"*Ab altitudine diei.*" Many, as Menochius, understand hereby the great dangers threatening: but I prefer the more literal interpretation of Calmet and Tirinus; according to which the verse is explained thus: During the whole day, from the rising of the sun, I am in a continual fear; but I hope from Thee, O Lord, the succour I need.

---

[1] This Psalm is also applicable to Jesus Christ, and to the Holy Church.

[2] *Height of the day.* S. Jerome translates this verse thus: In whatsoever day I shall be afraid, I will trust in Thee.

4. In Deo laudabo sermones meos, in Deo speravi: non timebo quid faciat mihi caro.

In God I will praise my words, in God have I put my trust: I will not fear what flesh can do unto me.

" *Sermones meos.*"[1] According to the Hebrew : *Verbum ejus.* The promises He has made me, or the word He has given me. ——" *Caro.*" The carnal man, which in regard to God is but weakness. (See verse 11.)

5. Tota die verba mea execrabantur : adversum me omnes cogitationes eorum, in malum.

All the day long they detested my words : all their thoughts *were* against me for evil.

All day long they slander my words, and all their thoughts are turned against me to consume me.

6. Inhabitabunt et abscondent : ipsi calcaneum meum observabunt.

They will dwell and hide *themselves :* they will watch my heel

They unite together and hide away in order to oppress me, and to this end they stand to observe my heel, that is, my steps.

7. Sicut sustinuerunt animam meam, pro nihilo salvos facies illos : in ira populos confringes.

As they have waited for my soul, for nought shalt Thou save them : in Thine anger Thou shalt break the people in pieces.

" *Sicut . . . meam.*" As in like manner they have waited for the opportunity to take away my life.——" *Pro nihilo . . . illos.*" So Thou wilt on no account save them. This is the explanation of S. Jerome.——S. Augustine, on the contrary, gives this interpretation : Thou wilt save them, of pure grace, without any merit on their part. The sense of S. Jerome agrees better with the words that follow : " *In ira populos confringes* ". In Thy just wrath, Thou wilt break to pieces this crowd of enemies who would destroy me.

8. Deus, vitam meam annuntiavi tibi : posuisti lacrymas meas in conspectu tuo.

O God, I have declared my life unto Thee : Thou hast set my tears in Thy sight.

My God, I lay before Thee all the afflictions of my life : I hope that Thou wilt have always my tears before Thine eyes.

9. Sicut et in *promissione tua : tunc convertentur inimici mei retrorsum.

As also in Thy promise : then shall mine enemies be turned back.

---

[1] According to Bellarmine, these words, when understood of David, signify : What the Lord declared concerning me personally (*Kings* xiii. 14 ; xvi. 1, 3, 12).

As Thou hast promised, I hope that my enemies filled with confusion, at seeing their designs brought to nought, will turn backwards.

10. In quacumque die invocavero te : ecce cognovi quoniam Deus meus es.

In what day soever I shall call upon Thee : behold, I know Thou art my God.

I shall not fail to call upon Thee every day ; for I have known well that Thou art my God, coming to my succour, as Thou hast, every time that I have called on Thee.

11. In Deo laudabo verbum, in Domino laudabo sermonem : in Deo speravi, non timebo quid faciat mihi homo.

In God will I praise *His* word ; in the Lord will I praise *His* speech : in God have I hoped ; I will not fear what man can do unto me.

I shall always praise in my God and my Lord His faithfulness to His promises ; and therefore, trusting in Him, I will not fear that man can do me any harm.

12. In me sunt Deus vota tua : quæ reddam, laudationes tibi.

Thy vows are upon me, O God : which I will pay, *even* praises unto Thee.

Bellarmine, with S. Jerome, explains this verse as follows : " *In me,*" that is, in my memory are always " *Vota tua* " the promises which I have made to Thee ; hence I will never cease to offer Thee the praises and the thanksgivings which are contained in these promises.

13. Quoniam eripuisti animam meam de morte, et pedes meos de lapsu : ut placeam coram Deo in lumine viventium.

For Thou hast delivered my soul from death, *and* my feet from falling : that I may be pleasing before God, in the light of the living.

" *Ut placeam . . .*" In order that I may be well-pleasing to Thee, by means of the light of grace, whereby Thy servants live in fidelity to Thee.

PSALM LVI.

The Psalmist gives utterance to his confidence in the protection of God, Whose praises he proclaims.

Unto the end, destroy not, for David, for an inscription of a title, when he fled from Saul into the cave (1 *Kings* xxiv.).[1]

1. Miserere mei Deus, miserere mei : quoniam in te confidit anima mea.

Have mercy upon me, O God, have mercy upon me : for my soul trusteth in Thee.

[1] This appears to be the tune to which it was sung.

2. Et in umbra alarum tuarum sperabo : donec transeat iniquitas.	And in the shadow of Thy wings will I hope : until iniquity pass away.

Sheltered under the shadow of Thy wings, I will not cease to hope, until I see the unjust persecution I suffer come to an end.

3. Clamabo ad Deum altissimum : Deum qui benefecit mihi.	I will cry unto God Most High : unto God that hath wrought good things for me.

4. Misit de cœlo, et liberavit me : dedit in opprobrium conculcantes me.	He hath sent from heaven, and delivered me : He hath made them a reproach that trod me under foot.

5. Misit Deus misericordiam suam, et veritatem suam : et eripuit animam meam de medio catulorum leonum : dormivi conturbatus.	God hath sent His mercy and His truth : and He hath delivered my soul from the midst of the young lions : I slept troubled.

God has sent from heaven His mercy which He had promised, and He has saved my life by withdrawing me from the midst of my enemies, who, like young lions, sought to slay me ; [1] still, I am unable as yet to sleep in peace, without being troubled with fears.

6. Filii hominum dentes eorum arma et sagittæ : et lingua eorum gladius acutus.	The sons of men, their teeth are weapons and arrows : and their tongue a sharp sword.

I fear ever this race of wicked men, who have their teeth and their tongues as sharp swords and darts, to wound me by their detractions and calumnies. This, according to Bellarmine, is the sense of the Hebrew.

7. Exaltare super cœlos Deus : et in omnem terram gloria tua.	Be Thou exalted, O God, above the heavens : and Thy glory above all the earth.

Exalt, O my God, Thy power above the heavens, and Thy glory over the whole earth, by delivering me from my enemies.

8. Laqueum paraverunt pedibus meis : et incurvaverunt animam meam.	They prepared a snare for my feet : and they bowed down my soul.

"*Incurvaverunt . . .*" They make me to bend under the weight of evils with which they oppress me.

9. Foderunt ante faciem meam foveam : et inciderunt in eam.	They dug a pit before my face : and they are fallen into it.

"*Foveam.*" A pit for me to fall in.

[1] An allusion to the danger incurred by David when he was surrounded by the troops of Saul in the desert of Maon (1 *Kings* xxxiii. 26).

10. Paratum cor meum Deus, paratum cor meum : cantabo, et psalmum
dicam.

My heart is ready, O God, my
heart is ready : I will sing, and give
praise.

My God, my heart is prepared, it is ready to suffer whatever
Thou shalt appoint for me : hence, in all that shall happen to
me, I will ever praise and sing Thy glory.[1]

11. Exurge gloria mea, exurge
psalterium et cithara : exurgam diluculo.

Arise, O my glory ; arise psaltery
and harp : I *myself* will arise early.

Arise, my soul,[2] and glory in the Lord ; and thou, my harp
and my lyre, wake up to praise the Lord, Whom I will ever
praise, even from the break of day.

12. Confitebor tibi in populis
Domine : et psalmum dicam tibi in
gentibus.

I will give praise unto Thee, O
Lord, among the people : I will sing
a psalm unto Thee among the nations.

13. Quoniam magnificata est usque
ad cœlos misericordia tua : et usque
ad nubes veritas tua.

For Thy mercy is greatly to be
praised, even unto the heavens : and
Thy truth unto the clouds.

I will say that from the earth even unto the heavens all is
full of Thy mercy and of Thy faithfulness.

14. Exaltare super cœlos Deus : et
super omnem terram gloria tua.

Be Thou exalted, O God, above
the heavens : and Thy glory above all
the earth.

See verse 7.

PSALM LVII.

The Psalmist describes the perverse conduct of the wicked,
and the chastisement wherewith God is wont to punish them.

Unto the end, destroy not, for David, for an inscription.

1. Si vere utique justitiam loqui-
mini : recta judicate filii hominum.

If in very deed ye speak justice :
judge right things, ye sons of men.

If, O men, you speak in praise of justice, see that you judge
in accordance therewith.

2. Etenim in corde iniquitates
operamini : in terra injustitias manus
vestræ concinnant.

For in your heart ye work iniquity:
your hands forge injustice in the
earth.

---

[1] This and the following verse are reproduced in *Ps.* cvii., with some
slight differences of expression.

[2] Bellarmine, following Theodoret, says that David calls the spirit or
gift of prophecy his glory.

But you determine in your heart wicked deeds, which your hands are at once ready unjustly to put into execution on earth.

3. Alienati sunt peccatores a vulva, erraverunt ab utero: locuti sunt falsa.

The wicked are estranged from the womb; from their birth they have gone astray : they have spoken lies.

"*Alienati.*" Strangers to justice.——"*Locuti* . . ." Are occupied in speaking falsehoods, ahd in deceiving their neighbour.

4. Furor illis secundum similitudinem serpentis : sicut aspidis surdæ, et obturantis aures suas.

Their madness is according to the likeness of a serpent : even like the deaf adder that stoppeth her ears.

"*Furor illis.*" Their fury against the just.

5. Quæ non exaudiet vocem incantantium : et venefici incantantis sapienter.

Which will not hearken to the voice of the charmers : nor of the wizard that charmeth wisely.

"*Incantantium* . . ." Of the charmers who wisely seek to charm it for its good.

6. Deus conteret dentes eorum in ore ipsorum : molas leonum confringet Dominus.

God shall break in pieces their teeth in their mouth : the Lord shall break the great teeth of the lions.

But God will pulverise their teeth in their mouth before they bite others, and will break the jaw-bones of these fierce lions.

7. Ad nihilum devenient tamquam aqua decurrens : intendit arcum suum donec infirmentur.

They shall come to nothing, like water running down : He hath bent His bow until they be weakened.

They shall be as a torrent that passes and is suddenly dried up, meaning that their designs will quickly come to nought : for the Lord will bend His bow, and will not cease to shoot arrows at them until they are discomfited.

8. Sicut cera, quæ fluit, auferentur : supercecidit ignis, et non viderunt solem.

Like wax that melteth they shall be taken away : fire hath fallen upon them, and they have not seen the sun.

"*Supercecidit* . . ." The fire of divine vengeance shall fall upon them, and they shall no more see the day.

9. Priusquam intelligerent spinæ vestræ rhamnum : sicut viventes, sic in ira absorbet eos.

Before your thorns could know the briar : He swalloweth them up, as alive, in His wrath.[1]

[1] *Before your thorns*, &c. Before they grow up, so as to become strong briars, they shall be consumed by divine justice.

S. Jerome's translation is : *Antequam crescant spinæ vestræ in rhamnum :* which is explained thus : Before your thorns become sharp like those of the briar, that is, before you come to execute the evil you design to do, the divine wrath will absorb ; swallow you down, as though alive, in punishment.[1]

10. Lætabitur justus cum viderit vindictam : manus suas lavabit in sanguine peccatoris.	The just shall rejoice when he seeth the vengeance : he shall wash his hands in the blood of the sinner.[2]

" *Vindictam.*" The justice of divine vengeance.——"*Manus suas . . .*" That is, as S. Augustine explains it, whilst seeing the blood, or the death of the sinner, he will preserve himself pure and innocent.

11. Et dicet homo : Si utique est fructus justo : utique est Deus judicans eos in terra.	And man shall say : Seeing verily there is fruit to the just : verily there is a God that judgeth them on the earth.

And then, seeing the fruit, or the profit which the just shall derive from the punishment of the sinner, every one will recognise that there is in the world a God Who knows how to judge over the earth, and to punish the wicked as they deserve.

PSALM LVIII.

DAVID, seeing himself hemmed in by the soldiers of Saul (1 *Kings* xix. 11), implores the help of God, and predicts the destruction of his enemies. This Psalm applies well to Jesus Christ persecuted by the Jews.

Unto the end, destroy not, for David, for an inscription of a title, when Saul sent and watched his house to kill him (1 *Kings* xix.).

1. Eripe me de inimicis meis Deus meus : et ab insurgentibus in me libera me.	Deliver me from mine enemies, O my God : and defend me from them that rise up against me.

[1] In the verses which precede there is a chain of striking comparisons : vv. 4, 5, the wicked become obstinate in evil like the adder, which is supposed to resist every means employed to charm or soften it ; 6, they are violent like furious lions, but God renders them incapable of doing harm ; 7, they advance like a torrent which threatens to swallow up everything on its way, but the waters flow away and disappear ; 8, they melt away like wax before the fire ; 9, they resemble a thorny shrub which is rooted up and buried in the ground before its thorns have acquired the strength to wound.

[2] *Shall wash his hands,* &c. Shall applaud the justice of God, and take occasion from the consideration of the punishment of the wicked to wash and cleanse his hands from sin.

2. Eripe me de operantibus iniquitatem : et de viris sanguinum salva
me.

Deliver me from them that work
iniquity : and save me from the men
of blood.

"*De viris sanguinum.*" From these cruel men who thirst
for my blood.

3. Quia ecce ceperunt animam
meam : irruerunt in me fortes.

For behold, they have caught my
soul : the mighty have rushed in
upon me.

Lo, my life is in their hands, for they are too strong for me ;
and already they have sallied forth against me.

4. Neque iniquitas mea, neque
peccatum meum Domine : sine iniquitate cucurri et direxi.

Neither is it my iniquity, nor my
sin, O Lord : without iniquity have I
run, and directed *my steps.*

Lord, thou knowest already that there is in me no iniquity,
nor any fault with which they can reproach me ; since I have
always walked and directed my steps free from any sin.

5. Exurge in occursum meum, et
vide : et tu Domine Deus virtutum,
Deus Israel.

Rise up Thou to meet me, and
behold : even Thou, O Lord, the God
of hosts, the God of Israel.

Lord, Thou seest already the peril in which I am ; arise to
my help, O mighty God, O God of Israel.

6. Intende ad visitandas omnes
Gentes : non misererais omnibus, qui
operantur iniquitatem.

Come forth and visit all the
nations : have no mercy upon all
them that work iniquity.

Set Thyself to examine all the nations, and show not pity
to any such as will not cease to be unjust.

7. Convertentur ad vesperam, et
famem patientur ut canes : et circui-
bunt civitatem.

They shall return at evening, and
shall suffer hunger like dogs : and
shall go round about the city.

Some understand this verse as follows : They will arrive
late in the evening, but, like stray dogs, they will suffer great
hunger, that is, they will have a great desire to be just in
order to find peace ; they will go round about the city of God,
but they shall not find mercy.——Others explain it better
thus : They will go and return from morning till evening,
they will even surround the city, seeking like dogs to satisfy
their hunger, and to oppress the just, but they will be dis-
appointed. (See verse 16.)

8. Ecce loquentur in ore suo, et
gladius in labiis eorum : quoniam
quis audivit?

Behold, they shall speak with
their mouth, and a sword *is* in their
lips : for who, *say they,* hath heard
us !

So their mouth will speak of nought else than of laying snares and killing, saying at the same time: Who knows of it?

9. Et tu Domine deridebis eos: ad nihilum deduces omnes Gentes.

But Thou, O Lord, shalt laugh at them: Thou shalt bring all the nations to nothing.

But Thou, O Lord, wilt make them an object of ridicule, and wilt destroy all their wicked people.

10. Fortitudinem meam ad te custodiam, quia Deus susceptor meus es: Deus meus, misericordia ejus prævceniet me.

I will keep my strength unto Thee, for Thou art my protector : My God, His mercy shall prevent me.

"*Fortitudinem ... custodiam.*" By means of Thy help I shall preserve my strength.——"*Misericordia ...*" And I hope that Thy mercy will ever go before me.

11. Deus ostendet mihi super inimicos meos, ne occidas eos : nequando obliviscantur populi mei.

God shall let me look down upon mine enemies : slay them not, lest at any time my people forget.

God will make me know the vengeance He will take on my enemies : I pray Thee, O Lord, to punish them, but do not destroy them, so that my subjects, having always their chastisement before their eyes, may not forget Thy justice.

12. Disperge illos in virtute tua : et depone eos protector meus Domine:

Scatter them by Thy power : and bring them down, O Lord my protector :

"*Depone eos.*" That is : Reduce them to such a state that they may not be able any more to raise their heads to injure me.

13. Delictum oris eorum, sermonem labiorum ipsorum : et comprehendantur in superbia sua.

For the sin of their mouth, and the word of their lips : and let them be taken in their pride.

Let this be the punishment of their slanderous mouth and of their wicked discourse : May they be taken and so confounded in their very pride.

14. Et de execratione et mendacio annuntiabuntur in consummatione : in ira consummationis, et non erunt.

And for their cursing and lying they shall be declared at an end by *Thy* consuming wrath : and they shall be no more.

Miserable men ! In the day of God's wrath they will appear consumed by their evil speaking and their lies, through which they will be lost.

15. Et scient quia Deus dominabitur Jacob : et finium terræ.

And they shall know that God will rule Jacob : and all the ends of the earth.

Then they shall know that there is a God, when He shall exercise the dominion that He has over the people of Jacob, and over all the ends of the earth.

16. Convertentur ad vesperam, et famem patientur ut canes: et circui-bunt civitatem.

They shall return at evening, and shall suffer hunger like dogs: and shall go round about the city.

Meanwhile, they continue from morning to evening laying snares for the just, to devour them like hungry dogs, and they surround the city in order that the prey may not be able to escape them. (See verse 7.)

17. Ipsi dispergentur ad mandu-candum: si vero non fuerint saturati, et murmurabunt.

They shall be scattered abroad to eat: and shall murmur if they be not filled.

They scatter themselves in different parts in order to devour the just; and if they do not succeed in satiating themselves with their blood, they do not cease from at least taking away their good name.

18. Ego autem cantabo fortitu-dinem tuam: et exultabo mane mise-ricordiam tuam.

But I will sing of Thy strength: and will extol Thy mercy in the morning.

"*Mane.*" From morning till evening.

19. Quia factus es susceptor meus: et refugium meum in die tribulationis meæ.

For Thou art become my support: and my refuge in the day of my trouble.

20. Adjutor meus tibi psallam, quia Deus susceptor meus es: Deus meus misericordia mea.

Unto Thee, O my helper, will I sing: for Thou, O God, art my de-fence; my God, my mercy.

Thou, my God, art my helper and defender in all my wants, and therefore will I ever sing Thy praises, calling Thee my God and my Mercy.[1]

PSALM LIX.

DAVID, after many victories over his enemies, implores the help of God against the Edomites. (2 *Kings* viii.-x. ; 1 *Par.* xviii.) This Psalm may be well applied to the Church in her persecutions and victories.

[1] Bellarmine remarks, with S. Augustine, that "*Misericordia mea*" means much more than "*Salus mea, Vita mea, Spes mea,*" and similar appellations; for it is to the Mercy of God that we owe existence, life, deliverance from evil, and progress in good; it is by the Mercy of God that we are predestined, called, justified, and shall at last be glorified.

Unto the end, for them that shall be changed, for the inscription of a
title, to David himself, for doctrine, when he set fire to Mesopotamia of
Syria and Sobal, and Joab returned, and slew of Edom, in the vale of the
salt-pits, twelve thousand men.

1. Deus repulisti nos, et destruxisti   O God, Thou hast cast us off, and
nos : iratus es, et misertus es nobis.   hast destroyed us : Thou hast been
                                             angry, and hast had mercy upon us.

O great God ! it seems that Thou hast deprived us of Thy
protection, since Thou hast let us see ourselves defeated ; but,
though Thou didst at first show Thyself angry with us, Thou
hast in the end had compassion on us.

2. Commovisti terram, et contur-   Thou hast moved the earth, and
basti eam : sana contritiones ejus,   hast troubled it : heal Thou the
quia commota est.   breaches thereof, for it has been
                                      moved.

Thou hast shaken the earth, and turned it upside down : it
now remains for Thy mercy to repair the ruins made by this
great shock.

3. Ostendisti populo tuo dura :   Thou hast shown Thy people hard
potasti nos vino compunctionis.   things : Thou hast made us drink the
                                      wine of sorrow.

Thou hast given proof of chastising us severely ; Thou hast
made us to taste of the bitter wine of compunction (or, according to the Hebrew, of fear), and *that* in order to see us holily
contrite.

4. Dedisti metuentibus te signifi-   Thou hast given a warning to them
cationem : ut fugiant a facie arcus : that fear Thee : that they may flee
                                      from before the bow :

Thou hast given a sign of warning to those who fear Thee,
that they may preserve themselves from the arrows of Thy
wrath at the sight of the already bended bow.

5. Ut liberentur dilecti tui : sal-   That Thy beloved may be deli-
vum fac dextera tua, et exaudi me.   vered : save me with Thy right hand,
                                      and hear me.

Thus hast Thou done in order to save those who love Thee ;
favourably hear me, then, and let Thy hand save me.[1]

6. Deus locutus est in sancto suo :   God hath spoken in His holy *place*:
Lætabor, et partibor Sichinam : et   I will rejoice, and I will divide
convallem tabernaculorum metibor.   Sichem ; and will mete out the vale
                                      of tabernacles.

God has declared from His Sanctuary that one day I shall
have the joy of dividing at my will the country of Sichem or

[1] This verse and the following form the second part of *Ps.* cvii., with
some difference of expression.

Samaria, and of measuring the plains of the valley of Tents, beyond the Jordan, to distribute them at my pleasure.

7. Meus est Galaad, et meus est Manasses : et Ephraim fortitudo capitis mei.	Galaad is mine, and Manasses is mine: and Ephraim *is* the strength of my head.

Already do I see mine, that is, beneath my sway, Galaad, Manasse, and Ephraim, which are the strength of my head. ——Under these names are meant the provinces occupied by the tribes of Israel, which David called the strength of his head, that is, of his crown.

8. Juda rex meus : Moab olla spei meæ.	Juda is my king : Moab is the pot of my hope.

"*Juda rex meus.*" It is in the tribe of Juda that my throne is established, because God has willed that the kings should be chosen from this tribe.——"*Moab olla spei meæ.*" David calls Moab " the pot of his hope," because the province of Moab was abundant, as a platter filled with meat, and therefore his hope. He means to say : I hope to satiate my people with the spoils of the Moabites.

9. In Idumeam extendam calceamentum meum : mihi alienigenæ subditi sunt.	Into Edom will I stretch forth my shoe : to me the strangers are made subject.

I shall stretch out my foot over Edom, and I shall see a people of foreigners become my subjects.[1]

10. Quis deducet me in civitatem munitam ? quis deducet me usque in Idumæam?	Who will bring me into the strong city? who will lead me into Edom?

Who will lead me into Edom, and make me master of that kingdom whose capital city is very strong ?

11. Nonne tu Deus, qui repulisti nos : et non egredieris Deus in virtutibus nostris?	Wilt not Thou, O God, who hast cast us off : and wilt not Thou, O God, go out with our armies

Will it not be Thou, my God, Who seemed at first to abandon us ? And wilt Thou not Thyself go forth at the head of our troops to make us victorious ?

---

[1] " *Alienigenæ.*" It is thus the Septuagint calls the Philistines because they had no affinity with the Israelites, whereas the Edomites were descended from Esau, or Edom, the brother of Jacob, and the Ammonites and Moabites from Lot, the nephew of Abraham. (See *Ps.* lxxvi. 4.) According to Menochius the meaning of the verse is : I will go to take possession of Edom, for already the Philistines obey me.

12. Da nobis auxilium de tribulatione : quia vana salus hominis.

Give us help from trouble : for
vain is the help of man.

Give us, Lord, Thy help to deliver us from tribulation :
because in vain can we hope for our salvation in human
succours, if Thou dost not aid us.

13. In Deo faciemus virtutem : et
ipse ad nihilum deducet tribulantes
nos.

Through God we shall do mightily:
and He shall bring to nought them
that afflict us.

In placing our hope in God we shall obtain the victory,
since He will destroy all the enemies that trouble us.

PSALM LX.

A PRAYER full of confidence to obtain help from God ; according to S. Hilary and S. Jerome, it is well suited for all who
are in affliction.

Unto the end, in hymns, for David.

1. Exaudi Deus deprecationem
meam : intende orationi meæ.

Hear, O God, my supplication : be
attentive unto my prayer.

2. Affinibus terræ ad te clamavi :
dum anxiaretur cor meum, in petra
exaltasti me.

Unto Thee have I cried from the
ends of the earth: when my heart
was in anguish, Thou hast exalted
me on a rock.

From the lowest depths of the earth, O Lord, I have cried
to Thee, and when my heart was anguished by fear, Thou
didst lift me upon a rock, that is, Thou hast placed me as
though upon a high rock, where I see myself safe from my
enemies.[1]

3. Deduxisti me, quia factus es
spes mea : turris fortitudinis a facie
inimici.

Thou has conducted me ; for Thou
hast been my hope : a tower of
strength against the face of the
enemy.

Thou hast led me by a sure way, because Thou hast made
Thyself my hope ; and Thou hast become for me as a strong
tower in the face of my enemies.

4. Inhabitabo in tabernaculo tuo
in sæcula : protegar in velamento
alarum tuarum.

In Thy tabernacle I shall dwell
for ever : I shall be protected under
the covert of Thy wings.

In this place that Thou hast given me I shall always dwell
securely, since there I shall be protected under the shadow
of Thy wings.

---

[1] *Ps.* xxvi. 10.

5. Quoniam tu Deus meus exaudisti orationem meam : dedisti hereditatem timentibus nomen tuum.

For thou, my God, hast heard my prayer : Thou hast given an inheritance unto them that fear Thy name.

" *Dedisti hæreditatem.*" Thou hast never refused the inheritance.

6. Dies super dies regis adjicies : annos ejus usque in diem generationis et generationis.

Thou wilt add days to the days of the king : his years even to generation and generation.

" *Annos ejus . . .* " Thou wilt even make his reign to endure from generation to generation.

7. Permanet in æternum in conspectu Dei : misericordiam et veritatem ejus quis requiret ?

He abideth for ever in the sight of God : His mercy and truth who shall search out ?

He will never cease to keep himself in the presence of his God ; and who shall be ever able to see His goodness and His faithfulness fail ?

8. Sic psalmum dicam nomini tuo in sæculum sæculi : ut reddam vota mea de die in diem.

So will I sing a psalm unto Thy name for ever and ever : that I may pay my vows from day to day.

" *Ut reddam . . .* " In order to render Thee all the days of my life the thanks that I owe Thee.

PSALM LXI.

DAVID encourages himself and his followers to have confidence in God in the midst of persecution, and to have patience in adversity.

Unto the end, for Idithun, a Psalm of David.[1]

1. Nonne Deo subjecta erit anima mea ? ab ipso enim salutare tuum.

Shall not my soul be subject to God ? for from Him is my salvation.

2. Nam et ipse Deus meus, et salutaris meus : susceptor meus, non movebor amplius.

For He is my God and my Saviour: *He is* my protector ; I shall be moved no more.

" *Non movebor amplius.*" Who will be able to move and cast me down ?

3. Quousque irruitis in hominem : interficitis universi vos : tamquam parieti inclinato et maceriæ depulsæ.

How long do ye rush in upon a man ? ye all destroy, as a leaning wall, and a tottering fence.

[1] Idithun was one of the three masters of music in the Temple (1 *Par.* vi. 44).

15

"*In hominem.*" Upon the man : Meaning himself.——
You are all killing me, at least by the desire you have to take
my life, and consider me as a leaning wall that is ready to fall.

4. Verumtamen pretium meum cogitaverunt repellere, cucurri in siti : ore suo benedicebant, et corde suo maledicebant.

But they have thought to cast away my price : I ran in thirst : they blessed with their mouth, but cursed with their heart.

"*Pretium meum.*" They have devised to take away my
honour, which is so precious to me. Thus S. Ambrose and S.
Augustine understand *Pretium.*——"*Cucurri in siti.*" For
this honour I so much toiled and sweated.——Bossuet explains
it thus : I fled like a thirsty stag pursued by the hunters.——
"*Benedicebant.*" They praised me.

5. Verumtamen Deo subjecta esto anima mea : quoniam ab ipso patientia mea.

But be thou, O my soul, subject to God : for from Him is my patience.

"*Ab ipso . . .*" Thou wilt receive from Him patience to
suffer all.

6. Quia ipse Deus meus, et salvator meus: adjutor meus non emigrabo.

For He is my God and my Saviour : *He is* my helper, I shall not be moved.

"*Non emigrabo.*" Therefore, I will not quit my kingdom ;
or the same as "*Non movebor*" (verse 2), I shall not be driven
out ; or I shall not fall from the state I am in.

7. In Deo salutare meum, et gloria mea : Deus auxilii mei, et spes mea in Deo est.

In God is my salvation and my glory : *He is* the God of my help, and my hope is in God.

8. Sperate in eo omnis congregatio populi, effundite coram illo corda vestra : Deus adjutor noster in æternum.

Trust in Him, all ye congregation of people : pour out your hearts before Him : God is our helper for ever.

"*Omnis congregatio populi.*" All you who are gathered
together to follow me.

9. Verumtamen vani filii hominum, mendaces filii hominum in stateris : ut decipiant ipsi de vanitate in idipsum.

But vain are the sons of men, the sons of men are liars in the balances : that by vanity they may together deceive.[1]

"*Mendaces . . . stateris.*" Liars in their judgment of things.
——"*In idipsum.*" This is, according to S. Jerome's translation : *Simul.* That with vanity they may mutually deceive
one another.

----

[1] *Are liars in the balances,* &c. They will be found to be of no weight,
and to be mere lies, deceit, and vanity.

10. Nolite sperare in iniquitate, et rapinas nolite concupiscere : divitiæ si affluant, nolite cor apponere.

Trust not in iniquity, and covet not robberies : if riches increase, set not your heart upon them.

" *Rapinas nolite concupiscere.*" Desire not to enrich your-·selves by rapine.——"*Divitiæ si affluant.*" And even should riches come to you abundantly in the way of justice and honesty.

11. Semel locutus est Deus, duo hæc audivi, quia potestas Dei est, et tibi Domine misericordia : quia tu reddes unicuique juxta opera sua.

God hath spoken once, these two things have I heard, that power belongeth to God, and mercy to Thee, O Lord : for Thou wilt render to every man according to his works.

God hath taught us, as I have heard, two things : that He has power to punish the wicked, and has mercy to console the just ; thus Thou, O Lord, renderest to each one as he deserves according to his works.

PSALM LXIII.

DAVID seeks help from God against the calumnies of his persecutors, and he hopes that their designs will serve for their ruin, and for the good of the just. In the mystical sense, this Psalm applies to the Passion of Jesus Christ.

Unto the end, a Psalm for David.

1. Exaudi Deus orationem meam cum deprecor : a timore inimici eripe animam meam.

Hear my prayer, O God, when I make supplication to Thee : deliver my soul from the fear of the enemy.

2. Protexisti me a conventu malignantium : a multitudine operantium iniquitatem.

Thou hast protected me from the assembly of the malignant : from the multitude of the workers of iniquity.

3. Quia exacuerunt ut gladium linguas suas : intenderunt arcum rem amaram, ut sagittent in occultis immaculatum.

For they have whetted their tongues like a sword : they have bent their bow a bitter thing, to shoot in secret the undefiled.

"*Rem amaram.*" Referring to the cruel plotting.

4. Subito sagittabunt eum, et non timebunt: firmaverunt sibi sermonem nequam.

They will shoot at him on a sudden, and will not fear : they are resolute in words of wickedness.

"*Firmaverunt ...*" They are fixed in their wicked design to destroy him.

5. Narraverunt ut absconderent laqueos : dixerunt : Quis videbit eos ?

They have talked of hiding snares : they have said : Who shall see them ?

They have agreed together to hide their snares, saying: Who will be able to know of them?

6. Scrutati sunt iniquitates: defecerunt scrutantes scrutinio.

They have searched after iniquities: they have failed in their search.

"*Iniquitates.*" According to Bossuet: *Vias nocendi:* Their ways of injuring.——They have gone on studying the means to do injury; but in this research they have found themselves foiled, and their labour lost.——These words are applied to the false witnesses brought forward against Jesus Christ.

7. Accedet homo ad cor altum: et exaltabitur Deus.

Man shall come to a deep heart:[1] and God shalt be exalted.

Bossuet well explains this verse: When the wicked man cannot find fault with the just on the score of his actions, he tries to give a wrong interpretation to the secret thoughts of his heart (signified by "*cor altum*"); but God, Who defends the innocent, will be exalted by punishing the wicked.

8. Sagittæ parvulorum factæ sunt plagæ eorum: et infirmatæ sunt contra eos linguæ eorum.

The arrows of children are their wounds: and their tongues are made weak against them.

Just as the arrows discharged by children inflict only slight wounds, so the plots and calumnies of the wicked will have no effect; and, therefore, the arrows discharged by their tongues have become powerless to injure the objects of their calumny, and have fallen back upon themselves. This is according to the rendering of S. Jerome: *Et corruent in semetipsos plagis suis.*

9. Conturbati sunt omnes qui videbant eos: et timuit omnis homo.

All that saw them were troubled: and every man was afraid.

Those who have seen their chastisement were seized with surprise; and every one will henceforth fear to follow them.

10. Et annuntiaverunt opera Dei: et facta ejus intellexerunt.

And they declared the works of God: and understood His doings.

In this all have recognised the hand of God, and have published it abroad.

11. Lætabitur justus in Domino, et sperabit in eo: et laudabuntur omnes recti corde.

The just shall rejoice in the Lord, and shall hope in Him: and all the upright in heart shall be praised.

---

[1] *A deep heart.* The deep thoughts and contrivances of the wicked, which God defeats and overrules by His wisdom and power.

PSALM LXV.

A THANKSGIVING of the people to God for having delivered them from their enemies. It applies also to the Gentiles set free from the power of Satan.

Unto the end, a Canticle of a Psalm of the Resurrection.

1. Jubilate Deo omnes terra, psalmum dicite'nomini ejus : date gloriam laudi ejus.

O sing joyfully unto God, all the earth, sing ye a psalm unto His name: give glory unto His praise.

2. Dicite Deo quam terribilia sunt opera tua Domine ! in multitudine virtutis tuæ mentientur tibi inimici tui.

Say unto God, How terrible are Thy works, O Lord ! in the greatness of Thy strength Thine enemies shall lie unto Thee.[1]

" *Mentientur* . . . " Thy very enemies, at the sight of Thy power, will come to submit themselves to Thy rule, but feignedly.

3. Omnis terra adoret te, et psallat tibi : psalmum dicat nomini tuo.

Let all the earth adore Thee, and sing unto Thee : let it sing a psalm unto Thy name.

4. Venite, et videte opera Dei : terribilis in consiliis super filios hominum.

Come and see the works of God : *Who* is terrible in His counsels over the sons of men.

5. Qui convertit mare, in aridam, in flumine pertransibunt pede : ibi lætabimur in ipso.

Who turneth the sea into dry land, in the river they shall pass on foot : there shall we rejoice in Him.

Allusion is made to the passage of the Red Sea and the Jordan in the exodus from Egypt.

6. Qui dominatur in virtute sua in æternum, oculi ejus super gentes respiciunt : qui exasperant non exaltentur in semetipsis.

Who by His power ruleth for ever, His eyes behold the nations : let not them that provoke *Him* be exalted in themselves.

He rules even over the whole world by His power : His eyes watch over all the nations, that the wicked who dare to offend Him may not wax proud in themselves.

7. Benedicite Gentes Deum nostrum : et auditam facite vocem laudis ejus.

O bless our God, ye Gentiles : and make the voice of His praise to be heard.

8. Qui posuit animam meam ad vitam : et non dedit in commotionem pedes meos.

Who hath kept my soul in life : and hath not suffered my feet to be moved.

[1] *Lie unto Thee.* Render forced homage—false professions of submission.

"*Ad vitam,*" *i.e.,* *Ad vivendum.* The sense of this verse is : He hath preserved my life, and hath not suffered my feet to stumble, or that I should fall over any precipice.

9. Quoniam probasti nos Deus : igne nos examinasti, sicut examinatur argentum.

For Thou, O God, hast proved us : Thou hast tried us by fire, as silver is tried.

Thou hast tried us with tribulations, as silver is tried in the fire.

10. Induxisti nos in laqueum, posuisti tribulationes in dorso nostro: imposuisti homines super capita nostra.

Thou hast brought us into a net, Thou hast laid afflictions on our back : Thou hast set men over our heads.

Thou hast suffered us to be taken in the snare by our enemies. Thon hast loaded our shoulders with afflictions ; and Thou hast placed cruel men over us.

11. Transivimus per ignem et aquam : et eduxisti nos in refrigerium.

We have passed through fire and water : and Thou hast brought us out into refreshing places.

12. Introibo in domum tuam in holocaustis : reddam tibi vota mea, quæ distinxerunt labia mea.

I will go into Thy house with burnt-offerings : I will pay Thee my vows, which my lips have uttered.

13. Et locutum est os meum : in tribulatione mea.

And my mouth hath spoken : when I was in trouble.

12, 13. I will go into Thy temple to offer to Thee the sacrifices, and to render Thee the thanksgivings which I owe Thee, according to the vows that I made to Thee, which my lips uttered, and which my mouth spoke when I was in tribulation.

14. Holocausta medullata offeram tibi cum incenso arietum : offeram tibi boves cum hircis.

I will offer unto Thee burnt-offerings full of marrow, with the incense of rams : I will offer unto Thee bullocks with goats.

My words in tribulation were : O Lord, I will offer to Thee victims, fat and full of marrow, that is, not only sacrifices of external works, but also of inward affections of the heart.—— "*Cum incenso arietum . . .*" Rams too fragrant with incense ; I will offer to thee also a sacrifice of bulls and of he-goats.

15. Venite, audite, et narrabo, omnes qui timetis Deum : quanta fecit animæ meæ.

Come and hear, all ye that fear God : and I will tell you what great things He hath done for my soul.

16. Ad ipsum ore meo clamavi : et exaltavi sub lingua mea.

I cried unto Him with my mouth : and I extolled Him with my tongue.

17. Iniquitatem si aspexi in corde meo : non exaudiet Dominus.   If I have looked at iniquity in my heart : the Lord will not hear me.

If I had regarded with attachment any iniquity in my heart, the Lord would not have heard me.

18. Propterea exaudivit Deus : et attendit voci deprecationis meæ.   Therefore hath God heard me : and hath attended to the voice of my supplication.

"*Propterea.*" But because I was far from doing this.

19. Benedictus Deus : qui non amovit orationem meam, et misericordiam suam a me.   Blessed be God, Who hath not turned away my prayer : nor His mercy from me.

May God be for ever blessed, since He has not suffered me to forget to pray to Him, because through my praying to Him He has not removed His mercy from me.——This led S. Augustine to write that golden sentence of his : " When thou seest that thy prayer is not removed from thee, be sure that neither is His mercy removed from thee ".

PSALM LXVII.

THIS Psalm represents in figure Jesus Christ, Who, having overcome death, ascended gloriously into heaven. It also foreshadows the holiness of the Church, and the help promised to it by God, who established it in strength, and made it glorious by so many victories. The Psalmist makes mention of divers prodigies of the Old Testament history, which prefigured those that occurred afterwards under the New Law. The Psalm is very obscure.[1]

Unto the end, a Psalm of a Canticle for David himself.

1. Exurgat Deus, et dissipentur inimici ejus : et fugiant qui oderunt eum, a facie ejus.   Let God arise, and let His enemies be scattered : and let them that hate Him flee from before His face.

2. Sicut deficit fumus, deficiant : sicut fluit cera a facie ignis, sic pereant peccatores a facie Dei.   As smoke vanisheth, so let them vanish away : as wax melteth before the fire, so let the wicked perish at the presence of God.

---

[1] This Psalm is thought to have been composed for the translation of the Ark of the Covenant to Jerusalem (2 *Kings* vi.). The first verse is a reproduction of the prayer of Moses in the desert, when the Ark was raised to begin the journey : " Arise, O Lord, and let Thy enemies be scattered, and let them that hate Thee flee from before Thy face" (*Numb.* x. 35).

3. Et justi epulentur, et exultent in conspectu Dei : et delectentur in lætitia.

And let the just feast, and rejoice before God : and be delighted with gladness.

"*Et justi.*" But let the just, on the other hand.—— "*Delectentur in lætitia.*" Let them be filled with delight in the joy of their victory.

4. Cantate Deo, psalmum dicite nomini ejus : iter facite ei, qui ascendit super occasum : Dominus nomen illi.

Sing ye to God, sing a psalm to His name : make a way for Him Who ascendeth upon the west :[1] the Lord is His name.

Sing, O faithful, to the honour of God, and praise His Name with hymns and canticles.——"*Iter facite ei ...*" Make a way for Him Who ascends over the West, the setting of the sun, that is, over the darkness of the grave ; for His Name is the Lord ; hence all things are under His dominion.

5. Exultate in conspectu ejus : turbabuntur a facie ejus, patris orphanorum, et judicis viduarum.

Rejoice ye before Him : but the wicked shall be troubled at His presence, Who is the father of orphans, and the judge of widows.

Rejoice with delight in His presence : when He shall judge the world, sinners shall tremble with fear ; but you shall stand rejoicing, since He is the Father of orphans, and the Judge who defends widows. This signifies that at the Last Judgment He will console all those who have been afflicted here on earth.

6. Deus in loco sancto suo : Deus, qui inhabitare facit unius moris in domo :

Even God in His holy place : God Who maketh men of one manner[2] to dwell in a house :

God sits in His sanctuary in heaven ; and there in His house He makes His servants to dwell : "*Unius moris,*" of one manner ; that is, at one in unity of virtue and sentiments.

7. Qui educit vinctos in fortitudine : similiter eos, qui exasperant, qui habitant in sepulchris.

Who bringeth out with strength : them that were bound ;[3] He causeth likewise them that rebel to dwell in sepulchres.

[1] *Who ascendeth upon the West.* S. Gregory understands these words of Jesus Christ, Who after His going down, like the sun, in the West, by His Passion and Death, ascended more glorious, and carried all before Him. S. Jerome renders it, *Who ascendeth through the deserts.*

[2] *Of one manner.* That is, agreeing in faith and love, and following the same discipline. It is verified in the servants of God living together in His *House,* which is the Church (1 *Tim.* iii. 15).

[3] *Them that were bound.* The power and mercy of God appears, in bringing out of their captivity those that were *bound* in sins.

He Who by His power sets free those who are held captive by their passions; and likewise those who have embittered Him by their faults, and have dwelt in the sepulchre, the abode of death, that is, in His displeasure.

8. Deus cum egredereris in conspectu populi tui: cum pertransires in deserto:	O God, when Thou didst go forth in the sight of Thy people : when Thou didst pass through the desert :
9. Terra mota est, etenim cœli distillaverunt a facie Dei Sinai: a facie Dei Israel.	The earth was moved, and the heavens dropped at the presence of the God of Sinai : at the presence of the God of Israel.

8, 9. O great God, as Thou didst go forth in the sight of Thy people set free from Egypt, and didst go before them in the desert, in a cloud of light; then all the earth was moved, because the heavens showered down manna in the presence of the God of Sinai and of Israel.

10. Pluviam voluntariam segregabis Deus hereditati tuæ: et infirmata est, tu vero perfecisti eam.	Thou shalt set aside for Thine inheritance a free rain, O God : and it was weakened, but Thou hast made it perfect.

Thus likewise dost Thou, O Lord, of Thine own free will, store up a plentiful shower, a great outpouring of grace for Thy inheritance, that is, for Thy new Church ; so that, however infirm she may be, Thou knowest how to heal her and make her perfect.

11. Animalia tua habitabunt in ea: parasti in dulcedine tua pauperi, Deus.	In it shall Thy animals dwell : in Thy sweetness, O God, Thou hast provided for the poor.

There Thy flock shall abide, for which, because of itself it is utterly poor, Thou, O supreme God, hast prepared, in Thy goodness, abundant pastures.

12. Dominus dabit verbum evangelizantibus : virtute multa.	The Lord shall give the word to them that preach good tidings : with great power.

The Lord will inspire words to those who will announce the New Law (the preachers of the Gospel), giving them a great power to convert entire nations.

13. Rex virtutum dilecti dilecti: et speciei domus dividere spolia.	The king of powers *is* of the beloved, of the beloved : and the beauty of the house shall divide the spoils.[1]

1 *The king of powers.* That is, the mighty King, is on the side of Christ, *His most beloved* Son ; and His *beautiful House*, viz., the Church in which God dwells for ever, shall by her spiritual conquests *divide the spoils* of many nations.

"*Rex virtutum dilecti dilecti.*" According to the Hebrew :
Reges exercituum confœderabuntur. The most powerful kings
of the earth will become subjects of the Well, or Most Beloved
(for such is the meaning of the Hebrew phrase : *Dilecti dilecti*),
that is, of the Redeemer, Who will be greatly beloved by them.
·——"*Et speciei…*" And He in order to render His House, that
is, His Church, beautiful, will give her the power to divide the
spoils of those kings converted by means of the Evangelists or
Apostles, who divided amongst themselves all the kingdoms
of the world, to lead them to embrace the Faith.

14. Si dormiatis inter medios cleros, pennæ columbæ deargentatæ : et posteriora dorsi ejus in pallore auri.

If you sleep in the midst of lots : yet shall you be as the wings of a dove covered with silver, and the hinder parts of her back with the paleness of gold.

Bellarmine justly remarks that this verse is very obscure ;
accordingly, it is necessary to explain it in detail.——"*Si
dormiatis.*" If you who preach the word of God sleep, that is,
if you repose.——"*Inter medios cleros.*" The word *Clerus* in
Greek signifies Lot, or Inheritance, meaning : In the midst of
the Church. This explanation is given by Bellarmine. But
S. Jerome, S. Augustine, Theodoret, and others, understand
by the word *Cleros*, the Old and the New Testaments, and explain the first part of the verse thus : If you repose in the
midst of the two Testaments.——"*Pennæ columbæ deargentatæ.*"
The Church, or the union of the faithful, will be like a dove
with its wings silvered with the purity of wisdom.——"*Et
posteriora dorsi ejus in pallore auri.*" And with its back gilded
by the fervour of charity, which makes it all beautiful.

15. Dum discernit cœlestis reges super eam, nive dealbabuntur in Selmon : mons Dei, mons pinguis.

When He that is in heaven judgeth kings in her, they shall be white as snow on Selmon : the mountain of God is a rich mountain.

16. Mons coagulatus, mons pin-guis : ut quid suspicamini montes coagulatos ?

A high mountain, a rich mountain : why do you suspect high mountains?

15, 16. "*Dum reges.*" While the heavenly King, that is, Christ,
will divide and send forth His preachers, raised to the dignity
of kings by the spiritual power given them over souls.——
"*Super eam.*" Over the Church scattered throughout the
kingdoms of the earth.——"*Nive dealbabuntur in Selmon.*"
Then the nations, set free from the blackness of their sins, will
become whiter than the snow of Mount Selmon.——"*Mons Dei*

... *coagulatus.*" The mountain of God, the Church, is a fat, or rich, mountain, a coagulated, that is, a very rich mountain ; for the milk of divine grace, with which it abounds, does not run off, but remains there coagulated and firm.——" *Ut quid* ... *coagulatos ?*" O men ; why do ye think that there are other coagulated mountains, that is, any other Church as fat and rich as this one ?

17. Mons, in quo beneplacitum est Deo habitare in eo : etenim Dominus habitabit in finem.

A mountain in which God is well pleased to dwell : for there the Lord shall dwell for ever.

18. Currus Dei decem millibus multiplex, millia lætantium : Dominus in eis in Sina in sancto.

The chariot of God is attended by ten thousands : thousands of them that rejoice : the Lord is among them in Sinai, in the holy place.

The chariot of the Lord is borne by many thousands of Angels, in great jubilee ; it was thus the Lord was borne upon these celestial spirits, when He descended upon the holy mountain of Sinai.

19. Ascendisti in altum, cepisti captivitatem : accepisti dona in hominibus :

Thou hast ascended on high: Thou hast led captivity captive : Thou hast received gifts for men :

S. Paul refers to this passage (*Ephes.* iv. 8) when he says : "*Ascending on high, He led captivity captive ; He gave gifts to men*". And then (verse 9) he adds : "*Now, that He ascended, what is it, but because He also descended first into the lower parts of the earth ?*" The verse is therefore thus explained : Thou, O Saviour of the world, coming forth from the sepulchre, didst ascend to the highest heavens, and didst take with Thee those who were captives here below ; and in heaven, Thou didst receive the gifts from Thy Father, to dispense them to men. This accords with S. Paul's explanation : "*He gave gifts to men*".

20. Etenim non credentes : inhabitare Dominum Deum.

Yea *for* those also that do not believe : that the Lord God might dwell in their midst.

For Thou hast bestowed Thy gifts on those who before did not believe that the Lord dwells in His holy mountain, that is, in His Church.

21. Benedictus Dominus die quotidie : prosperum iter faciet nobis Deus salutarium nostrorum.

Blessed be the Lord day by day : the God of our salvation will make our journey prosperous.

22. Deus noster, Deus salvos faciendi: et Domini Domini exitus mortis.

Our God is the God of salvation: and of the Lord our Lord are the issues of death.

He is our God, Whose property it is to save us; and it is His own gift to set us free from death.——"*Exitus mortis.*" According to Bellarmine and Menochius : *Evasio mortis:* Escape from death. *Ereptio et liberatio mortis:* Rescue and deliverance from death.

23. Verumtamen Deus confringet capita inimicorum suorum: verticem capilli perambulantium in delictis suis.

But God shall crush the heads of His enemies : the hairy scalp of them that walk on in their sins.

"*Verticem capilli.*" Denoting the top of the hair of the head ; which means, that He will bring down the summit of their proud locks, or the crest, of those who walk with pride in their sins, and do not walk in the law of God.

24. Dixit Dominus: Ex Basan convertam: convertam in profundum maris:

The Lord said : I will turn them from Basan : I will turn them into the depth of the sea :

"*Ex Basan convertam.*" Mattei translates the Hebrew thus : *Ex Basan reducam.* That is : My people, I will deliver thee from the Basanites, or the people of Basan ; and I will cast that people into the depths of the sea, as I did with Pharao.

25. Ut intingatur pes tuus in sanguine : lingua canum tuorum ex inimicis, ab ipso.

That thy foot may be dipped in the blood of thine enemies : and the tongue of thy dogs be red with the same.

26. Viderunt ingressus tuos Deus : ingressus Dei mei : Regis mei qui est in sancto.

They have seen Thy goings : O God, the goings of my God : of my King Who is in *His* sanctuary.

Then, O God, did they see Thy glorious march ; and Thy triumphs, my God and my King, Who art now in the holy place, that is, according to Bellarmine and Menochius, in Heaven, or in the Church.

27. Prævenerunt principes conjuncti psallentibus : in medio juvencularum tympanistriarum.

Princes went before joined with singers : in the midst of young damsels playing on timbrels.

"*Principes.*" The heads of the people.

28. In ecclesiis benedicite Deo Domino : de fontibus Israel.

In the churches bless ye God the Lord : from the fountains of Israel.

"*De fontibus Israel.*" According to the Chaldee version : *De semine Israel:* From the race of Israel. This reading is adopted by S. Hilary, Theodoret, Euthymius, Vatable, and Tirinus, who cites these authors. The sense of the verse is : Give praise in your Churches to the Lord God, even to Christ the Lord, Who hath sprung from Israel.

29. Ibi Benjamin adolescentulus : in mentis excessu.	There *is* Benjamin[1] a youth : in ecstasy of mind.

30. Principes Juda, duces eorum : principes Zabulon, principes Nephthali.	The princes of Juda *are* their leaders : the princes of Zabulon, the princes of Nephtali.

29, 30. "*Ibi.*" There in that triumph, described in verses 26-28.——"*Benjamin adolescentulus.*" The tribe of Benjamin, who was the youngest, the last of the children of Jacob.—— "*In mentis excessu.*" In a transport of joy, as though in ecstasy and beside himself.——S. Hilary, S. Jerome, Theodoret, Bellarmine, and others apply this passage to the Apostles, who were almost all from one of the four tribes here named : S. Paul was of the tribe of Benjamin ; S. James, S. John, and the other relations of our Lord were of the tribe of Juda ; and Galilee, the country of the Apostles, comprised especially the whole tribe of Zabulon and of Nephtali.

31. Manda Deus virtuti tuæ : confirma hoc Deus, quod operatus es in nobis.	Command Thy strength, O God : confirm, O God, what Thou hast wrought in us.

Ordain, O great God, according to Thy power, and confirm that which at other times Thou hast wrought for our good.

32. A templo tuo in Jerusalem : tibi offerent reges munera.	From Thy temple in Jerusalem : kings shall offer presents unto Thee.

"*A templo tuo.*" Mattei translates : *Post templum tuum,* and Bossuet : *Propter templum tuum.*——The verse then is thus explained : After Thy temple shall have been built at Jerusalem, or : Because of Thy temple, which shall be built at Jerusalem, kings will offer Thee their gifts.

33. Increpa feras arundinis, congregatio taurorum in vaccis populorum : ut excludant eos, qui probati sunt argento.	Rebuke the wild beasts of the reeds, the troop of bulls with the kine of the people : *who seek* to exclude them who are tried with silver.

"*Feras arundinis.*" Bellarmine says by this we are to understand the wild animals that hide among rushes.[2]——

[1] By Benjamin, the Holy Fathers understand S. Paul, who was of that tribe, named here *a youth,* because he was the last called to the apostleship.

[2] That is, the devils who hide themselves in order to surprise their prey.

"*In vaccis.*" According to the Hebrew : *In vitulis:* Calves.
——The verse therefore means : Frighten our enemies, who,
as wild beasts, and like an assemblage or a troop of savage
bulls, together with the calves of the people, that is, the
dissolute young men, will seek to exclude from the Temple
those who have been well proved, as silver. This is the
explanation given by Bossuet, Menochius, and Tirinus.

34. Dissipa gentes, quæ bella volunt : venient legati ex Ægypto : Æthiopia præveniet manus ejus Deo.	Scatter Thou the nations that delight in wars : ambassadors shall come out of Egypt : Ethiopia shall soon stretch out her hands unto God.[1]

"*Æthiopia . . . Deo.*" According to the Hebrew : Ethiopia
will make her hands run, will eagerly stretch out her hands
to God. Hence, S. Jerome translates : *Æthiopia festinet dare
manus Deo ;* and Father Mariana's interpretation is : *Junget
manus pacem petens.* The sense of the verse then is : Thou
wilt scatter, O Lord, the nations that wish for war : then
ambassadors from Egypt and Ethiopia will come running, with
joined hands, to ask for peace.

35. Regna terræ, cantate Deo : psallite Domino :	Sing unto God, ye kingdoms of the earth : sing ye unto the Lord :

36. Psallite Deo, qui ascendit super cœlum cœli : ad Orientem.	Sing ye unto God, Who mounteth above the heaven of heavens : unto the east.

"*Cœlum cœli.*" A Hebraism, signifying the highest heaven.
——"*Ad Orientem.*" Towards the East, that is, towards the
Mount of Olives, situated at the East of Jerusalem. It is thus
explained by Menochius and Tirinus, following S. Hilary and
S. Jerome.——Accordingly, the sense is : Give praise to God,
Who ascends from the Mount of Olives to the highest heaven.

37. Ecce dabit voci suæ vocem virtutis, date gloriam Deo super Israel : magnificentia ejus, et virtus ejus in nubibus.	Behold, He will give unto His voice the voice of power : give ye glory unto God for Israel : His magnificence and His power *are* in the clouds.

"*Ecce . . . virtutis.*" Behold, He will give to His word a
voice of virtue, that is, of power and efficacy.——"*Deo super
Israel.*" To the God of Israel, Whose greatness and power will
make themselves known in the clouds.——"*In nubibus.*"

---

[1] *Ambassadors shall come,* &c. It is a prophecy of the conversion of the
Gentiles, and by name of the Egyptians and Ethiopians.

According to the Hebrew: *In cœlis.* According to S. Augustine and Theodoret, this may be understood of the Day of Judgment, when Jesus Christ will come "in the clouds of heaven" ; then "He will give unto His voice the voice of power". He will speak with so great power, that He will cause a great terror by the sentence which He will pronounce against the reprobate.

38. Mirabilis Deus in sanctis suis, Deus Israel ipse dabit virtutem, et fortitudinem plebi suæ : benedictus Deus.

God is wonderful in His saints : power and strength unto His people : blessed be God.

God is admirable in His Saints. The God of Israel will give a virtue and strength to His people, which will make them victorious over their enemies. Therefore, let this great God be for ever blessed.

LAUDS FOR WEDNESDAY.

PSALM L.

PSALM LXIV.

THE people ask and hope for their return from Babylon to Jerusalem. The Jews, slaves of the Chaldeans, are a figure of the Gentiles, slaves of the devil. This Psalm well applies to the just, who sigh for the end of their exile here on earth.

To the end, a Psalm of David. The Canticle of Jeremias and Ezechiel to the people of the captivity, when they began to go out.[1]

1. Te decet hymnus Deus in Sion: et tibi reddetur votum in Jerusalem.

A hymn becometh Thee, O God, in Sion: and unto Thee shall the vow be paid in Jerusalem.

Thou, my God, art worthy to be praised in Sion, and in Jerusalem shall worthy homage be paid to Thee.

2. Exaudi orationem meam : ad te omnis caro veniet.

O hear my prayer : unto Thee shall all flesh come.

If Thou wilt hear me, we will come unto Thee with all the people.

3. Verba iniquorum prævaluerunt super nos : et impietatibus nostris tu propitiaberis.

The words of the wicked have prevailed against us : and Thou wilt pardon our transgressions.

"*Verba:*" A Hebraism for *Opera:* The works.——Accordingly, the verse is thus explained : The unjust deeds or plots of the enemy have prevailed against us ; but Thou, O Lord, wilt have compassion on our sins, which have reduced us to slavery, and Thou wilt take us out of these great miseries.

[1] *Of the captivity.* This is not in the Hebrew, but is found in the ancient translation of the *Septuagint.*

4. Beatus, quem elegisti, et assumpsisti: inhabitabit in atriis tuis.

Blessed is he whom Thou hast chosen, and taken to Thee: he shall dwell in Thy courts.

Happy is the man whom Thou choosest for Thine own, and whom Thou hast taken under Thy protection ; he shall dwell securely in Thy temple.

5. Replebimur in bonis domus tuæ : sanctum est templum tuum, mirabile in æquitate.

We shall be filled with the good things of Thy house: holy is Thy temple, wonderful in justice.

There in Thy house we shall be filled with good things: this Thy temple is all holy, and admirable for the love of justice which it inspires.——It is said : "Of justice," because the Saints are admitted into this house, whilst the wicked are excluded from it.

6. Exaudi nos Deus salutaris noster: spes omnium finium terræ, et in mari longe.

Hear us, O God our Saviour, *Who art* the hope of all the ends of the earth, and in the sea afar off.

Hearken to us, O God, our Saviour, Thou Who art the Hope of all nations, even of those who dwell at the uttermost limits of the earth and the sea, that is, in the most distant isles.

7. Præparans montes in virtute tua, accinctus potentia : qui conturbas profundum maris sonum fluctuum ejus.

Thou Who preparest the mountains by Thy strength, being girded with power : Who troublest the depth of the sea, the noise of its waves.

Thou, O God, armed with Thy power, hast prepared, that is, hast established, the mountains. Thou stirrest up the sea from its depths, and causest its billows to roar.

8. Turbabuntur Gentes, et timebunt qui habitant terminos a signis tuis : exitus matutini et vespere delectabis.

The Gentiles shall be troubled, and they that dwell in the uttermost borders shall be afraid at Thy signs : Thou shalt make the outgoings of the morning and of the evening to be joyful.

"*A signis tuis.*" When they behold the signs of Thy wrath. ——"*Exitus*..."[1] On the other hand, Thou shalt delight with Thy benefits the goings forth of the morning and of the evening, that is, of Thy servants who are in the East and in the West, where the sun rises and where it sets.

9. Visitasti terram et inebriasti eam : multiplicasti locupletare eam.

Thou hast visited the earth, and hast watered it plenteously : Thou hast copiously enriched it.

[1] "*Vespere.*" In the Greek this is in the genitive case.

16

"*Inebriasti eam.*" That is, Thou hast poured upon it abundance of rain.

10. Flumen Dei repletum est aquis, parasti cibum illorum : quoniam ita est præparatio ejus.

The river of God is filled with water, Thou hast prepared their food : for so is its preparation.

The river which Thou causest to run through the country is full of water, so as not to fail for Thy providing food for Thy people : since in this way art Thou wont to prepare the earth to bring forth its fruit.

11. Rivos ejus inebria, multiplica genimina ejus : in stillicidiis ejus lætabitur germinans.

Fill up plentifully the streams thereof, multiply its fruits : it shall spring up and rejoice in its showers.

"*Rivos.*" According to the Hebrew : *Sulcos :* Furrows. It is thus S. Jerome translates.——Thou wilt satiate its furrows with water, and Thou wilt multiply its plants : the showers of rain shall be such that the earth will rejoice therein, and abound with fruit.

12. Benedices coronæ anni benignitatis tuæ : et campi tui replebuntur ubertate.

Thou shalt bless the crown of the year of Thy goodness : and Thy fields shall be filled with plenty.

Throughout the circle of the year, Thou wilt bless it with the signs of Thy goodness ; and the fields will be, by Thee, filled with rich harvests.

13. Pinguescent speciosa deserti : et exultatione colles accingentur.

The beautiful places of the wilderness shall grow fat : and the hills shall be girded about with joy.

Even the very deserts shall become fertile and pleasant : and the hills shall be girded with joy, that is, they shall be clothed with smiling verdure.

14. Induti sunt arietes ovium, et valles abundabunt frumento : clamabunt, etenim hymnum dicent.

The rams of the flock are clothed, and the vales shall abound with corn : they shall shout, yea, they shall sing a hymn.

These fields and these hills will be afterwards clothed, that is, covered with flocks : the valleys will abound with corn, and then all will resound with voice of jubilee and hymns of praise to God.

PSALMS LXII. AND LXVI.

THE CANTICLE OF ANNA,
Mother of SAMUEL.

IN this Canticle, Anna (1 *Kings* i. 28., ii. 1-10), inspired by the Holy Ghost, renders thanks to God for having freed her from the reproach of sterility, and predicts very clearly the mystery of the Incarnation and the glories of the Church. This Canticle may be used by every Christian to thank the Lord for all the benefits which he has received, and especially for the grace of Redemption.

1. Exultavit cor meum in Domino: et exultatum est cornu meum in Deo meo :

My heart hath rejoiced in the Lord : and my horn is exalted in my God :

My heart has exulted with joy in the Lord ; and my glory, as mother, has been exalted by the power of my God :

2. Dilatatum est os meum super inimicos meos : quia lætata sum in salutari tuo.

My mouth is enlarged over my enemies : because I have joyed in Thy salvation.

My mouth is enlarged over my enemies, who insulted me : being now able to answer them, that Thou hast consoled me, by rejoicing my heart with Thy salvation, that is, with the favour which I have received from Thee.

3. Non est sanctus, ut est Dominus : neque enim est alius extra te ; et non est fortis sicut Deus noster.

There is none holy as the Lord is, for there is no other beside Thee : and there is none strong like our God.

4. Nolite multiplicare loqui sublimia : gloriantes.

Do not multiply to speak lofty things : boasting.

5. Recedant vetera de ore vestro : quia Deus scientiarum Dominus est, et ipsi præparantur cogitationes.

Let old matters depart from your mouth : for the Lord is a God of all knowledge, and to Him are thoughts prepared.

"*Recedant vetera.*" The Hebrew word here, as Du Hamel remarks, not only means *Vetera*, Old, but also *Dura*, Hard.—— The verse, then, may be thus explained : Let your hard and cutting words of the past cease ; for God is the Lord of wisdom, and all our thoughts ought to be prepared for, that is, should be directed to, Him.

6. Arcus fortium superatus est : et infirmi accincti sunt robore.

The bow of the mighty is overcome : and the weak are girt with strength.

7. Repleti prius pro panibus se locaverunt : et famelici saturati sunt.

They that were full before have hired out themselves for bread : and the hungry are filled.

8. Donec [1] sterilis peperit plurimos: et quæ multos habebat filios, infirmata est.

So that the barren hath borne many : and she that hath many children is weakened.

"*Infirmata est.*" Has become weak, that is, sterile.

9. Dominus mortificat et vivificat: deducit ad inferos et reducit.

The Lord killeth and maketh alive : He bringeth down to hell and bringeth back again.

10. Dominus pauperem facit, et ditat : humiliat, et sublevat.

The Lord maketh poor and maketh rich : He humbleth and He exalteth.

11. Suscitat de pulvere egenum ; et de stercore elevat pauperem :

He raiseth up the needy from the dust : and lifteth up the poor from the dunghill :

12. Ut sedeat cum principibus : et solium gloriæ teneat.

That he may sit with princes : and hold the throne of glory.

13. Domini enim sunt cardines terræ : et posuit super eos orbem.

For the poles of the earth are the Lord's : and upon them He hath set the world.

14. Pedes sanctorum suorum servabit, et impii in tenebris conticescent : quia non in fortitudine sua roborabitur vir.

He will keep the feet of His saints, and the wicked shall be silent in darkness : because no man shall prevail by his own strength.

"*Servabit.*" That is, that they may not stumble.——
"*Fortitudine sua.*" By his own strength alone.

15. Dominum formidabunt adversarii ejus : et super ipsos in cœlis tonabit.

The adversaries of the Lord shall fear Him : and upon them shall He thunder in the heavens.

The enemies of the Lord will tremble, when He shall make His voice of thunder to be heard above them.

16. Dominus judicabit fines terræ, et dabit imperium regi suo : et sublimabit cornu Christi sui.

The Lord shall judge the ends of the earth, and He shall give empire to His king, and shall exalt the horn of His Christ.

The Lord will judge all the earth, and will give it over to be governed by the King of His choice ; and He will exalt the glory of His Christ, that is, of the Messias.

PSALMS CXLVIII., CXLIX., CL.

CANTICLE OF ZACHARY.

[1] "*Donec.*" According to the Greek : *Quia.*——In this passage, vv. 6 to 12, may be noticed several figures found also in *Ps.* cxii. and in the Canticle *Magnificat.*

MATINS FOR THURSDAY.

PSALM LXVIII.

The Holy Fathers and interpreters say unanimously that this Psalm refers to our Divine Redeemer ill-treated by the Jews ; for this reason it is several times cited in the New Testament.

Unto the end, for them that shall be changed : for David.

1. Salvum me fac Deus : quoniam intraverunt aquæ usque ad animam meam.

Save me, O God : for the waters are come in even unto my soul.

" *Aquæ.*" The bitter waters of affliction.

2. Infixus sum in limo profundi : et non est substantia.

I stick fast in the deep mire : and there is no sure standing.

" *Non est substantia.*" S. Jerome's translation is : *Non possum consistere.* That is, according to the explanation of Menochius : There is no consistence or solidity where I can find footing.

3. Veni in altitudinem maris : et tempestas demersit me.

I am come into the depth of the sea : and a tempest hath overwhelmed me.

" *Altitudinem maris.*" The deep sea.——" *Tempestas . . .*" The tempest has engulphed me in its billows, that is, I am overwhelmed with bitterness.

4. Laboravi clamans : raucæ factæ sunt fauces meæ : defecerunt oculi mei, dum spero in Deum meum.

I am weary with crying : my jaws are become hoarse : mine eyes have failed, whilst I hope in my God.

" *Defecerunt oculi . . .*" My eyes have failed me in keeping them fixed upon my God, from Whom I hope for help.

5. Multiplicati sunt super capillos capitis mei : qui oderunt me gratis.

They who hate me without a cause:[1] are multiplied above the hairs of my head.

6. Confortati sunt qui persecuti sunt me inimici mei injuste : quæ non rapui, tunc exolvebam.

Mine enemies who have wrongfully persecuted me are grown strong : then did I pay that which I took not away.

My unjust persecutors have armed themselves doubly against me, and they have made me pay for that which I have not taken from any one. Behold Jesus Christ, Who, in dying, satisfies for sins that are not His own.

7. Deus tu scis insipientiam meam : et delicta mea a te non sunt abscondita.

O God, Thou knowest my foolishness : and my offences are not hid from Thee.

Thou knowest, O God, the folly with which I am wrongly accused by men ; nor are My offences hidden from Thee, that is, the sins of men that I have taken on Myself to atone for.——— This agrees with the words of Isaias (liii. 2) : "He shall bear their iniquities."

8. Non erubescant in me qui expectant te Domine : Domine virtutum.

Let not them who look for Thee, O Lord the Lord of hosts : be ashamed for me.

Let them not blush, that is, let them not be ashamed, on My account [2] who wait for Thee, that is, those who trust in Thee, O Lord, Who art the Lord of Hosts.——"*Virtutum.*" According to the Hebrew : *Exercituum.*

9. Non confundantur super me : qui quærunt te, Deus Israel.

Let them not be confounded on my account : who seek Thee, O God of Israel.

"*Super me.*" According to Bellarmine : *Mei causa.*

10. Quoniam propter te sustinui opprobrium ; operuit confusio faciem meam.

Because for Thy sake have I borne reproach : shame hath covered my face.

11. Extraneus factus sum fratribus meis : et peregrinus filiis matris meæ.

I am become a stranger unto my brethren : and an alien unto my mother's children.

"*Matris meœ.*" Of My mother, the Synagogue.[3]

---

[1] *John* xv. 25.

[2] "*In me.*" According to Bellarmine : *Propter me.*

[3] "The world knew Him not. He came unto His own, and His own received Him not." "As to this man, we know not from whence he is." (*John* i. 10, 11 ; ix. 29.)

12. Quoniam zelus domus tuæ comedit me : et opprobria exprobrantium tibi, ceciderunt super me.

For the zeal of Thine house hath eaten me up : and the reproaches of them that reproached Thee are fallen upon me.[1]

"*Quoniam.*" This has come to pass to Me because.——
"*Comedit me.*" Has devoured Me, or, according to the Chaldee, has consumed Me : *Consumpsit me.*

13. Et operui in jejunio animam meam : et factum est in opprobrium mihi.

And I shut up my soul in fasting : and it was made a reproach unto me.

This verse is very obscure.——"*Operui . . . meam.*" According to the Hebrew : *Flevi in jejunio animæ meæ.* The sense of the verse is : I whelmed Myself with My tears in My fast, and My enemies made of it a matter of scorn and contumely against Me.

14. Et posui vestimentum meum cilicium : et factus sum illis in parabolam.

And I made hair-cloth my garment : and I became a by-word to them.

"*In parabolam.*" A proverb, and a laughing-stock for their derision.

15. Adversum me loquebantur qui sedebant in porta : et in me psallebant qui bibebant vinum.

They that sat in the gate spake against me : and they that drank wine made me their song.

"*Qui sedebant in porta,*" *i.e.*, the magistrates, who had their station in the public place of judgment.——"*Et in me . . .*" And the drunkards sang scurrilous songs against Me, as they drank their wine.

16. Ego vero orationem meam ad te Domine : tempus beneplaciti Deus.

But as for me, my prayer *is* to Thee, O Lord : *for* the time of *Thy* good pleasure, O God.

"*Tempus beneplaciti.*" S. Jerome's translation is : *Tempus reconciliationis est.*——But I, O Lord, direct My prayer to Thee, for behold now the time of Thy good pleasure has arrived, that is, the time destined for the peace and reconciliation of men.

17. In multitudine misericordiæ tuæ exaudi me : in veritate salutis tuæ.

In the multitude of Thy mercy, hear me : in the truth of Thy salvation.

In Thy great mercy hear Me ; in the truth of Thy salvation, that is, according to the faithfulness of the promise which Thou hast made to save mankind.

[1] *John* ii. 17 ; *Rom.* xv. 3.

18. Eripe me de luto, ut non infigar : libera me ab iis, qui oderunt me, et de profundis aquarum.

Draw me out of the mire, that I may not stick fast: deliver me from them that hate me, and out of the deep waters.

19. Non me demergat tempestas aquæ, neque absorbeat me profundum : neque urgeat super me puteus os suum.

Let not the water-flood drown me, nor the deep swallow me up : and let not the pit shut her mouth upon me.

"*Neque urgeat.*" According to Bellarmine and others : *Non claudat.* This is to be understood of the sepulchre from which Jesus Christ willed to rise, and to pass to life eternal.

20. Exaudi me Domine, quoniam benigna est misericordia tua : secundum multitudinem miserationum tuarum respice in me.

Hear me, O Lord, for Thy mercy is kind : look upon me according to the multitude of Thy tender mercies.

21. Et ne avertas faciem tuam a puero tuo : quoniam tribulor, velociter exaudi me.

And turn not away Thy face from Thy servant: for I am in trouble, O hear me speedily.

22. Intende animæ meæ, et libera eam : propter inimicos meos eripe me.

Draw nigh unto my soul, and deliver it : save me because of mine enemies.

Consider the anguish of My soul, and deliver it : to the confusion of My enemies.

23. Tu scis improperium meum, et confusionem meam : et reverentiam meam.

Thou knowest my reproach, and my confusion, and my shame.

Thou knowest the scorn that I suffer, My confusion, and My ignominy.——"*Reverentiam.*" According to the Hebrew : *Ignominiam.* And so S. Jerome translates it.

24. In conspectu tuo sunt omnes qui tribulant me : improperium expectavit cor meum, et miseriam.

In Thy sight are all they that afflict me : my heart hath looked for reproach and misery.

"*In conspectu tuo sunt.*" Are in Thy sight, that is, are well known to Thee.——"*Improperium . . .*" Being, as I am, in their hands, I only expect insults and miseries from them.

25. Et sustinui qui simul contristaretur, et non fuit : et qui consolaretur, et non inveni.

And I looked for one that would grieve with me, but there was none : and for one that would comfort me, and I found him not.

26. Et dederunt in escam meam fel : et in siti mea potaverunt me aceto.

And they gave me gall for my food: and in my thirst they gave me vinegar to drink.[1]

1 *Matt.* xxvii. 34, 48.

27. Fiat mensa eorum coram ipsis in laqueum : et in retributiones, et in scandalum.

Let their table become as a snare before them : and a retribution, and a stumbling-block.[1]

Their table, in retribution for their cruelty, shall become unto them a snare, and an occasion of their ruin.——Jesus Christ here predicts, under the form of imprecation, the evils that were to fall on the Jews. For this reason the text is given a future tense ; it is thus Menochius and other commentators understand it.

28. Obscurentur oculi eorum ne videant : et dorsum eorum semper incurva.

Let their eyes be darkened that they see not : and their back bend Thou down always.

Their eyes will remain darkened, so that they will not see the precipice·over which they have fallen ; Thou wilt cause them to bend the back for ever, that is, Thou wilt always keep them under the yoke of strange masters.

29. Effunde super eos iram tuam : et furor iræ tuæ comprehendat eos.

Pour out Thine indignation upon them : and let Thy wrathful anger take hold of them.

Thou wilt pour out Thy wrath upon them, and the strength of Thy anger will come upon them one day.

30. Fiat habitatio eorum deserta : et in tabernaculis eorum non sit qui inhabitet.

Let their habitation be made desolate : and let there be none to dwell in their tents.

31. Quoniam quem tu percussisti, persecuti sunt : et super dolorem vulnerum meorum addiderunt.

For they have persecuted him whom Thou hast smitten : and they have added to the pain of my wounds.

Thou My God hast stricken Me, Thine Only beloved Son, for the sins of the human race ; as it is written in *Isaias* (liii. 8) : "*For the wickedness of my people have I struck Him.*" To these stripes of My Father the Jews have added pain upon pain to My wounds.

32. Appone iniquitatem super iniquitatem eorum : et non intrent in justitiam tuam.

Add Thou iniquity unto their iniquity : and let them not attain to Thy justice.

On this verse Bellarmine makes the following wise remark : *God is said to do, when He permits to be done, that which, without His permission, would not be done.* The sense of the verse, then, is : Thou, my God, permittest these wicked men to add iniquity to iniquity, and that they should not enter into Thy justice, that is, that they should not be admitted to receive from Thee justification.

[1] *Rom.* xi. 9.

33. Deleantur de libro viventium: et cum justis non scribantur.

Let them be blotted out of the book of the living : and with the just let them not be written.

"*De libro viventium.*" That is, from the number of the elect.

34. Ego sum pauper et dolens : salus tua Deus suscepit me.

But I am poor and sorrowful : Thy salvation, O God, hath set me up.

" *Salus tua suscepit me.*" [1] Thy salvation hath taken Me, or withdrawn Me, from so many pains, by causing Me to rise again. Or, as others explain the text, in a prophetic sense : I am that poor and suffering Man Who shall be saved from these pains by Thy salvation, that is, by Thy power.

35. Laudabo nomen Dei cum cantico : et magnificabo eum in laude :

I will praise the name of God with a song : and I will magnify Him with praise.

36. Et placebit Deo super vitulum novellum : cornua producentem et ungulas.

And it shall please God better than a young calf ; that putteth forth horns and hoofs.

And this my sacrifice of praise will please God more than that of a young calf.——" *Cornua . . .* " That begins to have horns and hoofs. [2]

37. Videant pauperes et lætentur: quærite Deum, et vivet anima vestra.

Let the poor see and rejoice ; seek ye God, and your soul shall live.

The poor and afflicted will see it and will rejoice ; O men, seek God and thus your souls will live for ever.

38. Quoniam exaudivit pauperes Dominus : et vinctos suos non despexit.

For the Lord hath heard the poor: and hath not despised His prisoners.

" *Vinctos suos . . .* " He does not despise His captives, that is, those who are loaded with the chains of their sins.

39. Laudent illum cœli et terra : mare, et omnia reptilia in eis.

Let the heavens and the earth praise Him ; the sea, and all creeping things therein.

Therefore let the heavens and the earth, the sea, and all creatures that live in heaven and on earth, praise God.

40. Quoniam Deus salvam faciet Sion : et ædificabuntur civitates Juda.

For God will save Sion : and the cities of Juda shall be built up.

1 In this last part of the Psalm, the Psalmist, continuing to speak in the person of Jesus Christ, foretells the glory of the Saviour and the establishment of the Church.

2 That is, which has all the qualities of a choice victim.

By Sion is understood the Church in general, and by the cities of Juda, the particular Churches. Thus Bossuet and others explain it.

41. Et inhabitabunt ibi : et heredi-tate acquirent eam.	And they shall dwell there : and acquire it by inheritance.

In this happy land men redeemed shall dwell, and shall possess it as their own inheritance.

42. Et semen servorum ejus pos-sidebit eam ; et qui diligunt nomen ejus, habitabunt in ea.	And the seed of His servants shall possess it : and they that love His name shall dwell therein.

And all the progeny of His servants shall possess this blessed land, which shall be always inhabited by those who love the glory of the Lord.

PSALM LXIX.

THIS Psalm, save some differences of expression, is a repetition of the seven last verses of Psalm xxxix. "*Expectans, expectavi*" (page 168). It is the prayer that Jesus Christ was to make on the Cross ; it is thus understood by most of the Latin interpreters. It may serve as a model to the faithful in their prayers, especially when they find themselves in grave dangers.

Unto the end, a Psalm for David, to bring to remembrance that the Lord saved him.

1. Deus in adjutorium meum in-tende ; Domine ad adjuvandum me festina.	Come unto my help, O God : O Lord, make haste to help me.

2. Confundantur, et revereantur : qui quærunt animam meam :	Let them be ashamed and put to confusion that seek after my soul :

"*Qui quærunt* ... " Who seek to take My life.

3. Avertantur retrorsum, et eru-bescant : qui volunt mihi mala :	Let them be turned backward, and blush for shame : that wish me evil :

4. Avertantur statim erubescen-tes ; qui dicunt mihi ; Euge, euge.	Let them be presently turned away blushing for shame : that say to me, Aha, aha.

"*Euge, euge.*" Well done, well done, we have struck Him down.——Instead of this word, S. Jerome translates : *Vah ! Vah !* a word (as Bossuet remarks) not of praise, but of mockery, just as cheers and cries of *hear ! hear !* are sometimes made in derision.

5. Exultent et lætentur in te omnes qui quærunt te: et dicant semper: Magnificetur Dominus: qui diligunt salutare tuum.

Let all those that seek Thee rejoice, and be glad in Thee: and let such as love Thy salvation say always, the Lord be magnified.

"*Qui diligunt...*" Who love the salvation which Thou hast promised. Or, as Bossuet explains: Those who wish to be saved by Thee.

6. Ego vero egenus, et pauper sum: Deus adjuva me.

But I am poor and needy: help me, O God.

7. Adjutor meus, et liberator meus es tu: Domine ne moreris.

Thou art my helper and my deliverer: O Lord, make no delay.

"*Ne moreris.*" Do not delay to help Me.

PSALM LXX.

DAVID asks help from God in the persecution raised against him by Absalom, his son. This Psalm will serve for all the faithful, when they are afflicted by temptations, in order to trust in God and ask His help.

A Psalm for David. Of the sons of Jonadab, and the former captives.[1]

1. In te Domine speravi, non confundar in æternum: in justitia tua libera me, et eripe me.

In Thee, O Lord, have I hoped, let me never be put to confusion: deliver me in Thy justice, and rescue me.

In Thee, O Lord, have I placed my hopes; I hope that I shall not be confounded for ever; deliver me from confusion in honour of Thy justice.

2. Inclina ad me aurem tuam: et salva me.

Incline Thine ear unto me: and save me.

Give ear to my prayers, and save me from the dangers that threaten me.

3. Esto mihi in Deum protectorem, et in locum munitum: ut salvum me facias.

Be Thou unto me a God, a protector, and a place of strength: that Thou mayest save me.

4. Quoniam firmamentum meum: et refugium meum es tu.

For thou art my support: and my refuge.

Since Thou art my firm support and my only refuge.

---

[1] *Of the sons of Jonadab.* The Rechabites, of whom see *Jeremias* **xxxv**. By this addition of the seventy-two interpreters, we gather that this Psalm was usually sung in the synagogue, in the person of the Rechabites, and of those who were first carried away into captivity.

5. Deus meus eripe me de manu peccatoris : et de manu contra legem agentis et iniqui.

Deliver me, O my God, out of the hand of the sinner: and out of the hand of the transgressor, and of the unjust.

"*Contra legem . . .*" Of him who unjustly acts against Thy law.

6. Quoniam tu es patientia mea Domine : Domine spes mea a juventute mea.

For Thou art my patience, O Lord : my hope, O Lord, from my youth.

"*Patientia.*" S. Jerome translates : *Expectatio.* According to the Hebrew, it is *Spes.*——Hence the verse may be explained with Bellarmine : Thou art my patience, that is, Thou art that Lord from Whom I expect, with patience, my deliverance, since, from my youth up, Thou hast been my only hope.

7. In te confirmatus sum ex utero : de ventre matris meæ tu es protector meus.

By Thee have I been supported from the womb : from my mother's womb Thou art my protector.

"*In te confirmatus sum.*" According to the Hebrew : *Super te innixus sum ;* or as S. Jerome's translation is : *A te sustentatus sum.*——The sense is : In Thee I have been confirmed, that is, I have found my support and my prop.

8. In te cantatio mea semper : tamquam prodigium factus sum multis : et tu adjutor fortis.

Of Thee shall my song be alway : I am become unto many as a wonder, but Thou art a strong helper.

My chant shall always be occupied with Thee, that is, I will always celebrate Thy goodness with praises ; I am admired by many as a prodigy, through the benefits Thou hast conferred upon me ; and Thou art looked upon as a strong defence of those whom Thou protectest.

9. Repleatur os meum laude, ut cantem gloriam tuam : tota die magnitudinem tuam.

Let my mouth be filled with praise, that I may sing of Thy glory : and of Thy greatness all the day long.

10. Ne projicias me in tempore senectutis : cum defecerit virtus mea, ne derelinquas me.

Cast me not off in the time of old age : when my strength shall fail, do not Thou forsake me.

11. Quia dixerunt inimici mei mihi : et qui custodiebant animam meam, consilium fecerunt in unum.

For mine enemies have spoken against me : and they that watched for my life took counsel together.

"*Qui custodiebant . . .*" S. Jerome translates: *Qui observabant animam meam inierunt consilium pariter.* Those who spied out my life, my way of living, have conspired against me.—— Others understand it of the guards whom David kept about his person, and explain it thus : Those who before guarded my life, are now united to plot my ruin.

12. Dicentes: Deus dereliquit eum, persequimini, et comprehendite eum : quia non est qui eripiat.

Saying, God hath forsaken him : pursue and take him, for there is none to deliver him.

13. Deus ne elongeris a me : Deus meus in auxilium meum respice.

Be not Thou far from me, O God : O my God, make haste to help me.

"*In auxilium...*" S. Jerome's translation is better : *In auxilium meum festina.* Haste to my help.

14. Confundantur, et deficiant detrahentes animæ meæ : operiantur confusione, et pudore qui quærunt mala mihi.

Let mine adversaries that seek my hurt be confounded, and come to nothing ; let them be covered with confusion and shame.

"*Detrahentes.*" The slanderers who blacken my character.

15. Ego autem semper sperabo : et adjiciam super omnem laudem tuam.

But I will always hope : and will add to all Thy praise.[1]

But I will always hope in Thee, my Lord ; and I will add fresh praises to all those that I have given Thee. For, according to Bossuet, Bellarmine, and Menochius, there is here an ellipsis which requires to be thus supplied.

16. Os meum annuntiabit justitiam tuam : tota die salutare tuum.

My mouth shall show forth Thy justice : Thy salvation all the day long.

"*Salutare tuum.*" I will publish, for Thy glory, the salvation I have received from Thee.

17. Quoniam non cognovi litteraturam, introibo in potentias Domini : Domine memorabor justitiæ tuæ solius.

Because I have not known learning, I will go in to the powers of the Lord : O Lord, I will be mindful of Thy justice alone.

"*Non cognovi litteraturam.*" I am little versed in worldly wisdom.——Interpreters generally understand the word *Litteraturam* as though David meant to say : I have never made profession of that infamous cunning in which my enemy Achitophel abounds.——"*Introibo in potentias Domini.*" I shall enter willingly into the power of the Lord, that is, I shall set myself to praise the divine power.——"*Memorabor...*" I shall have nothing else before my eyes but the memory of Thy justice.

18. Deus docuisti me a juventute mea : et usque nunc pronuntiabo mirabilia tua.

Thou hast taught me, O God, from my youth : and till now I will declare Thy wondrous works.

"*Et usque nunc...*" Wherefore, I will never cease to celebrate the wonderful graces which Thou hast done unto me.

---

[1] *Will add to all Thy praise, i.e.*, will praise Thee continually.

19. Et usque in senectam et senium : Deus ne derelinquas me.

And unto old age and grey hairs : [1] O God, forsake me not.

20. Donec annuntiem brachium tuum : generationi omni, quæ ventura est :

Until I show forth Thine arm to all the generation that is to come :

Until I succeed in proclaiming Thy arm, that is, Thy great power, to all the generations that shall come to inhabit this earth.

21. Potentiam tuam, et justitiam tuam Deus usque in altissima, quæ fecisti magnalia : Deus quis similis tibi ?

Thy power, and Thy justice, O God, even to the highest, the great things Thou hast done : O God, who is like unto Thee ?

Thus, also, I will announce Thy power and Thy justice, together with all the most sublime marvels which Thou hast wrought ; and where, O my God, can he be found who is like unto Thee ?

22. Quantas ostendisti mihi tribulationes multas, et malas : et conversus vivificasti me : et de abyssis terræ iterum reduxisti me :

How great troubles hast Thou shown me, many and grievous : and turning Thou hast brought me to life : and hast brought me back again from the depths of the earth :

What great afflictions, many, sore, and bitter, hast Thou made me endure ! Appeased once more, Thou hast, so to say, restored to me life ; and again, Thou hast brought me back, and drawn me forth from the abysses of the earth, that is, from the depth of miseries.

23. Multiplicasti magnificentiam tuam : et conversus consolatus es me.

Thou hast multiplied Thy greatness : and turning to me Thou hast comforted me.

Thou hast multiplied Thy magnificence upon me, that is, Thou hast, in many ways, shown the greatness of Thy goodness towards me ; and hast turned again to comfort me.—— "*Conversus.*" A Hebraism, which signifies that the action is repeated.

24. Nam et ego confitebor tibi in vasis psalmi veritatem tuam : Deus psallam tibi in cithara, sanctus Israel.

For I will also praise Thee, Thy truth with the instruments of psaltery : O God, I will sing unto Thee with the harp, Thou holy One of Israel.

"*In vasis psalmi.*" According to Menochius and Bossuet : *In musicis instrumentis.* The Hebrew text has : *With the instrument of the psaltery,* which comes to the same.—— "*Veritatem tuam.*" The faithfulness of Thy promises.

[1] Thus Malvenda and Menochius understand "*Senium.*" S. Alph. *Paraphrase.*

25. Exultabunt labia mea cum cantavero tibi : et anima mea, quam redemisti.

My lips shall greatly rejoice, when I shall sing unto Thee : and my soul which Thou hast redeemed.

" *Et anima mea* ... " And this my soul shall exult, which Thou hast redeemed, that is, hast set free from so many dangers.

26. Sed et lingua mea tota die meditabitur justitiam tuam : cum confusi et reveriti fuerint qui quærunt mala mihi.

Yea, and my tongue shall speak of Thy justice all the day long : when they shall be confounded and put to shame that seek my hurt.

" *Meditabitur.*"   That is : Shall praise whilst meditating upon.

PSALM LXXI.

In this Psalm David speaks of his son Solomon, whom he made heir of the kingdom of Israel, which was a figure of the spiritual kingdom of Jesus Christ ; thus speak unanimously the Fathers and commentators.   Indeed, it seems to me that the whole or nearly the whole Psalm ought to be applied to Jesus Christ : there are, moreover, some expressions in it, especially in the verses 5, 11, 12, and 17, which can only refer to our Divine Redeemer and to His coming, as well as to the vocation of the Gentiles, all which the holy King David saw clearly by the prophetic light.[1]

A Psalm on Solomon.

1. Deus judicium tuum regi da : et justitiam tuam filio regis :

Give to the king Thy judgment, O God : and Thy justice unto the king's son :

Give, my God, to the king Thy judgment, that is, the grace to judge justly, and grant to the son of David, Thy justice, that is, a righteous justice like Thine own.

2. Judicare populum tuum in justitia : et pauperes tuos in judicio.

To judge Thy people with justice : and Thy poor with judgment.

" *In judicio.*"   With righteousness.

3. Suscipiant montes pacem populo : et colles justitiam.

Let the mountains receive peace for the people : and the hills justice.

---

[1] The name of Solomon signifies Pacific, a name most suitable for Him Who is the Son of David by excellence, the Prince of Peace, of whom Solomon was the figure.   Hence it is generally acknowledged that this Psalm, taken as a whole, is applicable only to the Divine Messias.

"*Montes.*" This word is variously understood. Maldonatus understands it as though it were *Undique;* and meaning : May peace be enjoyed everywhere, even on the mountains. ——Emmanuel Sa interprets "mountains" here to mean, the chief men or rulers. Malvenda by "mountains" understands the whole kingdom abounding with mountains. It is in this way Bossuet, with Bellarmine and Menochius, explains the verse : May peace and justice descend from heaven and rest upon the kingdom of Israel. Lastly, Mariana, and with him Tirinus, says: Mountains, that is, where robbers and wild beasts are wont to be. This last interpretation, as Lallemant thinks, seems to be the most probable.——Accordingly the sense of the verse would be : May the mountains and the hills receive peace for the good of the people, that is : may even the people of the mountains, who are wont to be fierce and turbulent, taste the sweetness of peace and enjoy the fruits of the justice of the prince.

4. Judicabit pauperes populi, et salvos faciet filios pauperum : et humiliabit calumniatorem.

He shall judge the poor of the people : and He shall save the children of the poor : and He shall humble the oppressor.

"*Judicabit.*" That is, He will defend their cause.—— "*Calumniatorem.*" According to the Hebrew : *Oppressorem.*

5. Et permanebit cum sole, et ante lunam : in generatione et generatione.

And He shall continue with the sun, and before the moon, throughout all generations.

"*Ante lunam.*" S. Jerome's translation following the Hebrew is : *Ultra lunam.* Beyond the moon. That is : Till there be no moon. His kingdom shall endure throughout all generations, as long as the sun and the moon, and even beyond that. (See verse 7.)

6. Descendet sicut pluvia in vellus : et sicut stillicidia stillantia super terram.

He shall come down like rain upon the fleece : and as showers falling gently upon the earth.

He will descend as the dew descended on the fleece of Gedeon ; and as a gentle rain which descends in drops on an arid land.——"*Vellus.*" About this word there is a great diversity of opinion. Malvenda, Menochius, Bellarmine, Tirinus, and others understand by it the fleece, or skin covered with wool, upon which Gedeon asked might be collected all the dew that fell from heaven. (*Judges* vi. 36, 37.) Others, as Maldonatus, Mariana, Bossuet, Mattei, with Marino and

Lallemant, are of opinion that the word *Vellus* here means
something cut or shorn ; whence Lallemant translates the
passage thus : His coming to the throne will be like a rain
that waters a meadow newly mown.——But the first interpretation agrees better with that of S. Ambrose, Rupertus,
and Procopius, who understand by the fleece the Mother of
God, and by the dew the Divine Word, Who came down
gently as the dew into the womb of the Virgin Mary by the
operation of the Holy Ghost. Moreover, the verse taken in
this sense, has a better connection with the following: "In
His days shall justice spring up, and abundance of peace".
Which certainly is to be understood of the coming of the
Messias.

7. Orietur in diebus ejus justitia,
et abundantia pacis : donec auferatur
luna.

In His days shall justice spring
up, and abundance of peace : until
the moon be taken away.

"*In diebus ejus.*" Under His reign.——"*Donec auferatur
luna.*" This happy state will last until the end of the world.
(See v. 5.)

8. Et dominabitur a mari usque
ad mare : et a flumine usque ad terminos orbis terrarum.

And He shall rule from sea to sea:
and from the river unto the ends of
the earth.

"*A flumine.*" S. Augustine, Theodoret, &c., understand by
the river, the Jordan, because it was there, at the Baptism of
Jesus Christ, the Eternal Father's voice was heard saying :
"This is My beloved Son in Whom I am well pleased".
(*Matt.* iii. 17.)

9. Coram illo procident Æthiopes:
et inimici ejus terram lingent.

Before Him the Ethiopians shall
fall down : and His enemies shall
lick the ground.

"*Terram lingent.*" Shall lick the earth, that is, shall bow
down to kiss the earth that is under His feet.

10. Reges Tharsis, et insulæ
munera offerent : reges Arabum, et
Saba dona adducent :

The kings of Tharsis and the
islands shall offer presents : the
kings of the Arabians and of Saba
shall bring gifts :

"*Regis Tharsis et insulæ.*" The Kings of India and the
inhabitants of the Isles.

11. Et adorabunt eum omnes reges
terræ : omnes gentes servient ei.

And all kings of the earth shall
adore Him : all nations shall do Him
service.

These verses from verse 5th can only apply to Jesus Christ.

12. Quia liberabit pauperem a potente: et pauperem, cui non erat adjutor.

For He shall deliver the poor from the mighty: and the needy that had no helper.

"*Pauperem a potente.*" The poor, that is, the weak,[1] from the hands of the powerful.

13. Parcet pauperi et inopi: et animas pauperum salvas faciet.

He shall spare the poor and needy: and He shall save the souls of the poor.

"*Parcet.*" According to the Chaldee : *Miserebitur.* He will have compassion on, that is, He will spare and pardon.

14. Ex usuris et iniquitate redimet animas eorum : et honorabile nomen eorum coram illo.

He shall redeem their souls from usuries and wrong: and their name shall be honourable in His sight.

"*Ex usuris.*" According to the Chaldee : *Ab oppressione.* From oppression.——"*Et iniquitate.*" That is : And from injustice.——"*Honorabile.*" That is : Well-pleasing to Him.

15. Et vivet, et dabitur ei de auro Arabiæ, et adorabunt de ipso semper: tota die benedicent ei.

And He shall live, and to Him shall be given of the gold of Arabia : for to Him they shall always pray, they shall bless Him all the day.

"*Vivet.*" He shall live, that is, His reign shall be everlasting.——"*Vivet, et dabitur ei.*" According to the Hebrew : *Vivet et dabit ei.* Hence, Maldonatus interprets the passage thus : The poor delivered by Him shall live, and out of gratitude will give to Him gold of Arabia.——"*Adorabunt de ipso.*" S. Jerome's translation of the Hebrew is : *Orabunt de eo.* Emmanuel Sa thus comments on these words : *De eo*, that is, *Pro eo.* The people will pray continually for Him, for His cause, and the prosperity of His reign.[2]

16. Et erit firmamentum in terra in summis montium, superextolletur super Libanum fructus ejus: et florebunt de civitate sicut fœnum terræ.

And there shall be a firm foundation on the earth, on the tops of mountains : above Libanus shall its fruit be exalted : and *they* of the city shall flourish like the grass of the earth.

"*Firmamentum.*" The Hebrew text, S. Jerome, Bellarmine, Mattei, Lallemant, and all the interpreters of the Compilation

---

[1] By "*Pauperem*," Bellarmine understands the human race after its fall, despoiled of all its goods, and incapable of help from any creature. By "*A potente*," he understands the devil, whose miserable slave man had become.

[2] *Adorabant de ipso semper.* Bellarmine's explanation is : Those redeemed by Jesus Christ will adore the true God according to Christ's own rite, teaching, and institution.

of Venice, attest that *Firmamentum* is put here for *Frumentum*.
Accordingly, the verse is thus explained : There will be such
an abundance of wheat on earth, and even on the summits of
the mountains, that its fruit will rise above Lebanon, that is,
the ears will rise higher than the cedars of Lebanon ; and the
inhabitants of the City of God, which is the Church, shall
flourish or spring up like the herb of the field.

17. Sit nomen ejus benedictum in sæcula : ante solem permanet nomen ejus.	Let His name be blessed for ever· more : His name continueth before the sun.

"*Nomen ejus.*" The name of this new King.——"*Ante
solem.*" According to the Hebrew : *Coram sole;* and as S.
Jerome translates : *Ultra solem.*——"*Permanet.*" According
to S. Jerome, Menochius, Bossuet, &c., this verb is to be
understood in the future. Hence the meaning is : His name
shall endure longer than the sun.

18. Et benedicentur in ipso omnes tribus terræ : omnes gentes magnificabunt eum.	And in Him shall all the tribes of the earth be blessed : all nations shall magnify Him.
19. Benedictus Dominus Deus Israel : qui facit mirabilia solus.	Blessed be the Lord the God of Israel : Who alone doeth wondrous things.
20. Et benedictum nomen majestatis ejus in æternum : et replebitur majestate ejus omnis terra : fiat, fiat.	And blessed be the name of His majesty for ever : and the whole earth shall be filled with His majesty. Amen. Amen.

The praises of David the son of Jesse are ended.[1]

PSALM LXXII.

MISERABLE is the happiness of the wicked, and blessed are the
afflictions of the just, since the end of the one class will be
very different from that of the other. We learn hence not to
be astonished when we see the wicked prosper and the good
afflicted.

A Psalm for Asaph.

1. Quam bonus Israel Deus : his, qui recto sunt corde !	How good is God unto Israel : unto them that are of an upright heart !

[1] *Are ended.* By this it appears that this Psalm, though placed here, was
in order of time the last of those which David composed.

" *Israel.*" To Israel, or towards the people of Israel. Lallemant has understood this proper name as though in the
genitive ; but in the Greek it is preceded by the article in the
dative, and so in the Hebrew text, of which the literal sense
is : Truly, God is good to Israel. It is thus that Bossuet,
with several others, explains it.

2. Mei autem pene moti sunt   But my feet were almost gone :
pedes : pene effusi sunt gressus mei.   my steps had wellnigh slipt.

That is to say : My belief was almost shaken ; and I had
almost turned aside from the way, through the emotion and
trouble that I felt.

3. Quia zelavi super iniquos :   Because I was jealous of the
pacem peccatorum videns.   wicked : when I saw the prosperity
                            of sinners.

" *Super iniquos.*" S. Jerome's translation is : *Contra iniquos.*
For I was wroth against the wicked at seeing the peace in
which sinners lived, on account of the prosperity which they
enjoy, or to speak more correctly, which they flatter themselves that they enjoy.

4. Quia non est respectus morti   For there is no regard to their
eorum : et firmamentum in plaga   death : nor *is there* strength in their
eorum.   stripes.

" *Quia . . . eorum.*" S. Jerome translates : *Quod non recogi-
taverint de morte sua.* Because they have not reflected on their
death.——" *Et firmamentum . . .*" This passage is obscure,
and is differently explained by interpreters. The word
Firmamentum presents the greatest difficulty ; but Gordona
remarks that if the particle *Non* be repeated, by understanding *Et* as *Nec*, the sense becomes easy. Thus : *Nec est firmamentum in plaga eorum.* Nor is there firmness in their
wound : That is, if any evil happens to them, it quickly
passes, it is light and has no firmness.——Hence the most
natural explanation seems to be this : And in their wound,
that is, when they feel themselves tormented by the fear of
death, their affliction has no strength or firmness, and does
not last long.

5. In labore hominum non sunt: They are not in the labour of men:
et cum hominibus non flagellabuntur.   neither shall they be scourged with
                            other men.

They are not in the travail of men, that is, they are exempt
from poverty, from fatigues, and other evils which afflict the

generality of men; so that they are not scourged, that is, they
do not suffer with other men.

6. Ideo tenuit eos superbia: operti sunt iniquitate et impietate sua.	Therefore pride hath held them fast: they are covered with their iniquity and their wickedness.

7. Prodiit quasi ex adipe iniquitas eorum: transierunt in affectum cordis.	Their iniquity hath come forth, as it were from fatness:[1] they have passed into the desire of their hearts.

"*Prodiit ... eorum.*" Their iniquity has been produced by
fatness, that is, by the abundance of their good things of
the earth. Such is the explanation of Menochius.——"*Transierunt in affectum cordis.*" According to the Hebrew: *Transierunt cogitationes cordis.* That is: All things happen to
them beyond their hopes; they have come to surpass their
desires by obtaining more than they wished and hoped for.

8. Cogitaverunt, et locuti sunt nequitiam: iniquitatem in excelso locuti sunt.	They have thought and spoken wickedness: they have spoken iniquity on high.

They have meditated and uttered their wickedness, that is,
they have employed their thoughts and their words to put in
execution their evil designs; and they have not been ashamed
to publish their iniquity "*in excelso,*" as from a high place—
from the house tops—to make it known to all the world.

9. Posuerunt in cœlum os suum: et lingua eorum transivit in terra.	They have set their mouth against heaven: and their tongue hath passed through the earth.

They have opened their mouth even against heaven, that is,
according to Bellarmine, against God and His Saints; and
they have not abstained either from employing their tongue
on earth against men.——Malvenda's comment is: As
though the Psalmist would say: They spare neither God nor
man.

10. Ideo convertetur populus meus hic: et dies pleni invenientur in eis.	Therefore will my people return hither: and full days shall be found in them.

Wherefore my people shall turn and see that for these
impious men, notwithstanding their iniquity, there are days
full of worldly satisfaction. Thus Bellarmine and Lallemant
explain the verse.

[1] *Fatness.* Abundance, and temporal prosperity.

11. Et dixerunt: Quomodo scit Deus? et si est scientia in excelso?

And they said: How doth God know? and is there knowledge in the Most High?

And the men of my people say : How can it be that God, in Whom is the science and knowledge of all that comes to pass on earth, should know this, and, it may be added, should permit it ?

12. Ecce ipsi peccatores, et abundantes in sæculo: obtinuerunt divitias.

Behold, these are sinners : and yet prospering in the world they have obtained riches.

"*Abundantes in sæculo.*" Behold these sinners abound in riches in this world, so that they are esteemed as those who enjoy peace on earth.——In the Hebrew, *Pacifici sæculi.*

13. Et dixi : Ergo sine causa justificavi cor meum : et lavi inter innocentes manus meas :

And I said : Then have I cleansed my heart in vain : and washed my hands among the innocent :

"*Sine causa justificavi.*" According to the Hebrew : *Frustra mundavi.*——"*Inter innocentes.*" That is, with the innocent.——Therefore, I said : Is it then in vain that I have purified and justified my heart, and have cleansed my hands together with the innocent.

14. Et fui flagellatus tota die: et castigatio mea in matutinis.

And I have been scourged all the day : and my chastisement hath been in the mornings.

And all the while I am scourged, that is, I am afflicted with woes the whole day long ; and my affliction commences in the morning, from the dawn of day.

15. Si dicebam, Narrabo sic: ecce nationem filiorum tuorum reprobavi.

If I said ; I will speak thus : behold, I should condemn the generation of Thy children.

S. Jerome thus translates this verse : *Et dixi ; si narravero sic, ecce generationem filiorum tuorum reliqui.*——The sense of the verse is : But afterwards I said : If I spoke thus, I should do wrong, and I should come to abandon the nation, that is, the society of Thy children, in fact, to disapprove of the religion of Thy faithful.

16. Existimabam ut cognoscerem hoc : labor est ante me.

I studied that I might know this thing : it is a labour in my sight.

I thought to be able to understand this conduct of Thy Providence ; but I perceived that my labour was in vain.—— "*Ante me,*" that is, above my comprehension.

17. Donec intrem in sanctuarium Dei: et intelligam in novissimis eorum.

Until I go into the sanctuary of God: and understand concerning their last ends.

" *In sanctuarium.*" According to Bossuet : *In arcanum*, or according to Malvenda : *In sacratiora adyta*. The sense of the verse is : Until by means of prayer, I entered into the sanctuary of God, that is, into the secret judgments of God ; and then I came to understand the end of sinners ; what will be the miserable end of their happiness here on earth.

18. Verumtamen propter dolos posuisti eis : dejecisti eos dum allevarentur.

But indeed Thou hast set it as a snare for them : when they were lifted up, Thou hast cast them down.

" *Posuisti eis.*" Menochius says that here we must supply *Mala*, as being understood, and which some of the Greek texts have.——The sense then is : Nevertheless, because of the deceits which they employ to exalt themselves, Thou hast prepared punishments for them ; Thou hast caused their feet to fail them, and hast cast them down whilst they sought to raise themselves to power here on earth.

19. Quomodo facti sunt in desolationem, subito defecerunt: perierunt propter iniquitatem suam.

How are they brought to desolation ! they have suddenly ceased to be : they have perished by reason of their iniquity.

20. Velut somnium surgentium Domine : in civitate tua imaginem ipsorum ad nihilum rediges.

As the dream of them that awake, O Lord: so in Thy city Thou shalt bring their image to nothing.

" *Velut somnium surgentium.*" S. Jerome translates : *Quasi somnium evigilantis.*——" *In civitate tua.*" According to Menochius : *In civitate superna.*——The sense then is : O Lord, at the end of all things, these miserable men shall be afflicted, as those are afflicted who, after dreaming that they have come to a great fortune, find themselves on awaking in the same poverty as before ; and whereas Thy faithful servants shall be honoured, in Thy city of heaven, they on the contrary shall be excluded from it : and the great figure they have made in the world will be brought to nothing.

21. Quia inflammatum est cor meum, et renes mei commutati sunt : et ego ad nihilum redactus sum, et nescivi.

For my heart hath been inflamed: and my reins have been changed : and I am brought to nothing, and I knew not.

" *Inflammatum . . . sunt.*" According to the Septuagint : *Lætatum est cor meum, et renes mei dilatati sunt ;* and, as Mattei says, the same version is found in S. Ambrose, as also in the ancient Psalters.——The passage, then, is explained thus : Wherefore my heart was inflamed with joy, and my reins were stirred through gladness, when I saw my fears vanish. ——" *Et ego ad nihilum redactus sum, et nescivi.*" And at the same time I was brought to nought, that is, I became aware of my own nothingness, of which I was before ignorant.

22. Utjumentum factus sum apud te : et ego semper tecum.

I am become as a beast before Thee : and I am always with Thee.

S. Jerome translates : *Et ego insipiens et nescius quasi jumentum.*——I confess that hitherto I have been like a beast of burden, not knowing the truth of my nothingness; and, therefore, from henceforth, I desire to be always united to Thee, Who art my only good.

23. Tenuisti manum dexteram meam : et in voluntate tua deduxisti me : et cum gloria suscepisti me.

Thou hast held me by my right hand: and by Thy will Thou hast conducted me, and with Thy glory Thou hast received me.

Thou hast held my right hand, that is, Thou hast kept me up, so that I might not be lost; Thou hast led me to live according to Thy will ; Thou hast covered me with glory, in making known to me "the secret reasons of Thy Providence and justice ". Thus Bossuet with S. Jerome.

24. Quid enim mihi est in cœlo ? et a te quid volui super terram ?

For what have I in heaven but Thee? and beside Thee what do I desire upon earth?

25. Defecit caro mea, et cor meum : Deus cordis mei, et pars mea Deus in æternum.

My flesh and my heart hath failed : but Thou art the God of my heart, and the God that is my portion for ever,

My flesh and my heart have failed, that is, can no longer resist the attractions of Thy love, which draws me to Thee ; Thou art the God of my heart, it is for Thee alone to possess it eternally ; Thou alone must be my portion and all my good.

26. Quia ecce, qui elongant se a te, peribunt: perdidisti omnes, qui fornicantur abs te.

For behold, they that depart from Thee shall perish: Thou hast destroyed all them that are faithless unto Thee.

Those who withdraw from Thee will in the end perish, since Thou sendest justly to perdition those who love other objects than Thee. It is thus Menochius, Sa, Mariana, and Tirinus understand the expression : " *Qui fornicantur abs te*".[1]

[1] See *Ps.* xv. 37.

27. Mihi autem adhærere Deo bonum est : ponere in Domino Deo spem meam :

But it is good for me to hold fast unto my God : to put my hope in the Lord God :

But as for me, my only good is to adhere and unite myself entirely to my God, and to place in Him all my hopes.

28. Ut annuntiem omnes prædicationes tuas : in portis filiæ Sion.

That I may declare all Thy praises : in the gates of the daughter of Sion.

And thus I hope, one day, O Lord, to publish Thy glories in Jerusalem, which is called the daughter of Sion.[1]

PSALM LXXIII.

THE Jewish people address to God pious complainings, because of their captivity and the destruction of the Temple ; and, at the same time, prayers for their religion and kingdom, calling to mind the wonders worked by God in their behalf, and the benefits received from Him. Bellarmine and others think that the Psalmist speaks here of the persecution of Antiochus at the time of the Machabees. This Psalm can be used against the persecutions that the Church suffers at the hands of her enemies.

Understanding for Asaph.

1. Ut quid Deus repulisti in finem : iratus est furor tuus super oves pascuæ tuæ ?

O God, why hast Thou cast us off for ever? why is Thy wrath enkindled against the sheep of Thy pasture ?

2. Memor esto congregationis tuæ : quam possedisti ab initio ;

Remember Thy congregation : which Thou hast possessed from the beginning ;

" Ab initio." Menochius understands by this the time when the people of Israel had no other king but God : Quæ nullum habuit regem ante te.

3. Redemisti virgam hereditatis tuæ : mons Sion, in quo habitasti in eo.

The sceptre of Thine inheritance which Thou hast redeemed : Mount Sion in which Thou hast dwelt.

" Virgam." According to S. Augustine, Theodoret, Symmachus, Euthymius, Bellarmine, and Mattei : Sceptrum or Regnum.——The verse is thus explained : Thou didst redeem the sceptre of Thine inheritance, that is, the kingdom of the Promised Land, by driving out the enemies who occupied it ; there is Mount Sion, where Thou hast vouchsafed to dwell for our good.

[1] See *Ps.* ix. 14.

4. Leva manus tuas in superbias eorum in finem : quanta malignatus est inimicus in sancto !

Lift up Thy hands against their pride unto the end : *see* what things the enemy hath done wickedly in the sanctuary !

Raise the hands of Thy dread power, to utterly strike down their haughtiness ; Thou knowest how many and great evils this hostile people has wrought in the holy place ; that is, in the Holy City, or in the Holy Temple.

5. Et gloriati sunt qui oderunt te : in medio solemnitatis tuæ.

And they that hate Thee have made their boasts: in the midst of Thy solemnity.

Those who hated Thee have gloried in their insults committed in the Temple at the very time that solemnities were being offered to Thy name.——"*In medio* . . ." According to Menochius : " Whilst the sacred solemnities were going on ".

6. Posuerunt signa sua, signa : et non cognoverunt sicut in exitu super summum.

They have set up their ensigns [1] for signs: and they knew not both in the going out, and on the highest top.

"*Posuerunt signa sua, signa.*" They have placed their signs, that is, their banners, on the summit of the Temple.——" *Et non cognoverunt.*" According to S. Jerome, Theodoret, Tirinus, &c. : *Neque curarunt quantus honor deberetur templo tuo.* And had no thought of how great honour was due to Thy Temple. ——"*Sicut in exitu super summum.*" They have not scrupled to treat the highest, that is, the holiest place, *sicut in exitu*, that is, according to Mattei, as a common thoroughfare ; or, according to Lallemant, as the vilest place to be found in all the city.

7. Quasi in silva lignorum securibus exciderunt januas ejus in idipsum : in securi, et ascia dejecerunt eam.

As with axes in a wood of trees, they have cut down at once the gates thereof : with axe and hatchet they have brought it down.

As if they had been in the forest cutting wood, thus they have joined together in hacking down the gates of the Temple; and with hatchets and axes they have hewn down the thresholds thereof.

8. Incenderunt igni Sanctuarium tuum : in terra polluerunt tabernaculum nominis tui.

They have set on fire Thy sanctuary : they have defiled the dwelling-place of Thy name on the earth.

[1] *Their ensigns,* &c. They have fixed their colours on the gates, and on the highest top of the Temple : and *they knew not*, that is, they regarded not the sanctity of the place. This Psalm manifestly foretells the time of the Machabees, and the profanation of the Temple by Antiochus.

"*In terra . . .*" They have profaned the Tabernacle consecrated to Thy name, levelling it to the ground.

9. Dixerunt in corde suo cognatio eorum simul ; Quiescere faciamus omnes dies festos Dei a terra.

They said in their heart, the *whole* kindred of them together : Let us make to cease all the festival days of God from the land.

10. Signa nostra non vidimus, jam non est Propheta : et nos non cognoscet amplius.

Our signs we have not seen, there is now no prophet : and He will know us no more.

We have no longer to be seen amongst us the wonders that were once wrought in our midst ; there is now no longer any prophet ; and it seems that the Lord will not know us any more for His people.

11. Usquequo Deus improperabit inimicus ? irritat adversarius nomen tuum in finem ?

How long, O God, shall the enemy reproach ? *is* the adversary to blaspheme Thy name for ever ?

How long, O our God, wilt Thou suffer the enemy to revile us and to provoke to anger Thy name ? Must we see this go on for ever ?

12. Ut quid avertis manum tuam, et dexteram tuam ? de medio sinu tuo in finem ?

Why dost Thou turn away Thy hand ? and Thy right hand out of the midst of Thy bosom for ever ?

And why holdest Thou Thy hand afar off, and almost wholly idle, in Thy bounteous bosom, without pouring upon us Thy accustomed graces ?

13. Deus autem Rex noster ante sæcula : operatus est salutem in medio terræ.

But God is our king from everlasting : He hath wrought salvation in the midst of the earth.

"*In medio terræ.*" Mazzocchi says this is a Hebraism, and means the same as *In terra*. On earth.

14. Tu confirmasti in virtute tua mare : contribulasti capita draconum in aquis.

Thou, by Thy strength, didst stablish the sea : Thou didst crush the heads of the dragons in the waters.

Here the Psalmist begins to relate the wonders wrought in behalf of his people.——Thou by Thy virtue, that is, by Thy power, didst make the sea firm and stable, after having divided it for the passage of the Hebrews ; and Thou didst lay low, submerged in those waters, the heads of the dragons, that is, the chiefs of the Egyptians ; as Euthymius and others explain the passage.

15. Tu confregisti capita draconis: dedisti eum escam populis Æthiopum.

Thou hast broken the heads of the dragon : Thou hast given him to be meat for the people of the Ethiopians.

Thou didst break the pride of the dragon, that is, of this hostile people, who, being sunk, was made by Thee, the prey of the Ethiopians, who reaped its spoils.——According to Malvenda, Menochius, and Bellarmine, by the Ethiopians are meant properly the Arabians who inhabit the shores of the Red Sea, and are called Ethiopians in Scripture.

16. Tu dirupisti fontes, et torrentes: Tu siccasti fluvios Ethan.

Thou hast broken up the fountains and the torrents : Thou hast dried up the rivers of Ethan.[1]

" *Dirupisti fontes et torrentes.*" According to Bellarmine : *Dirupta petra, fecisti scaturire fontes et torrentes.*——When Thy people passed through the desert, Thou from a dry rock broken by Moses didst cause to spring forth fountains and torrents of water.——" *Siccasti fluvios Ethan.*" Thou didst dry up the river Ethan. Bellarmine, Menochius, Lallemant, and Panigarola understand here the river Jordan ; but Mattei says that it is in vain to seek what is this river *Ethan*, and that this word is rather an adjective, which means RAPID. In fact, S. Jerome translates : *Flumina fortia* : Strong rivers. Bellarmine, Menochius, and Tirinus also give this meaning. Other interpreters, however, have preferred to leave the word as it is, untranslated, as Rotigni and Mattei remark with Bellarmine.

17. Tuus est dies, et tua est nox : tu fabricatus es auroram et solem.

Thine is the day, and the night is Thine : Thou hast made the daybreak and the sun.

" *Tuus ... nox.*" That is, Thou hast made both the day and the night.

18. Tu fecisti omnes terminos terræ : æstatem et ver tu plasmasti ea.

Thou hast set all the borders of the earth : Thou hast made the summer and the spring.

" *Æstatem et ver.*" By the summer and the spring is meant the whole year ; because anciently, say the learned, the year was divided into only two parts. In fact, according to the Hebrew, instead of " *Ver* " it is *Hyemem* : Winter.

---

[1] *Ethan*, that is strong or mighty rivers. The drying up of the Red Sea and the Jordan is mentioned in contrast with the drawing of water from the rock.

19. Memor esto hujus, inimicus improperavit Domino: et populus insipiens incitavit nomen tuum.

Remember this, the enemy hath reproached the Lord: and a foolish people hath blasphemed Thy name.

"*Hujus.*" Some refer this pronoun to what has gone before, as if the Psalmist said : O Lord, remember this, namely, these works of Thine. But others more commonly, with Bellarmine, refer it to that which follows, in this sense : Have before Thine eyes what I am about to say to Thee.

20. Ne tradas bestiis animas con-fitentes tibi: et animas pauperum tuorum ne obliviscaris in finem.

Deliver not up unto beasts the souls that confess Thee : and forget not for ever the souls of Thy poor.

Abandon not to the power of these wild beasts, as are these our enemies, the lives of those who are faithful to Thee, and forget not for ever us Thy poor servants.

21. Respice in testamentum tuum : quia repleti sunt, qui obscurati sunt terræ domibus iniquitatum.[1]

Have regard unto Thy covenant : for they that are the vile of the earth are made rich with dwellings of ini-quity.

"*Testamentum tuum.*" That is, the covenant which Thou hast made with our fathers.——"*Iniquitatum,*" *i.e., Inique.* Thus Tirinus and others here understand.——And hence this interpretation : Consider how these vile men have pos-sessed themselves unjustly of our houses and of all our property. This second part of the verse is very obscure, as Mattei and others remark.

22. Ne avertatur humilis factus confusus: pauper et inops laudabunt nomen tuum.

Let not the humble be turned away with confusion : the poor and needy shall praise Thy name.

Permit not, O Lord, that Thy people, after having been so humiliated, should be brought to confusion ; it is poor and needy ; but raised up by Thee, it will know well how to praise Thy name and to give Thee thanks.

23. Exurge Deus, judica causam tuam : memor esto improperiorum tuorum, eorum quæ ab insipiente sunt tota die.

Arise, O God, judge Thine own cause : remember Thy reproaches with which the foolish man hath reproached Thee all the day long.

"*Causam tuam.*" This cause which is not only ours, but in truth Thine own.

24. Ne obliviscaris voces inimi-corum tuorum : superbia eorum, qui te oderunt, ascendit semper.

Forget not the voices of Thine enemies : the pride of them that hate Thee riseth up continually.

"*Voces.*" The blasphemies.

---

[1] "*Qui obscurati sunt terræ.*" According to Bellarmine: "*Qui obscuri sunt in terra, viles et barbari homines*".

PSALM LXXIV.

THIS Psalm contains a prayer to God that He will hasten to succour the good and to punish the wicked. It seems to be composed in the form of a dialogue between God and His captive people. It is fitted to encourage the just and to frighten the wicked.

Unto the end, Corrupt not,[1] a Psalm of a Canticle for Asaph.

1. Confitebimur tibi Deus: confitebimur, et invocabimus nomen tuum.

We will praise Thee, O God: we will praise Thee, and we will call upon Thy name.

2. Narrabimus mirabilia tua: cum accepero tempus, ego justitias judicabo.

We will tell of Thy wondrous works: when I shall take a time, I will judge justly.

"*Cum accepero tempus.*" That is: When the fitting time shall have come. (Here it is God Who speaks.)——"*Justitias judicabo.*" That is: I will determine what is just. *Quod justum est decernam.* Thus Tirinus explains it with S. Jerome and Theodoret.

3. Liquefacta est terra, et omnes qui habitant in ea: ego confirmavi columnas ejus.

The earth is melted, and all that dwell therein: I have established the pillars thereof.

"*Liquefacta est terra.*" S. Jerome translates: *Dissolvetur terra.*——Then in the time of My vengeance the earth shall be dissolved, and all its inhabitants with it through the terror they shall feel; but I will set up again its columns, that is, its foundations or solidity.——The verse is obscure, and different interpretations are given of it.

4. Dixi iniquis: Nolite inique agere: et delinquentibus: Nolite exaltare cornu.

I said unto the wicked: Deal not wickedly: and unto the sinners: Lift not up the horn.

(Some think that God continues to speak; but Lallemant, with more probability, says that it is the Psalmist who speaks here.)——I said to the wicked: Be no longer wicked, exult not, that is, glory not in your pride.——"*Cornu.*" According to Bellarmine: *Superbiam:* Pride.

5. Nolite extollere in altum cornu vestrum: nolite loqui adversus Deum iniquitatem.

Lift not up your horn on high: speak not iniquity against God.

[1] *Corrupt not.* This is believed to have been the beginning of some ode or hymn, to the tune of which this Psalm was to be sung.

"*Cornu vestrum.*" According to the Chaldee : *Gloriam vestram:* Pride not yourselves of your glory.

6. Quia neque ab Oriente, neque ab Occidente, neque a desertis montibus : quoniam Deus judex est.	For *greatness is* neither from the East, nor from the West, nor from the desert hills : for God is the judge.

"*Neque ab Oriente . . .*" According to Bossuet and Mattei, here should be supplied : *Veniet nobis auxilium.* And thus the sense is : At the time of punishment, there shall come to you no help, neither from the East nor from the West, &c. For God Himself being the Judge, no one can hinder the execution of His judgments.——Others explain thus : In vain will you hope to fly for refuge in the East, &c., since God, Who will be your Judge, is in all places.——But the former interpretation is more common, and pleases me better.

7. Hunc humiliat, et hunc exaltat : quia calix in manu Domini vini meri plenus misto.	He putteth down one, and lifteth up another : for in the hand of the Lord there is a cup of strong wine full of mixture.

"*Veni meri plenus misto.*" Full of pure wine, that is, of justice, and also, at the same time, of mixture, that is, of pity, so as to temper justice with mercy, as says S. Jerome (*In Malach.* iii.).

8. Et inclinavit ex hoc in hoc : verumtamen fæx ejus non est exinanita : bibent omnes peccatores terræ.	And He hath poured it out from this to that : but the dregs thereof are not emptied : all the sinners of the earth shall drink.

"*Inclinavit.*" According to the Hebrew : *Effudit, propinavit.* From this cup thus tempered, the Lord pours in turn one and the other on men, giving them at one time graces, at another punishments.——"*Verumtamen fœx . . .*" But let sinners know that the dregs, that is, the bitterest part of this cup, is not entirely emptied; the wicked shall all drink of it.——Bellarmine remarks that for sinners the greater part of their pains, besides those of this life, is reserved for them at the Day of Judgment.

9. Ego autem annuntiabo in sæculum : cantabo Deo Jacob.	But I will declare for ever : I will sing to the God of Jacob.

But I will never cease from proclaiming this judgment reserved for sinners ; and I will always sing of the glories of the God of Jacob.

10. Et omnia cornua peccatorum confringam : et exaltabuntur cornua justi.	And I will break all the horns of sinners : but the horns of the just shall be exalted.

And I will ever strive to repress and break down the pride of sinners ; and will, on the other hand, publish the glory of the just, who shall be exalted.

PSALM LXXV.

THE Hebrew people praise and return thanks to God for the victory gained over their enemies. Some of the Fathers refer this Psalm to the victory obtained over the Assyrians by the defeat of the army of Sennacherib (4 *Kings* xix. 35), the title of it being in the Vulgate : *Canticum ad Assyrios.* But Grotius and Mattei think that David composed it after his victory over the Ammonites (2 *Kings* x.), and that afterwards Ezechias recited it after the defeat of the Assyrians. It may be used by Christians to thank God for having delivered them from their enemies.

Unto the end, in praises, a Psalm for Asaph : a Canticle to the Assyrians.

1. Notus in Judæa Deus : in Israel magnum nomen ejus ;

In Judea is God known : His name is great in Israel ;

2. Et factus est in pace locus ejus : et habitatio ejus in Sion.

And His place is in peace : and His abode in Sion.

"*In pace.*" According to the Hebrew : *In Salem.* The word *Salem* signifies Peace ; but here it denotes the city of Jerusalem. Lallemant, with others, has, therefore, well translated the verse : He has chosen His dwelling-place in Jerusalem, and His habitation on the mountain of Sion.

3. Ibi confregit potentias arcuum : scutum, gladium, et bellum.

There hath He broken the might of bows : the shield, the sword, and the battle.

There He has broken "the powers of the bows," that is, the bows of the hostile powers, and the shields, and the swords, and all the forces of their enemies who were making war.

4. Illuminans tu mirabiliter a montibus æternis: turbati sunt omnes insipientes corde.

Thou shinest wondrously from the everlasting hills : all the foolish of heart were troubled.

"*A montibus æternis.*" Almost all modern interpreters read according to the Hebrew : *A montibus prædæ,* or *rapinæ;* and this agrees with the translation of S. Jerome : *A montibus captivitatis.*——Whence it is thus explained : Thou, O Lord, hast caused a marvellous light to shine forth from the moun-

18

tains of plunder, that is, where our army seized on the spoils of the enemy.——" *Turbati sunt . . .*" S. Jerome's translation is: *Spoliati sunt superbi corde.* The proud remained conquered, and despoiled of everything.

5. Dormierunt somnum suum : et nihil invenerunt omnes viri divitiarum in manibus suis.	They have slept their sleep : and all the men of riches have found nothing in their hands.

These men, so proud of their power and of their riches, stricken by the sleep of death, have no longer found anything in their hands. This is the translation of Lallemant ; but, according to this sense, I should prefer to render the verse thus : To the rich of the earth, at the hour of death, all the riches they have possessed will seem like a dream, since then they will find nothing any more in their hands.——Others, however, following the Hebrew text, which, instead of " *Divitiarum,*" has " *Fortitudinis,*" explain the passage in quite a different manner, thus : They slept, and on awaking they found no strength in their hands, that is, they saw that their strength was gone.——Bossuet, quoting the translation of S. Jerome, where we read the word *Exercitus* for *Fortitudinis* or *Divitiarum,* gives still another interpretation : *Parte exercitus cæsa, et somnum mortis dormiente, reliqui, conterriti, nec pugnare potuerunt:* A part of the army being killed, the rest, seized with terror, were unable to fight any more.——For myself, I see no reason for departing from the first sense : that the word in the Hebrew text signifies *Fortitudinis* makes nothing against it ; for men of the world consider riches to be their strength : and this fully accords with the Hebrew text.

6. Ab increpatione tua Deus Jacob: dormitaverunt qui ascenderunt equos.	At Thy rebuke, O God of Jacob : they have all slumbered that mounted on horseback.

By reason of Thy wrath, or of Thy chastisement, O God of Jacob, even those were smitten with death who thought themselves the strongest, because they were mounted on horseback.

7. Tu terribilis es, et quis resistet tibi ? ex tunc ira tua.	Thou art terrible, and who shall resist Thee ? from that time is Thy wrath.

" *Ex tunc ira tua.*" According to Estius and others : *Cum ira tua fuerit commota.* When Thy anger is aroused.

8. De cœlo auditum fecisti judicium : terra tremuit et quievit,	Thou didst cause judgment to be heard from heaven : the earth trembled, and was still,

"*Judicium.*"   The sentence of punishment launched against the enemy.——"*Terra tremuit et quievit.*   The earth quaked with terror, and then at once there was calm.——But according to the Hebrew, instead of "*Quievit*" it is *Siluit.*   That is : The inhabitants of the earth trembled and kept silence through terror.

9. Cum exurgeret in judicium Deus : ut salvos faceret omnes mansuetos terræ.

When God arose to judgment : to save all the meek of the earth.

On seeing God arise to execute judgment or justice, in order to save all the meek of the earth, that is, His humble servants.

10. Quoniam cogitatio hominis confitebitur tibi : et reliquiæ cogitationis diem festum agent tibi.

For the thought of man shall give praise to Thee : and the remainders of the thoughts shall keep holyday to Thee.

This verse is obscure.   Lallemant explains it thus : Hence Thy servants who have received mercies from Thee, will never think of them, without thanking and praising Thee for them ; and the memory thereof will cause them to celebrate feasts in Thy honour.——But others more commonly, as Maldonatus, Malvenda, Grotius, Mariana, Rotigni, Mattei, &c., supported by the Hebrew text, which has a word signifying not *Cogitatio*, Thought, but *Ira*, Anger, explain it thus : For the fury of hostile man will cause us to praise Thy goodness and power, on seeing his defeat.——"*Et reliquiæ* . . . " And the remains of the enemy's fury will serve Thee for a feast, since it will move us to celebrate a festival in Thy honour, in order to praise Thee and return Thee thanks.

11. Vovete, et reddite Domino Deo vestro : omnes qui in circuitu ejus affertis munera,

Vow, and pay unto the Lord your God : bring presents, all ye that are round about Him,

Make also, out of gratitude, vows to the Lord your God, and then be faithful to fulfil them, all you who, surrounding His altar, have come to offer Him gifts.

12. Terribili et ei qui aufert spiritum principum : terribili apud reges terræ.

Unto Him that is terrible, even unto Him Who taketh away the spirit of princes : unto Him that is terrible unto the kings of the earth.

Bring gifts to this terrible God Who takes away life from princes ; or, following this translation from the Hebrew : *Coercet spiritum principum :* Who subdues the pride of princes; and Who makes Himself feared even by the kings of the earth.

PSALM LXXVI.

MANY interpreters are of opinion that this Psalm is a prayer of the people of God during their captivity at Babylon. It is suitable, as S. Augustine observes, for all who are in affliction, and who sigh to leave this land of exile and enter into their heavenly country.

Unto the end, for Idithun, a Psalm of Asaph.

1. Voce mea ad Dominum clamavi: voce mea ad Deum, et intendit mihi.

I cried unto the Lord with my voice: even unto God with my voice, and He gave ear unto me.

I cried aloud to the Lord, even to my God, and He vouchsafed to hearken to me.——"*Intendit mihi.*" The literal translation of the Hebrew is : *Aures mihi præbuit*, or, according to S. Jerome : *Exaudivit me*.

2. In die tribulationis meæ Deum exquisivi, manibus meis nocte contra eum : et non sum deceptus.

In the day of my trouble I sought God with my hands *lifted up* unto Him in the night : and I was not deceived.

3. Renuit consolari anima mea: memor fui Dei, et delectatus sum, et exercitatus sum, et defecit spiritus meus.

My soul refused to be comforted : I remembered God, and was delighted, and I mused : and my spirit swooned away.

The following is the explanation of Lallemant : My soul, plunged in sorrow, refused all consolation ; I remembered God, and this memory filled me with joy ; but the thought of my evils made me fall again into despondency.——But others, as Malvenda, Maldonatus, Rotigni, and Mattei, follow the Hebrew text, which, instead of the word "*Delectatus*," gives *Conturbatus*. S. Jerome understands it in the same sense : we read in his commentary : *Memor fui Dei, et conturbabar. Qui olim, quamvis afflictus, audito Dei nomine, respirabam, nunc, minis ejus territus divini nominis recordatione conturbor.* "I remembered God, and was troubled. I who formerly, however much afflicted when I heard the Name of God, would again breathe freely (or revive), now, terrified by His threats, am troubled at the recollection of the Divine Name."——And so, following this interpretation of S. Jerome, which seems to be the one most received, the passage is explained thus : I remembered God, and instead of being consoled by this remembrance, I was thereby still more troubled.——"*Exercitatus sum.*" S. Jerome translates thus : *Loquebar in memetipso.*

Which more clearly accords with the Hebrew. The sense, then, of this latter part of the verse is : And speaking, complaining, in myself, I remained anxious and restless through sadness, so that my spirit fainted within me.

4. Anticipaverunt vigilias oculi mei : turbatus sum, et non sum lo- cutus.

Mine eyes prevented the watches : I was troubled, and I spake not.

My eyes looked forward to the dawn, that is, I passed all the night without being able to sleep, because of the trouble I suffered, and without saying a word.

5. Cogitavi dies antiquos : et annos æternos in mente habui.

I thought upon the days of old : and I had in my mind the eternal years.

"*Annos æternos.*" S. Jerome translates : *Annos sæculorum.*—— I thought of the ancient days, and I had in my mind the ages of the past. David recalled to his memory, in order to comfort himself, the graces and favours which he had formerly received from God, and the benefits conferred upon his people.

6. Et meditatus sum nocte cum corde meo : et exercitabar, et scope- bam spiritum meum.

And I meditated in the night with mine own heart : and I mused, and searched my spirit.

"*Et meditatus sum.*" According to the Hebrew : *Recordabar cantici mei;* or, following the translation of S. Jerome : *Psalmorum meorum.* I meditated by night in my heart that time when I sang canticles ; and thus I exercised myself, and searched out my spirit, that is, I examined my conscience.—— "*Scopebam :*" I swept. S. Augustine, in his day, read : *Perscrutabar :* I searched through.

7. Numquid in æternum projiciet Deus? aut non apponet ut compla- citior sit adhuc ?

Will God then cast off for ever? or will He never more be favourable ?

"*Non apponet . . .*" Will He not give Himself to be more complacent, or, will He not show Himself more appeased and propitious ?——Such is the sense S. Jerome gives, according to the Hebrew. *Non propitiabitur ultra ?* And thus also Bellarmine, Bossuet, &c., understand it.

8. Aut in finem misericordiam suam abscindet : a generatione in generationem ?

Or will He cut off from His mercy for ever : from generation to genera- tion ?

9. Aut obliviscetur misereri Deus? aut continebit in ira sua misericordias suas ?

Or will God forget to show mercy? or will He in His anger shut up His mercies ?

" *Aut continebit . . .*"   So that, peradventure, His wrath will shut up the current of His mercies.

10. Et dixi nunc cœpi: hæc mu-   And I said, Now have I begun:
tatio dexteræ Excelsi.   this change is of the right hand of
the Most High.

"*Hæc mutatio.*"   Some understand this change in respect to God, following the translation of S. Jerome, who renders the verse thus : *Et dixi: Imbecillitas mea est hæc: Commutatio dexteræ Excelsi.*   That is : I said my weakness, or my wickedness, is the cause of the change of the right hand of the Most High, Who, from being clement, has changed, so as to become severe. —— But others, as Lallemant, with S. Augustine, understand the change to be wrought in the Psalmist, who speaks : " *Et dixi: Nunc cœpi*"; which is explained thus : I said that now I begin to breathe again by means of hope; or, according to others, I have now determined to change my life, and this change is the work of the right hand of the Most High, that is, of divine grace, *dispellentis* (writes S. Augustine) *priorem nebulam et caliginem :* of grace, which, delivering me from the cloud of darkness in which I before was, draws me to Himself with a new light.——S. Antony, the abbot, enjoined his disciples to repeat every morning, when renewing the good intention of giving themselves entirely to God, these words : " *Et dixi: Nunc cœpi*".

11. Memor fui operum Domini: I remembered the works of the
quia memor ero ab initio mirabilium   Lord : for I will be mindful of Thy
tuorum.   wonders from the beginning.

"*Quia.*"   According to the Hebrew :   *Certe, quin etiam.* And assuredly, I shall continue to remember the wonderful things which Thou, my God, hast wrought since the beginning of the world.

12. Et meditabor in omnibus operi-   And I will meditate on all Thy
bus tuis : et in adinventionibus tuis   works : and will be employed in Thy
exercebor.   doings.

"*In adinventionibus . . .*"   S. Jerome translates : *Adinventiones tuas loquar.*——And Bossuet explains the passage thus : *Sapientiæ tuæ . . . ad salutem nostram excogitata consilia.*—— I shall exercise myself in praising the loving inventions of Thy wisdom with a view to our salvation.

13. Deus in sancto via tua: quis   Thy way, O God, is in the holy
Deus magnus sicut Deus noster ? Tu   place : who is the great God like our
es Deus qui facis mirabilia.   God? Thou art the God that doest
wonders.

"*In sancto via tua.*" Bossuet : *Viœ tuœ sanctœ.* That is, following the explanation of Bellarmine : Thy designs and Thy works are always in holiness.

14. Notam fecisti in populis virtu- tem tuam : redemisti in brachio tuo populum tuum, filios Jacob et Joseph.	Thou hast made known Thy power among the nations : with Thine arm hast Thou redeemed Thy people, the children of Jacob and of Joseph.

" *Redemisti.*" Thou hast redeemed or delivered Thy people from the hand of their enemies.[1]

15. Viderunt te aquæ Deus, vide- runt te aquæ : et timuerunt, et tur- batæ sunt abyssi.	The waters saw Thee, O God, the waters saw Thee : and they were afraid, and the depths were troubled.

The waters saw Thee, O God Almighty ; they were stricken with terror, and out of reverence and awe they drew back to their abysses, that is, to their lowest depths.——Bellarmine explains this of the waters of the Red Sea, which at the command of God divided to give a passage for the Hebrews.

16. Multitudo sonitus aquarum : vocem dederunt nubes.	Great was the noise of the waters : the clouds sent out a sound.

Then there was heard a great sound, that is, the great roaring of the waves of the sea, when they rushed on the Egyptians to overwhelm them ; and the clouds also gave forth their voice, raining with fury on the enemy.

17. Etenim sagittæ tuæ transeunt: vox tonitrui tui in rota :	For Thine arrows pass by : the voice of Thy thunder in a wheel :

Lallemant translates : Thy lightnings flashed on all sides, and Thy thunderbolts broke up the wheels of the enemy's chariots.——But other interpreters render the sense better, thus : The hailstones struck like arrows, and the voice of Thy thunder, that is, the thunder made a noise like that of a

---

[1] " *Populum tuum, filios Jacob et Joseph.*" The name of Joseph is frequently found in the Psalms, with or instead of the Patriarch Jacob, as representing the entire people of God. Several reasons may be given for this : God, as well as Jacob, had a particular affection for Joseph, and preferred him to his brethren on account of his virtue : besides, the right of primogeniture, of which Ruben had rendered himself unworthy, was given to the family of Joseph (1 *Paral.* v. 1), and, in the division of the promised land, it formed two tribes instead of one, those of Ephraim and Manasses, whom Jacob (*Gen.* xlviii. 5) had adopted and raised to the rank of his own sons, in trans- ferring the birthright of Manasses to Ephraim. The tribe of Ephraim was established in the centre, and for a long time it had the privilege of possess- ing, at Silo, the Tabernacle with the Ark of the Covenant, as may be seen in the following Psalm. Moreover, Bellarmine says (*Ps.* lxxix. 1) that Joseph, who had fed the people of Israel in Egypt, was looked upon as their chief.

wheel creaking by reason of its rapid motion.——"*In rota.*"
Bossuet says : *Instar rotæ rapide discurrentis;* and thus also it
is explained by Maldonatus and Mariana.

18. Illuxerunt coruscationes tuæ   Thy lightnings lightened the world:
orbi terræ : commota est et con-   the earth shook and trembled.
tremuit terra.

Thy lightnings flashed with such dazzling brightness over
the earth, that it was convulsed and scared by them.

19. In mari via tua, et semitæ tuæ   Thy way is in the sea, and Thy
in aquis multis : et vestigia tua non   paths in many waters : and Thy foot-
cognoscentur.   steps shall not be known.

Thou hast found a way for Thyself in the sea, walking
through those great waters, as if they were beaten roads.
" *Vestigia tua . . .*"   S. Jerome, with the Chaldee : *Vestigia tua
non sunt agnita.*   Thy traces, that is, those of Thy people who
passed over dry shod, were not known by the enemy, who
remained submerged.

20. Deduxisti sicut oves populum   Thou didst lead Thy people like
tuum : in manu Moysi et Aaron.   sheep : by the hand of Moses and
                                  Aaron.

" *Deduxisti.*"   Thou didst lead safely through the desert.

PSALM LXXVII.

THIS Psalm recalls briefly all that God did in favour of His
people from the time of Moses to that of David.   In it the
Psalmist praises the goodness of the Lord, and reproaches the
ingratitude of the Hebrews.

Understanding for Asaph.

1. Attendite popule meus legem   Give ear, O My people, unto My
meam : inclinate aurem vestram in   law : incline your ears unto the words
verba oris mei.   of My mouth.

" *Legem meam.*"   My precepts, or My teaching.

2. Aperiam in parabolis os meum :   I will open My mouth in parables :
loquar propositiones ab initio.   I will utter sayings [1] from the begin-
                                   ning.

---

[1] It appears that the historical facts of ancient times, commemorated in
this Psalm, were figures of great truths appertaining to the time of the New
Testament.

"*In parabolis.*" The learned Mazzocchi (*Spicil. Bibl. in Num.* xxiii. 7) says that in Scripture the word *Parabola* is used for every sort of poetical composition; whence it is explained: I will open my mouth to sing in verse.——"*Loquar . . .*" S. Jerome translates: *Loquar ænigmata antiqua:* I will speak ancient enigmas. This agrees with *Matt.* xiii. 35, where, after quoting the first clause of this verse : "I will open My mouth in parables," the Evangelist renders the second clause thus : "I will utter things hidden from the foundation of the world ". I will declare to you the mysteries of ancient deeds, come to pass since the beginning of the world.

3. Quanta audivimus et cognovimus ea : et patres nostri narraverunt nobis.	How great things we have heard and known : and our fathers have told us.

"*Quanta audivimus.*" S. Jerome translates : *Quæ audivimus.* I will tell you what I have heard and known, and what our fathers have related to us.

4. Non sunt occultata a filiis eorum : in generatione altera.	They have not been hidden from their children : in another generation.

"*Non sunt occultata a filiis.*" According to the Hebrew : *Non occultabimus a filiis, sed generationi posteræ narrabimus.* We shall not keep this hid from their sons, but we shall announce it to the generations of posterity.

5. Narrantes laudes Domini, et virtutes ejus : et mirabilia ejus quæ fecit.	Declaring the praises of the Lord and His powers : and His wonders which He hath done.

6. Et suscitavit testimonium in Jacob : et legem posuit in Israel.	And He set up a testimony in Jacob : and made a law in Israel.

"*Et suscitavit.*" S. Jerome translates : *Statuit :* He established.——God established the covenant in Jacob, that is, among the posterity of Jacob, and placed, that is, gave His written law to the people of Israel.

7. Quanta mandavit patribus nostris nota facere ea filiis suis : ut cognoscat generatio altera.	The great things which He commanded our fathers, that they should make them known unto their children: that another generation might know them.

"*Quanta.*" According to the Hebrew : *Quæ:* Which.——"*Generatio altera.*" That is, all their posterity.

8. Filii qui nascentur, et exurgent : et narrabunt filiis suis.	The children that should be born, and should rise up : and declare them to their children.

He commanded that their children should narrate them to those who should be born.

9. Ut ponant in Deo spem suam, et non obliviscantur operum Dei : et mandata ejus exquirant.

That they may set their hope in God, and may not forget the works of God : and may seek His commandments.

" *Operum Dei.*" The works wrought by God for the good of His people.——"*Et mandata* . . ." And thus might seek with diligence to understand His commandments, in order to accomplish them.

10. Ne fiant sicut patres eorum : generatio prava et exasperans.

That they may not become like their fathers : a generation that is evil and provoking to wrath.

" *Prava et exasperans.*" According to the Hebrew : *Amara et rebellis :* Bitter and rebellious. Or, following the translation of S. Jerome : *Declinans et provocans :* Inconstant and irritating.

11. Generatio, quæ non direxit cor suum : et non est creditus cum Deo spiritus ejus.

A generation that set not their heart aright ; and whose spirit was not faithful to God.

" *Non est creditus* . . ." Whose spirit never trusted in its God. S. Jerome has : *Non credidit Deo spiritus ejus :* Believed not God.

12. Filii Ephrem intendentes et mittentes arcum : conversi sunt in die belli.

The sons of Ephraim who bend and shoot with the bow : have turned back in the day of battle.

" *Filii Ephrem* . . ." Those of the tribe of Ephraim,[1] so skilled in drawing the bow.

13. Non custodierunt testamentum Dei : et in lege ejus noluerunt ambulare.

They kept not the covenant of God : and would not walk in His law.

14. Et obliti sunt benefactorum ejus : et mirabilium ejus, quæ ostendit eis.

And they forgot His benefits : and His wonders that He had showed them.

[1] Bellarmine adds here a useful remark : David, in mentioning the tribe of Ephraim, means all the Israelites : it was the most powerful after the tribe of Juda, and in holy Scripture most frequently reproaches are addressed to the tribe of Ephraim, and praises to the tribe of Juda. Hence it is that the afflictions of the entire people are represented under the name of Ephraim rather than of the other tribes ; and, towards the end of this Psalm, vv. 73, 74, the tribe of Juda is chosen in preference to that of Ephraim. See the Prophet Osee.——Moreover, in the tribe of Ephraim was situated the town of Silo, which for a long time had the privilege of possessing the holy Tabernacle, a favour of which it was afterwards deprived, as is related v. 66. (See note to preceding Psalm, v. 14.)

15. Coram patribus eorum fecit mirabilia in terra Ægypti : in campo Taneos.

Wonderful things did He in the sight of their fathers : in the land of Egypt, in the field of Tanis.

"*Taneos.*"   Tanis, the capital city of Lower Egypt (Menochius).

16. Interrupit mare, et perduxit eos : et statuit aquas quasi in utre.

He divided the sea, and brought them through : and He made the waters to stand as in a vessel.

"*Quasi in utre.*" According to the Hebrew and S. Jerome : *Quasi cumulum ; Quasi acervum* : Piled up high in a heap.

17. Et deduxit eos in nube diei : et tota nocte in illuminatione ignis.

He led them also with a cloud by day : and all the night with a light of fire.

"*Diei.*"   "*In illuminatione.*"   S. Jerome, according to the Hebrew, translates : *Per diem. In lumine ignis.* "And the Lord went before them, to show the way by day in a pillar of cloud, and by night in a pillar of fire " (*Exod.* xiii. 21).

18. Interrupit petram in eremo : et adaquavit eos velut in abysso multa.

He burst open the rock in the wilderness : and gave them to drink, as out of the great deep.

He broke in twain a rock in the desert.——"*Adaquavit.*" According to the Hebrew : *Potum dedit.*——"*Velut in . . .*" He made flow from it an abyss, that is, a great torrent of water.   In the words of Menochius : As though they were on the bank of a very deep river.[1]

19. Et eduxit aquam de petra : et deduxit tamquam flumina aquas.

He brought forth water out of the rock : and made streams to run down as rivers.

20. Et apposuerunt adhuc peccare ei : in iram excitaverunt Excelsum in inaquoso.

And they added yet more sin against Him : they provoked the Most High to wrath in the place without water.

"*Apposuerunt adhuc peccare.*" According to the Hebrew : *Iterum peccaverunt*, or, as S. Jerome translates : *Addiderunt ultra peccare.*——"*In inaquoso.*" According to the Chaldee : *In arido deserto.*——And yet they went on to sin still more against God, and provoked the Most High to wrath, in that arid desert.

21. Et tentaverunt Deum in cordibus suis : ut peterent escas animabus suis.

And they tempted God in their hearts : by asking meat for their desires.

---

[1] Allusion to the first miracle of the water drawn from the rock (*Exod.* xvii.).

In the *Invitatorium*, *Ps.* xciv. v. 14, is explained what we read here. The Hebrews, in asking of God for bread and flesh in the midst of the desert (*Exod.* xvi. 3 ; *Numb.* xi. 4), wished to tempt Him, in order to see by this experiment if He were really able to provide for them with such food in a place deprived of everything.

22. Et male locuti sunt de Deo: dixerunt, Numquid poterit Deus parare mensam in deserto?

And they spake ill of God : they said, Can God furnish a table in the wilderness?

"*Parare mensam.*"   Prepare for us a table such as we desire.

23. Quoniam percussit petram, et fluxerunt aquæ : et torrentes inundaverunt.

Because He struck the rock, and the waters gushed out: and the streams overflowed.

24. Numquid et panem poterit dare : aut parare mensam populo suo?

Can He also give bread : or provide a table for His people ?

25. Ideo audivit Dominus, et distulit : et ignis accensus est in Jacob, et ira ascendit in Israel.

Therefore the Lord heard, and was angry : and a fire was kindled against Jacob, and wrath came up against Israel.

"*Distulit.*"   Mattei interprets : *Distulit implere :* Delayed to fulfil His promises.   But it appears to me better to say : He suspended the course of His benefits to those ungrateful men.——"*Jacob.*"   "*Israel.*"   The posterity, or people of Israel.

26. Quia non crediderunt in Deo: nec speraverunt in salutari ejus :

Because they believed not in God : and trusted not in His salvation :

27. Et mandavit nubibus desuper: et januas cœli aperuit.

And He commanded the clouds from above : and opened the doors of heaven.

"*Januas cœli aperuit.*"   This is said to show the abundance of manna that came down from heaven.

28. Et pluit illis manna ad manducandum : et panem cœli dedit eis.

And rained down manna upon them to eat ; and gave them the bread of heaven.

29. Panem Angelorum manducavit homo : cibaria misit eis in abundantia.

Man did eat the bread of Angels : He sent them food in abundance.

28, 29.   "*Manna.*"   Bellarmine observes that this name comes from the wonder excited in the people when they saw the earth covered with this extraordinary food, spread over the ground like hoar-frost, and said to one another : *Man Hu,* which signifies : What is this ! (*Exod.* xvi. 14, 15). He adds that manna was like the seed of the coriander.——"*Panem Cœli.*" Manna is thus called, because it came from heaven or from the atmosphere.——"*Panem Angelorum.*" Because it was formed by the operation of the Angels.

30. Transtulit Austrum de cœlo: et induxit in virtute sua Africum.	He withdrew the south wind from heaven : and by His power He brought in the south-west wind.

Lallemant translates thus : The Lord caused to cease the Auster or east wind, and made to blow in its place the Africus or south wind. But Bellarmine remarks that the east wind, Auster (or Eurus), denoted in the Hebrew text is not opposed to the Africus, but is rather next to and united with it ; hence Theodoret, Euthymius, and others do not give to the word *Transtulit* the sense of *Cessare fecit :* Made to cease ; but that of *Flare jussit*, commanded to blow ; as though it were said, following the explanation of S. Augustine : *Transtulit de cœlesti thesauro et emisit in terram :* He brought out, or transferred, from His heavenly store the east wind, and by His power He sent forth the south wind : and thus God ordained that these two winds together should bring the quails in the wilderness.

31. Et pluit super eos sicut pulverem carnes : et sicut arenam maris volatilia pennata.	He rained flesh also upon them as dust : and feathered fowls like as the sand of the sea.

32. Et ceciderunt in medio castrorum eorum : circa tabernacula eorum.	And they fell in the midst of their camp : round about their tents.

33. Et manducaverunt et saturati sunt nimis, et desiderium eorum attulit eis : non sunt fraudati a desiderio suo.	So they did eat, and were filled exceedingly, and He gave them their desire : they were not defrauded of that which they craved.

34. Adhuc escæ eorum erant in ore ipsorum : et ira Dei ascendit super eos.	As yet their meat was in their mouth : and the wrath of God came upon them.

"*Ascendit.*" Arose : the same expression as in verse 25. When the fire of anger is great, its flame rises on high.

35. Et occidit pingues eorum : et electos Israel impedivit.	And He slew the fat ones amongst them : and brought down the chosen men of Israel.

"*Pingues eorum.*" Bellarmine understands by this : The most voluptuous ; Lallemant : The strongest.——"*Electos Israel impedivit.*" This means, according to Lallemant, that He struck with death the choice or the pick of their youth ;

and according to Bellarmine, that the strongest amongst them were by God prevented from escaping death.

36. In omnibus his peccaverunt adhuc : et non crediderunt in mirabilibus ejus.

In all these things they sinned still : and they believed not for His wondrous works.

With all these punishments they did not cease from sin ; nor could such wonders induce them to fear the Lord and trust in Him.

37. Et defecerunt in vanitate dies eorum : et anni eorum cum festinatione.

And their days were consumed in vanity, and their years in haste.

And thus they consumed uselessly their days in the desert ; and their years were shortened.

38. Cum occideret eos, quærebant eum : et revertebantur, et diluculo veniebant ad eum.

When He slew them, then they sought Him : and they returned, and came to Him early in the morning.

" *Veniebant ad eum.*" They went to find Him, imploring pity.

39. Et rememorati sunt quia Deus adjutor est eorum : et Deus excelsus redemptor eorum est.

And they remembered that God was their helper : and the Most High God their redeemer.

And then they remembered the helps that God had given them, and the evils from which He had delivered them.

40. Et dilexerunt eum in ore suo : et lingua sua mentiti sunt ei :

And they loved Him with their mouth : and with their tongue they lied unto Him :

And they promised to love Him with their mouth ; but they were liars to God in what they had promised Him with their tongue.

41. Cor autem eorum non erat rectum cum eo : nec fideles habiti sunt in testamento ejus.

But their heart was not right with Him : nor were they faithful in His covenant.

42. Ipse autem est misericors, et propitius fiet peccatis eorum : et non disperdet eos.

But He is merciful, and will forgive their sins : and will not destroy them.

Nevertheless He willed to show them pity, and to have compassion on their sins, and He would not utterly destroy His people as they deserved.

43. Et abundavit ut averteret iram suam : et non accendit omnem iram suam :

Yea, many a time did He turn away His anger : and did not kindle all His wrath :

He willed to abound in mercy, turning aside, that is, moderating, and not enkindling all His wrath as their sins deserved.

44. Et recordatus est quia caro sunt: spiritus vadens, et non rediens.

And He remembered that they are flesh: a wind that goeth and returneth not.

God remembers, that is, He considers that these sinners are men of flesh, infirm and weak ; whose life is as a passing wind that lasts but a short time, which comes and goes but does not return.——Thus the young man passes on to old age, but does not return to youth.

45. Quoties exacerbaverunt eum in deserto: in iram concitaverunt eum in inaquoso ?

How often did they provoke Him in the desert: and move Him to wrath in the place without water ?

"*In inaquoso.*" When thirsty in that place, without water.

46. Et conversi sunt, et tentaverunt Deum: et sanctum Israel exacerbaverunt.

And they turned back and tempted God: and angered the Holy One of Israel.

And scarcely were they converted to Him when they returned to tempt Him ; and embittered anew this Holy God of Israel.

47. Non sunt recordati manus ejus: die qua redemit eos de manu tribulantis :

They remembered not His hand in the day: that He redeemed them from the hand of him that afflicted them :

"*De manu tribulantis.*" From the hand of their enemy, Pharao, who oppressed them.

48. Sicut posuit in Ægypto signa sua: et prodigia sua in campo Taneos :

How He wrought His signs in Egpyt: and His wonders in the field of Tanis :

They did not call to mind the prodigies wrought by God in Egypt, and especially in the field of Tanis (see verse 15).

49. Et convertit in sanguinem flumina eorum : et imbres eorum, ne biberent.

And He turned their rivers into blood: and their showers, that they might not drink.

"*In sanguinem.*" Into the colour of blood ; so that they had a horror of drinking thereof.——"*Flumina.*" Bellarmine says that by these rivers are to be understood the different branches of the Nile which run through Egypt.——"*Imbres.*" This properly is not rain, of which there is hardly any in that country, but every sort of water, especially the overflowing of the Nile.

50. Misit in eos cœnomyiam, et comedit eos : et ranam, et disperdidit eos.

He sent divers sorts of flies among them which devoured them : and frogs which destroyed them.

He sent upon them a multitude of flies, by which they were, so to say, eaten up ; and of frogs that devoured every-thing.——" Cœnomyiam." It is a question if this should be written Cœnomyia, the common fly ; or Cynomia, the dog-fly. The Vulgate has the first, but the Greek more commonly pre-fers the second : S. Jerome varies.

51. Et dedit ærugini fructus eorum: et labores eorum locustæ.

And He gave up their fruits unto the blast : and their labours unto the locust.

" Ærugini." Caterpillars and locusts, according to S. Jerome's explanation, devour the herbs like rust or mildew.

52. Et occidit in grandine vineas eorum : et moros eorum in pruina.

He destroyed also their vineyards with hail : and their mulberry-trees with hoar-frost.

" Moros." S. Jerome translates : Sycomoros, and S. Gregory (Mor. l. xxvii. c. 27) makes the remark : Sycomorus quippe ficus fatua dicitur : The word Sycamore etymologically meaning a foolish fig.——" Pruina." Mattei says that the Hebrew word signifies here great hail-stones.

53. Et tradidit grandini jumenta eorum : et possessionem eorum igni.

And He gave up their cattle unto the hail : and their substance unto the fire.

" Igni." By this fire, Mattei understands, with probability, frost ; which also burns the fields. He does this to avoid in-troducing another plague of Egypt, that of fire, of which Moses makes no mention.[1]

54. Misit in eos iram indignationis suæ : indignationem, et iram, et tri-bulationem : immissiones per angelos malos.

He sent upon them the fierceness of His anger ; indignation and wrath and trouble, which He sent by evil angels.

" Angelos malos." Made the executors of His divine ven-geance.

[1] We must, on the other hand, bear in mind what is written of the Seventh Plague : "The Lord sent thunder and hail, and lightning running along the ground.... And the hail and fire mixt with it drove on together" (Exod. ix. 23, 24). And yet more explicitly elsewhere : "The wicked ... were scourged ... by hail ... and consumed by fire. And which was wonder-ful, in water, which extinguisheth all things, the fire had more force.... The fire above its own power, burnt in the midst of water, to destroy the fruits of a wicked land.... Snow and ice endured the force of fire, and melted not, that they might know that fire burning in the hail, and flashing in the rain, destroyed the fruits of the enemies" (Wisdom xvi. 16-22).—Tr.

55. Viam fecit semitæ iræ suæ, non pepercit a morte animabus eorum: et jumenta eorum in morte conclusit. — He made a way for His anger: He spared not their souls from death; and their cattle he shut up in death.

Mattei translates: He opened the gates of His wrath, neither sparing their own lives, nor those of their cattle.

56. Et percussit omne primogenitum in terra Ægypti: primitias omnis laboris eorum in tabernaculis Cham. — He smote also all the first-born in the land of Egypt: the first-fruits of all their labour in the tents of Cham.

He moreover struck with death in the houses of Egypt all the first-born, who were the first-fruits of their labours. "*Primitias omnis laboris eorum.*" Men labour hard to bring up their first-born, and for this reason these are called the first-fruits of their labours.——"*In tabernaculis Cham.*" It was the descendants of Cham, son of Nöe, who peopled Egypt after the deluge.

57. Et abstulit sicut oves populum suum: et perduxit eos tamquam gregem in deserto. — And He took away His own people as sheep: and guided them in the wilderness like a flock.

"*Et abstulit.*" And thus God delivered His people.

58. Et deduxit eos in spe, et non timuerunt: et inimicos eorum operuit mare. — And He brought them out in hope, and they feared not: and the sea overwhelmed their enemies.

And He led the Israelites full of confidence and without fear, because their enemies were now sunk in the Red Sea; and thus their slavery was at an end.

59. Et induxit eos in montem sanctificationis suæ: montem, quem acquisivit dextera ejus. — He brought them also into the mountain of His sanctuary: the mountain which His right hand had purchased.

"*In montem sanctificationis suæ.*" This, as Bellarmine explains, signifies the Promised Land; a mountain, that is, a mountainous land, which God had chosen for Himself to be there honoured by His people; a mountain, or land, which He had acquired by His own right hand; having wrought so many miracles to help the Israelites in conquering and driving out the idolaters who inhabited it.

60. Et ejecit a facie eorum Gentes: et sorte divisit eis terram in funiculo distributionis. — And He cast out the heathen before them: and by lot divided unto them the land by a line of distribution.

"*Gentes.*" The hostile nations, or the Chanaanites, who inhabited the land.——"*In funiculo distributionis.*" The lands were measured with cords, according to the custom of those

19

times, to be then distributed by lots to the families of the
Israelites.

61. Et habitare fecit in taber-   And He made the tribes of Israel
naculis eorum : tribus Israel.   to dwell in their tents.

And He made the tribes of Israel to inhabit the dwelling-
places of their enemies.

62. Et tentaverunt, et exacerba-   Yet they tempted and provoked
verunt Deum excelsum : et testimonia   the Most High God : and they kept
ejus non custodierunt.   not His testimonies.

But, ungrateful that they were, they did not leave off tempting God and provoking His anger by their disobedience.

63. Et averterunt se, et non ser-   And they turned away, and kept
vaverunt pactum : quemadmodum   not the covenant : even like their
patres eorum, conversi sunt in arcum   fathers they were turned aside as a
pravum.   crooked bow.

64. In iram concitaverunt eum in   They provoked Him to anger on
collibus suis : et in sculptilibus suis   their hills : and moved Him to
ad æmulationem eum provocaverunt.   jealousy with their graven things.

So that on these hills of the Lord, destined for His worship,
they provoked His wrath, setting Him aside for the idols,
which they adore and place on an equality with Himself.

65. Audivit Deos, et sprevit : et   God heard, and despised *them :* and
ad nihilum redegit valde Israel.   He reduced Israel exceedingly *as it*
                                            were to nothing.

God heard the insults that they committed against Him,
and being very wrath He despised and brought Israel to
nought.

66. Et repulit tabernaculum Silo :   And he put away the tabernacle of
tabernaculum suum ubi habitavit in   Silo : His tabernacle where He dwelt
hominibus.   among men.

" *Silo.*"   A town of the tribe of Ephraim, where abode for
some time the Ark of the Covenant, which God caused to be
made in the wilderness, and where the Lord in some sense
dwelt amongst men ; since it was from thence He gave to
them His answers.

67. Et tradidit in captivitatem   And He delivered their strength
virtutem eorum : et pulchritudinem   into captivity : and their beauty into
eorum in manus inimici.   the hands of the enemy.

" *Virtutem eorum et pulchritudinem eorum.*"   The strength
and the glory of the people of Israel was the holy Ark, as
Menochius, Lallemant, and Bossuet, with S. Augustine, explain:
God permitted that it should become the spoil of the enemy,
viz., of the Philistines.

68. Et conclusit in gladio populum | And He shut up His people under
suum : et hereditatem suam sprevit. | the sword : and He despised His inheritance.

He suffered moreover that His people should be encompassed on all sides by the swords of their enemies ; and thus
He had to despise that people whom He had chosen as His
heritage, that is, to be to Him a peculiar and special people.

69. Juvenes eorum comedit ignis : | Fire consumed their young men :
et virgines eorum non sunt lamentatæ. | and their maidens lamented not.

" *Ignis.*" The fire of war, or rather of the divine wrath.——
" *Lamentatæ.*" Some explain this word in an active sense ;
but Bellarmine, Lallemant, and Mattei think, with more
reason, that it should be taken in the passive sense : thus the
meaning is : After the death of the young men, the young
maidens whom they were to marry had no one to lament
their sad lot ; because in the general massacre every one had
to bewail the losses in his own family, rather than those of
others ; and this explanation agrees well with the Hebrew
text, which S. Jerome renders thus : *Virgines ejus (populi)
nemo luxit :* No one mourned the virgins of the people.

70. Sacerdotes eorum in gladio | Their priests fell by the sword :
ceciderunt : et viduæ eorum non | and their widows did not mourn.
plorabantur.

" *Sacerdotes eorum.*" Ophni and Phinees, the two sons of
Heli who fell in the same slaughter (1 *Kings* iv. 2).——
" *Non plorabantur.*" S. Jerome translates : *Non sunt fletæ.*
None consoled nor even pitied them, because all were occupied
with weeping the death of their own relations.

71. Et excitatus est tamquam | And the Lord was awakened as
dormiens Dominus : tamquam potens | one out of sleep: and like a mighty
crapulatus a vino. | man that had been surfeited with wine.

But at length the Lord awoke, as wakes up a strong warrior
who, heavy with wine, has fallen into a deep sleep.——This is
the interpretation given by Bellarmine, Menochius, Gordona,
and Lallemant : they say that God, when He does not punish
the wicked, seems to sleep a deep sleep.——But Mattei justly
remarks that the parallel of a drunken man waking up from
sleep is ill becoming to God ; and he adds that the verse
contains not one but two similies ; the first is that of the
awaking: " *Excitatus tamquam dormiens* " ; the second is that
of the return God makes against His enemies, like a mighty
warrior, strengthened and whetted for fight by the wine

he has taken : *Tamquam potens miles exhilaratus a vino* ; and this agrees with the Hebrew text, which is rendered by : *Ovans* or *Exhilaratus:* Cheered or Refreshed, instead of " *Crapulatus.*"

72. Et percussit inimicos suos in posteriora : opprobrium sempiternum dedit illis.

And He smote His enemies on the hinder parts : He put them to a perpetual shame.

" *Inimicos.*" The Philistines.——" *In posteriora.*" That is : *In secretiori parte natium* (1 *Kings* v. 6). God punished their pride by sores so disgraceful, that they were a perpetual cause of shame to them.

73. Et repulit tabernaculum Joseph : et tribum Ephraim non elegit :

And He cast aside the tabernacle of Joseph : and chose not the tribe of Ephraim :

74. Sed elegit tribum Juda : montem Sion quem dilexit.

But He chose the tribe of Juda : the Mount Sion which He loved.

73, 74. " *Tabernaculum Joseph.*" That is, the Tabernacle containing the Ark of the Covenant, and which was at Silo, a city of the tribe of Ephraim, son of Joseph.[1]——" *Elegit tribum Juda* ... " He chose the tribe of Juda, to establish there His Tabernacle, and Mount Sion, which He loved, preferring it to all other places in Juda.

75. Et ædificavit sicut unicornium sanctificium suum in terra : quam fundavit in sæcula.

And He built His sanctuary as of unicorns : in the land which He founded for ever.

And on this Mount Sion, that is, at Jerusalem, a land that He established to last for ever, He hath built His chosen Sanctuary, firm and strong as the horn of the unicorn.—— Bellarmine says that Jerusalem, which was afterwards destroyed, is here a figure of the Church, which is to endure until the end of the world. Mattei adds that Mount Sion was compared to the unicorn because upon it was the Temple, which was the one only temple of Judæa.

76. Et elegit David servum suum, et sustulit eum de gregibus ovium : de post fœtantes accepit eum.

He chose David also His servant, and took him from the flocks of sheep : He brought him from following the ewes great with young.

77. Pascere Jacob servum suum : et Israel hereditatem suam :

To feed Jacob His servant ; and Israel His inheritance :

[1] See notes to verses 12 and 66.

76, 77. God took David from the humble condition of a shepherd, to place in his hand the royal sceptre and the government of His people, composed of the children of His servant Jacob.

| 78. Et pavit eos in innocentia cordis sui: et in intellectibus manuum suarum deduxit eos. | And he fed them in the innocence of his heart: and guided them by the skilfulness of his hands. |

And David governed this people with a right heart, and directed them with counsel and prudence in all the works which he did for their good.[1]

PSALM LXXVIII.

THE Psalmist describes the miserable state of the Jewish people, during the persecution of Antiochus Epiphanes, in the time of the Machabees. This is to be gathered from the First Book of the Machabees, the author of which quotes the second verse of this Psalm as a prophecy then accomplished (1 *Mach.* vii. 17). But S. Augustine applies it to the persecutions which the Church had to suffer under the pagan emperors.

A Psalm for Asaph.

| 1. Deus, venerunt Gentes in hereditatem tuam, polluerunt templum sanctum tuum: posuerunt Jerusalem in pomorum custodiam. | O God, the heathen are come into Thine inheritance, they have defiled Thy holy temple: they have made Jerusalem as a place to keep fruit. |

"*In hereditatem tuam.*" Against Thy people, which is Thy inheritance.——"*In pomorum custodiam.*" As though it were a hut of straw, or a peasant's shed put up for keeping the fruit of an orchard. But S. Jerome translates the Hebrew here : *In acervos lapidum.* They have made of it heaps of stones. In the First Book of Machabees we read as follows : " He took the spoils of the city and burnt it with fire, and threw down the houses thereof, and the walls thereof round about. ... And Jerusalem was not inhabited, but was like a desert." (1 *Mach.* i. 33, iii. 45.)

| 2. Posuerunt morticina servorum tuorum, escas volatilibus cœli: carnes sanctorum tuorum bestiis terræ. | The dead bodies of Thy servants have they given to be meat unto the fowls of the air: the flesh of Thy saints unto the beasts of the earth. |

[1] Bellarmine observes that this eulogium is applicable to David only in a limited sense; but it is perfectly verified in Him of Whom David was the figure, Jesus Christ, the King of future ages and the Good Shepherd of the flock of His faithful.

3. Effuderunt sanguinem eorum tamquam aquam in circuitu Jerusalem : et non erat qui sepeliret.

Their blood have they shed like water, round about Jerusalem : and there was no man to bury them.

4. Facti sumus opprobrium vicinis nostris : subsannatio et illusio his, qui in circuitu nostro sunt.

We are become a reproach unto our neighbours : a scorn and derision unto them that are round about us.

"*Qui in circuitu nostro sunt.*" Namely, the Moabites, the Edomites, the Ammonites, and other Gentiles.

5. Usquequo Domine irasceris in finem : accendetur velut ignis zelus tuus ?

How long, O Lord, wilt Thou be angry for ever : shall Thy jealousy be kindled like a fire ?

"*In finem.*" According to the Hebrew and the Chaldee : *In perpetuum.*——"*Zelus.*" Tirinus explains this to be, Indignation.——"*Velut ignis.*" Like fire which is not extinguished till it has reduced everything to ashes, says Bellarmine : *Qui crescere solet in immensum, et in cinerem omnia redigere.*

6. Effunde iram tuam in Gentes, quæ te non noverunt : et in regna quæ nomen tuum non invocaverunt :

Pour out Thy wrath upon the nations that have not known Thee : and upon the kingdoms that have not called upon Thy name :

"*Effunde . . . noverunt.*" Rather pour out anger on those Gentiles who have not been willing to know Thee.

7. Quia comederunt Jacob : et locum ejus desolaverunt.

For they have devoured Jacob : and have laid waste his dwelling-place.

"*Jacob.*" The children of Jacob, that is, Thy people.——
"*Locum ejus.*" Their country ; or, according to the Hebrew, their Temple.

8. Ne memineris iniquitatum nostrarum antiquarum, cito anticipent nos misericordiæ tuæ : quia pauperes facti sumus nimis.

O remember not our former iniquities : let Thy mercies speedily prevent us, for we are become exceeding poor.

"*Ne . . . antiquarum.*" Bellarmine thus explains : Punish us not for the old faults we have committed, and for our fathers' sins.——"*Anticipent . . . tuæ.*" Rather prevent by Thy mercy the ruin with which our enemies threaten us.

9. Adjuva nos Deus salutaris noster : et propter gloriam nominis tui Domine libera nos : et propitius esto peccatis nostris, propter nomen tuum :

Help us, O God our Saviour : and for the glory of Thy name, O Lord, deliver us : and forgive us our sins for Thy name's sake :

"*Salutaris noster.*" According to the Hebrew : *Salutis*

nostræ : O God of our salvation.——"*Propter gloriam nominis tui ... propter nomen tuum.*" Not for our merits, but for the glory of Thy name.——"*Libera nos.*" Deliver us from the miseries in which we are.——"*Propitius esto peccatis nostris.*" Pardon us our sins which have drawn this persecution upon us.

10. Ne forte dicant in Gentibus : ubi est Deus eorum ? et innotescat in nationibus coram oculis nostris,	Lest they should say among the heathen : Where is their God ? And let Him be made known among the nations before our eyes,

11. Ultio sanguinis servorum tu-orum, qui effusus est : introeat in conspectu tuo gemitus compeditorum.	By the revenging the blood of Thy servants, which hath been shed : O let the sighing of the prisoners come in before Thee.

10, 11. "*Deus eorum.*" Their God in Whom they so much trusted.——"*Innotescat ... servorum tuorum.*" Let Thy justice be manifest to all, by avenging the blood of Thy servants.

12. Secundum magnitudinem bra-chii tui : posside filios mortificatorum.	According to the greatness of Thine arm : preserve the children of them that have been put to death.

"*Posside filios.*" Preserve the children who have escaped from the slaughter.

13. Et redde vicinis nostris septu-plum in sinu eorum : improperium ipsorum, quod exprobraverunt tibi Domine.	And render unto our neighbours sevenfold into their bosom : the reproach wherewith they have re-proached Thee, O Lord.

"*Vicinis nostris.*" These enemies who are neighbouring to us. Some think these are the Edomites and Philistines ; some others, as Bellarmine, those who brought ruin on Jerusalem under Antiochus, king of Syria.——"*Septuplum in sinu eorum.*" Sevenfold, or many times as much, or simply the double, expressing a full and complete retribution in the centre of their hearts for all the reproaches which they have uttered against the Lord.

14. Nos autem, populus tuus, et oves pascuæ tuæ : confitebimur tibi in sæculum :	But we, Thy people, and the sheep of Thy pasture : will give thanks unto Thee for ever :

15. In generationem et genera-tionem : annuntiabimus laudem tuam.	We will show forth Thy praise : unto generation and generation.

PSALM LXXIX.

IN the literal sense, prayers of the Jewish captives in Babylon
to obtain their deliverance, and in the mystical sense, supplications of the faithful under the Old Law, begging God to
send speedily the Messias to deliver them from the slavery of
hell.

Unto the end, for them that shall be changed, a testimony for Asaph, a
Psalm.

1. Qui regis Israel, intende: qui   Give ear, O Thou that rulest
deducis velut ovem Joseph.   Israel: Thou that leadest Joseph
                     like a sheep.

"*Qui regis Israel.*" According to the Hebrew: *O Pastor
Israel*, or according to S. Jerome: *Qui pascis Israel.* O God
Who, as a shepherd, rulest and feedest the people of Israel.
——"*Intende.*" S. Jerome translates: *Ausculta:* Hear Thou
Who guidest as Thy flock the posterity of Joseph.——"*Ovem.*"
The Hebrew word, though singular, denotes a multitude, as
Menochius remarks.——"*Joseph.*" Menochius and Tirinus
give the reasons why, under the name of Joseph, are comprised
all the Israelites, descendants of Joseph and of his brethren.
(See *Ps.* lxxvi. v. 14.)

2. Qui sedes super Cherubim: Thou that sittest upon the cheru-
manifestare coram Ephraim, Benja-   bim: shine forth before Ephraim,
min, et Manasse.   Benjamin, and Manasses.

"*Qui ... Cherubim.*" That is: Thou to whom the first
Angels of heaven serve as a throne.——"*Manifestare.*" According to the Hebrew: *Splende, Inclaresce.* Make Thy power
to brilliantly shine forth.——"*Coram ...*" By these three
tribes are meant the whole people of Israel, according to the
explanation of Bellarmine and other authors.

3. Excita potentiam tuam, et veni: Stir up Thy might: and come and
ut salvos facias nos.   save us.

"*Excita potentiam tuam.*" S. Jerome translates: *Suscita
fortitudinem tuam:* Raise up, awake Thy power, O Lord; for,
as Bellarmine explains, it seems to be asleep, when Thou permittest our enemies to afflict us in this way; awaken it, then,
by coming to save us and delivering us from this captivity.

4. Deus converte nos: et ostende   Convert us, O God: and show us
faciem tuam, et salvi erimus.   Thy face, and we shall be saved.

"*Converte nos.*" According to the Hebrew : *Reduc nos:* Make us, O God of might, to recover our liberty ; look upon us with a joyous, benign countenance, and we shall be saved. This verse is well rendered thus by Mattei :

"Signor, da queste carceri,
  Deh per pietà richiamaci ;
Un sol tuo sguardo bastaci,
E sarem salvi e liberi."

Ah ! from these prisons forth,
  O Lord,
In pity lead us, home restored ;
Enough, one gracious look from
  Thee,
To save and set us captives free.

5. Domine Deus virtutum : quousque irasceris super orationem servi tui ?

O Lord God of hosts : how long wilt Thou be angry against the prayer of Thy servant ?

"*Servi tui.*" That is, Of Thy people : as Bossuet and others explain with S. Jerome.

6. Cibabis nos pane lacrymarum : et potum dabis nobis in lacrymis in mensura ?

How long wilt Thou feed us with the bread of weeping : and mete out to us tears for drink ?

How long wilt Thou feed us with tears instead of bread ? and wilt Thou give us of these same tears drink even to over-flowing ?——Bellarmine says that some misunderstand the phrase : "*In mensura,*" as though it meant : With moderation ; for the Hebrew word here means something great and multi-plied, that is, in very full measure.

7. Posuisti nos in contradictionem vicinis nostris : et inimici nostri sub-sannaverunt nos.

Thou hast made us to be a strife unto our neighbours : and our enemies have scoffed at us.

Thou hast exposed us to the insults of the nations round about us, so that we are become the mockery of our enemies.

8. Deus virtutum converte nos : et ostende faciem tuam, et salvi erimus.

O God of hosts, convert us : and show Thy face, and we shall be saved.

Repetition of verse 4.

9. Vineam de Ægypto transtulisti: ejecisti Gentes, et plantasti eam.

Thou hast brought a vine out of Egypt : Thou hast cast out the heathen, and planted it.

Thou hast brought Thy vine, *i.e.,* us Thy people, out of Egypt into the Land of Promise, after having driven therefrom the Gentiles ; and there Thou hast planted it, that is to say, the Synagogue, which is already the figure of the Christian Church.

10. Dux itineris fuisti in conspectu ejus: plantasti radices ejus, et implevit terram.

Thou didst go before it on the way: Thou plantedst the roots thereof, and it filled the land.

Lallemant translates thus : Thou didst convoy (wert conductor of) this vine in the journey, without ever losing sight of it.——But others more commonly continue the allegory, following the sense of the Hebrew text, viz., *Præparasti locum coram eu ;* or according to S. Jerome : *Præparasti ante faciem ejus.* Hence they translate : Thou hast prepared this land for this vine.——*Plantasti radices,* &c. : And Thou hast caused it to take such good root, that it has filled all this land.

11. Operuit montes umbra ejus : et arbusta ejus cedros Dei.[1]

The shadow of it covered the hills: and the branches thereof the cedars of God.

12. Extendit palmites suos usque ad mare : et usque ad flumen propagines ejus.

It stretched forth its shoots unto the sea : and its boughs unto the river.

11, 12. This vine (that is, the Church), has increased so greatly, that its shadow has covered the mountains, and its stems have reached as high as the cedars of Lebanon——" *Cedros Dei.*" Meaning the most lofty cedars, as were those of Lebanon.—— "*Mare.*" The Mediterranean.——"*Flumen.*" The Euphrates. ——These are the explanations of Bellarmine, Lallemant, and others.

13. Ut quid destruxisti maceriam ejus: et vindemiant eam omnes, qui prætergrediuntur viam ?

Why hast Thou broken down the hedge thereof : so that all they who pass by the way do pluck it?

14. Exterminavit eam aper de silva : et singularis ferus depastus est eam.

The boar out of the wood hath laid it waste : and a solitary wild beast hath devoured it.

" *Aper de silva.*" Euthymius, Bellarmine, Malvenda, Mattei, and others understand by the wild boar Nabuchodonosor ; and allegorically, according to S. Jerome, it is the devil.—— "*Singularis ferus.*" Bellarmine, Mattei, and others say that hereby, according to the Hebrew phrase, is meant the same wild boar.

15. Deus virtutum convertere : respice de cœlo, et vide, et visita vineam istam :

Turn Thee again, O God of hosts : look down from heaven, and see, and visit this vine :

" *Vide et . . .*" Consider our miseries, and visit with Thy compassion this vine thus brought to ruin.

---

[1] " *Arbusta.*" S. Jerome translates : *Rami :* Its branches.

16. Et perfice eam, quam plantavit dextera tua : et super filium hominis, quem confirmasti tibi.

And perfect that which Thy right hand hath planted : and look upon the son of man whom Thou hast made strong for Thyself.

"*Super filium hominis.*" According to the Chaldee : *Propter regem Christum.* Do Thou restore it, since Thy hand has planted it ; this we pray Thee for the love of the Son of man, that is, the Messias, Whom Thou hast confirmed, that is, hast established, as Thy Son.——It is thus that S. Jerome, S. Augustine, Theodoret, Euthymius, Bellarmine, &c., explain this verse.

17. Incensa igni, et suffossa : ab increpatione vultus tui peribunt.

Things set on fire[1] and dug down : they shall perish at the rebuke of Thy countenance.

"*Incensa ... suffossa.*" Behold Thy vine is already burnt and uprooted.——"*Ab increpatione...*" Some, as Estius, Sa, and Bossuet, explain this passage thus : But those that have thus laid it waste shall perish through the wrath of Thy angry countenance.——Others more commonly, as Malvenda, Menochius, Rotigni, Tirinus, and Mattei, with Vatablus, Genebrard, Maldonatus, and Mariana, apply it to the Jewish people in this sense : If Thy countenance continues to appear threatening, and to show forth Thy wrath, all those who belong to the Synagogue will perish.

18. Fiat manus tua super virum dexteræ tuæ : et super filium hominis, quem confirmasti tibi.

Let Thy hand be upon the man of Thy right hand : and upon the son of man whom Thou hast made strong for Thyself.

Cause Thou Thy power to be known upon the Man of Thy right hand ;[2] and upon the Son of man Whom Thou hast willed for Thy glory to send into the world to restore Thy vineyard.

19. Et non discedimus a te, vivificabis nos : et nomen tuum invocabimus.

And we depart not from Thee, Thou shalt quicken us : and we will call upon Thy name.

"*Discedimus.*" The Hebrew text has this in the future, as also the Chaldee in the sense of *Recedemus.*——And thus we

---

[1] *Things set on fire*, &c. So this vineyard of Thine, almost consumed already, must perish if Thou continue Thy rebukes.

[2] "*Virum dexteræ tuæ.*" Bellarmine and other interpreters understand by these words Jesus Christ, Whom God formed with His own hand, or by the operation of the Holy Ghost, in the womb of the Blessed Virgin. We may add that He was to take His seat at the right hand of the Eternal Father.

shall never depart from Thee, since Thou wilt give us the
strength to serve Thee ; and we shall not cease to call upon
Thy name.

20. Domine Deus virtutum converte nos : et ostende faciem tuam, et salvi erimus.

O Lord God of hosts, convert us : and show Thy face, and we shall be saved.

Repetition of verses 4 and 8.

LAUDS FOR THURSDAY.

PSALM L.

PSALM LXXXIX.

S. JEROME applies this Psalm to Moses, who represents to God the shortness and the miseries of human life, and prays Him to have compassion on His people. But others apply it to the Jews, who being captives in Babylon implore help from God.

A Prayer for Moses, the man of God. [1]

1. Domine, refugium factus es nobis: a generatione in generationem.

O Lord, Thou hast been our refuge: from generation to generation.

Lord, Thou hast been at all times our refuge, and Thou wilt be so to the end.

2. Priusquam montes fierent, aut formaretur terra, et orbis : a sæculo et usque in sæculum tu es Deus.

Before the mountains were made, or the earth and the world were formed : from everlasting and to everlasting Thou art God.

"*A sæculo...*" Thou hast ever been and wilt ever be the God that Thou art. [2]

3. Ne avertas hominem in humilitatem : et dixisti, Convertimini filii hominum.

Turn not man away to be brought low: Thou hast said, Be converted, O ye sons of men.

[1] Many with S. Athanasius (*Ep. ad Marcell.*) and S. Jerome (*Ep. ad Cypr.*) think that these words are to be understood literally, and consequently that Moses is the author of the Psalm. Bellarmine combats this opinion ; Bossuet defends it.

[2] "*Deus.*" Bellarmine thinks that this word is in the vocative case ; he notes also the force of the present tense : *Tu es*, as showing the eternity of God, without past or future.

Some explain this verse thus : Do not Thou suffer that
men should turn their back upon Thee to give themselves up
to worthless creatures ; for Thou hast said to them : O men,
turn ye unto Me, and I will make you feel the effects of My
mercy.——But others, as Maldonatus, Bossuet, Mattei, &c.,
follow the Hebrew, which says : *Convertis hominem in pulverem,
et dicis* (or, according to S. Jerome : *Convertes hominem usque
ad contritionem, et dices*): *Convertimini*, or *revertimini filii
Adam ;* and they explain the verse thus : Thou, O Lord, art
eternal ; but Thou hast ordained that all men should one day
return to the dust, out of which they are formed.——This
explanation is founded on the Hebrew text ; but the former,
which follows the Vulgate, appears more simple and natural.

4. Quoniam mille anni ante oculos
tuos : tamquam dies hesterna, quæ
præteriit ;

For a thousand years in Thy sight
are but as yesterday, which is past ;

Because, even if we were to live a thousand years, what
more would these be in Thy sight, that is, compared with Thy
eternity, than as yesterday which is already past.——Such is
the explanation which the learned commonly give, as Malvenda thus attests : *Omnes fere.*

5. Et custodia in nocte : quæ pro
nihilo habentur, eorum anni erunt.

And as a watch in the night : as
things that are counted as naught,
so shall their years be.

All these thousand years are no more than one of the four
watches into which the night is divided, and which are
counted as nothing ; what then do all the years of men count
when compared with eternity !

6. Mane sicut herba transeat,
mane floreat, et transeat : vespere
decidat, induret, et arescat.

In the morning *man* shall grow up
like grass ; in the morning he shall
flourish and pass away : in the evening he shall fall, grow dry, and
wither.

S. Jerome translates : *Mane floruit et abiit ; ad vesperum
conteretur atque siccabitur.* The life of man is like a blade of
grass that soon passes ; in the morning it flourishes, and in the
evening it falls, withers, and dries up.

7. Quia defecimus in ira tua : et
in furore tuo turbati sumus.

For in Thy wrath we have fainted
away : and are troubled in Thine
indignation.

Thus we, having by our sins provoked Thy wrath, find
ourselves in this sad lost state, and afflicted with the fear of

Thy anger.——This accords with the sense in which Bellarmine and many others explain this verse.

8. Posuisti iniquitates nostras in conspectu tuo : sæculum nostrum in illuminatione vultus tui.

Thou hast set our iniquities before Thine eyes : our life in the light of Thy countenance.

When God wills to punish the sinner, He keeps His eyes fixed on his faults ; when, on the contrary, He wills to show him mercy, He turns away His eyes in order not to see them : *Avertit faciem.* It is for this reason David says in Psalm l. : *Averte faciem.* . . . "Turn away Thy face from my sins."—— "*Sæculum* . . . " Thou hast set the whole course of our life in the light of Thy countenance, that is, even all our most secret faults are openly and clearly exposed to view in Thy full and perfect knowledge.——These explanations are given by Bellarmine, Lallemant, &c.

9. Quoniam omnes dies nostri defecerunt : et in ira tua defecimus.

For all our days are spent : and in Thy wrath we have fainted away.

For all our days have waned away, that is, our life has been shortened, and we ourselves faint under the weight of Thy wrath which we have excited by our sins.——This is the sense given by Bellarmine and Menochius.

10. Anni nostri sicut aranea meditabuntur : dies annorum nostrorum in ipsis, septuaginta anni.

Our years shall be considered as a spider :[1] the days of our years are threescore years and ten.

Our life is like the web, which the spider wastes its own self to make, and which is destroyed by the least touch. As to the number of our years, they do not generally exceed seventy ——"*Anni nostri sicut aranea meditabuntur.*" The Hebrew, according to Bellarmine, is : *Anni nostri sicut meditatio ;* and according to S. Jerome : *Consumpsimus annos nostros quasi sermonem loquens.* But these different renderings signify the same thing, namely, that our life passes away like a thought, a meditation, or like a word that is over the moment that it is uttered.

11. Si autem in potentatibus, octoginta anni : et amplius eorum, labor et dolor.

But if in the strong *they be* fourscore years: and what is more of them is labour and sorrow.

The number of our years does not generally go beyond threescore years and ten ; and should some who are stronger

[1] *As a spider.* As frail and weak as *a spider's* web. The spider, however, is not mentioned in the Hebrew text, which means rather meditation, or slight breathing.

attain to fourscore, after that time of life there is nothing but infirmity and sorrow.

12. Quoniam supervenit mansue-
tudo: et corripiemur.

For humiliation is come upon us: and we shall be corrected.

For when we shall reach that age, seeing ourselves near death, we shall correct the sentiments of pride, which we had during our life.——This explanation will agree with the Hebrew text, which is thus rendered : *Quoniam tonsio celeriter, et avolabimus.* For quickly is the cutting off, *i.e.* we are soon cut off, and we have fled away. And with S. Jerome : *Transibimus cito et avolabimus.* We have passed away quickly and have fled.

13. Quis novit potestatem iræ tuæ:
et præ timore tuo iram tuam dinume-
rare ?

Who knoweth the power of Thine anger: and for Thy fear who can number Thy wrath ?

Who has ever understood how great, O Lord, is the power of Thy wrath ? and who can measure the greatness of Thy indignation, which surpasses all that we can conceive, and all that is commonly believed ?

14. Dexteram tuam sic notam fac:
et eruditos corde in sapientia.

So make Thy right hand known : and the learned in heart in wisdom.

Make us to know the strength of Thy arm, and cause us to be fully informed of Thine avenging justice ; and thus made wise, we shall come to Thee.——S. Jerome translates it thus : *Sic ostende, et veniemus ad te corde sapienti.* Thus show to us, and we shall come to Thee with a wise heart.

15. Convertere Domine usquequo ?
et deprecabilis esto super servos tuos.

Return, O Lord, how long ? and be entreated in favour of Thy servants.

Turn to us with a gracious countenance ; how long wilt Thou show Thyself in anger ? Suffer Thyself to be moved by the prayers of Thy servants.

16. Repleti sumus mane misericordia tua : et exultavimus, et delec-
tati sumus omnibus diebus nostris.

We are filled in the morning with Thy mercy : and we have rejoiced, and are delighted all our days.

And thus we shall at once see ourselves filled with Thy mercy ; we shall exult with joy and we shall be glad all the days of our life.[1]

---

[1] S. Jerome translates : Fill us in the morning with Thy mercy, and we shall give praise and rejoice all our days. Gladden us for the days wherein Thou has afflicted us, and for the years in which we have seen evils.

17. Lætati sumus pro diebus, quibus nos humiliasti : annis, quibus
vidimus mala.

We have rejoiced for the days in
which Thou hast humbled us : for
the years in which we have seen evils

We have rejoiced because of the glad days which Thou hast
granted us in compensation for the past days in which Thou
hast humbled us, and for the years of tribulation that we have
suffered.

18. Respice in servos tuos, et in
opera tua : et dirige filios eorum.

Look upon Thy servants and upon
Thy works ; and direct their children.

Turn Thine eyes upon Thy servants, who are the work of
Thy hands (thus Menochius and Tirinus) ; look graciously
also upon their children, and direct them in the way of salvation.

19. Et sit splendor Domini Dei
nostri super nos, et opera manuum
nostrarum dirige super nos : et opus
manuum nostrarum dirige.

And let the brightness of the Lord
our God be upon us, and direct Thou
the works of our hands over us ; yea,
the work of our hands do Thou
direct.

And may the grace of our Lord God shine upon us ; thus,
O God, direct in us our actions and all that we do.

PSALMS LXII. and LXVI.

THE CANTICLE OF MOSES (*Exodus* xv.).

Moses composed this Canticle, that the people of Israel might
sing it in thanksgiving for the miraculous passage of the Red
Sea. He predicts in it the Israelites' possession of the promised land by the defeat of their enemies.

1. Cantemus Domino : gloriose
enim magnificatus est : equum et
ascensorem dejecit in mare.

Let us sing to the Lord ; for He is
gloriously magnified : the horse and
the rider He hath thrown into the
sea.

"*Gloriose enim* . . ." Because He hath gloriously displayed
to us His magnificence in drowning in the sea the horses and
riders of our enemies who pursued us.

2. Fortitudo mea et laus mea
Dominus : et factus est mihi in salutem ;

The Lord is my strength and my
praise : and He is become salvation
to me :

The Lord is our strength and the object of our praise ; He
has made Himself our Saviour.

20

3. Iste Deus meus, et glorificabo eum : Deus patris mei, et exaltabo eum.

He is my God, and I will glorify Him : the God of my father, and I will exalt Him.

He is my God, Whom I will ever glorify ; He is the God of our father Abraham, and I will always proclaim His glory.

4. Dominus quasi vir pugnator omnipotens nomen ejus: Currus Pharaonis et exercitum ejus projecit in mare :

The Lord is as a man of war, Almighty is His name : Pharao's chariots and his army He hath cast into the sea :

"*Dominus quasi vir pugnator.*" The Lord as a warrior has come forth to defend us.

5. Electi principes ejus submersi sunt in mari Rubro : abyssi operuerunt eos, descenderunt in profundum quasi lapis.

His chosen captains are drowned in the Red Sea: the depths have covered them, they are sunk to the bottom like a stone.

"*Electi principes ejus.*" The first princes, or chief personages, of the kingdom.

6. Dextera tua Domine magnificata est in fortitudine : dextera tua, Domine, percussit inimicum. Et in multitudine gloriæ tuæ deposuisti adversarios tuos :

Thy right hand, O Lord, is magnified in strength : Thy right hand, O Lord, hath slain the enemy. And in the multitude of Thy power, Thou hast put down Thy adversaries :

7. Misisti iram tuam, quæ devoravit eos sicut stipulam : et in spiritu furoris tui congregatæ sunt aquæ.

Thou hast sent Thy wrath, which hath devoured them like stubble : and with the blast of Thy anger the waters were gathered together.

"*Iram tuam.*" The fire of Thy wrath.——"*Congregatæ sunt aquæ.*" The waters have gathered together, that is, have risen up, on either side to give a passage to Thy servants.

8. Stetit unda fluens : congregatæ sunt abyssi in medio mari.

The flowing water stood : the depths were gathered together in the midst of the sea.

9. Dixit inimicus : Persequar et comprehendam, dividam spolia, implebitur anima mea :

The enemy said : I will pursue and overtake, I will divide the spoils, my soul shall have its fill :

"*Implebitur anima mea.*" I shall be fully satisfied.

10. Evaginabo gladium meum : interficiet eos manus mea.

I will draw my sword : my hand shall slay them.

11. Flavit spiritus tuus, et operuit eos mare : submersi sunt quasi plumbum in aquis vehementibus.

Thy wind blew, and the sea covered them : they sank as lead in the mighty waters.

"*Flavit spiritus tuus.*" The wind sent by Thee blew waves.

12. Quis similis tui in fortibus Domine? quis similis tui, magnificus in sanctitate, terribilis atque laudabilis, faciens mirabilia?

Who is like to Thee among the strong, O Lord? who is like to Thee, glorious in holiness, terrible and praiseworthy, doing wonders?

Who among the mighty [1] can be found like unto Thee, O Lord? who shall be like unto Thee, Who art so great in holiness, so terrible in power, and so worthy of all praise for Thy goodness? and who can work the admirable marvels which Thou dost?

13. Extendisti manum tuam, et devoravit eos terra: Dux fuisti in misericordia tua populo quem redemisti:

Thou stretchedst forth Thy hand, and the earth swallowed them: in Thy mercy Thou hast been a leader to the people whom Thou hast redeemed:

"*Devoravit eos terra.*" Lallemant translates: Our enemies have disappeared from the face of the earth. But the explanation which Rotigni gives seems better: The earth swallowed them up, that is, being cast by the sea on the shore, they were there covered by the sand.——"*Quem redemisti.*" Whom Thou hast delivered from the hands of their enemies.

14. Et portasti eum in fortitudine tua: ad habitaculum sanctum tuum.

And in Thy strength Thou hast carried them to the holy habitation.

From this verse to the end of the Canticle, Moses speaks of the entrance and establishment of the people in the Land of Promise.

15. Ascenderunt populi, et irati sunt: dolores obtinuerunt habitatores Philisthiim.

Nations rose up, and were angry: sorrows took hold of the inhabitants of Philisthiim.

The people of that land rose up enraged against Thy people; the Philistines had the grief of seeing themselves driven out from the country where they dwelt.

16. Tunc conturbati sunt principes Edom, robustos Moab obtinuit tremor: obriguerunt omnes habitatores Chanaan.

Then were the princes of Edom troubled, trembling seized on the stout men of Moab: all the inhabitants of Chanaan became stiff.

"*Obriguerunt.*" Were petrified with terror.

17. Irruat super eos formido et pavor: in magnitudine brachii tui:

Let fear and dread fall upon them: in the greatness of Thy arm:

Let the fear and the terror of the might of Thy arm seize upon them on every side.

---

[1] "*In fortibus.*" According to the Hebrew and Greek: *In diis*: Among the gods of the heathen.

18. Fiant immobiles quasi lapis, donec pertranseat populus tuus Domine : donec pertranseat populus tuus iste, quem possedisti.

Let them become immovable as a stone, until Thy people, O Lord, pass by, which Thou hast possessed.

Let them become immovable as rocks, that Thy people may pass the sea, the people which Thou hast won and possessed for thine own.——Lallemant applies this verse to the passage of the Red Sea ; but Rotigni applies it to the entrance of the people into the Land of Promise, spoken of in the following verse. Notwithstanding this reason, the first explanation seems to me more proper.[1]——" *Quem possedisti.*" This people whom Thou hast won for Thyself, and hast made Thine own possession.

19. Introduces eos, et plantabis in monte hereditatis tuæ : firmissimo habitaculo tuo quod operatus es Domine :

Thou shalt bring them in, and plant them in the mountain of Thy inheritance: in Thy most firm habitation which Thou hast made, O Lord:

Thou wilt bring in this Thy people, and wilt establish them on Mount Sion, which Thou hast chosen for Thine inheritance and for Thy fixed abode, having prepared it in order to found there Thy Temple.

20. Sanctuarium tuum Domine, quod firmaverunt manus tuæ : Dominus regnabit in æternum et ultra.

Thy sanctuary, O Lord, which Thy hands have established : the Lord shall reign for ever and ever.

This sanctuary which Thou, O Lord, hast established to make there Thy perpetual abode, will serve for Thee to reign in, throughout all ages, and world without end.——Here finishes the Canticle ; the two next verses are a summary of the history of the passage of the Red Sea, as recorded in Exodus.

21. Ingressus est enim eques Pharao cum curribus et equitibus ejus in mare : et reduxit super eos Dominus aquas maris.

For Pharao went in on horseback, with his chariots and horsemen into the sea : and the Lord brought back upon them the waters of the sea.

22. Filii autem Israel ambulaverunt per siccum : in medio ejus.

But the children of Israel walked on dry ground : in the midst thereof.

PSALMS CXLVIII., CXLIX., AND CL.

CANTICLE OF ZACHARY.

[1] We have been unable to discover any other commentator who holds the opinion of Lallemant.

MATINS FOR FRIDAY.

PSALM LXXX.

The people are reproved for their negligence in celebrating the praises of God, and are exhorted to celebrate them henceforth with devotion, and in thanksgiving for the benefits received from the Lord, since for this end the feasts are instituted. Every Christian can apply this Psalm to himself.

Unto the end, for the wine-presses, a Psalm for Asaph himself.

1. Exultate Deo adjutori nostro: jubilate Deo Jacob.

Rejoice unto God our helper: sing aloud unto the God of Jacob.

Exult with gladness praising God, for His loving protection; rejoice, glorifying the God of Jacob.

2. Sumite psalmum, et date tympanum: psalterium jucundum cum cithara.

Take a psalm, and bring hither the timbrel: the pleasant psaltery with the harp.

Take up the Psalm, that is, make a beginning of the canticle; up! strike merrily the timbrel, the psaltery, and the harp.

3. Buccinate in neomenia tuba: in insigni die solemnitatis vestræ:

Blow the trumpet in the new moon: on the noted day of your solemnity:

Sound the trumpet of the New Moon, which it is customary to sound on the great day of your festival.——"*Neomenia.*" We should here remark that the Hebrews celebrated every month the Feast of the New Moon; but the most solemn Feast of the New Moon was in September, when the trumpets were sounded, and hence it was called the Feast of Trumpets: *Dies clangoris est et tubarum.* (*Num.* xxix. 1.)——"*Vestræ.*" Your. According to the Hebrew: *Nostræ*: Our.

4. Quia præceptum in Israel est : et judicium Deo Jacob.

For it is a commandment in Israel : and a law of the God of Jacob.

In the Book of Numbers, x. 10.

5. Testimonium in Joseph posuit illud, cum exiret de terra Ægypti : linguam, quam non noverat, audivit.

He ordained it for a testimony in Joseph, when he came out of the land of Egypt : he heard a tongue which he knew not.

"*In Joseph.*" This precept was laid on the posterity of Joseph and his brethren, that is, on the people of Israel.[1]——
"*Linguam, quam non noverat.*" A language which he did not know, because this was the first time that God spake to His people.

6. Divertit ab oneribus dorsum ejus : manus ejus in cophino servierunt.

He removed his back from the burdens : his hands had served in baskets.

He withdrew their shoulders from the heavy burdens that oppressed them ; and their hands from carrying the baskets of mud and bricks. The Hebrew reads : *Liberavi ab onere dorsum ejus, et manus ejus a cophinis cessaverunt.*

7. In tribulatione invocasti me, et liberavi te : exaudivi te in abscondito tempestatis : probavi te apud aquam contradictionis.

Thou didst call upon Me in affliction, and I delivered thee : I heard thee in the secret place of the tempest :[2] I proved thee at the waters of contradiction.

Here it is God Who speaks.——"*Exaudivi te in abscondito tempestatis.*" This passage is variously interpreted. Mattei understands it as referring to the storm of chastisements that God poured on the enemies of His people ; but I prefer the view of Genebrardus, who explains it thus : I heard thee in the tempest of afflictions which thou sufferedst at the hands of the Egyptians, when it seemed to thee that I hid Myself away, and did not hear thy prayers. (This applies well to souls in a state of desolation, to whom it appears as if God does not hear them any more, whilst the Lord in the midst of this storm secretly, that is, without letting them know it, listens to them and helps them.)——"*Probavi ... contradictionis.*" And yet I tried them and found them to be unfaithful near the water of Meriba.——The Hebrew word *Meriba*, meaning Contradiction or strife, and so translated in the Vulgate, is the name of the place where the people, suffering from the want

[1] See note to *Ps.* lxxvi. 14.

[2] Heb. Of *thunder*. When thou soughtest to *hide* thyself from the *tempest*.

of water, contradicted Moses and first refused to obey him. Thus Mattei and others. (See *Exod.* xvii. 5-7 ; *Numb.* xx. 13.)[1]

8. Audi, populus meus, et contes-tabor te: Israel, si audieris me, non erit in te deus recens, neque adorabis deum alienum.

Hear, O My people, and I will testify unto thee : O Israel, if thou wilt hearken unto Me, there shall be no new god in thee, neither shalt thou adore a strange god.

" *Contestabor te.*" Bellarmine thus explains : *Testatum faciam tibi quid a te requiram.*——"*Neque adorabis deum alienum.*" S. Jerome translates : *Et non adores deum peregrinum.*——The sense of the verse is : Hear, My people, and I will make plain to thee what I require of thee : O Israel, if thou wilt obey Me, let there not be in thee any new god besides Me, nor shalt thou worship any strange god.

9. Ego enim sum Dominus Deus tuus, qui eduxi te de terra Ægypti: dilata os tuum, et implebo illud.

For I am the Lord thy God, Who brought thee out of the land of Egypt : open thy mouth wide, and I will fill it.

" *Dominus Deus tuus.*" Thy only Lord and God.—— " *Dilata os tuum, et implebo illud.*" That is : Enlarge thy desires, and ask of Me what thou wilt, I will satisfy thee fully.

10. Et non audivit populus meus vocem meam : et Israel non intendit mihi.

But My people heard not My voice: and Israel hearkened not to Me.

" *Non intendit.*" According to the Hebrew : *Non acquievit*; or according to S. Jerome : *Non credidit.* That is, would not rest satisfied with believing My word.

11. Et dimisi eos secundum desideria cordis eorum: ibunt in adinventionibus suis.

So I let them go according to the desire of their hearts: they shall walk in their own devices.

" *Secundum desideria cordis eorum.*" That is, according to their disordered appetites.——"*Ibunt in adinventionibus suis.*" S. Jerome translates : *Ambulabunt in consiliis suis.* They will walk to their ruin, through following their evil designs.

12. Si populus meus audisset me: Israel si in viis meis ambulasset:

If My people had heard Me: if Israel had walked in My ways:

" *In viis meis.*" In the way of My precepts.

13. Pro nihilo forsitan inimicos eorum humiliassem : et super tribu-lantes eos misissem manum meam.

I should soon have humbled their enemies : and laid my hand on them that troubled them.

---

[1] Properly speaking, the name of Water of Contradiction was the designa-tion of the place where was wrought the second miracle of the water gushing forth from the rock (*Numb.* xx. 13). With regard to the place of the first like miracle, it received the name of Temptation (*Exod.* xvii. 7).

Nothing would have been more easy to Me than to
humiliate their enemies ; and I could well have stretched
forth My hand to punish those who were oppressing them.

14. Inimici Domini mentiti sunt
ei : et erit tempus eorum in sæcula.   The enemies of the Lord have lied
unto Him : and their time shall be
for ever.

But those who were loved by the Lord have failed in keeping their word to Him, and have become His enemies ; and
therefore the punishment of their unfaithfulness shall be everlasting.[1]

15. Et cibavit eos ex adipe fru-
menti : et de petra melle saturavit
eos.   And He fed them with the fat of
wheat : and with honey out of the
rock He satisfied them.

And yet God had nourished them with the most choice
wheat, and had satisfied them with honey gathered from the
rocks, that is, in abundance, since the bees had even made
their honey in the midst of rocks.

PSALM LXXXI.

In this Psalm it is God Himself who speaks, except in the
first and last verses : He reproaches the princes and judges for
their evil administration of justice, and places before them
the moment of death, when they will themselves have to be
judged.   The last verse predicts the coming of Jesus Christ to
judge all men at the end of the world.

A Psalm for Asaph.

1. Deus stetit in synagoga deorum :
in medio autem deos dijudicat.   God hath stood in the assembly of
gods : but in the midst He judgeth
gods.

"*Deorum.*"   According to the Chaldee : *Judicum.*[2]   God is
present in the council of the judges of the earth : and standing in the midst of them He judges them, that is, He weighs
the judgments which they render.

2. Usquequo judicatisiniquitatem :
et facies peccatorum sumitis ?   How long will ye judge unjustly :
and accept the persons of the wicked ?

---

[1] They had promised to obey Him faithfully.   " And all the people answered with one voice : We will do all the words of the Lord, which He
hath spoken " (*Exod.* xxiv. 3).——" *Tempus :* " Their time of punishment.
S. Augustine.——Bellarmine says that in this and the next verse it is the
Psalmist who speaks.

[2] See *Exod.* xxi. 6, xxii. 28 ; *Ps.* xlix. 1.

Here God is speaking to the judges : How long will you give unjust sentences?——"*Facies peccatorum sumitis?*" Bellarmine says that *Sumere faciem alicujus in judicio*, is to judge, not according to the rule that justice demands, but according to the pleasure of him whom the judge wishes to favour. But Mattei says that *Sumere faciem peccatorum*, according to the proper sense of the Hebrew expression, means : *Erigere faciem peccatorum;* and, says he, when judges favour the wicked, they cause the wicked to hold up their head, that is, their pride.

3. Judicate egeno et pupillo : humilem et pauperem justificate.

Judge for the needy and fatherless : do justice unto the humble and poor.

Judge according to the justice which the poor man and the orphan deserve : and render justice to those of mean condition and to the needy.

4. Eripite pauperem: et egenum de manu peccatoris liberate.

Rescue the poor : and deliver the needy out of the hand of the sinner.

"*De manu peccatoris.*" From the hands of the sinner, who is more powerful and would oppress them.

5. Nescierunt, neque intellexerunt ; in tenebris ambulant: movebuntur omnia fundamenta terræ.

They have not known nor understood ; they walk on in darkness : all the foundations of the earth shall be moved.

But the wicked judges do not understand these maxims, because they walk in the dark, and put all the world in confusion by their unjust practices.

6. Ego dixi: Dii estis: et filii Excelsi omnes.

I have said : Ye are gods : and all of you the sons of the Most High.

O judges, I have set you up as gods of the earth, by giving you a share of My own power ; in virtue of this authority that you have received from the Most High, you are His sons.

7. Vos autem sicut homines moriemini : et sicut unus de principibus cadetis.

But ye shall die like men : and shall fall like one of the princes.

But take note that you are men, and as men you have all to die : and one day each one of you will fall from his post, as the princes who went before you have fallen.

8. Surge, Deus, judica terram : quoniam tu hereditabis in omnibus Gentibus.

Arise, O God, judge Thou the earth : for thou shalt inherit among all the nations.

"*Hereditabis in omnibus Gentibus.*" Thy reign shall extend over all the nations as Thy heritage, and at the last day all these must submit to Thy justice and power.

PSALM LXXXII.

A PRAYER which the Jewish people address to God, to obtain
His help against the Ammonites, the Moabites, and other
Gentiles, who threatened to ruin the Temple and the city.
The Psalm may be taken as a prayer of the Church, whenever
she suffers any particular persecution.

A Canticle of a Psalm for Asaph.

1. Deus, quis similis erit tibi? ne
taceas: neque compescaris, Deus:

O God, who shall be like unto
Thee? hold not thy peace: neither
be Thou still, O God:

"*Quis similis erit tibi?*" Who shall have power to do that
which Thou canst?——"*Neque compescaris.*" S. Jerome translates: *Ne quiescas.* Hide not Thy just indignation by keeping
silence and peace.

2. Quoniam ecce inimici tui sonuerunt: et qui oderunt te, extulerunt
caput.

For lo, Thine enemies have made a
noise: and they that hate Thee have
lifted up the head.

Because the enemy has already sounded the call to arms:
that is, as S. Jerome explains, they have made a tumult,
Tumultuati sunt.

3. Super populum tuum malignaverunt consilium: et cogitaverunt
adversus sanctos tuos.

They have taken a crafty counsel
against Thy people: and have devised
against Thy saints.

"*Super ... malignaverunt.*" S. Jerome translates: *Contra
populum tuum nequiter tractaverunt.* They have formed plans
of ruin against Thy people; and they have taken counsel to
oppress Thy saints, that is, those who adore Thee.

4. Dixerunt: Venite, et disperdamus eos de gente: et non memoretur
nomen Israel ultra.

They have said: Come and let us
destroy them, so that they be not a
nation: and let the name of Israel
be remembered no more.

"*Disperdamus eos de gente.*" According to Mattei, this is a
Hebraism, which means: Let us remove this people from the
world.

5. Quoniam cogitaverunt una-
nimiter: simul adversum te testamentum disposuerunt, tabernacula
Idumæorum et Ismahelitæ:

For they have planned with one
consent: they have made a covenant
together against Thee, the tents of
the Edomites and the Ishmaelites:

For they had conspired with one accord to destroy us, and
strike us down, and they have formed a league against Thee.
——"*Testamentum disposuerunt.*" The Hebrew and S. Jerome

translate : *Fœdus pepigerunt.*——" *Tabernacula.*" That is, the
tents or the camp, the troops.

| 6. Moab, et Agareni, Gebal, et Ammon, et Amalec ; alienigenæ cum habitantibus Tyrum. | Moab, and the Agarenes, Gebal, and Ammon, and Amalec : the Philistines, with them that dwell at Tyre. |

" *Alienigenæ.*" The strangers, or foreigners.[1]

| 7. Etenim Assur venit cum illis : facti sunt in adjutorium filiis Lot. | Assur also is joined with them : they have helped the children of Lot. |

" *Etenim Assur.*" S. Jerome translates : *Sed et Assur.* And
even the host of the Assyrians.——" *Filiis Lot.*" Mattei says
that hereby we can only understand the Ammonites, the descendants of Ammon, son of Lot.[2]

| 8. Fac illis sicut Madian, et Sisaræ : sicut Jabin in torrente Cisson: [3] | Do unto them as Thou didst unto Madian and unto Sisara : as Thou didst unto Jabin at the brook of Cison : |

| 9. Disperierunt in Endor: facti sunt ut stercus terræ. | *Who* perished at Endor : and they became as dung for the earth. |

When they were defeated.——" *Endor.*" The place of the
enemies' defeat, where their dead bodies serve as dung to
manure the ground.

| 10. Pone principes eorum sicut Oreb, et Zeb : et Zebee et Salmana : | Make their princes like Oreb, and Zeb : and as Zebee, and Salmana. |

" *Pone ... sicut.*" Treat their captains as Thou didst treat.——
" *Oreb, et Zeb.*" Captains of Zebee and Salmana,[4] kings of the
Madianites, slain by the Hebrews.

| 11. Omnes principes eorum : qui dixerunt : Heredidate possideamus Sanctuarium Dei. | All their princes, who have said : Let us possess the Sanctuary of God for an inheritance. |

Thus treat, O Lord, these princes who have dared to say :
Let us go to take possession of the Sanctuary of God, that is,
Jerusalem, as an inheritance which belongs to us.

---

[1] Thus it is in the Septuagint : in the Hebrew text and S. Jerome's translation it is *Palæstina*, the land of the Philistines, or Palestines (*Gen.* xxi. 33; *Ps.* lix. 9, lxxxvi. 4).

[2] Also the Moabites (*Gen.* xix. 37, 38), descendants of Moab, likewise son of Lot.

[3] " *Madian.*" The Madianites, defeated by Gedeon (*Jud.* vii. 20).——
" *Sisara.*" The general of Jabin king of Asor, killed by Jael (*Jud.* iv.).

[4] These kings were slain by Gedeon himself (*Jud.* vii. 24, viii. 21).

| 12. Deus meus, pone illos ut rotam: et sicut stipulam ante faciem venti. | O my God, make them like unto a wheel: and as the stubble before the wind. |

"*Pone illos ut rotam.*" Lallemant thus interprets these words : Send upon them a spirit of giddiness, to disconcert them.——Mattei gives the passage the following metrical rendering :

| "Sol che dal ciglio irato
Sfavilli un lampo, et li
vedrem qual ruota,
Girar confusi intorno." | Sun from Thine angry eye
Dart lightning rays, and we
Shall see them as a wheel
Whirl round confusedly. |

"*Sicut stipulam ante . . .*" Scatter them as a heap of straw is scattered before the wind.——Such is the explanation also given by Mattei.

| 13. Sicut ignis, qui comburit silvam: et sicut flamma comburens montes : | Like as the fire that burneth up the wood : and as the flame that consumeth the mountains : |
| 14. Ita persequeris illos in tempestate tua: et in ira tua turbabis eos. | So shalt Thou pursue them with Thy tempest : and shalt trouble them in Thy wrath. |

13, 14. "*Flamma comburens montes.*"[1] Genebrard and Rotigni understand this of volcanoes, as Vesuvius and Etna, which cause general devastation by the flames they send forth. Bellarmine understands it of the dry grass burning on the mountains ; but Lallemant and Mattei interpret it of the lightning which strikes the mountains and sets them on fire. ——S. Jerome translates : *Sic persequere eos in tempestate tua et in turbine tuo conturba eos.* So pursue them with the tempest of Thy vengeance, and confuse them with the whirlwind of Thy wrath.

| 15. Imple facies eorum ignominia : et quærent nomen tuum, Domine. | Fill their faces with shame : and they shall seek Thy name, O Lord. |

"*Quærent nomen tuum.*" That is, they will enter into themselves and be converted to Thee.——But others, more commonly explain it thus : They will ask to know Thy name, that is, Thy power : they will be instructed therein, and they will venerate it.

| 16. Erubescant, et conturbentur in sæculum sæculi : et confundantur, et pereant. | Let them be ashamed and troubled for ever and ever : and let them be confounded and perish. |

[1] The wooded mountains, or the woods on the mountains. Menochius, and Bossuet.

And if this is not enough to bring about their conversion, let them remain troubled with continual fear of Thy power all their lives, and let them die in confusion.

17. Et cognoscant quia nomen tibi Dominus: tu solus Altissimus in omni terra.

And let them know that the Lord is Thy name : Thou alone art the Most High over all the earth.

And let them know that to no other but to Thee belongs properly the name of Lord ; because Thou alone art King of kings throughout the earth.

PSALM LXXXIII.

THE Psalmist ardently desires to see the Temple of Jerusalem, and mourns over his being at a distance from it. And as this Temple was a type of heaven, we must believe that he sighed at the same time after the happiness of going to enjoy the sight of God in Paradise. The Psalm is admirably fitted to kindle our desires to leave this earth, and to enter into the abode of the blessed.[1]

Unto the end, for the wine-presses, a Psalm for the Sons of Core.

1. Quam dilecta tabernacula tua, Domine virtutum! concupiscit, et deficit anima mea in atria Domini.

How lovely are Thy tabernacles, O Lord of hosts! my soul longeth and fainteth for the courts of the Lord.

"*Atria Domini.*" (See verse 10).

2. Cor meum, et caro mea: exultaverunt in Deum vivum.

My heart and my flesh : have rejoiced in the living God.

That is : My soul and my body leap for joy in thinking of Thee, O living God.——Our God is called the living God in contrast with the gods of the Gentiles, who are but dead gods.

3. Etenim passer invenit sibi domum : et turtur nidum sibi, ubi ponat pullos suos.

For the sparrow hath found her a house : and the turtle a nest for herself, where she may lay her young.

4. Altaria tua, Domine virtutum : Rex meus, et Deus meus.

Even Thine altars, O Lord of hosts : my King and my God.

3, 4. For the sparrow has found its dwelling in some house, and the turtle a nest where to place its young in safety ; and I, my King and my God, cannot I shelter myself near Thy altars, that is, in Thy Temple, which would be to me a happy

[1] See *Ps.* xli.

refuge and a very nest? Thus Bellarmine, Maldonatus, and
Lallemant understand the passage.——Mattei gives this paraphrase :

"Il tuo altare era il mio nido,   Thy Altar to me was a nest,
Era il porto, O mio Signor."   O my Lord, and a haven of rest.

5. Beati, qui habitant in domo   Blessed are they that dwell in Thy
tua, Domine : in sæcula sæculorum house, O Lord : they shall praise
laudabunt te.   Thee for ever and ever.

"*In sæcula . . .*" They are occupied in nought else but in
ever praising Thee.

6. Beatus vir, cujus est auxilium   Blessed is the man whose help is
abs te : ascensiones in corde suo   in Thee : in his heart he hath dis-
disposuit, in valle lacrymarum, in posed to ascend by steps, in the vale
loco quem posuit.   of tears, in the place which he hath
                                    set.

S. Augustine thus explains this verse: Happy the man who
hopes for the succour that he needs from Thee ; having resolved in his heart to rise continually more and more to higher
degrees of perfection, so long as he shall abide in this vale of
tears, where God has placed him to gain merit.——But Mattei, with Bossuet, interprets it very differently. He says that
the Psalmist, sighing to return from Babylon to Jerusalem,
fancies himself already set free from his captivity, and exclaims : Happy he who hopes for and obtains Thy help ; for
behold he is already on his return home, passes by the valley
of Bocha, and is there refreshed with the water which Thou
causest to rain down. The same author then gives some
explanations, viz.: "*Ascensiones.*" This word, according to the
Hebrew, expresses the return to Jerusalem ; and this is what
the Psalmist represents to himself in spirit (*in corde suo*).——
"*Disposuit.*" This word joins on to those that follow, viz.:
"*In valle lacrymarum*," expressed in the Hebrew by the name
Bocha, which was an arid valley, called the Place of Tears :
Locus Flentium, sive Lacrymarum (Jud. ii. 5). In the Hebrew
the word is : *Bochim.*——"*In loco quem posuit.*" Here the
Hebrew word, instead of *Locus,* Place, means *Fons,* a Fountain
or well. So that the rendering will be : *Fons ibi ponetur;* and
the passage reads : He will pass through the valley of *Bocha ;*
there shall be set a fountain of water.

7. Etenim benedictionem dabit   For the lawgiver shall give a
legislator, ibunt de virtute in virtu- blessing : they shall go from strength
tem : videbitur Deus deorum in Sion.   to strength : the God of gods shall
                                    be seen in Sion.

Mattei, following the sense of the preceding verse, trans-lates thus: *Eo in loco fons ponetur; etenim propitia dabitur pluvia; hinc ibit de cœtu in cœtum, donec videbit Deum deorum in Sion.* That is: There, in that valley, there shall be water; for a kindly rain shall be granted : and thence he shall go from company to company, until he comes to see the great God in Sion. Thus the Psalmist, imagining himself refreshed in the valley of *Bocha* with water of healthful rain, and that he is marching on with the several companies of the Israelites who are returning to Jerusalem, rejoices as if, already in the Temple, he saw there the God of gods.——But those who follow the interpretation which was first given, explain the verse thus : For God, Who has given the Law, which is the way to attain to eternal life, will give them His blessing ; and thus they will advance from virtue to virtue, until they see the God of gods in the heavenly Sion.——The truth is, that these two verses, 6 and 7, are obscure, and the interpreters have made them still more so.

8. Domine Deus virtutum, exaudi orationem meam : auribus percipe Deus Jacob.

O Lord God of hosts, hear my prayer : give ear, O God of Jacob.

9. Protector noster aspice Deus : et respice in faciem Christi tui :

Behold, O God, our protector : and look upon the face of Thy Christ :

O God, Who art our Protector, look upon us with a gracious eye, and especially look upon our king, who is the type of the future Saviour.——"*Christi tui.*" According to Bossuet : *Regis, qui est Christi figura.* The king who is a figure of Christ.——But it may be well understood as applying prin-cipally to the Messias.

10. Quia melior est dies una in atriis tuis : super millia.

For one day in Thy courts : is better than a thousand.

"*In atriis tuis.*" These words denote the Temple, says Mariana. He thus speaks of the Temple in which there were various courts.——Tirinus remarks that the Temple signifies allegorically the Church, and anagogically, that is, in a higher spiritual sense, Heaven.

11. Elegi abjectus esse in domo Dei mei : magis quam habitare in tabernaculis peccatorum.

I had rather be despised in the house of my God : than to dwell in the tents of sinners.

"*In domo Dei mei.*" By this House of God, Bellarmine, with S. Augustine, understands Heaven ; but Bossuet, Mattei,

&c., understand the Temple, following the Hebrew text, which may be thus translated : *Mallem esse custos liminis domus tuæ:* I would rather be a doorkeeper of the Temple, that is, amongst its most lowly servants—according to what we read of the most humble offices of the Levites (1 *Par.* ix. 19-29).——"*In tabernaculis.*" This expression here denotes the great houses, palaces.

12. Quia misericordiam, et verita-   For God loveth mercy and truth :
tem diligit Deus : gratiam, et gloriam   the Lord will give grace and glory.
dabit Dominus.

That is : God is merciful and faithful to His promises ; and hence He is most willing to give us grace in this life and glory in the next.

13. Non privabit bonis eos, qui   He will not withhold good things
ambulant in innocentia : Domine   from them that walk in innocence ;
virtutum, beatus homo, qui sperat in   O Lord of hosts, blessed is the man
te.   that hopeth in Thee.

No, for He will not leave those without these good things, "*Bonis,*" grace and glory, which are the true and real good things.——"*Qui ambulant in innocentia.*" Who live keeping themselves far from sin.

PSALM LXXXIV.

In this Psalm mention is first made of the deliverance of the Jewish people from captivity, and afterwards of the redemption of the human race from the slavery of the devil. The fruits of this redemption are, moreover, predicted. We can make use of the Psalm to obtain these fruits, as the Holy Church does in the Office for Christmas.

Unto the end, for the Sons of Core, a Psalm.

1. Benedixisti Domine terram   Thou hast blessed Thy land, O
tuam : avertisti captivitatem Jacob.   Lord : Thou hast turned away the
   captivity of Jacob.

"*Benedixisti . . . tuam.*" According to the Hebrew : Thou hast been favourable to, or well pleased with. S. Jerome translates : *Placatus es, Domine, terræ tuæ.* At length, O Lord, Thou hast been appeased in respect to Thy land, and Thou hast blessed it.——"*Jacob,*" *i.e.,* his children or descendants.

2. Remisisti iniquitatem plebis   Thou hast forgiven the iniquity of
tuæ : operuisti omnia peccata eorum.   Thy people : Thou hast covered all
   their sins.

"*Operuisti . . .*" Thou hast covered all their sins, or, as Bellarmine well explains, Thou hast hid them from Thy Face, not to see and punish them.——When God covers sins, He cancels and forgives them, as if they had never been. (See what was said on *Ps.* xxxi. 1.)

3. Mitigasti omnem iram tuam: avertisti ab ira indignationis tuæ. | Thou hast softened all Thine anger: Thou hast turned away from the wrath of Thine indignation.

"*Avertisti.*" S. Jerome translates : *Conversus es ab ira furoris tui.* Thou hast put off Thy wrath, or, as Bellarmine explains it : Thou hast turned away from Thine anger and Thy indignation : *Avertisti te ab ira et indignatione tua.*

4. Converte nos Deus salutaris noster : et averte iram tuam a nobis. | Convert us, O God our Saviour : and turn away thine anger from us.

"*Deus salutaris noster.*" S. Jerome translates : *Deus Jesus noster.* Or, according to the Hebrew : *Deus salutis nostræ :* O God of our salvation.

5. Numquid in æternum irasceris nobis? aut extendes iram tuam a generatione in generationem. | Wilt Thou be angry with us for ever? or wilt thou stretch out Thy wrath from generation to generation?

6. Deus tu conversus vivificabis nos : et plebs tua lætabitur in te. | Thou shalt turn again, O God, and quicken us : and Thy people shall rejoice in Thee.

"*Deus tu conversus.*" S. Jerome translates : "*Nonne tu reverteris . . . ?* " That is : If Thou, O Lord, art appeased, and turnest Thine eyes towards us, Thou wilt give us life, by causing us to rise again from sin to grace, and Thy people will rejoice in Thee, singing Thy praises.

7 Ostende nobis Domine misericordiam tuam : et salutare tuum da nobis. | Show us Thy mercy, O Lord : and grant us Thy salvation.

"*Misericordiam tuam.*" The effects of Thy mercy.—— "*Salutare . . .*" That is, according to Bellarmine and Menochius : Give us salvation, by sending to us the Saviour, that is, the expected Messias.

8. Audiam quid loquatur in me Dominus Deus : quoniam loquetur pacem in plebem suam : | I will hearken what the Lord God shall say within me : for He will speak peace unto His people :

I will listen to what the Lord my God shall say to me in my heart ; because He will speak of the peace there is for His people, that is, of the reconciliation that Jesus Christ, their

21

Redeemer, will obtain for them, who is called by Isaias :
Princeps pacis (*Is.* ix. 6).

9. Et super sanctos suos: et in eos,   **And unto His saints: and unto**
qui convertuntur ad cor.   **them that are converted in heart.**

He will make me understand that He wills to save the just,
and even sinners, who entering into themselves will be converted seriously and with all their heart ; according to Bellarmine and Bossuet : *Qui serio resipiscunt.*

10. Verumtamen prope timentes   **Surely His salvation is nigh unto**
eum salutare ipsius: ut inhabitet   **them that fear Him: that glory may**
gloria in terra nostra.   **dwell in our land.**

" *Verumtamen.*" According to the Hebrew : *Certe, utique.*
Surely of a truth ; as Malvenda, Menochius, Sa, Tirinus, and
Lallemant observe.——"*Salutare ipsius.*" The salvation that
God will give them with the coming of the Messias.——"*Gloria.*"
That is : Jesus Christ : *Splendor gloriæ* (*Heb.* i. 3). Thus Mal-
donatus and Malvenda.

11. Misericordia, et veritas obvia-   **Mercy and truth have met to-**
verunt sibi : justitia, et pax osculatæ   **gether : justice and peace have kissed**
sunt.   **each other.**

Mercy and truth, that is, justice, will meet at the coming of
the Messias, so that then justice satisfied and peace bestowed
shall mutually embrace. —— S. Jerome and S. Augustine
understand by *Mercy,* the coming of the Saviour for the
Gentiles, to whom He was not promised ; and by *Truth,* the
faithfulness of the Messias with respect to the Jews, to whom
He was promised.——We have used the future, *will meet* and
will embrace, because in this Psalm the advent of the Messias
is foretold as something yet to come. The Psalmist speaks in
the past, because, as Bellarmine remarks, the poetical language
of the Orientals often expresses the future in the past tense,
to denote the certainty of the prophecy.

12. Veritas de terra orta est: et   **Truth is sprung out of the earth:**
justitia de cœlo prospexit.   **and justice hath looked down from**
heaven.

" *Veritas de terra orta est.*" That is, according to Lallemant :
Innocence will spring up again on earth.——Others explain
it thus : The inhabitants of the earth will embrace the truth,
that is, the true faith. But the best interpretation to my
mind is that of Bellarmine and Menochius, namely : Truth
shall spring from the earth, that is, from the virginal womb of
Mary ; so also S. Augustine understands it, of the Eternal

Word, who is the Truth itself, clothing Himself with human flesh in the womb of the Blessed Virgin Mary.

13. Etenim Dominus dabit benignitatem : et terra nostra dabit fructum suum.	For the Lord shall give goodness : [1] and our earth shall yield her fruit.

God, in His goodness, will send His Son to become man ; and our earth, that is, the Virgin Mary, will give us her fruit, Jesus Christ, Who was called by the Archangel Gabriel the Fruit of Mary's womb (*Luc.* i. 42) ; thus was accomplished the prophecy of Isaias : " Let the earth be opened, and bud forth a Saviour " (*Isa.* xlv. 8).

14. Justitia ante eum ambulabit : et ponet in via gressus suos.	Justice shall walk before him : and shall set His steps in the way.

That is, all His actions and all His steps during His life shall be conformed to rectitude and justice, in order that men, by following Him, may arrive at the country of the Blessed.

PSALM LXXXV.

FERVENT prayers which David addressed to God in his sufferings : for, according to the common opinion, David is the author of this Psalm. In it he describes at the same time the feelings and sentiments of Jesus Christ during His Passion, and predicts the conversion of the Gentiles. This Psalm may serve afflicted souls for imploring the divine help in their tribulations.

A Prayer of David himself.

1. Inclina Domine aurem tuam, et exaudi me : quoniam inops, et pauper sum ego.	Incline Thine ear, O Lord, and hear me : for I am needy and poor.

2. Custodi animam meam, quoniam sanctus sum : salvum fac servum tuum, Deus meus, sperantem in te.	Preserve my soul, for I am holy : O my God, save Thy servant, that trusteth in Thee.

" *Sanctus sum.*" S. Jerome translates : *Sanctus ego.* According to the Syriac version and the Psalter of Milan : *Sanctus es ;* but the interpreters read commonly : *Sanctus sum ;* and Mattei says that we ought not to depart from the Hebrew. Whence the verse is explained thus : Preserve my life, because I am Thy faithful servant, dedicated and devoted to Thy service, &c.

[1] *The Lord shall give goodness,* is a reference to the descent of the Holy Ghost on the Blessed Virgin ; and the consequence is the bringing forth of our Saviour.

3. Miserere mei Domine, quoniam ad te clamavi tota die: lætifica animam servi tui, quoniam ad te Domine animam meam levavi.

Have mercy upon me, O Lord, for unto Thee have I cried all the day: give joy to the soul of Thy servant, for unto Thee, O Lord, have I lifted up my soul.

"*Ad te clamavi.*" I have cried to Thee asking of Thee mercy. "*Ad te . . . levavi.*" Calmet explains : Because with ardour I have desired Thy help. But Mattei translates better: Because I have lifted up my heart to Thee.

4. Quoniam tu Domine suavis, et mitis: et multæ misericordiæ omnibus invocantibus te.

For Thou, O Lord, art sweet and mild: and plenteous in mercy unto all that call upon Thee.

"*Mitis.*" S. Jerome translates : *Propitiabilis.* Ready to be propitiated, to pardon.

5. Auribus percipe Domine orationem meam : et intende voci deprecationis meæ.

Give ear, O Lord, unto my prayer: and attend to the voice of my petition.

"*Intende . . .*" Deign to listen to that which I ask Thee.

6. In die tribulationis meæ clamavi ad te: quia exaudisti me.

I have called upon Thee in the day of my trouble: for Thou hast heard me.

"*Exaudisti me.*" That is, according to Bellarmine, Menochius, Sa, and Mariana : Thou hast been always willing to hear me.

7. Non est similis tui in diis Domine : et non est secundum opera tua.

Among the gods there is none like unto Thee, O Lord : and there is none *that can do works* like unto Thy works.

"*In diis.*" Amongst all the gods that men worship.

8. Omnes gentes quascumque fecisti venient, et adorabunt coram te Domine : et glorificabunt nomen tuum.

All the nations, whom Thou hast made, shall come and worship before Thee, O Lord: and shall glorify Thy name.

"*Venient.*" They will come, not by leaving the countries in which they dwell, but by embracing the faith.

9. Quoniam magnus es tu, et faciens mirabilia: tu es Deus solus.

For Thou art great, and doest wondrous things : Thou art God alone.

10. Deduc me Domine in via tua, et ingrediar in veritate tua: lætetur cor meum ut timeat nomen tuum.

Lead me, O Lord, in Thy way, and I will walk in Thy truth : let my heart rejoice that it may fear Thy name.

"*In via.*" In the way of Thy commandments.——"*Ingrediar in veritate tua.*" Make me to enter upon it, to walk in it, with firm step, without slipping. Mattei says that the word *Veritas* means in the Hebrew the perfection of anything that is done.

——"*Lætetur cor meum.*" According to the Chaldee : *Uni cor meum ;* that is, says Mattei : *Collige cor meum ;* and this agrees with S. Jerome's translation : *Unicum fac cor meum :* Unite, gather together to Thyself all the affections of my heart : make my heart to be for Thee alone, so that it may fear nothing else than to give Thee displeasure.

11. Confitebor tibi Domine Deus meus in toto corde meo : et glorificabo nomen tuum in æternum.	I will praise Thee, O Lord my God, with my whole heart : and I will glorify Thy name for ever.

And thus I shall praise Thee, &c.

12. Quia misericordia tua magna est super me : et eruisti animam meam ex inferno inferiori.	For great is Thy mercy toward me : and Thou hast delivered my soul out of the lower hell.

"*Quia.*" I shall praise Thee, because, &c.——"*Ex inferno inferiori.*" That is, according to some : From great dangers, which were for me a deep grave. But it is better to understand it, with Gordona, of the depth of hell where are the damned ; or of the abyss of sin, which, according to S. Jerome, is a kind of hell.

13. Deus, iniqui insurrexerunt super me, et synagoga potentium quæsierunt animam meam : et non proposuerunt te in conspectu suo.	O God, the wicked are risen up against me, and the assembly of the mighty have sought after my soul : and they have not set Thee before their eyes.

"*Synagoga . . . meam.*" My powerful enemies have assembled together in numbers to take away my life. "*Non proposuerunt . . .*" They have not set before their eyes, that Thou protectest the just and punishest the guilty. This passage is thus understood by Bellarmine and Lallemant, with S. Augustine.

14. Et tu Domine Deus miserator et misericors : patiens, et multæ misericordiæ et verax.	And Thou, O Lord, art a God full of compassion, and merciful : long suffering, and of much mercy, and true.

"*Verax.*" That is : Faithful to Thy promises.

15. Respice in me, et miserere mei : da imperium tuum puero tuo, et salvum fac filium ancillæ tuæ.	O look upon me, and have mercy on me : give Thy strength unto Thy servant, and save the son of Thine handmaid.

"*Imperium.*" According to the Hebrew, notes Mattei : *Robur.* Strength ; or following S. Jerome's translation : *Fortitudinem.* This passage, as Mariana, Sa, and Rotigni say, may easily apply to Jesus Christ, the Son of the Blessed

Virgin, who called herself the handmaid of the Lord : *Ecce ancilla Domini.*

16. Fac mecum signum in bonum, ut videant qui oderunt me, et confundantur : quoniam tu Domine adjuvisti me, et consolatus es me.	Show me a token for good, that they who hate me may see, and be confounded : because Thou, O Lord, hast helped me, and hast comforted me.

" *Signum in bonum.*" A token or sign of Thy goodwill towards me. Bellarmine, Menochius, Malvenda, &c.—— " *Confundantur ...* " That they may be confounded on seeing it, and when they hear that Thou, O Lord, lovest me, by having helped and consoled me.

PSALM LXXXVI.

A PRAISE of Sion, or of Jerusalem, which God chose for His dwelling-place. Jerusalem being a figure of the Church, the Holy Fathers and commentators agree that this Psalm speaks of the Catholic Church, founded on the holy mountains ; that is, on the Apostles, as S. Jerome, S. Augustine, Theodoret, Euthymius, &c., &c., explain, and as may be inferred from those words of S. Paul : Built upon the foundation of the Apostles (*Eph.* ii. 20).[1] This Psalm is as obscure as it is short.

For the Sons of Core, a Psalm of a Canticle.

1. Fundamenta ejus in montibus sanctis : diligit Dominus portas Sion super omnia tabernacula Jacob.	Her foundations are in the holy mountains: The Lord loveth the gates of Sion above all the dwellings of Jacob.

"*Fundamenta ejus*," *i.e.*, with Bellarmine, Mattei, and others : The foundations of the holy city which I contemplate in spirit. ——" *In montibus sanctis.*" On the high mountains of Sion and Moriah, where the Temple is built ; and therefore S. Jerome translates : *In montibus sanctuarii.*——" *Portas Sion.*" The city of Jerusalem.——" *Tabernacula Jacob.*" The habitation of Jacob, that is, according to Menochius, Bossuet, Mattei, Rotigni, &c. : The other cities of Judea.

2. Gloriosa dicta sunt de te : civitas Dei.	Glorious things are spoken of Thee : O city of God.

---

[1] We append here, with Bellarmine, this passage from S. John : "The wall of the city had twelve foundations, and in them, the twelve names of the twelve Apostles of the Lamb" (*Apoc.* xxi. 14).

Many glorious things have been said of thee, O city of God, that is, by the Prophets; thus Menochius, Mariana, and Tirinus.

3. Memor ero Rahab et Babylonis: scientium me.

I will be mindful of Rahab and of Babylon : that know me.

God here speaks.——" *Rahab.*" That is to say, Egypt.—— According to the Hebrew : *Recordabor superbum :* [1] but inter- preters, following the Chaldee, commonly understand it to mean Egypt.——" *Scientium me.*" Whose inhabitants shall know Me one day through the Faith, and shall adore Me. It is thus explained by Menochius, Lallemant, and several others.

4. Ecce alienigenæ, et Tyrus, et populus Æthiopum : hi fuerunt illic.

Behold the men of another race and Tyre : and the people of the Ethiopians, these were there.

" *Alienigenæ.*" The Philistines.[2] Thus Lallemant, Mariana, and all the interpreters understand it.——" *Fuerunt.*" The past tense is here used for the future : All these nations shall be there. This is a prophecy which has been well verified in the Church of Jesus Christ, by the conversion of the Gentiles, as Mattei remarks.

5. Numquid Sion dicet : Homo, et homo natus est in ea : et ipse fundavit eam Altissimus ?

Shall not Sion say a man, even a mighty man, is born in her : and the Highest Himself hath founded her.

This verse is more obscure than the others.——" *Numquid Sion dicet.*" Here Sion is not in the nominative case [as here rendered in the English version].——S. Jerome translates : *Ad Sion autem dicetur.* To Sion it shall be said ; Estius, with Symmachus, has : *De Sion* (of Sion) *autem dicetur* ; and Pagnini : *Et ipsi Sion* (to Sion herself) *dicetur.*——*Homo et homo.* A Hebraism which, as Mattei says, may have two senses : it may either signify a multiplicity of men, and thus Lallemant understands it ; or it may signify the excellence of man, as a wise man, a powerful man, &c., as S. Augustine, S. Jerome, Theodoret, Tertullian, Bellarmine, and others under- stand it.——Hence the verse is explained thus : What ! Is there, then, no one there to say to Sion, that is, to Jerusalem, that in the midst of her will be born a Man the most excelling,

[1] " *Rahab.*" S. Jerome translates *Superbiæ :* Pride ; and elsewhere *Superbum :* The proud one. See *Ps.* lxxxviii. 11 ; *Is.* li. 9.

[2] See *Ps.* lxxxii. 6.

Who will be the Most High, at once God and man at the same time, becoming man in the city founded by Himself? *In ea factus est homo et ipse eam fundavit.* In her was He made man, and He Himself founded her—as S. Augustine expresses it.

> **6. Dominus narrabit in scripturis populorum, et principum : horum, qui fuerunt in ea.**
>
> The Lord shall tell in His writings of peoples and of princes : of them that have been in her.

The Lord will announce it, that is, will make it known in the Sacred Scriptures, written for the instruction of the peoples, and especially in the writings of the Apostles, who are the Princes or the heads of the new Church. In these Scriptures, therefore, following the explanation of Menochius, will be registered the names of those distinguished men who have illustrated her.

> **7. Sicut lætantium omnium: habitatio est in te.**
>
> As of people all rejoicing : so is our habitation in Thee.

In a word, those who shall dwell in thee, O city of God, O Holy Church, will be all filled with joy on account of the peace which they shall enjoy.

PSALM LXXXVII.

UNDER the figure of a soul which, overwhelmed with sorrows, insults, and desolation, prays God to be delivered from them, this Psalm foretells the Passion of Jesus Christ ; as S. Augustine testifies : *Domini hic passio prophetatur.* In the midst of His most bitter sufferings and in His total dereliction, our Divine Saviour, as man, prays to His Eternal Father to succour Him ; thus Bellarmine and other commentators understand the Psalm, with S. Jerome and S. Augustine, who thus writes : *Oravit enim et Dominus, non secundum formam Dei, sed secundum formam servi ; secundum hanc enim et passus est.*[1] " For the Lord, too, prayed, not according to the form of God, but according to the form of a servant : for according to this, too, He suffered." This Psalm is well fitted for a soul in desolation, to obtain relief from God.

---

[1] See S. Aug. on this Psalm, No. 1, 2.

A Canticle of a Psalm for the Sons of Core : unto the end, for Maheleth, to answer, understanding of Eman the Ezrahite.[1]

| 1. Domine Deus salutis meæ : in die clamavi, et nocte coram te. | O Lord, the God of my salvation : I have cried in the day, and in the night before Thee. |

"*Deus salutis meæ.*" O God, from Whom I look for my salvation.

| 2. Intret in conspectu tuo oratio mea : inclina aurem tuam ad precem meam : | Let my prayer have entrance in Thy sight : incline Thine ear to my petition : |

| 3. Quia repleta est malis anima mea : et vita mea inferno appropinquavit. | For my soul is filled with evils : and my life hath drawn nigh unto hell. |

"*Inferno appropinquavit.*" Is near the grave, its end.—— This verse agrees with what Jesus Christ said in the Garden of Olives : *Tristis est anima mea usque ad mortem* (*Matt.* xxvi. 38). It is thus applied by S. Augustine.

| 4. Æstimatus sum cum descendentibus in lacum : factus sum sicut homo sine adjutorio, inter mortuos liber, | I am counted among them that go down into the pit : I am become as a man without help, free among the dead, |

"*Cum descendentibus in lacum.*" As one of those who are lowered into the grave.——"*Homo sine adjutorio.*" A dead man deprived of all help.——"*Inter mortuos liber.*" Here the word *liber* gives rise to different interpretations. S. Augustine applies it to Jesus Christ in two ways : first in the sense of, Free from sin : *Inter peccatores solus sine peccato :* Through among sinners (the dead), Himself alone without sin ; in contrast with other men, who have died by reason of sin : meaning in this sense, that He died not from necessity, but solely by an act of His free-will. This second explanation is adopted by Bellarmine and Bossuet : it seems to me more adequate according to the letter, when speaking of Jesus Christ as typified under the person of David.——Mattei says the words : *Inter mortuos liber*, signify : Separate from the other dead. He instances the case of King Azarias, who, on account of his leprosy, "dwelt in a free house apart"—*in domo libera* (4 *Kings* xv. 5) : *in domo separata* (2 *Par.* xxvi. 21) ; and Josephus the historian attests that the same king, when dead, was likewise buried by himself in a place apart : *seorsum*

[1] *Maheleth.* A musical instrument, or chorus of musicians, to answer one another.——*Understanding.* Or a Psalm of *instruction* composed by *Eman the Ezrahite*, or by David, in his name.

solus sepultus est. Mattei, explaining this passage with regard to the person of David, renders it thus : I am reputed as separate even from the other dead, as though unworthy to remain amongst them.

5. Sicut vulnerati dormientes in sepulchris, quorum non es memor amplius : et ipsi de manu tua repulsi sunt.	Like unto them that are wounded and sleep in the grave, whom Thou rememberest no more : and they are cast off from Thy hand.

" *Vulnerati.*" S. Jerome translates : *Interfecti.* I am treated like one of those who have been killed and lie in the tomb no longer remembered by Thee.——" *De manu* . . ." That is, according to Bellarmine and Tirinus : Deprived of all help from Thee.

6. Posuerunt me in lacu inferiori : in tenebrosis, et in umbra mortis.	They have laid me in the lower pit : in the dark places, and in the shadow of death.

" *Posuerunt.*" According to the Hebrew and S. Jerome : *Posuisti.* That is : Thou hast permitted my enemies to place me.——" *In tenebrosis* . . ." According to the Hebrew : *In tenebris et profunditatibus.* S. Jerome for : " *In umbra mortis,*" translates : *In profundis.* Bellarmine says that the sense is the same : he adds that the words *umbra mortis* mean properly a shadow so dense as to deprive of all light.——Menochius, moreover, says, that this verse, applied to Jesus Christ, may be understood of His descent into Limbo.

7. Super me confirmatus est furor tuus : et omnes fluctus tuos induxisti super me.	Thy wrath is strong over me : and all Thy waves Thou hast brought in upon me.

" *Furor.*" S. Augustine justly remarks that this word is better rendered by Indignation, because fury is usually predicated of those who are of an unsound or troubled mind.—— " *Omnes fluctus* . . . " Thou hast heaped upon me all the floods of ills.

8. Longe fecisti notos meos a me : posuerunt me abominationem sibi.	Thou hast put away mine acquaintance far from me : they have set me an abomination to themselves.

Thou hast removed far from me my most familiar friends ; they hold me as an object of abomination. This was truly accomplished in Jesus Christ, when He was abandoned by His disciples : " Then the disciples all leaving Him fled " (*Matt.* xxvi. 56), " and all His acquaintance . . . stood afar off " (*Luke* xxiii. 49).

9. Traditus sum, et non egredie-   I was delivered up, and came not
bar : oculi mei languerunt præ inopia.   forth : mine eyes languished for want.

" *Traditus sum.*" I have been given up into the power of
my enemies.——" *Non egrediebar.*" That is, as Bellarmine
explains : *Non volebam egredi.* I did not wish to withdraw
Myself, as it was decreed by My Father that I should suffer
for the salvation of men.——" *Oculi mei ...* " That is, according to the same commentator : My eyes have become faint,
and weakened, as though drained by reason of shedding tears.
So also Menochius.

10. Clamavi ad te Domine tota   All the day I cried unto Thee, O
die : expandi ad te manus meas.   Lord : I stretched out my hands unto
   Thee.

That is, to ask help from His Father : according to what
the Apostle writes : "Who in the days of His flesh, with a
strong cry and tears offering up prayers and supplications to
Him that was able to save Him from death " (*Heb.* v. 7).

11. Numquid mortuis facies mira-   Wilt Thou show wonders unto the
bilia : aut medici suscitabunt et con-   dead ? or shall physicians raise to life,
fitebuntur tibi ?   and give praise unto Thee ?

Wilt Thou perhaps work miracles by raising the dead ? or
can physicians raise them to life, that they may praise Thee ?

12. Numquid narrabit aliquis in   Shall any one in the grave declare
sepulchro misericordiam tuam : et   Thy mercy : and Thy truth in de-
veritatem tuam in perditione ?   struction ?

" *Veritatem tuam.*" Thy faithfulness to Thy promises.——
" *In perditione.*" After having already lost his life.

13. Numquid cognoscentur in tene-   Shall Thy wonders be known in
bris mirabilia tua : et justitia tua in   the dark : and Thy justice in the
terra oblivionis ?   land of forgetfulness ?

Can the admirable prodigies of Thy goodness and justice be
known in the darkness of the tomb, even in that place of
forgetfulness ?[1]

14. Et ego ad te Domine clamavi :   But I, O Lord, have cried unto
et mane oratio mea præveniet te.   Thee : and in the morning my prayer
   shall come early before Thee.

" *Mane ...* " I will not cease to present my prayers to
Thee from the break of day.

15. Ut quid Domine repellis ora-   Lord, why castest Thou off my
tionem meam : avertis faciem tuam   prayer ? why turnest Thou away Thy
a me.   face from me ?

[1] On verses 11-13, see *Cant. of Ezechias* 13, and *Ps.* cxiii. 26.

This may be understood of the prayer which Jesus Christ
made in the Garden of Olives : " May this chalice pass from
Me ! " a prayer which His Father did not hear because our
Redeemer wished effectively to die, to save man ; for, says
Bellarmine, had the Son prayed absolutely, the Father would
certainly have heard Him.

16. Pauper sum ego, et in labori-   I am poor, and in labours from my
bus a juventute mea: exaltatus   youth up : and being lifted up I have
autem, humiliatus sum et conturba- been humbled and troubled.
tus.

I am poor and I have been so from my youth, living always
in fatigues and sufferings ; and no sooner have I at times
received some relief, than immediately I have seen myself
humbled and weighed down by affliction.

17. In me transierunt iræ tuæ: Thy wrath hath come upon me:
et terrores tui conturbaverunt me.   and Thy terrors have troubled me.

" *Conturbaverunt me.*" S. Jerome translates : *Oppresserunt
me.* That is : I am crushed down under the strokes of Thy
justice, on account of the rigour with which all the sins of
men have deserved to be punished.

18. Circumdederunt me sicut aqua   They came round about me like
tota die : circumdederunt me simul. water all the day : they have com-
                              passed me about together.

These terrors of Thy justice have surrounded me like a
torrent the whole day long, and have all united together to
overwhelm me.

19. Elongasti a me amicum, et   Friend and neighbour Thou hast
proximum : et notos meos a miseria. put far from me : and mine acquaint-
                              ance, because of misery.

Thou hast permitted that even my friends and neighbours
should keep at a distance from me ; those even who were
familiar and intimate with me have withdrawn far off from
my misery.——" *A miseria.*" According to the Hebrew : *Ab
obscuritate, a tenebris.* Hence this explanation which Mattei
gives with Marco Marino : *Tenebris se abdunt ne videantur a
me :* They hide themselves, not to be seen by me and obliged
to help me in my misery.

PSALM LXXXVIII.

THIS Psalm may be divided into three parts. In the first
(verses 1-36) the Psalmist recalls the promises made by God

to David, to give a kingdom in perpetuity to his posterity. In the second (verses 37-44) he shows that these promises had not their entire accomplishment in the descendants of David according to the flesh, and in his earthly kingdom. In the third, he concludes by sighing after the coming of the Messias, in Whom all the promises were to be verified in a perfect sense, because He alone was to deliver His people from the afflictions which they suffered. It is for this reason the Church recites this Psalm in the Office for Christmas.

Of understanding, for Ethan the Ezrahite.

1. Misericordias Domini : in æter-num cantabo.

The mercies of the Lord : I will sing for evermore.

2. In generationem et genera-tionem : annuntiabo veritatem tuam in ore meo.

I will show forth Thy truth with my mouth : from generation to gene-ration.

"*Annuntiabo veritatem tuam.*" According to the Hebrew : *Notam faciam fidem tuam.* I will make known Thy faithful-ness to Thy promises.

3. Quoniam dixisti : In æternum misericordia ædificabitur in cœlis : præparabitur veritas tua in eis.

For Thou hast said : Mercy shall be built up for ever in the heavens : Thy truth shall be stablished in them.

"*In æternum misericordia ædificabitur.*" That is : Mercy shall be there for us an eternal building of graces.——"*Præ-parabitur.*" According to the Chaldee : *Stabilietur* : Shall be established.——"*Veritas tua.*" That is : Thy fidelity, or the accomplishment of Thy promises.

4. Disposui testamentum electis meis, juravi David servo meo : Usque in æternum præparabo semen tuum.

I have made a covenant with Mine elect ; I have sworn unto my servant David My servant : Thy seed will I stablish for ever.

"*Disposui testamentum.*"   S. Jerome translates : *Percussi fœdus.*——"*Electis meis.*" With My elect, namely, Abraham, Isaac, and the other Patriarchs, as the commentators generally understand it. "*Præparabo.*" [S. Jerome translates : *Stabi-liam*]. I have promised (2 *Kings* vii. 12) with an oath to my servant David, that I will establish for ever My Kingdom in his seed. This promise has been verified in the person of Jesus Christ, as is the teaching of S. Jerome, S. Augustine, Theodoret, &c.——Mattei justly observes that the kingdom of David was made perpetual in Jesus Christ, his descendant, who continued and will continue eternally to hold the spiritual empire of the Church.

5. Et ædificabo in generationem, et generationem : sedem tuam.	And I will build up thy throne : from generation to generation.

David, My servant, I will establish for thee a royal throne through all ages. Bellarmine remarks with reason that this has been only properly verified in our Saviour, of whom David was the figure.

6. Confitebuntur cœli mirabilia tua Domine : etenim veritatem tuam in ecclesia sanctorum.	The heavens shall praise Thy wonders, O Lord : and Thy truth in the church of the saints.

"*Etenim.*" According to the Hebrew : *Et, Etiam.*——"*Veritatem tuam.*" Thy faithfulness in the promises Thou hast made.——"*In ecclesia sanctorum.*" The pious in their assemblies.

7. Quoniam quis in nubibus æquabitur Domino : similis erit Deo in filiis Dei ?	For who in the clouds can be compared unto the Lord : or who among the sons of God shall be like unto God ?

"*In nubibus.*" That is : The heavens.——"*In filiis Dei.*" According to the Chaldee : Among the Angels.

8. Deus, qui glorificatur in consilio sanctorum : magnus et terribilis super omnes, qui in circuitu ejus sunt.	God Who is glorified in the assembly of the saints : great and terrible above all them that are about Him.

"*Sanctorum.*" That is : Of the Angels.

9. Domine Deus virtutum quis similis tibi? potens es Domine, et veritas tua in circuitu tuo.	O Lord God of hosts, who is like unto Thee? Thou art mighty, O Lord, and Thy truth is round about Thee.

"*Veritas . . .*" That is : Thy faithfulness always accompanies Thee.——Mattei understands this part of the verse thus : Thou art mighty, and therefore dost Thou promise much, and Thou art faithful to fulfil Thy promises.

10. Tu dominaris potestati maris : motum autem fluctuum ejus tu mitigas.	Thou rulest the power of the sea : and appeasest the motion of the waves thereof.

"*Potestati maris.*" S. Jerome translates : *Superbiæ maris.* The pride of the sea.

11. Tu humiliasti sicut vulneratum, superbum : in brachio virtutis tuæ dispersisti inimicos tuos.	Thou hast humbled the proud, as one that is slain : with the arm of Thy strength Thou hast scattered Thine enemies.

"*Vulneratum.*" The Hebrew according to Menochius means : Wounded mortally.——"*Superbum.*" In the Hebrew : *Rahab.* That is : King Pharao, or else Egypt.[1]——"*Dispersisti.*" Thou

[1] *Ps.* lxxxvi. 3.

hast scattered thine enemies by drowning them in the Red Sea ; according to the interpretation of Bellarmine.

12. Tui sunt cœli, et tua est terra, orbem terræ et plenitudinem ejus tu fundasti: Aquilonem et mare tu creasti.

Thine are the heavens, and the earth is Thine ; the world and the fulness thereof Thou hast founded : the north and the sea Thou hast created.

" *Plenitudinem ejus.*" That is, all that is contained within its orb.——" *Aquilonem et mare.*" Bellarmine, Menochius, Lallemant, and Mattei, with Symmachus, hereby understand the North and the South.[1]

13. Thabor et Hermon in nomine tuo exultabunt : tuum brachium cum potentia.

Thabor and Hermon shall rejoice in Thy name : Thine arm is an arm of might.

" *Thabor et Hermon.*" That is, as Lallemant explains : The East and the West.

14. Firmetur manus tua, et exaltetur dextera tua : justitia et judicium præparatio sedis tuæ.

Let Thy hand be strengthened, and Thy right hand exalted : justice and judgment are the preparation of Thy throne.

" *Firmetur.*" S. Jerome translates : *Roboretur.* Let the might of Thy hand be strengthened and shine forth.—— " *Præparatio.*" According to the Hebrew : *Basis ;* or as S. Jerome translates : *Firmamentum.* Justice and Thy righteous judgment are the foundation and stability of Thy throne.

15. Misericordia et veritas præcedent faciem tuam : beatus populus, qui scit jubilationem.

Mercy and truth shall go before Thy face : blessed is the people that knoweth gladness.

" *Veritas.*" Faithfulness to Thy promises.——" *Præcedent faciem tuam.*" That is : Are always before Thine eyes.—— " *Beatus.*" Happy the people that knows the joy that is felt in praising Thee. Thus Bellarmine, Menochius, Tirinus, and Bossuet.

16. Domine, in lumine vultus tui ambulabunt, et in nomine tuo exultabunt tota die : et in justitia tua exaltabuntur.

They shall walk, O Lord, in the light of Thy countenance, and in Thy name they shall rejoice all the day : and in Thy justice they shall be exalted.

That is, according to Bellarmine and Menochius : Those who praise Thee shall walk in the light of Thy countenance, that is, of Thy grace, in following the way of Thy precepts ; they

[1] *Ps.* cvi. 3.

shall exult with joy all the day long in celebrating Thy Name; and Thy justice, which will never fail to recompense Thy servants, shall raise them to a high degree of perfection.

17. Quoniam gloria virtutis eorum tu es: et in beneplacito tuo exalta-bitur cornu nostrum.	For Thou art the glory of their strength: and in Thy good pleasure shall our horn be exalted.

Because Thou art the glory of their virtue, since all their force and vigour come from Thy grace, and not from their own works; and of Thy pure good pleasure alone shall our strength be raised against the enemy.——"*In beneplacito tuo exaltabitur.*" S. Jerome translates: *In voluntate tua elevabis.* In Thy will shalt Thou raise up.——"*Cornu nostrum.*" According to the Chaldee: *Robur:* Our strength.

18. Quia Domini est assumptio nostra: et sancti Israel Regis nostri.	For our defence is of the Lord: and of the Holy One of Israel our King.

"*Assumptio.*" S. Jerome translates: *Protectio.*

19. Tunc locutus es in visione sanctis tuis, et dixisti: posui adjuto-rium in potente, et exaltavi electum de plebe mea.	Then Thou spokest in a vision to Thy saints, and saidst: I have laid help upon one that is mighty, and have exalted one chosen out of My people.

"*Sanctis tuis.*" To Thy holy Prophets. According to the Hebrew: *Sancto tuo;* by which may be understood the Prophet Samuel; but Malvenda, Lallemant, and Mattei say that the other Prophets may also be very well understood, in accordance with the Vulgate.[1]——"*In potente.*" In a mighty man, who is David.——"*Exaltavi.*" I have raised him to the throne.

20. Inveni David servum meum: oleo sancto meo unxi eum.	I have found David My servant: with My holy oil have I anointed him.

This one, whom I have found, is David, My faithful servant; and I will cause him to be anointed with My holy oil King of Israel; as was done by the hand of Samuel (1 *Kings* xvi. 13).

21. Manus enim mea auxiliabitur ei: et brachium meum comfortabit eum.	For My hand shall help him: and Mine arm shall strengthen him.

[1] Some interpreters translate the Hebrew in the singular; but S. Jerome translates it in the plural, and Bellarmine says: In the Greek it is: *Filiis tuis*; but S. Jerome (*Epist. ad Suniam et Fretellam*) says that all the inter-preters have rendered it: "*Sanctis tuis*," as it is in the Hebrew.

22. Nihil proficiet inimicus in eo : et filius iniquitatis non apponet nocere ei.	The enemy shall no way prevail over him : nor the son of iniquity have power to hurt him.

23. Et concidam a facie ipsius inimicos ejus : et odientes eum in fugam convertam.	And I will cut down his enemies before his face : and them that hate him I will put to flight.

24. Et veritas mea, et misericordia mea cum ipso : et in nomine meo exaltabitur cornu ejus.	And My truth and My mercy *shall* be with him : and in My name shall his horn be exalted.

" *Veritas mea.*" My faithfulness to My promises.——" *In nomine meo.*" That is : By My help.——The expressions in this verse and in the following, commentators say, apply better to the person of Jesus Christ.

25. Et ponam in mari manum ejus : et in fluminibus dexteram ejus.	I will set his hand also in the sea : and his right hand in the rivers.

That is, I will give him the dominion of the sea and of the rivers.——If this verse is taken as applying to David, by the sea may be understood the Persian Gulf, the Arabian Gulf, or Red Sea, and all the Erythræan Sea, where were the Edomites, the Amalekites, and the Arabians, all tributaries of David ; and by the rivers, the Euphrates, the Orontes, and others subject to David, when he took Syria, Mesopotamia, and Damascus. But Maldonatus, Bellarmine, Menochius, and many others apply the verse better to Jesus Christ, of whom David was the figure, and to whom God made subject the seas, the rivers, and the whole earth.

26. Ipse invocabit me : Pater meus es tu : Deus meus, et susceptor salutis meæ.	He shall cry unto Me : Thou art my Father : My God, and the support of my salvation.

Jesus Christ, speaking to God, calls Him "His Father," with respect to His divine nature, and "His God and protector of His salvation," with regard to His human nature. Such is the explanation given by Bellarmine and Menochius.

27. Et ego primogenitum ponam illum : excelsum præ regibus terræ.	And I will make him My first-born : high above the kings of the earth.

Bellarmine and Menochius say that Jesus Christ, as God, is the Only Begotten, and as man, is the First-born, because He was the Head of the predestined (*Eph.* i.). Others apply this verse to the person of David. Mattei justly remarks that in the spiritual sense, the expressions in the verse are only fully verified in Jesus Christ.

22

28. In æternum   servabo   illi   I will keep My mercy for him for
misericordiam meam: et testamen- ever : and My covenant faithful unto
tum meum fidele ipsi.   him.

S. Augustine applies this verse also to the person of Jesus
Christ, saying: *Propter ipsum fidele testamentum:* which means
that God, on account of the merits of Jesus Christ, kept His
promise to save mankind. But others commonly apply it to
David, in this sense : I will for ever keep my mercy towards
him ; and I will be faithful to the promises I have made him :
that is, to give him a Son who shall be Jesus Christ, through
Whom his reign shall become eternal, everlasting. This promise was made to David by the prophet Nathan (2 *Kings*
vii. 12). Such is the explanation given by Bellarmine and
Menochius.

29. Et ponam in sæculum sæculi   And I will make his seed to endure
semen ejus : et thronum ejus sicut for ever : and his throne as the days
dies cœli.   of heaven.

This verse corresponds with what we read in the Gospel :
" The Lord shall give unto Him the throne of David His
father : and He shall reign in the house of Jacob for ever, and
of His kingdom there shall be no end " (*Luke* i. 32, 33). It
corresponds, likewise, with the prophecy of Isaias : " He shall
sit upon the throne of David, and upon his kingdom ; to
establish it and strengthen it with judgment and with justice,
from henceforth and for ever " (*Is.* ix. 7). Jesus Christ was,
in fact, to reign over all Israel and over the whole earth, not
indeed with a temporal rule, which it was not His will to
exercise, but with a spiritual rule, of which the earthly kingdom of David was a figure. Hence the verse may be thus
explained : I will preserve his seed by giving him the Messias
for his son, through Whom I will make his throne to endure
as long as the heavens, that is, for ever. Gordona remarks
here that the temporal reign of David ended under Jechonias ;
whence he says this promise of an everlasting kingdom can
only be understood of Jesus Christ typified by David.

30. Si autem dereliquerint filii   But if his children forsake My
ejus legem meam : et in judiciis meis law : and walk not in My judgments :
non ambulaverint :

" *Ejus.*"   David's.——" *Judiciis.*"   Commandments.

31. Si justitias meas profanaverint: If they profane my ceremonies :
et mandata mea non custodierint :   and keep not my commandments :

32. Visitabo in virga iniquitates eorum: et in verberibus peccata eorum.

I will visit their iniquities with a rod: and their sins with stripes.

The Lord threatens the rod and stripes, and not the sword and death, to show that He will come to them as a father to correct, not as an executioner to take their life.

33. Misericordiam autem meam non dispergam ab eo : neque nocebo in veritate mea :

Yet My mercy I will not utterly take from him : nor will I suffer My truth to fail :

"*Misericordiam ... ab eo.*" That is : However much the descendants of David may offend Me, I will not deprive him of the promised Messias in his family.——"*Neque nocebo in veritate mea.*" According to the Hebrew : *Non mentiar in veritate mea:* I will not fail in the promise I have made to him.

34. Neque profanabo testamentum meum : et quæ procedunt de labiis meis non faciam irrita.

Neither will I break My covenant : nor will I make void the words that go forth from My lips.

35. Semel juravi in sancto meo, si David mentiar : semen ejus in æternum manebit.

Once have I sworn by My holiness : I will not lie unto David : his seed shall endure for ever.

"*Semel ... meo.*" Mattei observes that this is a recognised expression in the Scriptures ; thus we read : "The Lord God hath sworn by His holiness" (*Amos* iv. 2).——"*Si David mentiar.*" The same commentator says that in the imprecatory oaths the Hebrews left the second part of the imprecation to be understood ; so that "*Si mentiar*" means the same as *Non mentiar,* as if God said : If I lie, 1 am no longer God.—— "*Semen ejus in æternum manebit.*" His posterity shall never come to an end, since Jesus Christ shall reign for all eternity.

36. Et thronus ejus sicut sol in conspectu meo : et sicut luna perfecta in æternum : et testis in cœlo fidelis.

And his throne as the sun before Me ; and as the moon perfect for ever : and the faithful witness in heaven.

And his throne shall stand like the sun before Me for ever, and like the perfect moon, that is, when it shines out in its full.——"*Testis in cœlo fidelis.*" That is, according to Bellarmine and Menochius : Like the rainbow which appears in heaven as a faithful witness of the peace which God wishes to keep with men. But Lallemant explains it thus : And this throne placed in heaven for the Son of David shall be there for ever a faithful witness of the truth of My promise.

37. Tu vero repulisti et despexisti: distulisti Christum tuum.

But Thou hast rejected and despised Thine anointed: Thou hast been angry with him.

But Thou, O Lord, hast rejected and despised us by delaying to send the promised Messias.[1]——S. Augustine says here: *Ergo, Domine non imples quod promisisti?* But he then adds: *Manet omnino, Deus, quod promisisti; nam Christum tuum non abstulisti sed distulisti.* Art thou not, Lord, going to fulfil what Thou hast promised? Yea, assuredly: and Thou still keepest Thy promise, for Thou hast not cast off Thy Christ, though Thou hast put Him off, that is, hast delayed Him.

38. Evertisti testamentum servi tui: profanasti in terra sanctuarium ejus.

Thou hast overthrown the covenant of Thy servant: Thou hast profaned his sanctuary on the earth.[2]

"*Sanctuarium.*" According to the Hebrew: *Diadema.* The verse is thus explained: It seems as if Thou hadst revoked the covenant and the promise made to Thy servant David; for Thou hast permitted Thy sanctuary to be profaned on earth, by allowing the crown to pass into the hands of a Gentile king, who has seized upon the throne.——This happened when Joachin and Sedecias, descendants of David, were taken captive (4 *Kings* xxiv., xxv.). But S. Augustine, Bede, Cassiodorus, and others apply this text to the destruction of Jerusalem by Titus.

39. Destruxisti omnes sepes ejus: posuisti firmamentum ejus formidinem.

Thou hast broken down all his hedges: Thou hast made his stronghold a fear.

"*Destruxisti . . . ejus.*" Thou hast willed all the walls of the city or kingdom of David to be ruined, so that it remained as a vineyard without hedges.——"*Posuisti . . .*" According to the Hebrew: *Posuisti in munitionibus ejus contritionem;* or, as S. Jerome translates: *Posuisti munitiones ejus pavorem.* That is: In place of the fortresses of the kingdom Thou hast set fear. Thus Lallemant explains it with Bellarmine: *Fecisti ut in locum munitionis succederet formido.* Thou hast caused terror to take the place of defence.

---

[1] Here begins the second part of the Psalm.

[2] *Overthrown the covenant,* &c. All this seems to relate to the time of the captivity of Babylon, in which, for the sins of the people and their princes, God seemed to have set aside for a while the covenant He made with David. ——*Sanctuary.* His crown, casting it to the ground. The Septuagint here uses the word rendered *sanctuary* for *ornament.*

40. Diripuerunt eum omnes transeuntes viam : factus est opprobrium vicinis suis.

All that passed by the way have spoiled him : he is become a reproach unto his neighbours.

"*Eum.*" The kingdom.——"*Vicinis suis.*" To the neighbouring nations.

41. Exaltasti dexteram deprimentium eum : lætificasti omnes inimicos ejus.

Thou hast set up the right hand of them that oppress him : Thou hast made all his enemies to rejoice.

"*Exaltasti dexteram.*" Thou hast increased the strength.

42. Avertisti adjutorium gladii ejus : et non es auxiliatus ei in bello.

Thou hast turned away the help of his sword : and hast not assisted him in battle.

S. Augustine, applying this passage to the destruction of the Jewish people, and to the ruin of their kingdom, for having put to death Jesus Christ, exclaims : *Terram perdidit, pro qua Dominum occidit !* It has lost that land, for which it killed the Lord.

43. Destruxisti eum ab emundatione : et sedem ejus in terram collisisti.

Thou hast made his glory to cease : and Thou hast cast his throne down to the ground.

Thou hast destroyed in this people their cleanliness or comeliness, that is, thou hast despoiled them of their splendour ; thus Lallemant explains this first clause of the verse.[1] ——But S. Augustine interprets it otherwise ; he says that the Jews, through not believing in Jesus Christ, remained deprived of the grace which would have purified them : *Soluti sunt ab emundatione* ; for believing in Him by faith was alone able to cleanse their hearts from their sins.——"*Et sedem...*" And Thou hast dashed to the ground in pieces his royal throne. Thus was fulfilled the prophecy implied in the words of Jacob : "The sceptre shall not be taken away from Juda," &c. (*Gen.* xlix. 10).

44. Minorasti dies temporis ejus : perfudisti eum confusione.

The days of his time hast Thou shortened : Thou hast covered him with confusion.

S. Augustine says that the Jews believed their kingdom would last for ever : *Putabant se in æternum regnaturos.*

---

[1] According to Bellarmine the Hebrew text is more clear : he translates it literally thus : Thou hast made his comeliness (or brightness, or glory) to cease, and hast brought down his throne to the ground. By *Munditiam* he understands the splendour of the regal ornaments. S. Jerome has : *Quiescere fecisti munditiam ejus.*

45. Usquequo Domine avertis in finem: exardescet sicut ignis ira tua?

How long, O Lord, turnest Thou away unto the end? shall Thine anger burn like fire?

"*Avertis.*"[1] According to the Hebrew *Absconderis.* Wilt Thou hide Thyself?——"*In finem?*" Is it to be until our ruin is complete?——The verse may be thus explained: How long, O Lord, wilt Thou refuse to look graciously upon us? Is thine anger, then, like fire, which is not quenched until it has utterly consumed whatever it lays hold of?——Thus Lallemant explains the words with Bellarmine.

46. Memorare quæ mea substantia: numquid enim vane constituisti omnes filios hominum?

Remember what my substance is: for hast Thou made all the children of men in vain?

"*Memorare quæ mea substantia.*" [Bellarmine translates the Hebrew thus: *Memorare ergo quanti temporis sim.* That is: Consider how short the time is that remains for me to live.] ——S. Augustine, explaining these words with reference to Jesus Christ, makes David say: Remember, O Lord, what is my substance, that is, that Thy Son is to take flesh from my blood.

47. Quis est homo, qui vivet, et non videbit mortem: eruet animam suam de manu inferi?

Who is the man that shall live, and shall not see death: that shall deliver his soul from the hand of hell?

"*Eruet* . . . " And who is there that shall be exempt from, or shall escape, the tomb?

48. Ubi sunt misericordiæ tuæ antiquæ Domine: sicut jurasti David in veritate tua?

Where are Thine ancient mercies, O Lord: as Thou swearedst unto David in Thy truth?

"*In veritate tua.*" That is: According to Thy faithfulness.

49. Memor esto Domine opprobrii servorum tuorum: (quod continui in sinu meo) multarum gentium:

Be mindful, O Lord, of the reproach of Thy servants (which I have borne in my bosom) of many nations:

Remember, O Lord, the reproach that Thy servants receive from many nations; of which reproach my own heart is full; as Mattei explains: *Quibus opprobriis plenus est sinus meus.*

50. Quod exprobraverunt inimici tui Domine: quod exprobraverunt commutationem Christi tui.

Wherewith Thine enemies have reproached, O Lord: wherewith they have reproached the change of Thine anointed.

"*Commutationem.*" According to the Hebrew: *Claudicationem:* Limping, Halting.——That is: These Thy enemies,

---

[1] Here begins the third part of the Psalm.

O Lord, upbraid us, and for what? They upbraid us because Thy Christ, or the Messias, comes limping with too slow a pace.——When the Gentiles insulted the Jews, the latter answered them that the Messias would soon come to deliver them from their miseries ; but the Gentiles, continuing their reproaches, rejoined : How is this? Is your Messias lame that He never arrives?

51. Benedictus Dominus in æter-   Blessed be the Lord for evermore.
num. Fiat, fiat.   Amen, amen.

That is : But may the Lord be blessed for ever, for He cannot fail in His promises ; let us, then, humbly pray Him to accomplish with all speed the promise He has made to send us the Saviour.

PSALM XCIII.

THIS Psalm speaks of the Providence of God in punishing the wicked and rewarding the good, though by His just judgment it often happens that the wicked prosper in this world and the good are afflicted. From the beginning of the Psalm to verse 14 the Psalmist expresses the complaints of the just who are grieved at seeing the prosperity of the wicked : afterwards he rebukes the just for their little faith, and exhorts them to patience and confidence in God.

A Psalm of David himself on the fourth day of the week.

1. Deus ultionum Dominus: Deus   God is the Lord to Whom ven-
ultionum libere egit.   geance belongeth : the God of ven-
                                   geance hath acted freely.

The Lord is the God of vengeance, that is, the punisher of crimes ; He punishes them, and there is no one who is able to hinder Him.——In the Hebrew this verse is in the imperative mood, and S. Jerome translates it thus : *Deus ultionum, Domine: Deus ultionum ostendere.* O God, Lord of vengeance, show forth the power that Thou hast to punish the wicked.[1]

2. Exaltare qui judicas terram: Lift up Thyself, Thou that judgest
redde retributionem superbis.   the earth : render a reward to the
                                   proud.

" *Exaltare.*" Let Thy power shine forth and be known.——
" *Redde . . .* " Render unto the proud the punishment they deserve.——S. Augustine observes here that the Psalmist

[1] *Cant. of Moses,* v. 50 ; or *Deut.* xxxii. 35. *Rom.* xii. 19.

under the imperative form is simply predicting. *Prophetia est prædicentis, non audacia jubentis:* Here is the prophecy of one who predicts, not the presumptuousness of one who commands.

3. Usquequo peccatores Domine : usquequo peccatores gloriabuntur ?

How long shall sinners, O Lord : how long shall sinners boast themselves ?

" *Gloriabuntur.*" Glory in their sins.

4. Effabuntur, et loquentur iniquitatem : loquentur omnes, qui operantur injustitiam ?

How long shall they utter, and speak iniquity : *how long shall they* speak who work injustice ?

" *Loquentur.*" Have the boldness to make known and speak of their sins to others.

5. Populum tuum Domine humiliaverunt: et hereditatem tuam vexaverunt.

Thy people, O Lord, they have brought low : and they have afflicted Thine inheritance.

" *Humiliaverunt.*" According to the Hebrew : *Attriverunt.* Have worn down, trampled upon. That is : They have oppressed and ill-treated this people which is Thy inheritance.

6. Viduam, et advenam interfecerunt : et pupillos occiderunt.

They have slain the widow and the stranger : and they have put the fatherless to death.

They have not hesitated to kill whosoever came in their way : widows and orphans, and even strangers whom they did not know.

7. Et dixerunt: Non videbit Dominus : nec intelliget Deus Jacob.

And they have said : The Lord shall not see : neither shall the God of Jacob understand.

" *Nec intelliget Deus.*" According to S. Augustine : *Deus nec avertit ut sciat.* God does not pay attention to know these things.

8. Intelligite insipientes in populo: et stulti aliquando sapite.

Understand, ye unwise among the people : and ye fools, be wise at last.

" *Stulti* . . . " For once undeceive yourselves of your folly.

9. Qui plantavit aurem, non audiet ? aut qui finxit oculum, non considerat ?

He that planted the ear, shall He not hear ? or He that formed the eye, doth he not consider ?

" *Plantavit.*" That is : Hath formed.——" *Considerat.*" S. Jerome translates : *Videbit.* Shall He not see ?

10. Qui corripit gentes, non arguet ? qui docet hominem scientiam ?

He that chastiseth nations, shall He not rebuke ? He that teacheth man knowledge ?

"*Corripit.*" S. Jerome and S. Augustine translate : *Erudit.*
Instructs. That is ; Shall He Who instructs the nations be
unable to rebuke ? and He who gives to man the knowledge of
things, not Himself know them ? As S. Augustine says :
Ipse non scit, qui te fecit scire ? Does not He know, He Who
made thee know ?

11. Dominus scit cogitationes hominum : quoniam vanæ sunt.	The Lord knoweth the thoughts of men : that they are vain.

"*Vanæ.*" Vain : or, as Mattei prefers, Evil ; he says that
in the language of the Bible vanity means sin.

12. Beatus homo, quem tu erudieris Domine : et de lege tua docueris eum.	Blessed is the man whom Thou shalt instruct, O Lord : and shalt teach him out of Thy law.

13. Ut mitiges ei a diebus malis : donec fodiatur peccatori fovea.	That Thou mayest give him rest from the evil days: till a pit be dug for the wicked.

12, 13. "*Ut mitiges ei.*" According to the Hebrew : *Ut
quietem des illi:* That Thou mayest give him rest. Or, as S.
Jerome translates : *Ut quiescat:* That he may rest. Hence it
is explained thus : Happy is he whom Thou dost teach and
instruct, with the view to mitigate his pains in the time of
tribulation.——"*Donec...*" Till the pit of the grave be dug
for the sinner, that is, till death arrives ; meaning that the
sinner, though he be not afflicted in this life, yet has to die.

14. Quia non repellet Dominus plebem suam : et hereditatem suam non derelinquet.	For the Lord will not cast off His people : neither will He forsake His own inheritance.

"*Plebem suam et hereditatem suam.*" His people who are
faithful to Him, and His inheritance which is the same faithful people.

15. Quoadusque justitia conver- tatur in judicium : et qui juxta illam omnes qui recto sunt corde.	Until justice be turned into judg- ment :[1] and all the upright in heart are near it.

Many different interpretations are given of this verse ; but
the following appears to me clear : God does not abandon His
faithful servants until justice be resolved into judgment, and
according to this same justice all those who are upright in
heart shall be judged. This sense appears to me to be that of
S. Jerome's translation, although it is expressed in different
terms, viz. : *Quoniam ad justitiam revertetur judicium, et sequen-*

[1] By being put in execution.

tur illud omnes recti corde.   Because judgment shall return to justice, and all the upright in heart shall follow it (that is, judgment).

16. Quis consurget mihi adversus malignantes? aut quis stabit mecum adversus operantes iniquitatem?

Who shall rise up for me against the evil-doers? or who shall stand with me against the workers of iniquity?

"*Consurget mihi . . . Stabit mecum.*" S. Jerome repeats: *Stabit pro me.* Will stand up for me: on my side, in my favour.

17. Nisi quia Dominus adjuvit me: paulominus habitasset in inferno anima mea.

Unless the Lord had been my helper: my soul had almost dwelt in hell.

If it had not been the Lord Who helped me, I should have narrowly escaped having now my abode in the grave.——But S. Augustine understands "*In inferno*" to be the real hell of the damned: he thus explains: *Prope rueram in illam fossam quæ paratur peccatoribus.* I was on the point of falling into that pit which is prepared for sinners.

18. Si dicebam: Motus est pes meus: misericordia tua Domine adjuvabat me.

If I said: My foot slippeth: Thy mercy, O Lord, held me up.

"*Motus est pes meus.*" That is, I am in danger of falling.

19. Secundum multitudinem dolorum meorum in corde meo: consolationes tuæ lætificaverunt animam meam.

According to the multitude of my sorrows in my heart: Thy comforts have given joy to my soul.

20. Numquid adhæret tibi sedes iniquitatis: qui fingis laborem in præcepto?

Doth the seat of iniquity cleave unto Thee: Who ordainest diligence in Thy precepts?

What! wouldst Thou then have a throne like to that of unjust judges, Thou who feignest that there is labour and irksomeness in the precept, that is, Who pretendest that Thy precepts cannot be fulfilled without fatigue and affliction?—— Estius says that the word which is here, "*Laborem,*" in the Hebrew signifies, Affliction. And so also Bellarmine, whose explanation seems to be the best.

21. Captabunt in animam justi: et sanguinem innocentem condemnabunt.

They will hunt after the life of the just: and will condemn innocent blood.

The wicked will conspire against the life of the just man, and will condemn the innocent to death.

22. Et factus est mihi Dominus in refugium : et Deus meus in adjutorium spei meæ.

But the Lord is my refuge : and my God is the help of my hope.

23. Et reddet illis iniquitatem ipsorum : et in malitia eorum disperdet eos : disperdet illos Dominus Deus noster.

And He will bring back upon them their iniquity : and in their malice He will destroy them : the Lord our God will destroy them.

He will make their iniquity to fall back upon themselves, and confused by their own malice He will scatter them ; the Lord our God knows well how so scatter them.

PSALM XCV.

THIS Psalm is substantially the second part of the one found in 1 *Paral.* xvi. 7-36, which David composed when the Ark was transferred from the house of Obededom to the Tabernacle erected on Mount Sion, which is a figure of the Catholic Church. In this Psalm the Israelites are invited to praise God ; and especially are Christians called on to serve with fidelity our Lord Jesus Christ. With S. Jerome, S. Augustine, S. Ambrose, and with the generality of commentators, Bellarmine says that the chief aim of David in this Psalm was to foretell the coming and the reign of the Messias.

A Canticle for David himself, when the house was built after the captivity.[1]

1. Cantate Domino canticum novum : cantate Domino, omnis terra.

O sing unto the Lord a new song : sing unto the Lord, all the earth.

2. Cantate Domino, et benedicite nomini ejus : annuntiate de die in diem salutare ejus.

Sing unto the Lord, and bless His name : tell forth His salvation from day to day.

"*Salutare ejus.*" According to the Hebrew : *Salutem ejus;* and the Chaldee : *Redemptionem ejus.* That is : The salvation which He has wrought by Redemption.

3. Annuntiate inter Gentes gloriam ejus : in omnibus populis mirabilia ejus.

Tell forth His glory among the Gentiles : His wonders among all peoples.

"*Mirabilia ejus.*" The wondrous things which He has wrought in our behalf.

4. Quoniam magnus Dominus, et laudabilis nimis : terribilis est super omnes deos.

For the Lord is great, and highly to be praised : He is to be feared above all gods.

[1] Alluding to that time, and then ordered to be sung : but principally relating to the building of the Church of Christ, after our redemption from the captivity of Satan.

5. Quoniam omnes dii Gentium dæmonia: Dominus autem cœlos fecit.

For all the gods of the Gentiles are devils: but the Lord made the heavens.

"*Dæmonia.*" According to the Hebrew : *Dii vani, falsi nihil.* Vain, false gods, nothing.

6. Confessio, et pulchritudo in conspectu ejus : sanctimonia et magnificentia in sanctificatione ejus.

Praise and beauty are before Him : holiness and majesty in His sanctuary.

"*Confessio, et pulchritudo in conspectu ejus.*" According to the Hebrew : *Gloria et decor coram eo ;* and Mattei says that in the Bible the word *Confessio* is taken for the praise that is given to God.[1] That is : In the presence of God all is worthy of praise, and all is beautiful.——"*Sanctimonia.*" Sanctity and grandeur shine in Him, Who is Himself the Holy One by essence.——By "*In sanctificatione ejus*" Mattei understands : *In ipso sancto :* In Him, the Holy One by essence. We may also translate these words according to the Hebrew : *In Sanctuario ejus.* In His Temple, or Tabernacle.

7. Afferte Domino patriæ gentium, afferte Domino gloriam et honorem: afferte Domino gloriam nomini ejus.

Bring unto the Lord, O ye kindred of the Gentiles, bring unto the Lord glory and honour : bring unto the Lord glory unto His name.

"*Patriæ gentium.*" Estius, according to the Hebrew, says that we should read : *Familiæ gentium.* So also Menochius, Tirinus, and others, with S. Jerome, who translates : *Familiæ populorum.*——Come, O families of the Gentiles, come to give glory and honour to the Lord ; come to celebrate the glory of His Name.

8. Tollite hostias, et introite in atria ejus : adorate Dominum in atrio sancto ejus.

Bring sacrifices and come into His courts : adore ye the Lord in His holy court.

"*Hostias.*" Bellarmine and Menochius say that the Hebrew *Mincha,* denotes an unbloody offering, and specially one made of flour : this points to the Holy Eucharist. Jansenius of Ghent, Tirinus, Rotigni, Sa, and others make the same remark.

9. Commoveatur a facie ejus universa terra : dicite in Gentibus quia Dominus regnavit.

Let all the earth be moved at His presence : tell ye among the Gentiles that the Lord hath reigned.

"*Commoveatur.*" S. Jerome translates : *Paveat.*——"*Regnavit.*" S. Justin (*Dial. cum Tryph.*), S. Augustine, and S. Leo read : *Regnavit a ligno.* Hath reigned from the Wood.

[1] *Ps.* ciii. 2.

But the Church no longer makes use of this reading, except in the Hymn *Vexilla Regis*, where she sings : *Regnavit a ligno Deus.*[1]——Let the whole earth fear or be in awe before His presence : Say to the Gentiles that the Lord has established His reign.

10. Etenim correxit orbem terræ qui non commovebitur : judicabit populos in æquitate.

For He hath established the world, and it shall not be moved : He will judge the people with equity.

"*Correxit.*" According to the Hebrew and Chaldee : *Firmavit.* Has made firm, or established.

11. Lætentur cœli, et exultet terra, commoveatur mare, et plenitudo ejus: gaudebunt campi, et omnia, quæ in eis sunt.

Let the heavens rejoice, and let the earth be glad : let the sea be moved, and the fulness thereof : the fields shall be joyful, and all things that are therein.

"*Plenitudo ejus.*" All that is in the sea, as the islands, the fishes, &c.——"*Omnia, quæ in eis sunt.*" All that is found in the fields, as the flocks and herds, the plants, &c.

12. Tunc exultabunt omnia ligna silvarum a facie Domini, quia venit : quoniam venit judicare terram.

Then shall all the trees of the woods rejoice before the face of the Lord, for He cometh : for He cometh to judge the earth.

13. Judicabit orbem terræ in æquitate : et populos in veritate sua.

He shall judge the world with equity : and the people with His truth.

"*In æquitate.*". . ."*In veritate sua.*" That is, with an exact and righteous judgment as regards both the good and the wicked.

PSALM XCVI.

MATTEI says that the Fathers saw in this Psalm the first and the second coming of the Redeemer into the world : whence he concludes that the spiritual is the principal sense of the Psalm.

For the same David, when his land was restored again to him.

1. Dominus regnavit, exultet terra : lætentur insulæ multæ.

The Lord hath reigned ; let the earth rejoice : let the multitude of the isles be glad.

That is : Behold, the Lord has already come to govern and to judge the world : let then all the earth and all the isles of the sea rejoice.

[1] Also in the Response of *Commem de Cruce Temp. Pasch.*

2. Nubes, et caligo in circuitu ejus : justitia, et judicium correctio sedis ejus.

Clouds and darkness *are* round about him : justice and judgment *are* the foundation of His throne.

"*Correctio.*" According to the Hebrew : *Firmamentum,* which signifies that the firmness of His tribunal will consist in the justice of His judgments.

3. Ignis ante ipsum præcedet : et inflammabit in circuitu inimicos ejus.

Fire shall go forth before Him : and shall burn up His enemies on every side.

Fire will burn up everything at the last day ; as S. Peter writes : "The earth and the works which are in it shall be burnt up " (2 *Pet.* iii. 10).

4. Illuxerunt fulgura ejus orbi terræ : vidit, et commota est terra.

His lightnings shone upon the world : the earth saw and was moved.

"*Illuxerunt.*" [Here, and in the following verses the past tense is used for the future.]——The lightnings will be seen flashing over the whole earth.

5. Montes sicut cera fluxerunt a facie Domini : a facie Domini omnis terra.

The mountains melted like wax before the face of the Lord : yea, all the earth, at the presence of the Lord.

6. Annuntiaverunt cœli justitiam ejus : et viderunt omnes populi gloriam ejus.

The heavens declared His justice : and all peoples saw His glory.

"*Annuntiaverunt.*" The heavens with marvellous signs will publish His justice.

7. Confundantur omnes, qui adorant sculptilia : et qui gloriantur in simulacris suis.

Let them all be confounded that adore graven things : and that glory in their idols.

"*Confundantur.*" Then shall be put to confusion.——"*In simulacris suis.*" In the protection of the idols they invoke.

8. Adorate eum omnes angeli ejus : audivit, et lætata est Sion.

Adore Him, all ye His Angels : Sion heard, and was glad.

"*Audivit* . . ." Sion, the faithful people, the Church, hearing of these things, was full of joy. (See verse 1.)

9. Et exultaverunt filiæ Judæ : propter judicia tua Domine.

And the daughters of Juda rejoiced : because of Thy judgments, O Lord.

"*Filiæ Judæ.*" The same faithful people.——"*Propter judicia tua.*" Knowing that Thou art to judge the world.

10. Quoniam tu Dominus altissimus super omnem terram : nimis
exaltatus es super omnes deos.

For Thou Lord art most high over
all the earth : Thou art exalted exceedingly above all gods.

"*Omnes deos.*" That is, according to Mattei : All the judges
of the earth.

11. Qui diligitis Dominum, odite
malum : custodit Dominus animas
sanctorum suorum, de manu peccatoris liberabit eos.

Ye that love the Lord, hate evil :
the Lord preserveth the souls of His
saints ; He will deliver them out of
the hand of the sinner.

"*Sanctorum suorum.*" Of His servants.——"*De manu
peccatoris.*" According to the Hebrew : *De manu impiorum.*
From the hands of the ungodly.

12. Lux orta est justo : et rectis
corde lætitia.

Light is risen to the just : and
gladness to such as are right of heart.

The gift of light is granted to the just man, and that of joy
to all those who are right of heart.

13. Lætamini justi in Domino : et
confitemini memoriæ sanctificationis
ejus.

Rejoice in the Lord, O ye just :
and exult in the remembrance of His
holiness.

"*Confitemini* . . ." Praise Him, being ever mindful of the
gift of sanctification you have received from Him.

LAUDS FOR FRIDAY.

PSALM L.

PSALM CXLII.

DAVID, driven from Jerusalem by Absalom, sees in this persecution a just chastisement for his sins : he gives utterance in
this Psalm to sentiments of repentance, and prays to God for
mercy.[1]

A Psalm of David, when his son Absalom pursued him (2 Kings xvii.).

1. Domine exaudi orationem meam:
auribus percipe obsecrationem meam
in veritate tua : exaudi me in tua
justitia.

Hear my prayer, O Lord : give ear
to my supplication in Thy truth :
hearken unto me for Thy justice'
sake.

"*In veritate tua.*" According to Thy faithful promise.——
"*In tua justitia.*" According to the goodness which Thou
showest to the truly penitent. Thus S. Chrysostom understands the word.

2. Et non intres in judicium cum
servo tuo : quia non justificabitur in
conspectu tuo omnis vivens.

And enter not into judgment with
Thy servant : for in Thy sight shall
no man living be justified.

"*Non justificabitur ...*" For there is no one, who living on
earth, can be called just before Thee.

3. Quia persecutus est inimicus
animam meam : humiliavit in terra
vitam meam.

For the enemy hath persecuted
my soul : he hath brought my life
down unto the ground.

For the enemy, that is, the devil, has persecuted my soul,
in tempting me to those offences which I have committed
against Thee ; and thus he has humbled my life here on earth;
making me to become vile in Thine eyes.

[1] This is the seventh Penitential Psalm.

4. Collocavit me in obscuris sicut mortuos sæculi: et anxiatus est super me spiritus meus, in me turbatum est cor meum.

He hath made me to dwell in darkness as those that have been long dead: and my spirit is vexed within me; my heart within me is troubled.

He has placed me in darkness, making me like a man of the world, who no more sees the light, by which to walk as he ought : " *Et anxiatus*," &c. And my spirit is restless with anxiety at the sight of my misery, and my heart within me is afflicted and troubled.

5. Memor fui dierum antiquorum, meditatus sum in omnibus operibus tuis: in factis manuum tuarum meditabar.

I remembered the days of old ; I meditated on all Thy works: I have mused upon the works of Thy hands.

I was mindful of the days of old and reflected on all the wonderful works wrought in our behalf by Thy Almighty hand.

6. Expandi manus meas ad te : anima mea sicut terra sine aqua tibi :

I stretched forth my hands unto Thee : my soul gaspeth unto Thee, as a land where no water is ;

I have stretched forth my hands towards Thee, to obtain mercy ; for my soul is become as dried up earth, it is unable to serve Thee, seeing itself deprived of the water of Thy grace.

7. Velociter exaudi me Domine: defecit spiritus meus.

Hear me speedily, O Lord : my spirit hath fainted away.

Make haste to hear me, O Lord, and strengthen me with Thy grace, for I feel my spirit fainting within me.

8. Non avertas faciem tuam a me : et similis ero descendentibus in lacum.

Turn not away Thy face from me : lest I be like unto them that go down into the pit.

" *Descendentibus in lacum.*" Who are cast into the pit of the dead.

9. Auditam fac mihi mane misericordiam tuam : quia in te speravi.

Make me to hear Thy mercy in the morning : for in Thee have I hoped.

Make me soon to hear the voice of Thy mercy, telling me that Thou hast pardoned me ; for in Thee alone have I placed all my hope of salvation.

10. Notam fac mihi viam, in qua ambulem : quia ad te levavi animam meam.

Make me to know the way wherein I should walk : for to Thee have I lifted up my soul.

" *Ad te levavi animam meam.*" That is : I have resolved to detach myself from all earthly affections to please Thee alone.

23

11. Eripe me de inimicis meis Domine, ad te confugi : doce me facere voluntatem tuam, quia Deus meus es tu.

Deliver me from mine enemies, O Lord, unto Thee have I fled : teach me to do Thy will, for Thou art my God.

"*Deus meus es tu.*" Thou art my God, and therefore Thou deservest that I should not do anything but what Thou willest.

12. Spiritus tuus bonus deducet me in terram rectam : propter nomen tuum Domine, vivificabis me in æquitate tua.

Thy good spirit shall lead me into the right land : for Thy name's sake, O Lord, Thou shalt quicken me in Thy justice.

Thy good spirit, that is, the Holy Ghost, will conduct me whilst here on earth by the right way, and I hope, for the glory of Thy name, that Thou wilt grant me vigour and strength to live according to Thy justice, that is, to lead the life of the just.——"*In æquitate tua.*" According to the Hebrew : *In justitia tua.*

13. Educes de tribulatione animam meam : et in misericordia tua disperdes inimicos meos.

Thou shalt bring my soul out of trouble : and in Thy mercy Thou shalt destroy mine enemies.

I hope that Thou wilt deliver my soul from eternal tribulation.

14. Et perdes omnes qui tribulant animam meam : quoniam ego servus tuus sum.

And Thou shalt destroy all them that afflict my soul : for I am Thy servant.

PSALMS LXII. AND LXVI.

CANTICLE OF HABACUC.

THE Prophet, having learnt by revelation the chastisement in store for his people by the captivity of Babylon, prays for them, and foretells their deliverance by Cyrus king of Persia. S. Jerome, Theodoret, Theophylact, Rupert, Euthymius, Jansenius of Ghent, Cornelius a Lapide, and others commonly, are of opinion that in this Canticle is plainly typified the human race which was to be ransomed from the slavery of Satan by Jesus Christ.

1. Domine audivi auditionem tuam: et timui.

O Lord, I heard what Thou madest me hear : and was afraid.

O Lord, I have understood all that Thou hast revealed to me, and am left in terror thereby.

2. Domine opus tuum: in medio   O Lord, Thy work: in the midst of
annorum vivifica illud: the years bring it to life:

" *Vivifica.*" According to Du Hamel : *Perfice :* Perfect.——
Lallemant gives this explanation: Complete Thy work, the
deliverance of the Jews from the captivity of Babylon, and in
mercy shorten the time of their chastisement.——But this
passage is better understood in the figurative sense, thus :
Bring to perfection, O Lord, the work of man's redemption by
means of the Messias : grant that it may have its full force
and effect within the space of years which Thou hast determined.[1]

3. In medio annorum notum facies: In the midst of the years Thou
cum iratus fueris, misericordiæ re-   shalt make it known : when Thou
cordaberis.   art angry, Thou wilt remember
    mercy.

In the midst of those years appointed ; that is, forestalling
the term of those years and the time fixed, Thou wilt make
manifest the work of the deliverance of the Jews from the
captivity of Babylon. (This is in the literal sense ; but in the
mystical sense is signified the redemption of mankind.) And
though angry at the sons of men, still Thou wilt be mindful
of Thy mercy, and wilt not withhold it from us. *Licet peccatis
hominum · iratus,* says Du Hamel, *misericordiam tuam non
subtrahes.*

4. Deus ab Austro veniet: et   God will come from the South :
sanctus de monte Pharan :   and the Holy One from Mount
    Pharan :

God will come from the South to deliver His people, as the
Holy One of Israel came of old on Sinai appearing from
Mount Pharan (*Deut.* xxxiii. 2). So too from Persia and Media
lying to the South, came Cyrus and Darius to deliver the Jews
from Babylon.——In the figurative sense this verse, as understood by S. Jerome, Theodoret, Theophylact, and others cited
by Tirinus, applies to the Messias who was to be born at
Bethlehem, situated to the South of Jerusalem.——"*Sanctus de
monte Pharan.*" Tirinus says that hereby is meant the Holy
Ghost, who descended on Mount Pharan and communicated
the spirit of prophecy to the seventy judges of the people
(*Num.* xi. 25).

5. Operuit cœlos gloria ejus: et   His glory covered the heavens: and
laudis ejus plena est terra.   the earth is full of His praise.

[1] " When the fulness of the time was come " (*Gal.* iv. 4).

His glory overspread the heavens, causing their brightness to pale, and the whole earth was filled with His praises.—— Du Hamel explains these words as referring in their mystical sense to the glory with which the future Messias, the Word Incarnate, would fill all heaven, and to the praise which the Angels would render to Him here on earth, as we read in S. Luke (ii. 13, 14): "*Gloria in altissimis Deo, et in terra pax.*"

6. Splendor ejus ut lux erit: His brightness shall be as the cornua in manibus ejus: light; horns are in His hands.

He shall appear resplendent with light as the sun, and His hands shall be armed with power. —— "*Splendor . . . erit.*" This may mean, in the literal sense, that at the coming of Cyrus the light of freedom should shine for the Jews, and in the figurative sense, that at the coming of the Messias, of whom Cyrus was a type, the true Light should shine forth on the world, according to what is said in S. John (i. 9): "That was the true light which enlighteneth every man."——"*Cornua in manibus ejus.*" The words *cornu* and *cornua* in Scripture mean strength. Tirinus and Du Hamel, with S. Cyprian and S. Augustine, thus apply this passage to Jesus Christ: All His strength to conquer the devil and the world shall be in His hands pierced upon the Cross. S. Augustine says: "*Quid fortius manu hac, quæ mundum vicit, non ferro armata, sed ferro transfixa?*" What is there stronger than that hand which conquered the world, not armed, but transfixed with iron? (*In Ps. xxxiv. s. 1, n. 1*).

7. Ibi abscondita est fortitudo There is His strength hid: death ejus: ante faciem ejus ibit mors.[1] shall go before His face.

In the figurative sense: There, that is, in His pierced hands, is hidden His power; so that before His power death will fly, conquered by His Death.——*Mors ipsa morte Christi victa est*, writes Du Hamel.[2]

8. Et egredietur diabolus ante And the devil shall go forth before pedes ejus: stetit, et mensus est His feet: He stood and measured terram. the earth.

At the entrance of the people into the Land of Promise the Lord was preceded by the devil, the executor of His vengeance, whereupon, the enemies being vanquished, He

---

[1] As Van Steenkiste observes, Death is here set forth under the person of the devil, the arch-enemy of the human race.

[2] "*Absorpta est mors in victoria*" (*Cor. xv. 54*).

distributed their lands to His people.——" *Egredietur diabolus ante pedes ejus.*" This is explained figuratively : The devil shall be utterly vanquished, and shall go forth with shame to be led in triumph before the feet of Jesus Christ, his conqueror, Who will despoil him of his power, according to the words of S. Paul : "Despoiling the principalities and powers, He led them forth confidently, with open show, triumphing over them in Himself " (*Col.* ii. 15).——"*Stetit et* . . ." Then Jesus as Conqueror, seated at the right hand of His Father, as Du Hamel says, and looking over the earth, divided it among His Apostles, that they might fill it with the light of the Gospel : *Qui sedens ad dexteram Patris, terram Apostolis suis divisit, ut Evangelii luce eam complerent.*

| 9. Aspexit, et dissolvit Gentes : et contriti sunt montes sæculi. | He beheld, and melted the nations : and the ancient mountains were crushed to pieces. |

With His looks He broke asunder the nations ; and the great ones of the world, who seemed like mountains, were brought to nought.——In the figurative sense : He looked upon the earth and the nations, and giving them the light of faith, He set them free from the yoke of Satan : and as for the princes of the world, who as mountains were lifted up, they were brought low and shattered at the coming of Jesus Christ.

| 10. Incurvati sunt colles mundi : ab itineribus æternitatis ejus. | The hills of the world were bowed down : by the journeys of His eternity. |

These proud hills of the world have been laid low beneath the feet of the Eternal.——In the figurative sense : These princes of the world shall bow down before the Redeemer, bending the knee to adore Him, as they consider that on Him depends the course of eternal ages.——"*Ab itineribus æternitatis ejus.*" According to the Hebrew : *Itinera sæculi æterni ejus sunt.* His are the journeys, the goings forth, of the eternal age.

| 11. Pro iniquitate vidi tentoria Æthiopiæ : turbabuntur pelles terræ Madian. | I saw the tents of Æthiopia for their iniquity : the curtains of the land of Madian shall be troubled. |

I saw the tents of the Ethiopians cast down for their wickedness, and the tabernacles of the Madianites thrown to the earth.——In the mystic sense : As the hosts of the Ethiopians and of the Madianites were seen destroyed on account of their wicked doings against God's people, so shall those who oppose the Gospel be likewise punished. Thus Du Hamel and Rotigni.

12. Numquid in fluminibus iratus es Domine? aut in fluminibus furor tuus? vel in mari indignatio tua?

Wast Thou angry, O Lord, with the rivers? or was Thy wrath upon the rivers? or Thy indignation in the sea?

Lord, would it not seem that Thou wert angry with the rivers and with the sea which obstructed the passage of Thy people?

13. Qui ascendes super equos tuos: et quadrigæ tuæ salvatio.

Who will ride upon Thy horses: and Thy chariots are salvation.

But Thou didst save Thy people, and didst deliver them from the Egyptians, mounting upon the clouds, as on horses which draw the chariot.

14. Suscitans suscitabis arcum tuum: juramenta tribubus quæ locutus es.

Thou wilt surely take up Thy bow: according to the oaths which Thou hast spoken to the tribes.

Thou wilt waken up Thy bow, which was as though sleeping, that is, Thou wilt resume the bow of Thy power, and wilt fulfil the promises which Thou hast sworn to the tribes of Israel. Thus Tirinus, Du Hamel, Rotigni, and Albert Hugo explain it.

15. Fluvios scindes terræ: viderunt te, et doluerunt montes: gurges aquarum transiit.

Thou wilt divide the rivers of the earth: the mountains saw Thee, and were grieved: the great body of waters passed away.

Thou didst cut in twain the course of the Jordan that Thy people might pass over. Its waters saw Thee, that is, understood Thy behest, and raising themselves like mountains, remained suspended in the air, as though grieving to see themselves stopped in their course: and thus Thy people crossed over the river.[1]

16. Dedit abyssus vocem suam: altitudo manus suas levavit.

The deep put forth its voice: the deep lifted up its hands.

The abyss of those waters as they flowed back gave forth its voice, and in lifting themselves on high, the waters seemed to raise up their hands to implore Thy permission to return again to their course.

17. Sol, et luna steterunt in habitaculo suo: in luce sagittarum tuarum, ibunt in splendore fulgurantis hastæ tuæ.

The sun and the moon stood still in their habitation: in the light of Thy arrows, they shall go in the brightness of Thy glittering spear.

[1] "And the priests that carried the Ark of the Covenant went on before them. And as soon as they came into the Jordan . . . the waters that came down from above stood in one place, and swelling up like a mountain were seen afar off . . . but those that were beneath ran down into the sea . . . until they wholly failed" (*Jos.* iii. 14-16).

At Josue's voice in the battle with the Madianites, Thou didst cause the sun and the moon to stand still in their course (*Jos.* x. 13), and didst make his army to march by the glare of Thy lightnings, and by the glitterings of Thy spear from which thunderbolts flashed.

18. In fremitu conculcabis terram : et in furore obstupefacies Gentes.

In Thy anger Thou wilt tread the earth under foot : in Thy wrath Thou wilt astonish the nations.

Thou didst tread underfoot, that is, Thou didst go through, the earth with the roar of thunderings and of lightnings ; and the hostile nations were astonished and in dismay at Thy wrath.

19. Egressus es in salutem populi tui : in salutem cum Christo tuo.

Thou wentest forth for the salva- tion of Thy people: for salvation with Thy Christ.

Thou wentest forth to save Thy people together with Thy Christ.——"*Cum Christo tuo.*" Such was Cyrus, who came to set free the people from captivity, as Isaias had foretold : "Thus saith the Lord to My Anointed (*Christo Meo*) Cyrus, whose right hand I have taken hold of, to subdue nations before his face" (*Is.* xlv. 1). Cyrus was a type of Jesus Christ, Who has saved us by His merits, as remark S. Jerome, S. Augustine (*De Civ. D.* l. 18, c. 32), and others.——The verse is translated thus according to the sixth Greek version : *Egres-sus es ut salvares populum per Jesum Christum tuum.*

20. Percussisti caput de domo impii : denudasti fundamentum ejus usque ad collum.

Thou struckest the head of the house of the wicked : Thou hast laid bare his foundation even to the neck.

Thou hast struck the head of the house of the impious one, that is, king Balthassar, the head of the Chaldæans, and Thou hast utterly ruined him (*Dan.* v.).——In the mystical sense : Thou hast laid prostrate the devil, the head of impiety.—— "*Denudasti...*" Tirinus thus interprets this: *Denudatum ever-tisti ab imo sursum.* Thou hast despoiled him of his empire, and hast upset him from top to bottom, that is, Thou hast taken from him all his tyrannical power. It is thus, Lord, Thou hast willed to save Thy people by means of Jesus Christ.

21. Maledixisti sceptris ejus, capiti bellatorum ejus : venientibus ut turbo ad dispergendum me.

Thou hast cursed their sceptres, the head of his warriors : them that came out as a whirlwind to scatter me.

Thou hast cursed his empire, that, viz., of king Balthassar, along with the head of his soldiers, who are come as a whirl-wind to destroy Thy people.[1]——This is understood mysti-cally of the curse pronounced on the devil, who held sway over the human race, and on his associates, who all contrived our ruin.

22. Exultatio eorum : sicut ejus, qui devorat pauperem in abscondito.

Their joy was like that of him that devoureth the poor man in secret.

Their joy was like that of a wicked man who robs and murders some poor man in a secret place, where no one can come to his help.

23. Viam fecisti in mari equis tuis : in luto aquarum multarum.

Thou madest a way in the sea for Thy horses : in the mud of many waters.

Thou didst open a passage in the Red Sea, making the horses of Thy people pass upon its muddy bed, in the midst of the piled-up masses of waters.——Tirinus observes that here, pro-perly speaking, the Canticle ends, and that the Prophet adds what follows.

24. Audivi, et conturbatus est venter meus : a voce contremuerunt labia mea.

I have heard, and my bowels were troubled : my lips trembled at the voice.

The Prophet, knowing by revelation what God's people would have to suffer before their deliverance, says : I heard this prediction and my heart was troubled : at what was told me my lips quivered, so that I was unable to utter a word. Thus Lallemant.

25. Ingrediatur putredo in ossibus meis : et subter me scateat.

Let rottenness enter into my bones: and swarm under me.

26. Ut requiescam in die tribula-tionis : ut ascendam ad populum ac-cinctum nostrum.

That I may rest in the day of tribulation : that I may go up to our people that are girded.

So that I may find myself at rest in the tomb on the day of such great tribulation, and thus be united to our people who have already fought the fight against the enemy.——But the reading of the old Vulgate is: *Ad populum peregrinationis meœ.*

---

[1] According to Cornelius a Lapide and others, the Prophet here refers especially to Pharao ; and throughout the Canticle celebrates the wonders God had wrought in bringing the people from Egypt, because thereby were represented those that were to be worked in the deliverance of the Jews from Babylon ; and that both these deliverances prefigured the mystery of Redemption, which the Prophet had principally in view.

To the people of my pilgrimage. That is: To the people who looked on the present life as a pilgrimage, as I myself consider it.

27. Ficus enim non florebit: et non erit germen in vineis.

For the fig-tree shall not blossom : and there shall be no spring in the vines.

For in the time of distress the fig-tree shall not blossom, and there shall not be a vine-shoot in the vineyards.——This may mean in the mystical sense : that in the desolation to which the Jews shall be brought in punishment for having put their Saviour to death, they will cease to produce any fruit of good works, having lost the kingdom of God which shall be given to the Christian people who will bring forth fruits of holiness, according to the words of Jesus Christ : "Therefore, I say to you that the kingdom of God shall be taken from you, and shall be given to a nation yielding the fruits thereof" (*Matt.* xxi. 43).

28. Mentietur opus olivæ : et arva non afferent cibum.

The labour of the olive-tree shall fail : and the fields shall yield no food.

"*Mentietur opus olivæ.*" The olive crop shall lie, that is, shall disappoint expectation.

29. Abscindetur de ovili pecus : et non erit armentum in præsepibus.

The flock shall be cut off from the fold : and there shall be no herd in the stalls.

S. Augustine (*De Civ. D.* 1. 18, c. 32) applies this passage to the Jews, who, after having put Jesus Christ to death, were to remain without pastors, without Temple, and without spiritual food.

30. Ego autem in Domino gau- debo : et exultabo in Deo Jesu meo.

But I will rejoice in the Lord : and I will rejoice in God my Jesus.

"*In Deo Jesu meo.*" That is, in the God of my salvation, as it is in the Hebrew, according to Pagnini, Vatablus, and others. Some, however, says Tirinus, interpret the Hebrew in the sense of the Septuagint, which agrees with the Chaldee and Syriac, viz.: *In Deo Jesu*, that is, *Salvatore*, or *Redemptore meo*. And thus S. Augustine and others understand it.

31. Deus Dominus fortitudo mea : et ponet pedes meos quasi cervorum.

The Lord God is my strength : and he will make my feet like the feet of harts.

This is understood of the return of the Jews from the captivity of Babylon. In the mystical sense it is applied to the Gentiles hastening to come to God when set free by Jesus Christ from the bondage of Satan.

32. Et super excelsa mea deducet me victor : in psalmis canentem.	And He, the conqueror, will lead me upon my high places : singing Psalms.

He, my God, the Vanquisher of enemies, will lead me up to the high places of Mount Sion, there to sing His glories.—— In the spiritual sense, according to S. Jerome : He will bring me to heaven, there to glorify Him with hymns of praise and thanksgiving.

PSALMS CXLVIII., CXLIX., CL.

CANTICLE OF ZACHARY.

MATINS FOR SATURDAY.

PSALM XCVII.

THE Psalmist thanks God for having delivered the Jewish people from captivity; and under this figure he foretells the coming of Jesus Christ and the Redemption of mankind.

A Psalm for David himself.

1. Cantate Domino canticum novum : quia mirabilia fecit.

Sing unto the Lord a new song : for He hath done wonderful things.

"*Quia mirabilia fecit.*" For the marvels He has wrought in behalf of His servants.

2. Salvavit sibi dextera ejus : et brachium sanctum ejus.

His right hand and His holy arm : hath wrought salvation for Him.

This verse may well be applied to Jesus Christ.——"*Sibi.*" Bellarmine says that this word, according to the Hebrew, is to be understood as though it were *Ipsa;* which gives this meaning : It is His own right hand that has saved the world. But S. Augustine refers the pronoun *Sibi* to Jesus Christ, as to the end proposed, thus : Christ has saved men for Himself, that is, for His own glory.——"*Et brachium sanctum ejus.*" And all has been the work of His holy arm.

3. Notum fecit Dominus salutare suum : in conspectu Gentium revelavit justitiam suam.

The Lord hath made known His salvation : He hath revealed His justice in the sight of the Gentiles.

"*Salutare suum.*" The salvation which He has provided for the world.——"*Revelavit justitiam suam.*" He has, by means of His Apostles, manifested His justice, that is, His faithfulness in the accomplishment of the promised Redemption.

4. Recordatus est misericordiæ suæ : et veritatis suæ domui Israel.

He hath remembered His mercy : and His truth toward the house of Israel.

God is said to remember, when He fulfils a promise that He has made ; now He had promised the people of Israel to come and save mankind ; and He remembered his mercy and faithfulness (*veritatis*, truth) by accomplishing this promise.

5. Viderunt omnes termini terræ : salutare Dei nostri.

All the ends of the earth have seen : the salvation of our God.

The whole earth, even to its furthest bounds, has seen the salvation wrought by our God.

6. Jubilate Deo, omnis terra : cantate, et exultate, et psallite.

Sing joyfully unto God, all the earth : sing, rejoice, and give praise.

All ye on earth exult with jubilee, and sing forth canticles in His praise.

7. Psallite Domino in cithara, in cithara et voce psalmi : in tubis ductilibus, et voce tubæ corneæ.

Give praise unto the Lord upon the harp, upon the harp and with voice of psalms : with the long trumpets, and sound of the cornet.

" *Voce psalmi.*" That is, as explained by Bellarmine, Menochius, and Lallemant : *Sonitu psalterii.* With the sound of the psaltery.——" *In tubis ductilibus.*" These, according to Menochius, were long, straight metal trumpets shaped and attuned by the hammer.——" *Tubæ corneæ* " or *buccinæ* were trumpets made of horn.

8. Jubilate in conspectu Regis Domini : moveatur mare, et plenitudo ejus : orbis terrarum, et qui habitant in eo.

Sing joyfully before the Lord our King : let the sea be moved, and the fulness thereof : the compass of the earth, and they that dwell therein.

9. Flumina plaudent manu, simul montes exultabunt a conspectu Domini : quoniam venit judicare terram.

The rivers shall clap their hands, the mountains shall rejoice together at the presence of the Lord : for He cometh to judge the earth.

" *Plaudent manu.*" As is done to praise any one.——" *Judicare terram.*" To govern the earth by good and righteous laws.

10. Judicabit orbem terrarum in justitia : et populos in æquitate.

He shall judge the world with justice : and the people with equity.

" *Judicabit.*" He will govern.——" *In æquitate.*" According to the Hebrew, as Bellarmine remarks : " *In rectitudine :* " Rectitude, or righteousness.

PSALM XCVIII.

DAVID calls upon the people to praise and invoke God on Mount Sion, which is a figure of the Holy Church wherein we ought to invoke and praise Jesus Christ.

A Psalm for David himself.

1. Dominus regnavit, irascantur populi : qui sedet super Cherubim, moveatur terra.

The Lord hath reigned, though the nations rage :[1] He that sitteth on the Cherubim, though the earth be moved.

The Lord hath established His reign in spite of the idolatrous nations who are enraged thereat. He has His throne above the Cherubim, however much thereby the earth be troubled : this signifies that none can resist His power.

2. Dominus in Sion magnus : et excelsus super omnes populos.

The Lord is great in Sion : and high above all peoples.

The God Who is adored on Mount Sion is great and high above all the peoples.

3. Confiteantur nomini tuo magno: quoniam terribile, et sanctum est : et honor regis judicium diligit.

Let them give praise to Thy great name : for it is terrible and holy : and the King's honour loveth judgment.[2]

Let all, O Lord, praise and fear Thy great Name ; for it is terrible on account of its exceeding power and holiness ; and the honour of a king, that is, his dignity or authority, requires him to love justice, that is, to exercise righteous judgment by rendering to everyone according to his deserts.

4. Tu parasti directiones : judicium et justitiam in Jacob tu fecisti.

Thou hast prepared equity : Thou hast done judgment and justice in Jacob.

Thou, O Lord, hast made most righteous laws for the direction of the conduct and lives of men, as Thou hast already shown amongst the people of Israel, acting with justice and judgment, that is, always judging justly.

5. Exaltate Dominum Deum nostrum, et adorate scabellum pedum ejus : quoniam sanctum est.

Exalt ye the Lord our God, and adore His footstool : for it is holy.[3]

" Scabellum pedum ejus." By God's footstool is meant the

---

[1] Though the whole earth be stirred up to oppose the reign of Christ, He shall still prevail.

[2] Loveth judgment. Requireth discretion.

[3] God was considered as seated on the wings of Cherubim, stretched out over the Propitiatory, or Mercy-seat (2 Kings vi. 2). Hence the Ark is called God's footstool (1 Par. xxviii. 2). But the Holy Fathers understand this text of the adoration of the Humanity of Jesus Christ personally united to the Divinity, and as paid by the Church to His Body and Blood in the Sacred Mysteries : inasmuch as the Humanity of Christ is, as it were, the footstool of His Divinity.

Ark of the Covenant supporting the Propitiatory, which was holy on account of the relation it had to God.

6. Moyses, et Aaron in sacerdotibus ejus: et Samuel inter eos, qui invocant nomen ejus.

Moses and Aaron among His priests: and Samuel among them that call upon His name.

There, before this Ark, were seen Moses and Aaron his priests, and Samuel also amongst those who were invoking His holy name.

7. Invocabant Dominum, et ipse exaudiebat eos: in columna nubis loquebatur ad eos.

They called upon the Lord, and He heard them: He spake to them in the pillar of cloud.

"*In columna nubis.*" According to S. Augustine, by the pillar of cloud we are to understand the obscure way in which God spoke to His people of old.

8. Custodiebant testimonia ejus: et præceptum quod dedit illis.

They kept His testimonies: and the commandment which He gave them.

"*Testimonia ejus.*" That is, according to Bellarmine, all the precepts given to all in common.——"*Præceptum* . . . " The special precept [for the priests and rulers], to govern and instruct the people.

9. Domine Deus noster, tu exaudiebas eos: Deus tu propitius fuisti eis, et ulciscens in omnes adinventiones eorum.

Thou didst hear and answer them, O Lord our God: Thou wast a merciful God to them, though Thou tookest vengeance on all their inventions.

"*Propitius fuisti* . . . " S. Augustine and Menochius thus explain this passage: Thou wast propitious to them in pardoning their faults, but without letting their sins go unpunished.——Theodoret and Euthymius, and with them Malvenda, explain it thus: Thou wast propitious in pardoning the people for their sake (*i.e.,* Moses, Aaron, Samuel, &c.), but without letting go unpunished the calumnies and injuries they had to suffer from this people.——Bellarmine says that both these interpretations are probable.

10. Exaltate Dominum Deum nostrum, et adorate in monte sancto ejus: quoniam sanctus Dominus Deus noster.

Exalt ye the Lord our God, and adore at His holy mountain: for the Lord our God is holy.

"*Sanctus Dominus Deus.*" God is holy by essence, and therefore worthy of all possible adoration and service.

PSALM XCIX. OR PSALM XCI.[1]

[1] See supra page 58, and infra page 414.

PSALM C.

DAVID gives excellent instruction to superiors, and especially to princes, how to live well : and here every father of a family will find rules for his conduct.

A Psalm for David himself.

1. Misericordiam et judicium cantabo tibi, Domine :

Mercy and judgment I will sing : unto Thee, O Lord :

O Lord, I will ever praise Thy mercy and Thy justice.

2. Psallam, et intelligam in via immaculata : quando venies ad me.

I will sing, and I will understand in the unspotted way : when Thou shalt come unto me.[1]

"*Immaculata.*" According to the Hebrew : *Perfecta.*——I will sing Thy praises upon the psaltery, and will apply myself to know the immaculate and perfect way, that therein I may walk ; but when wilt Thou come to my help ?

3. Perambulabam in innocentia cordis mei : in medio domus meæ.

I walked in the innocence of my heart : in the midst of my house.

"*Perambulabam.*" Some explain this verse and the following one in the past tense, as they are in the Vulgate and in the Greek ; but the Hebrew has them in the future, and thus S. Jerome, Theodoret, and Euthymius translate : *Ambulabo :* I will walk.——"*Domus meæ.*" That is, of those belonging to my house, my household.

4. Non proponebam ante oculos meos rem injustam : facientes prævaricationes odivi.

I set not before mine eyes any unjust thing : I hated the workers of iniquities.

I will never propose to do anything unjust ; I will hate, or have in abomination, all transgressors of Thy law.

5. Non adhæsit mihi cor pravum : declinantem a me malignum non cognoscebam.

The perverse heart did not cleave unto me : and the wicked that turned aside from me, I would not know.

"*Non adhæsit mihi cor pravum.*" S. Jerome translates : *Cor pravum recedet a me.*——I will never associate with those who have their heart perverse : and if any of those wicked persons keeps away from me, that is, does not wish me for a friend by changing his conduct, I will not know him, that is, I will show that I do not wish to know him.

[1] *I will understand,* &c. That is, I will apply my mind, to know and to follow the *perfect way of* Thy commandments: relying on Thy *coming to me* by Thy grace.——Some, as Bellarmine, prefer this reading without an interrogation.

6. Detrahentem secreto proximo suo : hunc persequebar.

The man that in private slandered his neighbour : him did I punish.

As for him who secretly rends the character of his neighbour, I will keep him at a distance, or I will even persecute him by reproaching him with his vice.

7. Superbo oculo, et insatiabili corde : cum hoc non edebam.

With him that had a proud eye, and an ambitious heart : I would not eat.

I will never sit at table with those who have a proud eye, that is, who look on others with contempt ; nor with the insatiable of heart, that is, with the ambitious and avaricious.

8. Oculi mei ad fideles terræ, ut sedeant mecum : ambulans in via immaculata, hic mihi ministrabat.

Mine eyes were upon the faithful of the earth, that they may sit with me : the man that walked in the perfect way, he served me.

My eyes shall be attentive to keep the company of the faithful men who live with me here on earth, and I will not have myself served or helped in my needs by any save those who live apart from vice.

9. Non habitabit in medio domus meæ qui facit superbiam : qui loquitur iniqua, non direxit in conspectu oculorum meorum.

He that worketh pride shall not dwell in the midst of my house : he that speaketh unjust things did not prosper before mine eyes.

The proud man shall not dwell in my house, and he who speaks unjustly, by lies or detraction, shall not remain long in my sight, that is, I will drive him out of the house.——" *Non direxit.*" According to the Hebrew : *Non firmabitur.* Shall not be established.

10. In matutino interficiebam omnes peccatores terræ : ut disperderem de civitate Domini omnes operantes iniquitatem.

In the morning I put to death all the wicked of the land : that I might cut off all the workers of iniquity from the city of the Lord.

" *Interficiebam.*" S. Jerome translates, according to the Hebrew and Chaldee : *Perdam.*——I will make haste to exterminate all the wicked from the country, taking care that they are punished : and thus I shall banish from the city of the Lord all those who lead bad lives and seek to have companions in evil.

PSALM CI.

The Psalmist describes one who humbles himself, and who prays to God for himself and for His people. S. Augustine is of opinion that this Psalm refers to Jesus Christ praying for us; there can be no doubt that in some verses the Messias and His Coming are spoken of.[1]

The prayer of the poor man, when he was anxious, and poured out his supplication before the Lord.

1. Domine, exaudi orationem meam : et clamor meus ad te veniat.

Hear my prayer, O Lord : and let my cry come unto Thee.

2. Non avertas faciem tuam a me : in quacumque die tribulor, inclina ad me aurem tuam.

Turn not away Thy face from me : in the day when I am in trouble, incline Thine ear unto me.

3. In quacumque die invocavero te : velociter exaudi me.

In what day soever I shall call upon Thee : O hearken unto me speedily.

4. Quia defecerunt sicut fumus dies mei : et ossa mea sicut cremium aruerunt.

For my days are vanished like smoke : and my bones are dried up like fuel for the fire.

"*Cremium.*" Du Hamel says : *Cremium est id omne quod facile crematur.* Whatever easily burns.

5. Percussus sum ut fœnum, et aruit cor meum : quia oblitus sum comedere panem meum.

I am smitten as grass, and my heart is withered : for I have forgotten to eat my bread.

My heart is stricken as grass by Thy hand, and my spirit has continued in such aridity that I have forgotten to take my food.[2]

6. A voce gemitus mei : adhæsit os meum carni meæ.

Through the voice of my groaning : my bones have cleaved unto my flesh.

My sobs and tears have been such as to cause my very skin to cleave to my bones.

7. Similis factus sum pellicano solitudinis : factus sum sicut nycticorax in domicilio.

I am become like a pelican in the wilderness : and like a night-raven in the house.

"*Pellicano.*" The pelican loves solitude. According to Mattei, this bird is said to exist, but in reality no one has any knowledge of it.——"*Nycticorax.*" S. Jerome translates : *Bubo.* The Owl, which makes its dwelling in ruins and deserted places.——"*Domicilio.*" Mariana says : *Vox hebræa ruinas vel parietinas significat.* The Hebrew word signifies ruins or crumbling walls.

[1] The fifth Penitential Psalm.
[2] Others understand it thus : Because I forgot, or neglected to take spiritual nourishment to sustain my soul.
24

8. Vigilavi: et factus sum sicut passer solitarius in tecto.

I have watched, and am become like a sparrow : that sitteth alone on the house-top.

I have passed whole nights without sleep under the pressure of my woes, and I am become like to a solitary sparrow which complains upon the roof, that is, my sadness keeps me to the most retired parts of my house.

9. Tota die exprobrabant mihi inimici mei: et qui laudabant me adversum me jurabant.

Mine enemies reviled me all the day long : and they that praised me have sworn together against me.

"*Qui laudabant me.*" Who formerly used to show me honour.——"*Jurabant.*" According to Du Hamel: *Conjurabant.* Conspired together.

10. Quia cinerem tamquam panem manducabam : et potum meum cum fletu miscebam.

For I have eaten ashes as it were bread : and mingled my drink with weeping.

"*Quia . . . manducabam.*" So that the bread that I ate seemed to me insipid as ashes.

11. A facie iræ et indignationis tuæ : quia elevans allisisti me.

Because of Thine indignation and wrath : for Thou hast lifted me up and cast me down.

Herein I live in affliction at the sight of Thy indignation, for I see that, after lifting me up, Thou hast cast me down. ——"*Elevans allisisti me.*" S. Jerome translates : *Levasti me, et allisisti me.*

12. Dies mei sicut umbra declina-verunt : et ego sicut fœnum arui.

My days have gone down like a shadow : and I am withered like the grass.

13. Tu autem, Domine, in æternum permanes : et memoriale tuum in generationem et generationem.

But Thou, O Lord, endurest for ever : and Thy memorial unto all generations.

"*In æternum permanes.*" That is : Thou art, and Thou wilt be always the same.——"*Memoriale tuum.*" According to the Chaldee : *Memoria tua.* Mattei says that the Hebrew may be so translated ; and Menochius explains it thus: *Tui memoria, et mentio, et laus.* The memory, the mention, and the praise of Thee shall pass on from generation to generation.

14. Tu exurgens misereberis Sion : quia tempus miserendi ejus, quia venit tempus.

Thou shalt arise, and have mercy upon Sion : for it is time that Thou have mercy upon her ; yea, the time is come.

Thou, as though rising from a sound sleep, shalt take pity on Sion ; for the time fixed in Thy decrees has come.——

"*Tempus.*" According to the Hebrew : *Tempus definitum.* The set time.

15. Quoniam placuerunt servis tuis lapides ejus : et terræ ejus miserebuntur.

For Thy servants have delighted in her stones : and they shall have pity on the earth thereof.

Here, says Mariana, is meant the city of Jerusalem, when destroyed by her enemies.——The verse is thus explained : For Thy servants take pleasure in the stones, that is, the heaps of stones which are now all that is left of the city ; and have a pious veneration even for the dust of her ruins.——"*Terræ ejus.*" The Hebrew, according to Menochius, Bossuet, and Mattei, here signifies *Pulveris ejus.* The dust of her ruins.

16. Et timebunt Gentes nomen tuum, Domine : et omnes reges terræ gloriam tuam.

And the Gentiles shall fear Thy name, O Lord : and all the kings of the earth Thy glory.

"*Gloriam tuam.*" That is : They shall know and fear Thy power.

17. Quia ædificavit Dominus Sion : et videbitur in gloria sua.

For the Lord hath built up Sion : and He shall be seen in His glory.

Thus shall it happen when God shall build up Sion anew ; and He shall be seen in His glory, that is, in His temple ; according to Maldonatus, Mariana, and Mattei.

18. Respexit in orationem humilium : et non sprevit precem eorum.

He hath had regard unto the prayer of the lowly : and hath not despised their petition.

19. Scribantur hæc in generatione altera : et populus, qui creabitur, laudabit Dominum :

Let these things be written for another generation : and the people that shall be created shall praise the Lord :

Let these works of the Lord be written, that their memory may pass to future generations. And the new people to be one day created shall give Him lasting praise.——Mattei remarks that this is to be understood of Christians who, re-generated by Baptism, are called by S. Paul : *Nova creatura* (*Gal.* vi. 15).

20. Quia prospexit de excelso sancto suo : Dominus de cœlo in terram aspexit :

For He hath looked down from His high and holy place : out of heaven hath the Lord looked upon the earth :

21. Ut audiret gemitus compeditorum : ut solveret filios interemptorum :

That He might hear the groaning of them that are in fetters : that He might deliver the children of the slain :

According to the Hebrew and S. Jerome's translation : *Ut audiret gemitum vincti, ut solveret filios mortis.* To hear the groaning of the prisoners, to loose the children of death. As Mattei remarks, these two versions are the same in sense ; meaning, according to the Hebrew phrase : Those doomed to death ; that is, men deprived of grace before the Redemption.

22. Ut annuntient in Sion nomen Domini: et laudem ejus in Jerusalem.	That they may declare the name of the Lord in Sion : and His praise in Jerusalem.

23. In conveniendo populos in unum : et reges ut serviant Domino.	When the people assembled together : and the kings to serve the Lord.

"*In unum.*" In one Church, in one same faith. Du Hamel thus comments : *Hæc ad Ecclesiam sub Christo referuntur.* This applies to the Church under Christ. Bellarmine, Malvenda, Mariana, and Menochius say the same.——"*Et reges...*" And even kings shall unite to serve the Lord.

24. Respondit ei in via virtutis suæ : Paucitatem dierum meorum nuntia mihi.	He answered him in the way of his strength :[1] Declare unto me the fewness of my days.

Bellarmine and Mattei say that this verse is very obscure, as indeed it is.——According to Bellarmine and Menochius the Psalmist here answers God "*in via virtutis suæ,*" that is, in the time of the vigour of his years,[2] and prays to Him, saying : "*Paucitatem dierum...*" O Lord, make me to know the shortness of my days ; that is, according to the commentators : If my life shall be too short for me to see the end of these evils on the day of man's redemption.

25. Ne revoces me in dimidio dierum meorum : in generationem et generationem anni tui.	Call me not away in the midst of my days : Thy years are unto generation and generation.

"*Ne revoces me.*" S. Jerome translates : *Ne rapias me.* Ah ! for mercy's sake, do not withdraw me from the world in the midst of my days ; for Thou, whose years are eternal, canst add to the number of my years.

---

[1] *He answered him in the way of his strength.* The Psalmist addressed God, after the manner of human strength, which is but weakness, and inquires into the shortness of life.

[2] Bellarmine understands the Psalmist's answer as referring to what God had said v. 19 sq. "*Scribantur*" etc. He explains "*In via virtutis suæ,*" thus : *In flore ætatis suæ, cum esset in via virtutis suæ robustissima.*

26. Initio tu, Domine, terram fundasti : et opera manuum tuarum sunt cœli.

Thou, Lord, in the beginning didst lay the foundation of the earth : and the heavens are the works of Thy hands.

S. Paul applies these words and the two following verses to Jesus Christ (*Heb.* i. 10-12).

27. Ipsi peribunt, tu autem permanes : et omnes sicut vestimentum veterascent.

They shall perish, but Thou enmanes: and they all shall grow old as a garment.

"*Permanes.*" S. Jerome translates : *Stabis.* Thou shalt ever remain the same.——"*Veterascent.*" S. Jerome translates : *Atterentur.* They shall come to an end, as a garment worn out with long use.

28. Et sicut opertorium mutabis eos, et mutabuntur : tu autem idem ipse es, et anni tui non deficient.

And as a vesture shalt Thou change them, and they shall be changed : but Thou art the same, and Thy years shall not fail.

And Thou shalt change these heavens, even as one changes a mantle that is worn.——"*Opertorium.*" S. Jerome translates : *Pallium,* a cloak.——Mattei here admires the images of the Oriental poetry. But Thou shalt ever be the self-same, and Thy years shall never fail, since they are eternal.

29. Filii servorum tuorum habitabunt : et semen eorum in sæculum dirigetur.

The children of Thy servants shall continue : and their seed shall be directed for ever.

"*Habitabunt.*" Shall dwell there, that is, in the holy city. ——"*Semen eorum . . .*" Thou wilt ever have a care of their posterity.

PSALM CII.

THE Psalmist celebrates the mercy of God ; and finding himself incapable of praising the Lord and thanking Him as He deserves, he invites the Angels and all creatures to do so in his name.

For David himself.

1. Benedic, anima mea, Domino : et omnia, quæ intra me sunt nomini sancto ejus.

Bless the Lord, O my soul : and let all that is within me bless His holy name.

"*Et omnia . . .*" And let all my powers give glory to His holy name.

2. Benedic, anima mea, Domino : et noli oblivisci omnes retributiones ejus.

Bless the Lord, O my soul : and forget not all His benefits.

3. Qui propitiatur omnibus iniqui- Who forgiveth thee all thine
tatibus tuis: qui sanat omnes iniquities: Who healeth all thine
infirmitates tuas. infirmities.

He is propitious, that is, He pardons thee all thy sins.
Thus nearly all interpret.——"*Omnes* . . ." That is, as Mattei
remarks: All thy infirmities, both corporal and spiritual.

4. Qui redimit de interitu vitam Who redeemeth thy life from
tuam: qui coronat te in misericordia destruction: Who crowneth thee
et miserationibus. with mercy and compassion.

"*De interitu.*" S. Jerome translates: *De corruptione;* and,
according to the Chaldee: *De gehenna.* That is, He delivers
thy corporal life from the death of the body, and thy spiritual
life from the death of the soul, whether it be from sin, or, as
we may also understand it, from hell.——"*Coronat te.*" According to Estius and others: Surrounds thee on all sides.

5. Qui replet in bonis desiderium Who satisfieth thy desire with
tuum: renovabitur ut aquilæ juven- good things: thy youth shall be
tus tua. renewed like the eagle's.

"*Renovabitur* . . ." He will make thy youth to be renewed,
as the wings and strength of the eagle are renewed.——This
may likewise be understood, as Mattei says, of the renovation
of the soul by means of baptism and conversion to penance,
according to the words of S. Paul: "Stripping yourselves of
the old man with his deeds and putting on the new, him who
is renewed," &c. (*Col.* iii. 9, 10).

6. Faciens misericordias Dominus: The Lord doth mercies and judg-
et judicium omnibus injuriam patien- ment: for all that suffer wrong.
tibus.

He, the Lord, is pleased to show mercy and to do justice to
all those who are wrongfully persecuted.

7. Notas fecit vias suas Moysi: He hath made His ways known un-
filiis Israel voluntates suas. to Moses: His will unto the children
  of Israel.

"*Vias suas.*" That is: The dispositions of His Providence.

8. Miserator, et misericors Domi- The Lord is full of compassion and
nus: longanimis, et multum miseri- mercy: long suffering and plenteous
cors. in mercy.

"*Miserator, et misericors.*" The divine attribute of mercy in
God shows itself in acts of compassion, which are the effects of
His mercy.——"*Longanimis.*" He is slow to anger and to
punish, He is patient and bears, but only up to a certain point.

9. Non in perpetuum irascetur: He will not always be angry:
neque in æternum comminabitur. neither will He threaten for ever.

If He be angry with any one and threaten to abandon him, He will not persevere in threatening if he soon amends his life.

10. Non secundum peccata nostra fecit nobis : neque secundum iniqui-tates nostras retribuit nobis.

He hath not dealt with us after our sins : nor rewarded us according to our iniquities.

Ah ! let us never cease to thank Him, seeing that He has not treated us as our sins deserved, nor has punished us accord-ing to our wickedness.

11. Quoniam secundum altitudi-nem cœli a terra : corroboravit misericordiam suam super timentes se.

For as the heaven is high above the earth : so hath He strengthened His mercy toward them that fear Him.

12. Quantum distat ortus ab occi-dente : longe fecit a nobis iniquitates nostras.

As far as the east is from the west : so far hath he removed our iniquities from us.

13. Quomodo miseretur pater filio-rum, misertus est Dominus timenti-bus se : quoniam ipse cognovit fig-mentum nostrum.

As a father hath pity upon his children, so hath the Lord pity upon them that fear Him : for He knoweth whereof we are made.

"*Figmentum nostrum.*" That is : Our weakness.

14. Recordatus est quoniam pulvis sumus: homo, sicut fœnum dies ejus, tamquam flos agri sic efflorebit.

He remembereth that we are but dust : man's days are as the grass, as the flower of the field so shall he flourish.

He is mindful that we are but dust, and that man, living on this earth, is like the grass, which to-day flowers in the field and to-morrow withers and dies.

15. Quoniam spiritus pertransibit in illo, et non subsistet : et non cog-noscet amplius locum suum.

For the wind shall pass over it, and it shall not be : and one shall know its place no more.

He is mindful that in this life the spirit is not lasting or permanent in man, but is passing, and on its way to its eter-nity.——"*Non cognoscet amplius locum suum.*" He does not return to know his place any more, that is, to begin over again his past years.

16. Misericordia autem Domini ab æterno : et usque in æternum super timentes eum :

But the mercy of the Lord is from everlasting to everlasting : upon them that fear Him :

17. Et justitia illius in filios filio-rum : his qui servant testamentum ejus:

And His justice upon children's children : unto such as keep His covenant :

"*Justitia illius.*"   His beneficent justice.——"*Testamentum ejus.*"   His covenant, His law.

| 18. Et memores sunt mandatorum ipsius : ad faciendum ea. | And are mindful of His commandments : to do them. |

| 19. Dominus in cœlo paravit sedem suam : et regnum ipsius omnibus dominabitur. | The Lord hath prepared His throne in heaven: and His kingdom shall rule over all. |

"*Paravit.*"   Hath established.——"*Regnum . . .*"   That is : All will have to obey His rule.

| 20. Benedicite Domino, omnes Angeli ejus : potentes virtute, facientes verbum illius, ad audiendam vocem sermonum ejus. | Bless the Lord, all ye His angels : ye that are mighty in strength, and fulfil His commandment, hearkening to the voice of His words. |

"*Facientes . . .*"   Who instantly execute His orders so soon as you hear His voice.

| 21. Benedicite Domino, omnes virtutes ejus : ministri ejus, qui facitis voluntatem ejus. | Bless the Lord all ye His hosts : ye ministers of His that do His will. |

Bless Him all ye hosts of His heavenly court, who are the ministers of His will.

| 22. Benedicite Domino, omnia opera ejus : in omni loco dominationis ejus benedic, anima mea, Domino. | Bless the Lord, all ye His works : in every place of His dominion bless the Lord, O my soul. |

PSALM CIII.

This Psalm, says Du Hamel, gives a figurative description of the glory of the Lord in the works of nature ; the Psalmist praises in it the wisdom and power which God has shown forth in the creation of heaven and earth.   The author of the arguments of the Psalms in the Compilation of Venice adds that in this one we may learn how to contemplate nature, and the manifold variety of created things.

| 1. Benedic, anima mea, Domino : Domine Deus meus, magnificatus es vehementer. | Bless the Lord, O my soul : O Lord my God, Thou art exceeding great. |

"*Vehementer.*"   S. Jerome translates : *Nimis :* Beyond all measure, exceedingly.——Thou hast magnified Thyself, that is, Thou hast made Thy greatness known by Thy works in a wonderful manner.

| 2. Confessionem, et decorem induisti : amictus lumine sicut vestimento | Thou hast put on praise and beauty : and art clothed with light as with a garment: |

"*Confessionem.*" According to the Hebrew : *Gloriam.* Glory.[1]

3. Extendens cœlum sicut pellem : qui tegis aquis superiora ejus.

Who stretchest out the heaven like a tent : Who coverest the higher places thereof with water.

"*Pellem.*" A skin. According to the Hebrew : *Tentorium.* ——"*Aquis.*" That is : With clouds ; according to Estius. —— Mattei says that this part of the heavens is really covered with waters.[2]

4. Qui ponis nubem ascensum tuum: qui ambulas super pennas ventorum.

Who makest the clouds Thy chariot : Who walkest upon the wings of the winds.

Thou ridest upon a cloud, as on a chariot which goes whither Thou willest ; Thou walkest flying on the winds, as though they were birds which had their wings extended.

5. Qui facis angelos tuos spiritus : et ministros tuos, ignem urentem.

Who makest Thine angels spirits : and Thy ministers a burning fire.

Thou causest Thy Angels to become as spirits or winds, and makest these Thy ministers to be as a burning flame. Thus S. Augustine (*in loc.*) and S. Gregory (*Hom.* 34 *in Evang.*). And this agrees with what S. Paul says (*Heb.* i. 7), when the Apostle absolutely interprets this verse of the Angels.[3]

[1] *Ps.* xcv. 6.

[2] *Gen.* i, 6 ; *Ps.* cxlviii. 4.

[3] This verse has been wrongly understood by some to mean simply that God uses the winds and the lightnings as His messengers : *angels* : according to what we read in *Exod.* xiv. 21, xv. 10, *Jona* i. 4, *Gen.* xix. 24, 25, *Ps.* cxlvii. 16-18, cxlviii. 8. It is against this view that S. Alphonsus, referring to the authority of S. Augustine and S. Gregory, and peremptorily to that of S. Paul, affirms that the Angels, properly speaking, are intended in this passage.——Cornelius a Lapide, on *Heb.* i. 7, well shows that the explanation, as given by the holy doctor, is the true and genuine sense of the words. He observes that the Greek word for " Angels," both in the Septuagint and in the New Testament, is preceded by the article, whilst that for " Spirits " is not ; thus marking the former word to be the subject, and the latter the predicate. The learned commentator then, following S. Jerome, S. Chrysostom, Theodoret, Euthymius, S. Thomas, Bellarmine, and others, explains the verse thus : God makes His Angels swift and subtile, as spirits or winds ; and again the same Angels, who are His ministers, God makes as a flame of fire, that is, of a nature most intensely active and ardent. This accords with the rendering of the Chaldee : " Who makes His angels swift as winds, and His ministers strong as burning fire." In Hebrew the note of comparison for *sicut, as,* is often to be understood, *e.g. Ps.* x. 1, where, according to the Hebrew, it is : " Flee to your mountains (as) a sparrow."—— It has been thought well to say so much, because it will doubtless readily occur to those conversant with the Breviary, that in the passage of S. Gregory referred to by S. Alphonsus, which is found in the V. Lection on the Feast of S. Michael, the holy Pontiff thus comments on this verse · " As though the

6. Qui fundasti terram super stabilitatem suam : non inclinabitur in sæculum sæculi.

Who didst found the earth upon its own basis : it shall not be moved for ever and ever.

"*Stabilitatem suam.*" S. Jerome translates : *Bases suas;* so also the Chaldee.——That is, as Lallemant well explains it, Thou hast made it firm by its own weight ; so that, as Mattei adds, it supports itself.

7. Abyssus, sicut vestimentum, amictus ejus : super montes stabunt aquæ.

The deep, like a garment, is its clothing : above the mountains shall the waters stand.

"*Abyssus.*" Mattei says that this word, in the language of the Bible, signifies an accumulation of waters.——"*Stabunt.*" According to the Hebrew : *Stabant.* Stood.——The verse is explained thus : Thou didst once upon a time cover the earth with waters, as with a vestment ; in such a manner that these waters were higher than the mountains (*Gen.* vii. 20).[1]

8. Ab increpatione tua fugient : a voce tonitrui tui formidabunt.

At Thy rebuke they shall flee : at the voice of Thy thunder they shall be afraid.

Then, at the sound of Thy voice, that is, of Thy command, as at the roar of threatening thunder, these waters withdrew, seized as though with terror, to the place assigned to them, which was the sea.——In the Hebrew the verbs are still in the past, and so they are generally interpreted.

9. Ascendunt montes, et descendunt campi : in locum quem fundasti eis.

The mountains rise up, and the plains go down : into the place which Thou hast laid for them.

At this Thy command it seemed as though the mountains rose up and the plains descended to the place which Thou didst destine for them.

Psalmist said plainly : Those whom the Lord has always as Spirits, He also, when He so wills, makes Angels." And S. Augustine expresses himself in the same sense. This, whilst differing from the interpretation given above and adopted by S. Alphonsus as the primary and genuine meaning of the verse, may be regarded as the expression of a truth nearly connected with the subject-matter of the verse, or contained in its full and complete sense, but not necessarily intended to be the exact rendering of its precise terms.—— Nay, Theodoret, who interprets the words in the same way as S. Alphonsus does, paraphrases them so as to include the thought of S. Gregory and of S. Augustine : "Spirits," he says, "by their own nature endowed with the highest intelligence, are, by the divine power and will, made to become like burning fire, and prompt to avenge the insults done to God : by which comparison are shown forth their power and swiftness."——"Who uses the ministry of His angels to stir up winds, and to send forth lightnings" (Maldonatus).—*Tr.*

[1] The passage is understood not only of the deluge, but also of the state of the earth and the waters at the beginning of Creation (*Gen.* i. 2-9).

10. Terminum posuisti, quem non transgredientur : neque convertentur operire terram.

Thou hast set a bound which they shall not pass over : neither shall they return to cover the earth.

That is, the waters now confined in the sea.

11. Quia emittis fontes in convallibus : inter medium montium pertransibunt aquæ.

Thou sendest forth springs in the valleys : the waters shall flow in the midst of the hills.

12. Potabunt omnes bestiæ agri : expectabunt onagri in siti sua.

All the beasts of the field shall drink : the wild asses shall look for it in their thirst.

"*Onagri.*" Wild asses, by which may be understood all wild animals.

13. Super ea volucres cœli habitabunt : de medio petrarum dabunt voces.

Over them the birds of the air shall dwell : they shall give forth their voices from the midst of the rocks.

"*Super ea.*" According to the Chaldee : *Juxta eos.* Above, or beside, these fountains or springs of water.——"*De medio petrarum.*" According to the Hebrew : *Inter ramos.* Amongst the branches : or, as S. Jerome translates : *De medio nemorum.* In the midst of the neighbouring groves.

14. Rigans montes de superioribus suis : de fructu operum tuorum satiabitur terra :

Thou waterest the hills from the heights above : the earth shall be filled with the fruit of Thy works :

Thou waterest the mountains with the upper waters, which descend from the clouds ; and thus the earth by the work of Thy providence shall be fully satisfied, that is, shall abound in fruits.

15. Producens fœnum jumentis : et herbam servituti hominum :

Bringing forth grass for cattle: and herb for the service of men.

16. Ut educas panem de terra : et vinum lætificet cor hominis :

That Thou mayest bring bread out of the earth : and that wine may cheer the heart of man :

"*Vinum . . .*" Here S. Chrysostom makes this reflection : "Some say : Away with wine. We should rather say : Away with drunkenness : for wine is the work of God, but drunkenness the work of the devil" (*Ad pop. Ant., Hom.* 1).

17. Ut exhilaret faciem in oleo : et panis cor hominis confirmet.

To make the face cheerful with oil : and that bread may strengthen man's heart.

We should here remark that, according to Theodoret, Maldonatus, Tirinus, and others, the Orientals were used to

anoint the face with oil to show a cheerful countenance. The
sense, then, is : Thou causest the earth to bring forth the
olives flowing with oil to anoint the face and make it look
joyous : and grain to make bread wherewith to sustain the
life of man.

18. Saturabuntur ligna campi, et cedri Libani, quas plantavit : illic passeres nidificabunt.	The trees of the field shall be filled, and the cedars of Libanus which He hath planted : there the sparrows shall make their nests.

"*Saturabuntur.*" Shall be sated with these waters of fountains and of rains.——"*Ligna campi.*" Mattei understands
hereby wild plants.——"*Passeres.*" The sparrows and the
other birds.

19. Herodii domus dux est eorum: montes excelsi cervis : petra refugium herinaciis.	The highest of them is the home of the heron : the high hills are a refuge for the harts, *and* the rock for the conies.

"*Herodii.*" It is uncertain what kind of bird this name
denotes; according to S. Jerome it is the kite; but Menochius,
Lallemant, and others, following the Chaldee, say it is the
stork.——"*Herodii domus dux est eorum.*" According to the
Hebrew : *Herodii abies est domus ejus.* As for the stork, the
fir tree is her house.——The verse, then, is thus rendered :
The stork has its dwelling on the lofty fir tree, the highest
mountains are the home of the harts, and the hollow rocks
afford refuge to the rabbits, or rather hares, according to the
Greek. (See Mattei.)

20. Fecit lunam in tempora : sol cognovit occasum suum.	He hath made the moon for seasons : the sun knoweth his going down.

"*Fecit lunam in tempora.*" He hath made the moon, whereby
to reckon the different times and seasons. The Hebrews were
used to regulate their calendar by the moon. Hence it is
written : "The moon in all her season is for a declaration of
times and a sign of the age. From the moon is the sign of
the festival day. . . . The month is called after her name"
(*Ecclus.* xliii. 6-8).——"*Sol* . . ." The sun runs his course to
his setting ; or, as Malvenda explains it, the sun knows how
to go through his course without the variations incident to the
moon.

21. Posuisti tenebras, et facta est nox ; in ipsa pertransibunt omnes bestiæ silvæ.	Thou hast appointed darkness, and it is night : wherein all the beasts of the woods shall come forth.

Thou hast ordained that to sunset darkness should succeed : and night is made : when all the beasts of the forest come forth from their lairs.

22. Catuli leonum rugientes, ut rapiant: et quærant a Deo escam sibi.

The young lions roaring after their prey ; and seeking their meat from God.

The lions come forth roaring with their young cubs to seek for prey in the forests ; and by their roaring they seem to ask of God their food.

23. Ortus est sol, et congregati sunt : et in cubilibus suis colloca-buntur.

The sun ariseth, and they are gathered together : and they shall lie down in their dens.

At sunrise they collect together to go back to their dens.

24. Exibit homo ad opus suum : et ad operationem suam usque ad vesperum.

Man shall go forth to his work : and to his labour until the evening.

And then man sallies forth and goes to his labour, and is busy with his work until the evening.

25. Quam magnificata sunt opera tua, Domine ! omnia in sapientia fecisti : impleta est terra possessione tua.

How great are Thy works, O Lord ! Thou hast made all things in wisdom : the earth is filled with Thy riches.

Oh, how exceeding great, how magnificent when known, are Thy works, O Lord ! Thou hast created them all with con-summate wisdom ; the earth is filled with Thy possessions. ——"*Possessione tua.*" According to the Greek : *Creatura tua.* With Thy creatures. Menochius and Mattei explain thus : The earth is filled with Thy works, with the goods which Thou hast created.

26. Hoc mare magnum, et spatio-sum manibus : illic reptilia, quorum non est numerus.

So is this great sea, which stretcheth wide its arms : therein are creeping things, without number.

"*Reptilia.*" Properly, Reptiles, animals without legs, that crawl on their bellies. Here the word denotes every kind of fish.

27. Animalia pusilla cum magnis : illic naves pertransibunt.

Living things both small and great: there *also* ships shall go.

Living things small and great sport in this vast deep ; there also sail the ships.

28. Draco iste, quem formasti ad illudendum ei : omnia a te expectant, ut des illis escam in tempore.

This sea-dragon which Thou hast formed to play therein : all wait upon Thee to give them food in season.

"*Draco.*" S. Jerome writes : *Leviathan*. Others, as Lallemant, and perhaps all commonly say that it is the whale ; but
according to Mattei this is not certain ; all that is certain is
that some sea-monster is signified.——"*Ad illudendum ei.*"
According to the Hebrew : *Ut luderet in eo.* And in this sense
it is understood by Maldonatus, Estius, Sa, Malvenda, Mattei,
&c., to play therein.

29. Dante te illis, colligent:
aperiente te manum tuam, omnia
implebuntur bonitate.

What Thou givest to them they
shall gather up : when Thou openest
Thy hand, they shall all be filled
with good.

30. Avertente autem te faciem,
turbabuntur : auferes spiritum eorum, et deficient, et in pulverem
suum revertentur.

But if Thou turnest away Thy
face, they shall be troubled : Thou
shalt take away their breath, and
they shall fail, and shall return to
their dust.

But shouldst Thou turn away Thy face, *i.e.*, withdraw Thy
gracious looks, they will languish ; Thou wilt take away their
life and they will cease to be, and thus they return to the
dust, whence Thou didst draw them.

31. Emittes spiritum tuum, et crea-
buntur : et renovabis faciem terræ.

Thou shalt send forth Thy spirit,
and they shall be created : and Thou
shalt renew the face of the earth.

Thou wilt send forth the breath of life into other animals
to which Thou wilt give being, and thus Thou wilt renew the
face of the earth.——Du Hamel applies this in a mystical sense
to the Holy Ghost, Who by His grace renews the face of the
earth, that is, of the souls living in this world; and thus the
Holy Church makes use of this verse in her Liturgy at Pente-
cost.

32. Sit gloria Domini in sæculum:
lætabitur Dominus in operibus suis.

May the glory of the Lord endure
for ever: the Lord shall rejoice in His
works.

Let then the Lord be glorified for ever ; and let us act in
such sort that He may rejoice in us, who are His works, and
that He may not be saddened by our faults.

33. Qui respicit terram, et facit
eam tremere : qui tangit montes, et
fumigant.

He looketh upon the earth, and
maketh it tremble : He toucheth the
mountains, and they smoke.

Let us beware of provoking that Lord Who, with a single
glance, makes the earth to tremble ; and by touching the
mountains causes them to smoke with His thunder and lightning, as He did on Mount Sinai : "And all Mount Sinai was
in a smoke " (*Exod.* xix. 18).

34. Cantabo Domino in vita mea : psallam Deo meo quamdiu sum.

I will sing unto the Lord as long as I live : I will sing praise unto my God while I have my being.

35. Jucundum sit ei eloquium meum : ego vero delectabor in Domino.

May my speech be pleasing unto Him : but I will take delight in the Lord.

May my canticles be pleasing to Him ; for I will seek no other delight but to take pleasure in the Lord.

36. Deficiant peccatores a terra, et iniqui ita ut non sint : benedic, anima mea, Domino.

Let sinners be consumed out of the earth, and the unjust, so that they be no more : bless the Lord, O my soul.

Let sinners and the unjust disappear from the earth, so that they may no longer exist; and thou, my soul, continue always to bless the Lord.

PSALM CIV.

THE Psalmist exhorts the Jews to praise God and to give Him thanks for the benefits bestowed on their fathers.[1]

Alleluia.

1. Confitemini Domino, et invocate nomen ejus : annuntiate inter Gentes opera ejus.

Give glory to the Lord, and call upon His name : make known His deeds among the nations.

2. Cantate ei, et psallite ei : narrate omnia mirabilia ejus.

Sing unto Him, yea sing praises unto Him : tell of all His wondrous works.

3. Laudamini in nomine sancto ejus : lætetur cor quærentium Dominum.

Glory ye in His holy name : let the heart of them rejoice, that seek the Lord.

Render yourselves worthy of praise by your zeal in procuring glory to His holy name.[2]

4. Quærite Dominum, et confirmamini : quærite faciem ejus semper.

Seek ye the Lord, and be strengthened : seek His face evermore.

[1] The first fifteen verses of this Psalm form part of the Canticle of David 1 *Paral.* xvi. 8-22), but with some differences of expression.

[2] " *Laudamini.*" S. Jerome translates the Hebrew : *Exultate*; and Bellarmine : *Laudate vos ipsos* ; which the learned Cardinal thus explains ; Congratulate yourselves or glory, not in yourselves or in your virtue, but in this, that the holy Name of God has been manifested to you, according to the advice of the Apostle : "He that glorieth, may glory in the Lord" (1 *Cor.* i. 31). In Paralipomenon we read simply : "Praise ye His holy name" (1 *Par.* xvi. 10).

Seek the Lord, and be constant in seeking Him ; study to be, in spirit, always in His presence.

5. Mementote mirabilium ejus, quæ fecit: prodigia ejus, et judicia oris ejus.

Remember His marvellous works which He hath done : His wonders, and the judgments of His mouth.

"*Judicia oris ejus.*" The commandments, or the law, delivered by His mouth.

6. Semen Abraham, servi ejus: filii Jacob electi ejus.

O ye seed of Abraham His servant: ye children of Jacob His chosen.

I say this to you who are the posterity of Abraham, and the servants of the Lord; to you children of Jacob, who are the chosen people of the Lord.[3]

7. Ipse Dominus Deus noster: in universa terra judicia ejus.

He is the Lord our God : His judgments are in all the earth :

"*In universa . . .*" That is, He governs the whole earth.

8. Memor fuit in sæculum testamenti sui : verbi, quod mandavit in mille generationes :

He hath remembered His covenant for ever: the word which He commanded to a thousand generations :

He has always been mindful of His covenant with His servants, and of the promise which He made them in words which expressed His will, to make all future generations have part therein.

9. Quod disposuit ad Abraham : et juramenti sui ad Isaac.

Which He made with Abraham : and His oath that He sware unto Isaac.

10. Et statuit illud Jacob in præceptum : et Israel in testamentum æternum :

And He appointed the same unto Jacob for a law : and to Israel for an everlasting testament :

"*Præceptum.*" That is, as an inviolable law. According to the Hebrew: *Statutum, Decretum.*——"*Testamentum æternum.*" A covenant or compact which was to be always observed.

11. Dicens : Tibi dabo terram Chanaan : funiculum hereditatis vestræ.

Saying : Unto thee will I give the land of Chanaan : the lot of your inheritance.

These were the words of promise in the Covenant.—— "*Terram Chanaan.*" The Land of Promise, where the Chanaanites dwelt.——"*Funiculum . . .*" This land shall be pos-

[1] "*Servi ... Electi.*" According to the Greek, these words are in the plural.

sessed by your children as an inheritance distributed in lots, measured with a line of cord.[1]

| 12. Cum essent numero brevi: paucissimi et incolæ ejus : | When they were but a small number : yea very few, and sojourners therein : |

"*Incolæ.*" According to the Hebrew: *Peregrini, Advenæ.*—— This promise was made to the Hebrews when they were few in number and strangers in the land of Chanaan.

| 13. Et pertransierunt de gente in gentem : et de regno ad populum alterum. | And they passed from nation to nation : and from one kingdom to another people. |

And the Patriarchs, Abraham, Isaac, and Jacob, had to pass from one country to another, as from Palestine to Egypt (*Gen.* xii., xx., xxvi., xxviii., xxxi., xlvi.).

| 14. Non reliquit hominem nocere eis ; et corripuit pro eis reges. | He suffered no man to do them wrong : and He reproved kings for their sakes. |

"*Corripuit.*" He corrected, *i.e.*, chastised kings who ill-treated them.

| 15. Nolite tangere christos meos : et in prophetis meis nolite malignari. | Saying : Touch not Mine anointed : and do My prophets no harm. |

"*Christos meos, Prophetis meis.*" My anointed, My Prophets ; that is, the Patriarchs.[2]

| 16. Et vocavit famem super terram: et omne firmamentum panis contrivit. | And He called a famine upon the land : and He brake in pieces all the support of bread. |

"*Vocavit.*" That is : He brought.——"*Firmamentum panis.*" That is : The staff or support of human life, which consists in bread.[3]

| 17. Misit ante eos virum : in servum venumdatus est Joseph. | He sent a man before them : Joseph, who was sold for a slave. |

He ordained that Joseph, who had been sold by his brethren, should be taken before them into Egypt, and thus deliver them from famine.

---

[1] The promises of God to Abraham, Isaac, and Jacob may be seen in *Gen.* xii. 7, xiii. 15, xvii. 7, xxvi. 3, xxviii. 13.——*Funiculum.* See *Ps.* lxxvii. 60.

[2] Abraham, Isaac, and Jacob, called Christs, or Anointed, and Prophets, because they were specially consecrated to the service of God, exercised the functions of the priesthood, and foretold the future (*Gen.* xx. 7 ; xxvii. 49).

[3] "*Firmamentum.*" According to the Hebrew : *Baculum:* The Staff. "After I shall have broken the staff of your bread" (*Levit.* xxvi. 26).

25

18. Humiliaverunt in compedibus pedes ejus, ferrum pertransiit
animam ejus: donec veniret verbum
ejus.

They humbled his feet in fetters:
the iron pierced his soul, until his
word came.

In Egypt, Joseph was humiliated and cast into prison, with
fetters on his feet.——"*Ferrum pertransiit animam ejus.*" According to the Greek text, *Anima* instead of *Animam.* The
Hebrew may be understood either way; but Bellarmine says
that in the Vulgate the sense is clearer, and that thus S.
Jerome, S. Augustine, and others explain the passage; viz.,
The pain caused by the iron fetters afflicted the soul of Joseph.
——"*Donec veniret verbum ejus.*" That is, until the accomplishment of his prophecy concerning the release from prison
of Pharao's chief butler, which release was followed by his
own (*Gen.* xl. 12, 20, 21; xli. 14).

19. Eloquium Domini inflammavit
eum: misit rex, et solvit eum;
princeps populorum, et dimisit eum.

The word of the Lord inflamed
him: the king sent and loosed him;
the prince of the people, and let him
go free.

The word of the Lord, that is, the spirit of prophecy with
which Joseph felt himself inspired, was as a torch which
inflamed him, that is, which encouraged him to make this
prediction. Whereupon King Pharao sent to free him from
chains, and this prince of many peoples set him at liberty.

20. Constituit eum dominum
domus suæ: et principem omnis
possessionis suæ:

He made him Lord of his house:
and ruler of all his possession.

Pharao made him master of his household, that is, set him
over all his kingdom, that he might govern it as lord and
prince.

21. Ut erudiret principes ejus sicut
semetipsum: et senes ejus prudentiam doceret.

That he might instruct his princes
as himself: and teach his ancients
wisdom.

That he might instruct the great men of his kingdom and
the ancients of his council with that prudence with which he
was gifted.

22. Et intravit Israel in Ægyptum: et Jacob accola fuit in terra
Cham.

Israel also came into Egypt: and
Jacob was a sojourner in the land of
Cham.

"*Israel, Jacob.*" Jacob, together with his family.——"*Terra
Cham.*" Egypt. We have already said (see *Ps.* lxxvii. 56)
that this country was peopled by the descendants of Cham,
son of Noe; it was Mesraïm, son of Cham, who first established himself in Egypt.

23. Et auxit populum suum vehementer: et firmavit eum super
inimicos ejus.

And He increased His people exceedingly : and made them stronger
than their enemies.

24. Convertit cor eorum ut odirent
populum ejus : et dolum facerent in
servos ejus.

He turned their heart to hate his
people : [1] and to deal deceitfully
with His servants.

That is, by multiplying the Israelites, and thus establishing
them in Egypt, God gave occasion to the Egyptians to be
exasperated against His faithful people, to persecute them and
to seek every means of oppressing His servants.

25. Misit Moysen servum suum ;
Aaron quem elegit ipsum.

He sent Moses His servant : Aaron
the man whom He had chosen.

Wherefore the Lord sent His servant Moses, and Aaron his
brother, whom He chose to be his fellow-helper.——" *Ipsum.*"
Bellarmine remarks that the Hebrew may be rendered *Ei ;*
but he says, with S. Augustine, that the word *Ipsum* in
Hebrew is used simply for elegance, and therefore adds
nothing to the sense.

26. Posuit in eis verba signorum
suorum : et prodigiorum in terra
Cham.

He gave them power to show His
signs : and His wonders in the land
of Cham.

"*Verba signorum.*" The words of His miracles. A Hebraism,
which means : The power to work miracles.

27. Misit tenebras, et obscuravit :
et non exacerbavit sermones suos.

He sent darkness, and made it
dark : and grieved not His words.[2]

In this and in the eight following verses, David describes
the miraculous prodigies wrought to punish the Egyptians.
——"*Misit tenebras.*" This darkness lasted three days (*Exod.*
x. 22).——"*Non exacerbavit sermones suos.*" Some would take
out the particle *Non ;* but, according to Bellarmine, this correction is inadmissible ; for the Vulgate here agrees with the
Hebrew text [of which the rendering is : *Non repugnarunt
sermonibus ejus*]. That is : Moses and Aaron did not resist the
orders of God, Who had commanded them to work those
wonders.

[1] *He turned their heart,* &c. Not that God moved the Egyptians to hate
His people ; but that the Egyptians took occasion of envying them, from the
sight of the benefits which God bestowed upon them.
[2] *Grieved not His words.* That is, He was not wanting to fulfil His words.
——(But we must here observe that the English version in referring these
words to God instead of to Moses—and with him to Aaron—gives a rendering of the Vulgate that is opposed to the Hebrew, S. Jerome, and the
Septuagint.)—*Tr.*

28. Convertit aquas eorum in sanguinem : et occidit pisces eorum.

He turned their waters into blood : and slew their fish.

29. Edidit terra eorum ranas : in penetralibus regum ipsorum.

Their land brought forth frogs : in the inner chambers of their kings.

Their land produced such a quantity of frogs that they penetrated even into the most private chambers of the king himself.

30. Dixit, et venit cœnomyia : et cinifes in omnibus finibus eorum.

He spake, and there came divers sorts of flies : and gnats[1] in all their coasts.

The Lord spoke, and there came a vast quantity of flies and gnats, which spread themselves in all their confines.

31. Posuit pluvias eorum grandinem : ignem comburentem in terra ipsorum.

He gave them hail for rain : a burning fire in their land.

"*Grandinem ignem comburentem.*" Hailstones which burned like fire.

32. Et percussit vineas eorum, et ficulneas eorum : et contrivit lignum finium eorum.

And He destroyed their vineyards and their fig-trees : and He brake in pieces the trees of their coasts.

33. Dixit, et venit locusta, et bruchus : cujus non erat numerus :

He spake, and the locust came : and the bruchus[2] without number :

"*Bruchus.*" The caterpillar.

34. Et comedit omne fœnum in terra eorum : et comedit omnem fructum terræ eorum.

And did eat up all the grass in their land : and devoured all the fruit of their ground.

35. Et percussit omne primogenitum in terra eorum : primitias omnis laboris eorum.

He smote also all the first-born in their land : the first-fruits of all their labour.

36. Et eduxit eos cum argento et auro : et non erat in tribubus eorum infirmus.

And He brought them out with silver and gold : and there was not one sick among their tribes.

"*Cum argento et auro.*" Laden with silver and gold.

37. Lætata est Ægyptus in profectione eorum : quia incubuit timor eorum super eos.

Egypt was glad when they departed : for the fear of them lay upon them.

"*Incubuit.*" They stood in fear of further chastisements if the Israelites did not depart.

---

[1] *Gnats.* The word in the text signifies a kind of fly common in Egypt.

[2] *Bruchus.* An insect of the locust kind.

38. Expandit nubem in protectionem eorum: et ignem ut luceret eis per noctem.

He spread a cloud for their protection : and fire to give them light by night.

The Lord in the day spread a cloud above them to protect them from the heat of the day, and a pillar of fire to give them light in the night. But here we must take notice, with Bellarmine, that this cloud is not the pillar spoken of in Exodus : "And the Lord went before them to show the way by day in a pillar of cloud" (*Ex.* xiii. 21). The pillar was to go before them to show them the way and not to be spread out over their heads. The cloud, moreover, spread out above them could not take the shape of a pillar. Hence, adds Bellarmine, we are justified in saying that, besides the pillar of cloud which went before the Israelites, and which once we read went behind them to protect them against the Egyptians (*Exod.* xiv. 19), there was another cloud spread out over them to shelter them from the heat during their journey. This explanation is supported by the Hebrew text, which S. Jerome thus renders: *Expandit nubem in tentorium.* He spread out a cloud for a tent or covering; as well as by the following words in the Book of Wisdom : "She (that is, Wisdom) conducted them in a wonderful way: and she was to them for a covert by day, and for the light of stars by night" (*Wisd.* x. 17).

39. Petierunt, et venit coturnix : et pane cœli saturavit eos.

They asked, and the quail came : and He filled them with the bread of heaven.

The Israelites asked for means to feed on flesh and bread, and the Lord sent amongst them an abundance of quails, and He satiated them with manna, which He caused to fall from heaven.

40. Dirupit petram, et fluxerunt aquæ : abierunt in sicco flumina :

He opened the rock, and waters flowed : rivers ran down in the dry land :

They were thirsty, and the Lord, by the hand of Moses, broke a rock, whence ran waters, seen flowing as torrents in that arid desert.

41. Quoniam memor fuit verbi sancti sui: quod habuit ad Abraham puerum suum.

For He remembered His holy word: which He had spoken to His servant Abraham.

42. Et eduxit populum suum in exultatione : et electos suos in lætitia.

And He brought forth His people with joy: and His chosen with gladness.

43. Et dedit illis regiones Gentium: et labores populorum possederunt.

And He gave them the lands of the Gentiles; and they possessed the labours of the people.

"*Labores . . .*" They came into possession of the labours of those nations, that is, of the cities which they had built, and of the fields which they had cultivated.

44. Ut custodiant justificationes ejus: et legem ejus requirant.[1]

That they might observe His precepts: and seek after His law.

PSALM CV.

THE Psalmist exhorts the Israelites to give thanks to God for the wonders wrought in their behalf from the time they left Egypt to the time of the Judges, and reproaches them for their ingratitude to the Lord. The thought of our ingratitude should still more be a matter of confusion to us Christians, who have received from God far greater benefits.

Alleluia.

1. Confitemini Domino quoniam bonus: quoniam in sæculum misericordia ejus.

Give glory to the Lord, for He is good: for His mercy endureth for ever.

"*Quoniam bonus.*" Since He is goodness itself.——"*In sæculum.*" S. Jerome translates : *In æternum.*

2. Quis loquetur potentias Domini? auditas faciet omnes laudes ejus?

Who shall declare the mighty works of the Lord? who shall set forth all His praises?

"*Loquetur.*" According to the Chaldee : *Eloqui poterit.* Who shall be able to express the power of the Lord? Who shall show forth, or make known all the praises that belong to Him?

3. Beati, qui custodiunt judicium: et faciunt justitiam in omni tempore.

Blessed are they that keep judgment: and do justice at all times.

"*Judicium.*" Judgment, equity, or the law of God.

4. Memento nostri, Domine, in beneplacito populi tui: visita nos in salutari tuo.

Remember us, O Lord, with the favour of Thy people : O visit us with Thy salvation.

[1] "*Justificationes.*" By which is to be understood the commandments of God, which are called *justifications,* because the keeping of them makes man just.

5. Ad videndum in bonitate electorum tuorum, ad lætandum in lætitia gentis tuæ : ut lauderis cum hereditate tua.

That we may see the good of Thy chosen, that we may rejoice in the joy of Thy nation : that Thou mayest be praised with Thine inheritance.

In the Hebrew, according to S. Jerome and the other interpreters, instead of the plural, "*Nostri,*" &c., is found the singular, viz.: *Mei, Me, Videam, Læter.*——"*Memento . . . tui.*" S. Jerome translates : *Recordare mei Domine in repropitiatione populi tui.*——The passage may be thus explained : Remember me, O Lord, in Thy good pleasure, that is, according to S. Jerome, graciousness and goodness, which Thou hast so often shown towards Thy people.——"*In salutari tuo.*" According to the Hebrew : *In salute tua ;* and according to the Chaldee : *In redemptione tua.* That is : Visit us (or me) by sending us salvation, or redemption, through Jesus Christ, as S. Augustine explains it. For He is the Saviour ; . . . since of Him the aged Simeon said : "Because my eyes have seen Thy salvation."—— "*Ad videndum in bonitate.*" According to the Hebrew : *Ut videam bonum,* or, according to St. Jerome, *Bona.* Be mindful of me, O Lord, that I may see the good things prepared for Thy elect.——"*Ad lætandum in lætitia gentis tuæ.*" That is, still according to the Hebrew in the singular : That I may rejoice in the joy, or that I may have part in the joy of Thy faithful people.——"*Ut lauderis cum hæreditate tua.*" That is : So that Thou mayest be for ever praised by this people and by me, who are Thine own inheritance.

6. Peccavimus cum patribus nostris ; injuste egimus, iniquitatem fecimus.

We have sinned with our fathers : we have acted wickedly : we have wrought iniquity.

7. Patres nostri in Ægypto non intellexerunt mirabilia tua : non fuerunt memores multitudinis misericordiæ tuæ.

Our fathers understood not Thy wonders in Egyyt : they remembered not the multitude of Thy mercies.

They did not understand or appreciate the wonders wrought by Thee in Egypt for their deliverance ; and too soon they forgot Thy many mercies towards them.

8. Et irritaverunt ascendentes in mare : mare Rubrum.

And they provoked to wrath : going up to the sea, even the Red sea.

"*Ascendentes in mare.*" According to the Hebrew : *Juxta mare.* That is : They provoked Thy anger near that same Red Sea, I say, where they had received so many benefits.

9. Et salvavit eos propter nomen suum : ut notam faceret potentiam suam.

And He saved them for His own name's sake : that He might make His power to be known.

And yet, notwithstanding, God willed to save them for the honour of His name, in order to make known His power.

10. Et increpuit mare Rubrum, et exsiccatum est : et deduxit eos in abyssis sicut in deserto.

He rebuked the Red sea also, and it was dried up : and He led them through the depths as through a wilderness.

Here the Psalmist returns to speak of the benefits done them in their progress through the Red Sea.——"*Increpuit mare Rubrum.*" S. Jerome translates : *Comminatus est mari Rubro.* God threatened the Red Sea to make it obey, that is, He bade the Red Sea to dry up, and it dried up, its waters withdrawing on either side to make a way for the Israelites.

11. Et salvavit eos de manu odientium : et redemit eos de manu inimici.

And He saved them from the hand of them that hated them : and He redeemed them from the hand of the enemy.

12. Et operuit aqua tribulantes eos : unus ex eis non remansit.

And the water covered them that afflicted them : there was not one of them left.

13. Et crediderunt verbis ejus : et laudaverunt laudem ejus.

And they believed His words : and they sang His praises.

Then the Hebrews gave credit to His words, and chanted His praises. They then sang the Canticle of Moses (*Exod.* xv.).

14. Cito fecerunt, obliti sunt operum ejus : et non sustinuerunt consilium ejus.

They had quickly done, they forgot His works : and they waited not for His counsel.

"*Cito fecerunt . . . ejus.*" They very soon made a change, that is, they went and forgot all the wonders God had wrought for them.——"*Non sustinuerunt.*" They would not await His counsel. S. Jerome translates : *Non expectaverunt voluntatem ejus.* They would not wait for the execution of His will.

15. Et concupierunt concupiscentiam in deserto : et tentaverunt Deum in inaquoso.

And they coveted exceedingly in the desert : and they tempted God in the place without water.

And whilst they were in the desert they gave themselves up to their disorderly appetites, and they tempted God in that place of aridity.——"*In inaquoso.*" S. Jerome translates : *In solitudine.*

16. Et dedit eis petitionem ipsorum : et misit saturitatem in animas eorum.

And He gave them their request : and sent fulness into their souls.

"*Misit saturitatem . . .*" That is, God sent them flesh, which they had craved and asked for so as even to cause satiety or surfeit to their souls.

17. Et irritaverunt Moysen in castris : Aaron sanctum Domini.	They angered Moses also in the camp : and Aaron, the holy one of the Lord.

"*Irritaverunt.*" According to the Hebrew : *Inviderunt*, and the Chaldee : *Invidia commoti sunt.* Allusion is here made to the envy which Nathan and Abiron, named in the next verse, had conceived against Moses and Aaron on seeing them constituted leaders of the people, and which led them to address Moses and Aaron in these words : " Why lift you up yourselves above the people of the Lord?"——"*Aaron sanctum Domini.*" Aaron, consecrated to God as His priest.

18. Aperta est terra, et deglutivit Dathan : et operuit super congregationem Abiron.	The earth opened and swallowed up Dathan : and covered the congregation of Abiron.

The earth swallowed them both up, together with all those assembled there, who had joined their party of revolt (*Numb.* xvi. 32).

19. Et exarsit ignis in synagoga eorum : flamma combussit peccatores.	And a fire was kindled in their company : the flame burned up the wicked.

"*In synagoga eorum.*" The multitude of those who murmured the day following (*Numb.* xvi. 41, 47, 50).

20. Et fecerunt vitulum in Horeb : et adoraverunt sculptile.	They made also a calf in Horeb : and they adored the graven thing.

Here the Psalmist alludes to another rising of the Israelites, when they worshipped the golden calf (*Exod.* xxxii.).—— "*In Horeb.*" Near Mount Horeb, or Sinai.

21. Et mutaverunt gloriam suam : in similitudinem vituli comedentis fœnum.	And they changed their glory : into the likeness of a calf that eateth grass.

"*Gloriam suam.*" Some understand these words to mean the glory of the Israelites ; but according to the Chaldee it is : *Gloriam Domini sui ;* and hence, as Estius says, the sense of the verse is : And they transferred the glory which was due to God, by giving it to the image of a calf, that feeds on grass.

22. Obliti sunt Deum, qui salvavit eos, qui fecit magnalia in Ægypto, mirabilia in terra Cham : terribilia in mari Rubro.	They forgot God, Who saved them, Who had done great things in Egypt, wondrous works in the land of Cham : terrible things in the Red sea.

23. Et dixit ut disperderet eos : si non Moyses electus ejus stetisset in confractione in conspectu ejus :

And He said that He would destroy them : had not Moses His chosen stood before Him in the breach :

Wherefore God declared He would destroy His people (*Exod.* xxxii. 10) ; and so He would have done if Moses, whom He had chosen to be their leader, had not interposed in His presence as their mediator.——"*In confractione.*" According to the Hebrew : *In ruptura,* or *divisione,* and S. Jerome translates : *Medius ; (stetisset medius contra faciem illius).*

24. Ut averteret iram ejus, ne disperderet eos : et pro nihilo habuerunt terram desiderabilem :

To turn away His wrath lest He should destroy them : and they despised the land of desire :

"*Ut averteret.*" Moses, I say, interposed to turn away, &c. ——"*Terram desiderabilem.*" The Land of Promise, so worthy of their desires, which God had destined for them.

25. Non crediderunt verbo ejus, et murmuraverunt in tabernaculis suis ; non exaudierunt vocem Domini.

They believed not His word, and they murmured in their tents : they hearkened not unto the voice of the Lord.

26. Et elevavit manum suam super eos : ut prosterneret eos in deserto :

And He lifted up His hand over them : to overthrow them in the desert :

27. Et ut dejiceret semen eorum in nationibus : et dispergeret eos in regionibus.

And to cast down their seed among the nations : and to scatter them in the countries.

"*Manum suam.*" His hand armed with the sword of justice. ——Bellarmine here well remarks that the first of these chastisements spoken of in verse 26 was inflicted in the desert itself, where all the murmurers twenty years old and upwards were condemned to die (*Numb.* xiv. 29) ; the second, namely, the dispersion, spoken of in verse 27, had its accomplishment later on, at first by means of the king of Babylon, and more fully afterwards by Titus and Vespasian.

28. Et initiati sunt Beelphegor : et comederunt sacrificia mortuorum.

They also were initiated to Beelphegor : and ate the sacrifices of the dead.

Here David mentions another sin of the Israelites, which they committed when, led away by the daughters of Moab, they began to worship their idol Beelphegor (*Numb.* xxv.). Calmet, in a dissertation at the commencement of the Book of Numbers, shows that Beelphegor is the same as Adonis.—— "*Sacrificia mortuorum.*" S. Jerome translates : *Victimas mor-*

tuorum. That is : Sacrifices offered to dead gods. The verse may be thus explained : They added the sin of being initiated, or of consecrating themselves in honour of the idol Beelphegor, and they ate of the sacrifices offered to the dead gods of the Gentiles ; whilst our true God is a living God.

29. Et irritaverunt eum in adin- ventionibus suis : et multiplicata est in eis ruina.	And they provoked Him to anger with their devices : and destruction was multiplied among them.

"*In adinventionibus suis.*" With their depraved inventions, that is, with their superstitions.——"*Multiplicata est in eis ruina.*" According to the Hebrew : *Erupit in eos plaga.* That is : A great slaughter was made of them on account of this sacrilege ; the number of those that perished on this occasion amounted to twenty-four thousand (*Numb.* xxv. 9).

30. Et stetit Phinees, et placavit: et cessavit quassatio.	Then stood up Phinees and ap- peased Him : and the slaughter ceased.

Then Phinees, grandson of Aaron, burning with zeal for God, slew one of the transgressors of the law with his accom- plice.——"*Stetit.*" He stood firm for the honour of the law. ——"*Placavit.*" S. Jerome translates the Hebrew : *Dijudicavit.* Executed judgment, or judged and punished the guilty one, and thus, according to the Chaldee : *Oravit,* or *Oratione placa- vit,* He interposed by praying for his people, and appeased the anger of God.——"*Cessavit quassatio.*" That is, according to some : The disorder or tumult ceased. But the sense of the Chaldee is : *Cessavit mors ;* and S. Jerome translates in the same sense : *Est retenta pecussio :* The slaughter ceased. This last interpretation is the best ; for we read in Numbers : *Cessavitque plaga a filiis Israel.* And the scourge ceased from the children of Israel (*Numb.* xxv. 8).

31. Et reputatum est ei in justi- tiam: in generationem et genera- tionem usque in sempiternum.	And it was reputed to him unto justice : unto generation and genera- tion for evermore.

This act of Phinees was imputed to him for merit, as a work of justice and of true zeal. He received in recompense the dignity of the high priesthood (*Numb.* xxv. 13), which continued in his family for more than thirteen centuries, according to Mattei, with Mariana, Menochius, &c.——"*In sempiternum.*" That is : He received this reward for as long as the Mosaic law should last ; *Quamdiu lex duraret,* says Sa.

| 32. Et irritaverunt cum ad aquas contradictionis; et vexatus est Moyses propter eos: quia exacerbaverunt spiritum ejus. | They angered Him also at the waters of strife: and Moses was afflicted for their sakes: because they provoked his spirit. |

Again the Israelites sinned against God when, suffering from want of water in the desert (*Numb.* xx.), they broke out into unjust murmurings. Moses then, though he had received from God the command to speak to the rock, hesitated somewhat, having conceived a certain feeling of diffidence; however, he struck the rock and water flowed from it in great abundance. God, displeased with Moses on account of his hesitation, punished him by making him die before entering the Promised Land.——"*Ad aquas contradictionis.*" That is : In the place where, on account of want of water, there arose a contradiction and a contest against Moses.——"*Vexatus est Moyses propter eos.*" Moses was grieved by the refractoriness of the people.——"*Exacerbaverunt spiritum ejus.*" They so embittered his soul, that he hesitated to execute the order which God had given him to speak to the rock.

| 33. Et distinxit in labiis suis : non disperdiderunt Gentes, quas dixit Dominus illis. | And he faltered with his lips :[1] they did not destroy the nations of which the Lord spake unto them. |

God distinctly with His own mouth rebuked the Hebrews, reproving them for not having exterminated the idolatrous nations, as He had commanded them.[2]

| 34. Et commixti sunt inter Gentes, et didicerunt opera eorum : et servierunt sculptilibus eorum : et factum est illis in scandalum. | And they were mingled among the heathens, and learned their works : and they served their idols : and it became a stumbling-block unto them. |

[1] *He faltered with his lips.* Moses, because instead of speaking to the rock, as God had commanded, said to the people, with a certain hesitation in his faith, "Hear, ye rebellious and incredulous : Can we from this rock bring out water for you?" (*Numb.* xx. 10).

[2] "*Distinxit in labiis suis.*" S. Alphonsus, in referring these words to God Himself, and not to Moses, as the English version does, adopts the opinion of Bellarmine, who admits that the other interpretation is that of S. Augustine, Theodoret, and Euthymius (and according to Calmet also of Heraclitus, S. Chrysostom, Genebrardus, Tirinus, and of others, *passim*). Bellarmine sustains his view by intrinsic reasons : he says that the words both in Greek and Hebrew here for *distinguere in labiis* do not signify in other places of Scripture : *to doubt* or *hesitate*, but to pronounce plainly and absolutely ; thus *v.g.* in *Ps.* lxv. 14, *Lev.* v. 4, and *Numb.* xxx. 4, where it is used in connection with promises, vows, and oaths. He adds that the Latin : *distinguere labiis* or *distincte loqui*, rather implies perspicuity than ambiguity. He concludes thus : "I am therefore of opinion, with all deference to better judgment, that in this verse begins the history, as given in *Judges*, and that by : *Distinxit* ... is meant : God pronounced openly, and rebuked the Hebrews for not having exterminated the Gentiles.——Menochius gives the same interpretation as Bellarmine.—*Tr.*

"*Opera eorum.*" All their abominations.——"*Servierunt.*" Adored.——"*Factum . . .*" Served for their great ruin.

35. Et immolaverunt filios suos : et filias suas dæmoniis.	And they sacrificed their sons : and their daughters to devils.

And they went so far as even to sacrifice, &c.

36. Et effuderunt sanguinem innocentem : sanguinem filiorum suorum et filiarum suarum, quas sacrificaverunt sculptilibus Chanaan.	And they shed innocent blood, even the blood of their sons and of their daughters : which they sacrificed unto the idols of Chanaan.

37. Et infecta est terra in sanguinibus, et contaminata est in operibus eorum : et fornicati sunt in adinventionibus suis.	And the land was polluted with blood, and was defiled with their works : and they went aside after their own inventions.

"*In sanguinibus et . . . in operibus eorum.*" With these detestable sacrifices of blood, and with their abominable works.——"*Fornicati sunt . . .*" They fornicated by their superstitions, that is, they fell away from their faith to God.—— In the Bible apostasy from the faith is called Fornication, or treason like to that of unfaithful spouses, who are false to their plighted troth.

38. Et iratus est furore Dominus in populum suum : et abominatus est hereditatem suam.	And the Lord was angered exceedingly against His people : and He abhorred His own inheritance.

"*Hereditatem suam.*" Those who were formerly His inheritance.

39. Et tradidit eos in manus Gentium : et dominati sunt eorum qui oderunt eos.	And He gave them over into the hands of the nations : and they that hated them had dominion over them.

40. Et tribulaverunt eos inimici eorum, et humiliati sunt sub manibus eorum : sæpe liberavit eos.	And their enemies afflicted them, and they were humbled under their hands : many times did He deliver them.

And these enemies so persecuted them, that they were humbled very lowly under their hands.——"*Sæpe . . .*" And yet, notwithstanding all, the Lord oftentimes delivered them.

41. Ipsi autem exacerbaverunt eum in consilio suo : et humiliati sunt in iniquitatibus suis.	But they provoked Him with their counsel : and were brought low for their iniquities.

"*Ipsi autem.*" But they, in spite of all that He did for them.——"*In consilio suo.*" According to the Hebrew : *In consilio ipsorum.* By the purpose, as Menochius explains, which they formed of serving idols.——"*Humiliati sunt in iniquitatibus suis.*" According to Mattei, we are by this not to understand that they were humbled in their wickedness, but that they grew more wicked in their humiliations.

42. Et vidit cum tribularentur : et audivit orationem eorum.

And He saw when they were afflicted : and He heard their prayer.

Nevertheless the Lord, seeing them thus afflicted, was moved to have pity on them and lent His ear to their prayers.

43. Et memor fuit testamenti sui : et pœnituit eum secundum multitudinem misericordiæ suæ.

He was mindful also of His covenant : and repented according to the multitude of His mercies.

" *Testamenti sui.*" That is, of the promises made to their fathers.——" *Pœnituit eum.*" According to the Chaldee : *Conversus est ab ira sua.* He turned aside from His anger, as though He felt sorrow for having punished them.

44. Et dedit eos in misericordias : in conspectu omnium qui ceperant eos.

And He moved to pity : all those that had made them captives.

That is, according to Maldonatus, Mariana, Tirinus, and Mattei : He caused them to meet with compassion from their enemies, who held them captives.[1]

45. Salvos nos fac, Domine Deus noster : et congrega nos de nationibus :

Save us, O Lord our God : and gather us from among the nations :

" *Congrega . . .* " Gather us together by delivering us from the midst of the Gentiles, where we are scattered.

46. Ut confiteamur nomini sancto tuo : et gloriemur in laude tua.

That we may give thanks unto Thy holy name : and may glory in Thy praise.

In order that we may come to return Thee thanks, and to bless Thy holy name ; and that our glory may be to praise Thee.

47. Benedictus Dominus Deus Israel a sæculo et usque in sæculum : et dicet omnis populus : Fiat, fiat.

Blessed be the Lord the God of Israel from everlasting to everlasting: and let all the people say : So be it, so be it.

Then shall we sing : Blessed be, &c.

PSALM CVI.

In the literal sense this Psalm sets forth the tribulations that the Israelites had to suffer during their captivity and in the desert ; and they are exhorted to return thanks to God for

[1] Others translate thus : He showed His mercy towards them in the sight of all those, &c. Such is the meaning which S. Augustine and Bellarmine consider the most probable.

having delivered them therefrom. In the figurative sense it represents the miseries from which Jesus Christ has delivered Christians. In it, moreover, the Psalmist announces the ruin of the Synagogue, the vocation of the Gentiles, and the establishment of the Church.[1]

Alleluia.

1. Confitemini Domino quoniam bonus: quoniam in sæculum misericordia ejus.

Give glory to the Lord, for He is good: for His mercy endureth for ever.

Praise the Lord, for He is truly good and merciful; and His mercy shall never fail.

2. Dicant qui redempti sunt a Domino, quos redemit de manu inimici: et de regionibus congregavit eos.

Let them that have been redeemed by the Lord say so, whom He hath redeemed from the hand of the enemy: and gathered out of the lands.

3. A solis ortu, et occasu: ab Aquilone, et mari.

From the rising and from the setting of the sun: from the north and from the sea.

Let those declare it whom the Lord has released from the hands of their enemies; whom He has reunited from the several countries where they were scattered, that is, from the East and from the West, from the North and from the South. ——"Mari." That is: From the South, for the ocean, or great sea, is in the South.

4. Erraverunt in solitudine in inaquoso: viam civitatis habitaculi non invenerunt.[2]

They wandered in a wilderness, in a place without water: they found not on the way a city to dwell in.

5. Esurientes, et sitientes: anima eorum in ipsis defecit.

Hungry and thirsty: their soul fainted in them.

4, 5. These Hebrews wandered in the desert, a barren land and without water, and were unable to discover the way that led to the city of their own habitation. They suffered hunger and thirst, so that their life came to fail them.

6. Et clamaverunt ad Dominum cum tribularentur: et de necessitatibus eorum eripuit eos.

And they cried unto the Lord in their trouble: and He delivered them out of their distresses.

1 The Psalmist begins by an invitation to praise the goodness and mercy of God. He then describes four examples of recourse to the Lord in affliction, and at the end of each repeats his invitation; see verses 6-8, 13-15, 19-21, 28-31. He concludes by an eulogium and a prophecy of the all-powerful and ever-merciful Providence of the Most High towards His servants or His Church.

2 Ps. lxxxviii. 12.

Finding themselves in such distress, they cried to the Lord for succour : and the Lord delivered them from the pains which they suffered in their necessity.

7. Et deduxit eos in viam rectam : And He led them into the right way : **ut irent in civitatem habitationis.** that they might go to a city to dwell in.

And God put them in the right way, that they might reach the city where they were to dwell.

8. Confiteantur Domino miseri- Let the mercies of the Lord give **cordiæ ejus : et mirabilia ejus filiis** glory unto Him : and His wonderful **hominum.** works unto the children of men.

"*Confiteantur . . . ejus.*" That is : Let them, then, in honour of the Lord, gratefully acknowledge and praise His mercies which He has shown to them.

9. Quia satiavit animam inanem : For He hath satisfied the empty **et animam esurientem satiavit bonis.** soul : and hath filled the hungry soul with good things.

For in a marvellous manner He provided food in the desert, and with it satisfied those who were famishing.

10. Sedentes in tenebris, et umbra Such as sat in darkness and in **mortis : vinctos in mendicitate, et** the shadow of death : bound in want **ferro.** and in iron.

He succoured them when they were in dark prisons, which were as the shadow of death,[1] and seemed to them the image of death ; miserable, in want of everything, and bound with iron chains.

11. Quia exacerbaverunt eloquia Because they had resisted the **Dei : et consilium Altissimi irritave-** words of God : and made void the **runt.** counsel of the Most High.

"*Eloquia.*" The commands.——"*Consilium.*" That is, the will.

12. Et humiliatum est in laboribus And their heart was humbled with **cor eorum : infirmati sunt, nec fuit** labours : they were weakened, and **qui adjuvaret.** there was none to help them.

Then was their heart humbled by labours, that is, the pride of their heart was brought low by the hardships which they suffered in the midst of all their afflictions ; they grew too weak to resist their enemies, and there was no one to help them to deliver themselves from their hands.

---

[1] " *Umbra mortis.*" See *Ps.* xliii. 21.

13. Et clamaverunt ad Dominum cum tribularentur: et de necessitatibus eorum liberavit eos.

Then they cried unto the Lord in their affliction : and He delivered them out of their distresses.

Repetition of verse 6.

14. Et eduxit eos de tenebris, et umbra mortis : et vincula eorum disrupit.

And He brought them out of darkness, and the shadow of death : and brake their bones in sunder.

"*De tenebris et umbra mortis.*" See verse 10.

15. Confiteantur Domino misericordiæ ejus: et mirabilia ejus filiis hominum.

Let the mercies of the Lord give glory unto Him : and His wonderful works unto the children of men.

Repetition of verse 8.

16. Quia contrivit portas æreas: et vectes ferreos confregit.

For He hath broken the gates of brass : and burst the bars of iron in sunder.

For He has shattered to pieces the gates of brass which shut them in, and He has riven asunder the chains, iron bars, and bolts of their prisons.

17. Suscepit eos de via iniquitatis eorum : propter injustitias enim suas humiliati sunt.

He took them out of the way of their iniquity : for they were brought low for their transgressions.

He rescued them from the midst of their iniquity, which had brought on them such severe chastisements ; since it was for their sins they had been thus humbled.

18. Omnem escam abominata est anima eorum : et appropinquaverunt usque ad portas mortis.

Their soul abhorred all manner of meat : and they drew nigh even unto the gates of death.

By reason of their infirmity, or sickness, they had a loathing and disgust of, &c.

19. Et clamaverunt ad Dominum cum tribularentur : et de necessitatibus eorum liberavit eos.

And they cried unto the Lord in their affliction : and He delivered them out of their distresses.

Repetition of verses 6 and 13. We should here remark that the Psalmist does not repeat this verse so often without design ; he would thereby make us well understand the compassion which God has for our miseries, and, at the same time, the efficacy of prayer, which makes the Lord not know how to refuse help to him who asks it of Him.

20. Misit verbum suum, et sanavit eos: et eripuit eos de interitionibus eorum.

He sent His word, and healed them : and delivered them from destruction.

"*Misit . . . suum.*" He gave forth His word.——"*De interi-tionibus eorum.*" That is, from death.

21. Confiteantur Domino miseri-cordiæ ejus : et mirabilia ejus filiis hominum.

Let the mercies of the Lord give glory unto Him : and His wonderful works unto the children of men.

Repetition of verses 8 and 15.

22. Et sacrificent sacrificium laudis : et annuntient opera ejus in exultatione.

And let them offer the sacrifice of praise : and declare His works with joy.

"*Opera ejus.*" His great and mighty works.

23. Qui descendunt mare in navi-bus : facientes operationem in aquis multis.

They that go down to the sea in ships : that do business in the great waters.

24. Ipsi viderunt opera Domini : et mirabilia ejus in profundo.

These men have seen the works of the Lord : and His wonders in the deep.

23, 24. "*Descendunt.*" Since the surface of the sea is lower than that of the earth.——"*Facientes . . .*" Carrying on their business of merchandise by the highway of these vast waters.——"*Ipsi . . .*" These men have seen by their own experience the admirable works which the Lord does in that deep, that is, in the sea.

25. Dixit, et stetit spiritus pro-cellæ : et exaltati sunt fluctus ejus.

He spoke the word, and a storm of wind arose : and the waves thereof were lifted up.

26. Ascendunt usque ad cœlos, et descendunt usque ad abyssos : anima eorum in malis tabescebat.

They mount up to the heavens, and they go down to the depths : their soul melted away with evils.

25, 26. The Lord commands the wind that makes the storm, to go forth : straightway the wind goes forth : thereupon the waves of the sea mount to the heavens, and then sink again into the deep.[1]   The spirit of those on board fails them through fear.

27. Turbati sunt, et moti sunt sicut ebrius : et omnis sapientia eorum devorata est.

They were troubled, and reeled like a drunken man : and all their wisdom was swallowed up.

"*Sicut ebrius.*" As a drunken man, who knows not what he does.——"*Omnis sapientia . . .*" In the midst of their confusion they have lost all their wisdom, that is, all their seaman's craft.

---

[1] Others take the seamen to be the subject of these verbs, but the sense is the same.

28. Et clamaverunt ad Dominum cum tribularentur : et de necessitatibus eorum eduxit eos.

And they cried unto the Lord in their affliction : and He brought them out of their distresses.

Repetition of verses 6, 13, 19.

29. Et statuit procellam ejus in auram : et siluerunt fluctus ejus.

And He turned the storm into a gentle breeze : and its waves were still.

" *Procellam ejus.*" The wind of the storm.——" *Siluerunt.*" Were silent, *i.e.,* calm and still.

30. Et lætati sunt quia siluerunt : et deduxit eos in portum voluntatis eorum.

And they rejoiced that they were stilled : and He brought them unto the haven where they would be.

" *Voluntatis suæ.*" In which they wished to take refuge.

31. Confiteantur Domino misericordiæ ejus : et mirabilia ejus filiis hominum.

Let the mercies of the Lord give glory unto Him : and His wonderful works unto the children of men.

Thus the Jews, freed from the storm of slavery and brought into the port of their own country, should confess the mercies of the Lord towards them, and the wonders which He works in behalf of the children of men.

32. Et exaltent eum in ecclesia plebis : et in cathedra seniorum laudent eum.

And let them exalt Him in the church of the people : and praise Him in the seat of the elders.

" *Exaltent.*" Let them praise Him greatly.——" *In ecclesia plebis.*" That is, in the congregation of the people met together to praise God.——" *In cathedra seniorum.*" In the assembly of the ancients, that is, of the chiefs of the people.

33. Posuit flumina in desertum : et exitus aquarum in sitim :

He hath turned rivers into a wilderness : and the sources of water into dry ground :

Rivers, moreover, and places abounding with water, He has caused to dry up and to become as an arid desert.

34. Terram fructiferam in salsuginem : a malitia inhabitantium in ea.

A fruitful land into barrenness : for the wickedness of them that dwell within.

And land formerly productive of much fruit, He has rendered sterile, as if it had been strewn with salt, in punishment of the sins of the inhabitants.

35. Posuit desertum in stagna aquarum : et terram sine aqua in exitus aquarum.

He hath turned a wilderness into pools of waters : and a dry land into water springs.

On the other hand He has turned, &c.[1]

36. Et collocavit illic esurientes : et constituerunt civitatem habita- tionis.

And He placed there the hungry: and they made a city to dwell in.

And He has placed there those who were languishing with misery ; so that they have established there in course of time a city for them to dwell in.

37. Et seminaverunt agros, et plantaverunt vineas ; et fecerunt fructum nativitatis.

And they sowed fields and planted vineyards : and they yielded fruit of birth.

And they sowed the fields and planted vineyards, and saw the fruit born of their labours.

38. Et benedixit eis, et multi- plicati sunt nimis : et jumenta eorum non minoravit.

And He blessed them, and they were multiplied exceedingly : and their cattle He suffered not to decrease.

The Lord gave them His blessing, and they multiplied exceedingly, the men and their beasts, causing them to thrive in great numbers.

39. Et pauci facti sunt : et vexati sunt a tribulatione malorum, et dolore.

Then they became few, and they were afflicted through the trouble of evils and sorrow.

But afterwards, in punishment for their sins, they were reduced to few in number, and were afflicted with great tribulations and sorrows.

40. Effusa est contemptio super principes : et errare fecit eos in invio, et non in via.

Contempt was poured forth upon their princes : and He caused them to wander in the waste, where there was no path.

Contempt was cast also upon their princes, that is, the Lord made the chiefs who ruled them to be despised, by allow- ing them to fall into many mistakes, when they strayed from the path of justice and prudence.

41. Et adjuvit pauperem de inopia : et posuit sicut oves familias.

And He helped the poor out of poverty ; and made him families like a flock of sheep.

[1] Bellarmine, with S. Augustine, applies this last part, even in its literal sense, or at least in its allegorical and prophetic sense, to the Synagogue and the Church ; and this is mentioned by S. Alphonsus in the heading of the Psalm. Indeed, it is easy to recognise, in these striking figures, the fields of the Synagogue, once so favoured, now sterile and abandoned, whilst the deserts and uncultivated lands of the Gentile world, receiving the seed of the Gospel with the waters of grace, are peopled with saints, and produce in abundance fruits of salvation.

Nevertheless, moved with pity for the poor, He helped them in their misery, and multiplied their families anew, like flocks of sheep.

42. Videbunt recti, et lætabuntur: et omnis iniquitas oppilabit os suum.

The just shall see, and shall rejoice: and all iniquity shall stop her mouth.

The just shall see these mercies and rejoice thereat; whilst the wicked for shame of their iniquity shall not dare to open their mouth.

43. Quis sapiens, et custodiet hæc: et intelliget misericordias Domini?

Who is wise, and will keep these things: and will understand the mercies of the Lord?

He that is wise will keep good memory of these things; and will understand how far reach the mercies of the Lord.

PSALM CVII.

DAVID thanks God for the benefits he has received and prays for victory over the Edomites. This Psalm has already been explained—viz., the first five verses in Psalm lvi. 10-14 (p. 216), and the verses 6-14 in Psalm lix. 5-13 (pp. 222-3). However, for the convenience of the reader, we shall reproduce the explanation of it here, but more succinctly.

A Canticle of a Psalm for David himself.

1. Paratum cor meum, Deus, paratum cor meum : cantabo, et psallam in gloria mea.

My heart is ready, O God, my heart is ready : I will sing, and will give praise, with my glory.

My God, my heart is disposed to will whatever Thou ordainest; in all I will bless Thee and sing Thy praises.

2. Exurge, gloria mea, exurge, psalterium, et cithara : exurgam diluculo.

Arise, my glory; arise, psaltery and harp : I will arise in the morning early.

Arise, my glory, that is, my soul, which loves to praise God; awake, my harp and my lyre, to praise Him at early morn.[1]

3. Confitebor tibi in populis, Domine : et psallam tibi in nationibus.

I will praise Thee, O Lord, among the people : and I will sing unto Thee among the nations.

"*Psallam...*" I will sing Thy glories among the nations.

1 "*Gloria mea.*" Bellarmine says with Theodoret, that David calls his glory the spirit or the gift of prophecy.

4. Quia magna est super cœlos misericordia tua : et usque ad nubes veritas tua.

For Thy mercy is great above the heavens : and Thy truth even unto the clouds.

For all, from earth even to the heavens, is full of Thy mercy and faithfulness.

5. Exaltare super cœlos, Deus, et super omnem terram gloria tua : ut liberentur dilecti tui.[1]

Be Thou exalted, O God, above the heavens, and Thy glory over all the earth : that Thy beloved may be delivered.

6. Salvum fac dextera tua, et exaudi me : Deus locutus est in sancto suo.

Save with Thy right hand and hear me : God hath spoken in His holiness.

7. Exultabo, et dividam Sichimam : et convallem tabernaculorum dimetiar.

I will rejoice, and I will divide Sichem : and I will mete out the Vale of Tabernacles.

6, 7. Hear me, O Lord, and let Thy right hand save me. God hath declared from His sanctuary that I shall one day have the joy of dividing the country of Sichem, or Samaria, at my pleasure, and of measuring the lands of the valley of Tents, beyond the Jordan, to distribute them at my will.

8. Meus est Galaad, et meus est Manasses : et Ephraim susceptio capitis mei.

Galaad is mine, and Manasses is mine : and Ephraim the protection of my head.

Behold, Galaad is already mine, &c.——"*Susceptio*..." The strength of my head. Under these names are designated the provinces of the several tribes.

9. Juda rex meus : Moab lebes spei meæ.

Juda is my king : Moab the pot of my hope.

In the tribe of Juda is my kingdom [or throne].—— "*Moab*..." That is to say, Moab is a province so abundant as to make me hope fully to satisfy my people.

10. In Idumæam extendam calceamentum meum : mihi alienigenæ amici facti sunt.

Over Edom will I stretch out my shoe : those of another race are become my friends.

I shall stretch my foot into Edom, and I shall see the people that are strangers[2] (that is, the Philistines) become my subjects.

11. Quis deducet me in civitatem munitam ? quis deducet me usque in Idumæam ?

Who will bring me into the strong city : who will lead me into Edom ?

Who will lead me to take possession of the strong city which is the centre of Edom ?

[1] "*Ut liberentur* . . ." See *Ps.* lix. 5.   [2] *Ps.* lxxxvi. 4.

12. Nonne tu, Deus, qui repulisti nos : et non exibis, Deus, in virtutibus nostris ?

Wilt not Thou, O God, Who hast cast us off? and wilt not Thou, O God, go forth with our armies ?

Shall it not be Thou, my God, Who at first didst repel us ? Wilt not Thou Thyself go forth with our troops to give us victory ?

13. Da nobis auxilium de tribulatione : quia vana salus hominis.

O grant us help in trouble: for vain is the help of man.

" *Quia vana salus hominis.*" For in vain can we hope for help from others.

14. In Deo faciemus virtutem : et ipse ad nihilum deducet inimicos nostros.

Through God we shall do mightily: and He will bring our enemies to nought.

Placing our hopes in God, we shall obtain the victory ; for He will exterminate those who afflict us.

PSALM CVIII.

This Psalm is variously applied by various interpreters. Some apply it to Saul speaking against Doeg and such like evil-minded men. Others to David, predicting, in form of imprecation, the chastisements reserved for Doeg and Achitophel, his enemies. Others, as Mattei, with Marino and Mingarella, suppose that the imprecations are uttered against David and Jesus Christ by their enemies. But commonly the Fathers and the other interpreters consider these imprecations as pronounced against Judas and the other enemies of our Saviour ; this is the interpretation which we follow, especially with S. Augustine.

Unto the end. A Psalm for David.

1. Deus, laudem meam ne tacueris: quia os peccatoris, et os dolosi super me apertum est.

O God, be not Thou silent in my praise : for the mouth of the wicked and the mouth of the deceitful man is opened against me.

My God, hide not My praise, that is, make known My innocence, for the mouth of an impious man and traitor is opened against Me.[1]——" *Super me.*" S. Jerome translates :

---

[1] It is Jesus Christ Who speaks. He said : "Glorify Thou Me, O Father" (*John* xvii. 5). Amongst the Jews some attacked Him openly, as when they called Him Beelzebub (*Matt.* x. 25) ; others sought to surprise Him, as when they said : " Master, we know that Thou art a true speaker " (*Matt.* xxii. 16). Judas was to betray Him with a kiss, and all were about to overwhelm Him with outrages, whilst declaring Him worthy of death.

Contra me. S. Augustine thus explains: *Odium, quod dolo tegebatur, erupit in vocem:* The hatred, treacherously concealed, broke forth in words.

2. Locuti sunt adversum me lingua dolosa, et sermonibus odii circumdederent me: et expugnaverunt me gratis.	They have spoken against me with deceitful tongues: they have compassed me about with words of hatred, and have fought against me without a cause.

" *Lingua dolosa.*" This, remarks S. Augustine, happened when a certain Jew addressed Jesus Christ as Good Master, saying, " Good Master, what shall I do," &c. (*Mark* x. 19.)

3. Pro eo ut me deligerent, detrahebant mihi: ego autem orabam.	In place of loving me, they oppose me: but I gave myself unto prayer.

" *Detrahebant.*" They defamed Me. S. Jerome translates: *Adversabantur;* They opposed, contradicted Me.——" *Orabam.*" S. Augustine adds: *Pro eis ipsis.* At the same time, I prayed for these very men.

4. Et posuerunt adversum me mala pro bonis: et odium pro dilectione mea.	And they repaid me evil for good: and hatred for my love.

5. Constitue super eum peccatorem; et diabolus stet a dextris ejus.	Set Thou the sinner over him:[1] and may the devil stand at his right hand.

" *Peccatorem.*" That is, according to Emmanuel Sa and Mariana, a wicked judge.——S. Augustine applies this verse to Judas, and by the sinner he understands Satan himself; which he thus explains: *Diabolo subditus sit, qui Christo subditus esse noluit.* Let him be subject to the devil, who refused to be subject to Christ. And in fact we know from S. John that Judas was possessed by Satan. " After the morsel," that is to say, after Holy Communion, " Satan entered into him." (*John* xiii. 27.)

6. Cum judicatur, exeat condemnatus: et oratio ejus fiat in peccatum.	When he is judged, let him go out condemned: and may his prayer be turned to sin.

When he shall be judged at the divine tribunal, may he thence go forth condemned; and may his prayer be imputed to him as sin, that is, as Lallemant wisely explains, if he ventures to speak in self-defence, may it be ascribed to him as a fresh crime, on account of his temerity.

---

[1] *Set Thou the sinner over him,* &c. Give the devil power over him. The imprecations contained in this Psalm are to be taken as prophetic denunciations, and not properly as curses.

7. Fiant dies ejus pauci : et episco-   Let his days be few : and his
patum ejus accipiat alter.   bishopric let another take.

Let the days of his life be shortened.——"*Et episcopatum.*"
Some understand by this, his place of honour or administration ; but Bossuet justly remarks, hereby must be understood
the Apostolate : and in this sense the passage was interpreted
by S. Peter, *Acts* i. 20. Whence the Apostles, then assembled
in council, prayed thus to the Lord : "Show which of these
two Thou hast chosen, to take the place of this ministry and
apostleship, from which Judas hath by transgression fallen "
(vv. 20-25). And then the lot fell upon S. Matthias.

8. Fiant filii ejus orphani : et uxor   Let his children be fatherless ; and
ejus vidua.   his wife a widow.

Here we must remark that S. Chrysostom, Theodoret, and
Euthymius are of opinion that Judas was never married.
Moreover, Genebrardus and Tirinus think that these imprecations against Judas did not all have their effect in his person,
but those only which could reach him. On the other hand,
Menochius, following S. Augustine, says that they were verified
with regard to the Jewish people, of whom Judas is here the
figure : for by the destruction of Jerusalem the Synagogue
became a widow, and the Jews, her children, were made
orphans.[1]

9. Nutantes transferantur filii ejus,   Let his children be carried about
et mendicent : et ejiciantur de habi-   vagabonds, and beg : and let them be
tationibus suis.   cast out of their dwellings.

These further imprecations have had their accomplishment
since the destruction of Jerusalem.——"*Nutantes transferantur*
(S. Jerome translates : *Instabiles vagentur*) ... *mendicent.*" Let
his children be rovers and vagabonds, and go about begging.

10. Scrutetur fœnerator omnem   Let the usurer search all his sub-
substantiam ejus : et diripiant alieni   stance : and let strangers plunder his
labores ejus.   labours.

"*Scrutetur.*" According to the Chaldee : *Colliget.*——Let
the usurer distrain all his goods, and strangers plunder all the
fruits of his labours.——Here Menochius remarks, that " In
the destruction of Jerusalem the Roman soldiers made such a
close search after the riches and property of the Jews, that
they even ripped up the bodies of some and searched their
bowels, hoping to find gold which they might have swallowed,
as Josephus testifies." (*De Bello Judaico,* l. 6, c. 15.)

[1] We may add that since that time the Jews have had no High Priest.

11. Non sit illi adjutor : nec sit qui misereatur pupillis ejus.

Let there be none to help him : nor to have compassion on his fatherless children.

12. Fiant nati ejus in interitum : in generatione una deleatur nomen ejus.

Let his posterity be cut off : in one generation may his name be blotted out.

May death carry off his children : and his name be blotted out, that is, the name of the father, in one generation : meaning to say, May the father's name not pass to a second generation, as Lallemant well explains.[1]

13. In memoriam redeat iniquitas patrum ejus in conspectu Domini : et peccatum matris ejus non deleatur.

May the iniquity of his fathers be remembered in the sight of the Lord : and let not the sin of his mother be blotted out.

"*Iniquitas patrum ejus.*" May the iniquity of their fathers come back to remembrance in the sight of the Lord, to be punished in him or in his people ; as S. Augustine explains, applying here the words of the Gospel : " That upon you may come all the just blood that hath been shed upon the earth from the blood of Abel…" (*Matt.* xxiii. 35.)——"*Matris ejus,*" *i.e.*, says S. Augustine, Jerusalem.

14. Fiant contra Dominum semper, et dispereat de terra memoria eorum : pro eo quod non est recordatus facere misericordiam.

May they be before the Lord continually, and let the memory of them perish from the earth : because he remembered not to show mercy.

15. Et persecutus est hominem inopem, et mendicum : et compunctum corde mortificare.

But persecuted the poor man and the beggar : and the broken-hearted to put him to death.

14, 15. May their iniquity be always before the Lord, that is, in His sight, and may their memory perish upon earth, in punishment for their having had no thought to show pity to Me, that is, Jesus Christ. (On the contrary) this people has persecuted a needy and poor man, and has sought to put to death one that was afflicted in soul and oppressed with grief.

16. Et dilexit maledictionem, et veniet ei : et noluit benedictionem, et elongabitur ab eo.

And he loved cursing, and it shall come unto him : and he would not have blessing, and it shall be far from him.

[1] Bellarmine applies this and the preceding verses to the Jewish nation after the ruin of Jerusalem, and he shows in this the fulfilment of the prophecy of Osee : "The children of Israel shall sit many days, without king, and without prince, and without sacrifice, and without altar, and without ephod" (*Osee* iii. 4). Thenceforward the Jews no longer formed one family, one people, or one kingdom ; they were so many separate units scattered amongst foreign nations, without king, without leader, without altar, and without High Priest.

"*Dilexit maledictionem.*" S. Augustine applies this to the time when the Jewish people cried out : "His blood be upon us and upon our children" (*Matt.* xxvii. 25).

17. Et induit maledictionem sicut vestimentum : et intravit sicut aqua in interiora ejus, et sicut oleum in ossibus ejus.	And he put on cursing like a garment : and it went like water into his entrails, and like oil into his bones.

18. Fiat ei sicut vestimentum, quo operitur : et sicut zona, qua semper præcingitur.	May it be unto him like the garment which covereth him : and like a girdle wherewith he is girded continually.

17, 18. That is, as S. Augustine explains : May cursing wrap round his body like a garment, and penetrate within his soul as water ; and like oil insinuate itself also in his bones. So may cursing cover him always as a mantle, and always bind about him as a girdle.

19. Hoc opus eorum, qui detrahunt mihi apud Dominum : et qui loquuntur mala adversus animam meam.	This is the work of them who oppose me before the Lord : and who speak evils against my soul.

"*Hoc opus.*" S. Jerome translates: *Hæc est retributio.*[1] That is, this is the punishment which God inflicts in retribution on those who malign Me and who invent calumnies against Me to take away My life.

20. Et tu, Domine, Domine, fac mecum propter nomen tuum : quia suavis est misericordia tua.	But Thou, O Lord, do with me for Thy name's sake : for Thy mercy is sweet.

And do Thou, I say, My Lord, deal with Me, that is, succour Me, for the glory of Thy name : for Thy mercy is sweet,[2] bent on helping the afflicted.

21. Libera me, quia egenus et pauper ego sum : et cor meum conturbatum est intra me.	Do Thou deliver me, for I am poor and needy : and my heart is troubled within me.

And since Thou art so merciful, deliver Me, for I am poor and forsaken, and My heart is all afflicted and sorrowful within Me. S. Augustine refers this passage to what Jesus Christ said in the garden : "My soul is sorrowful even unto death" (*Matt.* xxvi. 38).

22. Sicut umbra cum declinat, ablatus sum : et excussus sum sicut locustæ.	I am taken away like the shadow when it declineth : and I am shaken off as locusts.

---

[1] The word *opus* is used elsewhere in the sense of wages. See *Lev.* xix. 13.

[2] S. Jerome : *Bona.*

"*Ablatus.*" According to the Chaldee: *Consumptus.* As the shadow fades away towards evening, soon to vanish altogether, so do I see Myself worn away, flitting and tossed about as the locust. S. Augustine, Theodoret, Tirinus, &c., speak of the locust as hopping from place to place ; and thus, says Du Hamel, did it happen to Jesus Christ, "Who was cast about from one tribunal to another."

23. Genua mea infirmata sunt a jejunio: et caro mea immutata est propter oleum.

My knees are weakened through fasting: and my flesh is changed for want of oil.

"*Propter oleum.*" S. Jerome translates : *Absque oleo.* Without oil. We should then understand that ill and infirm condition of body was brought on not by the use of oil, but through being debarred from this use ; for Estius, Sa, Mariana, Malvenda, Tirinus, and Mattei say that unctions with the use of oil were customary among the Hebrews, and that their health suffered if they failed to use them. Hence, Mattei asserts that to understand here that flesh was lost by the use of oil is a most evident error. Besides, in the Chaldee : "*Et caro mea immutata est propter oleum*" would read : "*Et caro mea macilenta est absque pinguedine*" : My flesh is lean without fat ; meaning My flesh is become lean for want of food that produces fatness. And with still more point may the words be explained by the Hebrew text which is thus rendered : *Caro mea immutata est a pinguedine,* that is, My flesh has been changed from being fat, and is become lean, according to the explanation of Bellarmine and Menochius. I fail to see how in any other sense this verse can be, with propriety, applied to Jesus Christ.

24. Et ego factus sum opprobrium illis : viderunt me, et moverunt capita sua.

I became also a reproach unto them : they saw me, and shook their heads.

"*Et . . . illis.*" And I became with them an object of mockery.——"*Moverunt capita sua.*" They shook their heads to insult Me. This was verified, as Bellarmine remarks, when the enemies of Jesus Christ blasphemed Him as He was on the cross : "And they that passed by, blasphemed Him, wagging their heads" (*Matt.* xxvii. 39).

25. Adjuva me, Domine Deus meus : salvum me fac secundum misericordiam tuam.

Help me, O Lord my God : save me according unto Thy mercy.

26. Et sciant quia manus tua hæc : et tu, Domine, fecisti eam.	And let them know that this is Thy hand : and that Thou, O Lord, hast done it.

That is, as Menochius explains it : Let them know that all that I have suffered, I have suffered by Thy will, according to the words of Isaias : " For the wickedness of My people have I struck Him " (*Is.* liii. 8).

27. Maledicent illi, et tu bene-dices : qui insurgunt in me, confun-dantur : servus autem tuus lætabitur.	They will curse, and Thou wilt bless : let them that rise up against me be confounded : but Thy servant shall rejoice.

" *Maledicent illi.*" They will curse Me. And thus S. Paul wrote : " Christ hath redeemed us from the curse of the law, being made a curse for us " (*Gal.* iii. 13). Du Hamel comments on the last words thus: *Nostram in Se suscipiens maledic-tionem.* Taking on Himself our curse.——" *Tu benedices.*" Thou wilt bless Me.——" *Confundantur . . .* " May they remain confounded, and be converted, as S. Augustine understands it, and Thy servant will be consoled.

28. Induantur, qui detrahunt mihi, pudore : et operiantur sicut diploide confusione sua.	Let them that oppose me be clothed with shame : and let them be covered with their confusion as with a double cloak.

" *Qui detrahunt mihi.*" Those who malign Me.——" *Dip-loide.*" With a double cloak, that is, according to S. Augustine, both within and without, internally and externally.

29. Confitebor Domino nimis in ore meo : et in medio multorum laudabo eum.	I will give great thanks unto the Lord with my mouth : and in the midst of many will I praise Him.

" *Nimis . . . In medio multorum.*" S. Jerome translates : *Vehementer.*——*In medio populorum . . .* I will praise the Lord as much as I possibly can, with My mouth ; and I will sing His praises in the midst of the people.

30. Quia astitit a dextris pauperis : ut salvam faceret a persequentibus animam meam.	For He hath stood at the right hand of the poor : to save my soul from them that persecute me.

For He hath stood at My side, Who am poor, to defend Me and to save My life from the hands of My persecutors. Bellar-mine understands this of the resurrection of Jesus Christ, whereby He resumed the life which the Jews had taken from Him.

LAUDS FOR SATURDAY.

PSALM L.

PSALM XCI.

DAVID exhorts the people to praise God for the protection which He gives to the just, and for the chastisements which He inflicts on sinners in order to correct them. David is thought to have composed this Psalm after his victory over Absalom.[1]

A Psalm of a Canticle on the Sabbath day.[2]

1. Bonum est,[3] confiteri Domino : et psallere nomini tuo, Altissime.

It is good to give praise unto the Lord : and to sing to Thy name, O Thou Most High.

It is just, Lord, to give glory to Thee, O God Most High, to sing the glories of Thy name, to render thanks, and to praise Thee for Thy benefits.

2. Ad annuntiandum mane misericordiam tuam : et veritatem tuam per noctem.

To show forth Thy mercy in the morning : and Thy truth in the night.

It is good and fitting that, after having celebrated Thy mercy

---

[1] St. Alphonsus gives almost the same explanation of this Psalm also at Matins for Saturday (p. 366), when it is sometimes recited. This we then omitted. We now add all that the holy Doctor there says, which is not found here in the original text.

[2] According to Bellarmine, to be sung on the Sabbath, in order to teach the people that they should praise God on that day, and especially for His creating and governing the world.

[3] "*Bonum est.*" It is good, *i.e.*, it is just, profitable, pleasant, and honourable to give praise to the Lord, not only with heart and tongue, but also with musical instruments. It is just, because due ; profitable, because meritorious ; pleasant, because sweet to one who loves to praise the Beloved ; honourable, since we may say it is, properly speaking, the occupation of the celestial spirits.—*Bellarmine.*

in the morning, we should praise at night Thy faithfulness to Thy promises.

3. In decachordo psalterio: cum cantico, in cithara.
Upon an instrument of ten strings, upon the psaltery: with a song upon the harp.

Praise Him, singing a Canticle with sound of the ten-stringed psaltery and of the harp: thus Bellarmine and others. But Menochius, Mariana, and Sa will have "the ten-stringed psaltery" to be two different musical instruments, in this following S. Jerome, who translates: *In decachordo et in psalterio,* thus making them two. This, moreover, is closer to the Hebrew text, the sense of which is : *In decachordo et nablo* ; hence, according to this second explanation, the rendering will be : Praise Him, singing hymns to the sound of the decachordon, the psaltery, and the harp.

4. Quia delectasti me, Domine, in factura tua : et in operibus manuum tuarum exultabo.
For Thou hast given me, O Lord, delight in Thy doings : and in the works of Thy hands shall I rejoice.

For Thou, O Lord, hast made me feel a great joy at the sight of Thy creation, so that I ever exult with delight when I consider the works of Thy hands. Mattei says, with reason, that : *" In factura tua "* is synonymous with : *" In operibus manuum tuarum."*

5. Quam magnificata sunt opera tua ! nimis profundæ factæ sunt cogitationes tuæ.
O Lord, how great are Thy works ! Thy thoughts are exceeding deep.

" Magnificata." According to the Chaldee : *Magnifica,* magnificent.——*" Cogitationes tuæ."* Thy thoughts ; or according to Sa and Mariana, Thy counsels ; or with Menochius, the designs of Thy Providence.——O how great, O Lord, are these Thy works ! Thy most sweet thoughts, intentions, or dispositions, in forming so many creatures, so perfect according to their order, are too deep, that is to say, too hidden and mysterious, for our scant intelligence.

6. Vir insipiens non cognoscet : et stultus non intelliget hæc.
The unwise man shall not know : nor will the fool understand these things.

The ignorant and foolish man knows and understands nothing of all this.

7. Cum exorti fuerint peccatores sicut fœnum : et apparuerint omnes, qui operantur iniquitatem.
When the wicked shall spring up as the grass : and all the workers of iniquity shall appear.

8. Ut intereant in sæculum sæculi : tu autem Altissimus in æternum, Domine.

That they may perish for ever and ever : but Thou, O Lord, art Most High for evermore.

7, 8. *"Apparuerint."* According the Hebrew : *Floruerint.*
——Hardly are sinners, and all such as live wickedly, born, come forth, and multiplied as the grass of the field, which grows up thick apace, and have made a fair show here in the world with their dignities and riches, than they shall have perished for ever : but Thou, Lord, on the contrary, shalt be ever the same Most High that Thou art.

9. Quoniam ecce inimici tui, Domine, quoniam ecce inimici tui peribunt : et dispergentur omnes, qui operantur iniquitatem.

For behold Thine enemies, O Lord, for behold Thine enemies shall perish : and all the workers of iniquity shall be scattered.

All the wicked shall, in the end, be destroyed.

10. Et exaltabitur sicut unicornis cornu meum : et senectus mea in misericordia uberi.

But my horn shall be exalted like that of the unicorn : and my old age in plentiful mercy.

My strength, or glory, by Thy grace, shall greatly increase and rise on high, as on the head of the unicorn rises its single horn which is its strength and its glory ; and my old age shall go by privileged and consoled by Thy mercy, abounding in gifts, in helps, and comforts.

11. Et despexit oculus meus inimicos meos : et in insurgentibus in me malignantibus audiet auris mea.

Mine eye also hath looked down upon mine enemies : and mine ear shall hear *of the downfall* of the malignant that rise up against me.

My eyes shall see my enemies cast down, so that, far from fearing them, I shall despise them, and my ears shall be fain to hear of the chastisement inflicted on those who are risen against me in their malice to plot my ruin.

12. Justus ut palma florebit : sicut cedrus Libani multiplicabitur.

The just shall flourish like the palm-tree : he shall grow up like a cedar of Libanus.

The just man shall flourish and shall endure as the palm-tree, which, preserving its foliage, remains always green, and shall grow to a great height like a cedar of Lebanon.

13. Plantati in domo Domini : in atriis domus Dei nostri florebunt.

They that are planted in the house of the Lord : shall flourish in the courts of the house of our God.

All the just planted in the house of the Lord, and cultivated by Him shall flourish, that is, they will always preserve their vigour and their beauty.[1]

14. Adhuc multiplicabuntur in senecta uberi: et bene patientes erunt, ut annuntient :	They shall still increase in a fruitful old age : and it shall be well with them ;
15. Quoniam rectus Dominus Deus noster : et non est iniquitas in eo.	That they may show that the Lord our God is upright : and there is no iniquity in Him.

14, 15. They shall grow and increase even in their old age, which shall be abundant in fruits of virtue : and they shall have strength to celebrate Thy glories.——"*Bene patientes.*" According to the Hebrew : *Florentes* [*virides*]. Green and flowering ; S. Jerome translates : *Frondentes.* Leafy. Meaning, as Bellarmine explains, that by means of their temperament or character full of strength, they will be well able to bear up against fatigues ; and be flourishing and vigorous in virtue, to the end that they may announce—for, according to Bellarmine, this word "*Annuntient*" belongs to the next verse, —and make known to all by word and example that the Lord our God is right and just in all things ; and that there is no iniquity or injustice in Him, because He allows the wicked to prosper ; for, in His own time, He will reward the just and punish sinners as they deserve.

PSALMS LXII. AND LXVI.

CANTICLE OF MOSES.

MOSES, shortly before his death, recites this Canticle, by God's order, in presence of the people.[2]   In it he recounts the benefits done to the Israelites, their faults, and the chastisements sent by God to reclaim them.

1. Audite, cœli, quæ loquor : audiat terra verba oris mei.	Hear, O ye heavens, the things I speak : let the earth give ear to the words of my mouth.

Hear, O ye heavens, the things I shall say ; and let the earth hearken to the words of my mouth.

2. Concrescat ut pluvia doctrina mea : fluat ut ros eloquium meum.	Let my doctrine gather as the rain : let my speech distil as the dew.

[1] Planted in God's Church by the right faith, watered with the Sacraments and the word of God, rooted and grounded in charity, they will bring forth the flowers of virtue, and fruits of good works.—*Bellarmine.*

[2] *Deut.* xxxi., xxxii. 10.

"*Concrescat.*" According to the Hebrew : *Stillet ut pluvia verbum meum.* Let my doctrine distil as the rain ; and let my speech drop down as dew into the minds of those who hear me.

3. Quasi imber super herbam, et quasi stillæ super gramina : quia nomen Domini invocabo :

As a shower upon the herb, and as drops upon the grass : because I will invoke the name of the Lord :

May my words be received as the grass receives the rain, and as tender plants receive the shower that falls by drops upon them ; since I will invoke the name of the Lord, that my words may be of profit.

4. Date magnificentiam Deo nostro: Dei perfecta sunt opera, et omnes viæ ejus judicia :

Give ye magnificence to our God. The works of God are perfect, and all His ways are judgments.

"*Judicia.*" Equity, Justice itself.

5. Deus fidelis, et absque ulla iniquitate, justus et rectus: peccaverunt ei, et non filii ejus in sordibus :

God is faithful, and without any iniquity, He is just and right. They have sinned against Him, and are none of His children in their filth.

God is faithful to His promises, and in Him there is no iniquity, for He is just and righteous ; but, for all that, the Israelites have turned their back upon Him, and by their shameful actions have made themselves unworthy to be called His children.

6. Generatio prava atque perversa: hæccine reddis Domino, popule stulte et insipiens ?

They are a wicked and perverse generation. Is this the return thou makest to the Lord, O foolish and senseless people?

7. Numquid non ipse est pater tuus : qui possedit te, et fecit, et creavit te ?

Is not He thy Father, that hath possessed thee, and made thee, and created thee ?

"*Possedit te.*" That is : Hath chosen thee out of all nations for His own property.

8. Memento dierum antiquorum : cogita generationes singulas :

Remember the days of old, think upon every generation :

"*Generationes singulas.*" All the generations that are past.

9. Interroga patrem tuum, et annuntiabit tibi : majores tuos, et dicent tibi.

Ask thy father, and he will declare to thee : thy elders and they will tell thee.

Ask of your fathers, and they will recount to you what they have seen ; question your elders, and hear what they will tell you.

10. Quando dividebat Altissimus gentes: quando separabat filios Adam,

When the Most High divided the nations : when He separated the sons of Adam,

11. Constituit terminos populorum: juxta numerum filiorum Israel.

He appointed the bounds of people according to the number of the children of Israel.

He fixed the boundaries of the people who were to be the first to dwell in the Land of Promise, according to the number of the children of Israel who should possess that land.

12. Pars autem Domini, populus ejus: Jacob funiculus hereditatis ejus.

But the Lord's portion is His people : Jacob the lot of His inheritance.

For the portion which the Lord reserved to Himself, as specially His own, was the people of His choice ; He thus destined Jacob to be His inheritance.——In Holy Scripture the portion of inheritance is called *Funiculus*, a line ; because the portions were used to be marked out by a line of cord.

13. Invenit eum in terra deserta : in loco horroris, et vastæ solitudinis :

He found him in a desert land, in a place of horror, and of waste wilderness :

14. Circumduxit eum, et docuit : et custodivit quasi pupillam oculi sui.

He led him about, and taught him: and He kept him as the apple of His eye.

Hence he led him about by divers ways, and instructed him in His laws, &c.

15. Sicut aquila provocans ad volandum pullos suos ; et super eos volitans,

As the eagle enticing her young to fly, and hovering over them.

" *Et super* . . ." Does so, by flying herself above them [*i.e.*, over their nest].

16. Expandit alas suas, et assumpsit eum : atque portavit in humeris suis.

He spread His wings, and hath taken him, and carried him on His shoulders.

Thus the Lord spreads His wings over His people, &c.

17. Dominus solus dux ejus fuit : et non erat cum eo deus alienus.

The Lord alone was his leader : and there was no strange god with Him.

The Lord alone would be his leader, and would have no strange god with Him.

18. Constituit eum super excelsam terram : ut comederet fructus agrorum,

He set him upon high land : that he might eat the fruits of the fields,

" *Excelsam.*" Most excellent.

19. Ut sugeret mel de petra : oleumque de saxo durissimo :

That he might suck honey out of the rock, and oil out of the hardest stone.

That is, that he might draw honey even from the rocks where the bees made their combs, and gather oil from the olives, which bore fruit, though planted amongst the hardest rocks.

20. Butyrum de armento, et lac de ovibus cum adipe agnorum, et arietum filiorum Basan.

Butter of the herd, and milk of the sheep, with the fat of lambs, and of the rams of the breed of Basan.

"*Cum adipe* ..." Together with the fat of lambs that is : And that he might have the flesh of the fat lambs and sheep from the land of Basan. For, as we know, the Israelites were forbidden to eat the fat alone. (*Levit.* vii. 23.) The country of Basan had very rich pastures, and therefore the best and fattest flocks.

21. Et hircos cum medulla tritici : et sanguinem uvæ biberet meracissimum.

And goats with the marrow of wheat : and might drink the purest blood of the grape.

That he might likewise feed on fat goats, or kids, together with bread of the finest flour ; and drink most generous wine.

22. Incrassatus est dilectus, et recalcitravit : incrassatus, impinguatus, dilatatus.

The beloved grew fat, and kicked : he grew fat, and thick, and gross.

23. Dereliquit Deum factorem suum : et recessit a Deo salutari suo.

He forsook God Who made him : and departed from God his Saviour.

22, 23. This people, so beloved by God, after being thus fattened on His gifts, has kicked, struck out his heels against Him, by disobeying His precepts ; in fine, having grown fat, and big, and bloated, he forsook his God Who created Him, and separated himself from that God Who alone could save him.

24. Provocaverunt eum in diis alienis : et in abominationibus ad iracundiam concitaverunt.

They provoked Him by strange gods : and stirred Him up to anger with their abominations.

"*Provocaverunt eum in diis alienis.*" These ungrateful ones provoked Him to anger, by worshipping strange gods.

25. Immolaverunt dæmoniis et non Deo : diis, quos ignorabant :

They sacrificed to devils and not to God : to gods whom they knew not.

26. Novi recentesque venerunt : quos non coluerunt patres eorum.

That were newly come up : whom their fathers worshipped not.

They brought into the world certain new-fangled and unheard-of gods, whom their fathers had never adored.

27. Deum, qui te genuit, dereliquisti: et oblitus es Domini creatoris tui.

Thou hast forsaken the God that begot thee: and hast forgotten the Lord that created thee.

O foolish people ! thou hast forsaken that God Who gave thee thy being, &c.

28. Vidit Dominus, et ad iracundiam concitatus est: quia provocaverunt eum filii sui et filiæ.

The Lord saw, and was moved to wrath: because His own sons and daughters provoked Him.

The Lord saw, and was inflamed with indignation, because those who thus offended Him were His own sons and daughters.

29. Et ait: Abscondam faciem meam ab eis: et considerabo novissima eorum.

And He said : I will hide My face from them, and will consider what their last end shall be.

" *Considerabo . . . *" I will have before My eyes their last excesses ; these were the outrages and torments which the Jews inflicted on Jesus Christ, for which they were left abandoned in their obstinate unbelief.

30. Generatio enim perversa est : et infideles filii.

For it is a perverse generation : and unfaithful children.

They have rendered themselves undeserving of My mercy.

31. Ipsi me procaverunt in eo qui non erat deus : et irritaverunt in vanitatibus suis :

They have provoked Me with that which was no god : and have angered Me with their vanities.

32. Et ego provocabo eos in eo qui non est populus : et in gente stulta irritabo illos.

And I will provoke them with that which is no people : and will vex them with a foolish nation.

31, 32. They have provoked Me by adoring as God, what was not God ; and they have made Me indignant by setting themselves to honour vain and false deities. And I, on My part, will be to them the occasion of their affliction, by substituting for them a people which is not My people, and a foolish nation which knows Me not.[1]

33. Ignis succensus est in furore meo : et ardebit usque ad inferni novissima.

A fire is kindled in My wrath : and shall burn even to the lowest hell.

A wrath is kindled within Me against them, and it shall

[1] *Rom.* x. 19

burn them even to the lowest hell, where they shall be for ever condemned.

34. Devorabitque terram cum germine suo: et montium fundamenta comburet.

And shall devour the earth with her increase, and shall burn the foundations of the mountains.

My wrath shall consume their country, even to the herbs that grow there, &c.

35. Congregabo super eos mala: et sagittas meas complebo in eis.

I will heap evils upon them: and will spend My arrows among them.

"*Sagittas* . . ." That is : I will discharge against them all the arrows of My wrath.

36. Consumentur fame : et devorabunt eos aves morsu amarissimo.

They shall be consumed with famine : and birds shall devour them with a most bitter bite.

"*Aves.*" Birds of prey, such as vultures.

37. Dentes bestiarum immittam in eos : cum furore trahentium super terram, atque serpentium.

I will send the teeth of beasts upon them : with the fury of creatures that trail upon the ground and of serpents.

I will send against them wild beasts that shall crumble them with their teeth, and serpents that shall drag them along upon the ground with rage.

38. Foris vastabit eos gladius, et intus pavor : juvenem simul ac virginem, lactentem cum homine sene.

Without, the sword shall lay them waste, and terror within : both the young man and the virgin, the suckling child with the man in years.

All shall be the object of My vengeance.

39. Dixi, Ubinam sunt? cessare faciam ex hominibus memoriam eorum.

I said : Where are they ? I will make the memory of them to cease from among men.

"*Dixi.*" After that, I will say : Where are they now ?

40. Sed propter iram inimicorum distuli : ne forte superbirent hostes eorum.

But for the wrath of the enemies I have deferred it ; lest perhaps their enemies might be proud.

But I have delayed the chastisement on account of the hatred borne Me by their enemies ; lest, peradventure, these should become proud.

41. Et dicerent : Manus nostra excelsa, et non Dominus : fecit hæc omnia.

And should say : Our mighty hand, and not the Lord, hath done all these things.

42. Gens absque consilio est, et sine prudentia: Utinam saperent, et intelligerent, ac novissima providerent.

They are a nation without counsel, and without wisdom. O that they would be wise, and would understand, and would provide for their last end.

This hostile nation, moreover, has neither discernment nor prudence ; would to God that they had wisdom enough to understand, and prudence enough to provide for the last things, *i.e.*, for death and judgment.

43. Quomodo persequatur unus mille : et duo fugent decem millia?

How should one pursue after a thousand, and two chase ten thousand ?

44. Nonne ideo, quia Deus suus vendidit eos; et Dominus conclusit illos?

Was it not because their God had sold them, and the Lord had shut them up ?

43, 44. They ought indeed to say : How can it be that a single one of us goes against a thousand Hebrews, and two of us can put ten thousand to flight? This could not happen were it not that their God had sold them, that is, had ceased to have care of them, and because the Lord had so hemmed them in as to be unable to go forth and deliver themselves from their straits.

45. Non enim est Deus noster ut dii eorum : et inimici nostri sunt judices.

For our God is not as their gods : our enemies themselves are judges.

" *Et . . .*" Of this, &c.

46. De vinea Sodomorum, vinea eorum : et de suburbanis Gomorrhæ :

Their vines are of the vine-yard of Sodom, and of the suburbs of Gomorrha :

Here Tirinus observes that Moses returns to the Israelites, and assigns the cause of their chastisement : namely, because their vine [1] has become like the vine of the Sodomites, and like those in the suburbs of Gomorrha, which bear only the fruits of iniquity.

47. Uva eorum uva fellis : et botri amarissimi.

Their grapes are grapes of gall, and their clusters most bitter.

48. Fel draconum vinum eorum : et venenum aspidum insanabile.

Their wine is the gall of dragons, and the venom of asps, which is incurable.

49. Nonne hæc condita sunt apud me : et signata in thesauris meis ?

Are not these things stored up with Me, and sealed up in My treasures ?

Perhaps, says God, all these things are not stored up with Me and sealed up amongst the treasures of My judgments ?

[1] *Ps.* lxxxix. 9.

50. Mea est ultio, et ego retribuam in tempore : ut labatur pes eorum :

Revenge is Mine, and I will repay them in due time, that their foot may slide.

To Me it belongs to punish sins, and when the time arrives I will send the chastisement whereby they shall fall into the pit that is prepared for them, their feet stumbling against the stone, that is, as Rotigni explains, Jesus Christ the Corner-stone set by God for their salvation. The Jews, by rejecting their Saviour, fell into perdition.

51. Juxta est dies perditionis : et adesse festinant tempora.

The day of destruction is at hand, and the time makes haste to come.

Already this day of perdition is near, and the time of destruction hurries on.

52. Judicabit Dominus populum suum : et in servis suis miserebitur :

The Lord will judge His people, and will have mercy on His servants.

53. Videbit quod infirmata sit manus : et clausi quoque defecerunt, residuique consumpti sunt.

He shall see that their hand is weakened, and that they who were shut up have also failed, and they that remained are consumed.

But this shall not come to pass until the Jews shall be re-duced to such weakness, that those even who guarded the citadels shall themselves have yielded, and the others shall have perished.

54. Et dicet : Ubi sunt dii eorum : in quibus habebant fiduciam ?

And He shall say : Where are their gods, in whom they trusted ?

55. De quorum victimis comede-bant adipes : et bibebant vinum libaminum.

Of whose victims they ate the fat, and drank the wine of their drink-offerings.

They partook of the fat of victims offered to such deities, and drank the wine consecrated to them.—The Gentiles con-secrated wine to their gods, and such consecrations were called Libations.

56. Surgant, et opitulentur vobis : et in necessitate vos protegant.

Let them arise and help you, and protect you in your distress.

Let these your gods arise and help you ; and let them protect you in the extremities to which you are reduced.

57. Videte quod ego sim solus : et non sit alius deus præter me :

See ye that I alone am, and there is no other god besides Me :

Acknowledge that I alone am the true God, &c.

58. Ego occidam, et ego vivere faciam : percutiam, et ego sanabo : et non est qui de manu mea possit eruere.

I will kill, and I will make to live : I will strike, and I will heal, and there is none that can deliver out of My hand.

I cause to die and I cause to live ; I strike and I heal ; and none can escape My hands.

59. Levabo ad cœlum manum meum, et dicam: Vivo ego in æternum.

I will lift up My hand to heaven, and I will say : I live for ever.

60. Si acuero ut fulgur gladium meum : et arripuerit judicium manus mea :

If I shall whet My sword as the lightning, and My hand take hold on judgment :

59, 60. " *Vivo . . .* " A form of oath which God pronounces to confirm the threat that follows : I will sharpen My sword keen as the lightning, and My hand shall grasp it to deal justice.

61. Reddam ultionem hostibus meis ; et his, qui oderunt me, retribuam.

I will render vengeance to My enemies, and repay them that hate Me.

I will take revenge on My enemies ; and I will inflict condign punishment on those who hate Me.

62. Inebriabo sagittas meas sanguine : et gladius meus devorabit carnes.

I will make My arrows drunk with blood, and My sword shall devour flesh.

I will make My arrows drunk, that is, soaked with their blood ; and My sword shall devour their flesh, that is, make of them immense slaughter.

63. De cruore occisorum : et de captivitate, nudati inimicorum capitis.

Of the blood of the slain, and of the captivity, of the bare head of the enemies.

That is, as Tirinus explains : My vengeance shall strike them all, but in different ways ; some shall be put to death, others shall be made slaves, and others shall have their heads shaved.——In ancient times the victors shaved the heads of the vanquished to disgrace and make a laughing-stock of them, as it is related the Scipios did in Africa.

64. Laudate, Gentes, populum ejus : quia sanguinem servorum suorum ulciscetur :

Praise His people, ye nations, for He will revenge the blood of His servants :

Praise, O ye nations, the people of the Lord ; for He well knows how to avenge the blood of His servants.

65. Et vindictam retribuet in hostes eorum : et propitius erit terræ populi sui.

And will render vengeance to their enemies, and He will be merciful to the land of His people.

He will avenge them of their enemies ; and He will be propitious, that is, He will bless the land where His people shall dwell.

PSALMS CXLVIII., CXLIX., CL.

THE CANTICLE OF ZACHARY.

VESPERS FOR SUNDAY.

PSALM CIX.

THE Psalmist here speaks of the reign of Jesus Christ, of His eternal and temporal generation, of His Priesthood, and of His Passion. This Psalm must be understood literally of our Divine Saviour, since it is recorded in the Gospel that He applied it to Himself (*Matt.* xxii. 44), in order to convince the Jews that He was truly the Son of God: after drawing from them the avowal that the Messias must be the Son of David, He asked them how it was, then, David called Him his Lord: "The Lord said unto my Lord," and thereupon followed up the argument by asking them how the same Messias Whom David called his Lord, was his Son : " If David then call Him Lord, how is He his Son ? " The Jews did not answer that the Messias could not be the Lord of David, as true God ; but they would not allow that Jesus was the Messias or Christ of Whom David had spoken. We Christians all believe that Jesus Christ was the true Messias. This ought to convince the Arians, who deny that Jesus Christ is true Son of God and true God as His Father : how in fact can they deny this verity, seeing that David called Him his Lord, Who was to be his Son ?

A Psalm of David.

1. Dixit Dominus Domino meo : Sede a dextris meis.

The Lord said unto my Lord: Sit Thou at My right hand.

"*Dixit . . . meo.*" That is : The Eternal Father said to Jesus Christ. For "*Dominus Domino*" the Hebrew reads : *Jehova Ladoni. Jehova* is a name which belongs to God alone : meaning HE WHO IS. The Hebrews, through reverence, did not pronounce the name of God. *Adonai* signifies Lord. Since David would have us here understand that the

Father spoke to the Son not only as God, but also as man, he therefore makes use of the word *Adoni*, which is equally applicable to the Messias as God and as man ; whereas, if he had, in speaking of Christ, used the name of *Jehova*, he would have been understood as speaking of Him as God only, and not as man.——"*Sede a dextris meis.*"　"*Sede :* " Be seated, signifies supreme authority given to Jesus Christ, as sitting at the right hand of God, "*A dextris meis,*" signifies an equality of position, an elevation equal to that of the Father. And in reality Jesus Christ has the same dominion and power as His Father, not only as God, but also as man, since His Most Sacred Humanity has been raised to this exaltation in virtue of His hypostatic union with the Word, according to the words of S. Paul : "Who, being in the form of God, thought it not robbery to be equal with God ... Jesus Christ is in the glory of God the Father." (*Phil.* ii. 6-11.) There is no doubt but that : "Is in the glory of God," is the same as : "*Sit Thou at My right hand;*" that is : *In the majesty of God.* So S. Mark (xvi. 19), speaking of our Saviour ascended into heaven, says : "He was taken into heaven, and sitteth at the right hand of God." S. Ambrose thus comments : "He hears as Man, He sits as the Son of God." (*De David. Apol.* 2.)

2. Donec ponam inimicos tuos : scabellum pedum tuorum.
Until I make Thine enemies : Thy footstool.

That is: Thou shalt reign at My right hand, even during the time that Thou shalt subdue Thine enemies ; according to what S. Paul writes : "For He must reign until He hath put all His enemies under His feet." (1 *Cor.* xv. 25.) The word "*Donec*" is said by commentators to mean, *As long as ;* for, as Mattei says, "*Donec*" does not always imply the termination of what is spoken of.[1]

3. Virgam virtutis tuæ emittet Dominus ex Sion : dominare in medio inimicorum tuorum.
The Lord will send forth the sceptre of Thy power out of Sion : rule Thou in the midst of Thine enemies.

Here David speaks to Jesus Christ, and says to Him : The Lord, that is, Thy Eternal Father, will cause to come forth from Sion, or from Jerusalem, the sceptre of Thy power, and Thy reign shall extend over the whole earth.——This accords with the command given by Jesus Christ to His disciples to go and preach the faith, beginning with Jerusalem : "That penance and remission of sins should be preached in His name

[1] *Heb.* x. 12, i. 13 ; *Acts* ii. 34.

... beginning at Jerusalem" (*Luke* xxiv. 47).——Mattei observes that by " *Virgam* " many of the Holy Fathers understand the Cross (which is the sceptre of Jesus Christ), faith in which, preached at first in Sion, afterwards made its way way to the Gentiles.

| 4. Tecum principium in die virtu- tis tuæ in splendoribus sanctorum : ex utero ante luciferum genui te. | Thine shall be dominion in the day of Thy power, amid the brightness of the Saints ; from the womb before the day-star have I begotten Thee. |

There are in this verse several words difficult to understand: of these, Commentators give various explanations ; but not to perplex the reader, I shall offer only one.——*Tecum principium.*" Some understand by " *Principium*," the Divine Word Himself, Who is also in truth the " *Principium*," the First Principle, the Beginning, according to the words of Jesus Christ : " As Thou, Father in Me, and I in Thee " (*John* xvii. 21).[1] But "*Principium*" is commonly explained as *Principatus:* Principality, or Dominion ; and this agrees with the rendering of the Septuagint. Thus Tertullian understands it, who writes: *Principium pro principatu sumitur* (*Adv. Hermog.*, c. 9).—— " *In die virtutis tuæ.*" Mattei, according to the authority, as he says, of several Holy Fathers, explains this of eternity : *Ab æterno.* But others, with great probability, apply it to the day of the last judgment, when Jesus Christ will display His power over all creatures : and this is the explanation of S. Augustine, Theodoret, Lallemant, and many others.—— " *In splendoribus sanctorum.*" That is : When the eternal Judge shall be surrounded by the Saints, who will shine forth as so many suns : " Then shall the just shine as the sun " (*Matt.* xiii. 43).——"*Ex utero . . .*" This is to be understood, according to S. Thomas, of the eternal generation of the Word : I have begotten Thee before the star called Lucifer, that is, putting a part for the whole, before all creatures ; and I have begotten Thee from My womb : " *Ex utero*," *i.e.*, from My substance, as S. Jerome explains : *De sua natura, de sua substantia.*——The sense, then, of the verse is this : My Son, Thy Princedom over all created things shall appear, when Thou shalt sit on Thy throne in the midst of the Saints, who shall shine as stars or suns, to judge the world ; for I have begotten Thee of My substance before the existence of the stars and of all other creatures, even from eternity.

[1] See *John* viii. 25.

5. Juravit Dominus, et non pœni-   The Lord hath sworn, and He will
tebit eum : Tu es sacerdos in æternum not repent : Thou art a priest for ever
secundum ordinem Melchisedech.   after the order of Melchisedech.

The Lord hath sworn, and will never repent of it ; it is an
oath and an immutable decree. He hath said : Thou art
Priest eternal, according to the order of Melchisedech, in con-
tradistinction to the priests according to the order of Aaron,
who were subject to change and death.——Jesus Christ is a
Priest for ever, because even in heaven He offers the merits
of His Passion for the salvation of men, so long as they shall
live on this earth ; and even after the end of the world, He
will ever continue to offer them on behalf of men, in thanksgiving for the graces bestowed on them by God. There is
also this difference between the sacrifices of the Old Law, that
in it animals were offered ; whilst that of Melchisedech, in
which bread and wine were offered, was a figure of the Sacrifice
of Mass, wherein Jesus Christ is the principal Sacrificer.

6. Dominus a dextris tuis : con-   The Lord upon Thy right hand :
fregit in die iræ suæ reges.   hath overthrown kings in the day of
                                     His wrath.

The Lord shall always be at Thy side, and in the day of His
just vengeance He will overthrow the power of those kings
who are Thy enemies.——Here Mattei justly remarks that,
according to the Hebrew, instead of "A dextris tuis," it is
Super dextera tua. Hence these words mean here, not that
Jesus Christ is to sit at the right hand of God, as some understand them, but that the Eternal Father, "Dominus," "the
Lord at Thy right hand," will give to Jesus Christ the strength
to vanquish all His enemies.

7. Judicabit in nationibus implebit He shall judge among the nations ;
ruinas : conquassabit capita in terra He shall fill them with ruins : He
multorum.   shall smite in sunder the heads in
                                     the land of many.

Jesus Christ shall judge the rebellious nations, and will
carry into effect the chastisements with which they have been
threatened ; He shall shiver in pieces on the earth the proud
heads that rose up against Him.

8. De torrente in via bibet : prop- He shall drink of the brook in the
terea exaltabit caput.   way : therefore shall He lift up His
                                     head.

Mattei, together with Marcus Marinus, thus explains this
verse : He shall cause the blood of His foes to flow like a
torrent, in which He will quench His thirst.——But others

give this explanation : Nevertheless, this God made Man shall first, during His mortal life, drink of the water of the torrent, that is, the chalice of His Passion, which, like a torrent of pains, shall overwhelm Him to death ; but in consequence of this death, He shall lift up His head, for thereby He shall be exalted to a throne of glory, according to the words of the Apostle : "We see Jesus ... for the suffering of death, crowned with glory and honour : that, through the grace of God, He might taste death for all" (*Heb.* ii. 9). Blessed Death, which has restored life to all men ![1]

PSALM CX.

PRAISE to God for His perfections, and for the wonders which He has wrought in behalf of His people.

Alleluia.

1. Confitebor tibi Domine in toto corde meo : in consilio justorum, et congregatione.

I will praise Thee, O Lord, with my whole heart : in the assembly of the just, and in the congregation.

"*In consilio ... et congregatione.*" According to the Hebrew : *In secreto et synagoga;* the sense is, in private gatherings of few, and in public assemblies of the people.

2. Magna opera Domini : exquisita in omnes voluntates ejus.

Great are the works of the Lord : sought out are they according unto all His pleasure.

All the works of the Lord are great ; for in all, His infinite wisdom and power shine forth : and all are perfect, since they all correspond to the intentions of His Holy Will.

3. Confessio et magnificentia opus ejus : et justitia ejus manet in sæculum sæculi.

His work is His praise and His honour : and His justice endureth for ever and ever.

All His works are so many motives for us to praise Him and magnify Him ; He it is who does all things, and everything that He does is always just.

4. Memoriam fecit mirabilium suorum, misericors et miserator Dominus : escam dedit timentibus se.

A memorial hath the merciful and gracious Lord made of His marvellous works : He hath given meat unto them that fear Him.

The Lord, Who is merciful and (according to the Hebrew word) tender as a Father, has left the memorial of His admir-

[1] *Philip.* ii. 8, 9 ; *Luke* xxiv. 26.

able prodigies, which He has wrought in favour of His people, especially in the miraculous food (the Manna) which He gave to our fathers, who had the gift of His holy fear.——Every one knows that this Manna was a figure of the Holy Eucharist, that most admirable work which Jesus Christ left on earth as a memorial of the Death which He suffered for us.

5. Memor erit in sæculum testamenti sui : virtutem operum suorum annuntiabit populo suo :

He shall ever be mindful of His covenant : He shall show forth to His people the power of His works :

" *Virtutem.*" The worth, the priceless value.

6. Ut det illis hereditatem gentium : opera manuum ejus veritas, et judicium.

That He may give them the heritage of the Gentiles : the works of His hands are truth and judgment.

" *Hereditatem gentium.*" The Land of Promise in possession of the Gentiles.——" *Opera . . .*" In a word, His works show forth to us His fidelity and His justice.

7. Fidelia omnia mandata ejus : confirmata in sæculum sæculi : facta in veritate et æquitate.

All His commandments are faithful : they stand fast for ever and ever, they are done in truth and equity.

All His precepts are ever righteous and unchangeable, &c.

8. Redemptionem misit populo suo : mandavit in æternum testamentum suum.

He hath sent redemption unto His people : He hath commanded His covenant for ever.

He hath sent redemption to His people, that is, the Redeemer, as S. Augustine and Euthymius explain, and He has made a covenant with them which shall never be broken.

9. Sanctum et terribile nomen ejus : initium sapientiæ timor Domini.

Holy and terrible is His name : the fear of the Lord is the beginning of wisdom.

His Name is holy and terrible ; we must, therefore, greatly fear to violate this covenant, and be careful to preserve the fear of the Lord, since this is the beginning of wisdom.

10. Intellectus bonus omnibus facientibus eum : laudatio ejus manet in sæculum sæculi.

A good understanding have all they that do thereafter : His praise endureth for ever and ever.

They have a good intelligence, that is, they rightly understand this salutary fear who act up to it ; hence, he who keeps this fear shall be for ever praised.——" *Facientibus eum.*" According to the Hebrew : *Facientibus ea*, that is, *mandata*, the commandments. Mattei says that it is the same in substance, though the Hebrew makes us better understand that speculative fear is not enough if we would have the wisdom of

the Saints, but that we must live practically according to this
fear, in order to be truly wise. Many have the fear of God,
but, because they lead a bad life, they are the greatest fools in
the world.[1]

PSALM CXI.

The character of the just man and his temporal happiness
according to the promises which God made in the Old Law
for the present life; but we, in the New Law, must understand
them as spoken of the spiritual happiness which God bestows
on the just in this life and in the next.

Alleluia. Of the returning of Aggeus and Zacharias.

1. Beatus vir, qui timet Dominum:
in mandatis ejus volet nimis.

Blessed is the man that feareth
the Lord: he shall delight exceedingly in His commandments.

He who fears God as he ought, that is, with a fear not
servile but filial, takes all his delight in observing His precepts. S. Jerome says: *Anxie mandata ejus non facit, sed vult.*
The just man obeys not by force, but with a good will, and
finds his pleasure in obeying.

2. Potens in terra erit semen ejus:
generatio rectorum benedicetur.

His seed shall be mighty upon
earth: the generation of the upright
shall be blessed.

His progeny shall be numerous and powerful on the earth;
for the posterity of the good are always seen to be blessed by
the Lord.

3. Gloria et divitiæ in domo ejus:
et justitia ejus manet in sæculum
sæculi.

Glory and riches shall be in his
house: and his justice endureth for
ever and ever.

His house shall enjoy honours and riches; and with all his
honours and riches he will firmly persevere in his holy life,
and will not feel regret at leaving them, because the reward
due to his justice shall be everlasting in the life to come.

4. Exortum est in tenebris lumen
rectis: misericors, et miserator, et
justus.

Unto the upright there hath risen
up light in the darkness: he is merciful, and compassionate, and just.

The light that comes from the Lord shall not fail the

[1] According to the Septuagint: *Eam,* referring to *Sapientia.*——"*Ejus*"
may be taken either as referring to "*Intellectus,*" and this sense the holy
Doctor adopts; or to, the Lord, understood; this latter is the interpretation
of St. Chrysostom, and of the English version.—*Tr.*

righteous in the darkness of their afflictions, for He is full of
mercy and goodness, and the just rewarder of His servants.

5. Jucundus homo qui miseretur
et commodat, disponet sermones suos
in judicio : quia in æternum non commovebitur.

Acceptable is the man who is merciful and lendeth : he shall order his
words with judgment, for he shall
not be moved for ever.

"*Jucundus.*" Mattei says that, according to the Hebrew,
this word here signifies *Beatus*, Blessed.——Happy is the man
who exercises mercy towards the poor, in at least lending
them what they stand in need of; he will regulate his words
and his temporal affairs, or will manage his possessions, "*In
judicio,*" with such wise prudence, that he shall never be
moved or disturbed from his prosperity.

6. In memoria æterna erit justus :
ab auditione mala non timebit.

The just man shall be in everlasting remembrance : he shall not be
afraid for evil tidings.

The just man shall live for ever in the memory of men ;
and he will not fear to lose his character by the calumnies of
his enemies.

7. Paratum cor ejus sperare in Domino, confirmatum est cor ejus : non
commovebitur donec despiciat inimicos suos.

His heart is ready to hope in the
Lord : his heart is strengthened, he
shall not be moved until he look down
upon his enemies.

He keeps a mind determined never to lose confidence in the
Lord ; his heart stands firm, stayed on God, and he shall not
be moved by his enemies, for at length he will be able to
despise them, when he sees them vanquished.

8. Dispersit, dedit pauperibus :
justitia ejus manet in sæculum sæculi : cornu ejus exaltabitur in gloria.

He hath dispersed abroad, he hath
given to the poor : his justice endureth for ever and ever : his horn shall
be exalted in glory.

He has distributed and given generously of his goods to the
poor : his justice, that is, his good deeds, his merits, shall be
ever before the eyes of God, to be recompensed eternally in
heaven, and he shall be exalted in power and in glory.

9. Peccator videbit, et irascetur,
dentibus suis fremet et tabescet :
desiderium peccatorum peribit.

The wicked shall see it and shall
be wroth : he shall gnash with his
teeth and pine away : the desire of
the wicked shall perish.

The wicked, at seeing this, will be angry, he will gnash
with his teeth for rage, and pine away with spite and envy;
he would wish to deprive the just man of this happiness; but
the desires of the wicked shall vanish as smoke.

PSALM CXII.

THE Psalmist invites the just to praise God for the care that He takes of all His creatures, even of the meanest.

Alleluia.

1. Laudate pueri Dominum : laudate nomen Domini.	Praise the Lord, ye children : praise ye the name of the Lord.

Praise the Lord, you who are His servants ; praise His great Name.[1]

2. Sit nomen Domini benedictum : ex hoc nunc, et usque in sæculum.	Blessed be the name of the Lord : from this time forth for evermore.
3. A solis ortu usque ad occasum : laudabile nomen Domini.	From the rising up of the sun unto the going down of the same : the name of the Lord is worthy to be praised.
4. Excelsus super omnes Gentes Dominus : et super cœlos gloria ejus.	The Lord is high above all nations : and His glory above the heavens.

The Lord is sovereign, supreme over all the nations : His glory surpasses that of the heavens.

5. Quis sicut Dominus Deus noster, qui in altis habitat : et humilia respicit in cœlo et in terra ?	Who is like unto the Lord our God, Who dwelleth on high: and regardeth the things that are lowly in heaven and on earth ?

Who can ever compare with the Lord our God, Whose goodness is such that, from the highest heaven where He dwells, He does not disdain to look upon the creatures that are the most lowly in heaven and on earth ?

6. Suscitans a terra inopem : et de stercore erigens pauperem :	Who raiseth up the needy from the earth : and lifteth the poor out of the dunghill :
7. Ut collocet eum cum principibus : cum principibus populi sui.	That He may set him with the princes : even with the princes of His people.
8. Qui habitare facit sterilem in domo : matrem filiorum lætantem.	Who maketh the barren woman to dwell in her house : the joyful mother of children.

He it is Who, beholding the spouse full of sadness in her house, at seeing herself barren, without offspring, makes her become the joyful mother of many children. This verse applies well to Jesus Christ, Who, when the Church was bereaved of children by the perversion of the Jews, made her, by His redemption, the mother of all the faithful.

[1] " *Pueri.*" According to the Hebrew : *Servi :* His servants.

PSALM CXIII.

THE wonders wrought by God to deliver His people from the slavery of Egypt. The folly of the Gentiles, who trusted in their idols. The faithful people are exhorted to place their confidence in our true God, and to persevere in His service.[1]

Alleluia.

1. In exitu Israel de Ægypto: domus Jacob de populo barbaro.

When Israel came out of Egypt: the house of Jacob from among a strange people:

2. Facta est Judæa sanctificatio ejus: Israel potestas ejus.

Judea was made His sanctuary: and Israel His dominion.

1, 2. When the people of Israel were delivered from the yoke of the Egyptians, who oppressed them, then the Jewish nation was sanctified and consecrated to the service of God, Who willed thenceforth to reign alone over them.[2]

3. Mare vidit, et fugit: Jordanis conversus est retrorsum.

The sea saw it, and fled: Jordan was turned back.

The Red Sea beheld the Hebrews pursued by the Egyptians, and fled, that is, drew back to afford an open passage to the people of God. The river Jordan turned back, that is, its waters stopped in their course, and lifted themselves up on high, that the faithful people might pass over, as we read in *Jos.* iii. 13.

4. Montes exultaverunt ut arietes: et colles sicut agni ovium.

The mountains skipped like rams: and the little hills like the lambs of the flock.

Then did the mountains exult with joy.——Others apply this verse to the trembling of the mountains when the Law was given to Moses. I prefer the first sense as agreeing better with the following verse.

5. Quid est tibi mare quod fugisti: et tu Jordanis, quia conversus es retrorsum?

What aileth thee, O thou sea, that thou fleddest: and thou, Jordan, that thou wast turned back?

6. Montes exultastis sicut arietes: et colles sicut agni ovium.

Ye mountains, that ye skipped like rams: and ye little hills, like the lambs of the flock?

[1] The Hebrew divides this into two Psalms.

[2] *Barbaro."* That is, speaking another language not understood. (1 *Cor.* xiv. 11.)——*"Facta est Judæa."* According to the Hebrew : *Factus est Juda.* Juda or the Jewish people.——Others understand the second verse in the sense that God chose the land of Judæa, there to establish His Sanctuary, His Temple, and Worship, and chose the people of Israel to exercise or represent His power on earth.

5, 6. But why, O sea, didst thou fly, &c.

7. A facie Domini mota est terra : a facie Dei Jacob.

At the presence of the Lord the earth was moved : at the presence of the God of Jacob ;

8. Qui convertit petram in stagna aquarum : et rupem in fontes aquarum.

Who turned the rock into a standing water : and the stony hill into a flowing stream.

9. Non nobis Domine, non nobis : sed nomini tuo da gloriam.

Not unto us, O Lord, not unto us : but unto Thy name give the glory.

10. Super misericordia tua, et veritate tua : nequando dicant Gentes : Ubi est Deus eorum?

For Thy mercy, and for Thy truth's sake : lest the Gentiles should say, Where is their God?

Protect us for Thy mercy's sake, and according to the faithfulness of Thy promises, lest the impious should say, in case Thou should'st abandon us : Where now is their God to help them ?

11. Deus autem noster in cœlo : omnia quæcumque voluit, fecit.

But our God is in heaven : He hath done all things whatsoever He would.

But our God is in heaven : He causes to happen whatsoever He wills.

12. Simulacra gentium, argentum, et aurum : opera manuum hominum.

The idols of the Gentiles are silver and gold : the work of the hands of men.

13. Os habent, et non loquentur : oculos habent, et non videbunt.

They have mouths, and speak not : eyes have they, and see not.

14. Aures habent, et non audient : nares habent, et non odorabunt.

They have ears, and hear not : noses have they, and smell not:

15. Manus habent, et non palpabunt ; pedes habent et non ambulabunt : non clamabunt in gutture suo.

They have hands, and feel not : they have feet and walk not : neither shall they speak through their throat.

" *Non clamabunt.*" They are unable to call out.

16. Similes illis fiant qui faciunt ea : et omnes qui confidunt in eis.

Let them that make them become like unto them : and all such as put their trust in them.[1]

Let those who with their own hands make to themselves such gods, and all those who put their trust in them, become like unto them.

17. Domus Israel speravit in Domino : adjutor eorum et protector eorum est.

The house of Israel hath hoped in the Lord : He is their helper and protector.

[1] A prediction under the form of an imprecation.

" *Adjutor . . .*" He alone is, &c.

18. Domus Aaron speravit in Domino : adjutor eorum et protector eorum est.

The house of Aaron hath hoped in the Lord : He is their helper and protector.

19. Qui timent Dominum speraverunt in Domino : adjutor eorum et protector eorum est.

They that fear the Lord have hoped in the Lord : He is their helper and protector.

20. Dominus memor fuit nostri : et benedixit nobis.

The Lord hath been mindful of us : and hath blessed us.

" *Benedixit nobis.*" He has blessed us, loading us with graces.

21. Benedixit domui Israel : benedixit domui Aaron.

He hath blessed the house of Israel : He hath blessed the house of Aaron.

22. Benedixit omnibus qui timent Dominum : pusillis cum majoribus.

He hath blessed all that fear the Lord : both small and great.

23. Adjiciat Dominus super vos : super vos, et super filios vestros.

May the Lord add blessings upon you : upon you, and upon your children.

24. Benedicti vos a Domino : qui fecit cœlum, et terram.

Blessed be ye of the Lord : Who hath made heaven and earth.

25. Cœlum cœli Domino : terram autem dedit filiis hominum.

The heaven of heavens is the Lord's : but the earth hath He given to the children of men.

" *Cœlum cœli.*" The Empyrean, as Lallemant and others explain it. The Lord has created the empyrean heaven for Himself, that is, to reign there ; and He has given the earth to men for their habitation, that they may there gain merit to be raised to the empyrean.

26. Non mortui laudabunt te Domine : neque omnes qui descendunt in infernum.

The dead shall not praise thee, O Lord : neither all they that go down into hell.

" *In infernum.*" Into the grave. That is : After death, no one can do good works any more.

27. Sed nos qui vivimus, benedicimus Domino : ex hoc nunc et usque in sæculum.

But we that live bless the Lord : from this time forth for evermore.

That is : We who enjoy the life of grace, let us bless the Lord now at the present time, and let us hope to bless Him for all eternity.

THE CANTICLE OF THE BLESSED VIRGIN MARY
(*Luke* i. 46-55).

THE most Holy Virgin extols the goodness of God in having

chosen her to be the Mother of the Divine Incarnate Word, and for having redeemed the world by the means of Jesus Christ. This Canticle may be divided into three parts : in the first, the Blessed Virgin thanks the Lord for the favours which she has herself received from His goodness ; in the second, she praises Him for the benefits granted to the Hebrew people ; in the third, she glorifies Him for the grace which He has bestowed upon all men in giving them Jesus Christ for their Saviour.

1. Magnificat anima mea Domi-   My soul doth magnify the Lord.
num.

"*Magnificat*." According to the sense of the Greek text : Extols, proclaims the greatness of.

2. Et exultavit spiritus meus : in   And my spirit hath rejoiced : in
Deo salutari meo.   God my Saviour.

"*Salutari*." According to the Greek : *Salvatore;* and the Hebrew [in parallel passages] : *Jesu.* The most Blessed Virgin found all her delight in rejoicing in her God ; and such also should be ours.

3. Quia respexit humilitatem an-   Because He hath regarded the
cillæ suæ : ecce enim ex hoc beatam humility of His handmaid : for behold
me dicent omnes generationes.   from henceforth all generations shall
                                     call me blessed.

"*Humilitatem*." According to the Greek : *Vilitatem: Abjectionem.* Meanness, Littleness, Lowliness. The most humble Mary could not mean by this word the virtue of humility ; for if so, she would be praising herself ; whereas Humility, says Euthymius, alone amongst the virtues does not know itself. ——"*Ecce enim* ..." For behold from this time forth all nations and all ages shall call me Blessed.——This prophecy has been perfectly verified ; for there is not one among Catholics who does not in an especial manner venerate this great Mother of God.

4. Quia fecit mihi magna qui   Because He that is mighty hath
potens est : et sanctum nomen ejus. done great things to me : and holy is
                                     His name.

For, indeed, the Almighty, Whose name is Holy, has wrought great and marvellous things in me, making me Virgin and Mother of my Creator.

5. Et misericordia ejus a progenie   And His mercy is from generation
in progenies : timentibus eum.   unto generations to them that fear
                                     Him.

" *Timentibus eum.*" Extends itself to all those who fear Him with a filial fear.

6. Fecit potentiam in brachio suo : dispersit superbos mente cordis sui.

He hath shown might in His arm : He hath scattered the proud in the conceit of their heart.

God has shown forth the might of His arm, by putting to the rout the proud, that is, the haughty princes of the earth (we may also here understand the rebel Angels), and defeating all their wicked designs whereby they sought to oppress the innocent.

7. Deposuit potentes de sede : et exaltavit humiles.

He hath put down the mighty from their seat, and hath exalted the humble.

" *Potentes de sede.*" These proud princes from their thrones.

8. Esurientes implevit bonis : et divites dimisit inanes.

He hath filled the hungry with good things : and the rich He hath sent empty away.

" *Esurientes.*" The poor.——"*Divites . . .*" The rich are left spoiled of everything.

9. Suscepit Israel puerum suum : recordatus misericordiæ suæ.

He hath received Israel His servant : being mindful of His mercy.

10. Sicut locutus est ad patres nostros : Abraham, et semini ejus in sæcula.

As He spoke to our fathers : to Abraham and to His seed for ever.

9, 10. He hath taken under His protection Israel His servant, that is, His chosen people, being mindful of the promise which, in His mercy, He had made to him to send the Messias to redeem him, as thus He spoke and promised to our fathers, especially to Abraham and to all his descendants.

VESPERS FOR MONDAY.

PSALM CXIV.

DAVID gives thanks to God for having delivered him from the persecution of Absalom. The person of David is here the figure of a Christian soul, which, after suffering many dangerous temptations, finds itself victorious at the hour of death, and is on the point of going to enjoy God in heaven.

Alleluia.

1. Dilexi quoniam exaudiet Dominus : vocem orationis meæ.

I have loved the Lord : for He will hear the voice of my prayer.

I have loved and I love my Lord ; for He has heard, and I hope will always hear, my prayer.

2. Quia inclinavit aurem suam mihi : et in diebus meis invocabo.

For He hath inclined His ear unto me : and in my days will I call upon Him.

He has inclined His ears to my voice ; therefore, I will never cease to call upon Him all the days of my life, confiding in His mercy.

3. Circumdederunt me dolores mortis : et pericula inferni invenerunt me.

The sorrows of death have compassed me : and the perils of hell have taken hold upon me.

Lallemant and Mattei explain this verse as referring to the fears and dangers of losing the life of the body, and understand "*Inferni*" to mean the grave ; but Bellarmine interprets it thus : Deadly temptations have surrounded me which would draw me to eternal death. This sense is brought out more clearly by the words which follow : "*Et pericula inferni . . .*" And these temptations have brought me near to the danger of being condemned to hell.

| 4. Tribulationem et dolorem inveni : et nomen Domini invocavi. | I found trouble and sorrow : and I called upon the name of the Lord. |
| 5. O Domine libera animam meam: misericors Dominus, et justus, et Deus noster miseretur. | O Lord, do Thou deliver my soul : the Lord is merciful and just, and our God showeth mercy. |

4, 5. In this state I found nothing on all sides but afflictions and sorrows ; then I had recourse to the Lord, and called upon His name, saying : My God, deliver my soul from these perils. The Lord is as merciful as He is just ; He is that God Who shows mercy to those who have recourse to Him.

| 6. Custodiens parvulos Dominus : humiliatus sum, et liberavit me. | The Lord preserved the little ones : I was humbled, and He delivered me. |

"*Parvulos.*" The little ones who are humble.——"*Humiliatus . . .*" No sooner did I humble myself than He delivered me.

| 7. Convertere anima mea in requiem tuam : quia Dominus benefecit tibi. | Turn, O my soul, into thy rest : for the Lord hath been bountiful unto thee. |

"*In requiem tuam.*" To the place of thy repose, that is, to the heavenly country, as Bellarmine, with S. Basil, understand it.——"*Benefecit tibi.*" According to the Hebrew : *Retribuit super te.* The Lord will recompense thee according to thy good works, by giving thee eternal life, which is a crown of justice. Thus again Bellarmine, with S. Basil, interprets the words.

| 8. Quia eripuit animam meam de morte : oculos meos a lacrymis, pedes meos a lapsu. | For He hath delivered my soul from death : mine eyes from tears, and my feet from falling. |
| 9. Placebo Domino : in regione vivorum. | I will please the Lord : in the land of the living. |

I hope, then, to find myself in the land of the living, far from hell, where all are dead, and far from this world, where so many are also miserably dead through sin, and there I shall be happy, occupied for ever in pleasing the Lord.

PSALM CXV.

The same subject as that of the preceding Psalm ; but this is more full of thanksgiving to God for the benefits which the Psalmist acknowledges he has received from His goodness.[1]

---

[1] This in the Hebrew is joined with the foregoing Psalm.

Alleluia.

1. Credidi, propter quod locutus sum: ego autem humiliatus sum nimis.

I believed, and therefore did I speak: but I was humbled exceedingly.

This verse is clearly explained by S. Paul : " But having the same spirit of faith, as it is written : *I believed, for which cause I have spoken;* we also believe, for which cause we speak also" (2 *Cor.* iv. 13). Hence this explanation : Resting on faith, I have hoped in God ; and I therefore said : O Lord, Thou art my hope ; and this I said on beholding myself so deeply humiliated and afflicted.

2. Ego dixi in excessu meo : Omnis homo mendax.

I said in mine excess : All men are liars.

The following is the explanation given by Bellarmine, with Euthymius : In my ecstasy, when my spirit was raised to the knowledge of the land of the living, I said that every man is a liar, that is, that when men talk of this world's happiness they only speak lies.

3. Quid retribuam Domino : pro omnibus quæ retribuit mihi.

What shall I render unto the Lord : for all the things that He hath rendered unto me?

4. Calicem salutaris accipiam : et nomen Domini invocabo.

I will take the chalice of salvation : and call upon the name of the Lord.

By the chalice of salvation, S. Basil, S. Chrysostom, S. Jerome, S. Augustine, Theodoret, and Euthymius, according to Bellarmine, understand the chalice of the Passion of Jesus Christ, of which He Himself spoke thus : " The chalice which My Father hath given Me, shall I not drink it ? " (*John* xviii. 11). Hence this explanation : Having nothing to render the Lord for the graces which He has bestowed upon me, I will offer Him in thanksgiving the sufferings of Jesus Christ, to which I will unite those that I endure ; and I will invoke always the name of the Lord, that He may enable me to bear my pains with patience.

5. Vota mea Domino reddam coram omni populo ejus : pretiosa in conspectu Domini mors sanctorum ejus.

I will pay my vows unto the Lord, in the presence of all His people : precious in the sight of the Lord is the death of His saints.

"*Pretiosa ...*" I will proclaim that the death of the Saints is precious in the sight of God.

6. O Domine, quia ego servus tuus : ego servus tuus, et filius ancillæ tuæ.

O Lord, I am Thy servant : I am Thy servant, and the son of Thine handmaid.

That is : I have paid my vows to Thee, for I am Thy servant, &c.

7. Dirupisti vincula mea : tibi sacrificabo hostiam laudis, et nomen Domini invocabo.

Thou hast broken my bonds in sunder : I will offer unto Thee the sacrifice of praise, and will call upon the name of the Lord.

"*Nomen* ..." I will call upon no other name than that of my Lord.

8. Vota mea Domino reddam in conspectu omnis populi ejus : in atriis domus Domini, in medio tui Jerusalem.

I will pay my vows unto the Lord in the sight of all His people : in the courts of the house of the Lord, in the midst of thee, O Jerusalem.

PSALM CXVI.

ALL the peoples are invited to praise the mercy and the faithfulness of the Lord, for having united them together in one and the same Church. This is the sense which the Apostle gives to this Psalm (*Rom.* xv. 8-11).

Alleluia.

1. Laudate Dominum omnes Gentes : laudate eum omnes populi :

O praise the Lord, all ye nations : praise Him, all ye people.

2. Quoniam confirmata est super nos misericordia ejus : et veritas Domini manet in æternum.

For His mercy is confirmed upon us : and the truth of the Lord endureth for ever.

That is, He has multiplied upon us the effects of His mercy; and His faithfulness in the promises, which He has made to us, shall never fail.

PSALM CXIX.

DAVID beseeches Almighty God to defend him from the calumnies of his enemies, and bewails the length of his exile during the persecution of Saul. This Psalm is suitable to every Christian who looks forward to the end of his exile here on earth.

A Song of Degrees.[1]

1. Ad Dominum cum tribularer clamavi : et exaudivit me.

When I was in trouble I cried unto the Lord : and He heard me.

[1] This Psalm, and those that follow till Ps. cxxxiii. inclusively, in number fifteen, are called *Songs of Degrees*, and in the Breviary the *Gradual Psalms*, from the word *gradus*, signifying steps, ascensions, or degrees ; either because

2. Domine libera animam meam a labiis iniquis: et a lingua dolosa.

O Lord, deliver my soul from wicked lips: and from a deceitful tongue.

3. Quid detur tibi, aut quid apponatur tibi: ad linguam dolosam?

What shall be given unto thee, or what shall be added unto thee: to a deceitful tongue?

What greater evil canst thou have to fear, to be given or added unto thee, O my soul, than that of a deceitful tongue?

4. Sagittæ potentis acutæ: cum carbonibus desolatoriis.

Sharp arrows of the mighty One: with destroying coals of fire.

The shafts that go forth from the mouth of a man of power are so sharp and hurtful, that they are as burning coals dealing destruction all around.

5. Heu mihi, quia incolatus meus prolongatus est: habitavi cum habitantibus Cedar: multum incola fuit anima mea.

Woe is me, that my sojourn is prolonged; I have dwelt with the inhabitants of Cedar: my soul hath long been a sojourner.

"*Incolatus meus.*" My exile.——"*Habitavi ... Cedar.*" That is, I am constrained to dwell amongst barbarians. *Cedar*, says Bellarmine, is a Hebrew word, which means *Swarthiness.*—— "*Multum ...*" It is now long time that my soul suffers thus sojourning as a stranger amongst them.

6. Cum his qui oderunt pacem eram pacificus: cum loquebar illis, impugnabant me gratis.

With them that hated peace I was peaceable: when I spake unto them they fought against me without cause.

With those who hate peace, I who love peace have had to dwell; and if I began to speak of peace, they fought against me without cause.

PSALM CXX.

HERE the Psalmist makes a just man speak, who lifts his eyes to the blessed mountains where is seated the Holy City, and whence he hopes for divine help.

they were appointed to be sung on the fifteen *steps*, by which the people went up to the Temple; or that in the singing of them the voice was to be raised by certain *steps* or *degrees;* or that they were to be sung by the people returning from their captivity and going up to Jerusalem, which was seated amongst mountains. They may be understood of the degrees by which Christians spiritually ascend to virtue and perfection, and to the true Temple of God in the heavenly Jerusalem.

A Song of Degrees.

1. Levavi oculos meos in montes : unde veniet auxilium mihi.

I have lifted up mine eyes unto the hills : from whence my help shall come.

"*Montes*..." The holy mountains, whence is to come to me the succour that I hope for.

2. Auxilium meum a Domino : qui fecit cœlum et terram.

My help is from the Lord : Who hath made heaven and earth.

3. Non det in commotionem pedem tuum : neque dormitet qui custodit te.

Let Him not suffer thy foot to be moved : neither let Him slumber that keepeth thee.

The Lord will not suffer thee to fall, when thou hast recourse to Him ; nor does He sleep Who has taken thee to His keeping.

4. Ecce non dormitabit, neque dormiet : qui custodit Israel.

Behold, He that keepeth Israel : shall neither slumber nor sleep.

5. Dominus custodit te, Dominus protectio tua : super manum dexteram tuam.

The Lord is thy keeper : the Lord is thy defence upon thy right hand.

6. Per diem sol non uret te : neque luna per noctem.

The sun shall not burn thee by day : nor the moon by night.

By day thou shalt not have to fear the burning of the sun, nor by night the noxious influences of the moon.

7. Dominus custodit te ab omni malo : custodiat animam tuam Dominus.

The Lord preserveth thee from all evil : may the Lord preserve thy soul.

8. Dominus custodiat introitum tuum, et exitum tuum : ex hoc nunc, et usque in sæculum.

May the Lord preserve thy coming in and thy going out : from this time forth for evermore.

May He protect thee in all thy doings, from the beginning to the end, now and for ever.

MAGNIFICAT.

VESPERS FOR TUESDAY.

PSALM CXXI.

THE joy of the Jews, on hearing that they are about to be
released from the captivity of Babylon. Christians should by
this Psalm enkindle anew their desires for heaven.

A Song of Degrees.

1. Lætatus sum in his, quæ dicta sunt mihi : in domum Domini ibimus.

I was glad at the things that were said unto me : We will go into the house of the Lord.

2. Stantes erant pedes nostri : in atriis tuis Jerusalem.

Our feet were standing in thy courts : O Jerusalem.

We rejoice, O Jerusalem, at seeing our feet as though already
arrived at the threshold of thy gates.

3. Jerusalem, quæ ædificatur ut civitas : cujus participatio ejus in idipsum.[1]

Jerusalem, which is built as a city : that is in unity with itself.

"*Jerusalem.*" It is of thee, O Jerusalem, that I speak.——
Whose participation is *in idipsum,* i.e., *simul participatur ab
omnibus :* is mutually shared together by all, as Bellarmine
explains it ; since by means of holy charity all things friends
possess become the joy of each.

4. Illuc enim ascenderunt tribus, tribus Domini : testimonium Israel ad confitendum nomini Domini.

For thither did the tribes go up, *even* the tribes of the Lord : the testimony of Israel, to praise the name of the Lord.

"*Illuc ... tribus.*" For to thee, according to the promise,
will the numerous tribes go up.——"*Testimonium Israel.*"
This is understood of the law by which the Israelites were
obliged to go up at certain fixed periods to worship God in the

---

[1] "*Ejus.*" Here redundant, as is common in Hebrew.

Temple; but on applying it to heaven, it has reference to the souls of the just, who will ascend thither to be solely occupied in praising the Lord.

5. Quia illic sederunt sedes in judicio : sedes super domum David.

For there are the set seats of judgment : the seats over the house of David.

For there shall be the supreme tribunal of justice, and the throne of the kingdom given to the house of David.

6. Rogate quæ ad pacem sunt Jerusalem : et abundantia diligentibus te :

Pray ye for the things that are for the peace of Jerusalem : and plenteousness be to them that love thee.

Pray for the prosperity of Jerusalem. May those who love thee, O holy city, possess in thee the abundance of every good.

7. Fiat pax in virtute tua : et abundantia in turribus tuis.

Let peace be in thy strength : and plenteousness in thy towers.

8. Propter fratres meos, et proximos meos : loquebar pacem de te :

For my brethren and companions' sake : I spake peace concerning thee.

The hope of seeing myself united to my brethren and my friends causes me to speak of the peace enjoyed within thee.

9. Propter domum Domini Dei nostri : quæsivi bona tibi.

Because of the house of the Lord our God : I have sought good things for thee.

And because thou art the house of the Lord our God, I desire for thee an abundance of every good.

PSALM CXXII.

THE people of Israel pray to the Lord to deliver them from the captivity of Babylon. In like manner does the Church, in her persecutions, implore deliverance from God.

A Song of Degrees.

1. Ad te levavi oculos meos : qui habitas in cœlis.

Unto Thee have I lifted up mine eyes : O Thou that dwellest in the heavens.

2. Ecce sicut oculi servorum : in manibus dominorum suorum,[1]

Behold, as the eyes of servants : are on the hands of their masters ;

---

[1] " *In manibus.*" Here and in verse 3, S. Jerome translates : *Ad manum.* Bellarmine thus explains the simile : As servants or slaves when being beaten by their masters, in sadness and fear keep their eyes on the hand of those who are chastising them, as though by their very look begging them to have pity and to cease from striking them, so our eyes, &c.—— Tirinus explains otherwise : Servants look to the hand of their masters to experience their liberality and help.

3. Sicut oculi ancillæ in manibus dominæ suæ : ita oculi nostri ad Dominum Deum nostrum donec misereatur nostri.

As the eyes of the maiden are on the hands of her mistress: so are our eyes unto the Lord our God, until He have mercy upon us.

4. Miserere nostri Domine, miserere nostri : quia multum repleti sumus despectione.

Have mercy upon us, O Lord, have mercy upon us : for we are greatly filled with contempt.

5. Quia multum repleta est anima nostra : opprobrium abundantibus, et despectio superbis.

Yea, our soul is greatly filled : *us* a reproach unto the rich, and a contempt unto the proud.

"*Multum . . . est.*" Is overwhelmed with such like contempts.

PSALM CXXIII.

A THANKSGIVING of the Jews to God, after their deliverance from the captivity of Babylon. This Psalm is also very suitable to a soul delivered by God from some temptation.

A Song of Degrees.

1. Nisi quia Dominus erat in nobis, dicat nunc Israel : nisi quia Dominus erat in nobis,

If the Lord had not been with us, now may Israel say : If the Lord had not been with us,

2. Cum exurgerent homines in nos : forte vivos deglutissent nos.

When men rose up against us : peradventure they had swallowed us up alive.

Confess now, O Israel : If the Lord, &c.

3. Cum irasceretur furor eorum in nos : forsitan aqua absorbuisset nos :

When their fury was enkindled against us : perchance the waters had swallowed us up.

"*Aqua.*" That is, this their rage like to a torrent of water.

4. Torrentem pertransivit anima nostra : forsitan pertransisset anima nostra aquam intolerabilem.

Our soul hath passed through a torrent : peradventure our soul would have passed through overwhelming waters.

We have passed, happily, through that torrent ; but without the assistance of God we could never have passed through so great a flood.

5. Benedictus Dominus : qui non dedit nos in captionem dentibus eorum.

Blessed be the Lord : Who hath not given us up to be a prey unto their teeth.

6. Anima nostra sicut passer erepta est : de laqueo venantium :

Our soul hath been delivered : as a sparrow out of the snare of the fowlers.

7. Laqueus contritus est : et nos liberati sumus.

The snare is broken : and we are delivered.

29

8. Adjutorium nostrum in nomine Domini : qui fecit cœlum et terram.

Our help is in the name of the Lord : Who hath made heaven and earth.

The help has come to us from, &c.

PSALM CXXIV.

THE Psalmist gives the Jews, now released from captivity, assurance that God will never fail to assist them against their enemies, as long as they trust in Him.

A Song of Degrees.

1. Qui confidunt in Domino, sicut mons Sion : non commovebitur in æternum, qui habitat in Jerusalem.

They that trust in the Lord shall be as Mount Sion : he shall not be moved for ever that dwelleth in Jerusalem.

"*Sicut mons Sion.*" Shall remain firm as Mount Sion.——
"*Non commovebitur . . .*" Whosoever dwells in Jerusalem shall never be disturbed by his enemies.

2. Montes in circuitu ejus : et Dominus in circuitu populi sui, ex hoc nunc, et usque in sæculum.

The hills stand round about her : even so is the Lord round about His people from this time forth for evermore.

The city shall be defended by the mountains that surround it, and His people shall ever be protected by the Lord, Who will stand round about them.

3. Quia non relinquet Dominus virgam peccatorum super sortem justorum : ut non extendant justi ad iniquitatem manus suas.

For the Lord will not leave the rod of sinners over the lot of the just : that the just may not stretch forth their hands unto wickedness.

For God will not suffer sinners to bear sway over the inheritance of the just, lest the just stretch out their hands to evil deeds.

4. Benefac Domine bonis : et rectis corde.

Do well, O Lord, unto those that are good : and unto them that are right of heart.

"*Benefac.*" Replenish with good things.

5. Declinantes autem obligationes, adducet Dominus cum operantibus iniquitatem : pax super Israel.[1]

But such as turn aside unto deceits the Lord shall number with the workers of iniquity : but peace shall be upon Israel.

[1] "*Obligationes.*" According to Bellarmine, in the Hebrew and Greek, as also it is in the Chaldee : *Obliquitates, Tortuositates :* Crooked ways. S. Jerome has : *Pravitates suas.*

On the other hand, the Lord will treat those who fail in their duties as He treats the wicked ; but Israel shall always enjoy peace.

PSALM CXXV.

THE sighs of the Jews for release from the captivity of Babylon. This Psalm may be of service to sinners who wish to be delivered from the slavery of sin, and to the just who sigh for the end of their exile here on earth.

A Song of Degrees.

1. In convertendo Dominus captivitatem Sion: facti sumus sicut consolati.

When the Lord turned again the captivity of Sion: we became like men consoled.

S. Jerome translates according to the Hebrew text : *Cum converteret Dominus captivitatem Sion, facti sumus quasi somniantes;* and the verse is explained thus : When the Lord shall bring forth Sion, that is, His people, from captivity, we, beholding ourselves freed, shall be filled with so great consolation, that we shall seem to be in a dream.

2. Tunc repletum est gaudio os nostrum : et lingua nostra exultatione.

Then was our mouth filled with gladness : and our tongue with joy.

Then we shall be so full of joy that our tongue will break forth in canticles of gladness.

3. Tunc dicent inter Gentes : Magnificavit Dominus facere cum eis.

Then shall they say among the Gentiles : The Lord hath done great things for them.

4. Magnificavit Dominus facere nobiscum : facti sumus lætantes.

The Lord hath done great things for us : we are become joyful.

And we, too, shall say : The Lord hath wrought great things in our behalf, and for this cause we thus rejoice.

5. Converte Domine captivitatem nostram : sicut torrens in Austro.

Turn again our captivity, O Lord : as a river in the South.

Deliver us, then, O Lord, from our captivity, and grant that we may be consoled, as those are consoled who dwell in the region of the South when there comes to them an abundance of water.[1]

[1] Others, with Bellarmine, explain the verse differently. Grant that we return from exile in full numbers and with speed, as a torrent that carries everything with it, when under the influence of the South wind it is filled with rains and the melted snow.

6. Qui seminant in lacrymis : in exultatione metent.

They that sow in tears : shall reap in joy.

" *Qui seminant.*" Thus those who now sow.

7. Euntes ibant et flebant : mittentes semina sua.

They went forth on their way and wept : scattering their seed.

8. Venientes autem venient cum exultatione : portantes manipulos suos.

But returning, they shall come with joy : carrying their sheaves with them.

VESPERS FOR WEDNESDAY.

PSALM CXXVI.

THE Jews, on their return from Babylon, wish to rebuild the city of Jerusalem and the Temple, but are hindered by the incursions of their enemies; the Psalmist exhorts them to trust in God.

A Song of Degrees of Solomon.

1. Nisi dominus ædificaverit domum; in vanum laboraverunt qui ædificant eam.

Unless the Lord build the house: they labour in vain that build it.

2. Nisi Dominus custodierit civitatem: frustra vigilat qui custodit eam.

Unless the Lord keep the city: he watcheth in vain that keepeth it.

3. Vanum est vobis ante lucem surgere: surgite postquam sederitis, qui manducatis panem doloris.

In vain do ye rise before the light: rise not till ye have rested, O ye that eat the bread of sorrow.

In vain do you rise before daybreak, if God does not come to your aid ; moreover, you ought not to rise until you have taken your repose, since you have eaten the bread of sorrow, that is, you have lived in the midst of such great evils.

4. Cum dederit dilectis suis somnum: ecce hereditas Domini filii: merces, fructus ventris.

When He hath given sleep to His beloved : Lo, children are an heritage from the Lord ; and the fruit of the womb a reward.

" Cum dederit ... somnum." After the Lord shall have given to His beloved, that is, to His people, sleep, viz., peace by means of the promised Redeemer.——" Ecce ... filii." Then shall appear the inheritance of Jesus Christ the Lord, an inheritance which shall consist in the multitude of the children born in His Church according to the prophecy : " Ask of Me, and I will give Thee the Gentiles for Thine inheritance (Ps. ii. 8).——" Merces, fructus ventris." The recom-

pense of Christ the Lord shall be the fruit of the womb, that
is, these same children shall be the recompense of Jesus Christ
according to another prophecy : " If He shall lay down His
life for sin, He shall see a long-lived seed " (*Is.* liii. 10). This
is well expressed in the Greek version in this sense : The
multitude of children shall be the inheritance of the Lord,
and the recompense of Jesus Christ, Who was properly the
fruit of Mary's womb.

5. Sicut sagittæ in manu potentis: ita filii excussorum.	Like as arrows in the hand of the mighty One : so are the children of those that have been cast out.

These children, tormented by persecutions, shall be against
their enemies as so many arrows in the hand of a strong man.

6. Beatus vir qui implevit desiderium suum ex ipsis : non confundetur cum loquetur inimicis suis in porta.	Blessed is the man whose desire is satisfied with them : he shall not be confounded when he speaketh with his enemies in the gate.

Blessed is the man who shall see his desire satisfied by the
birth of so many children ; he shall not suffer confusion when
he shall have to treat with his enemies before the gate of the
city,[1] that is, according to Bellarmine, at the last judgment,
which shall take place at the great gate, or at the assize of the
whole world, when Jesus Christ shall confound the demons,
who thought to drag the entire human race down to hell.

PSALM CXXVII.

THE Psalmist announces to the Jews, after their return from
Babylon, the blessings which they will receive from God, if
they keep His laws. These blessings, being temporal, belong,
properly speaking, to the just under the Old Law.

A Song of Degrees.

1. Beati omnes, qui timent Dominum : qui ambulant in viis ejus.	Blessed are all they that fear the Lord : that walk in His ways.

"*In viis ejus.*"   In the way of His commandments.

2. Labores manuum tuarum quia manducabis : beatus es, et bene tibi erit.	For thou shalt eat the labours of thy hands : blessed art thou, and it shall be well with thee.

The labours of thy hands shall be blessed, for thou shalt

---

[1] See *Ps.* lxviii. 14.

taste of their fruits ; thou shalt be happy and rest well con-
tented with them.

3. Uxor tua sicut vitis abundans :
in lateribus domus tuæ.[1]

Thy wife shall be as a fruitful vine :
on the walls of thy house.

Thy wife, living retired in her house, shall be fruitful in
children as a vine abundant with grapes.

4. Filii tui sicut novellæ olivarum:
in circuitu mensæ tuæ.

Thy children as olive plants :
round about thy table.

5. Ecce sic benedicetur homo : qui
timet Dominum.

Behold, thus shall the man be
blessed : that feareth the Lord.

6. Benedicat tibi Dominus ex
Sion : et videas bona Jerusalem
omnibus diebus vitæ tuæ.

May the Lord bless thee out of
Sion : and mayest thou see the good
things of Jerusalem all the days of
thy life.

"*Ex Sion.*" From Mount Sion, that is, from heaven.

7. Et videas filios filiorum tuorum : pacem super Israel.

Mayest thou see thy children's
children : and peace upon Israel.

"*Pacem . . .*" And a lasting peace in Israel.

PSALM CXXVIII.

MANY interpreters refer this Psalm to the time when the
Jews, freed from captivity, strove to rebuild Jerusalem. The
Psalmist exhorts the people to put their trust in the Lord,
Who had already delivered them from their past evils.

A Song of Degrees.

1. Sæpe expugnaverunt me a juventute mea : dicat nunc Israel.

Many a time have they fought
against me from my youth up : let
Israel now say.

The Psalmist makes the people of Israel speak, and say :
Many times from my youth up have I been combatted by my
enemies.

2. Sæpe expugnaverunt me a juventute mea : etenim non potuerunt
mihi.[2]

Many a time have they fought
against me from my youth up : but
they could not prevail against me.

3. Supra dorsum meum fabricaverunt peccatores : prolongaverunt
iniquitatem suam.

The wicked have wrought upon
my back : they have prolonged their
iniquity.

---

[1] "*In lateribus.*" S. Jerome translates : *In penetralibus* : In the inner part.

[2] "*Etenim.*" S. Jerome translates : *Sed :* But.

"*Fabricaverunt.*" According to the Hebrew, this word signifies properly the repeated strokes dealt by the smith on the anvil ; hence the more precise meaning would be : Sinners have struck on my back with repeated blows, and have prolonged their persecutions.

4. Dominus justus concidit cervices peccatorum : confundantur et convertantur retrorsum omnes qui oderunt Sion.

The just Lord hath hewn asunder the necks of sinners: let them all be confounded and turned back that have hated Sion.

"*Cervices.*" Their heads, that is, their pride.——"*Sion.*" The people of Israel.

5. Fiant sicut fœnum tectorum : quod priusquam evellatur, exaruit :

Let them be as grass upon the house-tops : which withereth before it be plucked up.

"*Fiant ... tectorum.*" Let them become as the grass which grows on the roofs of houses, &c.

6. De quo non implevit manum suam qui metit : et sinum suum qui manipulos colligit.

Wherewith the mower filleth not his hand : nor he that gathereth the sheaves, his bosom.

Of which grass the mower finds not enough wherewith to fill his hand, nor gathers sheaves sufficient to fill his bosom.

7. Et non dixerunt qui præteribant : Benedictio Domini super vos : benediximus vobis in nomine Domini.

And they that pass by say not : The blessing of the Lord be upon you : we have blessed you in the name of the Lord.

"*Non dixerunt.*" Say not to such mowers.

PSALM CXXIX.

In this Psalm the Jews are represented as not yet set free from the captivity of Babylon. This Psalm is suitable to every sinner who, groaning under the weight of his sins, implores aid from God.[1]

A Song of Degrees.

1. De profundis clamavi ad te Domine : Domine exaudi vocem meam.

Out of the depths have I cried unto Thee, O Lord : Lord, hear my voice.

[1] The Sixth Penitential Psalm.

O Lord, from the deep abyss of my miseries I cry out to Thee : Lord, hear my prayer.

2. Fiant aures tuæ intendentes: O let Thine ears consider well : the voice of my supplication.
in vocem deprecationis meæ.

Ah, do Thou, for pity's sake, graciously incline Thine ears to hearken to the voice of my supplication.

3. Si iniquitates observaveris Domine: Domine quis sustinebit? If Thou, O Lord, wilt mark iniquities : Lord, who shall abide it ?

If, O Lord, Thou dost set Thyself to take a strict account of my iniquities, who will be able to endure it ?

4. Quia apud te propitiatio est: et propter legem tuam sustinui te Domine. For with Thee there is merciful forgiveness : and because of Thy law, I have waited for Thee, O Lord.

But Thy mercy gives me courage, for in Thee there is an exhaustless fountain of compassion and goodness ; and what causes me to hope in Thee is, that Thou makest it a law to have pity on every sinner who in humility seeks Thy pardon.

5. Sustinuit anima mea in verbo ejus : speravit anima mea in Domino. My soul hath waited on His word : my soul hath hoped in the Lord.

My soul awaits the mercy of God, relying on His promise ; thus having hoped in the Lord, it will not be confounded.

6. A custodia matutina usque ad noctem : speret Israel in Domino. From the morning watch even until night : let Israel hope in the Lord.

From break of day, even until night, Israel will not cease to trust in the Lord.

7. Quia apud Dominum misericordia : et copiosa apud eum redemptio. For with the Lord there is mercy : and with Him is plenteous redemption.

Here the Psalmist points out the foundation of all our hopes, namely, the Blood of Jesus Christ, by which He was to redeem the human race. He says : For mercy with God is infinite ; and He is well able to redeem us, by abundant helps, from all our evils.

8. Et ipse redimet Israel : ex omnibus iniquitatibus ejus. And He shall redeem Israel : from all his inquities.

Therefore, Himself will redeem His people from all their sins.

PSALM CXXX.

DAVID, complaining that Saul and his followers unjustly
accused him of pride and ambition, calls God to witness
against this calumny.

A Song of Degrees of David.

1. Domine non est exaltatum cor
meum : neque elati sunt oculi mei.

O Lord, my heart is not lifted up :
nor are mine eyes lofty.

"*Domine.*"   O Lord, Thou knowest that.——"*Neque* ..."
Nor have my eyes shown proud looks.

2. Neque ambulavi in magnis :
neque in mirabilibus super me.

Neither have I walked in great
matters ; nor in things too wonderful
for me.

That is, I have not indulged in great thoughts and lofty
conceits, nor such as are above my condition.

3. Si non humiliter sentiebam :
sed exaltavi animam meam.

If I have not been humbly minded :
but have lifted up my soul.

4. Sicut ablactatus est super matre
sua : ita retributio in anima mea.

As a child that is weaned upon his
mother's breast ; so let my reward be
in my soul.

3, 4. If, instead of thinking humbly of myself, I have been
exalted in mind above what was becoming, I am content to be
punished, and treated as a babe that lies wailing on its
mother's breast when deprived of milk.

5. Speret Israel in Domino : ex
hoc nunc, et usque in sæculum.

Let Israel hope in the Lord : from
this time forth for evermore.

Let Israel, then, hope in the Lord always, and never give
way to distrust.

VESPERS FOR THURSDAY.

PSALM CXXXI.

KING SOLOMON prays God to take up His dwelling in the Temple which is prepared for Him, and, at the same time, to perform the promises that the Lord made to David for his descendants. This Psalm is supposed to have been sung when Solomon had the Ark borne into the Temple which he had built.

A Song of Degrees.

1. Memento Domine David : et omnis mansuetudinis ejus.

O Lord, remember David : and all his meekness.

2. Sicut juravit Domino : votum vovit Deo Jacob.

How he sware unto the Lord : and vowed a vow to the God of Jacob.

3. Si introiero in tabernaculum domus meæ : si ascendero in lectum strati mei :

If I shall enter into the tabernacle of my house : if I shall go up into my bed :

4. Si dedero somnum oculis meis : et palpebris meis dormitationem,

If I shall give sleep to mine eyes : or slumber to mine eyelids,

5. Et requiem temporibus meis : donec inveniam locum Domino : tabernaculum Deo Jacob.

Or rest unto the temples of my head : until I find a place for the Lord, a tabernacle for the God of Jacob.

2-5. Whilst the holy Ark was still under a tent, David made to God this vow, which he confirmed with an oath : I promise not to enter into my house, nor to give myself any repose, until I have found a place for my Lord, which may be a dwelling worthy of the God of Jacob.

6. Ecce audivimus eam in Ephrata : invenimus eam in campis silvæ.

Lo, we heard of it in Ephrata : we found it in the fields of the wood.[1]

---

[1] *We heard of it in Ephrata.* When I was young and lived in Bethlehem, otherwise called *Ephrata*, I heard of God's Tabernacle and Ark, and had a devout desire of seeing it ; and accordingly I found it at Cariathurim, the city of the woods, where it was till it was removed to Jerusalem. (See 1 *Par.* xiii.)

We heard that the Ark was in Ephrata ; but, &c.

7. Introibimus in tabernaculum ejus : adorabimus in loco, ubi steterunt pedes ejus.

We will go into His tabernacle : we will worship in the place where His feet have stood.

But now we shall enter with joy into His own Tabernacle ; and we shall adore Him in this holy place, where He has set His feet, that is, where He has begun to dwell.

8. Surge Domine in requiem tuam : tu et arca sanctificationis tuæ.

Arise, O Lord, into Thy resting-place : Thou and the ark of Thy holiness.

Arise, then, O Lord, and enter into the place of Thy repose, and there also shall enter the Ark of Thy sanctification, that is, the Ark through which Thou hast been so much glorified.

9. Sacerdotes tui induantur justitiam : et sancti tui exultent.

Let Thy priests be clothed with justice : and let Thy saints rejoice.

"Justitiam." That is, Sanctity.——*"Et sancti ..."* And all Thy holy ministers serve Thee with gladness.

10. Propter David servum tuum : non avertas faciem Christi tui.

For Thy servant David's sake : turn not away the face of Thine Anointed.

For the love of David, Thy beloved servant, reject not Thy Christ, Who is his Son.

11. Juravit Dominus David veritatem, et non frustrabitur eam : De fructu ventris tui ponam super sedem tuam.

The Lord hath sworn the truth unto David, and He will not make it void : of the fruit of thy body I will set upon thy throne.

The Lord swore to David in truth, and this oath He will not fail to keep : I will place thy children on thy throne.

12. Si custodierint filii tui testamentum meum : et testimonia mea hæc, quæ docebo eos : [1]

If thy children will keep My covenant : and these My testimonies which I shall teach them,

"Testimonia mea." My precepts.

13. Et filii eorum usque in sæculum : sedebunt super sedem tuam.

Their children also shall sit upon thy throne : for evermore.

And if their sons shall do likewise, they in perpetuity shall sit upon this same throne of thine.

14. Quoniam elegit Dominus Sion : elegit eam in habitationem sibi.

For the Lord hath chosen Sion : He hath chosen her for His dwelling.

1 *" Testamentum."* S. Jerome translates : *Pactum :* Covenant.

15. Hæc requies mea in sæculum sæculi: hic habitabo, quoniam elegi eam.

This is My rest for ever and ever: here will I dwell, for I have chosen her.

The Lord, moreover, said : This is, &c.

16. Viduam ejus benedicens benedicam : pauperes ejus saturabo panibus.

With blessing I will bless her widows : I will satisfy her poor with bread.

" *Viduam . . . benedicam.*" Here I will bless the widow by succouring her abundantly.

17. Sacerdotes ejus induam salutari : et sancti ejus exultatione exultabunt.

I will clothe her priests with salvation: and her saints shall rejoice with exceeding joy.

Here I will vest with salvation, that is, I will sanctify, her priests ; and her sacred ministers shall live in joy.

18. Illuc producam cornu David : paravi lucernam Christo meo.

There will I bring forth a horn unto David : I have prepared a lamp for Mine Anointed.

Here I will cause the power of David to flourish ; for I have prepared a lamp, that is, a brilliant posterity, for This My Christ.

19. Inimicos ejus induam confusione : super ipsum autem efflorebit sanctificatio mea.

His enemies I will clothe with confusion : but upon him shall my sanctification flourish.

" *Sanctificatio mea.*" The sacred crown by which I have sanctified him.

PSALM CXXXII.

THE Psalmist exhorts all the ministers of the Sanctuary to live together in peace, and to praise God with one accord, by praying to Him for the people.

A Song of Degrees of David.

1. Ecce quam bonum, et quam jucundum : habitare fratres in unum.

Behold, how good and how pleasant it is : for brethren to dwell together in unity.

Oh ! how profitable and how sweet it is for brethren to dwell together in perfect union !

2. Sicut unguentum in capite : quod descendit in barbam, barbam Aaron,

Like the precious ointment upon the head : that ran down unto the beard, even the beard of Aaron,

3. Quod descendit in oram vestimenti ejus : sicut ros Hermon, qui descendit in montem Sion.

That ran down to the skirt of his garment : like as the dew of Hermon, that falleth upon Mount Sion.

This union is like the perfumed unguent which poured on the head of Aaron, flowed down by his beard even to the border, the skirt of his vestment ; it is like also to the dew that falls down upon the mountains of Hermon and of Sion, and renders them so fertile.

4. Quoniam illic mandavit Domi- nus benedictionem : et vitam usque in sæculum.　For there hath the Lord ordained blessing : and life for evermore.

Because, where such-like union reigns, God showers down blessings in abundance, and vouchsafes the joy of a life that is eternal.

PSALM CXXXIV.

THE Psalmist exhorts the ministers of the Temple to praise the Lord for His power, which distinguishes Him from the gods of the Gentiles, and to render Him thanks for the benefits He has bestowed upon His people.

Alleluia.

1. Laudate nomen Domini : laudate servi Dominum.　Praise ye the name of the Lord : O ye His servants, praise ye the Lord.

2. Qui statis in domo Domini : in atriis domus Dei nostri.　Ye that stand in the house of the Lord : in the courts of the house of our God.

1, 2. Servants of the Lord, and you His ministers who dwell in His Temple, praise the name of the Lord.

3. Laudate Dominum, quia bonus Dominus : psallite nomini ejus quo- niam suave.　Praise ye the Lord, for the Lord is good : sing ye to His name, for it is sweet.

" *Quia bonus.*"　For He is goodness itself.——" *Psallite . . .*" Extol the glories of His name, for it is sweet on account of the blessings which He pours on His creatures.

4. Quoniam Jacob elegit sibi Dominus : Israel in possessionem sibi.　For the Lord hath chosen Jacob unto Himself : and Israel for His own possession.

" *Jacob . . . Israel.*"　That is, the children of Israel.

5. Quia ego cognovi quod magnus est Dominus : et Deus noster præ omnibus diis.　For I know that the Lord is great : and our God is above all gods.

" *Ego cognovi.*"　Yea, right well do I know.——" *Omnibus diis.*"　All the other gods of the Gentiles.

6. Omnia quæcumque voluit, Dominus fecit in cœlo, et in terra : in mari, et in omnibus abyssis.

Whatsoever the Lord pleased He hath done, in heaven, and in earth : in the sea, and in all the deeps.

7. Educens nubes ab extremo terræ : fulgura in pluviam fecit.

He bringeth up clouds from the ends of the earth : He hath made lightnings for the rain.

He gathers the clouds from the extremity of the earth.——
" Fulgura . . ." From the storms, which send forth lightnings,
He forms showers to water the land.

8. Qui producit ventos de thesauris suis : qui percussit primogenita Ægypti ab homine usque ad pecus.

He bringeth the winds out of His treasures : He slew the first-born of Egypt, from man even unto beast.

He makes the winds issue forth from the places, where He
keeps them stored as in a treasure-house, to make use of them
when He wills ; He it is Who, in Egypt, struck with death
the first-born of men and of beasts.

9. Et misit signa, et prodigia in medio tui, Ægypte : in Pharaonem, et in omnes servos ejus.

He sent forth signs and wonders in the midst of thee, O Egypt : upon Pharao and all his servants.

" In Pharaonem . . ." When he willed to punish Pharao,
&c.

10. Qui percussit gentes multas : et occidit reges fortes :

He smote many nations : and slew mighty kings :

11. Sehon regem Amorrhæorum, et Og regem Basan : et omnia regna Chanaan.

Sehon, king of the Amorrhites, and Og, the king of Basan : and all the kingdoms of Chanaan :

10, 11. He it was, moreover, that brought low many nations,
and made kings to die, (" Fortes ") who gloried greatly in their
power and strength : even Sehon, &c.——" Et omnia . . ."
And all the other rulers of the Chanaanites.

12. Et dedit terram eorum hereditatem : hereditatem Israel populo suo.

And gave their land for an inheritance : for an inheritance unto His people Israel.

13. Domine, nomen tuum in æternum : Domine memoriale tuum in generationem et generationem.

Thy name, O Lord, is for ever : Thy memorial, O Lord, unto all generations.

" Nomen tuum." The glory of Thy name.——" Memoriale
tuum." The memory of Thee.

14. Quia judicabit Dominus populum suum : et in servis suis deprecabitur.

For the Lord will judge His people: and will be entreated for His servants.

" Judicabit." That is : With a just judgment, in punishing
the persecutors of His people.——" Deprecabitur." Bellarmine

says that this verb must be taken in a passive sense: that is :
Exorabitur. He will be favourably entreated : He will deal
in mercy with His servants, by showing Himself prompt to
hear and answer their prayers.[1]

15. Simulacra Gentium argentum, et aurum : opera manum hominum.	The idols of the Gentiles are silver and gold : the work of men's hands.

The idols of the Gentiles have no power at all,[2] since they
are but silver and gold, the works of the very men who adore
them.

16. Os habent, et non loquentur : oculos habent, et non videbunt.	They have a mouth, but they speak not : eyes have they, but they do not see.

17. Aures habent, et non audient : neque enim est spiritus in ore ipsorum.	Ears have they, but they hear not : neither is there any breath in their mouths.

" *Neque enim . . .*" Nor do they show any sign of life in
their face.

18. Similes illis fiant qui faciunt ea : et omnes, qui confidunt in eis.	Let them that make them be like unto them : and every one that trusteth in them.

19. Domus Israel benedicite Domino : domus Aaron benedicite Domino.	Bless the Lord, O house of Israel : bless the Lord, O house of Aaron.

" *Domus Israel.*" The family or people of Israel.

20. Domus Levi benedicite Domino : qui timetis Dominum, benedicite Domino.	Bless the Lord, O house of Levi : ye that fear the Lord, bless the Lord.

" *Qui timetis Dominum.*" All you who have His holy fear.

21. Benedictus Dominus ex Sion : qui habitat in Jerusalem.	Blessed be the Lord out of Sion : Who dwelleth in Jerusalem.

Blessed, in fine, be the Lord Who dwells in Jerusalem, and
Who pours forth His graces upon us from Mount Sion.

PSALM CXXXV.

THE Psalmist exhorts the Jews to thank God for all the
benefits that He has bestowed upon men, and especially upon
His own people.

---

[1] *Canticle of Moses, v.* 52 (Lauds for Saturday).　　　　[2] *Ps.* cxiii. 12-16.

Alleluia.

1. Confitemini Domino quoniam bonus : quoniam in æternum misericordia ejus.

O praise the Lord, for He is good : for His mercy endureth for ever.

" *Confitemini Domino.*"   Render thanks to the Lord.

2. Confitemini Deo deorum : quoniam in æternum misericordia ejus.

Praise ye the God of gods : for His mercy endureth for ever.

" *Deo deorum.*"   The true God of false gods.[1]

3. Confitemini Domino dominorum : quoniam in æternum misericordia ejus.

Praise ye the Lord of lords : for His mercy endureth for ever.[2]

4. Qui facit mirabilia magna solus : quoniam in æternum misericordia ejus.

Who alone doeth great wonders : for His mercy endureth for ever.

5. Qui fecit cœlos in intellectu : quoniam in æternum misericordia ejus.

Who made the heavens in understanding : for His mercy endureth for ever.

" *In intellectu.*"   With wisdom.

6. Qui firmavit terram super aquas : quoniam in æternum misericordia ejus.

Who established the earth above the waters : for His mercy endureth for ever.

7. Qui fecit luminaria magna : quoniam in æternum misericordia ejus.

Who made the great lights : for His mercy endureth for ever.

" *Luminaria magna.*"   The great luminaries to light up the world.

8. Solem in potestatem diei : quoniam in æternum misericordia ejus.

The sun to rule the day : for His mercy endureth for ever.

9. Lunam et stellas in potestatem noctis : quoniam in æternum misericordia ejus.

The moon and the stars to rule the night : for His mercy endureth for ever.

10. Qui percussit Ægyptum cum primogenitis eorum : quoniam in æternum misericordia ejus.

Who smote Egypt with their firstborn : for His mercy endureth for ever.

11. Qui eduxit Israel de medio eorum : quoniam in æternum misericordia ejus.

Who brought out Israel from among them : for His mercy endureth for ever.

" *Eorum.*"   The Egyptians.

12. In manu potenti, et brachio excelso : quoniam in æternum misericordia ejus.

With a mighty hand and with a stretched-out arm : for His mercy endureth for ever.

[1] And of all such as are called gods by any title whatsoever. See *Ps.* xlix. 1, lxxxi. 1.

[2] By this invitation to praise the Lord, thrice repeated, we profess the Blessed Trinity, One God in Three distinct Persons, the Father, and the Son, and the Holy Ghost.

30

He hath brought them forth with His powerful hand, and " *Brachio excelso* : " With His invincible arm.

13. Qui divisit mare Rubrum in divisiones : quoniam in æternum misericordia ejus.

Who divided the Red Sea into two parts : for His mercy endureth for ever.

14. Et eduxit Israel per medium ejus : quoniam in æternum misericordia ejus.

And brought out Israel through the midst thereof: for His mercy endureth for ever.

15. Et excussit Pharaonem, et virtutem ejus in mari Rubro : quoniam in æternum misericordia ejus.

And overthrew Pharao and his host in the Red Sea : for His mercy endureth for ever.

16. Qui traduxit populum suum per desertum : quoniam in æternum misericordia ejus.

Who led His people through the desert : for His mercy endureth for ever.

17. Qui percussit reges magnos : quoniam in æternum misericordia ejus.

Who smote great kings ; for His mercy endureth for ever.

18. Et occidit reges fortes : quoniam in æternum misericordia ejus.

And slew mighty kings : for His mercy endureth for ever.

19. Sehon regem Amorrhæorum : quoniam in æternum misericordia ejus.

Sehon king of the Amorrhites : for His mercy endureth for ever.

20. Et Og regem Basan : quoniam in æternum misericordia ejus.

And Og the king of Basan : for His mercy endureth for ever.

21. Et dedit terram eorum hereditatem : quoniam in æternum misericordia ejus.

And He gave their land for an inheritance : for His mercy endureth for ever.

22. Hereditatem Israel servo suo : quoniam in æternum misericordia ejus.

For an inheritance unto His servant Israel : for His mercy endureth for ever.

23. Quia in humilitate nostra memor fuit nostri : quoniam in æternum misericordia ejus.

For He was mindful of us in our affliction : for His mercy endureth for ever.

24. Et redemit nos ab inimicis nostris : quoniam in æternum misericordia ejus.

And He redeemed us from our enemies : for His mercy endureth for ever.

25. Qui dat escam omni carni : quoniam in æternum misericordia ejus.

Who giveth food to all flesh : for His mercy endureth for ever.

" *Omni carni*." All men and beasts.

26. Confitemini Deo cœli : quoniam in æternam misericordia ejus.

Give glory to the God of heaven : for His mercy endureth for ever.

Render thanks, therefore, &c.

27. Confitemini Domino dominorum : quoniam in æternum misericordia ejus.

Give glory to the Lord of lords : for His mercy endureth for ever.

Praise the Lord of lords, for He is ever merciful.

PSALM CXXXVI.

THE Jews, in the captivity of Babylon, bewail their miseries, and sigh for their return to Jerusalem. This Psalm is suitable for a Christian soul that mourns in this exile here below, and ardently desires to go to its heavenly country.

A Psalm of David, for Jeremias.[1]

1. Super flumina Babylonis, illic sedimus et flevimus : cum recordaremur Sion:

By the rivers of Babylon, there we sat and wept: when we remembered Sion :

On the banks of the rivers of Babylon we sat down, o'erpressed with sadness, and wept as we remembered thee, O Sion.

2. In salicibus in medio ejus : suspendimus organa nostra.

On the willows in the midst thereof : we hung up our harps.

" *Organa nostra.*" All instruments of music.

3. Quia illic interrogaverunt nos, qui captivos duxerunt nos : verba cantionum.

For there they that led us into captivity : required of us the words of our songs.

" *Interrogaverunt nos verba cantionum.*" Asked us to sing.

4. Et qui abduxerunt nos : Hymnum cantate nobis de canticis Sion.

And they that carried us away, said : Sing to us a hymn of the songs of Sion.

" *Hymnum* ... " Sing us one of those hymns, which you were used to sing in Sion.

5. Quomodo cantabimus canticum Domini : in terra aliena ?

How shall we sing the song of the Lord : in a strange land ?

But we made reply : How, &c.

6. Si oblitus fuero tui Jerusalem : oblivioni detur dextera mea.

If I forget thee, O Jerusalem : let my right hand be forgotten.

If ever I forget thee, O Jerusalem, in this bondage, where I now am, may my right hand become helpless.

7. Adhæreat lingua mea faucibus meis: si non meminero tui :

Let my tongue cleave to my jaws : if I do not remember thee :

8. Si non proposuero Jerusalem : in principio lætitiæ meæ.

If I make not Jerusalem : the beginning of my joy.

---

[1] *For Jeremias.* For the time of Jeremias and the captivity of Babylon ——If this Psalm, according to the title, was written by David, it is a prophecy. Calmet, however, says that in the Hebrew text and the Chaldee version it never had any title.

7, 8. May my tongue be dried up and cleave to the roof of my mouth, if I fail to be ever mindful of thee, O Jerusalem. May it so happen to me if I do not make Jerusalem the beginning of all my joy, that is, if I ever give myself to joy whilst I am afar from my country and fatherland.

9. Memor esto Domine filiorum Edom : in die Jerusalem.

Remember, O Lord, the children of Edom : in the day of Jerusalem.

10. Qui dicunt : Exinanite, exinanite : usque ad fundamentum in ea.

Who say, Down with it, down with it : even to the foundation thereof.

9, 10. Bear in mind, O Lord, the barbarity which the Edomites showed on the day when they took Jerusalem, and said : Destroy it, destroy it even to its foundations.

11. Filia Babylonis misera : beatus, qui retribuet tibi retributionem tuam, quam retribuisti nobis.

O miserable daughter of Babylon : blessed shall he be who shall repay thee the payment which thou hast paid to us.

12. Beatus, qui tenebit : et allidet parvulos tuos ad petram.

Blessed shall he be that shall take : and dash thy little ones against the rock.[1]

11, 12. O miserable Babylon ! blessed is he who shall pay back to thee those evils which thou hast brought upon us. Blessed is he who shall take thy little ones in his hands, and shall dash them to death against a rock.

[1] In the spiritual sense, we dash the little ones of Babylon against the rock, when we mortify our passions, and stifle their first movements, by a speedy recourse to the Rock, which is Christ.

VESPERS FOR FRIDAY.

PSALM CXXXVII.

DAVID thanks God for having heard his prayers, by delivering him from persecution.[1]

For David himself.

1. Confitebor tibi Domine in toto corde meo: quoniam audisti verba oris mei.	I will praise Thee, O Lord, with my whole heart: for Thou hast heard the words of my mouth.

I will ever give thanks to Thee, O Lord, with my whole heart, because Thou hast graciously hearkened to my supplications.

2. In conspectu Angelorum psallam tibi: adorabo ad templum sanctum tuum, et confitebor nomini tuo.	I will sing praise unto Thee in the sight of the Angels: I will worship towards Thy holy Temple, and give glory unto Thy Name.
3. Super misericordia tua, et veritate tua: quoniam magnificasti super omne, nomen sanctum tuum.	For Thy mercy, and for Thy truth: for Thou hast magnified Thy holy Name above all.

I will praise Thy mercy and Thy faithfulness to Thy promises, because Thou hast made known how great above everything else is Thy holy Name.[2]

---

[1] This Psalm, in the mystical sense, according to the Holy Fathers, celebrates the victories of Jesus Christ and His Church, and on that account, no doubt, was chosen for the Vespers of the Feasts of the Most Holy Redeemer and the Sacred Heart of Jesus.

[2] It is agreed on all hands that " *Sanctum tuum* " is to be taken as a substantive. In the Hebrew it is : *Verbum tuum :* Thy Word. In the Greek it is : Thy Holy, in the neuter, as expressed in the words of Gabriel to Mary. (*Luke* i. 35.) This, which accords with the Vulgate, was the rendering of S. Hilary, S. Augustine, S. Chrysostom, Theodoret, and other Fathers in their commentaries. According to Bellarmine, it is to be reconciled with the Hebrew by understanding " *Sanctum tuum* " to mean the Son of God, our Lord Jesus Christ ; and this S. Jerome himself says. (*In Epist. ad Suniam et Fretellam.*) Bellarmine thus paraphrases the passage : With my whole heart

4. In quacumque die invocavero te, exaudi me : multiplicabis in anima mea virtutem.

In what day soever I shall call upon Thee, hear Thou me : Thou shalt multiply strength in my soul.

O Lord, in whatsoever day I shall call upon Thee, hear me speedily, by manifold augmenting in me the strength which I need to be able to serve Thee always.

5. Confiteantur tibi Domine omnes reges terræ : quia audierunt omnia verba oris tui.

Let all the kings of the earth give glory unto Thee, O Lord : for they have heard all the words of Thy mouth.

" *Quia audierunt ...* " For they have been instructed in all the words which Thou hast said, and Thou hast brought them to pass.

6. Et cantent in viis Domini : quoniam magna est gloria Domini.

And let them sing in the ways of the Lord : for great is the glory of the Lord.

And let them praise the ways pursued by the Lord, for very great is His glory in fulfilling all His divine counsels.

7. Quoniam excelsus Dominus, et humilia respicit : et alta a longe cognoscit.

For the Lord is high, and looketh on the lowly : and the lofty He knoweth afar off.

Let them say that the Lord is most high above all, and yet that He does not disdain to look with gracious favour on things that are mean and low, that is, on the humble ; whilst He knows from afar off the things that are lofty, that is, He holds Himself aloof from the proud, and despises them.

8. Si ambulavero in medio tribulationis vivificabis me : et super iram inimicorum meorum extendisti manum tuam, et salvum me fecit dextera tua.

If I shall walk in the midst of tribulation, Thou wilt quicken me : and Thou hast stretched forth Thy hand against the wrath of mine enemies, and Thy right hand hath saved me.

If I find myself in the midst of tribulations, Thou wilt give me strength to bear them in peace ; when my enemies advanced upon me in rage, Thou didst stretch forth Thy hand, and it saved me.

9. Dominus retribuet pro me : Domine misericordia tua in sæculum : opera manuum tuarum ne despicias.

The Lord will repay for me : Thy mercy, O Lord, endureth for ever : O despise not the works of Thy hands.

will I praise Thee for this Thy great mercy and Thy faithfulness, whereby, as Thou didst promise to our Fathers, taking pity on mankind, Thou hast *magnified* Thy Christ, Who is *Thy Word*, and *Thy Holy One*, above every name, because Thou hast given Him a name which is above every name.—— According to the Hebrew it is : *Super omne nomen tuum* ; Above all Thy name, or every name of Thine. (*Phil.* ii. 9.)

" *Dominus . . . me.*" The Lord will avenge Himself on those who persecute me.——" *Domine . . . sæculum.*" Yea, my Lord, Thy mercy is everlasting.

PSALM CXXXVIII.

THE Psalmist shows us that God knows everything and provides for everything. He seeks, moreover, to induce us to unite ourselves to the just, whom God enriches with blessings, and to detach ourselves from sinners, whom His justice constrains Him to punish.

Unto the end. A Psalm of David.

1. Domine probasti me, et cognovisti me : tu cognovisti sessionem meam, et resurrectionem meam.

Lord, Thou hast proved me, and known me : Thou hast known my sitting down, and my rising up.

Thou hast known perfectly the time when I ought to sit down and when I should rise up, that is, when I should take repose and when I should work ; this, taken in a moral sense, may mean when I should be humbled and when exalted.—— Bellarmine says this verse may well be applied to Jesus Christ, speaking of His death and of His resurrection, as, indeed, the Church does apply it on Easter Sunday in the Introit.

2. Intellexisti cogitationes meas de longe : semitam meam, et funiculum meum investigasti.[1]

Thou hast understood my thoughts afar off : my path and my line hast Thou searched out.

" *Semitam . . . meum.*" The path that I ought to follow, the term at which I ought to arrive.

3. Et omnes vias meas prævidisti : quia non est sermo in lingua mea.

Thou hast foreseen also all my ways : for there is no speech in my tongue.[2]

Thou hast foreseen my ways, that is, my actions, before my tongue has uttered a word to reveal them.

4. Ecce Domine tu cognovisti omnia, novissima, et antiqua : tu formasti me, et posuisti super me manum tuam.

Behold, O Lord, Thou hast known all things, the newest and those of old : Thou hast formed me, and laid Thine hand upon me.

---

[1] " *De longe.*" Long before, from eternity.——" *Funiculum.*" S. Augustine translates : *Limitem.*

[2] Bellarmine says that here should be supplied : *Which Thou hast not foreseen :* that is, Unknown to Thee : or it means, When there is speech in my tongue ; yet my whole interior and my most secret thoughts are known to Thee.

Behold, O Lord, Thou hast known all things that concern me, whether old or new, since Thou hast formed me ; Thou hast busied Thy hands to create me, and make me Thy servant.[1]

5. Mirabilis facta est scientia tua ex me : confortata est, et non potero ad eam.

Thy knowledge is become wonderful unto me : it is high, and I cannot reach unto it.

Thy knowledge is too wonderful for my comprehension.—— "*Ex me.*" A Hebraism, says Bellarmine, for *Super me:* Above, beyond me ; this is explained by the words that follow : "*Confortata...*" That is : Thy knowledge is too high for me to be able to comprehend it.

6. Quo ibo a spiritu tuo ? et quo a facie tua fugiam ?

Whither shall I go from Thy spirit : or whither shall I flee from Thy face ?

"*A spiritu tuo.*" That is : Away from Thy knowledge, Thy ken.——"*A facie tua.*" Away from Thy gaze, so as to be out of Thy sight.

7. Si ascendero in cœlum, tu illic es : si descendero in infernum, ades.

If I ascend into heaven, Thou art there : if I descend into hell, Thou art present.

"*Illic es.*" Thou art already there.——"*Ades.*" There, too, art Thou present ; and this through Thine immensity.

8. Si sumpsero pennas meas dilu-culo : et habitavero in extremis maris :

If I take my wings early in the morning : and dwell in the uttermost parts of the sea,

9. Etenim illuc manus tua deducet me : et tenebit me dextera tua.

Even there also shall Thy hand lead me : and Thy right hand shall hold me.

8, 9. If at morning I take wings, and go to dwell in the farthest bounds of the sea, thence Thy hand will take me, and from it I shall be unable to free myself.

10. Et dixi : Forsitan tenebræ con-culcabunt me : et nox illuminatio mea in deliciis meis.

And I said : Perhaps darkness shall cover me : and night shall be my light in my pleasures.

"*Conculcabunt.*" S. Jerome translates : *Operient.*——"*Et nox...*" According to the Hebrew text : *Et nox lux est circa me:* Night is light around me.——Hence the verse is thus explained : If I should say that perhaps darkness will hide

[1] As Bellarmine explains : After having formed me, Thou hast not aban-doned me ; but Thou hast placed and hast constantly kept Thy hand upon me, to lead, protect, and preserve me ; without which I should have fallen back into nothingness.

me from Thine eyes, night to the eyes of God is not night, but is a light round about me that discovers to Him all my actions.——But, we may also observe, Menochius and Bellarmine explain this passage according to the rendering of the Vulgate, in this sense : If I should hide myself in the darkness of night in order not to be seen, whilst indulging in such shameful pleasures as shun the light of day, still I could not, for all that, withdraw myself from Thy gaze.

11. Quia tenebræ non obscurabuntur a te, et nox sicut dies illuminabitur : sicut tenebræ ejus, ita et lumen ejus.

But darkness shall not be dark to Thee ; and night shall be as light as the day : the darkness and the light thereof shall be alike *to Thee*.

Because darkness is not dark to Thee, since the night to Thee is as clear as the day ; so that Thou seest just the same in the darkness of night as in the light of day.

12. Quia tu possedisti renes meos : suscepisti me de utero matris meæ.

For Thou hast possessed my reins : Thou hast upholden me from my mother's womb.

"*Possedisti renes meos.*" That is : The most inward parts of my body ; and consequently my affections and my desires are in Thy hand.——"*Suscepisti.*" Thou hast protected.

13. Confitebor tibi, quia terribiliter magnificatus es : mirabilia opera tua, et anima mea cognoscit nimis.

I will praise Thee, for Thou art fearfully magnified : wonderful are Thy works, and my soul knoweth them right well.

O Lord, I will praise Thee always, because Thou hast fearfully, that is, by inspiring me with holy awe and reverential fear, made me know Thy greatness in Thy wonderful works, which my soul knows but too well.

14. Non est occultatum os meum a te, quod fecisti in occulto : et substantia mea in inferioribus terræ.

My bone is not hidden from Thee, which Thou hast made in secret : and my substance in the lower parts of the earth.

My bone is not hidden from Thee,[1] and all that Thou hast

---

[1] The text of the Italian is : *Non è nascosta a voi la mia bocca :* My mouth is not, &c. But we do not for a moment believe that this was the rendering intended by the holy Doctor : we hold that it must be an error that crept into the text, by occasion of the equivocal Latin word *Os*, either through inadvertence, and, so to say, a slip of the pen, or through a mistake on the part of some one perhaps employed to copy S. Alphonsus' manuscript, or to carry it through the press ; and that then through oversight this error was reproduced in the subseqent editions. There is, of course, no second opinion as to the word *Os* here in the Vulgate ; that it is *Os*, a bone, and not *Os*, a mouth. This is clear from the Hebrew text : the word there is variously

formed in secret within me, that is, my bowels and bones ; so that all the substance of my body is known to Thee, as is known whatever is hidden in the deepest bowels of the earth.

15. Imperfectum meum viderunt oculi tui, et in libro tuo omnes scribentur : dies formabuntur, et nemo in eis.

Thine eyes did see my imperfect being, and in Thy book all shall be written : the days shall be formed, and no one in them.

Thine eyes have seen what was imperfect in me, namely, my body when it was shapeless,[1] without distinction of members ; for in Thy book, that is, in Thy mind, all men are found written, so that Thou knowest what is to become of them.——The meaning is brought out better by what follows: "*Dies* . . .*"* Which Menochius thus explains : Days shall

---

rendered as *bone, substance, strength,* and *body ;* from the Septuagint, from S. Jerome's translation, and from all modern versions of the Vulgate, including the Italian Paraphrase of Panigarola, and the translation of Martini, as also from the commentaries of S. Augustine, S. Chrysostom, Theodoret, Bellarmine, Menochius, Bossuet, &c., which were all before the eyes of the Saint. We are of opinion, therefore, that the rendering S. Alphonsus intended to give was : *My bone is not hidden from Thee,* literally translating the first words of the Vulgate text ; and then he goes on to explain that what is implied in these words, according to S. Augustine, as hidden from man—all, viz., that was formed secretly within him by God, as his bowels and *bones* (which is drawn from the word *Os*)—is known to God. The mention of *mouth* here would be not only irrelevant, but quite at variance with the sense and context.——" *Os meum,*" or, says Bellarmine, if so we might term it, *Ossatura mea,* the whole system and structure of my bones, their formation and knitting together, what and how many they are. S. Chrysostom speaks also in the same sense.——" *In inferioribus terræ.*" According to the Chaldee : *In utero,* writes Bossuet. Besides the explanation given by the holy Doctor, these words, as Calmet remarks, are very generally explained to mean, metaphorically, the mother's womb. Thus Theodoret : " Everything, says the Psalmist, that relates to me Thou perfectly knowest : for Thou didst form me when yet hidden in my mother's womb, and just as though I were in the remotest part of the earth, Thou didst bring me forth to light. . . . Nothing can be hid from Thee, Who formest the nature of men in the secret workshop of Nature." So also Bellarmine, Menochius, Panigarola, &c.—— Calmet, comparing these words of the Psalmist with those of S. Paul concerning Jesus Christ : " He descended first into the lower parts of the earth " (*in inferiores partes terræ*) (*Eph.* iv. 9), says that some interpret these last of the Blessed Womb of Mary. Estius says that the interpretation of them to signify the descent of Christ from heaven to this earth by His Incarnation, is not rejected by S. Thomas, and is embraced by Cajetan and others. The words of the Angelic Doctor are : According to this interpretation, the Son of God is said to have descended to these parts of this earth in which we live, which we called lower, because below the heaven and the air, not by any local motion, but by the assumption of our lower and earthly nature [through His Incarnation in the Blessed Virgin's womb]. According to what is said by S. Paul : " *Semetipsum exinanivit,* &c., He debased Himself, taking the form of a servant, being made in the likeness of men." (*Philip.* ii. 9.) *Tr.*

[1] " *Imperfectum meum.*" S. Jerome translates : *Informem adhuc me.*

succeed to days, and not one of them shall be missing in Thy book, so as to escape Thy knowledge.

16. Mihi autem nimis honorificati sunt amici tui Deus : nimis confortatus est principatus eorum.

But to me Thy friends, O God, are made exceedingly honourable : their principality is exceedingly strengthened.

To my mind, or, it seems to me that, Thy friends, O Lord, are too much honoured, and their princedom is too highly exalted, since they are called by Thee to enjoy eternal glory, when they shall be made princes of the eternal Kingdom.

17. Dinumerabo eos, et super arenam multiplicabuntur : exurrexi, et adhuc sum tecum.

I will number them, and they shall be multiplied above the sand : I rose up, and am still with Thee.

"*Dinumerabo . . . multiplicabuntur.*" I shall try, then, to count the number of these Thy friends, who will be found more numerous than the sand of the sea.——"*Exurrexi.*" According to the Hebrew : *Evigilavi :* Have wakened from sleep.——"*Adhuc sum tecum.*" That is : I am united to Thee up to the present time, and I hope to continue thus united to the end.

18. Si occideris Deus peccatores : viri sanguinum declinate a me.

If Thou wilt slay the wicked, O God : ye men of blood, depart from me.

19. Quia dicitis in cogitatione : Accipient in vanitate civitates tuas.

Because ye say in thought : They shall receive Thy cities in vain.

18, 19. Seeing, on the other hand, that Thou my God wilt destroy the wicked, I say : Men of blood, depart from me.—— Because you say in your thought, that is, amongst yourselves : In vain, O Lord, will Thy servants occupy the cities which Thou hast given them.

20. Nonne qui oderunt te Domine oderam : et super inimicos tuos tabescebam ?

Have I not hated them, O Lord, that hated Thee ? and pined away because of Thine enemies ?[1]

"*Et super . . .*" And have I not pined away with sorrow, beholding the audacity of Thy enemies ?

21. Perfecto odio oderam illos : et inimici facti sunt mihi.

I have hated them with a perfect hatred : and they became as enemies unto me.

"*Perfecto.*" Utter, entire.

---

[1] *I have hated them.* Not with a hatred of malice, but out of zeal for the observance of God's commandments ; which he saw were despised by the wicked, who are to be considered the enemies of God.

22. Proba me Deus, et scito cor meum : interroga me, et cognosce semitas meas.

Prove me, O God, and know my heart : examine me, and know my paths.

23. Et vide, si via iniquitatis in me est : et deduc me in via æterna.

And see if there be in me the way of iniquity : and lead me in the eternal way.

22, 23. Prove me, my God, and search into all the affections of my heart ; interrogate me, that is, examine me and weigh all my ways, all my actions ; and if Thou seest that I am in the way of iniquity, do Thou lead me into the eternal way, that is, make me to walk by that way which will bring me to the possession of eternal goods.

PSALM CXXXIX.

DAVID implores help from God against Saul, and against those who spoke calumniously of him to that prince.[1]

Unto the end.   A Psalm of David.

1. Eripe me Domine ab homine malo : a viro iniquo eripe me.

Deliver me, O Lord, from the evil man : and rescue me from the unjust man.

2. Qui cogitaverunt iniquitates in corde : tota die constituebant prælia.

Who have devised iniquities in their hearts : all the day long they designed battles.

3. Acuerunt linguas suas sicut serpentis : venenum aspidum sub labiis eorum.

They have sharpened their tongues like serpents : the venom of asps is under their lips.

4. Custodi me Domine de manu peccatoris : et ab hominibus iniquis eripe me.

Keep me, O Lord, from the hand of the wicked : and deliver me from unjust men.

5. Qui cogitaverunt supplantare gressus meos : absconderunt superbi laqueum mihi.

Who are purposed to supplant my steps : the proud have hidden a net for me.

6. Et funes extenderunt in laqueum : juxta iter scandalum posuerunt mihi.

And they have stretched out cords for a snare : they have laid for me a stumbling-block by the wayside.

That is, they use every means in their power to make me fall into their hands.

7. Dixi Domino : Deus meus es tu : exaudi Domine vocem deprecationis meæ.

I said unto the Lord, Thou art my God : hear, O Lord, the voice of my supplication.

[1] This, says Bellarmine, is the opinion of Theodoret and of others ; but also, according to the ancient Fathers, S. Hilary, S. Jerome, S. Augustine, S. Chrysostom, this Psalm is a prayer of the Mystical Body of Jesus Christ against the devil and his abettors. It is doubtless in this sense the Church recites it at Vespers the three last days of Holy Week, as well as in the Office of the Commemoration of the Passion, and in that of the Five Wounds.

8. Domine, Domine virtus salutis meæ : obumbrasti super caput meum in die belli.

O Lord, Lord, the strength of my salvation : Thou hast overshadowed my head in the day of battle.

" *Virtus salutis meæ.*" The sole staff of my salvation.——" *Obumbrasti . . .*" Thou hast covered my head with Thy protection, in my combats.

9. Ne tradas me Domine a desiderio meo peccatori : cogitaverunt contra me, ne derelinquas me, ne forte exaltentur.

Give me not up, O Lord, against my desire to the wicked : they have plotted against me ; do not Thou forsake me, lest they triumph.

" *Ne tradas me . . . peccatori.*" Bellarmine renders these words thus : Suffer me not to be given over by my desire to the wicked, meaning the devil. The verse, then, is explained as follows : O Lord, permit not that, drawn by my concupiscence, I give myself over into the hands of the enemy. These enemies have no other thought than to injure me ; do not Thou abandon me, lest they should boast of having conquered me.

10. Caput circuitus eorum : labor labiorum ipsorum operiet eos.

The head of them compassing me about : the labour of their lips shall overwhelm them.

If Thou dost assist me, the whole force of their wiles, with which they seek to circumvent me in divers ways, and the evil they strive so hard to do me by their calumnies, all this will cover their own selves, by falling back upon them.

11. Cadent super eos carbones, in ignem dejicies eos : in miseriis non subsistent.

Burning coals shall fall upon them : Thou shalt cast them down into the fire : in their miseries they shall not be able to stand.

" *Carbones.*" Burning coals, that is, the afflictions which they devised for me.——" *In miseriis . . .*" Their miseries shall be such that they will not fail to be crushed by them.

12. Vir linguosus non dirigetur in terra : virum injustum mala capient in interitu.

A man full of words shall not be established in the earth : evil shall seize the unjust man unto destruction.

The man who makes an ill use of his tongue to lie, to detract, and to injure his neighbour, will never be able to lead a happy life on earth ; and the evils that shall afflict him, far from making him gain merit by patience, will only serve to sink him deeper in eternal death.

13. Cognovi quia faciet Dominus judicium inopis : et vindictam pauperum.

I know that the Lord will do justice to the needy : and will revenge the poor.

I know that the Lord takes care to protect the needy, and to avenge the wrongs of the poor.

14. Verumtamen justi confitebun- tur nomini tuo: et habitabunt recti cum vultu tuo.

But the just shall give glory to Thy Name: and the upright shall dwell with the light of Thy countenance.

"*Cum vultu tuo.*" That is : In that blessed Kingdom where they shall see Thy beautiful Face.

PSALM CXL.

THE Psalmist here implores the divine protection against his enemies, and prays God to preserve him from such faults as may hinder the effect of his prayer.

A Psalm for David.

1. Domine clamavi ad te, exaudi me : intende voci meæ, cum clama- vero ad te.

I have cried unto Thee, O Lord, hear me : and hearken unto my voice, when I cry unto Thee.

"*Clamavi ad te.*" I have cried to Thee for help.

2. Dirigatur oratio mea sicut incensum in conspectu tuo : elevatio manuum mearum sacrificium vesper- tinum.

Let my prayer be directed as incense in Thy sight : and the lifting up of my hands, as the evening sacri- fice.

May my prayer ascend to Thee, as the smoke of incense rises in Thy sight ; and when I lift my hands to Thee to im- plore Thy succour, may this be acceptable to Thee as the sacrifice that is offered to Thee at evening time.[1]

3. Pone Domine custodiam ori meo : et ostium circumstantiæ labiis meis.

Set a watch, O Lord, before my mouth : and a door round about my lips.

That is : Permit not that any inconsiderate word escape me that could cause Thee displeasure.

4. Non declines cor meum in verba malitiæ : ad excusandas excusationes in peccatis.

Incline not my heart to evil words : to make excuses in sins.

5. Cum hominibus operantibus iniquitatem : et non communicabo cum electis eorum.

With the men that work iniquity : I will have no dealings with the choicest of them.

4, 5. And if perchance through weakness I should offend Thee, suffer me not to speak maliciously by seeking to excuse

[1] Incense was to be burnt on the altar of incense twice each day, at morning and evening (*Exod.* xxx. 7, 8). Two lambs were to be offered like- wise (xxix. 38, 30).

my sins. This is what wicked men do ; but I do not wish to have part with them, nor to share in those disorders which are their chief delight.[1]

6. Corripiet me justus in misericordia, et increpabit me : oleum autem peccatoris non impinguet caput meum.

The just man shall correct me in mercy, and reprove me : but let not the oil of the sinner anoint my head.

That is : I prefer the charitable corrections and reproaches of the just when I go wrong, to the flatteries of the wicked.—— " Oleum . . ." That is : May the flattery of the wicked never be pleasing to me.

7. Quoniam adhuc et oratio mea in beneplacitis eorum : absorpti sunt juncti petræ judices eorum.

For my prayer[2] shall still be against the things that please them : their judges falling on the rock have been swallowed up.

This verse is very obscure : according to S. Chrysostom, it is thus explained : I will not only have no communication with the wicked, but moreover, my prayer to God is ("in beneplacitis eorum") that He will not allow me to find delight in those things that please them ; ("absorpti sunt," &c.) they will perish along with their judges, that is, their chiefs who lead them on to evil ; ("juncti petræ") these indeed have already perished, by striking against the rock which has caused their wreck.

8. Audient verba mea quoniam potuerunt : sicut crassitudo terræ erupta est super terram.

They shall hear my words, for they have prevailed :[3] as when the thickness of the earth is broken up upon the ground :

This verse is also very obscure ; it is thus explained : I hope nevertheless that they will hear my words ; ("quoniam ea verba potuerunt") for they are such as will have power to make them repent ; ("sicut . . . terram") and that as the stubborn hardened earth yields to the spade and is broken up, so their obstinacy will be broken and yield to my persuasions.

[1] "Cum electis." Bellarmine says that this is according to the Hebrew : Cum dulcibus cibis : With their dainties. St. Jerome translates : In deliciis : In their feastings, their pleasures.

[2] For my prayer, &c. So far from coveting their praises, who are never well pleased but with things that are evil, I shall continually pray to be preserved from such things as delight them.

[3] That is they are powerful and will prevail; or, as it is in the Hebrew, for they are sweet, that is, persuasive.

9. Dissipata sunt ossa nostra secus infernum : quia ad te Domine, Domine oculi mei : in te speravi, non auferas animam meam.

Our bones lie scattered nigh unto hell. But on Thee, O Lord, *my* Lord, are mine eyes : in Thee have I put my trust, take not away my soul.

Our bones have been scattered, that is, our strength is weakened, so that we find ourselves as it were on the brink of the grave ; but, O Lord, Lord, my eyes turn to Thee ; in Thee have I put my hopes, give me not up to death.

10. Custodi me a laqueo, quem statuerunt mihi : et a scandalis operantium iniquitatem.

Keep me from the snare, which they have laid for me : and from the stumbling-blocks of them that work iniquity.

11. Cadent in retiaculo ejus peccatores : singulariter sum ego donec transeam.

The wicked shall fall into his net : until I pass hence, I am alone.

These wicked ones shall be caught in the snares which they laid for me ; for myself, I hope to be in an especial manner protected by Thee, until I am out of danger.[1]

PSALM CXLI.

DAVID when hiding in the cave of Odollam, according to the Commentators, calls on God to deliver him from the great and imminent danger he is in.[2]

Of understanding for David.   A Prayer when he was in the cave.
(1 *Kings* xxiv.)

1. Voce mea ad Dominum clamavi : voce mea ad Dominum deprecatus sum :

I cried unto the Lord with my voice ; with my voice I made supplication unto the Lord.

"*Deprecatus sum.*"   That is, for succour.

2. Effundo in conspectu ejus orationem meam : et tribulationem meam ante ipsum pronuntio.

In His sight I pour out my prayer : and before Him I declare my trouble.

3. In deficiendo ex me spiritum meum : et tu cognovisti semitas meas.

When my spirit failed me : then Thou knewest my paths.

Seeing that with my feeble force I have no courage to resist,

---

[1] Bellarmine, amongst other interpretations of *Ejus*, prefers to understand it of the devil.

[2] This Psalm is mystically explained by most of the Holy Fathers of Jesus Christ in His Passion.   Thus verses 1-4 are applicable to His Agony in the garden ; 5-9 to His betrayal, apprehension, dereliction, and denial on the part of His disciples : verse 10 to His entombment and awaiting His Resurrection.

I have recourse to Thee, my God, Who knowest how perilous are the ways which I have to tread.

4. In via hac, qua ambulabam: absconderunt laqueum mihi.

In the way wherein I walked : they have hidden a snare for me.

5. Considerabam ad dexteram, et videbam : et non erat qui cognosceret me.

I looked on my right hand, and beheld : and there was no man that would know me.

I turned to my right hand to see if any one would help me ; and I found not even one who seemed to know me.

6. Periit fuga a me : et non est qui requirat animam meam.

Flight hath failed me : and there is no one that hath regard unto my soul.

All hope even of saving myself by flight is gone, and there is no one to have any care of my life.

7. Clamavi ad te Domine, dixi : Tu es spes mea, portio mea in terra viventium.

I cried unto Thee, O Lord, and said : Thou art my hope, my portion in the land of the living.

" *Portio mea.*" My portion, that is, my inheritance.

8. Intende ad deprecationem meam : quia humiliatus sum nimis.

Attend unto my supplication : for I am brought very low.

" *Intende.*" Give ear to.——" *Quia . . .*" For Thou seest me so greatly afflicted.

9. Libera me a persequentibus me : quia confortati sunt super me.

Deliver me from my persecutors : for they are stronger than I.

" *Quia confortati . . .*" Who are thus forward in persecuting me.

10. Educ de custodia animam meam ad confitendum nomini tuo : me expectant justi, donec retribuas mihi.

Bring my soul out of prison, that I may praise Thy name : the just wait for me, until Thou reward me.

Oh ! take me out of this prison, that I may be able to praise Thy Name ; the just await me, till Thou restore to me the freedom which I long for.

VESPERS FOR SATURDAY.

PSALM CXLIII.

David returns thanks to the Lord for his victory gained over Goliath, and for all the other benefits he had received, and he begs God to give him strength likewise to vanquish the Philistines.

A Psalm of David against Goliath.[1]

1. Benedictus Dominus Deus meus, qui docet manus meas ad prælium: et digitos meos ad bellum.

Blessed be the Lord my God : Who teacheth my hands to fight, and my fingers to war.

2. Misericordia mea, et refugium meum : susceptor meus, et liberator meus :

My mercy and my refuge : my upholder and my deliverer.

3. Protector meus, et in ipso speravi : qui subdit populum meum sub me.

My protector in Whom I have hoped : Who subdueth my people under me.

" *Qui subdit . . .*" Because Thou hast made my people subject to my rule.

4. Domine quid est homo, quia innotuisti ei ? aut filius hominis, quia reputas eum ?

Lord, what is man, that Thou makest Thyself known unto him ? or the son of man, that Thou makest account of him ?

5. Homo vanitati similis factus est : dies ejus sicut umbra prætereunt.

Man is like to vanity : his days pass away as a shadow.

Man is not vanity, since he is Thy creation, but his littleness is such that he is like unto vanity ; the days of his life pass by as a shadow.

6. Domine inclina cælos tuos, et descende : tange montes, et fumigabunt.

Bow down Thy heavens, O Lord, and come down : touch the mountains, and they shall smoke.

[1] The Holy Fathers say that under these figures we may see Jesus Christ and His Church triumphing over the devil and his agents ; and also the just man fighting against his spiritual enemies, interior and exterior.

"*Descende...*" Come down to defend me from my enemies; place Thy powerful hand on these proud mountains, and they shall pass away in smoke.[1]

7. Fulgura coruscationem, et dissipabis eos : emitte sagittas tuas, et conturbabis eos :

Send forth lightning, and Thou shalt scatter them : shoot out Thine arrows, and Thou shalt trouble them.

"*Fulgura coruscationem.*" Cause Thy lightnings to flash. ——"*Conturbabis eos.*" Thou wilt put them to confusion.

8. Emitte manum tuam de alto, eripe me, et libera me de aquis multis : de manu filiorum alienorum.

Put forth Thy hand from on high ; take me out and deliver me from many waters : and from the hand of the strange children.

Stretch forth Thy hand from the height of heaven ; save me and deliver me from the hands of these foreign foes,[2] who rush forward like a torrent of water to swallow me up.

9. Quorum os locutum est vanitatem : et dextera eorum dextera iniquitatis.

Whose mouth hath spoken vanity : and their right hand is the right hand of iniquity.

Their mouth utters words only of vanity and pride ; and their hands work nought but iniquity.

10. Deus canticum novum cantabo tibi : in psalterio decachordo psallam tibi.

Unto Thee, O God, will I sing a new song : on the psaltery and an instrument of ten strings will I sing praises unto Thee.

My God, I will sing to Thee a new song in thanksgiving, and will celebrate Thy praises on a psaltery of ten strings.

11. Qui das salutem regibus : qui redemisti David servum tuum de gladio maligno : eripe me.

Who givest salvation to kings : Who hast redeemed Thy servant David from the malicious sword : deliver me.

"*Qui...regibus.*" Thou art He that savest kings.——"*De gladio...*" That is, from the persecutions of the malicious : continue, then, to deliver me from perils.

12. Et erue me de manu filiorum alienorum, quorum os locutum est vanitatem : et dextera eorum, dextera iniquitatis :

And rescue me out of the hand of strange children ; whose mouth hath spoken vanity : and their right hand is the right hand of iniquity;

"*Quorum os...*" Whose mouth knows only to speak of vanity, and their hands are skilled only in working iniquity.

---

[1] *Ps.* xvii. 11 ; ciii. 33.

[2] "*Filiorum alienorum.*" That is, a foreign race, or the Philistines, who are called : "*Alienigenæ.*" See *Psalm* lxxxii. 6.

13. Quorum filii, sicut novellæ plantationes : in juventute sua.

Whose sons are as new plants : in their youth.

14. Filiæ eorum compositæ : circumornatæ ut similitudo templi.

Their daughters decked out : adorned round about after the similitude of a temple.

15. Promptuaria eorum plena : eructantia ex hoc in illud.

Their storehouses full : flowing over from one into another.

Their store-rooms are full and superabounding with all manner of victuals.

16. Oves eorum fœtosæ abundantes in egressibus suis : boves eorum crassæ.

Their sheep fruitful in young, abounding in their goings out : their oxen well fed.

Their sheep are fruitful with lambs at their bringing forth, and their herds are fat.

17. Non est ruina maceriæ, neque transitus : neque clamor in plateis eorum.

There is no breach of wall, nor passage : neither any crying in their streets.

Their walls stand firm and strong, their lands are well fenced in, and no cries nor lamentations are heard in their public places.

18. Beatum dixerunt populum, cui hæc sunt : beatus populus, cujus Dominus Deus ejus.

They have called the people happy that hath these things : *but* happy is that people whose God is the Lord.

And say they, blessed the people that enjoys these good things ! but no, let us say : Blessed is the people that has the Lord for their God !

PSALM CXLIV.

The Psalmist celebrates the perfections of God, but more especially His goodness and mercy.

Praise, for David himself.

1. Exaltabo te Deus meus Rex : et benedicam nomini tuo in sæculum, et in sæculum sæculi.

I will extol Thee, O God, my King : and I will bless Thy name for ever : yea, for ever and ever.

I will always praise Thee, my God and King ; and I will bless for all eternity Thy holy Name.

2. Per singulos dies benedicam tibi : et laudabo nomen tuum in sæculum, et in sæculum sæculi.

Every day will I bless Thee : and I will praise Thy name for ever, yea for ever and ever.

3. Magnus Dominus et laudibilis nimis : et magnitudinis ejus non est finis.

Great is the Lord, and greatly to be praised : and of His greatness there is no end.

Too (excessively) great and worthy of praise is the Lord ; and His greatness has no bounds.

4. Generatio et generatio laudabit opera tua : et potentiam tuam pro-nuntiabunt.

Generation and generation shall praise Thy works : and they shall declare Thy power.

5. Magnificentiam gloriæ sancti-tatis tuæ loquentur ; et mirabilia tua narrabunt.

They shall speak of the magni-ficence of the glory of Thy holiness : and shall tell of Thy wondrous works.

6. Et virtutem terribilium tuorum dicent : et magnitudinem tuam nar-rabunt.

And they shall speak of the might of Thy terrible acts : and shall declare Thy greatness.

"*Virtutem . . . dicent.*" They shall publish the might of Thy terrible judgments.

7. Memoriam abundantiæ suavi-tatis tuæ eructabunt : et justitia tua exultabunt.

They shall publish the memory of the abundance of Thy sweetness : and shall rejoice in Thy justice.

They shall recall anew to others the memory of Thy abun-dant sweetness, and shall rejoice at Thy just judgments.

8. Miserator et misericors Domi-nus : patiens, et multum misericors.

The Lord is gracious and merciful : patient and plenteous in mercy.

9. Suavis Dominus universis : et miserationes ejus super omnia opera ejus.

The Lord is sweet to all : and His tender mercies are over all His works.

"*Super . . .*" Shines above all His works.

10. Confiteantur tibi Domine omnia opera tua : et sancti tui benedicant tibi.

Let all Thy works, O Lord, praise Thee ; and let Thy saints bless Thee.

11. Gloriam regni tui dicent : et potentiam tuam loquentur.

They shall speak of the glory of Thy kingdom : and shall tell of Thy power.

12. Ut notam faciant filiis homi-num potentiam tuam : et gloriam magnificentiæ regni tui.

To make Thy might known unto the sons of men : and the glory of the magnificence of Thy kingdom.

13. Regnum tuum, regnum omni-um sæculorum : et dominatio tua in omni generatione et generationem.

Thy kingdom is a kingdom of all ages : and Thy dominion endureth throughout all generations.

14. Fidelis Dominus in omnibus verbis suis : et sanctus in omnibus operibus suis.

The Lord is faithful in all His words : and holy in all His works.

"*Verbis.*" That is : Promises.[1]

15. Allevat Dominus omnes qui corruunt : et erigit omnes elisos.

The Lord lifteth up all them that fall : and setteth up all them that are cast down.

[1] This verse is not found in the present Hebrew text. Bellarmine and Bossuet see in this omission an evident proof of the alteration of that text.

"*Allevat.*" According to the Hebrew : *Sustentat.* He sustains all those who are in danger of falling, and raises up all that are fallen ; because those who have fallen are never left without means on the part of God to raise themselves, if they have the will.

16. Oculi omnium in te sperant Domine : et tu das escam illorum in tempore opportuno.

The eyes of all hope in Thee, O Lord : and Thou givest them their meat in due season.

The eyes of all are turned to Thee, and hope in Thee for succour.

17. Aperis tu manum tuam : et imples omne animal benedictione.

Thou openest Thine hand : and fillest every living creature with blessing.

"*Benedictione.*" That is : With Thy benefits.

18. Justus Dominus in omnibus viis suis : et sanctus in omnibus operibus suis.

The Lord is just in all His ways : and holy in all His works.

"*In omnibus viis suis.*" In all the dispositions of His Providence.

19. Prope est Dominus omnibus invocantibus eum : omnibus invocantibus eum in veritate.

The Lord is nigh unto all them that call upon Him : to all that call upon Him in truth.

"*In veritate.*" That is : With confidence.

20. Voluntatem timentium se faciet, et deprecationem eorum exaudiet : et salvos faciet eos.

He will do the will of them that fear Him : and He will hear their prayer, and save them.

"*Et salvos . . .*" And will save them from evils.

21. Custodit Dominus omnes diligentes se : et omnes peccatores disperdet.

The Lord keepeth all them that love Him : but all the wicked He will destroy.

"*Peccatores.*" Obstinate sinners.

22. Laudationem Domini loquetur os meum : et benedicat omnis caro nomini sancto ejus in sæculum, et in sæculum sæculi.

My mouth shall speak the praise of the Lord : and let all flesh bless His holy name for ever, yea for ever and ever.

My mouth shall speak of naught else but the praises of the Lord ; and I desire that all men should ever bless His holy Name.

PSALM CXLV.

THE Psalmist speaks to the Jews, captives in Babylon ; he exhorts them to hope in God alone, for their deliverance.

Alleluia, of Aggeus and Zacharias.

1. Lauda anima mea Dominum, laudabo Dominum in vita mea: psallam Deo meo quamdiu fuero.

Praise the Lord, O my soul: while I live will I praise the Lord; I will sing to my God as long as I shall have my being.

"*Laudabo*..." Yes, I will praise Him throughout my life ; and as long as I shall live I will sing the glories of my God.

2. Nolite confidere in principibus : in filiis hominum, in quibus non est salus.

Put not your trust in princes : in the children of men, in whom there is no salvation.

Beware of putting your trust in the powerful of this world ; they are but men, and therefore cannot give you salvation.

3. Exibit spiritus ejus, et revertetur in terram suam : in illa die peribunt omnes cogitationes eorum.

His spirit shall go forth ; and he shall return unto his earth : in that day all their thoughts shall perish.

They are but men, I say ; one day their spirit will go forth, and their body will return to the earth from which they were formed : then all their projects will come to an end.

4. Beatus cujus Deus Jacob adjutor ejus, spes ejus in Domino Deo ipsius : qui fecit cœlum et terram, mare, et omnia, quæ in eis sunt.

Blessed is he who hath the God of Jacob for his helper, whose hope is in the Lord his God: Who made heaven and earth, the sea, and all things that are in them.

5. Qui custodit veritatem in sæculum, facit judicium injuriam patientibus : dat escam esurientibus.

Who keepeth truth for ever: Who executeth judgment for them that suffer wrong: Who giveth food to the hungry.

He is faithful in keeping His word for ever firm ; He does justice to those who suffer unjustly, and provides food for the hungry.

6. Dominus solvit compeditos : Dominus illuminat cæcos.

The Lord looseth them that are fettered : the Lord giveth sight to the blind.

7. Dominus erigit elisos : Dominus diligit justos.

The Lord lifteth up them that are cast down : the Lord loveth the just.

8. Dominus custodit advenas, pupillum et viduam suscipiet : et vias peccatorum disperdet.

The Lord keepeth the strangers ; He will support the fatherless and the widow: and the ways of sinners He will destroy.

The Lord has care of strangers who are far from their country.——"*Vias*." The designs.

9. Regnabit Dominus in sæcula, Deus tuus Sion : in generationem et generationem.

The Lord shall reign for ever: Thy God, O Sion, unto generation and generation.

O Sion, the Lord thy God shall reign for ever and ever.

PSALM CXLVI.

CONTINUATION of the subject of the preceding Psalm.

Alleluia.

1. Laudate Dominum quoniam bonus est psalmus : Deo nostro sit jucunda decoraque laudatio.

Praise ye the Lord, for it is good to sing praises : let the praise of our God be joyful and comely.

Let all praise the Lord, because to praise Him is good, that is, profitable to ourselves and pleasing to God ; but see that your praises are acceptable to God, pleasing and becoming, that is, worthy of His majesty.

2. Ædificans Jerusalem Dominus : dispersiones Israelis congregabit.

The Lord buildeth up Jerusalem : He will gather together the dispersed of Israel.

The Lord will rebuild Jerusalem ; and will reunite the people of Israel who are scattered among the Gentiles.

3. Qui sanat contritos corde : et alligat contritiones eorum.

Who healeth the broken of heart : and bindeth up their bruises.

"*Contritos.*"	That	is :	The	afflicted.——"*Contritiones.*"
Wounds.

4. Qui numerat multitudinem stellarum : et omnibus eis nomina vocat.

Who telleth the number of the stars : and calleth them all by their names.

He knows well the number of the stars, and He gives to all of them their name.

5. Magnus Dominus noster et magna virtus ejus : et sapientiæ ejus non est numerus.

Great is our Lord, and great is His power : and of His wisdom there is no measure.

6. Suscipiens mansuetos Dominus : humilians autem peccatores usque ad terram.

The Lord lifteth up the meek : and bringeth the wicked down even to the ground.

"*Suscipiens.*"	Protects.

7. Præcinite Domino in confessione : psallite Deo nostro in cithara.

Sing ye to the Lord with praise : sing unto our God upon the harp.

"*Psallite.*" Sing psalms in honour of our God with the sound of the harp.

8. Qui operit cœlum nubibus : et parat terræ pluviam.

Who covereth the heaven with clouds : and prepareth rain for the earth.

9. Qui producit in montibus fœnum : et herbam servituti hominum.

Who maketh grass to grow on the mountains : and herbs for the service of men.

10. Qui dat jumentis escam ipsorum : et pullis corvorum invocantibus eum.

Who giveth to beasts their food :
and to the young ravens that call
upon Him.

"*Invocantibus eum.*" That by their cries seem to call upon
Him.

11. Non in fortitudine equi voluntatem habebit : nec in tibiis viri beneplacitum erit ei.

He shall not delight in the
strength of the horse : nor take
pleasure in the legs of a man.

He has no will to help the man who trusts to the strength
or fleetness of his horse ; nor him who glories and confides in
the agility and speed of his legs.

12. Beneplacitum est Domino
super timentes eum : et in eis, qui
sperant super misericordia ejus.

The Lord taketh pleasure in them
that fear Him : and in them that
hope in his mercy.

"*Sperant.*" Place all their confidence in.

PSALM CXLVII.

THE Psalmist exhorts the people of God to thank Him for His
benefits. This Psalm regards the Jews now returned from
captivity, and in the sweet enjoyment of peace.[1]

Alleluia.

1. Lauda Jerusalem Dominum :
lauda Deum tuum Sion.

Praise the Lord, O Jerusalem :
praise thy God, O Sion.

"*Lauda Deum . . .*" And thou, Sion, give glory to thy God.

2. Quoniam confortavit seras por-
tarum tuarum : benedixit filiis tuis
in te.

For He hath strengthened the
bars of thy gates : He hath blessed
thy children within thee.

"*Benedixit.*" That is : He hath filled with good things.

3. Qui posuit fines tuos pacem : et
adipe frumenti satiat te.

Who hath made peace in thy
borders : and filleth thee with the
fat of corn.

"*Adipe frumenti.*" Choice wheat.

4. Qui emittit eloquium suum
terræ : velociter currit sermo ejus.

Who sendeth forth His speech
upon the earth : His word runneth
very swiftly.

He sends His commands to the earth ; and they arrive
promptly.

5. Qui dat nivem sicut lanam :
nebulam sicut cinerem spargit.

Who giveth snow like wool : He
scattereth mists like ashes.

[1] In the Hebrew this Psalm is joined to the foregoing.

"*Dat ... lanam.*" That is : He showers down snow from heaven in such quantities to benefit the earth, that its flakes form as it were a quilt of wool.——"*Nebulam.*" Hoar-frost.[1]

6. Mittit crystallum suam sicut buccellas : ante faciem frigoris ejus quis sustinebit?

He sendeth his crystal [2] like morsels : who shall stand before the face of His cold ?

Moreover He covers the earth with ice as with pieces of crystal ; how shall he who is exposed to such great cold be able to endure it ?——"*Ante faciem.*" A Hebraism, says Bellarmine, for : *Coram*, i.e., In its presence.

7. Emittet verbum suum, et liquefaciet ea : flabit spiritus ejus, et fluent aquæ.

He shall send out His word, and shall melt them : His wind shall blow, and the waters shall run.

Then the Lord will issue another command and will cause the snow to melt, for He will send forth the South wind, and the snows will thaw into water.

8. Qui annuntiat verbum suum Jacob : justitias et judicia sua Israel.

Who declareth His word unto Jacob : His justice and judgments unto Israel.

9. Non fecit taliter omni nationi : et judicia sua non manifestavit eis.

He hath not done in like manner to every nation : and His judgments He hath not made manifest to them. Alleluia.

8, 9. "*Verbum, justitias, judicia.*" That is : His will, His precepts, His commandments.——"*Omni nationi.*" To the other nations.

---

[1] "*Nebulam.*" S. Jerome translates : *Pruinam :* Hoar-frost.

[2] *Crystal ;* that is, *ice.*

COMPLINE.

PSALM IV.

COMMENTATORS suppose that David composed this Psalm after his having been delivered from the hands of Saul, or of Absalom. It is applied in a mystical sense to Jesus Christ, Who is the end of the Law and of the Prophets.

Unto the end, in verses. A Psalm for David.

1. Cum invocarem exaudivit me Deus justitiæ meæ : in tribulatione dilatasti mihi.

When I called upon Him, the God of my justice heard me : when I was in straits, Thou didst set me at liberty.

When I called upon my God, He heard me, He Who is the defender of my innocence. Yea, Lord, when I was in tribulation, Thou didst enlarge my heart by Thy consolations.

2. Miserere mei : et exaudi orationem meam.

Have mercy on me : and hear my prayer.

Continue, then, my Lord, always to have pity on me, and hearken to my prayers whenever I have recourse to Thee.

3. Filii hominum usquequo gravi corde? ut quid diligitis vanitatem, et quæritis mendacium ?

O ye sons of men, how long will ye be dull of heart? why do ye love vanity, and seek after lying ?

" *Usquequo gravi corde ?* " How long do you wish to have your heart thus heavy, that is, so bowed down to earth, and inclined to earthly passions?——" *Mendacium.*" Lies that deceive you.

4. Et scitote quoniam mirificavit Dominus sanctum suum : Dominus exaudiet me cum clamavero ad eum.

Know ye also that the Lord hath exalted His holy one : the Lord will hear me when I cry unto Him.

Know that the Lord has made His holy one admirable, that is, me His servant, whom He has sanctified as King and

Prophet ; He will, therefore, continue to hearken to me whenever I shall have recourse to Him in prayer.

5. Irascimini, et nolite peccare :   Be ye angry, and sin not: the
quæ dicitis in cordibus vestris, in things ye say in your hearts, be sorry
cubilibus vestris compungimini.   for upon your beds.

Be angry, but without committing sin, that is, be angry
with a just anger, that is to say, when the honour of God or
your own duty require it, and then, without perturbation. S.
Paul thus says : " Be angry, and sin not. Let not the sun go
down upon your anger" (*Ephes.* iv. 26).——" *Quæ dicitis in
cordibus vestris, in cubilibus vestris compungimini.*" And if your
conscience reproaches you for having yielded to some fit of
passion, then, at night, in the retirement of your chambers,
ask pardon of God with compunction.——"*Compungimini.*"
According to the Chaldee : *Deum apud vos cogitate.* Think
with yourselves on God.

6. Sacrificate sacrificium justitiæ,   Offer up the sacrifice of justice,[1]
et sperate in Domino : Multi dicunt: and trust in the Lord : many say :
Quis ostendit nobis bona ?   Who showeth us good things ?

Offer to God the sacrifice of justice, that is, of a just life,
and then put all your trust in the Lord.——" *Quis ostendit nobis
bona ?* " Commentators refer these words to the followers of
David, who, seeing themselves persecuted with him, said :
When shall we recover peace ?——According to Bellarmine,
we can explain them in two ways, either by supposing them
as coming from the mouth of worldlings, who make but little
account of heavenly goods, and say : Who has ever come back
from the other world to tell us of these goods, which we do
not see ? Or else : What is this holiness, which you so much
recommend to us?—and who will show us the way to
obtain it ?

7. Signatum est super nos lumen   The light of Thy countenance, O
vultus tui Domine : dedisti lætitiam Lord, is signed upon us : Thou hast
in corde meo.   given gladness in my heart.

" *Signatum est.*" According to the Hebrew : *Eleva :* Lift
up ; or : *Elevatum est ut signum :* Is lifted up as a sign ; which
comes to the same thing. The sense, then, of the verse is :
Thou hast shown us, O Lord, the light of Thy face, that is,
Thy benignity, or goodness, and thereby Thou hast rejoiced
my heart.

That is, the sacrifice prescribed by the law.

8. A fructu frumenti, vini, et olei sui : multiplicati sunt.

By the fruit of their corn, and wine, and oil : are they multiplied.

That is : I behold, O Lord, my enemies multiplying and thriving with their abundance of corn, of wine, of oil, that is to say, with the good things which they enjoy.

9. In pace in idipsum : dormiam et requiescam ;

In peace in the self-same : I will sleep, and I will rest :

But for me, confiding in Thy goodness, I shall continue to sleep and to repose in peace.

10. Quoniam tu Domine singulariter in spe constituisti me.

For Thou, O Lord, alone : hast established me in hope.

"*Singulariter.*" In a singular manner. According to the Greek : *Solitarie.* This is as much as to say : Thou takest care of me, as if Thou hadst none else but me to look after.

PSALM XXX.

DAVID, driven out of Jerusalem by his son Absalom, begs succour from God. Jesus Christ applies to Himself part of the sixth verse of this Psalm, and hence it appears that the persecution of David was a figure of His own.[1]

Unto the end. A Psalm for David, in an ecstasy.

1. In te Domine speravi, non confundar in æternum : in justitia tua libera me.

In Thee, O Lord, have I hoped, let me never be confounded : deliver me in Thy justice.

" *Non* . . . *æternum.*" Hence I hope never to see myself confounded.——" *In justitia* . . ." Wherefore, deliver me from confusion by Thy justice [with which Thou dost punish the guilty and dost protect the innocent]. (See p. 126.)

2. Inclina ad me aurem tuam : accelera ut eruas me.

Bow down Thine ear unto me : make haste to deliver me.

Incline Thy ears to my prayers, and speedily deliver me from dangers.

3. Esto mihi in Deum protectorem, et in domum refugii : ut salvum me facias.

Be Thou unto me a God, a protector : and a house of refuge to save me.

[1] This Psalm xxx. has its place as the fifth Psalm in Matins for Monday, where it is more fully explained. Here only the first six verses are given. (See Matins for Monday, pp. 126, 127.)

4. Quoniam fortitudo mea, et refugium meum es tu : et propter nomen tuum deduces me, et enutries me.

For Thou art my strength and my refuge : and for Thy Name's sake Thou wilt lead me and nourish me.

For Thou art my strength and my asylum, and Thou wilt save me from evils and provide for me in need for the glory of Thy Name.

5. Educes me de laqueo hoc quem absconderunt mihi : quoniam tu es protector meus.

Thou wilt bring me out of this snare, which they have hidden from me : for Thou art my protector.

"*Quem . . . mihi.*" Which in secret my enemies have pre pared for me.

6. In manus tuas commendo spiritum meum : redemisti me Domine Deus veritatis.

Into Thy hands I commend my spirit : Thou hast redeemed me, O Lord God of truth.

"*Redemisti . . .*" Lord, Thou hast redeemed me, Thou Who art my true God. These words, however, cannot be understood as personally applicable to Jesus Christ, since He was not redeemed, but was Himself the Redeemer.

PSALM XC.

HE who places all his hopes in God is exhorted to have no fear of dangers. This Psalm has a dramatic form ; at one time it is the Psalmist, at another the just man, and sometimes Almighty God Himself Who speaks.

The praise of a Canticle.

1. Qui habitat in adjutorio Altissimi : in protectione Dei cœli commorabitur.[1]

He that dwelleth in the help of the Most High, shall abide under the protection of the God of heaven.

He who lives in the confidence of the help of the Most High, shall dwell securely, &c.

2. Dicet Domino : Susceptor meus es tu, et refugium meum : Deus meus sperabo in eum.

He shall say unto the Lord : Thou art my upholder and my refuge : my God, in Him will I hope.

"*Dicet.*" He will be ever saying.——"*Deus . . .*" My God, I will say always : I will place my hopes in God alone.

3. Quoniam ipse liberavit me de laqueo venantium : et a verbo aspero.

For He hath delivered me from the snare of the hunters : and from the sharp word.

---

[1] "*In adjutorio.*" S. Jerome translates : *In abscondito :* In the secret or hiding-place. The Septuagint has : Help.

" *Venantium.*" That is : Of enemies who sought to make me their prey.[1]——"*A verbo aspero.*" Some interpret this of every calamity ; Bellarmine, with others, understands it of the condemnation of the reprobate, that is, of the sentence of eternal death.

4. Scapulis suis obumbrabit tibi : et sub pennis ejus sperabis.	He shall overshadow thee with His shoulders : and under His wings shalt thou trust.

If Thou trustest in the Lord, He will cover thee with His shoulders, that is, with His wings ; and under the wings of His protection thou mayest hope to be sheltered from every danger.

5. Scuto circumdabit te veritas ejus : non timebis a timore nocturno.	His truth shall compass thee with a shield : thou shalt not be afraid for the terror of the night ;
6. A sagitta volante in die, a negotio perambulante in tenebris : ab incursu, et dæmonio meridiano.	For the arrow that flieth in the day ; for the plague that walketh in the darkness : for the assault of the evil one in the noon-day.

5, 6. " *Veritas.*"——The faithfulness of His promises.—— " *Non timebis . . . nocturno.*" Under which thou wilt not be afraid of any alarms by night, that is, of the secret plots of thy enemies.——"*A sagitta . . . die.*" Nor of the arrows that shall be shot at thee unexpectedly during the day, that is, sudden and unforeseen dangers.——"*A negotio perambulante in tenebris.*" All hurtful things brought about by unknown causes.——"*Ab incursu et dæmonio meridiano.*" Nor of any assault of the devil, made with open attack in the middle of the day.——In a word, as S. Augustine says, if God protects thee, thou wilt not have to fear any evil planned against thee, by day or by night, in public or in private, whether on the part of men or of demons.

7. Cadent a latere tuo mille, et decem millia a dextris tuis : ad te autem non appropinquabit.	A thousand shall fall at thy side, and ten thousand at thy right hand : but it shall not come nigh thee.

Thou shalt see thy enemies fall around thee, on one side a thousand, and ten thousand at the right, without their being able to come near to hurt thee.[2]

---

[1] " *Liberavit.*" This in the Hebrew and Greek is in the future tense.

[2] Bellarmine, with S. Augustine, explains it thus : Amongst thy fellow-combatants in life thou wilt see a great number fall on thy left hand, that is, in adversity, and a still greater number at thy right, that is, in prosperity, without thyself receiving any injury.

8. Verumtamen oculis tuis considerabis : et retributionem peccatorum videbis.

But with thine eyes shalt thou behold : and shalt see the reward of the wicked.

With thine eyes thou shalt see clearly the protection of God over thee, and the vengeance which He will take of thy unjust persecutors.

9. Quoniam tu es Domine spes mea : altissimum posuisti refugium tuum.

For Thou, O Lord, art my hope : thou hast made the Most High thy refuge.

And whereas thou hast trusted in the Lord, saying : O Lord, Thou art my hope ; thou hast procured for thyself a most high refuge, that is, one most safe, wherein thou hast nought to fear.[1]

10. Non accedet ad te malum : et flagellum non appropinquabit tabernaculo tuo.

There shall no evil approach unto thee : neither shall the scourge come nigh thy dwelling.

Know that there, no evil shall happen to thee, &c.

11. Quoniam Angelis suis mandavit de te : ut custodiant te in omnibus viis tuis.

For He hath given His Angels charge over thee : to keep thee in all thy ways.

12. In manibus portabunt te : ne forte offendas ad lapidem pedem tuum.

In their hands they shall bear thee up : lest haply thou dash thy foot against a stone.

11, 12. For the Lord hath commended thee to His Angels, that they may guard thee in all thy ways ; if ever thou art in some perilous road, they will bear thee up in the palm of their hand, so that thy feet may not chance to stumble against any stone of scandal, that is, any dangerous occasion of sin.[2]

13. Super aspidem et basiliscum ambulabis : et conculcabis leonem et draconem.

Thou shalt walk upon the asp and the basilisk : the lion and the dragon shalt thou trample under foot.

That is : Thou wilt be secure, and shalt have nothing to fear from any evil encounters.——In a spiritual sense, by the asp is understood the demon, who inspires despair ; by the basilisk, the demon who inspires presumption ; by the lion, pride ; and by the dragon, attachment to earthly goods.

[1] "*Altissimum.*" According to the Hebrew and Greek, this word is here substantive : The Most High.

[2] Bellarmine thus explains the metaphors in this verse : The *hands of the Angels* are their intelligence and will ; the *stones* are the difficulties to be met with in the course of life, as scandals, temptations, persecutions, &c.; the *feet* are, with S. Augustine and S. Bernard, human affections, especially love and fear.

COMPLINE. **497**

14. Quoniam in me speravit, liberabo eum : protegam eum, quoniam
cognovit nomen meum.

Because he hath hoped in Me, I
will deliver him : I will protect him,
because he hath known My Name.

"*Quoniam . . . eum.*" Because the just man has put his trust
in Me, he shall be delivered by Me.——"*Cognovit.*" He has
known and invoked.

15. Clamabit ad me, et ego exaudiam eum : cum ipso sum in tribulatione : eripiam eum et glorificabo
eum.

He shall cry unto Me, and I will
hear him : I am with him in trouble:
I will deliver him, and I will glorify
him.

"*Clamabit ad me.*" He shall cry to Me for help.——
"*Eripiam . . .*" I will take him out of his tribulation, and
will crown him with glory.

16. Longitudine dierum replebo
eum : et ostendam illi salutare meum.

I will fill him with length of days :
and will show him My salvation.

I will give him a long life, and will make him to enjoy the
health and salvation that I shall bestow upon him in this life,
and eternal salvation which I reserve for him in the next.[1]

PSALM CXXXIII.

The Psalmist exhorts the Priests and Levites to praise God,
and to pray to Him for the people.

A Song of Degrees.[2]

1. Ecce nunc benedicite Dominum:
omnes servi Domini :

Behold, now, bless ye the Lord :
all ye servants of the Lord,

Bless now and always.

2. Qui statis in domo Domini : in
atriis domus Dei nostri,

Ye that stand in the house of the
Lord : in the courts of the house of
our God.

3. In noctibus extollite manus
vestras in sancta : et benedicite
Dominum.

Lift up your hands by night to the
holy places : and bless ye the Lord.

At night lift up your hands to the Sanctuary, and cease not
to bless the Lord.

---

[1] Bellarmine remarks that in the three last verses there are eight promises made on the part of God, four of which regard this present life:
Liberabo eum, Protegam eum, Exaudiam eum, Cum ipse sum ; and the four others
relate to the next life : *Eripiam eum, Glorificabo eum, Longitudine dierum
replebo eum, Ostendam illi salutare meum,* and this last is the vision of God
Himself.

[2] This Psalm is the last of the fifteen Gradual Psalms.

32

4. Benedicat te Dominus ex Sion : qui fecit cœlum et terram.

May the Lord bless thee out of Sion : Who hath made heaven and earth.

" *Te.*" This pronoun applies to the assembly of those whom the Psalmist exhorts to praise God.——" *Ex Sion.*" From Mount Sion, where He takes up His abode.

THE CANTICLE OF SIMEON.

THE holy old man Simeon uttered this Canticle when he took into his arms the Infant Jesus, Whom the Blessed Virgin brought to present Him in the Temple.

1. Nunc dimittis servum tuum Domine : secundum verbum tuum in pace :

Now dost Thou dismiss Thy servant, O Lord : according to Thy word in peace.

Now, O Lord, dost Thou let Thy servant depart in peace from this life, according to Thy promise.[1]

2. Quia viderunt oculi mei : salutare tuum.

Because my eyes have seen Thy salvation.

" *Salutare tuum.*" The Saviour Whom Thou hast sent.

3. Quod parasti : ante faciem omnium populorum :

Which Thou hast prepared before the face of all peoples.

Whom Thou hast set forth in the sight of all the peoples.

4. Lumen ad revelationem Gentium : et gloriam plebis tuæ Israel.

A light to the revelation of the Gentiles : and the glory of Thy people Israel.

He is the light that is come to illumine the Gentiles, and to give glory to Thy people Israel.

[1] Cornelius à Lapide says that this Canticle is recited every evening to remind us of death before sleep, which is the image of death, and in order that we may prepare for it by desiring it.

NOTE.

The translator observes in his work the following *corrigenda :—*

ERRATA.

INDEX TO THE PSALMS.

_____

INDEX TO THE CANTICLES.

TABLE OF CONTENTS.

CONTENTS. 507

LAUDS FOR SUNDAY.

PSALM   PAGE

XCII. Dominus regnavit, decorem 57

XCIX. Jubilate Deo omnis terra, servite . . . 58

LXII. Deus, Deus meus, ad te 59

LXVI. Deus misereatur nostri 61

Canticle of the Three Children. Benedicite . 62

CXLVIII. Laudate Dominum de cœlis 64

CXLIX. Cantate Domino canticum novum : laus ejus . 66

CL. Laudate Dominum in sanctis 68

Canticle of Zachary. Benedictus Dominus . 69

PRIME, TERCE, SEXT, NONE.

LIII. Deus, in nomine tuo salvum 71

CXVII. Confitemini Domino quoniam ... Dicat nunc . 72

XXIII. Domini est terra 77

XXIV. Ad te, Domine, levavi animam 78

XXV. Judica me, Domine, quoniam 81

XXII. Dominus regit me 83

XXI. Deus, Deus meus, respice 85

CXVIII. Beati immaculati in via 91

MATINS FOR MONDAY.

XXVI. Dominus illuminatio 117

XXVII. Ad te, Domine, clamabo 119

XXVIII. Afferte Domino, filii Dei 121

XXIX. Exaltabo te, Domine, quoniam 124

XXX. In te, Domine, speravi 126

XXXI. Beati, quorum remissæ sunt 130

XXXII. Exultate justi in Domino 134

XXXIII. Benedicam Dominum in omni tempore . . 136

XXXIV. Judica, Domine, nocentes me 139

XXXV. Dixit injustus, ut delinquat 143

XXXVI. Noli æmulari in malignantibus 146

XXXVII. Domine, ne in furore tuo ... Quoniam . . 152

508   CONTENTS.

LAUDS FOR FRIDAY.

MATINS FOR SATURDAY.

LAUDS FOR SATURDAY.

VESPERS FOR SUNDAY.

VESPERS FOR MONDAY.

512 CONTENTS.

COMPLINE.

THE END.

www.ingramcontent.com/pod-product-compliance
Lightning Source LLC
Chambersburg PA
CBHW030242100426
42812CB00002B/288